MW00444121

An Introduction to American Law

An Introduction to American Law

Second Edition

Gerald Paul McAlinn
PROFESSOR OF LAW
KEIO LAW SCHOOL

Dan Rosen
PROFESSOR OF LAW
CHUO LAW SCHOOL

John P. Stern
PROFESSOR OF LAW
NIHON UNIVERSITY LAW SCHOOL

CAROLINA ACADEMIC PRESS
Durham, North Carolina

ISBN 13: 9781594607141
LCCN: 2010927266

Carolina Academic Press
700 Kent Street
Durham, North Carolina 27701
Telephone (919) 489-7486
Fax (919) 493-5668
www.cap-press.com

Printed in the United States of America

This book is dedicated generally to the many students who have studied American law with us in Japan. They have tirelessly and diligently struggled with copied materials and roughly edited cases.

To Sachiko, Ken & Miki

Gerald Paul McAlinn

For Daniel and Allison

Dan Rosen

To Sakumi, George and Ken

John P. Stern

Contents

Preface

If necessity is the mother of invention, efficiency is the father of the textbook. Native speakers of American English, enrolled in a traditional three-year American law school, have scores of legal textbooks from which to choose. The authors' experience, however, is mainly with the "have-nots" of legal textbook readership: students of American law outside of the United States, including those for whom English is not a native language; American undergraduates taking courses in pre-law programs; paralegal professionals handling American law materials; and graduate students in majors other than American law. It is our experience that few English-language textbooks currently in print offer the mix of coverage, instruction, and vocabulary to appeal to this readership. We decided to create a textbook to serve these non-traditional American law textbook readers better than our existing set of photocopied materials.

This book is meant for readers who want to understand the contemporary American legal system at a more than superficial level, but who are not yet studying to become American lawyers. Our approach has been to present the fundamental rules, court cases, concepts, and trends of each key subject in American law in a narrative tailored to the reader without an American legal background. Each chapter covers a major area of law; summarizes the leading doctrines; analyzes recurring, current and developing trends; highlights areas of contemporary debate; offers streamlined versions of precedent-setting cases; raises questions for further discussion; and lists important vocabulary words. Since we have tried to make it possible to finish the entire textbook in one semester, we have necessarily shortened the treatment of some subjects and left out other subjects entirely. However, there is ample opportunity for debate and extended discussion as a result of the materials and cases on such controversial and timely topics as same-sex marriage, reproductive rights, intellectual property, privacy, the jury system, and the role of the courts in a democratic society. Of course the teacher is welcome to supplement the textbook and expand its treatment of any subject.

We have departed significantly from existing practice in editing cases and in the use of footnotes. We have deleted virtually all references to governing authority and cut out much supplementary material. In order to achieve our goals, we have at times heavily edited court cases without use of formal editing marks such as brackets and ellipses, and have frequently left out subsections and headnotes included in the opinion. Our experience has been that these marks are distracting to most students and incomprehensible to non-native readers of English. These editorial marks have a purpose: to make sure that when counsel quotes precedent to a court the precedent is quoted precisely, without misleading quotation out of context. However, brackets, ellipses and the like are not needed when a case is being introduced, in shortened form, to a student who can, if desired, usually view the entire text of the case opinion for free on the Internet. Our students have also found footnotes distracting, particularly since many of the journals cited are not yet easily available for reading outside of a well-stocked law library. So, we have cited cases, reference works, and quotations with enough attribution to allow a student to find the original source if desired, but without full *Bluebook* details.

Law is an instrument of society and an agent of change. American society in particular is in constant motion. The authors fully expect that some cases and doctrines of American law will change in importance in the years following publication of this textbook. However, we are confident that this textbook will give students the necessary background in process and substance to understand future changes in American law.

Tokyo, June 2010

Gerald Paul McAlinn
Dan Rosen
John P. Stern

Acknowledgments

The authors would like to acknowledge with gratitude the following individuals who read and provided insightful comments on various chapters of the first edition of this book: Lawton W. Hawkins, Elizabeth E. Hoyt, Steven B. Givens, W. Temple Jorden, Jeffrey Lubbers, and Kenneth L. Port. We owe a debt of gratitude to Dennis Flesch, a student in the Temple Law Program in Japan, for his invaluable work proofreading and cite checking this second edition. We would like to offer our special thanks to Meg Daniel for her invaluable assistance in helping us to finalize the book by reading the manuscript in its entirety for consistency and generating the Index and Table of Cases.

The Carolina Academic Press and our editors Linda Lacy, Zoë Oakes, Karen Clayton, and Keith Sipe, have been supportive, prompt, and flexible. What more could an author want?

A Note on Reading Cases

Embarking on the study of American law without a preliminary understanding of the case law system is an impossible task. Cases are what set the common law apart from other legal traditions and systems, most notably the civil law. They are the grist for the mill of common law. This book will introduce many general principles of American law throughout the text, but the reader will develop the greatest sense and feel for the American legal process through reading the excerpted cases. Careful readers will also observe that central themes permeate the book, and that certain cases are cross-referenced in one or more chapters.

In the common law system, every case serves at least two separate and distinct functions: satisfying the requirements of justice and helping predict future results. The justice function is served when the case decides the matter disputed between the litigants and provides them with a statement of the reasons for the decision. People bring lawsuits because they want to assert a right or to affirm the legality of their point of view. This function could conceivably be served by a simple decision announcing the winner of the suit. However, this would leave the parties feeling uncertain as to why they won or lost and would ultimately undermine the integrity and stature of the courts as the principal forum for justice and the rule of law. To avoid such dissatisfaction, judges render reasoned (some more so than others) decisions explaining why one party has won and the other has lost. Losing parties are rarely satisfied with the results, but at least they can go away feeling they have had their proverbial day in court and their positions have been heard. Giving a fair and balanced statement of the facts, setting forth the applicable rules of law, and then the decision in a single written opinion enhances transparency, allows for focused appeals, and promotes the fundamental value of fairness.

Second, a well-reasoned opinion will also serve as a guidepost to resolving future disputes. Cases make law. A lawyer who reads the opinions in his or her area of expertise and jurisdiction develops a keen awareness of the rules, policies, and material facts that lead to certain results. When consulted by a client about a specific problem, the lawyer can use the existing case law to make an informed judgment about the strengths and weaknesses of the proposed case. This can then be translated into advice intended to prevent unnecessary litigation and to avoid lawsuits without merit.

The common law system is based on two core principles, namely, *stare decisis* (meaning, "let the decision stand") and respect for precedent. The principle of *stare decisis* holds that lower courts within the jurisdiction of a higher court are bound to follow the legal rulings of the higher court unless the facts of the case at hand are distinguishable to a degree to justify divergence. A lower court can rest assured that its efforts to break free of binding precedent will be reviewed by the appellate courts and either accepted as a new rule or reversed in light of the existing rules. Learning to distinguish cases is an important skill for an American lawyer.

The cases contained in this book have been selected out of hundreds and sometimes even thousands of possible choices for their representative nature. They are not presented because they are the last and final word on the principles of law for which they are being cited. What the authors hope to achieve is for the lay reader to be able to get the flavor of the American legal process. This means coming to understand how the facts relate to and merge with the general principles of applicable law to form new rules capable of addressing the contemporary issues of society.

The cases have been severely edited to make them more accessible to the non-law school reader. We have deleted virtually all references to governing authority and deleted much extraneous material. Citations have been provided in the text for all of the cases for those readers who desire to read the full text of any of the opinions we have selected. Most of the federal materials can now be found on the Internet at a variety of free sites. A partial list of useful sites is as follows:

Findlaw: http://www.findlaw.com

Legal Information Institute: http://www.law.cornell.edu/

The Library of Congress: http://thomas.loc.gov/

U.S. Supreme Court: http://www.supremecourt.gov/opinions

Global Legal Information Network: http://www.loc.gov/law

Google Scholar Legal: http://scholar.google.com

Many state and local bar associations, as well as state and federal district and appellate courts maintain free online databases.

Finally, it is important to remember when reading the cases in this book that each represents a slice of real life. The disputes were between real people with real concerns, often such that they were willing to pursue their cases through multiple levels of trial and appeal. Extract the principles of law that are to be learned from reading the cases and develop a sense of judicial reasoning by all means, but do not neglect to consider the human conditions and foibles that led the parties to go to court in the first place. It is said that the common law is "living law" because of its ability to adapt to the changing conditions in society. We hope that the reader will share our excitement about the law as a result of reading through the cases we have selected.

Table of Cases

Primary case names are in **bold font** followed by a citation, a comma and the page numbers separated by a hyphen where the excerpted case appears.

An Introduction to American Law

Chapter 1

Basic Principles of American Law

"It is one of the great merits and advantages of the common law, that instead of a series of detailed practical rules, established by positive provisions, and adapted to the precise circumstances of particular cases, which would become obsolete and fail, when the practice and course of business, to which they apply, should cease and change, the common law consists of a few broad and comprehensive principles.... The consequence ... is, that when a new practice or new course of business arises, the rights and duties of parties are not without a law to govern them."

Shaw, C.J. in *Norway Plains Co. v. Boston & Maine Railroad*, 67 Mass 263 (1854)

Law is defined as a system of rules and regulations, promulgated by a controlling authority, and enforceable by sanction. It operates on many levels throughout society, and comes in many forms. In societies with a written constitution, the constitution is the highest source of law followed closely by statutes and judicial opinions. Some nations give international treaties a superior place over statutes in domestic law, while others such as the U.S. give treaties equal weight with domestic statutes and provide that the last in time takes precedence. Law can be national and local; federal or state. It can take the form of local ordinances or even informal directives from government officials that are not strictly law but must be followed all the same.

Historically, law was seen as being largely a matter of domestic concern, limited by territorial boundaries and strongly supported by the principle of sovereignty. The concept of sovereignty provides that each nation is supreme within its own territory. Rapid globalization of the world's economy combined with the ease of travel and communications in the modern era has seen traditional borders begin to erode. How can any legal system purport to assert exclusive jurisdiction over the Internet? How can a nation institute one-sided trade barriers, or deprive its people of basic human rights, in the face of international condemnation? The United Nations and virtually every country has grappled with these thorny issues as global norms and expectations emerge. Recognition of the need to harmonize legal principles across national borders has taken root, even though it cannot be said to have yet produced much fruit and there remains substantial opposition in many quarters to a truly global legal regime.

The Civil Law and Common Law Traditions

There are two principal legal traditions in the world, namely, the Civil Law System and the Common Law System. If we were to divide up the world based on legal tradition, we would see that most of Europe (except England, Scotland, Wales and Ireland), Latin America and much of Asia (except for Hong Kong, Singapore and Malaysia) subscribe to civil law. Countries that derive their legal heritage from England, such as the U.S., Canada, Ireland, Australia, New Zealand, India, and much of Africa follow the common law tradition. These are not the only systems. If one were to undertake a systematic review of world legal systems, it would be necessary to consider legal systems based on religion, feudalism, custom, communism, socialism, and other organizing social principles.

The focus of this book is on introducing our readers to the broad parameters and underlying traditions of the U.S., as a leading member of the common law nations. Comparisons will be made to civil law principles, but only incidental to the study of American law. The common law is often referred to as "judge made" law and, as you read the materials that follow, you will develop a sense of how American judges approach problems and find solutions.

America is a land of immigrants. Law is among the most important institutions for ensuring harmony when the people do not share common traditions and values. Time and again, the courts are asked to resolve disputes over basic social values and to develop a rule of law that is just and fair. The U.S. is also a geographically vast nation. It is not surprising, therefore, to learn that legal rules can vary from state to state. Federal law allows for a measure of uniformity where it is applicable, but large areas of the law remain outside of federal jurisdiction. Americans are, for the most part, not troubled by these regional differences in law and custom, provided the basic principles of American justice are in evidence.

The civil law tradition is said to rest, in contrast, on a philosophy of embodying all of the important rules of law into unified written codes. Civil law drafters believe that a comprehensive body of written codes is possible. Once the laws are formalized, the role of the courts and lawyers is to identify the appropriate section of the appropriate code and apply it to the case at hand. Civil judges are not expected or encouraged to interpret the codes. Written codes have many advantages, especially regarding predictability and accessibility. However, the process of amending codes is time-consuming and necessarily lags behind social developments. This often causes the codes to appear antiquated and out of date. To a lawyer trained in the common law, the reliance on a uniform application of the codes seems to lack a full appreciation of the multitude of factual variations.

As you study American law in greater depth, you will realize there is no lack of statutory law or written codes in the U.S. This can be explained, at least in part, by the great complexity of modern society. We now live in a post-industrial, high technology society where it is no longer possible to argue that there is any "common" understanding among people as to what rules should govern all behavior or how various matters should be resolved. That may have been a realistic expectation in feudal England where the common law developed, but it is certainly strained by the pressures of a diverse and sophisticated, technology enabled society.

An introductory study of the civil law would reveal far more similarities than differences in the legal results produced by both systems. In the final analysis, law in every society must guide behavior and resolve disputes between people. Culture, history, and tradition differ among nations for sure, but we are all human and there are only a limited number of ways that behavior can be dictated and rational results achieved. For example, both systems make it a crime to commit murder, both provide for the payment of damages for private wrongs in tort, and both enforce contracts.

So, what then are the major differences between the civil law and common law? The differences can be found, as already suggested, in the role of the courts and lawyers in forging new laws and promoting social change through law. The civil law system is based on what is known as the inquisitorial model. This model posits that the law is fixed by the codes, and the role of the judge is to determine the facts. There are no juries; attorneys are there to assist the judge. In contrast, the common law system is based on the adversarial model. This adversarial system relies on each party having a lawyer to vigorously represent the best interests of the client. The role of the judge is to act as referee during the bout between the advocates and then to inform the jury of the applicable legal principles, or to apply them directly if no jury is involved. As the facts are determined through the adversarial system, the legal rules must be modified and extended to fit the circumstances. This makes the common law flexible and evolutionary at the same time as it searches back into its traditions and origins for guiding principles. The distinctions are a subtle as they are profound and account for much of the difference in operation between the civil and common law systems.

There are two side effects of the adversarial system that merit observation. One is positive and the other less so. The positive aspect is that courts and lawyers are actively engaged in defining the rights and duties of members of society in the context of real factual disputes that will have implications for many people beyond the litigants. Every person (and every social issue it seems) is entitled to his or her proverbial day in court. The less positive result is that contentious social issues tend to be framed in the extreme and pitted against others in a zero sum game. The exercise of a right by A means the deprivation of a right arguably belonging to B. One scholar has called this tension the "clash of absolutes." A legal system that placed less reliance on the courts and lawyers to resolve such issues might display a more temperate approach to conflict resolution. This too would, of course, have its costs in terms of individual rights.

With that general introduction, we will now turn to an exploration of the background and context in which American law exists. Our journey begins with the Declaration of Independence. The Declaration set off the American Revolution and it contains the historical predicates and political foundation on which the new nation was formed. The Constitution that it produced abounds with principles aimed at eliminating for all time the long list of abuses suffered at the hands of a tyrant king.

The Constitution of the United States of America

The United States has the oldest written constitution still in continuous use in the world. Beyond that, despite the country's many faults, America has achieved a high degree of both economic and social prosperity under that basic document. Unlike the constitutions of most countries, the Constitution of the United States is based on a deep and abiding distrust of government. Power is divided and subdivided through a system of "checks and balances" in a way that no one part can accomplish much by itself. Even the courts, whose judges are guaranteed independence by life tenure, depend on the Congress and the President for their budget, jurisdiction, and appointment. At first glance, this arrangement seems like a recipe for failure. Indeed, observers from abroad often conclude that the American government spends much of its time fighting within itself, leaving little opportunity for the passage of legislation. As an institution, government with a capital "G" seems inefficient at best, and hopelessly deadlocked at worst.

The Constitution was written in 1787, during a hot summer in Philadelphia. At the outset, it was not intended to be a constitution at all. Rather, the delegates from the various states had been called together simply to improve on the existing Articles of Confederation. The Articles of Confederation, adopted in 1777, created a loose structure within which the thirteen states, previously colonies, could cooperate with one another. The revolutionary experience had convinced the people of the need to work together, but the colonial experience had soured them on any sort of strong, national government—especially one with a powerful leader at the top.

With the revolutionary war won, the Confederation had to face the facts of its own future. The individual states competed sharply for advantages over one another. Trade barriers, designed to protect insiders and disadvantage outsiders, degenerated into domestic trade wars. The Articles of Confederation had not created a national government powerful enough to take charge and correct all the infighting. Indeed, the national government—such as it was—could not even raise money effectively. It had no power to tax (taxation without representation being one of the leading complaints against England); only the power to request funds from the various states. They often said no. Moreover, the Articles had done nothing at all to resolve the debate over whether slavery could continue to exist in the United States. As it turned out, the Constitution also failed to resolve that great matter, contributing to the tragic Civil War.

When the convention of delegates convened in May 1787, one of the first rules it made for itself was secrecy. Nothing that occurred within the meetings was to be communicated to the outside, even to members of Congress. There was much speculation as to what was going on inside the building, most of it erroneous. Few people surmised that the "improvements" being discussed involved a completely new form of government under a new constitution.

The Structure of the Constitution

It can safely be said that every viable constitution must accomplish two things. It must establish a form of government, and it must provide for the protection of individual rights against what has been called the "tyranny of the majority." The structure of the U.S. Constitution is elegant in its simplicity. Article I sets out the powers of the Congress. Article II establishes the power of the President. Article III creates the Courts. The Constitution goes on, in Article IV, to ensure cooperation among the states. Article V allows amendments to be adopted, while Article VI boldly states that the Constitution, and the laws of the United States made under it, is supreme to the constitutions and laws of the states. This section of Article VI is known as the "Supremacy Clause." Article VII simply states the basis for adoption of the document. With these seven articles, the government of the United States was made, fulfilling the first task of a new constitution.

With the form of government established, the Founding Fathers turned to a set of ten amendments to address the issue of individual rights. These were agreed upon essentially at the same time as the overall document, and were insisted upon by various states which feared that the newly empowered national government would impose its will oppressively upon the people. For various reasons, the amendments were not adopted at the same time as the Constitution, and had to be added later in the form of Amendments I through X. These amendments are commonly known as the "Bill of Rights," and they guarantee the fundamental rights of the people. You will find detailed discussions of these rights liberally sprinkled throughout the following chapters, and especially in Chapters 4 and 10.

The Tenth Amendment deserves a special note at this point because it states that the national government has only the powers given to it by the Constitution. Everything else is reserved to the states or the people. Thus, the principle was born that the United States government is a government of enumerated and "limited powers." The relationship of the national and the state governments was the central issue at the time the Constitution was written, and it certainly remains a central issue in constitutional jurisprudence today.

Article I

The lawmaking power of the national government is limited to the subjects set forth in Article I. However, the reach of those subjects has been a matter of judicial interpretation. For example, in order to solve the problem of trade wars among the states experienced under the Articles of Confederation, Article 1, section 8, clause 3 of the Constitution gives Congress the power to regulate interstate commerce. But what is "commerce"? And what of activity that occurs in one state but has effects in or on others? Is that "interstate"? Indeed, in the nationally-integrated (some would say, internationally-integrated) economy of the 21st century, an act anywhere could reasonably be said to have an economic effect everywhere. If that is so, what becomes of the federalism principle, allocating lawmaking power between the national government and the state governments? In the following cases, the Supreme Court examined the dimensions of federal commerce power.

United States v. Lopez
514 U.S. 549 (1995)

Rehnquist, C.J.

In the Gun Free School Zones Act of 1990, Congress made it a federal offense "for any individual knowingly to possess a firearm at a place that the individual knows, or has reasonable cause to believe, is a school zone." The Act neither regulates a commercial activity nor contains a requirement that the possession be connected in any way to interstate commerce. We hold that the Act exceeds the authority of Congress "[t]o regulate Commerce ... among the several States."

On March 10, 1992, respondent, who was then a 12th grade student, arrived at Edison High School in San Antonio, Texas, carrying a concealed .38 caliber handgun and five bullets. Acting upon an anonymous tip, school authorities confronted respondent, who admitted that he was carrying the weapon. He was arrested and charged under Texas law with firearm possession on school premises. The next day, the state charges were dismissed after federal agents charged respondent by complaint with violating the Gun Free School Zones Act of 1990.

We start with first principles. The Constitution creates a Federal Government of enumerated powers. As James Madison wrote, "[t]he powers delegated by the proposed Constitution to the federal government are few and defined. Those which are to remain in the State governments are numerous and indefinite." This constitutionally mandated division of authority "was adopted by the Framers to ensure protection of our fundamental liberties." A healthy balance of power between the States and the Federal Government will reduce the risk of tyranny and abuse from either front.

The Constitution delegates to Congress the power "[t]o regulate Commerce with foreign Nations, and among the several States, and with the Indian Tribes."

"[We] have identified three broad categories of activity that Congress may regulate under its commerce power. First, Congress may regulate the use of the channels of interstate commerce. '[T]he authority of Congress to keep the channels of interstate commerce free from immoral and injurious uses has been frequently sustained, and is no longer open to question.'" Second, Congress is empowered to regulate and protect the instrumentalities of interstate commerce, or persons or things in interstate commerce, even though the threat may come only from intrastate activities. Finally, Congress' commerce authority includes the power to regulate those activities having a substantial relation to interstate commerce, i.e., those activities that substantially affect interstate commerce.

Within this final category, admittedly, our case law has not been clear whether an activity must "affect" or "substantially affect" interstate commerce in order to be within Congress' power to regulate it under the Commerce Clause. We conclude, consistent with the great weight of our case law, that the proper test requires an analysis of whether the regulated activity "substantially affects" interstate commerce.

Section 922(q) [of the Gun Free School Zones Act] is a criminal statute that by its terms has nothing to do with "commerce" or any sort of economic enterprise, however broadly one might define those terms. Section 922(q) is not an essential part of a larger regulation of economic activity, in which the regulatory scheme could be undercut unless the intrastate activity were regulated. It cannot, therefore, be sustained under our cases upholding regulations of activities that arise out of or are connected with a commercial transaction, which viewed in the aggregate, substantially affects interstate commerce.

The Government argues that possession of a firearm in a school zone may result in violent crime and that violent crime can be expected to affect the functioning of the national economy in two ways. First, the costs of violent crime are substantial, and, through the mechanism of insurance, those costs are spread throughout the population. Second, violent crime reduces the willingness of individuals to travel to areas within the country that are perceived to be unsafe. The Government also argues that the presence of guns in schools poses a substantial threat to the educational process by threatening the learning environment. A handicapped educational process, in turn, will result in a less productive citizenry. That, in turn, would have an adverse effect on the Nation's economic well being. As a result, the Government argues that Congress could rationally have concluded that 922(q) substantially affects interstate commerce.

We pause to consider the implications of the Government's arguments. The Government admits, under its "costs of crime" reasoning, that Congress could regulate not only all violent crime, but all activities that might lead to violent crime, regardless of how tenuously they relate to interstate commerce. Similarly, under the Government's "national productivity" reasoning, Congress could regulate any activity that it found was related to the economic productivity of individual citizens: family law (including marriage, divorce, and child custody), for example. Under the theories that the Government presents in support of 922(q), it is difficult to perceive any limitation on federal power, even in areas such as criminal law enforcement or education where States historically have been sovereign. Thus, if we were to accept the Government's arguments, we are hard pressed to posit any activity by an individual that Congress is without power to regulate.

To uphold the Government's contentions here, we would have to pile inference upon inference in a manner that would bid fair to convert congressional authority under the Commerce Clause to a general police power of the sort retained by the States. Admittedly, some of our prior cases have taken long steps down that road, giving great deference to congressional action. The broad language in these opinions has suggested the possibility of additional expansion, but we decline here to proceed any further.

Breyer, J., dissenting

The issue in this case is whether the Commerce Clause authorizes Congress to enact a statute that makes it a crime to possess a gun in, or near, a school. In my view, the statute falls well within the scope of the commerce power as this Court has understood that power over the last half century.

For one thing, reports, hearings, and other readily available literature make clear that the problem of guns in and around schools is widespread and extremely serious. These materials report, for example, that four percent of American high school students (and six percent of inner city high school students) carry a gun to school at least occasionally, that 12 percent of urban high school students have had guns fired at them, that 20 percent of those students have been threatened with guns, and that, in any 6 month period, several hundred thousand schoolchildren are victims of violent crimes in or near their schools. And, they report that this widespread violence in schools throughout the Nation significantly interferes with the quality of education in those schools. Based on reports such as these, Congress obviously could have thought that guns and learning are mutually exclusive. And, Congress could therefore have found a substantial educational problem—teachers unable to teach, students unable to learn—and concluded that guns near schools contribute substantially to the size and scope of that problem.

Having found that guns in schools significantly undermine the quality of education in our Nation's classrooms, Congress could also have found, given the effect of education upon interstate and foreign commerce, that gun related violence in and around schools is a commercial, as well as a human, problem. Education, although far more than a matter of economics, has long been inextricably intertwined with the Nation's economy.

Specifically, Congress could have found that gun related violence near the classroom poses a serious economic threat (1) to consequently inadequately educated workers who must endure low paying jobs, and (2) to communities and businesses that might (in today's "information society") otherwise gain, from a well educated work force, an important commercial advantage of a kind that location near a railhead or harbor provided in the past. Congress might also have found these threats to be no different in kind from other threats that this Court has found within the commerce power, such as the threat that loan sharking poses to the "funds" of "numerous localities," and that unfair labor practices pose to instrumentalities of commerce. As I have pointed out, Congress has written that "the occurrence of violent crime in school zones" has brought about a "decline in the quality of education" that "has an adverse impact on interstate commerce and the foreign commerce of the United States."

* * *

Topics for Further Discussion

1. Both the majority and dissent believe that the powers of the national government are limited. What is the difference in their understanding of the limitation? As a result of this opinion, do you think guns in schools are unregulated? If not, who can regulate them and how?

2. The dissent by Justice Breyer suggests that the meaning of the Constitution may change over time. If that is so, what standards should be used to decide when it has

changed and how? On the other hand, if the meaning never changes, how can the Constitution respond to changes in society?

3. In general, education in the United States is regulated by each of the states. Although a national Department of Education does exist, its primary role is supporting education rather than regulating it. The national government indirectly engages in regulation by offering federal money to schools in return for their agreement to various federal guidelines, and certain constitutional rights and civil liberties are applicable in the school context.

Reno v. Condon
528 U.S. 141 (2000)

Rehnquist, C.J.

The Driver's Privacy Protection Act of 1994 regulates the disclosure of personal information contained in the records of state motor vehicle departments (DMVs). We hold that in enacting this statute Congress did not run afoul of the federalism principles enunciated in *New York v. United States*, 505 U.S. 144 (1992), and *Printz v. United States*, 521 U.S. 898 (1997).

The DPPA regulates the disclosure and resale of personal information contained in the records of state DMVs. State DMVs require drivers and automobile owners to provide personal information, which may include a person's name, address, telephone number, vehicle description, Social Security number, medical information, and photograph, as a condition of obtaining a driver's license or registering an automobile. Congress found that many States, in turn, sell this personal information to individuals and businesses.

The DPPA establishes a regulatory scheme that restricts the States' ability to disclose a driver's personal information without the driver's consent. The DPPA generally prohibits any state DMV, or officer, employee, or contractor thereof, from "knowingly disclos[ing] or otherwise mak[ing] available to any person or entity personal information about any individual obtained by the department in connection with a motor vehicle record."

The DPPA establishes several penalties to be imposed on States and private actors that fail to comply with its requirements. The Act makes it unlawful for any "person" knowingly to obtain or disclose any record for a use that is not permitted under its provisions, or to make a false representation in order to obtain personal information from a motor vehicle record. Any person who knowingly violates the DPPA may be subject to a criminal fine. Additionally, any person who knowingly obtains, discloses, or uses information from a state motor vehicle record for a use other than those specifically permitted by the DPPA may be subject to liability in a civil action brought by the driver to whom the information pertains. While the DPPA defines "person" to exclude States and state agencies, a state agency that maintains a "policy or practice of substantial noncompliance" with the Act may be subject to a civil penalty imposed by the United States Attorney General of not more than $5,000 per day of substantial noncompliance.

South Carolina law conflicts with the DPPA's provisions. Under that law, the information contained in the State's DMV records is available to any person or entity that fills out a form listing the requester's name and address and stating that the information will not be used for telephone solicitation. South Carolina's DMV retains a copy of all requests for information from the State's motor vehicle records, and it is required to release copies of all requests relating to a person upon that person's written petition. State law authorizes the South Carolina DMV to charge a fee for releasing motor vehicle information, and it requires the DMV to allow drivers to prohibit the use of their motor vehicle information for certain commercial activities.

The United States asserts that the DPPA is a proper exercise of Congress' authority to regulate interstate commerce under the Commerce Clause. The United States bases its Commerce Clause argument on the fact that the personal, identifying information that the DPPA regulates is a "thin[g] in interstate commerce," and that the sale or release of that information in interstate commerce is therefore a proper subject of congressional regulation. We agree with the United States' contention. The motor vehicle information which the States have historically sold is used by insurers, manufacturers, direct marketers, and others engaged in interstate commerce to contact drivers with customized solicitations. The information is also used in the stream of interstate commerce by various public and private entities for matters related to interstate motoring. Because drivers' information is, in this context, an article of commerce, its sale or release into the interstate stream of business is sufficient to support congressional regulation.

* * *

Topics for Further Discussion

1. Chief Justice Rehnquist wrote the majority opinions in the *Condon* case and in the *Lopez* case five years earlier. The cases reach different conclusions about the power of Congress to pass laws under the Commerce Clause. Why?

2. In revealing information from their state files, were states acting as government institutions or as businesses? Does that make a constitutional difference?

3. In the United States, drivers' licenses are issued by the individual states, not by the national government. Also, driving records, rules (provided they do not substantially burden interstate commerce), and enforcement are all within the powers of the states. On the other hand, as with education, the national government exercises some influence by offering federal highway funds to states, in return for their agreement to follow various federal guidelines.

* * *

These cases were not the Supreme Court's first attempt to define the limits of federal commerce power. The search goes back almost as far as the Constitution itself. In *Gibbons v. Ogden*, 22 U.S. 1 (9 Wheat.) (1824), the Court took up the question of whether steam ship travel constituted "commerce." One party had an exclusive franchise from the State of New York to navigate the State's waters. The other party decided to compete on the interstate route between New York and New Jersey. It defended itself in a lawsuit by contending that the state franchise improperly conflicted with the federal government's shipping licenses. Chief Justice John Marshall said that "commerce" means "intercourse." Thus, the federal government could properly assert its predominance over any commerce that concerned more than one state. Later cases took up the issue of when commerce within one state could be said to be interstate.

In *Swift v. United States*, 196 U.S. 375 (1905), Justice Oliver Wendell Holmes described commerce as a kind of current. Activities in one state would be subject to federal law if they were simply one part of a larger interstate current. Thus, meat packers in one state could be held accountable under federal antitrust law because the meat was destined to travel on to other places. The early 20th century found the Court trying to resolve issues of whether the stream of commerce had begun or ended. Production, for example, was deemed to be prior to the running of the stream. As a result, the working conditions of persons (even children) involved in making products was ruled to be beyond federal control.

The economic depression of the 1920s and 30s led to the election of Franklin Roosevelt as President, along with his promise of a "New Deal." The New Deal depended on federal economic legislation, which the Supreme Court almost uniformly struck down. The standoff reached its peak in *Carter v. Carter Coal Co.*, 298 U.S. 238 (1936), when the Court struck down federal regulation of labor issues in the coal industry. The coal industry, of course, was largely interstate and affected the entire country. The President responded by recommending to Congress a plan to allow him to appoint additional justices equal to the number of those who had reached age 70 and had served at least 10 years. Later that year, the Court changed its mind, ruling 5–4 that applying federal labor law to the steel industry was constitutional. After the President got his way, the so-called "court packing plan" fell away, no longer needed. From that time until the *Lopez* case presented above, the Court let Congress have its way with commerce. Even today, the limits on federal power are few.

In addition to "commerce," the subjects on which Congress may legislate are listed in Article I, section 8. Because the new Constitution was meant to correct the perceived defects in the Articles of Confederation, many of these subjects are financial. For example, Congress has the power to tax and to pay the debts of the nation under Article I, section 8, clause 1. This may seem obvious, but it was lacking before in the Articles of Confederation. Moreover, clause 2 allows the Congress to borrow money on behalf of the entire nation.

Other clauses permit Congress to establish an army and navy, and to pay for them. Article I also places the power to declare war in the Congress. The final clause of Article I, section 8 creates some additional breadth. It says that Congress can make other laws too, but only those that are "necessary and proper" for acting upon the specified powers. In other words, Congress cannot simply make a law about any subject it wishes, for example — marriage. However, Congress could make a law about the price of postage stamps because section 7 gives it the power to establish post offices.

Difficulties arise when both the federal government and state governments pass legislation that is, arguably, within their respective powers. The Supremacy Clause of the Constitution contained in Article VI clearly states that when Congress is operating within its authority under the Constitution, the laws it makes are supreme to those of any state. Sometimes, the state law may be considered unconstitutional because it interferes with a federal law. At other times, the question is whether Congress means to "preempt" the field.

The case is clear when federal legislation is properly authorized and it contains an explicit preemption clause. Often, however, the intent of Congress is ambiguous. It may be willing to live with concurrent state legislation, so long as the state law does not conflict with the federal law. In the end, courts are called upon to rule, and such rulings — ironically — often turn on judicial attempts to determine what Congress intended. Consider the following cases, paying particular attention to the specific question the Court is addressing.

Crosby v. Nat'l Foreign Trade Council
530 U.S. 363 (2000)

Souter, J.

The issue is whether the Burma law of the Commonwealth of Massachusetts, restricting the authority of its agencies to purchase goods or services from companies doing business with Burma, is invalid under the Supremacy Clause of the National Constitution owing to its threat of frustrating federal statutory objectives. We hold that it is.

I

In June 1996, Massachusetts adopted An Act Regulating State Contracts with Companies Doing Business with or in Burma (Myanmar). The statute generally bars state entities from buying goods or services from any person (defined to include a business organization) identified on a restricted purchase list of those doing business with Burma. Although the statute has no general provision for waiver or termination of its ban, it does exempt from boycott any entities present in Burma solely to report the news, or to provide international telecommunication goods or services, or medical supplies.

There are three exceptions to the ban: (1) if the procurement is essential, and without the restricted bid, there would be no bids or insufficient competition; (2) if the procurement is of medical supplies; and (3) if the procurement efforts elicit no comparable low bid or offer by a person not doing business with Burma, meaning an offer that is no more than 10 percent greater than the restricted bid. To enforce the ban, the Act requires petitioner Secretary of Administration and Finance to maintain a restricted purchase list of all firms doing business with Burma.

In September 1996, three months after the Massachusetts law was enacted, Congress passed a statute imposing a set of mandatory and conditional sanctions on Burma.

First, it imposes three sanctions directly on Burma. It bans all aid to the Burmese Government except for humanitarian assistance, counternarcotics efforts, and promotion of human rights and democracy. Second, the federal Act authorizes the President to impose further sanctions subject to certain conditions. He may prohibit United States persons from new investment in Burma, and shall do so if he determines and certifies to Congress that the Burmese Government has physically harmed, rearrested, or exiled Daw Aung San Suu Kyi (the opposition leader selected to receive the Nobel Peace Prize), or has committed large-scale repression of or violence against the Democratic opposition. Third, the statute directs the President to work to develop a comprehensive, multilateral strategy to bring democracy to and improve human rights practices and the quality of life in Burma.

On May 20, 1997, the President issued the Burma Executive Order. He certified that the Government of Burma had committed large-scale repression of the democratic opposition in Burma and found that the Burmese Government's actions and policies constituted an unusual and extraordinary threat to the national security and foreign policy of the United States, a threat characterized as a national emergency. The President then prohibited new investment in Burma by United States persons, any approval or facilitation by a United States person of such new investment by foreign persons, and any transaction meant to evade or avoid the ban. The order generally incorporated the exceptions and exemptions addressed in the statute. Finally, the President delegated to the Secretary of State the tasks of working with ASEAN and other countries to develop a strategy for democracy, human rights, and the quality of life in Burma, and of making the required congressional reports.

II

Respondent National Foreign Trade Council (Council) is a nonprofit corporation representing companies engaged in foreign commerce; 34 of its members were on the Massachusetts restricted purchase list in 1998. Three withdrew from Burma after the passage of the state Act, and one member had its bid for a procurement contract increased by 10 percent under the provision of the state law allowing acceptance of a low bid from a listed bidder only if the next-to-lowest bid is more than 10 percent higher.

In April 1998, the Council filed suit in the United States District Court for the District of Massachusetts, seeking declaratory and injunctive relief against the petitioner state officials charged with administering and enforcing the state Act (whom we will refer to simply as the State). The Council argued that the state law unconstitutionally infringed on the federal foreign affairs power, violated the Foreign Commerce Clause, and was preempted by the federal Act. After detailed stipulations, briefing, and argument, the District Court permanently enjoined enforcement of the state Act, holding that it unconstitutionally impinge[d] on the federal government's exclusive authority to regulate foreign affairs.

III

A fundamental principle of the Constitution is that Congress has the power to preempt state law. Even without an express provision for preemption, we have found that state law must yield to a congressional Act in at least two circumstances. When Congress intends federal law to occupy the field, state law in that area is preempted. And even if Congress has not occupied the field, state law is naturally preempted to the extent of any conflict with a federal statute. We will find preemption where it is impossible for a private party to comply with both state and federal law, and where under the circumstances of [a] particular case, [the challenged state law] stands as an obstacle to the accomplishment and execution of the full purposes and objectives of Congress. What is a sufficient obstacle is a matter of judgment, to be informed by examining the federal statute as a whole and identifying its purpose and intended effects.

A

First, Congress clearly intended the federal Act to provide the President with flexible and effective authority over economic sanctions against Burma. It is simply implausible that Congress would have gone to such lengths to empower the President if it had been willing to compromise his effectiveness by deference to every provision of state statute or local ordinance that might, if enforced, blunt the consequences of discretionary Presidential action.

And that is just what the Massachusetts Burma law would do in imposing a different, state system of economic pressure against the Burmese political regime. As will be seen, the state statute penalizes some private action that the federal Act (as administered by the President) may allow, and pulls levers of influence that the federal Act does not reach. But the point here is that the state sanctions are immediate. This unyielding application undermines the President's intended statutory authority by making it impossible for him to restrain fully the coercive power of the national economy when he may choose to take the discretionary action open to him, whether he believes that the national interest requires sanctions to be lifted, or believes that the promise of lifting sanctions would move the Burmese regime in the democratic direction. Quite simply, if the Massachusetts law is enforceable the President has less to offer and less economic and diplomatic leverage as a consequence.

B

Congress manifestly intended to limit economic pressure against the Burmese Government to a specific range. The State has set a different course, and its statute conflicts with federal law at a number of points by penalizing individuals and conduct that Congress has explicitly exempted or excluded from sanctions.

C

Finally, the state Act is at odds with the President's intended authority to speak for the United States among the world's nations in developing a comprehensive, multilateral strategy to bring democracy to and improve human rights practices and the quality of life in Burma. Congress called for Presidential cooperation with members of ASEAN and other countries in developing such a strategy, directed the President to encourage a dialogue between the government of Burma and the democratic opposition, and required him to report to the Congress on the progress of his diplomatic efforts. As with Congress's explicit delegation to the President of power over economic sanctions, Congress's express command to the President to take the initiative for the United States among the international community invested him with the maximum authority of the National Government, in harmony with the President's own constitutional powers. This clear mandate and invocation of exclusively national power belies any suggestion that Congress intended the President's effective voice to be obscured by state or local action.

Because the state Act's provisions conflict with Congress's specific delegation to the President of flexible discretion, with limitation of sanctions to a limited scope of actions and actors, and with direction to develop a comprehensive, multilateral strategy under the federal Act, it is preempted, and its application is unconstitutional, under the Supremacy Clause.

* * *

Geier v. American Honda Motor Co., Inc.
529 U.S. 861 (2000)

Breyer, J.

This case focuses on the 1984 version of a Federal Motor Vehicle Safety Standard promulgated by the Department of Transportation under the authority of the National Traffic and Motor Vehicle Safety Act of 1966. The standard, FMVSS 208, required auto manufacturers to equip some but not all of their 1987 vehicles with passive restraints. We ask whether the Act pre-empts a state common-law tort action in which the plaintiff claims that the defendant auto manufacturer, who was in compliance with the standard, should nonetheless have equipped a 1987 automobile with airbags. We conclude that the Act, taken together with FMVSS 208, pre-empts the lawsuit.

In 1992, petitioner Alexis Geier, driving a 1987 Honda Accord, collided with a tree and was seriously injured. The car was equipped with manual shoulder and lap belts which Geier had buckled up at the time. The car was not equipped with airbags or other passive restraint devices. Geier and her parents, also petitioners, sued the car's manufacturer, American Honda Motor Company, Inc., and its affiliates (hereinafter American Honda), under District of Columbia tort law. They claimed, among other things, that American Honda had designed its car negligently and defectively because it lacked a driver's side airbag. The Court of Appeals found that those claims conflicted with FMVSS 208, and that, under ordinary pre-emption principles, the Act consequently pre-empted the lawsuit.

Several state courts have held to the contrary, namely, that neither the Act's express pre-emption nor FMVSS 208 pre-empts a "no airbag" tort suit. All of the Federal Circuit

Courts that have considered the question, however, have found pre-emption. One rested its conclusion on the Act's express pre-emption provision. Others have instead found pre-emption under ordinary pre-emption principles by virtue of the conflict such suits pose to FMVSS 208's objectives, and thus to the Act itself. We granted *certiorari* to resolve these differences. We now hold that this kind of "no airbag" lawsuit conflicts with the objectives of FMVSS 208, a standard authorized by the Act, and is therefore pre-empted by the Act.

In reaching our conclusion, we consider three subsidiary questions. First, does the Act's express pre-emption provision pre-empt this lawsuit? We think not. Second, do ordinary pre-emption principles nonetheless apply? We hold that they do. Third, does this lawsuit actually conflict with FMVSS 208, hence with the Act itself? We hold that it does.

We first ask whether the Safety Act's express pre-emption provision pre-empts this tort action. The provision reads as follows: "Whenever a Federal motor vehicle safety standard established under this subchapter is in effect, no State or political subdivision of a State shall have any authority either to establish, or to continue in effect, with respect to any motor vehicle or item of motor vehicle equipment[,] any safety standard applicable to the same aspect of performance of such vehicle or item of equipment which is not identical to the Federal standard."

We need not determine the precise significance of the use of the word "standard," rather than "requirement," however, for the Act contains another provision, which resolves the disagreement. That provision, a "saving" clause, says that "[c]ompliance with" a federal safety standard "does not exempt any person from any liability under common law." The saving clause assumes that there are some significant number of common-law liability cases to save. And a reading of the express pre-emption provision that excludes common-law tort actions gives actual meaning to the saving clause's literal language, while leaving adequate room for state tort law to operate, for example, where federal law creates only a floor, i.e., a minimum safety standard. We have found no convincing indication that Congress wanted to pre-empt, not only state statutes and regulations, but also common-law tort actions, in such circumstances. Hence the broad reading cannot be correct. The language of the pre-emption provision permits a narrow reading that excludes common-law actions. Given the presence of the saving clause, we conclude that the pre-emption clause must be so read.

The basic question, then, is whether a common-law "no airbag" action like the one before us actually conflicts with FMVSS 208. We hold that it does.

In petitioners' and the dissent's view, FMVSS 208 sets a minimum airbag standard. As far as FMVSS 208 is concerned, the more airbags, and the sooner, the better. But that was not the Secretary's view. DOT's comments, which accompanied the promulgation of FMVSS 208, make clear that the standard deliberately provided the manufacturer with a range of choices among different passive restraint devices. Those choices would bring about a mix of different devices introduced gradually over time; and FMVSS 208 would thereby lower costs, overcome technical safety problems, encourage technological development, and win widespread consumer acceptance all of which would promote FMVSS 208's safety objectives.

In effect, petitioners' tort action depends upon its claim that manufacturers had a duty to install an airbag when they manufactured the 1987 Honda Accord. Such a state law would have required manufacturers of all similar cars to install airbags rather than other passive restraint systems, such as automatic belts or passive interiors. It thereby would have presented an obstacle to the variety and mix of devices that the federal regulation sought. It would have required all manufacturers to have installed airbags in respect to the entire District-of-Columbia-related portion of their 1987 new car fleet, even though FMVSS 208 at that time required only that 10% of a manufacturer's nationwide fleet be equipped with any passive restraint device at all. It thereby also would have stood as an obstacle to the gradual passive restraint phase-in that the federal regulation deliberately imposed. In addition, it could have made less likely the adoption of a state mandatory buckle-up law. Because the rule of law for which petitioners contend would have stood as an obstacle to the accomplishment and execution of the important means-related federal objectives that we have just discussed, it is pre-empted.

Stevens, J., dissenting

Airbag technology has been available to automobile manufacturers for over 30 years. There is now general agreement on the proposition "that, to be safe, a car must have an airbag." The question raised by petitioner's common-law tort action is whether that proposition was sufficiently obvious when Honda's 1987 Accord was manufactured to make the failure to install such a safety feature actionable under theories of negligence or defective design. The Court holds that an interim regulation motivated by the Secretary of Transportation's desire to foster gradual development of a variety of passive restraint devices deprives state courts of jurisdiction to answer that question. I respectfully dissent from that holding, and especially from the Court's unprecedented extension of the doctrine of pre-emption.

It is evident that Honda has not crossed the high threshold established by our decisions regarding pre-emption of state laws that allegedly frustrate federal purposes: it has not demonstrated that allowing a common-law no-airbag claim to go forward would impose an obligation on manufacturers that directly and irreconcilably contradicts any primary objective that the Secretary set forth with clarity in Standard 208.

Our presumption against pre-emption is rooted in the concept of federalism. It recognizes that when Congress legislates "in a field which the States have traditionally occupied, we start with the assumption that the historic police powers of the States were not to be superseded by the Federal Act unless that was the clear and manifest purpose of Congress." The signal virtues of this presumption are its placement of the power of pre-emption squarely in the hands of Congress, which is far more suited than the Judiciary to strike the appropriate state/federal balance (particularly in areas of traditional state regulation), and its requirement that Congress speak clearly when exercising that power.

Because neither the text of the statute nor the text of the regulation contains any indication of an intent to pre-empt petitioners' cause of action, and because I cannot agree with the Court's unprecedented use of inferences from regulatory history and commentary as a basis for implied pre-emption, I am convinced that Honda has not overcome the presumption against pre-emption in this case.

* * *

Topics for Further Discussion

1. In his dissent in the *American Honda* case, Justice Stevens argued against allowing the federal government to interfere with state police power. However, in the dissent he joined in the *Lopez* case, he contended that the federal government does have constitutional power to pass a law involving schools, an area traditionally within state power. What is the difference between these two cases?

2. Compare the second clause of Article VI the Constitution (the Supremacy Clause) with the Tenth Amendment. Are all laws passed by the national government supreme? If not, which ones are supreme and how can they be distinguished from those that are not?

3. In *Printz v. United States*, 521 U.S. 898 (1997), the Supreme Court was called upon to decide whether certain provisions of the Brady Act requiring state officials to assist in the enforcement of federal gun control regulations were an unconstitutional intrusion on the sovereignty of the states. The majority held as follows:

> Congress cannot compel the States to enact or enforce a federal regulatory program. Today we hold that Congress cannot circumvent that prohibition by conscripting the State's officers directly. The Federal Government may neither issue directives requiring the States to address particular problems, nor command the States' officers, or those of their political subdivisions, to administer or enforce a federal regulatory program. It matters not whether policymaking is involved, and no case-by-case weighing of the burdens or benefits is necessary; such commands are fundamentally incompatible with our constitutional system of dual sovereignty.

* * *

The Congress cannot make a law by itself since the President must agree pursuant to Article I, section 7, clause 2. If the President does not agree, and vetoes the proposed law, the Congress can overcome his objection if two-thirds of its members agree to the legislation. Congress is divided into two sections: the House of Representatives and the Senate. In order to pass an ordinary bill, a majority in each house must agree. In order to overcome a Presidential veto, the two-thirds majority must be obtained in each house separately. In other words, the requirement is not two-thirds of all members of Congress; it is two-thirds of the House of Representatives and two-thirds of the Senate.

The number of seats in the House of Representatives is based on state populations, and presently has 435 voting seats. States with many people have more representatives in the House than do sparsely-populated states. However, each state—no matter how large or small—gets two Senators. This system creates a balance between a rather pure form of democracy based on population (the House) and one that recognizes the interest of each state as a political entity (the Senate). Bitter battles are often fought over apportionment of House of Representatives' districts, the number of people in each district (which should be about the same as any other), and the shape of the district (which should not be artificially manipulated to favor or disfavor a particular group). No such challenges can be mounted in Senate elections since the number of Senators is not defined by the population or size of the states. As a result, the roughly 785,000 residents of Delaware (the least populous state) and the 34,000,000 residents of California (the most populous state) have the same number of Senators (two), but greatly different numbers of representatives in the House. Delaware has only one; California has 53 according to the 2000 census.

Ironically, the District of Columbia, the place where the head offices of all three branches of the federal government are located, has no voting member in the Congress. This is because it is not a state. Rather, it was created out of the land of other states for the purpose of being a neutral seat of government. D.C. residents have waged a long campaign to revise that interpretation, as they are the only American citizens who have no right to elect full members of Congress. As a result of their efforts, the District is allowed to send an advisory delegate to the House of Representatives, but that delegate is prohibited from voting on legislation.

Article II

This article sets forth the role of the President. Despite the power that the position holds today, it was intended at the outset for the office to be rather weak. Having just fought a war to cast off the power of the British Crown, the last thing the Americans wanted was a strong, powerful political leader. Only late in the Constitutional Convention did they decide that the President should be elected independently, instead of chosen by Congress.

Eventually, the delegates decided on a system in which the President is afforded power independent of the legislature, but is unable to take extreme action without the assent of Congress. For example, as noted in the summary of Article I, the President has the ability to veto a bill. However, the veto is not absolute. His objections can be overcome by a two-thirds majority of both Houses. This compromise reveals the ambivalence the drafters of the Constitution felt toward the office of the President. In a famous speech, Benjamin Franklin argued for restraining the powers of the presidency. "The first man put at the helm will be a good one," he said, but "[n]o body knows what sort may come afterwards." The "first man" he was referring to was, without question, George Washington, the Revolutionary War hero. His popularity was such that many people wanted him to become the new king. Washington wisely declined and became the first President. As Franklin pointed out, the Constitution would need to set rules that would endure long after Washington was gone.

And so, Article II created an office of a chief executive who is also the "Commander in Chief of the Army and Navy...." His stated powers are quite few, and often require assent of the Senate. For example, he can only make treaties with the consent of two-thirds of the Senate under Article II, section 2, clause 2. He can nominate ambassadors and judges and other high officials (such as his cabinet members), but even those nominees must be approved by a majority of the Senate. He can appoint lower-ranking government officials by himself, but only if the Congress gives him that authority by law.

In fact, much of the President's power comes from the ambiguity of Article II. Executive power has served as the basis for a wide range of presidential action, as has the "Commander in Chief" language. Presidents have sent the military into battle around the world many times without a formal congressional declaration of war. They also routinely make "executive agreements" with other countries. These "agreements" are, many times, hard to distinguish from treaties except for the fact that the Senate never gets a chance to agree or disagree. The President both makes and executes the agreements by himself.

Structurally, too, the President enjoys a great advantage. He is the one and only chief executive and the one and only Commander in Chief. On the other hand, Congress consists (currently) of 435 members of the House of Representatives and 100 Senators. Thus, the President speaks with one voice, but the Congress with 535 different voices, each with its own point of view and political party perspective. As a result, many Presidents have been able to assert control while members of Congress fought amongst themselves.

Presidents often rely on their power as "Commander in Chief" of the military to justify actions involving armed conflict. As the following two cases indicate, the courts will generally defer to those claims, but not always.

Hirabayashi v. United States
320 U.S. 81 (1943)

Stone, C.J.

Appellant, an American citizen of Japanese ancestry, was convicted in the district court of violating the Act of Congress, which makes it a misdemeanor knowingly to disregard restrictions made applicable by a military commander to persons in a military area prescribed by him as such, all as authorized by an Executive Order of the President.

The indictment is in two counts. The second charges that appellant, being a person of Japanese ancestry, had on a specified date, contrary to a restriction promulgated by the military commander of the Western Defense Command, Fourth Army, failed to remain in his place of residence in the designated military area between the hours of 8:00 o'clock p. m. and 6:00 a.m. The first count charges that appellant, on May 11 and 12, 1942, had, contrary to a Civilian Exclusion Order issued by the military commander, failed to report to the Civil Control Station within the designated area, it appearing that appellant's required presence there was a preliminary step to the exclusion from that area of persons of Japanese ancestry.

Appellant asserted that the indictment should be dismissed because he was an American citizen who had never been a subject of and had never borne allegiance to the Empire of Japan, and also because the Act of March 21, 1942, was an unconstitutional delegation of Congressional power. On the trial to a jury it appeared that appellant was born in Seattle in 1918, of Japanese parents who had come from Japan to the United States, and who had never afterward returned to Japan; that he was educated in the Washington public schools and at the time of his arrest was a senior in the University of Washington; that he had never been in Japan or had any association with Japanese residing there.

The evidence showed that appellant had failed to report to the Civil Control Station on May 11 or May 12, 1942, as directed, to register for evacuation from the military area. He admitted failure to do so, and stated it had at all times been his belief that he would be waiving his rights as an American citizen by so doing. The evidence also showed that for like reason he was away from his place of residence after 8:00 p.m. on May 9, 1942. The jury returned a verdict of guilty on both counts and appellant was sentenced to imprisonment for a term of three months on each, the sentences to run concurrently.

The curfew order which appellant violated, and to which the sanction prescribed by the Act of Congress has been deemed to attach, purported to be issued pursuant to an Executive Order of the President. In passing upon the authority of the military commander to make and execute the order, it becomes necessary to consider in some detail the official action which preceded or accompanied the order and from which it derives its purported authority.

On December 8, 1941, one day after the bombing of Pearl Harbor by a Japanese air force, Congress declared war against Japan. On February 19, 1942, the President promulgated Executive Order No. 9066. The Order recited that "the successful prosecution of the war requires every possible protection against espionage and against sabotage to national-defense material, national-defense premises, and national-defense utilities." By virtue of the authority vested in him as President and as Commander in Chief of the Army and Navy, the President purported to "authorize and direct the Secretary of War, and the Military Commanders whom he may from time to time designate, whenever he or any designated Commander deems such action necessary or desirable, to prescribe military areas in such places and of such extent as he or the appropriate Military Commander may determine, from which any or all persons may be excluded, and with respect to which, the right of any person to enter, remain in, or leave shall be subject to whatever restrictions the Secretary of War or the appropriate Military Commander may impose in his discretion."

On March 2, 1942, General J. L. DeWitt promulgated Public Proclamation No. 1. The proclamation recited that the entire Pacific Coast "by its geographical location is particularly subject to attack, to attempted invasion by the armed forces of nations with which the United States is now at war, and, in connection therewith, is subject to espionage and acts of sabotage, thereby requiring the adoption of military measures necessary to establish safeguards against such enemy operations." It stated that "the present situation requires as a matter of military necessity the establishment in the territory embraced by the Western Defense Command of Military Areas and Zones thereof"; it specified and designated as military areas certain areas within the Western Defense Command; and it declared that "such persons or classes of persons as the situation may require" would, by subsequent proclamation, be excluded from certain of these areas, but might be permitted to enter or remain in certain others, under regulations and restrictions to be later prescribed. Among the military areas so designated by Public Proclamation No. 1 was Military Area No. 1, which embraced, besides the southern part of Arizona, all the coastal region of the three Pacific Coast states, including the City of Seattle, Washington, where appellant resided. Military Area No. 2. designated by the same proclamation, included those parts of the coastal states and of Arizona not placed within Military Area No. 1.

An Executive Order of the President of March 18, 1942, established the War Relocation Authority, in the Office for Emergency Management of the Executive Office of the President; it authorized the Director of War Relocation Authority to formulate and effectuate a program for the removal, relocation, maintenance and supervision of persons designated under Executive Order No. 9066, already referred to; and it conferred on the Director authority to prescribe regulations necessary or desirable to promote the effective execution of the program.

Congress, by the Act of March 21, 1942, provided: "That whoever shall enter, remain in, leave, or commit any act in any military area or military zone prescribed, under the authority of an Executive order of the President, by the Secretary of War, or by any military commander designated by the Secretary of War, contrary to the restrictions applicable to any such area or zone or contrary to the order of the Secretary of War or any such military commander, shall, if it appears that he knew or should have known of the existence and extent of the restrictions or order and that his act was in violation thereof, be guilty of a misdemeanor and upon conviction shall be liable" to fine or imprisonment, or both.

Beginning on March 24, 1942, the military commander issued a series of Civilian Exclusion Orders pursuant to the provisions of Public Proclamation No. 1. Each such order related to a specified area within the territory of his command. The order applicable to appellant was Civilian Exclusion Order No. 57 of May 10, 1942. It directed that from and after 12:00 noon, May 16, 1942, all persons of Japanese ancestry, both alien and non-alien, be excluded from a specified portion of Military Area No. 1 in Seattle, including appellant's place of residence, and it required a member of each family, and each individual living alone, affected by the order to report on May 11 or May 12 to a designated Civil Control Station in Seattle.

Executive Order No. 9066, promulgated in time of war for the declared purpose of prosecuting the war by protecting national defense resources from sabotage and espionage, and the Act of March 21, 1942, ratifying and confirming the Executive Order, were each an exercise of the power to wage war conferred on the Congress and on the President, as Commander in Chief of the armed forces, by Articles I and II of the Constitution. We have no occasion to consider whether the President, acting alone, could lawfully have made the curfew order in question, or have authorized others to make it. For the President's action has the support of the Act of Congress, and we are immediately concerned with the question whether it is within the constitutional power of the national government, through the joint action of Congress and the Executive, to impose this restriction as an emergency war measure.

Congress and the Executive, including the military commander, could have attributed special significance, in its bearing on the loyalties of persons of Japanese descent, to the maintenance by Japan of its system of dual citizenship. Children born in the United States of Japanese alien parents, and especially those children born before December 1, 1924, are under many circumstances deemed, by Japanese law, to be citizens of Japan. No official census of those whom Japan regards as having thus retained Japanese citizenship is available, but there is ground for the belief that the number is large.

The large number of resident alien Japanese, approximately one-third of all Japanese inhabitants of the country, are of mature years and occupy positions of influence in Japanese communities. The association of influential Japanese residents with Japanese Consulates has been deemed a ready means for the dissemination of propaganda and for the maintenance of the influence of the Japanese Government with the Japanese population in this country.

As a result of all these conditions affecting the life of the Japanese, both aliens and citizens, in the Pacific Coast area, there has been relatively little social intercourse between them and the white population. The restrictions, both practical and legal, affecting the privileges and opportunities afforded to persons of Japanese extraction residing in the United States, have been sources of irritation and may well have tended to increase their isolation, and in many instances their attachments to Japan and its institutions.

Viewing these data in all their aspects, Congress and the Executive could reasonably have concluded that these conditions have encouraged the continued attachment of members of this group to Japan and Japanese institutions.

* * *

Hamdi v. Rumsfeld
542 U.S. 507 (2004)

O'Connor, J.

On September 11, 2001, the al Qaeda terrorist network used hijacked commercial airliners to attack prominent targets in the United States. Approximately 3,000 people were killed in those attacks. One week later, in response to these "acts of treacherous violence," Congress passed a resolution authorizing the President to "use all necessary and appropriate force against those nations, organizations, or persons he determines planned, authorized, committed, or aided the terrorist attacks" or "harbored such organizations or persons, in order to prevent any future acts of international terrorism against the United States by such nations, organizations or persons." Soon thereafter, the President ordered United States Armed Forces to Afghanistan, with a mission to subdue al Qaeda and quell the Taliban regime that was known to support it.

This case arises out of the detention of a man whom the Government alleges took up arms with the Taliban during this conflict. His name is Yaser Esam Hamdi. Born an American citizen in Louisiana in 1980, Hamdi moved with his family to Saudi Arabia as a child. By 2001, the parties agree, he resided in Afghanistan. At some point that year, he was seized by members of the Northern Alliance, a coalition of military groups opposed to the Taliban government, and eventually was turned over to the United States military. The Government asserts that it initially detained and interrogated Hamdi in Afghanistan before transferring him to the United States Naval Base in Guantanamo Bay in January 2002. In April 2002, upon learning that Hamdi is an American citizen, authorities transferred him to a naval brig in Norfolk, Virginia, where he remained until a recent transfer to a brig in Charleston, South Carolina. The Government contends that Hamdi is an "enemy combatant," and that this status justifies holding him in the United States indefinitely—without formal charges or proceedings—unless and until it makes the determination that access to counsel or further process is warranted.

In June 2002, Hamdi's father, Esam Fouad Hamdi, filed the present petition for a writ of *habeas corpus*. The elder Hamdi alleges in the petition that he has had no contact with his son since the Government took custody of him in 2001, and that the Government has held his son "without access to legal counsel or notice of any charges pending against him." The petition contends that Hamdi's detention was not legally authorized. It argues that, "[a]s an American citizen, ... Hamdi enjoys the full protections of the Constitution," and that Hamdi's detention in the United States without charges, access to an impartial tribunal, or assistance of counsel "violated and continue[s] to violate the Fifth and Fourteenth Amendments to the United States Constitution." The *habeas* petition asks that the court, among other things, (1) appoint counsel for Hamdi; (2) order respondents to cease interrogating him; (3) declare that he is being held in violation of the Fifth and Fourteenth Amendments; (4) "[t]o the extent Respondents contest any material factual allegations in this Petition, schedule an evidentiary hearing, at which Petitioners may adduce proof in support of their allegations"; and (5) order that Hamdi be released from his "unlawful custody." Although his *habeas* petition provides no details with regard to the factual circumstances surrounding his son's capture and detention, Hamdi's father has asserted in documents found elsewhere in the record that his son went to Afghanistan to do "relief work," and that he had been in that country less than two months before September 11, 2001, and could not have received military training. The 20-year-old was traveling on his own for the first time, his father says, and "[b]ecause of his lack of experience, he was trapped in Afghanistan once that military campaign began."

The Government filed a declaration from one Michael Mobbs (hereinafter "Mobbs Declaration"), who identified himself as Special Advisor to the Under Secretary of Defense for Policy. Mobbs set forth what remains the sole evidentiary support that the Government has provided to the courts for Hamdi's detention. The declaration states that Hamdi "traveled to Afghanistan" in July or August 2001, and that he thereafter "affiliated with a Taliban military unit and received weapons training." It asserts that Hamdi "remained with his Taliban unit following the attacks of September 11" and that, during the time when Northern Alliance forces were "engaged in battle with the Taliban," "Hamdi's Taliban unit surrendered" to those forces, after which he "surrender[ed] his Kalishnikov assault rifle" to them. The Mobbs Declaration also states that, because al Qaeda and the Taliban "were and are hostile forces engaged in armed conflict with the armed forces of the United States," "individuals associated with" those groups "were and continue to be enemy combatants."

The threshold question before us is whether the Executive has the authority to detain citizens who qualify as "enemy combatants." There is some debate as to the proper scope of this term, and the Government has never provided any court with the full criteria that it uses in classifying individuals as such. It has made clear, however, that, for purposes of this case, the "enemy combatant" that it is seeking to detain is an individual who, it alleges, was "'part of or supporting forces hostile to the United States or coalition partners'" in Afghanistan and who "'engaged in an armed conflict against the United States'" there. We therefore answer only the narrow question before us: whether the detention of citizens falling within that definition is authorized.

While the full protections that accompany challenges to detentions in other settings may prove unworkable and inappropriate in the enemy-combatant setting, the threats to military operations posed by a basic system of independent review are not so weighty as to trump a citizen's core rights to challenge meaningfully the Government's case and to be heard by an impartial adjudicator.

In so holding, we necessarily reject the Government's assertion that separation of powers principles mandate a heavily circumscribed role for the courts in such circumstances. Indeed, the position that the courts must forgo any examination of the individual case and focus exclusively on the legality of the broader detention scheme cannot be mandated by any reasonable view of separation of powers, as this approach serves only to condense power into a single branch of government. We have long since made clear that a state of war is not a blank check for the President when it comes to the rights of the Nation's citizens. Whatever power the United States Constitution envisions for the Executive in its exchanges with other nations or with enemy organizations in times of conflict, it most assuredly envisions a role for all three branches when individual liberties are at stake. Likewise, we have made clear that, unless Congress acts to suspend it, the Great Writ of *habeas corpus* allows the Judicial Branch to play a necessary role in maintaining this delicate balance of governance, serving as an important judicial check on the Executive's discretion in the realm of detentions. Thus, while we do not question that our due process assessment must pay keen attention to the particular burdens faced by the Executive in the context of military action, it would turn our system of checks and balances on its head to suggest that a citizen could not make his way to court with a challenge to the factual basis for his detention by his government, simply because the Executive opposes making available such a challenge. Absent suspension of the writ by Congress, a citizen detained as an enemy combatant is entitled to this process.

Any process in which the Executive's factual assertions go wholly unchallenged or are simply presumed correct without any opportunity for the alleged combatant to demonstrate otherwise falls constitutionally short. The "some evidence" standard has been employed by courts in examining an administrative record developed after an adversarial proceeding— one with process at least of the sort that we today hold is constitutionally mandated in the citizen enemy-combatant setting. This standard therefore is ill suited to the situation in which a *habeas* petitioner has received no prior proceedings before any tribunal and had no prior opportunity to rebut the Executive's factual assertions before a neutral decisionmaker.

Today we are faced only with such a case. Hamdi has received no process. An interrogation by one's captor, however effective an intelligence-gathering tool, hardly constitutes a constitutionally adequate factfinding before a neutral decisionmaker. Plainly, the "process" Hamdi has received is not that to which he is entitled under the Due Process Clause.

* * *

Topics for Further Discussion

1. Both the *Hirabayashi* case and the *Hamdi* case concerned American citizens. Do they both also involve wartime? When the President's "wartime" actions are supported by Congressional legislation, the courts are less likely to second-guess their content. What would be the constitutional reason for the courts to defer in such cases? What would the constitutional reasons be for not deferring?

2. Following the attacks on the World Trade Center in 2001, the U.S. military detained over 600 foreign nationals captured abroad at the Guantanamo Bay Naval Base in Cuba.

What if the detainees were not U.S. citizens and were not held on U.S. soil? Would the federal courts have power to review the detentions under these circumstances? This question was answered affirmatively in *Rasul v. United States*, 542 U.S. 466 (2004) ("Consistent with the historic purpose of the writ, this Court has recognized the federal courts' power to review applications for habeas relief in a wide variety of cases involving executive detention, in wartime as well as in times of peace.").

3. Congress reacted to these cases by passing the Detainee Treatment Act (DTA) at the end of 2005. Section 1005(e)(1) of the DTA provides in relevant part that "no court, justice, or judge shall have jurisdiction to hear or consider an application for a writ of habeas corpus filed by or on behalf of an alien detained by the Department of Defense at Guantanamo Bay, Cuba." The Supreme Court held in *Hamdan v. Rumsfeld*, 548 U.S. 557 (2006) that the DTA did not operate to divest the courts of jurisdiction over cases pending prior to the enactment of the statute. The Supreme Court also concluded that the military commissions formed to try alien detainees violated the Uniform Code of Military Justice and the Geneva Conventions.

4. As the cases indicate, claims of executive power often involve a conflict with the judicial branch. To what extent can the courts rule on another branch of government's understanding of its role? In the Watergate era, President Nixon claimed that tape recordings made in his office were protected by "executive privilege," and need not be turned over for prosecution of Nixon's aides. In *United States v. Nixon*, 418 U.S. 683 (1974), the Supreme Court ruled unanimously that a President's executive privilege is not absolute. The Court said the President must yield to the judicial branch's need for evidence in a criminal proceeding. The President complied with the ruling. Subsequently, as an ex-President, Nixon contested a Congressional act directing that presidential tapes and papers be turned over to the General Services Administration. The Supreme Court again ruled against him in *Nixon v. Administrator of General Services Administration*, 433 U.S. 425 (1977), holding the law's screening procedure made sure that any intrusion would be limited. More recently, Vice President Dick Cheney contended that he was not required to turn over certain information to investigators from Congress. The Supreme Court agreed with him in *Cheney v. U.S. District Court*, 124 S. Ct. 2576 (2004), a case that has been excerpted in Chapter 13.

Article III

Article III defines the power of the federal courts. "The judicial power," it states, "shall be vested in one Supreme Court, and in such inferior courts as the Congress may ... establish." Thus, it creates both independence and dependence in the same breath. Although not stated explicitly, "the judicial power" surely includes the ability to decide cases without regard to politics. Indeed, that is the reason why judges are given their jobs for life with a guarantee that their salary can never be cut.

The judicial power extends to cases involving the Constitution and laws made by Congress and the President. The doctrine of judicial review is firmly entrenched in American jurisprudence, but judges are required to defer to both the politically-made decisions of the elected branches, and the judicial precedents of the Supreme Court. Supreme Court Justices are not supposed to inject their own opinions or act as super-legislators. Beyond that, the very existence of federal courts other than the Supreme Court depends on Congress. They exist only because Congress wishes them to, and even then only under such jurisdictional rules as Congress may create.

Of course, the principal role of the courts is to decide how a particular law applies to a particular case. Often enough, the law (including the Constitution) is none too clear. This room for interpretation means that judges in fact enjoy a great degree of latitude in determining the meaning of laws. This has generated an ongoing debate about the proper way for judges to review governmental action. For example, should they put themselves in the role of legislators and try to imagine what the legislature intended? Or, should they simply look at the words that the legislators wrote? Or, should they also consider the context of the times and conditions under which the laws were written? Beyond that, judges are empowered to decide whether a statute or action violates the Constitution. American judges quite often tell the Congress or the Executive Branch "No." In other words, the law that Congress passed or the action that the Executive Branch took cannot be enforced because of Constitutional deficiencies.

Unlike most countries, the United States has a dual judicial system. The system created by the Constitution and Congress constitutes the federal courts. On the other hand, each state also has its own court system, often with three levels (a trial court, an appellate court and a court of last instance) similar to that of the federal system. Nevertheless, all judges—wherever they may be—are bound to obey the Constitution, the treaties of the United States, and all constitutional laws passed by the Congress. As noted in the discussion of Presidential power above, the President appoints judges of the federal courts with the advice and consent of the Senate. The selection (or popular election) of state court judges, and the length of their respective terms, is decided by the individual states.

In 2000, the Supreme Court of the United States took upon itself the task of deciding the winner of the Presidential election. Ballots in Florida had been contested, and the Florida Supreme Court ordered remedial action, including a recount requested by Democratic candidate Al Gore. Whichever candidate won Florida would become President. The Florida Supreme Court's decision interpreted Florida election law as to when ballots may be recounted. Ordinarily, election law matters (even those involving federal elections) are a state concern. Many observers expected the Supreme Court, with a large number of justices who were strong advocates of respecting the states' role in the federal system, not to become involved in the case. They were mistaken.

Bush v. Gore

531 U.S. 98 (2000)

Per curiam

On December 8, 2000, the Supreme Court of Florida ordered that the Circuit Court of Leon County tabulate by hand 9,000 ballots in Miami-Dade County. It also ordered the inclusion in the certified vote totals of 215 votes identified in Palm Beach County and 168 votes identified in Miami-Dade County for Vice President Albert Gore, Jr., and Senator Joseph Lieberman, Democratic Candidates for President and Vice President. The Supreme Court noted that petitioner, Governor George W. Bush asserted that the net gain for Vice President Gore in Palm Beach County was 176 votes, and directed the Circuit Court to resolve that dispute on remand. The court further held that relief would require manual recounts in all Florida counties where so-called "undervotes" had not been subject to manual tabulation. The court ordered all manual recounts to begin at once. Governor Bush and Richard Cheney, Republican Candidates for the Presidency and Vice Presidency, filed an emergency application for a stay of this mandate. On December 9, we granted the application, treated the application as a petition for a writ of *certiorari*, and granted *certiorari*.

The petition presents the following questions: whether the Florida Supreme Court established new standards for resolving Presidential election contests, thereby violating Art. II, § 1, cl. 2, of the United States Constitution and failing to comply with 3 U. S. C. § 5, and whether the use of standardless manual recounts violates the Equal Protection and Due Process Clauses. With respect to the equal protection question, we find a violation of the Equal Protection Clause.

The individual citizen has no federal constitutional right to vote for electors for the President of the United States unless and until the state legislature chooses a statewide election as the means to implement its power to appoint members of the Electoral College. History has now favored the voter, and in each of the several States the citizens themselves vote for Presidential electors. When the state legislature vests the right to vote for President in its people, the right to vote as the legislature has prescribed is fundamental; and one source of its fundamental nature lies in the equal weight accorded to each vote and the equal dignity owed to each voter.

The right to vote is protected in more than the initial allocation of the franchise. Equal protection applies as well to the manner of its exercise. Having once granted the right to vote on equal terms, the State may not, by later arbitrary and disparate treatment, value one person's vote over that of another.

Much of the controversy seems to revolve around ballot cards designed to be perforated by a stylus but which, either through error or deliberate omission, have not been perforated with sufficient precision for a machine to count them. In some cases a piece of the card—a chad—is hanging, say by two corners. In other cases there is no separation at all, just an indentation.

The Florida Supreme Court has ordered that the intent of the voter be discerned from such ballots. For purposes of resolving the equal protection challenge, it is not necessary to decide whether the Florida Supreme Court had the authority under the legislative scheme for resolving election disputes to define what a legal vote is and to mandate a manual recount implementing that definition. The recount mechanisms implemented in response to the decisions of the Florida Supreme Court do not satisfy the minimum requirement for non-arbitrary treatment of voters necessary to secure the fundamental right. Florida's basic command for the count of legally cast votes is to consider the "intent of the voter." This is unobjectionable as an abstract proposition and a starting principle. The problem inheres in the absence of specific standards to ensure its equal application. The formulation of uniform rules to determine intent based on these recurring circumstances is practicable and, we conclude, necessary.

Given the Court's assessment that the recount process underway was probably being conducted in an unconstitutional manner, the Court stayed the order directing the recount so it could hear this case and render an expedited decision. The contest provision, as it was mandated by the State Supreme Court, is not well calculated to sustain the confidence that all citizens must have in the outcome of elections. The State has not shown that its procedures include the necessary safeguards.

The Supreme Court of Florida has said that the legislature intended the State's electors to "participat[e] fully in the federal electoral process," as provided in 3 U. S. C. § 5. That statute, in turn, requires that any controversy or contest that is designed to lead to a conclusive selection of electors be completed by December 12. That date is upon us, and there is no recount procedure in place under the State Supreme Court's order that comports with minimal constitutional standards. Because it is evident that any recount seeking to meet the December 12 date will be unconstitutional for the reasons we have discussed, we reverse the judgment of the Supreme Court of Florida ordering a recount to proceed.

None are more conscious of the vital limits on judicial authority than are the members of this Court, and none stand more in admiration of the Constitution's design to leave the selection of the President to the people, through their legislatures, and to the political sphere. When contending parties invoke the process of the courts, however, it becomes our unsought responsibility to resolve the federal and constitutional issues the judicial system has been forced to confront.

Stevens, J., dissenting

The Constitution assigns to the States the primary responsibility for determining the manner of selecting the Presidential electors. When questions arise about the meaning of state laws, including election laws, it is our settled practice to accept the opinions of the highest courts of the States as providing the final answers. On rare occasions, however, either federal statutes or the Federal Constitution may require federal judicial intervention in state elections. This is not such an occasion.

The legislative power in Florida is subject to judicial review pursuant to Article V of the Florida Constitution, and nothing in Article II of the Federal Constitution frees the state legislature from the constraints in the state constitution that created it. Moreover, the Florida Legislature's own decision to employ a unitary code for all elections indicates that it intended the Florida Supreme Court to play the same role in Presidential elections that it has historically played in resolving electoral disputes. The Florida Supreme Court's exercise of appellate jurisdiction therefore was wholly consistent with, and indeed contemplated by, the grant of authority in Article II.

What must underlie petitioners' entire federal assault on the Florida election procedures is an unstated lack of confidence in the impartiality and capacity of the state judges who would make the critical decisions if the vote count were to proceed. Otherwise, their position is wholly without merit. The endorsement of that position by the majority of this Court can only lend credence to the most cynical appraisal of the work of judges throughout the land. It is confidence in the men and women who administer the judicial system that is the true backbone of the rule of law. Time will one day heal the wound to that confidence that will be inflicted by today's decision. One thing, however, is certain. Although we may never know with complete certainty the identity of the winner of this year's Presidential election, the identity of the loser is perfectly clear. It is the Nation's confidence in the judge as an impartial guardian of the rule of law.

* * *

Topics for Further Discussion

1. The Supreme Court majority employed an "Equal Protection" analysis to overturn the decision of the Florida Supreme Court on Florida law. Ordinarily, under equal protection, those who are treated less well under the law sue to receive the same treatment as others. These people would seem to be the voters whose votes were not counted in Florida. Instead, the Supreme Court used equal protection to protect voters whose votes had been counted. Is this a proper reason for the federal court to displace the decision of the Florida Supreme Court?

2. The Supreme Court issued a stay order on December 9, preventing a recount from going forward. If that was the reason why a recount could not be completed by the December 12

deadline, is the Court's argument less persuasive? A separate dissenting opinion indicated that December 12 was not, in fact, the deadline. According to state law, Florida's electors were to meet on December 18, allowing time for the U.S. Supreme Court to return the matter to Florida's jurisdiction to see if an appropriate recount could be conducted in time.

3. What would have happened if Vice President Gore and the Florida Supreme Court had refused to adhere to the Supreme Court's opinion on the grounds of illegitimacy? In fact, Mr. Gore did the opposite. Following the decision, he said, "Let there be no doubt, while I strongly disagree with the court's decision, I accept it. I accept the finality of this outcome which will be ratified next Monday in the Electoral College. And tonight, for the sake of our unity of the people and the strength of our democracy, I offer my concession."

Amendments

Amendments to the Constitution can be made in a number of ways. Most commonly, Article V allows for an amendment to the Constitution when passed by two-thirds majorities of the House and Senate and subsequently ratified by three-fourths of the state legislatures (currently 38 states). The intentional difficulty of the process has kept the number of amendments down to fewer than thirty in more than two hundred years.

After the Bill of Rights (the First Amendment through and including the Tenth Amendment), the most important amendments are called "The Reconstruction Amendments" passed just after the Civil War. The Thirteenth Amendment (1865) eliminates slavery. The Fourteenth Amendment (1868) guarantees "equal protection of the laws" to any "person" (not just citizens) as well as "due process of law." Over time, these phrases have been interpreted numerous times to create affirmative rights. The Fifteenth Amendment (1870) guarantees the unimpeded right to vote to every citizen, regardless of race. Women, however, were not included in this right to vote until the passage of the Nineteenth Amendment in 1920. An amendment near the end of the 20th century that would have explicitly eliminated legal differences based on gender failed to gather the support of enough states in time and, thus, did not take effect. As a result, the constitutional rights of women have largely come through interpretation of other constitutional provisions, most notably the Fifth and Fourteenth Amendments, and civil rights statutes.

Key Terms and Concepts

Adversarial System
Checks and Balances
Commerce Clause
Executive Privilege
Federalism
Inquisitorial System
Judicial Review
"Necessary and Proper"
Preemption
Separation of Powers
Supremacy Clause

Chapter 2

The Jury System

"I consider [trial by jury] as the only anchor ever yet imagined by man, by which a government can be held to the principles of its constitution."

Thomas Jefferson, Letter to Thomas Paine (1789)

The American legal system provides for three kinds of juries: (1) a trial jury, meaning a body of persons selected from the citizens of the area served by the court and sworn to try and determine by verdict questions of fact in a trial; (2) a grand jury, meaning a body of persons selected from the citizens of the jurisdictional area served by the court and sworn to determine whether the prosecutor has enough evidence to charge someone with a serious crime; and (3) a jury of inquest or coroner's jury; meaning a jury called by a coroner (government medical investigator) to determine whether an unexplained death requires a criminal investigation. This chapter will discuss trial juries and grand juries.

The U.S. Constitution guarantees a jury trial for certain civil cases in federal courts (Seventh Amendment), a grand jury for serious crimes in federal courts (Fifth Amendment) and for certain criminal cases in all courts (Sixth and Fourteenth Amendments). If a party has a right to a jury trial, and if the party asks for a jury trial when required, and if the case goes to trial, a jury will be selected. In a trial in the United States, this means a group of six to twelve persons (plus reserve jurors), selected at random from a large group of citizens for one trial only. This jury will make their decision in secret without participation by the judge, and its conclusions normally need not be justified to anyone.

The jury system is hundreds of years older than the United States. The first permanent English-speaking settlers in North America arrived in 1607 with a charter from King James I providing for their right to trial by jury. One of the acts that King George III listed in the Declaration of Independence as justifying rebellion against Great Britain was that of "depriving us in many cases, of the benefits of trial by jury." While the jury system seems natural to citizens of the United States, it often seems strange or inefficient to persons from other countries, including countries that once had the right to trial by jury. Some features of the American jury system may be unique reflections of American society, but other issues of the jury system arise whenever a society designs a system of justice.

The Roles of Judge and Jury in American Law

Countries in which there is no jury trial, or in which there is a system of professional judges and specially-trained "lay judges," often criticize the American jury system. Some of these attacks reflect misunderstandings, but others raise important questions about government and the administration of justice.

"Professional Judges Should Decide the Law"

Here U.S. courts agree 100%. Only judges decide the law in an American court. The jury in an American court does not decide the law, it decides the facts. The judge (with the influence of lawyers for each party) tells the jury in the form of jury instructions what the law is, the jury decides what the facts are (based on presentations by the lawyers in court), and then the jury applies the facts to the law during their secret deliberations.

"Professional Judges Should Decide the Facts"

Non-American commentators often assume that a judge who has graduated from the most prestigious university and who belongs to the proper social, political or economic class is more qualified to judge facts than the average citizen because the judge has shown that he is a pillar of society. But what are the facts in a typical civil case? They may be: "What did the plaintiff say to the defendant?" or "How fast was the truck going when it hit the car?" or "Which of the three doctors left the scissors inside the patient during surgery?" or "Which witness is lying?" or "How much money should the plaintiff get to compensate her for the scar on her face"? The facts often are unclear, or are subject to many interpretations. The jurors will always have a wider range of shared human experience and general knowledge about life and human nature than any one judge. And even if the judge had a Nobel Prize in physics, he would not necessarily be more able than the jury to determine how fast the truck was going, merely by listening to the evidence. The jury may also have specific personal skills to use in deciding the case. In one 1985 antitrust case between two huge U.S. telephone companies, in which the jury was required to determine damages based on complicated economic factors, *The Washington Post* newspaper reported that the jury included an engineer, a hearing system designer, an accountant, a purchasing agent, an aircraft mechanic, a chemist, a bank loan officer, a secretary, a college employee, an office clerk and a housewife. This jury undoubtedly brought more business, organizational, and economic experience to the verdict than any one judge could have done.

Still, the idea that ordinary persons are unable to comprehend complicated facts and arguments is common in many countries with a tradition of government by elite officials. United States courts are not immune to the same arguments. In the *SRI v. Matsushita* case below, SRI sued Matsushita, claiming that SRI's patent on complicated technology had been infringed. SRI requested a jury trial, but the district court decided that patent disputes were different and conducted a bench (judge-only) trial, awarding judgment to Matsushita. SRI appealed, and the U.S. Court of Appeals for the Federal Circuit reversed the District Court for errors of patent law. The excerpts from the case that follows deal only with the jury trial issue.

SRI Int'l v. Matsushita Electric Corp. of America
775 F.2d 1107 (Fed. Cir. 1985)

Markey, C.J.

Despite the clear directive of the Seventh Amendment—that "the right to jury trial shall be preserved"—one federal appellate court and three federal district courts have remanded or struck jury demands in "complex" civil cases, relying on a judge-created "complexity exception."

Proponents of a "complexity exception" say legally or factually complex matters, e.g., those appearing in some antitrust, securities, or patent cases, are "too complex" for juries to comprehend, and those cases should therefore be tried by a single judge.

Nor has anyone yet spelled out definitive, reliable criteria on which to determine clear boundaries for "simple," "complex but not too complex," and "too complex."

A second line of argument for a "complexity exception" is that trying a complex case before an "incompetent" jury denies the due process protection of the Fifth and Fourteenth Amendments. Proponents of that view argue that a jury "incapable" of understanding the evidence, or the legal rules to be applied, provides no "constitutional" safeguard against an "erroneous" result. The argument confuses the route with the destination, for "due process" is just that, a process. It is an important and constitutionally required process. It is not a result.

That juries have been eliminated from most civil litigation in Great Britain is of little if any relevance to the present discussion. The training and recruitment of judges in that country differs substantially from our own, and there is no Seventh Amendment requirement that the right to jury trial be preserved.

One commentator, apparently recognizing that not all judges are inevitably more competent than all juries, has suggested that the "complexity exception" should encompass judges. Empirical support is simply lacking for the assumption that the process provided in a properly conducted jury trial is necessarily less "due" than that provided in a bench trial.

However some may view what they see as a "better system," and however one may weigh its effect on the due process clauses of the Fifth and Fourteenth Amendments, judges are nowhere authorized to exercise their personal predilection by revising or repealing the Seventh Amendment.

The call for injection of "expertise" into our jurisprudence can be as alluring, and as fatal, as the sirens' song. Exhibiting no desire to convert our jurisprudence into "juriscience," Congress has repeatedly rejected calls for "specialized" courts limited to decision making solely on technological considerations, and has cautiously limited reliance on "expertise" to its employment by administrative agencies.

The Ninth Circuit, in which sits the district court in this case, has repeatedly rejected calls for a "complexity exception," stating that "we do not believe any case is so overwhelmingly complex that it is beyond the abilities of a jury." The Seventh and Fifth Circuits have reserved judgment on the constitutionality of a complexity exception and have declined to apply it. No circuit has affirmed an actual jury denial on the ground of complexity.

We discern no authority and no compelling need to apply in patent infringement suits for damages a "complexity" exception denying litigants their constitutional right under the Seventh Amendment. There is no peculiar cachet which removes "technical" subject matter from the competency of a jury when competent counsel have carefully marshaled and presented the evidence of that subject matter and a competent judge has supplied carefully prepared instructions.

In the case at bar, the district court indicated that this court had distinguished between fact issues "appropriate" for a jury and those "appropriate" for a judge. There is, however, no such distinction in the Seventh Amendment. Fact issues are no less such because they are "complex" or "ultimate." The district court, in announcing its decision to deny a jury trial and employ a bench trial, said "these questions" could be resolved in that way "more economically and expeditiously." But whether judicial economy and expedition might be served is irrelevant. The Seventh Amendment contains no "economy" exception.

* * *

Topics for Further Discussion

1. Chief Judge Markey commented in the notes to his opinion:

> We have found no suggestion that persons charged with crime should be denied their Sixth Amendment right to a jury trial, though some criminal trials involve highly complex matters of law and fact. It appears at least incongruous to suggest that a person may with due process be deprived of life or liberty following a complex criminal trial by jury, but cannot with due process be deprived of a property interest following a complex civil trial by jury.... Judges in 1791 were among the very few who were educated. The Seventh Amendment brings the people into our jurisprudential system. In almost 200 years, while society grew more complex, the education and work experience of the people advanced as well. It is clear that juries will necessarily differ in "competence," but it is at best incongruous to suggest that a society that sends its citizens routinely into space could never produce a jury competent to determine a case some judge might consider too "complex" for people with "common experience" to decide.

Are there subjects that are "too complex" for 12 ordinary people to understand?

2. How does the jury system in complex trials affect the skills a lawyer needs to win a case?

"Trial by a Judge Is More Impartial"

Some say that a single judge is more likely to be less prejudiced for or against parties than the average citizen. It is probably more accurate to say that in a trial by judge there are fewer prejudiced people to find the facts, but not necessarily less prejudiced people. American jurors are repeatedly lectured on doing their duty as jurors, without allowing their personal prejudices to guide them, by the judge, the lawyers, and society in general. Good lawyers can eliminate the most prejudiced people before they become jurors. Even if one juror dislikes persons of a certain skin color, or thinks corporations make too much money, or believes that the police are too strong, that person is only one of six to 12 jurors. Furthermore, during their secret discussions to decide the case, the other jurors commonly ask each member of the jury to defend their reasoning. There will probably be group pressure on a juror who refuses to change to the majority opinion due to prejudice rather than due to a discussion of the evidence and presentations in court.

American lawyers in general do not approve of the "professional juror" or "lay judge" system of some civil law countries in which "reliable" citizens "assist" the judge to reach a decision. From the American perspective, "lay judge" systems do not provide a true jury of the peers of the party and are subject to pressure from the professional judge as well as from public opinion. An American jury's discussions are secret even from the judge. Federal rules forbid a judge to ask about the content of federal jury discussions, except to determine whether there was any attempt to influence jurors by persons or sources outside the jury room.

Some think that the American jury is prejudiced against non-Americans, and that a judge is more likely to find in favor of an international party. However, a detailed study of lawsuits in federal courts, appearing in the *Harvard Law Review* of March 1996, found that foreign plaintiffs won 64.37% of trials, foreign defendants won 50.66% of trials, and American parties won 52.88% of trials. The authors of the study concluded that "The available data indicate that foreigners do very well in the federal courts. They win a higher percentage of their cases, whether as plaintiff or as defendant, than do their domestic counterparts. Thus, the data offer no support for the existence of xenophobic bias in American courts."

"Trial by a Judge Is More Efficient"

Most lawsuits are settled before trial, and most trials are not jury trials. When there is a jury trial, it is often time-consuming and expensive. Jurors must be selected and questioned, sometimes for many hours. They must be given a place to sit and to discuss the trial in private. If the trial is long or the judge orders the jury "sequestered," meaning "isolated from the public," each juror must be given meals and sometimes a hotel room until the end of the trial. Employees must be hired to take care of the jurors, and money must be spent on jury facilities. After all this expense, a jury sometimes cannot reach a verdict. Critics have said that bench trials (in which there is a judge but no jury) are more convenient and less expensive. In most civil suits, the parties actively consider the cost and length of a jury trial against the much lower cost and arguably more efficient procedures of a bench trial. The economics often convince a party not to request a jury trial. Courts in the United States regularly experiment with new ways to save money and time in jury trial administration.

"A Judge Is More Independent"

Commentators from the civil law countries sometimes believe that a well-educated, highly respected individual is more likely to be willing to make an unpopular decision than a group of ordinary people. In fact, a generally anonymous group of ordinary people who make their decision and disappear from public view are more likely to give an independent decision than a civil law judge worried about the effect of an unpopular decision on his reputation, family, and career. Citizens of the United States have never believed that a single government official, without control by the people, can be trusted to be independent. As Thomas Jefferson wrote in 1789: "We all know that permanent judges acquire an *esprit de corps*; that, being known, they are liable to be tempted by bribery; that they are misled by favor, by relationship, by a spirit of party, by a devotion to the Executive or Legislative."

"Trial by a Judge Upholds Respect for the Law"

European commentators sometimes ask how anyone can have respect for the law in the United States when the jury is dressed in ordinary clothes, includes people without a college education, who are poor, or members of a minority, or work with their hands for a living. These commentators feel that a judge in the starched robes and wig of a European jurist is much more likely to inspire respect for the judicial system. However, the American view is that a jury made up of ordinary people representing no particular class or party, deciding the lawsuits of their fellow citizens, is much more likely to inspire respect for the judicial system among all people, not just those of the top social, political or economic class.

History shows that the loss of the right to a jury trial is connected to the loss of other freedoms and ultimately a loss of support for the judicial process. Hitler and 3000 Nazi supporters marched through Munich in 1923; Germany abolished trial by jury in 1924. France surrendered its territory to the Nazis in 1940. The Vichy government of France gave up trial by jury in 1941. In Japan, a democratic government enacted trial by jury in 1923 and, 500 criminal jury trials later, a military government suspended jury trials in 1943. Russia had jury trials until 1917, but juries were abolished during the Soviet Union era. Under Soviet communism, judges were seen a tool of the State, often sending citizens to prison without a fair trial. After more than 70 years of communist rule, Russia has revived jury trials so citizens will trust their courts once again. Spain had jury trials before the fascist dictatorship of Generalissimo Franco, but abolished them for more than forty years. Spain's judges also became servants of the dictatorship. Like Russia, Spain and Japan have returned to jury trials to revive popular support for the rule of law. Xinhua, a wire service in the People's Republic of China, reported a speech to the National People's Congress, urging that "participation of jurors selected from the general public in court trials is an important way for people to take part in national governance, and will help build a clean and fair judicial system."

Right to Trial by Jury

A party must request a jury trial at the proper time in the civil or criminal case, or lose the right to trial by jury. When does the party have a right to a jury trial? We will examine the grounds of the right in civil and criminal trials.

Civil Cases

For civil suits, the party requesting a trial must first be in a federal court, or in the court of a state that provides for jury trial in civil suits. This follows from the fact that the Supreme Court has never required that the Seventh Amendment be "incorporated," that is, made binding on state governments as a fundamental right through the Fourteenth Amendment. The Seventh Amendment states that "In suits at common law ... the right of trial by jury shall be preserved." At the time the Seventh Amendment was adopted, most states, for historical reasons, had two parallel systems of justice, the system of "common law" courts, and the system of "equity" courts. However, nearly all states "merged" the two systems of law and equity into one system in the 20th century or earlier, making it difficult for a party in the 21st century to know what kind of "suits at common law" the Constitution meant in 1791. Adding to the problem of interpreting the Seventh Amendment is that more than two hundred years of American laws have created new causes of action and new kinds of lawsuits that did not exist in 1791. Some of these newly-created rights of action are of the type where a plaintiff probably would want the right to a jury trial: union collective bargaining, antitrust suits and discrimination in housing are three issues considered by the courts. In a stockholder's derivative suit, a shareholder sues a corporation's management on behalf of the corporation for breach of duty, combining what would probably have been both equitable and legal issues. *Ross v. Bernhard,* below, considers the right to a jury trial for the modern shareholder's derivative suit.

Ross v. Bernhard
396 U.S. 531 (1970)

White, J.

The Seventh Amendment to the Constitution provides that in "suits at common law, where the value in controversy shall exceed twenty dollars, the right of trial by jury shall be preserved." Whether the Amendment guarantees the right to a jury trial in stockholders' derivative actions is the issue now before us.

We hold that the right to jury trial attaches to those issues in derivative actions as to which the corporation, if it had been suing in its own right, would have been entitled to a jury.

We have noted that the derivative suit has dual aspects: first, the stockholder's right to sue on behalf of the corporation, historically an equitable matter; second, the claim of the corporation against directors or third parties on which, if the corporation had sued and the claim presented legal issues, the company could demand a jury trial. The claim pressed by the stockholder against directors or third parties "is not his own but the corporation's." The corporation is a necessary party to the action; without it the case cannot proceed. Although named a defendant, it is the real party in interest, the stockholder being at best the nominal plaintiff. The proceeds of the action belong to the corporation and it is bound by the result of the suit. The heart of the action is the corporate claim. If it presents a legal issue, one entitling the corporation to a jury trial under the Seventh Amendment, the right to a jury is not forfeited merely because the stockholder's right to sue must first be adjudicated as an equitable issue triable to the court.

Stewart, J., dissenting

The Seventh Amendment, by its terms, does not extend, but merely preserves the right to a jury trial "in Suits at common law." All agree that this means the reach of the Amendment is limited to those actions that were tried to the jury in 1791 when the Amendment was adopted. Suits in equity, which were historically tried to the court, were therefore unaffected by it. Since, as the Court concedes, a shareholder's derivative suit could be brought only in equity, it would seem to me to follow by the most elementary logic that in such suits there is no constitutional right to a trial by jury. Today the Court tosses aside history, logic, and over 100 years of firm precedent to hold that the plaintiff in a shareholder's derivative suit does indeed have a constitutional right to a trial by jury. This holding has a questionable basis in policy and no basis whatever in the Constitution.

* * *

Topics for Further Discussion

1. It has been said that in a federal civil suit, the Supreme Court determines whether a party can have a jury trial today by deciding whether that party could have had a jury trial in 1791. What problems do you see with this approach?

2. Why does Justice White say the shareholder is at best a nominal plaintiff in a derivative lawsuit?

Criminal Cases

The right to trial by jury in federal criminal cases is guaranteed several times by the Constitution: in Article III, section 2, clause 3 ("The trial of all crimes, except in cases of impeachment, shall be by jury") and in the Sixth Amendment ("In all criminal prosecutions, the accused shall enjoy the right to a speedy and public trial, by an impartial jury of the State and district wherein the crime shall have been committed"). Most state constitutions, following English law, require trial by jury in all criminal cases. However, the constitution of Louisiana, a state with a legal system based on French law, at one time required a jury trial only for crimes punishable by hard labor or the death penalty. The Supreme Court concluded in *Duncan v. Louisiana*, 391 U.S. 145 (1968) that the Constitution requires each state to offer the accused a jury trial in all serious criminal cases because "the deep commitment of the Nation to the right of jury trial in serious criminal cases as a defense against arbitrary law enforcement qualifies for protection under the Due Process Clause of the Fourteenth Amendment, and must therefore be respected by the States." As a result of *Duncan*, many of the cases before the Supreme Court have involved the question of which criminal penalties are "serious" enough to require a jury trial. Another line of cases concerns whether civil commitment proceedings to confine someone as mentally incompetent or as a sex offender are "serious criminal cases;" the courts have denied a constitutional right to a jury trial in each of these two examples. These cases and other issues relating to trial by jury in criminal cases are discussed in greater detail in Chapter 10.

Selection of the Trial Jury

The *Venire*

The list from which jurors are ultimately selected is called the *venire* (part of a Latin phrase meaning "to cause to come"). Jurors were at one time selected only from lists of voters in the court district, but this method meant that too few jurors were selected from classes of people less likely to be registered, including persons who had difficulty registering to vote, persons who moved frequently and could not satisfy the voter registration residence requirements, persons uninterested in politics, and persons from economic or social classes with low voter registration. As a result, many states have expanded the search for jurors to include persons found in the court district as a result of searching driver's license records. California, for example, at the time of this writing also searches utility company bills and the telephone directory to find a representative cross section of the population.

From the large number of potential jurors, certain persons are eliminated. Some states automatically exempt policemen, firemen, public officials, doctors, lawyers and others. The more recent trend is not to exempt automatically any person. Currently, the California Trial Jury Selection and Management Act, a typical modern law, states that "[n]o eligible person shall be exempt from service as a trial juror by reason of occupation, race, color, religion, sex, national origin, economic status, or sexual orientation, or for any other reason" except: (a) persons who are not U.S. citizens; (b) persons who are not at least 18 years old; (c) persons who are not residents of the court district; (d) persons who have lost the right to vote because they were convicted of a felony; (e) persons who do not understand English (but English-speaking persons with hearing, vision or other bodily disabilities are not automatically excluded); (f) persons already on another jury; and (g) persons legally incapable of handling their own affairs.

There are no automatic excuses in California-type juror selection laws, but the law does provide for "hardship" excuses. A person requested to serve on a jury can ask the judge or the jury commission official to excuse them based on the argument that jury service would constitute a "hardship" on them. Such "hardships" could include having no reasonable transportation to the court house, excessive travel costs or distances to the court house, extreme financial burden, undue risk to property from the juror's absence, physical or mental weakness for those over age seventy, public health and safety, or an inability to find someone who can substitute for the juror in caring for another person (such as a child or sick person). Obviously residents living in downtown San Francisco, a major city, would be less likely to convince a judge to grant them an excuse on the basis of "excessive travel" or "inability to find a substitute" care giver than a person living in a remote California mountain community. A person can also request a one-year postponement for temporary health problems, to take a paid vacation, or for other personal affairs that cannot be rescheduled.

The *Voir Dire*

Persons eligible to be jurors may receive a command from the court (a "summons") every few years to appear as jurors, and, if they do not have a valid excuse, they must appear at a specified time in a specified court room and wait. In order to reduce the burden of appearing on the jury list, many states have adopted a "One Day or One Trial" system, under which a juror will only be called to court one day, unless selected for a trial. Most states do not pay potential jurors anything to answer the summons and wait at the courtroom. After the first day, most states pay a token amount to jurors. California's $15 a day plus $0.34 per mile ($0.21 per kilometer) of travel expenses is typical of the attitude that jury duty is a citizen's duty, not work. Most states make it illegal to fire a worker because the worker took time off for jury duty.

The potential juror may go home without having been asked to serve on a jury. In many cases, however, the potential jurors will be called in a group and examined for their suitability to serve in a process called the *voir dire* (from an old French legal phrase meaning "to speak the truth"). In federal courts and some state courts, the judge does the questioning. In other courts, the attorney for each party can ask questions after the judge has finished. Jurors can be challenged (prevented from serving) either "for cause" or through "peremptory" challenges.

Challenge for cause is similar to the system in most countries with a jury trial, because it seeks to remove potential jurors who are likely to be biased. California's law lists the standard challenges for cause based on implied bias:

1. The potential juror is a relative of any party, of any officer of a corporation that is a party, of a witness, of a victim, or of an attorney in the case;

2. The potential juror is a landlord, tenant, employer, employee, principal, agent, debtor, creditor, partner, surety, shareholder or bondholder, attorney or client of either party, of any officer of a corporation that is a party, or any attorney of a party;

3. The potential juror has been a juror in a previous case involving either of the parties, or a similar crime or cause of action;

4. The potential juror has a personal interest in the outcome of the case, other than as a citizen or taxpayer;

5. The potential juror has already made a judgment based on knowledge of some of the facts of the case; and

6. The potential juror's state of mind shows bias against or dislike of either party.

California does not list blindness, deafness or speech impediments as a "cause" disqualifying a potential juror, and provides for the use of service providers such as sign language interpreters and readers if the disabled juror is not otherwise challenged.

Trials in the United States since the 18th century have allowed limited peremptory (arbitrary) challenges by an attorney for either side that can be used to eliminate a potential juror without the attorney having to specify a reason. Peremptory challenges originated in England as a way to question jurors about their sympathies in political trials; however, England abolished peremptory challenges in 1988. The adversary system requires that each attorney try to achieve the most advantage for his client, but most trial attorneys are uneasy with accepting the judgment of a random group of up to twenty four people (if the jury is twelve persons plus twelve alternates) in determining the fate of their client. Trial attorneys often believe that certain jurors will be "better" for their client than others. Among some of the beliefs are that "fat people favor the defense and thin people favor the plaintiff," "women are distrustful of other women," "bankers will vote to convict the accused person," "engineers only see things in black and white," "men engage in sin more than women and forgive faster," "young rich people are the worst jurors in a criminal trial because they fear crime, love property, and have not suffered enough to be sympathetic to the accused person." In California, for example, in a civil case with two parties, each side is allowed six peremptory challenges, while in a criminal case where the death penalty may be applied, each side is allowed twenty peremptory challenges.

As a result of the peremptory challenge system, trial lawyers often spend weeks analyzing the jurors, or potential jurors, in a case to determine when to use their limited peremptory challenges. An entire industry of "jury consultants" exists to use statistics, detective work, psychology, economics, and other areas of knowledge in an attempt to pick the ideal jury, or to prevent one's opponent from obtaining a favorable jury. Many American personal injury lawyers who appeal to juries for large damage awards regard selecting the proper jury, or avoiding a bad jury, as the most important phase of the trial. There is a joke that "[in] England the trial begins with the selection of the jury and in America the trial ends with the selection of the jury."

Peremptory challenges were not a joke to a black suspect who was convicted by an all-white jury after blacks were excluded from the jury through the prosecutor's peremptory challenges. In *Batson v. Kentucky*, 476 U.S. 79 (1986), the Supreme Court held that due process prevented peremptory challenges based solely on race. *Batson* has caused continuing litigation concerning when peremptory challenges can be used without violating the Constitution. In the case below, a man identified as J.E.B. (the plaintiff's name is protected to maintain privacy) was found to be the father of a child and required to pay child support as a result of a verdict from an all-female jury from which all men had been excluded due to the prosecutor's use of peremptory challenges. The Supreme Court also points out that in a criminal case, the adversary system does not require that the prosecutor "win" the case; it requires that the prosecutor use peremptory challenges to select a fair and impartial jury.

J. E. B. v. Alabama
511 U.S. 127 (1994)

Blackmun, J.

In *Batson v. Kentucky*, this Court held that the Equal Protection Clause of the Fourteenth Amendment governs the exercise of peremptory challenges by a prosecutor in a criminal trial. The Court explained that although a defendant has "no right to a 'jury composed in whole or in part of persons of his own race,'" the "defendant does have the right to be tried by a jury whose members are selected pursuant to nondiscriminatory criteria." Since *Batson,* we have reaffirmed repeatedly our commitment to jury selection procedures that are fair and nondiscriminatory. We have recognized that whether the trial is criminal or civil, potential jurors, as well as litigants, have an equal protection right to jury selection procedures that are free from state-sponsored group stereotypes rooted in, and reflective of, historical prejudice.

Today we are faced with the question whether the Equal Protection Clause forbids intentional discrimination on the basis of gender, just as it prohibits discrimination on the basis of race. We hold that gender, like race, is an unconstitutional proxy for juror competence and impartiality.

Respondent maintains that its decision to strike virtually all the males from the jury in this case "may reasonably have been based upon the perception, supported by history, that men otherwise totally qualified to serve upon a jury in any case might be more sympathetic and receptive to the arguments of a man alleged in a paternity action to be the father of an out-of-wedlock child, while women equally qualified to serve upon a jury might be more sympathetic and receptive to the arguments of the complaining witness who bore the child." We shall not accept as a defense to gender-based peremptory challenges "the very stereotype the law condemns."

Discrimination in jury selection, whether based on race or on gender, causes harm to the litigants, the community, and the individual jurors who are wrongfully excluded from participation in the judicial process. The litigants are harmed by the risk that the prejudice that motivated the discriminatory selection of the jury will infect the entire proceedings. The community is harmed by the State's participation in the group stereotypes and the inevitable loss of confidence in our judicial system that discrimination in the courtroom causes.

Our conclusion that litigants may not strike potential jurors solely on the basis of gender does not imply the elimination of all peremptory challenges. Neither does it conflict with a State's legitimate interest in using such challenges in its effort to secure a fair and impartial jury. Parties still may remove jurors who they feel might be less acceptable than others on the panel; gender simply may not serve as a proxy for bias.

Equal opportunity to participate in the fair administration of justice is fundamental to our democratic system. It not only furthers the goals of the jury system. It reaffirms the promise of equality under the law—that all citizens, regardless of race, ethnicity, or gender, have the chance to take part directly in our democracy.

Scalia, J., dissenting

Even if the line of our later cases guaranteed by today's decision limits the theoretically boundless *Batson* principle to race, sex, and perhaps other classifications (which presumably would include religious belief), much damage has been done. It has been done, first and foremost, to the peremptory challenge system, which loses its whole character when (in order to defend against "impermissible stereotyping" claims) "reasons" for strikes must be given. The right of peremptory challenge is "an arbitrary and capricious right; and it must be exercised with full freedom, or it fails of its full purpose." The loss of the real peremptory will be felt most keenly by the criminal defendant. And make no mistake about it: there really is no substitute for the peremptory. *Voir dire* (though it can be expected to expand as a consequence of today's decision) cannot fill the gap. The biases that go along with group characteristics tend to be biases that the juror himself does not perceive, so that it is no use asking about them. It is fruitless to inquire of a male juror whether he harbors any subliminal prejudice in favor of unwed fathers.

And damage has been done, secondarily, to the entire justice system, which will bear the burden of the expanded quest for "reasoned peremptories" that the Court demands. Every case contains a potential sex-based claim. Another consequence, as I have mentioned, is a lengthening of the *voir dire* process that already burdens trial courts.

* * *

Topics for Further Discussion

1. It has been said that England has taken the view that if a jury does not contain people with a financial, family, or other previous relationship to a party, then each party will receive a "fair" trial. In other words, a party is entitled to an impartial jury, not a jury of saints without any prejudices. What is your view?

2. Peremptory challenges were uncontroversial for most of American history but are now the subject of divided opinions. The first black Supreme Court Justice, Thurgood Marshall, stated in *Batson* that the goal of eliminating racial discrimination in jury selection "can be accomplished only by eliminating peremptory challenges entirely," while the second black Supreme Court Justice, Clarence Thomas, joined in the *J.E.B.* dissent position that without peremptory challenges, a defendant would have no way to combat unconscious prejudice by a potential juror.

3. In *Berghuis v. Smith,* 559 U.S. ___, 130 S. Ct. 1382 (2010), Smith, an African-American, was tried by a jury chosen from between 60 and 100 individuals, only 3 of whom, at most, were African-American. At that time, African-Americans constituted 7.28% of the jury-eligible population, and 6% of the pool from which potential jurors were drawn. An all-white jury convicted Smith of second-degree murder and felony firearm possession, and the court sentenced him to life in prison with the possibility of parole. The Supreme Court rejected Smith's objection to the panel's racial composition, commenting that "No 'clearly established' precedent of this Court supports Smith's claim that he can make out a prima facie case merely by pointing to a host of factors that, individually or in combination, might contribute to a group's underrepresentation."

The Grand Jury

Grand juries function differently from civil or criminal trial juries. Since grand juries conduct their business in secret (to spare the reputation of persons unjustly accused of crimes), most people are unaware of their high level of activity. According to the Administrative Office of the United States Courts, in a typical 12-month period there were 9,873 federal grand sessions convened, involving a total of 65,237 defendants, with an average of 20 jurors per session, who spent an average of 5.1 hours per session.

Grand juries began as a way to place a citizens' barrier between prosecutors who may abuse their powers and persons accused of death penalty or felony crimes. The Fifth Amendment requires that in federal government prosecutions, a grand jury of citizens agree that the government has sufficient evidence to move ahead with criminal charges against a defendant and issue an "indictment" (formal charges). The Supreme Court decided in 1884 that the Fifth Amendment requires only the federal government, and not the states, to provide a grand jury. Some states require a grand jury indictment for all crimes, some for all felonies, some for death penalty crimes only, and about half of the states make the use of the grand jury optional. Some states use grand juries for civil investigations, such as checking the functioning of prisons or the honesty of the state government's expense accounting.

The fact that grand jury hearings are secret, and the fact that defense counsel is not allowed to be present (because there is no "accused" person yet), makes using the grand jury attractive in a variety of situations. These include cases where children are called as witnesses and would be unable to tolerate the vigorous cross-examination of a regular trial; where the prosecutor wishes to test a weak or doubtful case against the judgment of citizens before proceeding with a trial; where the accused person is himself powerful and the strength of a citizens' indictment is needed to counter that power; where the secrecy of the grand jury would allow police to arrest defendants as soon as they are indicted and before they are able to harm witnesses or run away; where the prosecutor is relying on undercover agents whose identity he wishes to protect; and where the defendant cannot be located and the statute of limitations for prosecution is about to expire unless there is an indictment.

Jurors on a grand jury, which often is made up of more than twelve people, may be asked to serve for as much as twenty hours per week in any one given year. They are selected at random from the general list of jurors and can be removed for cause or excused for hardship reasons. The jurors are usually questioned only by the judge and, since defense counsel is not present, there are no peremptory challenges to grand jurors.

Conduct of Trial Arguments

The major stages in civil and criminal trials are covered in other chapters, so we will focus here on the effect a jury has on the conduct of a trial. One obvious factor is that, unlike a judge, jurors do not earn a living listening to court cases. American juries would never consent to serving for the months or years a civil law court may take to hear witnesses in a judge-only trial. Another obvious factor is that jurors are ordinary people; unlike a judge, they are usually not able to listen for hours to lawyers talking in difficult-to-understand legal language.

Evidence

A detailed study of the rules of evidence in American trials is beyond the scope of this book, but it should be mentioned that many important rules of evidence exist to regulate the information given to a jury of ordinary people, not legal scholars. One of the most famous rules of common law evidence is the "rule against hearsay," which supposedly exists to prevent ordinary people from being confused about statements in court. Federal Rule of Evidence 801 states: "'Hearsay' is a statement, other than one made by the declarant while testifying at the trial or hearing, offered in evidence to prove the truth of the matter asserted." For example, Student A takes the witness stand and testifies "Yesterday Student B telephoned me and said that she went to the hamburger restaurant because the pizza shop was closed." If Student A's testimony is being offered to prove that Student B went to the hamburger restaurant, or that the pizza shop was closed, a typical judge would advise the jury "That last statement is hearsay and you must disregard it." However, if the statement were offered to show that Student B's telephone worked yesterday, or that Student B was alive yesterday, it would not be hearsay and the judge would allow it.

If during the trial the jurors hear improper statements or evidence from one lawyer, it is impossible to get the jury to forget what they heard, even if the judge gives an instruction to "disregard the witness' last statement" or "disregard that remark." So, the lawyers for each side will try to "object" immediately to evidence, as it is being presented, that they feel should not be allowed into the trial. Typically the judge will either decide immediately "objection sustained" or "objection denied," but when the matter is complicated the judge will ask the lawyers to consult with him where the jury cannot hear what is said.

Since expert witnesses testify on matters beyond the every day knowledge of the jurors, courts have been concerned that jurors may be misled by expert testimony. Lawyers will if possible attack the expert's credibility or supply their own expert with a different view, but the Supreme Court has underlined the judge's role as "testimony gatekeeper" in the *Kumho Tire* case below. In *Kumho Tire*, Carmichael and others were injured when a tire on their auto exploded. Carmichael sued Kumho, the maker of the tire, and based much of the case against Kumho on the testimony of an engineer, Carlson, who said the tire was defective. Kumho asked the U.S. District Court judge to exclude Carlson's testimony on the ground that Carlson's methodology failed to satisfy Federal Rule of Evidence 702, which states: "If scientific, technical, or other specialized knowledge will assist the trier of fact..., a witness qualified as an expert ... may testify thereto in the form of an opinion." The District Court granted Kumho's request and entered summary judgment in favor of Kumho. Carmichael appealed.

Kumho Tire Co., Ltd. v. Carmichael
526 U.S. 137 (1999)

Breyer, J.

In *Daubert v. Merrell Dow Pharmaceuticals, Inc.*, 509 U.S. 579 (1993), this Court focused upon the admissibility of scientific expert testimony. It pointed out that such testimony is admissible only if it is both relevant and reliable. And it held that the Federal Rules of Evidence "assign to the trial judge the task of ensuring that an expert's testimony both rests on a reliable foundation and is relevant to the task at hand." This case requires us to decide how *Daubert* applies to the testimony of engineers and other experts who are not scientists. We conclude that *Daubert*'s general holding—setting forth the trial judge's general "gatekeeping" obligation—applies not only to testimony based on "scientific" knowledge, but also to testimony based on "technical" and "other specialized" knowledge. We also conclude that a trial court may consider one or more of the more specific factors that *Daubert* mentioned when doing so will help determine that testimony's reliability. Applying these standards, we determine that the District Court's decision in this case—not to admit certain expert testimony—was within its discretion and therefore lawful.

Kumho Tire moved the District Court to exclude Carlson's testimony on the ground that his methodology failed Rule 702's reliability requirement. The court then examined Carlson's methodology in light of the reliability-related factors that *Daubert* mentioned, such as a "theory's testability," whether it "has been a subject of peer review or publication," the "known or potential rate of error," and the "degree of acceptance ... within the relevant scientific community." The District Court found that all those factors argued against the reliability of Carlson's methods, and it granted the motion to exclude the testimony (as well as the defendants' accompanying motion for summary judgment).

... [a]s the Court stated in Daubert, the test of reliability is "flexible," and Daubert's list of specific factors neither necessarily nor exclusively applies to all experts or in every case.

* * *

Topics for Further Discussion

1. Expert testimony is widely used in major trials in the United States, whether before a jury or a judge. The expert in *Kumho Tire* had an academic degree in engineering, but many experts will not have academic degrees in their field because they rely on long practical experience in the subject (such as a real estate appraiser) or because the field of expertise is not studied in universities. The party producing the expert in federal court must "qualify" the expert, meaning that it must satisfy the court that the "expert" satisfies Federal Rule of Evidence 702. To win the case, the lawyer for the party must also convince the jury that it should believe the "expert's" opinion.

2. Experts in most civil cases are hired by one of the parties, not appointed by the court. The party retaining the expert must pay the expert's fees (often several thousand dollars a day) and expenses. Some commentators criticize the use of paid experts as a "battle of the hired guns."

The Jury Verdict

Jury Instructions

After the closing arguments, the jury must decide the facts of the case and the damages awarded. Suppose one witness said a truck was driving faster than the speed limit, but another witness said the truck was driving within the speed limit? Usually, a judge will give the jury "instructions" telling the jury, in general terms, how to examine all the evidence to reach a conclusion. These instructions are often standardized by jurisdiction and by issue or by the type of lawsuit or crime charged. Moreover, they are usually based on discussions among judges, lawyers, and legal scholars. For example, the instructions below, used in the federal Eighth Circuit, explain to jurors what it means when a plaintiff in a civil case must prove its case by a "preponderance of the evidence."

> In deciding what the facts are, you may have to decide what testimony you believe and what testimony you do not believe. You may believe all of what a witness said, or only part of it, or none of it.

> In deciding what testimony to believe, you may consider the witness' intelligence, the opportunity the witness had to have seen or heard the things testified

about, the witness' memory, any motives that witness may have for testifying a certain way, the manner of the witness while testifying, whether that witness said something different at an earlier time, the general reasonableness of the testimony, and the extent to which the testimony is consistent with any evidence that you believe.

In deciding whether or not to believe a witness, keep in mind that people sometimes hear or see things differently and sometimes forget things. You need to consider therefore whether a contradiction is an innocent misrecollection or lapse of memory or an intentional falsehood, and that may depend on whether it has to do with an important fact or only a small detail.

The party who has the burden of proving a fact must provide it by the preponderance of the evidence. To prove something by the preponderance of the evidence is to prove that it is more likely true than not true. It is determined by considering all of the evidence and deciding which evidence is more believable. If, on any issue in the case, the evidence is equally balanced, you cannot find that issue has been proved. The preponderance of the evidence is not necessarily determined by the greater number of witnesses or exhibits a party has presented.

You may have heard of the term "proof beyond a reasonable doubt." That is a stricter standard which applies in criminal cases. It does not apply in civil cases such as this. You should, therefore, put it out of your minds.

There are usually specific instructions asking the juries to reach a "verdict," that is, a finding on each of the claims in dispute or each of the crimes charged, and an award of damages or determination of sentence. In civil cases, lawyers for the parties will draft jury instructions for the judge's approval on specific areas of liability and damages.

Outside Influence on Juries

The previous discussion indicates the care the American legal system takes to try to guarantee that jurors will decide a case based only on evidence properly admitted into a trial. However, the fact that jurors come from the local community and live in a society of increasingly mobile communications means that the jury system sometimes fails to produce a verdict based on evidence received in open court. In one famous case (later to be the basis of the television series and several movies called "The Fugitive"), Doctor Sam Sheppard claimed to have found his wife beaten to death and gave vague statements about a possible murderer. Sheppard was tried for murder. Jurors during the trial were able to read newspapers, watch television news, listen to radio, telephone friends, and talk to reporters—almost all of which loudly stated that Sheppard was a guilty "monster." In *Sheppard v. Maxwell*, 384 U.S. 333 (1966), the Supreme Court concluded that "due process requires that the accused receive a trial by an impartial jury free from outside influences" and ordered Sheppard released from prison unless new charges were filed.

A half century after the events of the *Sheppard* case, an executive of Tyco International was accused in a New York City criminal trial of stealing $600 million from Tyco, including having the company pay for personal expenses such as his two million dollar birthday party. After the close of arguments, the jury quickly split into 11 persons for a verdict of guilty and one 79-year-old juror for a verdict of innocent. In order to preserve the jurors' privacy, newspapers rarely publish the names of jurors. However, the *Wall Street Journal*, a prestigious newspaper, claimed that the 79-year-old juror had made an

"OK" sign to the defense and with that excuse identified her as Mrs. Ruth Jordan. The next day, the *New York Post*, a local paper famous for sensational reporting, put a drawing of Mrs. Jordan on the cover page and called her the "hold-out granny" and a "batty blue-blood." Mrs. Jordan began receiving angry telephone calls and letters from the public. With the jury reportedly less than 15 minutes away from returning a guilty verdict against the Tyco executive, the judge declared a "mistrial" (defective trial) due to outside pressure on Mrs. Jordan. After a trial lasting six months, hearing 48 witnesses and recording 12,000 pages of testimony, both the prosecutor and the defendants had to prepare for a new trial.

Removing outside opinions from the judgment of the jury is not a new problem. For more than 100 years, juries in major criminal cases were "sequestered," meaning that during a trial they were sheltered from outside society, housed and fed at government expense, and prevented from communicating with any person outside the court except in the presence of a court official. New York stopped requiring sequestration three years before the *Tyco* case because there were complaints about the cost to the government and the hardship to the jurors of being isolated. Without sequestration, monitoring the flow of information to jurors requires a strong judge and reporters willing to sacrifice a headline for the general good of society.

Split Juries and Hung Juries

At the time the Constitution was written a jury was twelve persons, whose verdict had to be unanimous. By law, the federal government and over forty states require a unanimous verdict to convict in a criminal case. Some states, however, allow conviction by split vote in criminal cases and others allow a criminal trial jury of less than twelve persons. The Supreme Court decided that an Oregon criminal conviction by a jury voting ten persons to convict, two to acquit was acceptable (*Apodaca v. Oregon*, 406 U.S. 404 (1972)) but that a criminal conviction by a six-person Louisiana jury, voting five to one, was against the Constitution because such a small jury had to be unanimous (*Burch v. Louisiana*, 441 U.S. 130 (1979)). In civil cases, some jurisdictions require a simple majority vote, others a two-thirds vote to award the plaintiff damages. A jury that is unable to put together a sufficient number of votes on either side of a case is called a "hung jury." If a jury informs the judge that it is "unable to reach a verdict," the judge will typically lecture the jury to be more cooperative, to think seriously about their own position and to listen to the arguments of other jurors. If this direction does not work, the judge may call a recess to let the jurors take a short time off from discussions. If, after a long period, perhaps several days, the jury is totally unable to reach a verdict (unanimous, two-thirds or majority as required by state law), a judge will declare a "mistrial." This means the trial process suffered a fatal defect and the trial must usually be held again with new jurors.

Announcing the Verdict

If a jury reaches a verdict, the foreman (representative) of the jury notifies the court. The jurors return to the court room from their private conference room and sit down. The judge asks: "Ladies and gentlemen of the jury, have you reached a verdict?" The foreman of the jury replies: "We have, Your Honor." The foreman hands the verdict to the judge. Next the foreman will usually read what the jurors decided, which must answer each of the questions to the jury contained in the judge's instructions. In a civil case, the verdict should determine whether the defendant is liable to the plaintiff, and if so, the nature and amount of damages. In a criminal case, the verdict determines guilt or innocence on each charge, and, in certain circumstances, the penalty to be imposed.

Damage Awards

Civil Damages

Under the "American rule" for legal costs, each party in a civil suit pays its own court and legal costs unless they agree otherwise. This is in contrast to the "English rule" by which the loser pays the legal and court costs of both parties in a civil suit. Some argue that the "English rule" prevents unnecessary or unworthy lawsuits, others argue that the "American rule" allows people who are not rich to use the courts to remedy a wrong done to them without fear of bearing the costs of both sides should they lose.

Damages in an American civil case can be "nominal," "punitive," or "compensatory." Nominal damages are token damages of a very small amount, usually $1.00, to a party that the jury found was injured, but who could not prove any actual monetary damage. "Punitive" damages are penalties against defendants to discourage similar malicious or repeatedly negligent actions, and may be many times the actual damages the party suffered. "Compensatory" damages are, as the name suggests, damages awarded to compensate for actual harm. A party in a civil case must prove the nature and amount of each item of compensatory damages to the jury by a "preponderance of the evidence."

Compensatory damages always include actual loss and usually also include other economic and non-economic losses. The types of damages that can be awarded are determined by the law under which the plaintiff is suing, or by the statutory or common law of the jurisdiction. For example, California Civil Code section 1431.2 recently provided for an award of "objectively verifiable monetary losses" and "subjective, non-monetary losses" including: (i) medical expenses; (ii) loss of earnings; (iii) burial costs; (iv) loss of use of property; (v) costs of repair or replacement; (vi) costs of obtaining substitute domestic services (i.e., cost of hiring a maid if the person who normally cleans the house is injured due to fault of the defendant); (vii) loss of employment; (viii) loss of business or employment opportunities; (ix) pain and suffering; (x) inconvenience; (xi) mental suffering; (xii) emotional distress; (xiii) loss of society and companionship (i.e., injury to a friend or family member that prevents them from participating in life with the plaintiff); (xiv) loss of consortium (i.e., loss of sexual relations with one's spouse due to injury); and (xv) injury to reputation.

The Controversial Damage Award System

The amounts awarded by American juries often astonish outside observers. Corporate executives routinely complain about large damage awards in civil actions when they lose as defendants (but not when they win as plaintiffs). There are many reasons why American jury awards are larger than what is typical in many civil law countries, such as the following:

1. Many Kinds of Damages are Allowed. The California list of fifteen types of civil damages, above, includes many that are often not compensated outside of the U.S. (e.g., "mental suffering," "loss of companionship").

2. Juries Know the Current Value of Money. Many civil law codes are generations old and the damages they give no longer reflect current wages or costs of living. Some civil law judges who award damages came from wealthy families and went from studying at a university directly to being a judge, so they may not have a realistic idea of wages or costs. In contrast, the working or retired people in an American jury are extremely well aware of prices.

3. American Lawyers May Receive a Percentage of the Damage Award. American lawyers who make a living in court are generally skilled at demonstrating all the damage a party has suffered, and in getting the jury to think about the amount of damage every minute in the injured party's future. When American personal injury lawyers represent a person who has been physically injured, they often do so for 33% or more of the damages awarded, but for free if the person loses the lawsuit (a "contingency fee") Therefore, they have great incentive to make sure juries award the maximum damages.

4. The U.S. is Expensive. Some types of damages, such as medical expenses and professional fees, are much more expensive in the United States than in most of the world.

5. American Laws use Damage Awards for Enforcement. Some U.S. laws use large damage awards as a method of enforcement. For example, three times the actual damages can be awarded to the plaintiff in an antitrust suit, and a percentage of the contract amount is awarded to persons who report fraud in government contracting.

Punitive Damages

Punitive damages in the United States are the subject of much comment, but are not necessarily representative of American justice. Punitive damages are awarded in only a small percentage of cases. Nevertheless, some legal theorists claim that there should be a strict separation between the damages in civil suits (which should restore the plaintiff to his position before the wrong to the extent possible) and punishment in criminal suits (which should exist to deter behavior that society views as negative or for purposes of retribution). Punitive damages, which use private suits to try to deter behavior that is not criminal but does harm society, are troubling because they do not fit neatly into the two theoretical categories of award. Indeed, several countries refuse to enforce American punitive damage awards as against their local public policy, in which only the State is allowed to punish a party.

Studies have shown that the types of negative business action that resulted in punitive damages awards were: (1) fraudulent misconduct; (2) knowing violations of safety standards; (3) inadequate testing and manufacturing procedures; (4) failures to warn of known dangers before marketing; and (5) post-marketing failures to remedy known dangers. American business executives have been criticizing punitive damage awards for the past 150 years, saying that such awards are irrational and raise the cost of doing business to intolerable levels. These issues were brought into focus by *Liebeck v. McDonald's Restaurants, P.T.S., Inc.*, No. CV 93-02419, 1995 WL 360309 (D.N.M. Aug. 18, 1994), a case in which newspapers like the *Wall Street Journal* screamed "Coffee Spill Burns Woman; Jury Awards $2.9 Million."

At first hearing, the *Liebeck* case sounds as if it could justify various stereotypes about an American jury trial: a 79-year-old grandmother spilled McDonald's coffee on herself and was awarded $200,000 in compensatory and $2.7 million in punitive damages. What possible grounds could a jury have for awarding such huge amounts for a simple coffee accident? Did Granny Liebeck win because the jury decided that she was a nice, silver-haired lady who could use some extra money? As investigated by the *Wall Street Journal*, the jury had clear grounds for punishing McDonald's for repeated negligence. After spilling the hot coffee on herself, Mrs. Liebeck spent eight days in the hospital and had multiple skin grafts for severe, third-degree burns that took two years to heal. Before suing McDonald's, she asked only that McDonald's pay her actual medical expenses of $11,000; McDonald's offered just $800 as compensation for her "nuisance" complaint. McDonald's sold coffee heated to 180–190°F (82–88°C), much hotter than its competitors. A doctor testified that coffee takes less than three seconds to produce a third-degree burn at that temperature. In the ten years before the lawsuit, McDonald's received more than 700 reports of serious burns from its coffee, including burns to babies and children, settling with some customers for up to $500,000 in damages. McDonald's made $1.35 million per day on the sale of coffee. McDonald's had refused both a $300,000 settlement offer from Liebeck's attorney and a recommendation by a retired judge and mediator that McDonald's settle for $225,000.

The jury in the *Liebeck* case likely was convinced that it was dealing with a corporation that had repeatedly and knowingly violated safety standards, leading to the severe injury of ordinary customers, and had refused to compensate the injured customers in a fair manner or make its coffee safer by lowering the temperature. In order to deter the defendant from future dangerous conduct, the jury could not merely award $200,000: McDonald's made $1.35 million per day from the sale of the scalding coffee, so an award of less than one percent of yearly sales would not alter such conduct. If a high level of punitive damages were not awarded, McDonald's would not have had an economic incentive to make the coffee safer: the defendant would make more money by continuing to sell scalding coffee, refusing to settle with any injured customers, and paying the very few who sued and won. It is unlikely that criminal law would be of much help: a jury would be unlikely to find beyond a reasonable doubt that any of the low wage servers at a fast food restaurant, or the overworked manager, or the distant top executives at McDonald's, actually intended to commit criminal battery on Mrs. Liebeck for which they should be put in prison. The dilemma for those who allow only compensatory damages or criminal punishment is that they deprive consumers of an effective remedy for negligent behavior by wealthy defendants against ordinary people and small businesses. It often does not make economic sense for an individual to pay for the cost of a civil trial for a relatively small amount against a wealthy defendant, and it is difficult to convince a prosecutor to indict for actions such as coffee spills, defective automobile parts or abusive insurance practices, which may not even be crimes.

Although the award in the *Liebeck* case was attacked as outrageous by many commentators, the result of the jury's verdict may be to promote safer coffee. An article in the June 2004 issue of the *American Lawyer* commented on the effects of the *Liebeck* case:

> Coffee sellers listened. "It caused the industry to look at itself and its standards, and say, 'Are we sure we know what we are doing?'" recalls Ted Lingle, the executive director of the Specialty Coffee Association of America. "We are selling a product that represents a hazard, no one denies that," Lingle adds, "so the question then is, how do we keep it reasonably safe for the millions of consumers who enjoy it every day? And the answer is in more secure packaging."

Does the existence of the punitive damages system in the United States mean that juries are free to punish defendants with any amount of damages they please, given that punitive damages by definition are not based on calculated losses to the plaintiff? The Supreme

Court decided a case in which the amount of punitive damages was so high that it offended the due process of law to which the defendant was entitled. In the *State Farm* case below, Campbell was driving and decided to pass the six cars traveling ahead of him on a two-lane highway. Driver A was driving a car approaching from the opposite direction. To avoid a head-on collision with Campbell, who by then was driving on the wrong side of the highway toward oncoming traffic, Driver A suddenly turned, lost control of his automobile, and collided with a car driven by Driver B. Driver A was killed, Driver B was permanently disabled and Campbell escaped without harm. Campbell had automobile liability insurance with the State Farm insurance company covering up to $50,000 in damages. Although State Farm's investigators reported that Campbell was at fault in the injuries to Drivers A and B, State Farm decided to fight and declined offers by lawyers for Drivers A and B to settle the claims for the policy limit of $50,000 ($25,000 each). State Farm also ignored the advice of one of its own investigators and took the case to trial, assuring the Campbells that "their assets were safe, that they had no liability for the accident, that State Farm would represent their interests, and that they did not need to hire their own lawyer." When a jury determined that Campbell was 100% at fault, and a judgment was returned for $185,849 (far more than the amount offered in settlement), State Farm refused to appeal the verdict and told Campbell that he should sell his house to pay the judgment. Campbell sued State Farm for bad faith breach of contract, fraud and intentional infliction of emotional distress. A jury awarded Campbell $145 million in punitive damages and, ultimately, $1 million in compensatory damages. State Farm appealed against punitive damages that were 145 times larger than the actual loss Campbell suffered.

State Farm Mut. Automobile Ins. Co. v. Campbell
538 U.S. 408 (2003)

Kennedy, J.

We address once again the measure of punishment, by means of punitive damages, a State may impose upon a defendant in a civil case. The question is whether an award of $145 million in punitive damages, where full compensatory damages are $1 million, is excessive and in violation of the Due Process Clause of the Fourteenth Amendment to the Constitution of the United States.

Compensatory damages "are intended to redress the concrete loss that the plaintiff has suffered by reason of the defendant's wrongful conduct." By contrast, punitive damages serve a broader function; they are aimed at deterrence and retribution. "Punitive damages may properly be imposed to further a State's legitimate interests in punishing unlawful conduct and deterring its repetition." "Punitive damages are imposed for purposes of retribution and deterrence."

Although these awards serve the same purposes as criminal penalties, defendants subjected to punitive damages in civil cases have not been accorded the protections applicable in a criminal proceeding. We have admonished that "punitive damages pose an acute danger of arbitrary deprivation of property. Jury instructions typically leave the jury with wide discretion in choosing amounts, and the presentation of evidence of a defendant's net worth creates the potential that juries will use their verdicts to express biases against big businesses, particularly those without strong local presences."

In light of these concerns, we instructed courts reviewing punitive damages to consider three guideposts: (1) the degree of reprehensibility of the defendant's misconduct; (2)

the disparity between the actual or potential harm suffered by the plaintiff and the punitive damages award; and (3) the difference between the punitive damages awarded by the jury and the civil penalties authorized or imposed in comparable cases.

The most important is the degree of reprehensibility of the defendant's conduct. We have instructed courts to determine the reprehensibility of a defendant by considering whether: the harm caused was physical as opposed to economic; the tortious conduct evinced an indifference to or a reckless disregard of the health or safety of others; the target of the conduct had financial vulnerability; the conduct involved repeated actions or was an isolated incident; and the harm was the result of intentional malice, trickery, or deceit, or mere accident. The existence of any one of these factors weighing in favor of a plaintiff may not be sufficient to sustain a punitive damages award; and the absence of all of them renders any award suspect. It should be presumed a plaintiff has been made whole for his injuries by compensatory damages, so punitive damages should only be awarded if the defendant's culpability, after having paid compensatory damages, is so reprehensible as to warrant the imposition of further sanctions to achieve punishment or deterrence.

Applying these factors in the instant case, we must acknowledge that State Farm's handling of the claims against the Campbells merits no praise. The trial court found that State Farm's employees altered the company's records to make Campbell appear less culpable. State Farm disregarded the overwhelming likelihood of liability and the near-certain probability that, by taking the case to trial, a judgment in excess of the policy limits would be awarded. While we do not suggest there was error in awarding punitive damages based upon State Farm's conduct toward the Campbells, a more modest punishment for this reprehensible conduct could have satisfied the State's legitimate objectives, and the Utah courts should have gone no further.

For a more fundamental reason, however, the Utah courts erred in relying upon this and other evidence: The courts awarded punitive damages to punish and deter conduct that bore no relation to the Campbells' harm. A defendant should be punished for the conduct that harmed the plaintiff, not for being an unsavory individual or business. Due process does not permit courts, in the calculation of punitive damages, to adjudicate the merits of other parties' hypothetical claims against a defendant under the guise of the reprehensibility analysis, but we have no doubt the Utah Supreme Court did that here. Punishment on these bases creates the possibility of multiple punitive damages awards for the same conduct; for in the usual case nonparties are not bound by the judgment some other plaintiff obtains.

We have been reluctant to identify concrete constitutional limits on the ratio between harm, or potential harm, to the plaintiff and the punitive damages award. We decline again to impose a bright-line ratio which a punitive damages award cannot exceed. Our jurisprudence and the principles it has now established demonstrate, however, that, in practice, few awards exceeding a single-digit ratio between punitive and compensatory damages, to a significant degree, will satisfy due process.

Nonetheless, because there are no rigid benchmarks that a punitive damages award may not surpass, ratios greater than those we have previously upheld may comport with due process where "a particularly egregious act has resulted in only a small amount of economic damages." When compensatory damages are substantial, then a lesser ratio, perhaps only equal to compensatory damages, can reach the outermost limit of the due process guarantee. The precise award in any case, of course, must be based upon the facts and circumstances of the defendant's conduct and the harm to the plaintiff.

The third guidepost is the disparity between the punitive damages award and the "civil penalties authorized or imposed in comparable cases." The existence of a criminal penalty does have bearing on the seriousness with which a State views the wrongful action. The most relevant civil sanction under Utah state law for the wrong done to the Campbells appears to be a $10,000 fine for an act of fraud, an amount far less than the $145 million punitive damages award.

The punitive award of $145 million, therefore, was neither reasonable nor proportionate to the wrong committed, and it was an irrational and arbitrary deprivation of the property of the defendant. The proper calculation of punitive damages under the principles we have discussed should be resolved, in the first instance, by the Utah courts. The judgment of the Utah Supreme Court is reversed, and the case is remanded for proceedings not inconsistent with this opinion.

Scalia, J., dissenting

I adhere to the view that the Due Process Clause provides no substantive protections against "excessive" or "unreasonable" awards of punitive damages.

Thomas, J., dissenting

I would affirm the judgment below because I continue to believe that the Constitution does not constrain the size of punitive damages awards.

* * *

Topics for Further Discussion

1. In *State Farm*, the Supreme Court agreed that punitive damages can be imposed for purposes of retribution and deterrence. Does a Constitutional limit on the amount of punitive damages to less than ten times actual damages defeat the purposes of punitive damages?

2. Should punitive damages be awarded to the plaintiff, or to the state? Additional aspects of this question are taken up in Chapter 7.

3. In *Philip Morris USA v. Williams*, 549 U.S. 346 (2007), the Supreme Court again commented on the limits of a jury's ability to award punitive damages: "We can find no authority supporting the use of punitive damages awards for the purpose of punishing a defendant for harming others. We have said that it may be appropriate to consider the reasonableness of a punitive damages award in light of the potential harm the defendant's conduct could have caused. But we have made clear that the potential harm at issue was harm potentially caused the plaintiff. . . . We therefore conclude that the Due Process Clause requires States to provide assurance that juries are not asking the wrong question, i.e., seeking, not simply to determine reprehensibility, but also to punish for harm caused strangers."

4. The Tyco International executive was retried after his initial mistrial and sentenced to eight to twenty-five years in prison, *New York v. Kozlowski*, 846 N.Y.S.2d 44 (New York, 2007).

After the Verdict

Judges are extremely reluctant to upset the jury's verdict in any trial, but judges do have several ways to manage an improper verdict, all of which are exceptional.

In a civil case, a judge may enter "judgment not withstanding the verdict" (JNOV). In a JNOV, the judge directs the clerk to enter judgment for the party opposite that favored by the jury. The judge must believe that there was "no legally sufficient evidence for a reasonable jury" to find against the loser, and an appeals court will reverse the judgment if there is *any* rational evidence supporting the jury's verdict.

In a criminal case, neither the judge nor the prosecutor may challenge a verdict of "Not Guilty." A verdict of "Not Guilty" cannot be set aside or appealed, but the prosecutor may, of course, appeal various legal rulings by the judge in the trial prior to the verdict. In theory, a judge can also enter a ruling of "Not Guilty" if the jury finds the defendant "Guilty," but only after the extremely rare trial where there is no evidence that could satisfy *any* rational jury beyond a reasonable doubt. As one circuit court stated, a judge may not oppose a jury verdict even if the only evidence the jury had for conviction was testimony from a "lying, drug-dealing, paid government informant."

Some states and the federal government provide for a "poll" of jurors in criminal cases that require a unanimous verdict. The "poll" asks each juror only one question: "Is the verdict just announced your verdict?" The Federal Rules of Criminal Procedure provide in Rule 31 that "[after] a verdict is returned but before the jury is discharged, the court shall, on a party's request, or may on its own motion, poll the jurors individually. If the poll reveals a lack of unanimity, the court may direct the jury to deliberate further or may declare a mistrial and discharge the jury."

In both civil and criminal cases, the judge may grant a "new trial." A "new trial" is usually reserved for cases in which the verdict was ruined by circumstances over which the jury had no control. For example, the jury delivers a rush verdict because there is a fire in the jury room and they all want to escape, or after the verdict it is discovered that someone has threatened a juror with harm if they do not vote a certain way. Other reasons for a new trial include an error by the judge or attorneys that made it impossible for a party to get a fair hearing, or misconduct by a juror.

Jury Nullification

Since American juries are made up of ordinary people from the community who decide in secret, they obviously have an opportunity to apply their own values. At times, juries in criminal cases have appeared to disregard the instructions of the judge in reaching their verdict. Famous examples include trials in the Colonial Period when juries refused to convict Americans of crimes against the British government and trials in the Civil War period when juries refused to convict persons for assisting runaway slaves to freedom. A common contemporary example is when a prosecutor tries a defendant for the murder of the defendant's old, dying spouse or parent who is in constant pain and unable to enjoy life. Even if the deceased begged to be killed, and the defendant acted out of love for the deceased, a crime has been committed. Even so American juries routinely refuse to convict defendants in cases of genuine "mercy killings." However, even if juries can function as guarantors of justice against tyranny, unpopular laws reflecting personal morals, or against overly ambitious prosecutors, jury secrecy can also frustrate justice. It was common at one time for persons proven to have murdered black Americans to be acquitted by juries in the former Slave States.

The practice of a jury's disregarding the judge's instructions and voting their conscience, rather than on the facts and law, is called "jury nullification." It has had both critics and supporters among judges for the past 200 years of American history. Various views of jury nullification are given in *United States v. Dougherty*, below. During the Vietnam War, Dougherty and several others illegally entered and destroyed the Washington offices of Dow Chemical, the company making the Vietnam War fire weapon Napalm. Charged with burglary and criminal destruction of property, Dougherty demanded that the jury be told that they could vote their consciences. The judge denied Dougherty's demand and Doughtery appealed.

United States v. Dougherty
473 F.2d 1113 (D.C. Cir. 1972)

Leventhal, J.

The appellants say that the jury has a well-recognized prerogative to disregard the instructions of the court even as to matters of law, and that they accordingly have the legal right that the jury be informed of its power.

There has evolved in the Anglo-American system an undoubted jury prerogative-in-fact, derived from its power to bring in a general verdict of not guilty in a criminal case, that is not reversible by the court.

The pages of history shine on instances of the jury's exercise of its prerogative to disregard uncontradicted evidence and instructions of the judge. The jury is likely to call on its prerogative of lenity and equity, contrary to the judge's instruction, when the case is one where it can empathize with the defendant, feeling either that the jurors might well have been or come to be in the same position, or that in the large the defendant's conduct is not so contrary to general conduct standards as to be condemned. "The essential feature of a jury obviously lies in the interposition between the accused and his accuser of the common sense judgment of a group of laymen, and in the community participation and shared responsibility that results from that group's determination of guilt or innocence."

In the last analysis, our rejection of the request for jury nullification doctrine is a recognition that there are times when logic is not the only or even best guide to sound conduct of government. What makes for health as an occasional medicine would be disastrous as a daily diet. An explicit instruction to a jury conveys an implied approval that runs the risk of degrading the legal structure requisite for true freedom, for an ordered liberty that protects against anarchy as well as tyranny.

Bazelon, C.J., concurring in part and dissenting in part

My own view rests on the premise that nullification can and should serve an important function in the criminal process. I do not see it as a doctrine that exists only because we lack the power to punish jurors who refuse to enforce the law or to re-prosecute a defendant whose acquittal cannot be justified in the strict terms of law. The doctrine permits the jury to bring to bear on the criminal process a sense of fairness and particularized justice. The drafters of legal rules cannot anticipate and take account of every case where a defendant's conduct is "unlawful" but not blameworthy, any more than they can draw a bold line to mark the boundary between an accident and negligence. It is the jury—as spokesman for the community's sense of values—that must explore that subtle and elusive boundary. More than twenty-five years ago this Court recognized that "our collective conscience does not allow punishment where it cannot impose blame."

If a jury refuses to apply strictly the controlling principles of law, it may—in conflict with values shared by the larger community—convict a defendant because of prejudice against him, or acquit a defendant because of sympathy for him and prejudice against his victim. But it is hard for me to see how a nullification instruction could enhance the likelihood of that result. Does the judge's recitation of the instruction increase the likelihood that the jury will ignore the limitation that lies at its heart? I hardly think so.

As for the problem of unjust acquittal, it is important to recognize the strong internal check that constrains the jury's willingness to acquit. Where defendants seem dangerous, juries are unlikely to exercise their nullification power, whether or not an explicit instruction is offered.

One often-cited abuse of the nullification power is the acquittal by bigoted juries of whites who commit crimes (lynching, for example) against blacks. But the revulsion and sense of shame fostered by that practice fueled the civil rights movement, which in turn made possible the enactment of major civil rights legislation. That same movement spurred on the revitalization of the equal protection clause and, in particular, the recognition of the right to be tried before a jury selected without bias. The lessons we learned from these abuses helped to create a climate in which such abuses could not so easily thrive.

This case is significantly different from the classic, exalted cases where juries historically invoked the power to nullify. Here, the defendants have no quarrel with the general validity of the law under which they have been charged. They did not simply refuse to obey a government edict that they considered illegal, and whose illegality they expected to demonstrate in a judicial proceeding. Rather, they attempted to protest government action by interfering with others—specifically, the Dow Chemical Company. This is a distinction which could and should be explored in argument before the jury. If revulsion against the war in Southeast Asia has reached a point where a jury would be unwilling to convict a defendant for commission of the acts alleged here, we would be far better advised to ponder the implications of that result than to spend our time devising stratagems which let us pretend that the power of nullification does not even exist.

* * *

Topics for Further Discussion

1. Should "jury nullification" be encouraged, punished, or ignored by judges?

Status of the Jury Trial

Trial by jury presents ongoing issues of the administration of justice and the role of the average citizen, as well as the professional judge, in the judicial process. Most of the complaints about jury trials are not new, and in England they have led to a significant decrease in the right to jury trial. The United States is unlikely substantially to modify the jury trial from its present form. At one time, the English themselves would not have valued efficiency above the protection of jury trial. Writing in 1769, William Blackstone answered critics of jury inefficiencies in his *Commentaries on the Laws of England* by pointing out that efficient trials often end up as arbitrary trials:

> So that the liberties of England cannot but subsist, so long as [the jury system] remains sacred and inviolate, not only from all open attacks, (which none will be so hardy as to make) but also from all secret machinations, which may sap and undermine it; by introducing new and arbitrary methods of trial, by justices of the peace, commissioners of the revenue, and courts of conscience. And

however convenient these may appear at first, (as doubtless all arbitrary powers, well executed, are the most convenient) yet let it be again remembered, that delays, and little inconveniences in the forms of justice, are the price that all free nations must pay for their liberty in more substantial matters; … and that, though begun in trifles, the precedent may gradually increase and spread, to the utter disuse of juries in questions of the most momentous concern.

Key Terms and Concepts

Bench Trial
Hearsay
"Hung Jury"
Judgment NOV
Jury Nullification
Mistrial
Peremptory challenge
Sequestration
Venire
Voir dire

Chapter 3

The Legal Profession

"Discourage litigation. Persuade your neighbors to compromise whenever you can. Point out to them how the nominal winner is often a real loser—in fees, expenses, and waste of time. As a peacemaker the lawyer has a superior opportunity of being a good man. There will still be business enough."

Abraham Lincoln, Notes for a Law Lecture (July 1, 1850)

Every one of the one million lawyers in the United States knows the famous words of Shakespeare from *Henry VI*: "The first thing we do, let's kill all the lawyers." The quotation is paraded out whenever someone complains about America as an overly litigious society. When people have been injured, however, or when they want to prevent trouble, or make plans for the future of their property, or enter into a contract, or pay no more tax than is due, or do any countless number of other things, they look for the best lawyer they can find.

This reveals the paradox of American society's attitude toward lawyers. People love to complain about them, but they also rely on them for many of the most important matters of their lives. The State Bar of California reports more than 160,000 active practitioners as of the end of 2009. Japan, by contrast, has fewer than 25,000 licensed lawyers for the entire country.

Unlike England, where office lawyers (solicitors) and court lawyers (barristers) are separated, American lawyers are licensed to do both kinds of work. In fact, trying lawsuits in court (known as litigation) is only the tip of the iceberg for the legal profession. A large "full service" law firm will have many practice areas, such as Antitrust, Banking, Commercial, Corporate, Employment, Estate Planning, Insurance, Intellectual Property, International, Litigation, Mergers & Acquisitions, Real Estate, and Taxation. So-called "boutique" law firms may specialize in particular areas such as insurance defense work, telecommunications, or entertainment law. Not surprisingly, the specialties available in any geographical area will mirror the region's characteristics. Silicon Valley in California, home to many technology companies, has a large number of intellectual property lawyers. Houston, Texas, has many experts in oil and gas law. New York, where the New York Stock Exchange is located, has numerous attorneys who specialize in securities law. Washington, D.C., has many specialists in administrative law and government contracting.

In general, lawyers that represent parties in tort cases are separated into plaintiffs' and defendants' firms. In the same way, those involved in employment cases typically work for either employee or management side law offices. The reason for this separation is that working for "both sides" might require the law firm to take inconsistent positions in court: arguing a dismissed employee's interpretation of the law in one case and an employer's interpretation in another. As we will see later in the chapter, lawyers are also required to avoid conflicts of interest involving clients. If a firm represents a defendant employer in one matter, it would be prohibited from using any information it learned in representing a plaintiff against the same employer. Even if no conflict were present, plaintiffs and defendants might not be comfortable relying on lawyers who also work for "the other side," nor would they be happy if their lawyers were responsible for setting precedents that proved detrimental to their best interests.

Criminal defense lawyers tend to practice in firms that do only that kind of work. It is not at all uncommon for a defense lawyer to have worked as a prosecutor for many years before joining the defense bar. One reason for making the change may be economic: prosecutors are government employees and, thus, limited in salary. On the other hand, many (perhaps most) criminal defendants are not wealthy and have little money to pay for legal representation. In the end, both prosecutors and defense lawyers are committed to serving justice, and both are necessary for the system to function properly.

With so many lawyers, the size of law firms in the United States varies widely. The days of one-person law offices are far from over, but the increasing complexity of practice makes it difficult to practice alone. The largest firm in the country, indeed in the world, has more than 3,000 attorneys, with offices around the globe.

American lawyers are licensed to practice by the state or states where they have offices. The United States has no national examination for lawyers. The standards are set by the states, each of which has its own bar examination. A lawyer who wishes to practice in both New York and California must pass the bar examination in both states, unless the states have reciprocity arrangements in place. While some parts of the exams may be the same, other parts will differ to reflect local concerns. Oil and gas law, for example, is tested on the bar examination in Texas. It is not a part of the exam in New York, but New York Practice and Procedure is. Serving as a lawyer in a state requires one to demonstrate knowledge of its laws in order to qualify for a lawyer's license. It is not necessary to go to a law school in that state (although it might help in passing the bar exam) so long as the lawyer passes the state's bar exam.

Lawyers and the Public

Lawyers are not civil servants unless they work for the government. However, they are considered to be "officers of the court" with certain public responsibilities beyond what other licensed professionals, such as plumbers and carpenters, possess. As you read the following case, consider the nature of the relationship between lawyers and the public at large.

Florida Bar v. Went For It, Inc.
515 U.S. 618 (1995)

O'Connor, J.

Rules of the Florida Bar prohibit personal injury lawyers from sending targeted direct-mail solicitations to victims and their relatives for 30 days following an accident or disaster. This case asks us to consider whether such rules violate the First and Fourteenth Amendments of the Constitution. We hold that in the circumstances presented here, they do not.

In 1989, the Florida Bar completed a 2-year study of the effects of lawyer advertising on public opinion. After conducting hearings, commissioning surveys, and reviewing extensive public commentary, the Bar determined that several changes to its advertising rules were in order. In late 1990, the Florida Supreme Court adopted the Bar's proposed amendments with some modifications. Two of these amendments are at issue in this case. Rule 4-7.4(b)(1) provides that "[a] lawyer shall not send, or knowingly permit to be sent, ... a written communication to a prospective client for the purpose of obtaining professional employment if: (A) the written communication concerns an action for personal injury or wrongful death or otherwise relates to an accident or disaster involving the person to whom the communication is addressed or a relative of that person, unless the accident or disaster occurred more than 30 days prior to the mailing of the communication." Rule 4-7.8(a) states that "[a] lawyer shall not accept referrals from a lawyer referral service unless the service: (1) engages in no communication with the public and in no direct contact with prospective clients in a manner that would violate the Rules of Professional Conduct if the communication or contact were made by the lawyer." Together, these rules create a brief 30-day blackout period after an accident during which lawyers may not, directly or indirectly, single out accident victims or their relatives in order to solicit their business.

In March 1992, G. Stewart McHenry and his wholly owned lawyer referral service, Went For It, Inc., filed this action for declaratory and injunctive relief in the United States District Court for the Middle District of Florida challenging Rules 4.7-4(b)(1) and 4.7-8 as violative of the First and Fourteenth Amendments to the Constitution. McHenry alleged that he routinely sent targeted solicitations to accident victims or their survivors within 30 days after accidents and that he wished to continue doing so in the future. Went For It, Inc. represented that it wished to contact accident victims or their survivors within 30 days of accidents and to refer potential clients to participating Florida lawyers. In October 1992, McHenry was disbarred for reasons unrelated to this suit. Another Florida lawyer, John T. Blakely, was substituted in his stead.

Constitutional protection for attorney advertising, and for commercial speech generally, is of recent vintage. In *Virginia State Bd. of Pharmacy v. Virginia Citizens Consumer Council, Inc.*, 425 U.S. 748 (1976) we invalidated a state statute barring pharmacists from advertising prescription drug prices. One year later, however, the Court applied the Virginia State Board principles to invalidate a state rule prohibiting lawyers from advertising in newspapers and other media. In *Bates v. State Bar of Arizona*, 433 U.S. 350 (1977), the Court struck a ban on price advertising for what it deemed "routine" legal services: "the uncontested divorce, the simple adoption, the uncontested personal bankruptcy, the change of name, and the like." Expressing confidence that legal advertising would only be practicable for such simple, standardized services, the Court rejected the State's proffered justifications for regulation.

Nearly two decades of cases have built upon the foundation laid by *Bates*. It is now well established that lawyer advertising is commercial speech and, as such, is accorded a measure of First Amendment protection. We have always been careful to distinguish commercial speech from speech at the First Amendment's core. Mindful of these concerns, we engage in "intermediate" scrutiny of restrictions on commercial speech.

The Florida Bar asserts that it has a substantial interest in protecting the privacy and tranquility of personal injury victims and their loved ones against intrusive, unsolicited contact by lawyers. This interest obviously factors into the Bar's paramount (and repeatedly professed) objective of curbing activities that "negatively affec[t] the administration of justice." Because direct mail solicitations in the wake of accidents are perceived by the public as intrusive, the Bar argues, the reputation of the legal profession in the eyes of Floridians has suffered commensurately. The regulation, then, is an effort to protect the flagging reputations of Florida lawyers by preventing them from engaging in conduct that, the Bar maintains, "is universally regarded as deplorable and beneath common decency because of its intrusion upon the special vulnerability and private grief of victims or their families."

We have little trouble crediting the Bar's interest as substantial. On various occasions we have accepted the proposition that "States have a compelling interest in the practice of professions within their boundaries, and ... as part of their power to protect the public health, safety, and other valid interests they have broad power to establish standards for licensing practitioners and regulating the practice of professions." Our precedents also leave no room for doubt that the protection of potential clients' privacy is a substantial state interest.

The Florida Bar submitted a 106-page summary of its 2-year study of lawyer advertising and solicitation to the District Court. That summary contains data — both statistical and anecdotal — supporting the Bar's contentions that the Florida public views direct-mail solicitations in the immediate wake of accidents as an intrusion on privacy that reflects poorly upon the profession. As of June 1989, lawyers mailed 700,000 direct solicitations in Florida annually, 40% of which were aimed at accident victims or their survivors. A survey of Florida adults commissioned by the Bar indicated that Floridians "have negative feelings about those attorneys who use direct mail advertising." Significantly, 27% of direct-mail recipients reported that their regard for the legal profession and for the judicial process as a whole was "lower" as a result of receiving the direct mail.

The anecdotal record mustered by the Bar is noteworthy for its breadth and detail. With titles like "Scavenger Lawyers" and "Solicitors Out of Bounds," newspaper editorial pages in Florida have burgeoned with criticism of Florida lawyers who send targeted direct mail to victims shortly after accidents. The study summary also includes page upon page of excerpts from complaints of direct-mail recipients. For example, a Florida citizen described how he was "appalled and angered by the brazen attempt" of a law firm to solicit him by letter shortly after he was injured and his fiancée was killed in an auto accident. Another found it "despicable and inexcusable" that a Pensacola lawyer wrote to his mother three days after his father's funeral. Another described how she was "astounded" and then "very angry" when she received a solicitation following a minor accident. Still another described as "beyond comprehension" a letter his nephew's family received the day of the nephew's funeral. One citizen wrote, "I consider the unsolicited contact from you after my child's accident to be of the rankest form of ambulance chasing and in incredibly poor taste.... I cannot begin to express with my limited vocabulary the utter contempt in which I hold you and your kind."

Florida permits lawyers to advertise on prime-time television and radio as well as in newspapers and other media. They may rent space on billboards. They may send untargeted letters to the general population, or to discrete segments thereof. There are, of course, pages upon pages devoted to lawyers in the Yellow Pages of Florida telephone directories. These listings are organized alphabetically and by area of specialty. These ample alternative channels for receipt of information about the availability of legal representation during the 30-day period following accidents may explain why, despite the ample evidence, testimony, and commentary submitted by those favoring (as well as opposing) unrestricted direct-mail solicitation, respondents have not pointed to — and we have not independently found — a single example of an individual case in which immediate solicitation helped to avoid, or failure to solicit within 30 days brought about, the harms that concern the dissent. In fact, the record contains considerable empirical survey information suggesting that Floridians have little difficulty finding lawyers when they need one. Finding no basis to question the commonsense conclusion that the many alternative channels for communicating necessary information about attorneys are sufficient, we see no defect in Florida's regulation.

Speech by professionals obviously has many dimensions. There are circumstances in which we will accord speech by attorneys on public issues and matters of legal representation the strongest protection our Constitution has to offer. This case, however, concerns pure commercial advertising, for which we have always reserved a lesser degree of protection under the First Amendment. Particularly because the standards and conduct of state-licensed lawyers have traditionally been subject to extensive regulation by the States, it is all the more appropriate that we limit our scrutiny of state regulations to a level commensurate with the "subordinate position" of commercial speech in the scale of First Amendment values.

Kennedy, J., dissenting.

Attorneys who communicate their willingness to assist potential clients are engaged in speech protected by the First and Fourteenth Amendments. That principle has been understood since *Bates v. State Bar of Arizona.* The Court today undercuts this guarantee in an important class of cases and unsettles leading First Amendment precedents, at the expense of those victims most in need of legal assistance.

The Court neglects the fact that this problem is largely self-policing: potential clients will not hire lawyers who offend them. And even if a person enters into a contract with an attorney and later regrets it, Florida, like some other States, allows clients to rescind certain contracts with attorneys within a stated time after they are executed. The State's restriction deprives accident victims of information which may be critical to their right to make a claim for compensation for injuries. The telephone book and general advertisements may serve this purpose in part; but the direct solicitation ban will fall on those who most need legal representation: for those with minor injuries, the victims too ill-informed to know an attorney may be interested in their cases; for those with serious injuries, the victims too ill-informed to know that time is of the essence if counsel is to assemble evidence and warn them not to enter into settlement negotiations or evidentiary discussions with investigators for opposing parties. One survey reports that over a recent 5-year period, 68% of the American population consulted a lawyer.

The use of modern communication methods in a timely way is essential if clients who make up this vast demand are to be advised and informed of all of their choices and rights in selecting an attorney. The very fact that some 280,000 direct mail solicitations are sent to accident victims and their survivors in Florida each year is some indication of the efficacy of this device. Nothing in the Court's opinion demonstrates that these efforts do not serve some beneficial role. A solicitation letter is not a contract. Nothing in the record shows that these communications do not at the least serve the purpose of informing the prospective client that he or she has a number of different attorneys from whom to choose, so that the decision to select counsel, after an interview with one or more interested attorneys, can be deliberate and informed. And if these communications reveal the social costs of the tort system as a whole, then efforts can be directed to reforming the operation of that system, not to suppressing information about how the system works. The Court's approach, however, does not seem to be the proper way to begin elevating the honor of the profession.

* * *

Topics for Further Discussion

1. Justice O'Connor says this case "concerns pure commercial advertising." Is informing potential clients of the availability of legal services the same as advertising a product? Does Justice Kennedy agree that this case is one of commercial speech?

2. What is the basis of the majority's opinion upholding the Florida law: that the privacy of people should be protected or that the reputation of lawyers should be improved?

3. How would you go about finding a lawyer if you needed one? Do you think that ordinary people can find a lawyer easily? If making legal services available is a good thing, why would sending letters to potential clients be bad?

4. The introduction to the case mentions that one of the lawyers originally involved was disbarred for other reasons. Disbarment is the ultimate sanction for lawyers, involving the cancellation of the lawyer's license to practice law. Usually, disbarment involves some serious misconduct. The Court does not reveal the reason behind the disbarment in this case, but whatever it was it was not because of the issues raised in this matter.

Duties and Obligations of Lawyers

Lawyers in the United States are regulated by rules governing their conduct as professionals. Each state is free to make its own rules, but most such rules are based on two documents produced by the American Bar Association: the Model Rules of Professional Conduct passed in 1983, and the earlier Model Code of Professional Responsibility. Their basic themes are much the same, but the documents differ in some details. For our discussion, we will rely primarily on the Model Rules. Lawyer discipline is handled at the state bar association level, where disciplinary boards will accept complaints from clients and other lawyers, conduct hearings, and mete out appropriate punishment for wrongdoing.

Competence

The first Model Rule deals with the duty of the lawyer to represent the client adequately. It says, "A lawyer shall provide competent representation to a client. Competent representation requires the legal knowledge, skill, thoroughness and preparation reasonably necessary for the representation." This may seem like an obvious requirement, but it is one that—far too frequently—is not fulfilled. In an age of increased specialization, a universal definition of competence may be hard to establish. A tax attorney with many years of experience may be much better prepared to handle a dispute with the Internal Revenue Service, but the Rules do not require every lawyer to meet the highest standard of expertise. A lawyer may be convinced she can sufficiently take care of the client's interests, or be unwilling to refer a client to another lawyer, only to find out that she is in over her head. Quite understandably, lawyers do not like to turn away clients, especially paying ones. The cost of not doing so, however, may be even higher.

Lawyer Disciplinary Bd. v. Turgeon
557 S.E.2d 235 (W. Va. 2000)

Per curiam

A Hearing Panel Subcommittee of the Lawyer Disciplinary Board conducted extensive hearings on the allegations against the respondent, and now recommends to this Court a number of sanctions against the respondent, including a recommendation that the respondent's license to practice law be suspended for a period of 2 years.

After a thorough review of the record and arguments of counsel, we agree with the findings and recommendations of the Board.

The Board alleged that the respondent engaged in misconduct during the representation of 3 separate clients.

In 1991, Douglas Gunnoe was serving a 5-to-18 year imprisonment sentence for second-degree murder, for stabbing to death a counselor whom he met in a substance abuse program. While on work release for the second-degree murder, Mr. Gunnoe met Alicia McCormick, a woman who performed domestic violence counselor duties at the work release center. Mr. Gunnoe was employed doing maintenance at the apartment complex in which Ms. McCormick resided. Ms. McCormick was stabbed to death with a knife in her apartment on or about July 20, 1991. Mr. Gunnoe was charged with the offense, and he admitted to the police certain details of the crime. The respondent was appointed to represent Mr. Gunnoe.

In the course of representing Mr. Gunnoe, the Board asserted that the respondent violated Rule 1.1 of the *Rules of Professional Conduct,* which states: "A lawyer shall provide competent representation to a client. Competent representation requires the legal knowledge, skill, thoroughness and preparation reasonably necessary for the representation."

The respondent had very little experience defending criminal cases, particularly serious cases such as the Gunnoe matter. Consequently, the circuit court appointed additional, more experienced lawyers to assist the respondent, but the other lawyers were unable to participate in Mr. Gunnoe's defense because the respondent would not adjust his schedule so that the other lawyers might help. The respondent told one of these lawyers that he should not be participating in Mr. Gunnoe's defense, because the lawyer believed Mr. Gunnoe was guilty.

Through the course of two trials, the respondent engaged in long and repetitious cross-examinations that did not extract information helpful to the defense. The circuit judge stopped the first trial three times, took Mr. Gunnoe and the respondent into his chambers, and advised Mr. Gunnoe of the judge's concerns that the respondent was not representing him competently. When the first trial ended in a mistrial, the circuit judge removed the respondent as counsel because of his incompetence. Mr. Gunnoe and the respondent then consulted together at the counsel table, and the respondent apparently announced he would continue as Mr. Gunnoe's counsel, although not as court-appointed counsel.

During the course of Mr. Gunnoe's trials, the respondent apparently proffered odd defense theories to the prosecutor. At one point, the respondent suggested that the prosecutor look at the case as a suicide—even though Ms. McCormick suffered a stab wound which penetrated her back and almost exited out her front, and there were five stab wounds in her chest. The respondent also suggested that the prosecutor take the police report, remove any references to Mr. Gunnoe, and submit it to the FBI profiling unit so that they could determine the "real murderer"—even though Mr. Gunnoe had confessed to portions of the crime.

On the basis of evidence such as this, the Board concluded that the respondent had violated Rule 1.1 and had failed to provide Mr. Gunnoe with competent representation.

We find substantial evidence in the record to support the Hearing Panel Subcommittee of the Lawyer Disciplinary Board's findings of fact, and believe that the Office of Disciplinary Counsel proved the allegations contained in the various charges by clear and convincing evidence.

The Board found the respondent "ill-prepared" for the disciplinary proceedings, and found that he "spent a great deal of time riffling through boxes of papers looking for possible exhibits." Many of these exhibits were not helpful to his case, and the Board found the exhibits "harmed his case and credibility." The Board believed that while the respondent spent many hours in preparation for his case and the disciplinary hearings, "he has exhibited a lack of good judgment or knowledge as to how to handle these legal matters." In sum, the Board concluded—in both his representation of himself and others—that the respondent "has exhibited a pattern of not competent, ill-prepared legal work[.]" We agree with the Board's assessment.

It is therefore Ordered that:

1. The respondent, Marc P. Turgeon, is suspended from the practice of law for a period of 2 years. He must petition for reinstatement pursuant to Rule 3.32 of the *Rules of Lawyer Disciplinary Procedure.*

2. As a mandatory condition for reinstatement, the respondent must complete 12 hours of continuing legal education relating to ethics.

3. As a mandatory condition for reinstatement, the respondent must have in place a plan of supervised practice to last for a period of 2 years from the date of reinstatement. The supervision plan must have the respondent working very closely with a mentoring/supervising lawyer. The plan must be comprehensive, and must involve the supervising lawyer in every case the respondent is handling. It will not be sufficient for the respondent and supervising lawyer to meet on an occasional basis to have general discussions about the respondent's practice. The supervising lawyer must be familiar with the substantive law areas in which the respondent practices. The responsibility of locating a supervising attorney and drafting a supervision plan shall rest with the respondent, although the Office of Disciplinary Counsel must, within reason, approve of the supervising attorney selected and the contents of the plan. If the respondent and the Office of Disciplinary Counsel cannot agree upon a supervising attorney or the contents of the plan, the matter may be submitted to a Hearing Panel Subcommittee of the Lawyer Disciplinary Board. The supervising attorney must make regular reports to the Office of Disciplinary Counsel.

4. As a mandatory condition for reinstatement, the respondent must demonstrate by expert medical and psychological testimony that he is presently capable of practicing law.

5. The respondent must pay all costs of this proceeding.

* * *

Topics for Further Discussion

1. Where is the line between poor lawyering and incompetent lawyering? How can a court draw it, and how can a client and lawyer know it in advance?

2. If the lawyer truly was incompetent, was the discipline adequate?

3. What is the purpose of discipline in such a case? Of course, attorneys are also subject to being sued for malpractice.

Diligence and Communication

A lawyer's prime duty is to the client. Counsel is required to take care of the client's business promptly. In addition, the client must be kept informed of what is going on with the matter. A lawyer should give the client sufficient explanation so that he can make informed decisions about what to do. What this shows is that the client does not just place himself in the lawyer's hands. Rather, he enters into a cooperative professional contract in which the client, not the lawyer, has the right to make the ultimate choices.

Clients naturally tend to believe that their matters need and deserve immediate attention. Lawyers, at least successful ones, have a large number of clients. One of the difficulties of the job is taking care of all of their business in a timely fashion and keeping them informed. Legal issues often bring a great deal of anxiety to clients. Returning a client's phone call right away may not have any substantive impact on the case itself, but it will allow the client to feel some relief. A skillful lawyer must learn how to balance the demands of what *must* be done immediately with what *should* be done as soon as possible. The clearest and most egregious cases involve missing filing deadlines (a court imposed deadline or a statute of limitation), which can result in the client's case being barred from trial. The consequences of failing to pursue the best interests of the client diligently are much worse than not returning a phone call promptly.

In the Matter of Garnett
603 S.E.2d 281 (Ga. 2004)

Per curiam

Given the number and seriousness of Garnett's violations, we conclude that he should be disbarred for the conduct set forth below.

In Case No. S04Y1627, Garnett agreed to represent a client in a land dispute matter and the client paid Garnett $3,500. The only action Garnett took in the case, however, was to write one letter to the opposing party. He did not file a lawsuit, and he failed to return most of his client's phone calls. When he did speak to the client, Garnett falsely assured him that he would file the lawsuit soon. He did not refund the fees the client paid to him.

In Case No. S04Y1628, a client hired Garnett to represent her in a medical negligence case and paid Garnett to obtain relevant medical records, which he did. Garnett sent the records to an attorney who specializes in that area of law, but failed to perform any additional work for his client and did not answer her phone calls or letters. He took no action in the case, thus causing the statute of limitations to expire.

In Case No. S04Y1629, a client paid Garnett $3,500 to represent her in a civil case against the City of Warwick but Garnett did not return her phone calls and did not perform any work on her behalf for over three years, until she filed a grievance with the State Bar, at which time Garnett filed a complaint in her case.

In Case No. S04Y1630, the court appointed Garnett to represent a client in a criminal appeal. Garnett filed the appeal, but never informed his client about the affirmation of his conviction and did not communicate with his client until the client filed a grievance with the State Bar, at which time Garnett sent the client a copy of the appellate decision.

In Case No. S04Y1631, Garnett represented a client in a criminal trial and filed a notice of appeal on his behalf. Garnett did not inform his client about the affirmation of his conviction, did not maintain adequate contact with his client, and did not update him on the status of the appeal. The client did not find out about the result of his appeal until after he filed a grievance against Garnett.

Finally, in Case No. S05Y0028, Garnett was appointed to represent a client in a criminal action, but refused his client's request to enter a guilty plea. Garnett failed to obtain a copy of the transcript from a previous conviction as his client requested, and over the period of almost a year, responded only once to his client's letters and telephone calls. Garnett also failed to contact the client about his trial date or discuss his case with him prior to trial.

We have reviewed the records in these cases and note in aggravation of discipline that in addition to the disciplinary matters set forth herein, Garnett has had prior disciplinary action against him. These include a 1990 Investigative Panel reprimand, a 1991 three-month suspension, a 1993 Public Reprimand, and a 2003 Letter of Formal Admonition, which together suggest a pattern of neglect and abandonment. Based on his repeated violations of the rules governing the conduct of lawyers in this State, we hereby order that Garnett be disbarred from the practice of law in the State of Georgia.

* * *

Topics for Further Discussion

1. As the *Garnett* case demonstrates, there is considerable slack before a lawyer will be disbarred. Disciplinary boards are usually willing to consider mitigating circumstances that might lessen the punishment. Should lawyers be held to higher standards of professional conduct than other professionals?

2. Ineffective assistance of counsel is frequently the basis for appeal in criminal cases as discussed in Chapter 10.

Confidentiality

The attorney-client privilege is one of the most fundamental principles of American law. A client must feel free to discuss everything with her lawyer, without any worry that the information might be disclosed to someone else. In that way, the lawyer will be able to offer the best advice possible under the circumstances. The attorney has a duty to preserve the client's confidences and cannot be required to disclose them. Only the client herself can waive the privilege. Newspaper reporters have tried unsuccessfully to protect their sources, but courts have rejected any notion of extending such a privilege to them.

One difficult question is what kind of information is covered by the duty of confidentiality? The Model Rules speak of "information relating to representation of a client." While not a model of clarity itself, the standard suggests that lawyers should think of the duty broadly. It is not just secret information that may not be disclosed, and not just information that would injure the client's case. Rather it is any information relating to the representation. Often times, it is impossible to tell what might harm the client's interests so it is better to cover the situation with a blanket rule.

What should a lawyer do if he learns that a client plans to do harm to someone else? Comments to the Model Rules indicate he should remain quiet, except in extreme circumstances. Comment 9 to Rule 1.6 says, "[t]o the extent a lawyer is required or permitted to disclose a client's purposes, the client will be inhibited from revealing facts which would enable the lawyer to counsel against a wrongful course of action. The public is better protected if full and open communication by the client is encouraged than if it is inhibited." However, Rule 1.6(b)(1) says that a lawyer "may reveal such information to the extent the lawyer believes necessary to prevent the client from committing a criminal act that the lawyer believes is likely to result in imminent death or substantial bodily harm."

The choice of words is significant: "*may*" reveal, not *must* reveal. What if a client tells a lawyer that he intends to kill someone and then does so? Did the lawyer violate Rule1.6(b)(1) by not telling someone before the crime occurred? The answer would seem to be "no," since the rule is permissive and not mandatory.

The following case involves a lawyer's disclosure of information when he thought it would be helpful to the client. The client was convicted of murder, but there is no suggestion that he disclosed any information about such plans to the lawyer.

In re Disciplinary Proceedings Against O'Neil
661 N.W.2d 813 (Wis. 2003)

Per curiam

We review the recommendation of the referee that Attorney O'Neil receive a public reprimand for professional misconduct consisting of revealing information relating to his representation of a client without the client's consent, and that he be required to pay the costs of the proceeding.

We determine that a public reprimand is appropriate discipline for Attorney O'Neil's misconduct. We also order him to pay the costs of this proceeding.

Attorney O'Neil was admitted to practice law in Wisconsin in 1988 and practices in Green Bay. On November 21, 1995, this court suspended Attorney O'Neil's license to practice law for 12 months as the result of misconduct involving dishonesty, fraud, deceit, and misrepresentation. Attorney O'Neil's license was reinstated on February 26, 1997.

On May 6, 1999, Attorney O'Neil was retained by Erik Gracia to file a divorce action against his wife, Colleen Gracia. Mr. Gracia paid Attorney O'Neil a $1,000 retainer and provided him with copies of various financial records. Attorney O'Neil contacted the Brown County Family Court Commissioner's Office to schedule a date for a temporary hearing and prepared the necessary pleadings to commence a divorce action.

On May 11, 1999, Gracia filed the divorce petition and gave Attorney O'Neil the required filing fee. That same day, before the divorce petition was filed, Colleen Gracia was found dead. Newspaper accounts indicated that investigators initially thought the cause of her death was suicide, but two weeks later an autopsy established the cause of death as homicide by asphyxiation.

On May 12, 1999, Gracia called Attorney O'Neil to notify him of his wife's death and to request a refund of his retainer. Attorney O'Neil was out of the office that day but learned of Mrs. Gracia's death in a phone call to his office.

On May 14, 1999, Detective Zittel from the Green Bay Police Department contacted Attorney O'Neil's office and spoke to both Attorney O'Neil and his secretary. The police report indicates that Attorney O'Neil told the detective that Erik Gracia said the reason he wanted a divorce was that his wife had a boyfriend. The police report also indicates that Attorney O'Neil told the detective that Gracia said he and his wife were splitting up their property and that Gracia did not want any confrontation in the divorce and wanted the case to go smoothly.

The police report also indicates that Attorney O'Neil told Detective Zittel that when Erik Gracia came into his office his mother was with him. Attorney O'Neil also told the detective that when he spoke to Erik Gracia the day after his wife's death Gracia told Attorney O'Neil to stop the divorce and refund the retainer money. The police report further indicates that the detective asked Attorney O'Neil if he would jot down any conversations he might have in the future with Erik Gracia, and Attorney O'Neil said he would do so. Although Attorney O'Neil denied the accuracy of some statements attributed to him, he admitted meeting with the detective and discussing the matter with him. Attorney O'Neil did not request Gracia's consent to provide information relating to his representation of Gracia to the police.

On May 18, 1999, Gracia telephoned Attorney O'Neil and inquired about representation in defense of potential criminal proceedings. Attorney O'Neil referred Gracia to an attorney not associated with O'Neil's firm. This was the last contact Attorney O'Neil had with Gracia.

On June 8, 1999, the Brown County Circuit Court issued a subpoena for Attorney O'Neil's file for the Gracia divorce. The subpoena stated that, pursuant to an official felony criminal investigation, Attorney O'Neil was "requested" to furnish copies of "any file notes, records, and all other information concerning your work on behalf of Erik Garcia [sic] in his pending divorce action with Colleen Garcia [sic]." Attorney O'Neil did not request Gracia's consent to turn over the file or provide information to the police. On June 14, 1999, Attorney O'Neil turned over to police investigators the entire Gracia file, including notes, bank account records, and other financial information.

The police report indicates that during a June 14, 1999, interview Attorney O'Neil told a police investigator that when he initially met with Gracia, Gracia said he wanted Attorney O'Neil to set up custody arrangements and visitation with Colleen Gracia for their daughter and that Gracia did not want to talk to Colleen. Attorney O'Neil told the investigator he thought it was strange that Gracia could not at least talk to his wife about these things. Attorney O'Neil also told the investigator that Gracia said Colleen had taken a second job to help pay for daycare for their daughter and this made Gracia mad.

Attorney O'Neil told the police investigator that Gracia said he was not looking for any type of reconciliation with Colleen and that he just wanted to get divorced and get it over with. Attorney O'Neil told police that during his initial interview with Gracia he probably would have told Gracia he would be obligated to pay 17 percent of his income for child support, along with other expenses. Attorney O'Neil said Gracia neglected to tell him about his past record of domestic abuse. In looking over the financial form that Gracia had filled out Attorney O'Neil noted that Gracia made approximately $1100 a month after taxes and that his expenses were almost double his monthly income. While Attorney O'Neil denied making some of the statements attributed to him in the investigator's report, he admitted meeting with the police investigator on June 14, 1999, and discussing the Gracia divorce case.

Police investigators noted that one of the legal forms in the Gracia file had been signed by Gracia the day of Colleen's murder and had been notarized by Attorney O'Neil's secretary. Attorney O'Neil, without seeking Gracia's consent, gave the police investigators permission to talk with his secretary about the times and dates she had contact with Gracia in the O'Neil law office. The investigators did contact Attorney O'Neil's secretary who supplied them with the information they requested.

On July 28, 1999, criminal charges were filed against Gracia. He was subsequently convicted of first-degree intentional homicide in the death of his wife and is currently serving a life sentence.

The complaint filed by the Office of Lawyer Regulation (OLR) alleged that Attorney O'Neil never considered asserting the attorney-client privilege on behalf of Gracia, that he acknowledged he should have done so, and that he claimed to have provided the information to law enforcement investigators because he felt that by doing so he was best serving his client's interests. The complaint alleged that Gracia contended the statements made by Attorney O'Neil to law enforcement investigators were used in the decision to issue criminal charges and that financial information that was disclosed from the divorce file was used by the prosecution to help establish a motive for the crime.

The referee filed his report and recommendation on February 19, 2003. The referee's report notes that prior to the Gracia murder trial the Brown County District Attorney agreed not to use any of the information received from Attorney O'Neil when filing the original and amended criminal complaints and, in fact, no documents received from Attorney O'Neil were used at Gracia's trial. The referee's report also notes that neither Attorney O'Neil nor any member of his staff was called as a witness at the trial and none of the information disclosed by Attorney O'Neil was used in the prosecution of Gracia's case. The referee also notes that Gracia did not raise any issues about Attorney O'Neil's representation in his criminal appeal. In its opinion affirming Gracia's judgment of conviction the court of appeals pointed to the overwhelming circumstantial evidence of Gracia's guilt, including his inconsistent statements, DNA evidence, and admissions against interest.

The referee's report note that, in defense of his admitted violation of the rule, Attorney O'Neil suggested he was trying to help Gracia by divulging information in his client's file which showed that the divorce was amicable and that the Gracias were attempting to split up the marital property without a contest. The referee also notes that Attorney O'Neil claimed he did not know he was violating [the confidentiality rule] when he made the disclosures to police. The referee's report states that Attorney O'Neil said since the filing of the grievance he has become familiar with [the rule], has advised his staff with respect to the importance of confidentiality, and attended a seminar on the subject.

The referee concluded that by disclosing his client's file and discussing its contents with the Green Bay Police Department, Attorney O'Neil revealed information relating to representation of a client without the client's consent, in violation of [the confidentiality rule]. The referee concluded that although Attorney O'Neil was previously suspended from practicing law for 12 months, and although the violations committed in the instant case were unrelated to those resulting in the previous suspension, and there did not appear to be a pattern of misconduct, the time period between Attorney O'Neil being reinstated to practice and the commitment of the violation in this matter was only 27 months.

The referee concluded that although misconduct occurred, it was not of a significantly serious nature given the mitigating circumstances. The referee also concluded there was no need to protect the public from Attorney O'Neil since he has indicated he now understands [the rule] and has said he will conduct his practice accordingly. The referee also noted that Attorney O'Neil cooperated fully with the OLR and for the most part made full and free disclosures showing a cooperative attitude toward the proceedings. The referee recommended that Attorney O'Neil be given a public reprimand and that he be required to pay the costs of the proceeding, which totaled $11,438.82 as of March 12, 2003.

We adopt the referee's findings of fact and conclusions of law. Attorney O'Neil's misconduct with respect to his disclosure of information relating to representation of a client without the client's consent is a serious failing. As discipline for the professional misconduct we impose a public reprimand and order Attorney O'Neil to pay the costs of this proceeding, as recommended by the referee.

* * *

Topics for Further Discussion

1. The decision states that the lawyer contended that he did not know giving client information to the police in a murder investigation would violate the confidentiality rule. Is this a plausible defense? If O'Neil really did not understand the violation, should he have been allowed to practice law in the first place?

2. Why didn't the client challenge his murder conviction based on the lawyer's disclosure of information? If he had challenged the conviction, what would the specific grounds be?

3. Although the court described the lawyer's misconduct as serious, it did not suspend him from practicing law. Rather, it only issued a "public reprimand," meaning a public criticism of the attorney. What are the mitigating factors the court considered? Are future clients likely to know about this reprimand? If not, what good does it do?

Conflicts of Interest

As part of the lawyer's duty to the client, she may not be involved with other representations or activities that would conflict with the client's interests. Lawyers are required to avoid even the appearance of a conflict. This is related to the confidentiality requirement. For example, a lawyer may represent an auto manufacturer in a defense to a personal injury product defect lawsuit. As a result of the representation, she will learn a great deal about the company's design process. Later on, a different person claiming injury might want to hire her to represent him as plaintiff against the company. The lawyer must refuse, unless the conflict is disclosed to both parties and they give an informed waiver.

Entering into business transactions with clients is a particularly dangerous undertaking, although it may seem perfectly reasonable at the time. A lawyer representing a client in developing a piece of property may believe that the development offers a good chance for profit. At the same time, the client might like to minimize the amount he must pay the lawyer. Thus, they might want to consider giving the lawyer part ownership in return for his waiving his fees. Later, however, if the business goes bad, the interests of the lawyer and the client may come to differ.

The prohibition against conflict of interest even applies to others in the same law firm. Model Rule 1.10 says that if one of the lawyers in the firm would be disqualified from taking the case because of a conflict, all of them are disqualified. For this reason, when lawyers move from one firm to another, the new firm must make sure that hiring the attorney will not cause conflicts with its existing clients. Similarly, when a new potential client comes seeking help, the law firm must first search its records to confirm that taking on the representation will not conflict with its existing obligations. In some cases, if the new client is big enough, the firm may decide to give up its association with the old client. In doing so, however, it must ensure that the needs of the existing client are taken care of by other lawyers. Also, it may not use any information that it gained as a result of its previous relationship against the previous client.

As law firms become larger, the disqualification rules become all the more difficult to monitor. A firm with offices around the globe must maintain a sophisticated computer data base of clients and their matters that can be checked for conflicts in a timely manner. With so many lawyers in the United States, another attorney can always be found. That is not always the case in countries that have far fewer members of the bar. The number of lawyers who can handle complex international business transactions in foreign languages (especially English) may be few indeed. Such countries often tolerate law firms simultaneously representing competitors, perhaps insisting only on some separation between the attorneys actually responsible for the different clients. This is sometimes called a "Chinese Wall," deriving from analogy to the Great Wall of China.

Doe ex rel. Doe v. Perry Community School Dist.
650 N.W.2d 594 (Iowa 2002)

Streit, J.

Litigants in a civil sexual abuse case against a school district want the court to stop their lawyer's new law firm from representing the school district in the litigation. The law firm, Bradshaw, Fowler, Proctor & Fairgrave, P.C., argues it has implemented a screening mechanism sufficient to prevent the disclosure of confidential information between the disqualified associate, Jason Palmer, and the other members of the firm. The district court found adequate screening procedures were in place to ensure there was no actual conflict between the other members of the firm and its client. Because the representations by Palmer for the plaintiffs and the Bradshaw law firm for the defendants bear a substantial relationship to each other, we reverse and remand.

Russell Alan Gronewold, an eighth-grade teacher at Perry Middle School was convicted of sexually abusing Jane Doe, one of his fourteen-year-old students. Attorney Brent Cashatt of Smith, Schneider, Stiles, Hudson, Serangeli, Mallaney & Shindler served as Doe's guardian *ad litem* in the criminal case. Attorney Jason Palmer was an associate with the Smith law firm at that time and appeared as the Does' attorney.

Doe and her parents retained Cashatt, Palmer, and Jan Mohrfeld to represent them in their civil suit against Gronewold, the Perry Community School District, and principal Arthur Pixler. Palmer attended a pre-petition conference with the clients. He prepared a draft of the petition using the clients' file, including internal memoranda. Palmer signed the petition and it was filed on February 26, 2001.

On March 21, 2001, members of Bradshaw, Fowler, Proctor & Fairgrave, P.C., appeared on behalf of the school district and Pixler. Palmer joined the Bradshaw firm in August 2001. Because of the conflict between Bradshaw's current representation of the defendants and Palmer's prior representation of the Does, Palmer filed a motion to withdraw as counsel for the Does.

The Does filed a motion to disqualify the Bradshaw firm based upon Palmer's prior representation of the Does in the same lawsuit. The district court denied the motion. The court presumed confidences were divulged by the Does to Palmer in the prior representation which may be relevant to the current representation. However, the court found it was clear Bradshaw ensured there was no actual conflict by creating a "Chinese Wall." The court further noted to disqualify Bradshaw at this stage of the proceedings would deny the defendants counsel of their choice and place them at a disadvantage in the lawsuit. We granted the Does' application for interlocutory appeal.

This case presents an issue of first impression in Iowa. We must determine whether a screening mechanism known as a Chinese Wall is sufficient to allow a law firm to eliminate the conflict of an attorney who switched sides of representation during the same case. In general, an attorney must be disqualified from representing a party against a former client if the two representations bear a "substantial relationship" to each other. Here, Bradshaw contends its implementation of a Chinese Wall is sufficient to avoid disqualification of the entire law firm.

The Does do not need to show confidences were actually disclosed by Palmer to prove a conflict exists. To show the Bradshaw firm must be disqualified, the Does must only prove there is a substantial relationship between the former and the present representation. In determining whether a substantial relationship exists, we consider: (1) the nature and scope of the prior representation; (2) the nature of the present lawsuit; and (3) whether the client might have disclosed a confidence to her attorney in the prior representation which could be relevant to the present action. The former client must be given the presumption confidences were disclosed.

Bradshaw admits a substantial relationship exists between the two representations. Palmer's former representation of the Does and Bradshaw's current representation of the defendants involve the same case. Palmer filed a motion to withdraw from the current litigation because of his previous participation in the Does' case. The pending lawsuit includes allegations that the school district and principal knew Gronewold molested Doe but did nothing to stop the continual harassment and abuse. Such issues necessarily involve sensitive and confidential information. The Does likely disclosed confidences to Palmer in the prior representation which would certainly be relevant in Bradshaw's defense of the school district and principal. As such, we conclude there is a substantial relationship between the former and the present representations. This determination alone requires disqualification of the Bradshaw firm.

Because of the strong appearance of impropriety, once we conclude a substantial relationship exists between the two representations, disqualification cannot be avoided.

The extent of Palmer's involvement in the prior representation is clear. Palmer first appeared in this case as Does' attorney. On one occasion, Palmer met with Mr. and Mrs. Doe to discuss whether the Does should file a civil law suit. Palmer had telephone conversations with the Does. He signed pleadings and entered his appearance on behalf of the Does. Brent Cashatt, Jane Doe's guardian *ad litem,* testified "confidences were exchanged." Paige Fiedler joined the Smith attorneys in the lawsuit only a few days prior to the date the Does filed their lawsuit. Cashatt stated that prior to Fiedler taking over, Palmer had done most of the work on the case. Palmer drafted the petition in the civil suit. In drafting the petition, Palmer had access to the entire case file, including all internal memoranda, correspondence to and from the Does, and attorney notes from confidential meetings, and telephone calls with the Does. The Smith law firm ultimately filed Palmer's draft of the petition with some revisions. Though there is some question regarding whether Palmer drafted the exact petition filed, there is no doubt Palmer signed the filed petition.

Given these circumstances, we find a reasonable layperson would conclude Bradshaw's current representation would compromise the integrity of the trial and would harm the Does. This conflict before us did not arise as the result of Palmer's prior representation in a different, unrelated matter. Rather, Palmer's firm now stands as adversary against the Does in the very litigation in which Palmer first served as their trusted attorney. When Palmer left the Smith firm, he stopped advocating for the Does by taking a new position clearly adverse to their best interests.

To analogize to baseball, [Palmer] has not only switched teams, he has switched teams in the middle of the game after learning the signals. That [Palmer] has been benched by his new team does little to ameliorate the public perception of an unfair game.

For a lawyer to represent the Does today, and the defendant school district and principal tomorrow in the same litigation "creates an unsavory appearance of a conflict of interest that is difficult to dispel in the eyes of the lay public or even the bench and bar." Despite the attempted screening, continued representation constitutes a threat to the adversarial process and creates an undeniably strong appearance of impropriety.

Though Bradshaw concedes there is a substantial relationship between the prior and current representations, it attempts to minimize the degree of Palmer's involvement in the plaintiff's case and emphasizes the steps it took to lessen his contact with the defense. Specifically, Bradshaw argues the use of a Chinese Wall allows the firm to avoid imputed disqualification. Bradshaw contends it has taken precautionary measures to prevent disclosure of confidential information. The firm asserts Palmer, now at the Bradshaw firm, has no involvement in or access to the Does' case. Bradshaw contends it has taken and will continue to take "appropriate safeguards to completely isolate Mr. Palmer from involvement in or knowledge about this case."

The presence or absence of a Chinese Wall does not enter into our analysis of whether there is a substantial relationship between two representations. We consider whether a substantial relationship exists based upon the nature and scope of the prior representation, the nature of the present lawsuit, and whether confidences may have been disclosed. If we determine a substantial relationship exists, then unequivocally, the law firm must be disqualified. This is such a case. This is not a case where Palmer did not have involvement in the case prior to his switch to Bradshaw. As discussed above, Palmer's involvement was substantial, significant, and intimate. A Chinese Wall will not prevent the conclusion that a substantial relationship exists and Palmer's new firm cannot continue to represent the defendants.

It appears Bradshaw implemented the Chinese Wall only *after* the Does filed their petition to disqualify the firm. There is no evidence to suggest Bradshaw took any steps to prevent Palmer from divulging the Does' confidences to the other Bradshaw attorneys prior to that time. There is also little evidence to prove Bradshaw implemented procedures to prevent the other Bradshaw attorneys from discussing sensitive matters regarding the present lawsuit. We presume Palmer and the Bradshaw lawyers will act within the confines of our rules of ethics and professional responsibility. However, confidence in attorneys alone does not overcome the strong appearance of impropriety in cases such as this where the litigation involves sensitive and confidential matters.

We approve of the use of Chinese Walls under certain circumstances to overcome imputed disqualification of a law firm. Such circumstances do not exist in this case. There is a substantial relationship between the former and present representations. Accordingly, it is improper for Bradshaw to continue its representation and it must be disqualified. We conclude the district court abused its discretion in denying Does' petition to disqualify Bradshaw. We reverse and remand for further proceedings consistent with this opinion.

* * *

Topics for Further Discussion

1. The lawyer who changed law firms was an associate in the first firm and became an associate in the second. He was not a partner of the law firm. Should this make any difference?

2. Could the second law firm have done anything more to prevent being disqualified from representing the school district?

3. Ordinarily, a party may only appeal from a lower court judgment once the final judgment has been entered. In some cases, an interlocutory appeal (a provisional appeal) will be allowed to resolve a critical point in advance. The issue of who could represent the school district would affect the entire trial; thus, it was appropriate for an interlocutory appeal.

Simpson Performance Products, Inc. v. Robert W. Horn, P.C.

92 P.3d 283 (Wyo. 2004)

Voigt, J.

The appellant, Simpson Performance Products, Inc. (SPP), hired the appellee, Robert W. Horn (Horn), to conduct an investigation and to provide legal counsel regarding a possible lawsuit by SPP against the National Association of Stock Car Auto Racing (NASCAR). Upon completing his work, Horn submitted a bill to SPP for $40,383.29 for legal fees and costs. SPP paid Horn $20,000.00, but refused to pay the balance. Horn sued SPP to collect the outstanding amount. The district court found in favor of Horn. SPP now appeals, claiming that Horn is not entitled to the entire fee because his representation of E.J. "Bill" Simpson (Simpson), individually, violated Rule 1.9 of the Wyoming Rules of Professional Conduct for Attorneys at Law (Rule 1.9). Finding no violation of Rule 1.9, we affirm.

Horn represented SPP in investigating a possible lawsuit against NASCAR. He then represented Simpson, who had recently resigned as the CEO of SPP, in a lawsuit against NASCAR involving the same facts and cause of action. The issue presented by this case is whether Horn's representation of Simpson, his new client, was "materially adverse" to SPP, his former client, and therefore a violation of Rule 1.9.

SPP manufactures and sells automobile racing safety equipment such as fire-resistant driver suits, helmets, shoes, seatbelts and other products. In 1998, Simpson, the company's founder, sold a two-thirds interest in the company to Carousel Capital. Simpson retained his one-third share and remained involved with the company, acting as the Chairman of the Board of Directors and Chief Executive Officer.

On February 18, 2001, Dale Earnhardt died in a racing accident at the Daytona 500. Five days later, NASCAR held a press conference where a NASCAR representative displayed an SPP brand seatbelt and stated that it had broken in the crash. Further, the NASCAR representative asserted that had the seatbelt not failed, Earnhardt would have survived the accident.

The negative publicity resulting from the NASCAR press conference threatened SPP's reputation and financial well-being. SPP hired Epley and Associates, a public relations group, to assess the situation and to propose a plan to counter the negative publicity. Additionally, SPP considered a slander/false-light lawsuit against NASCAR, and was conditionally, SPP considered a slander/false-light lawsuit against NASCAR, and was concerned with a potential wrongful death suit by the Earnhardt family. Nelson Schwab (Schwab), Carousel Capital's managing partner, and Simpson agreed to hire two attorneys to "gather information and facts surrounding the accident in case there was a possible lawsuit." Robert Horn, a Jackson lawyer who had performed some prior work for Simpson, and Jim Voyles, a lawyer from Indianapolis, Indiana, were hired in March of 2001 to perform this task. No formal engagement letter was drafted; however, it was agreed that Horn would bill SPP "at 200 an hour for non-court time and 250 for court time, and that the cost of the case would be borne by Simpson Performance Products."

From March 28, 2001, to September 9, 2001, Voyles and Horn provided legal services to SPP. They actively participated in an investigation conducted by NASCAR into the cause of Dale Earnhardt's death. During that time, Horn billed approximately 200 hours and incurred expenses relating to three trips.

Simpson was saddened and distraught by the death of Earnhardt, who was a personal friend, and even more upset that SPP was being partly blamed for the tragedy. He was quite steadfast in his desire to sue NASCAR, and felt that a lawsuit was necessary to clear the company's name and protect its reputation. However, Schwab did not share Simpson's view. Schwab felt the only way to stabilize SPP and maintain its viability was to work with NASCAR and preserve that relationship. In August of 2001, Simpson resigned from SPP, reporting that his "relationship with them had become very strained." He stated, "I don't know if [the resignation] was in regard to us suing NASCAR. It was in regard to us protecting the name, the Simpson name, that I worked so hard to build a spotless reputation."

Having completed its investigation into the Earnhardt crash, NASCAR held another press conference on August 21, 2001, to report its results. Schwab, Horn, Voyles, Simpson, and other SPP representatives attended the press conference. The results of NASCAR's investigation indicated a number of factors, including a failure of the seatbelt, contributed to Earnhardt's death. Simpson felt that NASCAR's statement was inadequate and that SPP was not exonerated. Following the press conference, the group from SPP "huddled briefly" and agreed to meet in the next few days to decide how to respond.

On September 5, 2001, Horn and Voyles participated in a conference call with Schwab to discuss an appropriate course of action for SPP. The attorneys reported the conclusions they had reached as a result of their investigation, and offered their opinions about SPP's likelihood of success in a lawsuit against NASCAR. Schwab then indicated that SPP's relationship with NASCAR was improving and stated that he had discussed the possibility of the lawsuit with SPP corporate counsel and they predicted a remote chance of success. Schwab then told Voyles and Horn that SPP had no interest in pursuing a lawsuit against NASCAR.

When Schwab decided that SPP would not sue NASCAR, the purpose for which Horn had been hired—to participate in the investigation and evaluate the possibility of a lawsuit by SPP against NASCAR—was complete. Horn prepared a final bill totaling $40,383.29, which he submitted to SPP in October of 2001.

Two months after SPP decided it would not pursue an action against NASCAR, Simpson decided to sue NASCAR on his own. He contacted Voyles and Horn to inform them that he planned to sue and to ask their opinion. Simpson told them that he was going to send them a "pile of information" to look over to determine if there was a basis for his individual lawsuit. Horn and Voyles sought the assistance of Dick Cardwell, an Indianapolis lawyer with special expertise in libel issues, and the three attorneys began preparing the lawsuit for Simpson.

Although Simpson had resigned from SPP, there was continued discussion between Simpson and SPP about the possibility of his returning to the company in some capacity. Simpson was adamant that he would only return if SPP agreed to go forward with the lawsuit against NASCAR. Because of the continued negotiations between Simpson and SPP, the first draft of the lawsuit against NASCAR included both Simpson individually and SPP as named plaintiffs. When SPP received a draft of the complaint in late January 2002, or early February 2002, Schwab immediately called Horn and Voyles to inform them that SPP had no interest in the lawsuit, and issued a press release announcing that SPP was not suing NASCAR. On February 13, 2002, Simpson, as the lone plaintiff, filed the suit against NASCAR.

When SPP received Horn's bill, Chuck Davies (Davies), who was acting as the company's CEO following Simpson's resignation, was "uncomfortable" with the amount. On February 28, 2002, Horn received an email from Davies informing him that SPP would make no further payments. The email stated, "I think that the [$]20,000 we have paid you is the most we consider reasonable for the only bill you submitted in October representing work you said was for several earlier months." Davies later testified that he probably would have paid the entire amount had Horn not prepared the lawsuit for Simpson.

On March 19, 2002, Horn filed a lawsuit to collect the unpaid balance of his bill. Following a two-day trial, the district court took the matter under consideration. Less than one month later, a decision letter finding in favor of Horn was sent to the parties; and on April 21, 2003, the district court entered a judgment in the amount of $20,383.29 in favor of Horn. SPP filed a notice of appeal on May 13, 2003.

SPP claims that Horn violated Rule 1.9 when he represented Simpson in the lawsuit against NASCAR, and therefore he should be required to forfeit his fee. Horn contends that his representation of Simpson was not in violation of the rule inasmuch as the lawsuit against NASCAR was not "materially adverse" to the interests of SPP. Rule 1.9(a) reads:

> A lawyer who has formerly represented a client in a matter shall not thereafter represent another person in the same or a substantially related matter in which that person's interests are materially adverse to the interests of the former client unless the former client consents after consultation except that when the former client is a governmental entity, consent is not permitted.

When a lawyer violates Rule 1.9, a number of remedies are available to the aggrieved party: many seek disqualification of the attorney or his firm, others may pursue a malpractice action, and others file a grievance.

If the interests of Horn's present client Simpson, and his former client SPP, are not materially adverse, then Horn did not violate Rule 1.9; and if he did not violate Rule 1.9, then SPP is obligated to pay the entire amount of Horn's attorney's fees.

We must first ascertain what is meant by "materially adverse."

As the comments to Rule 1.7 indicate, most alleged conflicts of interest relating to former clients arise when a lawyer is representing a new client who is suing a former client. However, the question of whether representation is "materially adverse" to a former client becomes less clear in situations like the present, where the former client, although not directly involved in the litigation, may be affected by it in some manner.

SPP claims that Horn's representation of Simpson was materially adverse to it because Schwab had advised Horn that SPP did not want to pursue the lawsuit against NASCAR, and because it jeopardized SPP's relationship with NASCAR, its major customer. SPP fails to expound on this argument or point to any facts contained in the record demonstrating any harm the company has suffered, or will suffer, as a result of Horn's representation of Simpson. Contrary to SPP's assertion, the record indicates that the company's relationship with NASCAR has not been adversely affected.

Also, we find nothing in the record indicating that Horn's representation of Simpson compromised his continuing duty of loyalty and confidentiality to his former client, SPP.

SPP fails to point to any disclosure of confidential information or breach of Horn's duty of loyalty, and the irrebuttable presumption of disclosure does not arise in this case, as SPP has failed to demonstrate that its interests are materially adverse to Horn's representation of Simpson.

We refuse to speculate as to the possible effects, adverse or otherwise, that Horn's representation of Simpson may have had, or could have, on SPP. Based on the facts, as they exist in the record, we hold that Horn's representation of Simpson was not "materially" or "directly" adverse to SPP in violation of Rule 1.9.

Finding no violation of Rule 1.9, we affirm the decision of the district court.

* * *

Topics for Further Discussion

1. What was the relationship between the money SPP owed to the lawyer for his previous representation and the claim that his subsequent representation of Simpson was a conflict? Wouldn't the proper remedy for any violation be simply to have him disqualified from helping Simpson?

2. In the *Doe* case, the court said the strong appearance of impropriety was enough to disqualify the lawyer. In the *Horn* case, the court looked for some actual evidence of harm and found none. Are these approaches consistent?

Counseling and Mediation

The Model Rules contemplate a lawyer doing more than taking adversary positions on behalf of a client. They authorize the attorney to refer to moral and social matters, among others, in offering advice. Beyond that, they allow him to serve as an intermediary between clients, but only if both clients agree and the lawyer believes he can serve them both well. That may be possible theoretically, but—in actual practice—it is very difficult to achieve. The results of failure are that the lawyer will no longer be able to represent either party.

A divorce between spouses who wish to end their marriage without bitterness would seem to be a perfect candidate for this type of approach. Not only would it avoid the contentiousness that comes with divorce litigation, it would cut the legal fees at least in half, as both parties could share one lawyer. Unfortunately, the ideal often soon becomes tarnished. Which of the spouses earns a greater income? Should one pay some sort of financial support to the other? Assuming they agree on the need for and amount of money for the care of the children, how should it be structured? Including it as alimony—payment to the spouse—makes it taxable to the receiving party. The spouses may agree on the goals, but—at the outset—they may have no idea that the goals could be achieved in many different ways that favor one side or the other. Once they find out, their commitment to shared representation may soon fade, and both of them may be forced to start from the beginning with new attorneys.

Advocacy

More commonly, a lawyer is called upon to be an advocate for her client. As mentioned earlier, an attorney may not reveal information she receives from the client without the client's consent, but she may not participate in knowingly allowing misinformation to come into court. Model Rule 3.1 prohibits an attorney from taking frivolous positions. Rule 3.2 says a lawyer should make reasonable efforts to keep litigation moving along, and Rule 3.3 says a lawyer must be truthful in dealing with a court. That includes revealing laws or cases that may go against the client's position and not offering false evidence. Rule 3.4 requires fairness to the opposing party and counsel too. A recurring problem in America's courts is finding the line between zealous advocacy of a client and abuse of the other participants.

In re Discipline of Eicher
661 N.W.2d 354 (S.D. 2003)

Gilbertson, C.J.

This is a disciplinary proceeding against Benjamin J. Eicher, a member of the State Bar of South Dakota. The Disciplinary Board of the State Bar of South Dakota has recommended public censure. The Referee has recommended a public censure on some issues and a private reprimand on another. Eicher urges the Court to hold that he "committed no violations of the Rules of Professional conduct for which reprimand of any kind is appropriate."

Eicher is a 1985 graduate of the University of Nebraska School of Law. After passing the bar examination he was admitted to practice law in South Dakota. He specializes in litigation and insurance defense.

Koch Complaint

On April 16, 2002, Spearfish attorney Dedrich R. Koch filed a complaint with the Disciplinary Board concerning Eicher's conduct in a civil action, *Thomas v. Thomas*. In the course of the lawsuit, Koch, who represented Gail Thomas, and Eicher, who represented Shirley M. Thomas, filed various motions and pretrial briefs and memorandums for Circuit Judge Kern's consideration. Koch attached these to his complaint and told the Board: "Although I personally find Mr. Eicher's repeated threats and claims for sanctions to be unsupported, meritless and unprofessional, it is the personal attacks and insults hurled by Mr. Eicher at my client and me that I can not ignore. Vigorously attacking the allegations or criticizing the tactics of an opponent does not necessitate or allow the use of such blatantly offensive comments and I hope the disciplinary board will take the necessary steps to inform Mr. Eicher of the same."

In a document titled "Shirley Thomas' Reply to Gail Thomas' Brief in Support of Motion for Waste and Property Taxes" Eicher wrote, in part:

> Gail's attempt to avoid any burden at all from her great bounty (it is assumed that no one would even try to argue that receiving title to $100,000 in unencumbered property without paying the giver a penny for it constitutes a "great bounty"), is shockingly greedy, to put it bluntly.

Gail continues to not only want her pound of flesh from Shirley, but wants all of the blood associated with it.

Gail's greed is stunningly bold.

Then, to make certain that her fangs are fully bared for all to see, Gail hurls yet another dose of acidic bile at Shirley. Gail accuses Shirley of criminal misconduct.... Perhaps Gail plans to have Shirley arrested, and hauled from the courtroom on March 27 in shackles, too.

Gail's despicable greed should not be rewarded.

Gail's ... adamant persistence in trying to make Shirley accountable, belies an active, rancid animosity against Shirley which not only defies logic but apparently knows no bounds.

Following Judge Kern's oral bench decision which was adverse to Eicher's client, Eicher filed a "Memorandum of Law for Reconsideration." In it he chastised Judge Kern: "The Court attempted to issue its oral bench decision on March 27 in the scant moments left on the Court's clock at that specific time."

In this document Eicher also lectured the trial court about his view of Koch's legal ability:

Our present system is clogged with specious claims brought by novice lawyers. It is clogged with positions which have no basis in fact or law, as if "lawyering" means to disagree with whatever the other side says. The circuit court judges see enough of this. But, the Court should be well aware that for every example played out before it in open court, are hundreds of instances "behind the scenes" which never see the inside of a court file or the courtroom.

Formerly, there was a greater amount of mentoring by older, experienced lawyers to guide novice attorneys. However, without mentoring and without an eye toward quality practicing, Gail and her counsel simply fire away with a blunderbuss as much buckshot as possible—even if it is improper, unmerited, groundless or just plain wrong—with the comfort of knowing that all the Court will do is reject the position. Just like a child who grows up undisciplined because the parents failed to provide appropriately strict guidance, when lawyers dump their half-baked or completely uninvestigated contentions on the courtroom floor without any correction, then it's no wonder that they never learn to do things differently (i.e., correctly) next time.

Clayborne Complaint

On April 22, 2002, Rapid City attorney Courtney R. Clayborne filed a complaint with the Disciplinary Board concerning Eicher's conduct in a criminal court trial held February 8, 2002.

Eicher represented Shawna Martin who was accused of stealing money from her employer. Clayborne represented her employer and was the first witness called during Martin's criminal trial. Clayborne testified that he had spoken with Martin who admitted to him that she had taken money from her employer on two or three occasions.

He also testified that he had watched two videotapes supplied by Martin's employer which showed Martin stealing money.

Eicher, in open court and "as an officer of the court," moved to dismiss the charges because the State no longer had the videotapes of Martin in its possession. Eicher told the trial court that he had watched the videotapes and they showed Martin "didn't take anything." He claimed that the videotapes were "Defendant's best evidence" "because of what it shows and what it doesn't show. It's our best evidence because the other testimony would be that people are in and out of that [money] bag all the time." He argued, "It's manifest that when the State loses evidence, that is significant it is grossly prejudicial to the defendant[.]" It deprived him of evidence necessary to cross examine witnesses.

Eicher did not tell the trial court that he possessed copies of the videotapes. He received them from one of the employer's attorneys seven months earlier in a civil proceeding Martin initiated. During a break in the criminal trial Clayborne confronted Eicher and told him that it was unethical and misleading to fail to tell the court that he had copies of the videotape. Following the recess, Eicher told the court of Clayborne's accusation. He admitted that he had copies of the videotapes but did not bring them. He told the court that "I haven't misled the court about anything. The official tapes that are in evidence are not here." He also told the court, "[b]ut for [Clayborne] to accuse me of unethical conduct is about how low we've got to this thing."

Disciplinary Board

Following a hearing the Disciplinary Board entered findings of fact and conclusions of law. Included in its findings were: "[Eicher's] conduct demonstrates a persistent practice prejudicial to the administration of justice of directing exceptionally harsh, vindictive and insulting communication to opposing counsel that serve no purpose, but aim to harass opposing counsel and their clients and result in burdening the justice system with unnecessary expense and acrimony."

Referee

The Referee recommended that Eicher receive a private reprimand for his conduct in the Clayborne complaint and a public censure for the remaining violations of Rules of Professional Conduct. The Referee noted: "[Eicher] is an intelligent and articulate attorney with a resume replete with accomplishments, civil, legal, and religious. All of this notwithstanding, it appears to me that [Eicher] does not know, or refuses to acknowledge, the distinction between retaliation and appropriate response; between offensive personality and fair and reasoned comment; between vigorous representation and professional conduct. It is his obligation to know and follow."

Legal Analysis 1. The Koch Complaint

When Eicher became a member of the State Bar of South Dakota he took an oath to "abstain from all offensive personality, and advance no fact prejudicial to the honor or reputation of a party or witness, unless required by the justice of the cause with which I am charged[.]" "Each day of an attorney's life demands that these requirements be met anew." This constitutes a lawyer's duty, and a lawyer's responsibility to "use the law's procedures only for legitimate purposes and not to harass or intimidate others. A lawyer should demonstrate respect for the legal system and for those who serve it, including judges, other lawyers and public officials."

"[T]he legal profession has seen an increasing number of attorneys engaging in conduct that is personally and professionally offensive. State-bar disciplinary action results because of findings that an attorney has engaged in flagrant disrespect toward a court, opposing counsel, an adverse party, or the attorney's own client[.]"

Eicher's written comments to the trial court in the *Thomas* matter concerning Koch, Koch's client, and the trial court, went far beyond fair and reasoned comment protected by the First Amendment. Instead they constitute unprotected, unprofessional statements.

2. The Clayborne Complaint

During a criminal trial Eicher moved to dismiss the proceeding because the State failed to produce the original videotapes purporting to show his client taking money. Eicher claimed that the tapes provided exculpatory evidence and his ability to cross examine witnesses was impaired by the loss of the tapes. Eicher did not tell the court that he had a copy of the videotapes until Clayborne confronted him with this fact.

While Eicher did not directly lie to the trial court, he intentionally misled the court concerning the availability of what he claimed was essential evidence. "Clearly, the requirement of candor towards the tribunal goes beyond simply telling a portion of the truth." It requires every attorney to be fully honest and forthright.

We cannot overemphasize the importance of attorneys in this state being absolutely fair with the court. Every court ... has the right to rely upon an attorney to assist it in ascertaining the truth of the case before it. Therefore, candor and fairness should characterize the conduct of an attorney at the beginning, during, and at the close of litigation. There is no allowance for interpretation.

Eicher's professional obligation to represent his client does not exonerate him in this situation. "[T]here is a line that even the zealous advocate cannot cross." It is absolutely necessary that each member of the bar comprehends the great responsibility that every person who has the privilege to practice law must strive for: to be a person of unquestionable integrity as he or she deals with the rights of people before the bar. A practitioner of the legal profession does not have the liberty to flirt with the idea that the end justifies the means, or any other rationalization that would excuse less than complete honesty in the practice of the profession. Certainly, our Rules of Professional Conduct allow no such flirtation.

It is the duty of an attorney and counselor at law to employ, for the purpose of maintaining the causes confided to him, such means only as are consistent with truth and never to seek to mislead the judges by any artifice or false statement of fact or law.

Eicher intentionally misled the court and "crosse[d] the line into improper and unprofessional conduct."

Appropriate Discipline

Eicher refuses to acknowledge the impropriety of his actions. This, coupled with his penchant for blaming others and the repeated unprofessional attacks that have continued throughout this appeal underscore the need for discipline.

Eicher's egregious conduct involved in this case combined with his disciplinary history, lack of respect for the legal system, and complete lack of remorse is of such serious professional nature that it warrants a one hundred (100) day suspension from the practice of law. We feel that this adequately protects the public while allowing Eicher sufficient time to educate himself on the proper conduct of an attorney and moreover, justify to this Court that the public would be benefited by his re-admission to being a full-time practitioner.

History is replete with those who have overcome a weakness or character flaw and risen to what Attorney at Law Abraham Lincoln declared to be the "better angels of our nature." Perfection is not required-good moral character is.

* * *

Topics for Further Discussion

1. What is it that the lawyer did in the Koch complaint that was so bad? Is a lawyer required to be nice? If you were involved in litigation, would you want a nice lawyer or one who was more provocative?

2. In the Clayborne complaint, the court acknowledged that the lawyer did not actually lie. Why then was he found to have acted improperly?

3. The court ordered a 100-day suspension of the lawyer's license in order to protect the public. Who in the public is being protected?

Prosecutors and Judges

As employees of the public, prosecutors and judges have their own particular responsibilities in the judicial system. Model Rule 3.8 addresses prosecutors, directing them to refrain from bringing charges not supported by evidence, to inform the accused of the right to counsel, to exercise restraint in dealing with unrepresented people, and to provide the defense with information that would tend to negate guilt or mitigate the offense.

Judges have an entire model code of their own: the Model Code of Judicial Conduct. States have also enacted their own laws dealing with the subject of judicial ethics. They are primarily concerned with maintaining fairness, both in appearance and fact. Judges are elected in many states, rather than appointed, and this creates concerns when they make campaign speeches. In the following case, a public prosecutor running for election as a judge made campaign statements indicating that she had the support of the police, would favor victims, and would be tough on criminals.

In re Kinsey
842 So.2d 77 (Fla. 2003)

Per curiam

We review the recommendation of the Judicial Qualifications Commission ("JQC") that Judge Patricia Kinsey be disciplined. This case arose out of charges brought against Judge Kinsey alleging that she engaged in a pattern of improper conduct during the course of her 1998 election campaign for the office of County Court Judge for Escambia County. Formal proceedings were officially instituted against Judge Kinsey on September 9, 1999, when she was initially charged with eleven ethical violations, all based upon conduct occurring during her election campaign. These charges were amended on March 8, 2000, to include an additional allegation which related to a radio advertisement that was aired during the campaign. A hearing was held before the JQC on June 12–13, 2000, at which time the campaign brochures and radio excerpts were the primary evidence used to support the charges. The JQC found Judge Kinsey guilty or guilty in part of nine ethical violations

During Judge Kinsey's judicial campaign, she distributed numerous pamphlets which depicted a very "pro-law enforcement" stance. In charge 1, Kinsey disseminated a brochure which showed a full-page picture of her standing with ten heavily armed police officers and was captioned "Who do these guys count on to back them up?" Within the flyer, she stated, "[Y]our police officers expect judges to take their testimony seriously and to help law enforcement by putting criminals where they belong ... *behind bars!*"

Charge 2 is based upon another flyer entitled "*If you are a criminal, you probably won't want to read this!*" In this leaflet, she again stressed, "[Y]our police officers expect judges to take their testimony seriously and to help law enforcement by putting criminals where they belong ... *behind bars!*" The brochure also declared, "Above all else, Pat Kinsey identifies with the victims of crime."

A brochure entitled "*Let's Elect Pat Kinsey*" is the basis behind charge 3. In this leaflet, she informed the voting public that she believes, "We must support our hard-working law enforcement officers by putting criminals behind bars, not back on our streets."

Charge 5, which is drawn from the six brochures and a radio interview, asserts that Judge Kinsey deliberately attempted to cloak her campaign "in an umbrella of law enforcement." In a flyer entitled "*The Alternative for County Judge,*" she stated, "Pat Kinsey will support our valiant law enforcement officers ... not make their job harder." She also declared in this literature that, "Pat Kinsey will bend over backward to ensure that honest, law-abiding citizens are not victimized a second time by the legal system that is supposed to protect them." This charge also refers to statements in a brochure entitled "*A Vital Message From Law Enforcement,*" which declared, "victims have a right to expect judges to protect them by denying bond to potentially dangerous offenders."

Although some of these charges taken in isolation would not violate the judicial canons, taken together it becomes clear that Judge Kinsey was running on a platform which stressed her allegiance to police officers. Each of the charges addressed above involved implicit pledges that if elected to office, Judge Kinsey would help law enforcement. Through these statements, Judge Kinsey fostered the distinct impression that she harbored a prosecutor's bias and police officers could expect more favorable treatment from her as she promised to support police officers and help them put criminals behind bars. She also made pledges to victims of crime, promising to bend over backward for them and stressing the point that she identified with them "above all else," thus giving the appearance that she was already committed to according them more favorable treatment than other parties appearing before her. By disseminating materials which promised a different treatment based on the identity of the person appearing before her, it is beyond question that these promises affect her appearance of impartiality and fitness as a judge. While our judicial code does not prohibit a candidate from discussing his or her philosophical beliefs, in the campaign literature at issue Judge Kinsey pledged her support and promised favorable treatment for certain *parties and witnesses* who would be appearing before her (i.e., police and victims of crime). Criminal defendants and criminal defense lawyers could have a genuine concern that they will not be facing a fair and impartial tribunal. We do not find that these types of pledges and statements by a judicial candidate are protected by the First Amendment.

The panel found that based on the violations of the canons as addressed above, Judge Kinsey engaged in conduct unbecoming a candidate for a judicial post and brought the judiciary into disrepute by conveying the false and misleading impression of the judge's role, particularly in the handling of criminal cases. We agree. Judge Kinsey's campaign materials gave the misleading impression that a judge's role in criminal proceedings is to combat crime and support police officers as opposed to being an impartial tribunal where justice is dispensed without favor or bias.

Discipline

We next turn to the appropriate sanction for Judge Kinsey's misconduct. The JQC found that Judge Kinsey was guilty of serious violations and that a public reprimand alone was insufficient; accordingly, the JQC recommended that Judge Kinsey be publicly reprimanded and fined in the amount of $50,000 plus the costs of these proceedings. The amount of the fine represented approximately 50% of her yearly salary, or in other words, a six-month suspension without pay (which was the other option that the JQC considered imposing).

We agree with the JQC that Judge Kinsey is guilty of serious campaign violations that warrant a severe penalty. Accordingly, this Court agrees with the JQC's recommendation as to discipline and finds that a substantial fine is warranted in order to assure the public that justice is dispensed in a fair and unbiased manner and to warn any future judicial candidates that this Court will not tolerate improper campaign statements which imply that, if elected, the judicial candidate will favor one group of citizens over another or will make rulings based upon the sway of popular sentiment in the community.

* * *

Topics for Further Discussion

1. In *Republican Party of Minnesota v. White*, 536 U.S. 765 (2002), the U.S. Supreme Court considered a statute that prohibited a judicial candidate from "announc[ing] his or her views on disputed legal or political issues." A candidate for the state supreme court had criticized several of that court's decisions. The U.S. Supreme Court struck the law down as an unconstitutional infringement of freedom of speech. The Florida Supreme Court, in the *Kinsey* case, distinguished the Florida law from that involved in *White*.

Recusal

Judges who have a personal interest in a matter coming before them are obligated to step down and to transfer the case to a different judge. For example, a judge owning stock in a corporation is not permitted to handle a case concerning that company. When a judge voluntarily removes himself from a case it is called a recusal. Parties are also permitted to make a motion to remove a judge whom they believe to be prejudiced or otherwise unfit to preside over the case. The motion is not always successful as can be seen from the following opinion.

Cheney v. U.S. Dist. Court for Dist. of Columbia
124 S. Ct. 1391 (2004)

Memorandum of Justice Scalia

I have before me a motion to recuse in these cases consolidated below. The motion is filed on behalf of respondent Sierra Club. The other private respondent, Judicial Watch, Inc., does not join the motion and has publicly stated that it "does not believe the presently-known facts about the hunting trip satisfy the legal standards requiring recusal." Since the cases have been consolidated, however, recusal in the one would entail recusal in the other.

I

The decision whether a judge's impartiality can "'reasonably be questioned'" is to be made in light of the facts as they existed, and not as they were surmised or reported. The facts here were as follows: For five years or so, I have been going to Louisiana during the Court's long December–January recess, to the duck-hunting camp of a friend whom I met through two hunting companions from Baton Rouge, one a dentist and the other a worker in the field of handicapped rehabilitation. The last three years, I have been accompanied on this trip by a son-in-law who lives near me. Our friend and host, Wallace Carline, has never, as far as I know, had business before this Court. He is not, as some reports have described him, an "energy industry executive" in the sense that summons up boardrooms of ExxonMobil or Con Edison. He runs his own company that provides services and equipment rental to oil rigs in the Gulf of Mexico.

During my December 2002 visit, I learned that Mr. Carline was an admirer of Vice President Cheney. Knowing that the Vice President, with whom I am well acquainted (from our years serving together in the Ford administration), is an enthusiastic duck-hunter, I asked whether Mr. Carline would like to invite him to our next year's hunt. The answer was yes; I conveyed the invitation (with my own warm recommendation) in the spring of 2003 and received an acceptance (subject, of course, to any superseding demands on the Vice President's time) in the summer. The Vice President said that if he did go, I would be welcome to fly down to Louisiana with him. (Because of national security requirements, of course, he must fly in a Government plane.) That invitation was later extended—if space was available—to my son-in-law and to a son who was joining the hunt for the first time; they accepted. The trip was set long before the Court granted *certiorari* in the present case, and indeed before the petition for *certiorari* had even been filed.

We departed from Andrews Air Force Base at about 10 a.m. on Monday, January 5, flying in a Gulfstream jet owned by the Government. We landed in Patterson, Louisiana, and went by car to a dock where Mr. Carline met us, to take us on the 20-minute boat trip to his hunting camp. We arrived at about 2 p.m., the 5 of us joining about 8 other hunters, making about 13 hunters in all; also present during our time there were about 3 members of Mr. Carline's staff, and, of course, the Vice President's staff and security detail. It was not an intimate setting. The group hunted that afternoon and Tuesday and Wednesday mornings; it fished (in two boats) Tuesday afternoon. All meals were in common. Sleeping was in rooms of two or three, except for the Vice President, who had his own quarters. Hunting was in two- or three-man blinds. As it turned out, I never hunted in the same blind with the Vice President. Nor was I alone with him at any time during the trip, except, perhaps, for instances so brief and unintentional that I would not recall them—walking to or from a boat, perhaps, or going to or from dinner. Of course we said not a word about the present case. The Vice President left the camp Wednesday afternoon, about two days after our arrival. I stayed on to hunt (with my son and son-in-law) until late Friday morning, when the three of us returned to Washington on a commercial flight from New Orleans.

II

Let me respond, at the outset, to Sierra Club's suggestion that I should "resolve any doubts in favor of recusal." That might be sound advice if I were sitting on a Court of Appeals. There, my place would be taken by another judge, and the case would proceed normally. On the Supreme Court, however, the consequence is different: The Court proceeds with eight Justices, raising the possibility that, by reason of a tie vote, it will find itself unable to resolve the significant legal issue presented by the case. Thus, as Justices stated in their 1993 Statement of Recusal Policy: "[W]e do not think it would serve the public interest to go beyond the requirements of the statute, and to recuse ourselves, out of an excess of caution, whenever a relative is a partner in the firm before us or acted as a lawyer at an earlier stage. Even one unnecessary recusal impairs the functioning of the Court." Moreover, granting the motion is (insofar as the outcome of the particular case is concerned) effectively the same as casting a vote against the petitioner. The petitioner needs five votes to overturn the judgment below, and it makes no difference whether the needed fifth vote is missing because it has been cast for the other side, or because it has not been cast at all.

Even so, recusal is the course I must take—and will take—when, on the basis of established principles and practices, I have said or done something which requires that course. I have recused for such a reason this very Term. See *Elk Grove Unified School District v. Newdow*, 124 S.Ct. 384 (*cert.* granted, Oct. 14, 2003). I believe, however, that established principles and practices do not require (and thus do not permit) recusal in the present case.

A

My recusal is required if, by reason of the actions described above, my "impartiality might reasonably be questioned." 28 U.S.C. § 455(a). Why would that result follow from my being in a sizable group of persons, in a hunting camp with the Vice President, where I never hunted with him in the same blind or had other opportunity for private conversation? The only possibility is that it would suggest I am a friend of his. But while friendship is a ground for recusal of a Justice where the personal fortune or the personal freedom of the friend is at issue, it has traditionally not been a ground for recusal where official action is at issue, no matter how important the official action was to the ambitions or the reputation of the Government officer.

A rule that required Members of this Court to remove themselves from cases in which the official actions of friends were at issue would be utterly disabling. Many Justices have reached this Court precisely because they were friends of the incumbent President or other senior officials—and from the earliest days down to modern times Justices have had close personal relationships with the President and other officers of the Executive. John Quincy Adams hosted dinner parties featuring such luminaries as Chief Justice Marshall, Justices Johnson, Story, and Todd, Attorney General Wirt, and Daniel Webster. Justice Harlan and his wife often "'stopped in'" at the White House to see the Hayes family and pass a Sunday evening in a small group, visiting and singing hymns. Justice Stone tossed around a medicine ball with members of the Hoover administration mornings outside the White House. Justice Douglas was a regular at President Franklin Roosevelt's poker parties; Chief Justice Vinson played poker with President Truman.

B

The recusal motion claims that "the fact that Justice Scalia and his daughter [sic] were the Vice President's guest on Air Force Two on the flight down to Louisiana" means that I "accepted a sizable gift from a party in a pending case," a gift "measured in the thousands of dollars."

Let me speak first to the value, though that is not the principal point. Our flight down cost the Government nothing, since space-available was the condition of our invitation. And, though our flight down on the Vice President's plane was indeed free, since we were not returning with him we purchased (because they were least expensive) round-trip tickets that cost precisely what we would have paid if we had gone both down and back on commercial flights. In other words, none of us saved a cent by flying on the Vice President's plane. The purpose of going with him was not saving money, but avoiding some inconvenience to ourselves (being taken by car from New Orleans to Morgan City) and considerable inconvenience to our friends, who would have had to meet our plane in New Orleans, and schedule separate boat trips to the hunting camp, for us and for the Vice President's party.

The principal point, however, is that social courtesies, provided at Government expense by officials whose only business before the Court is business in their official capacity, have not hitherto been thought prohibited.

III

The core of Sierra Club's argument is as follows: "Sierra Club makes this motion because ... damage [to the integrity of the system] is being done right now. As of today, 8 of the 10 newspapers with the largest circulation in the United States, 14 of the largest 20, and 20 of the 30 largest have called on Justice Scalia to step aside.... Of equal import, there is no counterbalance or controversy: not a single newspaper has argued against recusal. Because the American public, as reflected in the nation's newspaper editorials, has unanimously concluded that there is an appearance of favoritism, any objective observer would be compelled to conclude that Justice Scalia's impartiality has been questioned. These facts more than satisfy Section 455(a), which mandates recusal merely when a Justice's impartiality "might reasonably be questioned.'"

The implications of this argument are staggering. I must recuse because a significant portion of the press, which is deemed to be the American public, demands it. The motion attaches as exhibits the press editorials on which it relies. Many of them do not even have the facts right.

IV

While Sierra Club was apparently unable to summon forth a single example of a Justice's recusal (or even motion for a Justice's recusal) under circumstances similar to those here, I have been able to accomplish the seemingly more difficult task of finding a couple of examples establishing the negative: that recusal or motion for recusal did not occur under circumstances similar to those here.

Of course it can be claimed (as some editorials have claimed) that "times have changed," and what was once considered proper—even as recently as Byron White's day—is no longer so. That may be true with regard to the earlier rare phenomenon of a Supreme Court Justice's serving as advisor and confidant to the President—though that activity, so incompatible with the separation of powers, was not widely known when it was occurring, and can hardly be said to have been generally approved before it was properly abandoned. But the well-known and constant practice of Justices' enjoying friendship and social intercourse with Members of Congress and officers of the Executive Branch has not been abandoned, and ought not to be.

V

Since I do not believe my impartiality can reasonably be questioned, I do not think it would be proper for me to recuse. That alone is conclusive; but another consideration moves me in the same direction: Recusal would in my judgment harm the Court. If I were to withdraw from this case, it would be because some of the press has argued that the Vice President would suffer political damage if he should lose this appeal, and if, on remand, discovery should establish that energy industry representatives were *de facto* members of NEPDG—and because some of the press has elevated that possible political damage to the status of an impending stain on the reputation and integrity of the Vice President. But since political damage often comes from the Government's losing official-action suits; and since political damage can readily be characterized as a stain on reputation and integrity; recusing in the face of such charges would give elements of the press a veto over participation of any Justices who had social contacts with, or were even known to be friends of, a named official. That is intolerable.

* * *

As in the *Cheney* case, the judge whose impartiality is in question makes the decision as to whether s/he should opt out. That is what happened initially in a case heard in the Supreme Court of Appeals of West Virginia. Judges of the West Virginia Court are elected. Blankenship, the president of the defendant coal company, spent $3 million to support the campaign of a candidate, Benjamin, knowing that the case would reach that court on appeal. The trial court jury had returned a damage award of $50 million against the company.

The candidate Blankenship supported was elected and, when the case did come before the court, he declined to recuse himself. He turned out to be one of the members of a 3–2 majority that reversed the lower court judgment. The plaintiff, Caperton, then sought relief in the Supreme Court of the United States for what he contended was a violation of Due Process.

Caperton v. A.T. Massey Coal Co.
129 S.Ct. 2252 (2009)

Kennedy, J.

It is axiomatic that "[a] fair trial in a fair tribunal is a basic requirement of due process." As the Court has recognized, however, "most matters relating to judicial disqualification [do] not rise to a constitutional level." The early and leading case on the subject is Tumey v. Ohio, 273 U. S. 510 (1927). There, the Court stated that "matters of kinship, personal bias, state policy, remoteness of interest, would seem generally to be matters merely of legislative discretion."

The *Tumey* Court concluded that the Due Process Clause incorporated the common-law rule that a judge must recuse himself when he has "a direct, personal, substantial, pecuniary interest" in a case. This rule reflects the maxim that "[n]o man is allowed to be a judge in his own cause; because his interest would certainly bias his judgment, and, not improbably, corrupt his integrity." The Federalist No. 10, p. 59 (J. Cooke ed. 1961) (J. Madison). Under this rule, "disqualification for bias or prejudice was not permitted"; those matters were left to statutes and judicial codes. Personal bias or prejudice "alone would not be sufficient basis for imposing a constitutional requirement under the Due Process Clause."

As new problems have emerged that were not discussed at common law, however, the Court has identified additional instances which, as an objective matter, require recusal. These are circumstances "in which experience teaches that the probability of actual bias on the part of the judge or decisionmaker is too high to be constitutionally tolerable."

This problem arises in the context of judicial elections, a framework not presented in the precedents we have reviewed and discussed.

Not every campaign contribution by a litigant or attorney creates a probability of bias that requires a judge's recusal, but this is an exceptional case. We conclude that there is a serious risk of actual bias—based on objective and reasonable perceptions—when a person with a personal stake in a particular case had a significant and disproportionate influence in placing the judge on the case by raising funds or directing the judge's election campaign when the case was pending or imminent. The inquiry centers on the contribution's relative size in comparison to the total amount of money contributed to the campaign, the total amount spent in the election, and the apparent effect such contribution had on the outcome of the election.

Applying this principle, we conclude that Blankenship's campaign efforts had a significant and disproportionate influence in placing Justice Benjamin on the case. Blankenship contributed some $3 million to unseat the incumbent and replace him with Benjamin. His contributions eclipsed the total amount spent by all other Benjamin supporters and exceeded by 300% the amount spent by Benjamin's campaign committee. Caperton claims Blankenship spent $1 million more than the total amount spent by the campaign committees of both candidates combined.

Massey responds that Blankenship's support, while significant, did not cause Benjamin's victory. In the end the people of West Virginia elected him, and they did so based on many reasons other than Blankenship's efforts. Massey points out that every major state newspaper, but one, endorsed Benjamin.

Whether Blankenship's campaign contributions were a necessary and sufficient cause of Benjamin's victory is not the proper inquiry. Much like determining whether a judge is actually biased, proving what ultimately drives the electorate to choose a particular candidate is a difficult endeavor, not likely to lend itself to a certain conclusion. This is particularly true where, as here, there is no procedure for judicial fact-finding and the sole trier of fact is the one accused of bias. Due process requires an objective inquiry into whether the contributor's influence on the election under all the circumstances "would offer a possible temptation to the average ... judge to ... lead him not to hold the balance nice, clear and true." Blankenship's campaign contributions—in comparison to the total amount contributed to the campaign, as well as the total amount spent in the election—had a significant and disproportionate influence on the electoral outcome. And the risk that Blankenship's influence engendered actual bias is sufficiently substantial that it "must be forbidden if the guarantee of due process is to be adequately implemented."

It was reasonably foreseeable, when the campaign contributions were made, that the pending case would be before the newly elected justice. The $50 million adverse jury verdict had been entered before the election, and the Supreme Court of Appeals was the next step once the state trial court dealt with post-trial motions. So it became at once apparent that, absent recusal, Justice Benjamin would review a judgment that cost his biggest donor's company $50 million. Although there is no allegation of a quid pro quo agreement, the fact remains that Blankenship's extraordinary contributions were made at a time when he had a vested stake in the outcome. Just as no man is allowed to be a judge in his own cause, similar fears of bias can arise when—without the consent of the other parties—a man chooses the judge in his own cause. And applying this principle to the judicial election process, there was here a serious, objective risk of actual bias that required Justice Benjamin's recusal.

Justice Benjamin did undertake an extensive search for actual bias. But, as we have indicated, that is just one step in the judicial process; objective standards may also require recusal whether or not actual bias exists or can be proved. Due process "may sometimes bar trial by judges who have no actual bias and who would do their very best to weigh the scales of justice equally between contending parties." The failure to consider objective standards requiring recusal is not consistent with the imperatives of due process. We find that Blankenship's significant and disproportionate influence — coupled with the temporal relationship between the election and the pending case — "offer a possible temptation to the average ... judge to ... lead him not to hold the balance nice, clear and true." On these extreme facts the probability of actual bias rises to an unconstitutional level.

* * *

Topics for Further Discussion

1. In the *Cheney* case, the Sierra Club sought to compel Vice President Cheney to produce documents regarding a meeting that was allegedly held in his office with various energy officials. The implication was that the Vice President was improperly engaged in helping his former industry colleagues. The Supreme Court held that the Vice President was not required to produce the documents. Do you agree with Justice Scalia that imposing a "no-friend" rule on the Court would be unreasonable?

2. What does Justice Scalia say the standards for recusal are for Supreme Court Justices? How about for the judges of other courts? Are these different from the standards the Court subsequently put forth in *Caperton*? The administrative law aspects of the *Cheney* case are discussed further in Chapter 13.

Key Terms and Concepts

Attorney-Client Privilege
Chinese Wall
Conflict of Interest
Disbarment
Model Code of Judicial Conduct
Model Code of Professional Responsibility
Model Rules of Professional Conduct
Recusal
Retainer
Statute of Limitations

Chapter 4

Constitutional Law: Individual Rights

"Bear in mind this sacred principle, that though the will of the majority is in all cases to prevail, that will, to be rightful, must be reasonable; that the minority possess their equal rights, which equal laws must protect, and to violate would be oppression."

Thomas Jefferson, 1st Inaugural Address (1801)

The United States is widely thought of as a country in which the individual ranks supreme. The rights of individuals are generally perceived to be more important than the well-being of the society as a whole. Like most stereotypes, this overstates the fact while containing some degree of truth. The rights of persons in the United States are not absolute to be sure, but they are taken very seriously. The strong emphasis on individual rights is a reflection of the history by which the nation was formed. Born out of the American Revolution (1776–1783), the Founding Fathers were bound and determined to protect their newfound civil liberties from a repeat of the long list of abuses and usurpations suffered at the hands of the King of England as vividly detailed in the Declaration of Independence (July 4, 1776). This chapter will illustrate how the concept of individual rights has evolved over the more than two centuries following the creation of the United States of America.

Due Process and Equal Protection: An Overview

The first ten amendments to the Constitution are commonly called "The Bill of Rights." Although these amendments took effect in 1791, two years after the Constitution was adopted, their passage was, in fact, a condition for ratification of the Constitution. An agreement was struck among the states to approve the Constitution based on the firm understanding that the Bill of Rights would be enacted by the first Congress.

The concern was that the new Constitution did not specifically set forth various important rights of individuals. Many of the people involved in the drafting of the Constitution argued that such a listing of rights was unnecessary. They had written a Constitution establishing a national government of limited powers, that is to say, a government lacking authority except as expressly granted by the Constitution. Everything beyond that, they argued, was off limits for government and so, quite naturally, remained within the rights of individuals and the states. Moreover, there was a legitimate concern that specifying certain rights could lead to the negative implication that the many other rights enjoyed by the people under the common law would be lost. It is mainly for this reason that England today still does not have a written constitution or a bill of rights. Notwithstanding these arguments, some states decided that they would settle for nothing less than a written guarantee in the form of the Bill of Rights.

As a result of the colonial experience, a strong national government was viewed with suspicion and distrust. The Bill of Rights was adopted to stand squarely between the inherent power of the federal government and the rights of the people to "Life, Liberty and the Pursuit of Happiness" as articulated in the Declaration of Independence. These protections were framed in terms of express limitations on the power of the federal government to restrict or deny certain fundamental rights.

The protection of these rights against the authority of state government (as opposed to Congress) was not included in the Constitution until after the American Civil War (1861–1865). The Thirteenth Amendment (1865) eliminated slavery. The Fourteenth Amendment (1868) made all persons born or naturalized in the U.S. (including former slaves) citizens. It also guaranteed all persons "due process" and "equal protection of the laws" in a manner similar to the Fifth Amendment guarantee against the federal government. The Fifteenth Amendment (1870) bestowed the right to vote on all persons (but not women), regardless of race or color.

The initial beneficiaries of these post-Civil War amendments were African-Americans, the majority of whom were slaves prior to the Emancipation Declaration issued by President Abraham Lincoln on September 22, 1862. African-Americans were given no rights against either national or state governments in the Constitution or the Bill of Rights. This point was made painfully clear in *Scott v. Sandford*, 60 U.S. 393 (1856), the famous *Dred Scott* case. Dred Scott and his family were slaves who ran away from their owner. Scott sued in the federal court to have his status as a free man affirmed. The Supreme Court stated that:

> The question is simply this: Can a negro, whose ancestors were imported into this country, and sold as slaves, become a member of the political community formed and brought into existence by the Constitution of the United States, and as such become entitled to all the rights, and privileges, and immunities, guarantied by that instrument to the citizen? One of which rights is the privilege of suing in a court of the United States in the cases specified in the Constitution.

In reaching the conclusion that Scott was not entitled to sue because of his race, Chief Justice Taney issued his infamous dictum that African-Americans "had no rights which the white man was bound to respect; and that the negro might justly and lawfully be reduced to slavery for his benefit. He was bought and sold and treated as an ordinary article of merchandise and traffic, whenever profit could be made by it."

At the time of the American Revolution, the main complaint of the colonials was the arbitrary and dictatorial practices of the British Empire. At that time and thereafter, African-Americans' main complaint was against the states—particularly those that allowed them to be held as slaves and owned as property. An attempt to outlaw slavery in 1787 would have been met with widespread resistance and almost surely prevented the passage of any constitution and the realization of the American nation. The men involved in writing and ratifying the Constitution, many of whom were slave owners, decided they must ignore the issue for the time, notwithstanding the lofty words of the Declaration of Independence proclaiming that: "We hold these truths to be self-evident, that all men are created equal, that they are endowed by their Creator with certain unalienable Rights, that among these are Life, Liberty and the Pursuit of Happiness." The decision to postpone the issue of abolishing slavery, along with the question whether states retained the right freely to withdraw from the nation, resulted in the Civil War, some eighty years later.

Against this backdrop, the Supreme Court has developed different standards for assessing the validity of challenges based on Due Process and Equal Protection. The chart below provides a summary that you should keep in mind as you read the cases in this chapter.

	DUE PROCESS	EQUAL PROTECTION
Fundamental Right	Strict Scrutiny	Strict Scrutiny
Ordinary Right	Rational Basis Test	Rational Basis Test
Suspect Classification (race, nationality, ethnicity, religion)		Strict Scrutiny
"Quasi-Suspect" Classification (gender, illegitimacy)		"Intermediate Scrutiny"
Non-Suspect Classification		Rational Basis Test

Due Process

The post-Civil War Amendments have not been limited to providing constitutional protections to African-Americans. Due process, despite its name, has been held to include "substantive due process," namely the rights of "life, liberty, and property." In practical terms, this has been understood to mean the right to be free from unwarranted government intrusion. The concept of substantive rights embedded in a provision concerning process may seem paradoxical, and critics have questioned its legitimacy for that very reason. This criticism notwithstanding, substantive due process has evolved to mean individuals possess various rights for which appropriate process is due.

"Life, liberty, and property" are guides to those rights; however, the courts—and the Supreme Court in particular—have assumed the responsibility of deciding *which* kinds of liberties are entitled to due process protection and *what* kind of process is due. This principle was enunciated nearly 100 years ago in the case of *Lochner v. New York,* 198 U.S. 45 (1905). The *Lochner* case involved a New York law making it a criminal offense for an employer to require or permit bakers to work more than sixty hours in one week. The Supreme Court struck the law down, writing as follows:

> It must, of course, be conceded that there is a limit to the valid exercise of the police power by the state. There is no dispute concerning this general proposition. Otherwise the 14th Amendment would have no efficacy and the legislatures of the states would have unbounded power, and it would be enough to say that any piece of legislation was enacted to conserve the morals, the health, or the safety of the people; such legislation would be valid, no matter how absolutely without foundation the claim might be. The claim of the police power would be a mere pretext, become another and delusive name for the supreme sovereignty of the state to be exercised free from constitutional restraint. This is not contended for. In every case that comes before this court, therefore, where legislation of this character is concerned, and where the protection of the Federal Constitution is sought, the question necessarily arises: Is this a fair, reasonable,

and appropriate exercise of the police power of the state, or is it an unreasonable, unnecessary, and arbitrary interference with the right of the individual to his personal liberty, or to enter into those contracts in relation to labor which may seem to him appropriate or necessary for the support of himself and his family? Of course the liberty of contract relating to labor includes both parties to it. The one has as much right to purchase as the other to sell labor.

This is not a question of substituting the judgment of the court for that of the legislature. If the act be within the power of the state it is valid, although the judgment of the court might be totally opposed to the enactment of such a law. But the question would still remain: Is it within the police power of the state? and that question must be answered by the court.

In general, the Court has looked through the other sections of the Bill of Rights for more specific examples of rights that are fundamental to a free society, but those sections do not exhaust the possibilities. Although the Court has offered a number of tests, one of the most common formulations is whether some right is considered essential to a system of ordered liberty. A good example can be found in the concurring opinion of Justice Stewart in *Rosenblatt v. Baer*, 383 U.S. 75 (1966), a case involving the balance between state libel laws and free speech. Justice Stewart wrote that protection of an individual's good name and reputation

reflects no more than our basic concept of the essential dignity and worth of every human being—a concept at the root of any decent system of ordered liberty. The protection of private personality, like the protection of life itself, is left primarily to the individual States under the Ninth and Tenth Amendments. But this does not mean that the right is entitled to any less recognition by this Court as a basis of our constitutional system.

The Equal Protection Clause, by contrast, has been construed to protect specific groups of persons from discrimination. The rights at issue in due process and equal protection cases are sometimes the same, but the theories are different. In general, due process complaints allege that the government may not deprive a person of the right in question, whether or not that person belongs to a protected class. Equal protection cases, on the other hand, contend that the government may not treat people differently with regard to the right because they are members of a protected class.

What rights do people have? In due process, the concept has changed over time. In the early 20th century, economic rights carried particular importance. Economic liberty was considered to be an essential element of "liberty" under the due process clause. At the time, it meant the ability of businesspeople to do as they liked. Hence, the Court's decision in *Lochner*. Of course, employers had much more bargaining power in such contracts, casting doubt on whether the employees' exercise of their economic liberty was, in fact, willingly made.

Later on, the Supreme Court adopted a different view, distinguishing between those rights it characterized as "fundamental" and others that are not. Fundamental rights are those that are included in the Bill of Rights, most of which have been "incorporated" against (made to apply to) the states, and others that are considered to be essential to a system of ordered liberty or deeply rooted in the nation's history and tradition. These include such well-known rights as speech, press and religion, as well as more controversial ones such as abortion, which the Court derived from a theory of privacy. Of course, it is the Court that decides which rights are "incorporated." Among those rights not incorporated, or not yet decided upon, by the Supreme Court, are the prohibition against forced quartering of soldiers (Third Amendment), the right to a jury trial in civil cases (Seventh Amendment), the reservation of unstated rights (Ninth Amendment), and — quite logically — the reservation of certain rights by the people or the states against the national government (Tenth Amendment).

When the Court believes a fundamental right is at stake, the government's action in depriving someone of it is judged with what is called "strict scrutiny." That is, the government's action will only be upheld if it is found to be necessary to achieve a compelling governmental interest. For other rights — including most economic matters such as regulation of wages, hours, and working conditions involved in *Lochner* — the Court now applies a "rational basis" test, requiring the government to show only that the action is rationally related to a legitimate government interest.

Abortion is the issue that has tested the boundaries of due process. In *Roe v. Wade,* 410 U.S. 113(1973), the Supreme Court relied on a fundamental right to privacy to strike down a state law preventing a woman from voluntarily ending her pregnancy. The Court adopted the privacy rationale despite the fact that privacy is nowhere mentioned in the Constitution, at least not directly. An earlier decision, *Griswold v. Connecticut,* 381 U.S. 479 (1965), invalidating restrictions on access to contraceptives, had given rise to the theory. The principal opinion in *Griswold* searched for a "liberty" interest that was being infringed and found it in what it called "penumbras, formed by emanations" of other guarantees in the Bill of Rights "that help to give them life and substance." These, Justice Douglas said, added up to a constitutional right called "privacy." The issue of abortion is discussed in greater detail in Chapter 12.

Two dissenting judges declined to certify privacy as constitutionally based. They said they could find no textual basis for it and, thus, no justification for employing it. This disagreement on constitutional interpretation continues to this day. The debate reflects a broader underlying conceptual dispute between those who believe judges should read the Constitution flexibly and those who insist that courts must enforce its actual words (and perhaps their historical meaning referred to as "original intent") but nothing more. The latter group, represented most prominently on the Supreme Court today by Justice Scalia, is called the "strict constructionists." The majority and dissenting opinions in the *Lawrence* case appearing below provide a good example of the positions taken by these two camps.

The judicial theory notwithstanding, the propriety of abortion itself is the subject of ongoing social debate. *Roe* moved that debate from the legislatures to the courtrooms of the country. The Supreme Court has interpreted, limited, or modified *Roe* from time to time but has never abandoned its core holding. On the other hand, the Court has changed its mind on the issue of sexual privacy rights among consenting adults, including homosexuals. In *Bowers v. Hardwick,* 478 U.S. 186 (1986), it held that the state could prohibit homosexual acts because they were not fundamental rights. Seventeen years later in *Lawrence,* the Court concluded that its decision in *Bowers* was wrong, and had to be overruled. The *Lawrence* case illustrates the difficulty that sometimes arises in distinguishing between due process and equal protection cases. The Court granted *certiorari* in the case to consider three questions:

1. Whether the law that criminalized sexual intimacy by persons of the same sex but not the same activity by persons of different sexes violated equal protection,

2. Whether the law violated the due process rights of adult consensual sexual intimacy in the home, and

3. Whether the *Bowers* decision should be overruled.

Lawrence v. Texas
539 U.S. 558 (2003)

Kennedy, J.

Liberty protects the person from improper government intrusions into a dwelling or other private places. In our tradition the State is not present in the home. And there are other spheres of our lives and existence, outside the home, where the State should not be a dominant presence. Freedom extends beyond spatial bounds. Liberty presumes an autonomy of self that includes freedom of thought, belief, expression, and certain intimate conduct. The instant case involves liberty of the person both in its spatial and more transcendent dimensions.

The question before the Court is the validity of a Texas statute making it a crime for two persons of the same sex to engage in certain intimate sexual conduct.

In Houston, Texas, officers of the Harris County Police Department were dispatched to a private residence in response to a reported weapons disturbance. They entered an apartment where one of the petitioners, John Geddes Lawrence, resided. The right of the police to enter does not seem to have been questioned. The officers observed Lawrence and another man, Tyron Garner, engaging in a sexual act. The two petitioners were arrested, held in custody over night, and charged and convicted. The applicable state law is the Texas Penal Code which provides: "A person commits an offense if he engages in deviate sexual intercourse with another individual of the same sex." The statute defines "[d]eviate sexual intercourse" as follows: "(A) any contact between any part of the genitals of one person and the mouth or anus of another person; or (B) the penetration of the genitals or the anus of another person with an object."

The petitioners were adults at the time of the alleged offense. Their conduct was in private and consensual.

We conclude the case should be resolved by determining whether the petitioners were free as adults to engage in the private conduct in the exercise of their liberty under the Due Process Clause of the Fourteenth Amendment to the Constitution. For this inquiry we deem it necessary to reconsider the Court's holding in *Bowers v. Hardwick*.

There are broad statements of the substantive reach of liberty under the Due Process Clause in earlier cases. In *Griswold* the Court invalidated a state law prohibiting the use of drugs or devices of contraception and counseling or aiding and abetting the use of contraceptives. The Court described the protected interest as a right to privacy and placed emphasis on the marriage relation and the protected space of the marital bedroom.

The facts in *Bowers* had some similarities to this case. A police officer, whose right to enter seems not to have been in question, observed Hardwick, in his own bedroom, engaging in intimate sexual conduct with another adult male. The conduct was in violation of a Georgia statute making it a criminal offense to engage in sodomy.

The Court began its substantive discussion in *Bowers* as follows: "The issue presented is whether the Federal Constitution confers a fundamental right upon homosexuals to engage in sodomy and hence invalidates the laws of the many States that still make such conduct illegal and have done so for a very long time." That statement, we now conclude, discloses the Court's own failure to appreciate the extent of the liberty at stake. To say that the issue in *Bowers* was simply the right to engage in certain sexual conduct demeans the claim the individual put forward, just as it would demean a married couple were it to be said marriage is simply about the right to have sexual intercourse. The laws involved in *Bowers* and here are, to be sure, statutes that purport to do no more than prohibit a particular sexual act. Their penalties and purposes, though, have more far-reaching consequences, touching upon the most private human conduct, sexual behavior, and in the most private of places, the home. The statutes do seek to control a personal relationship that, whether or not entitled to formal recognition in the law, is within the liberty of persons to choose without being punished as criminals.

This, as a general rule, should counsel against attempts by the State, or a court, to define the meaning of the relationship or to set its boundaries absent injury to a person or abuse of an institution the law protects.

It must be acknowledged, of course, that the Court in *Bowers* was making the broader point that for centuries there have been powerful voices to condemn homosexual conduct as immoral. The condemnation has been shaped by religious beliefs, conceptions of right and acceptable behavior, and respect for the traditional family. For many persons these are not trivial concerns but profound and deep convictions accepted as ethical and moral principles to which they aspire and which thus determine the course of their lives. These considerations do not answer the question before us, however. The issue is whether the majority may use the power of the State to enforce these views on the whole society through operation of the criminal law. "Our obligation is to define the liberty of all, not to mandate our own moral code."

Of even more importance, almost five years before *Bowers* was decided the European Court of Human Rights considered a case with parallels to *Bowers* and to today's case. An adult male resident in Northern Ireland alleged he was a practicing homosexual who desired to engage in consensual homosexual conduct. The laws of Northern Ireland forbade him that right. He alleged that he had been questioned, his home had been searched, and he feared criminal prosecution. The court held that the laws proscribing the conduct were invalid under the European Convention on Human Rights. *Dudgeon v. United Kingdom*, 45 Eur. Ct. H. R. (1981) & ¶ 52. Authoritative in all countries that are members of the Council of Europe (21 nations then, 45 nations now), the decision is at odds with the premise in *Bowers* that the claim put forward was insubstantial in our Western civilization.

In our own constitutional system the deficiencies in *Bowers* became even more apparent in the years following its announcement. The 25 States with laws prohibiting the relevant conduct referenced in the *Bowers* decision are reduced now to 13, of which 4 enforce their laws only against homosexual conduct. In those States where sodomy is still proscribed, whether for same-sex or heterosexual conduct, there is a pattern of nonenforcement with respect to consenting adults acting in private. The State of Texas admitted in 1994 that as of that date it had not prosecuted anyone under those circumstances.

Two principal cases were decided after *Bowers* cast its holding into even more doubt. In *Planned Parenthood of Southeastern Pa. v. Casey*, 505 U.S. 833 (1992), the Court reaffirmed the substantive force of the liberty protected by the Due Process Clause. The *Casey* decision again confirmed that our laws and tradition afford constitutional protection to personal decisions relating to marriage, procreation, contraception, family relationships, child rearing, and education. In explaining the respect the Constitution demands for the autonomy of the person in making these choices, we stated as follows:

> These matters, involving the most intimate and personal choices a person may make in a lifetime, choices central to personal dignity and autonomy, are central to the liberty protected by the Fourteenth Amendment. At the heart of liberty is the right to define one's own concept of existence, of meaning, of the universe, and of the mystery of human life. Beliefs about these matters could

not define the attributes of personhood were they formed under compulsion of the State.

Persons in a homosexual relationship may seek autonomy for these purposes, just as heterosexual persons do. The decision in *Bowers* would deny them this right.

The second post-*Bowers* case of principal relevance is *Romer v. Evans*, 517 U.S. 620 (1996). There the Court struck down class-based legislation directed at homosexuals as a violation of the Equal Protection Clause. *Romer* invalidated an amendment to Colorado's constitution which named as a solitary class persons who were homosexuals, lesbians, or bisexual either by "orientation, conduct, practices or relationships," and deprived them of protection under state antidiscrimination laws. We concluded that the provision was "born of animosity toward the class of persons affected" and further that it had no rational relation to a legitimate governmental purpose.

As an alternative argument in this case, counsel for the petitioners argue that *Romer* provides the basis for declaring the Texas statute invalid under the Equal Protection Clause. We conclude the instant case requires us to address whether *Bowers* itself has continuing validity. Were we to hold the statute invalid under the Equal Protection Clause some might question whether a prohibition would be valid if drawn differently, say, to prohibit the conduct both between same-sex and different-sex participants.

To the extent *Bowers* relied on values we share with a wider civilization, it should be noted that the reasoning and holding in *Bowers* have been rejected elsewhere, [including] The European Court of Human Rights in *P. G. & J. H. v. United Kingdom* (Sept. 25, 2001). Other nations, too, have taken action consistent with an affirmation of the protected right of homosexual adults to engage in intimate, consensual conduct. The right the petitioners seek in this case has been accepted as an integral part of human freedom in many other countries. There has been no showing that in this country the governmental interest in circumscribing personal choice is somehow more legitimate or urgent.

The doctrine of *stare decisis* is essential to the respect accorded to the judgments of the Court and to the stability of the law. It is not, however, an all powerful command. There has been no individual or societal reliance on *Bowers* of the sort that could counsel against overturning its holding once there are compelling reasons to do so. *Bowers* itself causes uncertainty, for the precedents before and after its issuance contradict its central holding.

The rationale of *Bowers* does not withstand careful analysis. In his dissenting opinion in *Bowers*, Justice Stevens came to these conclusions:

> Our prior cases make two propositions abundantly clear. First, the fact that the governing majority in a State has traditionally viewed a particular practice as immoral is not a sufficient reason for upholding a law prohibiting the practice; neither history nor tradition could save a law prohibiting miscegenation from constitutional attack. Second, individual decisions by married persons, concerning the intimacies of their physical relationship, even when not intended to produce offspring, are a form of "liberty" protected by the Due Process Clause of the Fourteenth Amendment. Moreover, this protection extends to intimate choices by unmarried as well as married persons.

Justice Stevens' analysis, in our view, should have been controlling in *Bowers* and should control here. *Bowers* was not correct when it was decided, and it is not correct today. It ought not to remain binding precedent. *Bowers v. Hardwick* should be and now is overruled.

The present case does not involve minors. It does not involve persons who might be injured or coerced or who are situated in relationships where consent might not easily be refused. It does not involve public conduct or prostitution. It does not involve whether the government must give formal recognition to any relationship that homosexual persons seek to enter. The case does involve two adults who, with full and mutual consent from each other, engaged in sexual practices common to a homosexual lifestyle. The petitioners are entitled to respect for their private lives. The State cannot demean their existence or control their destiny by making their private sexual conduct a crime. Their right to liberty under the Due Process Clause gives them the full right to engage in their conduct without intervention of the government. "It is a promise of the Constitution that there is a realm of personal liberty which the government may not enter." The Texas statute furthers no legitimate state interest which can justify its intrusion into the personal and private life of the individual.

Had those who drew and ratified the Due Process Clauses of the Fifth Amendment or the Fourteenth Amendment known the components of liberty in its manifold possibilities, they might have been more specific. They did not presume to have this insight. They knew times can blind us to certain truths and later generations can see that laws once thought necessary and proper in fact serve only to oppress. As the Constitution endures, persons in every generation can invoke its principles in their own search for greater freedom.

Scalia, J., dissenting

The Texas Penal Code undoubtedly imposes constraints on liberty. So do laws prohibiting prostitution, recreational use of heroin, and, for that matter, working more than 60 hours per week in a bakery. But there is no right to "liberty" under the Due Process Clause, though today's opinion repeatedly makes that claim. The Fourteenth Amendment expressly allows States to deprive their citizens of "liberty," so long as "due process of law" is provided.

We have held repeatedly, in cases the Court today does not overrule, that only fundamental rights qualify for so-called "heightened scrutiny" protection—that is, rights which are "deeply rooted in this Nation's history and tradition." All other liberty interests may be abridged or abrogated pursuant to a validly enacted state law if that law is rationally related to a legitimate state interest.

Bowers held, first, that criminal prohibitions of homosexual sodomy are not subject to heightened scrutiny because they do not implicate a "fundamental right" under the Due Process Clause.

The Court today does not overrule this holding. Not once does it describe homosexual sodomy as a "fundamental right" or a "fundamental liberty interest," nor does it subject the Texas statute to strict scrutiny. Instead, having failed to establish that the right to homosexual sodomy is "deeply rooted in this Nation's history and tradition," the Court concludes that the application of Texas's statute to petitioners' conduct fails the rational-basis test, and overrules *Bowers*' holding to the contrary.

Sodomy was a criminal offense at common law and was forbidden by the laws of the original 13 States when they ratified the Bill of Rights. In 1868, when the Fourteenth Amendment was ratified, all but 5 of the 37 States in the Union had criminal sodomy laws. In fact, until 1961, all 50 States outlawed sodomy, and today, 24 States and the District of Columbia continue to provide criminal penalties for sodomy performed in private and between consenting adults. Against this background, to claim that a right to engage in such conduct is 'deeply rooted in this Nation's history and tradition' or 'implicit in the concept of ordered liberty' is, at best, facetious."

The Court says: "We think that our laws and traditions in the past half century are of most relevance here. These references show an emerging awareness that liberty gives substantial protection to adult persons in deciding how to conduct their private lives in matters pertaining to sex." Constitutional entitlements do not spring into existence because some States choose to lessen or eliminate criminal sanctions on certain behavior. Much less do they spring into existence, as the Court seems to believe, because foreign nations decriminalize conduct.

I turn now to the ground on which the Court squarely rests its holding: the contention that there is no rational basis for the law here under attack. This proposition is so out of accord with our jurisprudence—indeed, with the jurisprudence of any society we know—that it requires little discussion.

The Texas statute undeniably seeks to further the belief of its citizens that certain forms of sexual behavior are "immoral and unacceptable." The Court embraces instead Justice Stevens' declaration in his *Bowers* dissent, that "the fact that the governing majority in a State has traditionally viewed a particular practice as immoral is not a sufficient reason for upholding a law prohibiting the practice." This effectively means the end of all morals legislation.

The matters appropriate for this Court's resolution are only three: Texas's prohibition of sodomy neither infringes a "fundamental right" (which the Court does not dispute), nor is unsupported by a rational relation to what the Constitution considers a legitimate state interest, nor denies the equal protection of the laws. I dissent.

* * *

Topics for Further Discussion

1. The Court concluded the case should be decided on due process grounds and, as a result, chose not to discuss the equal protection theory. The reason, it said, is because if it relied on equal protection, some persons might believe the state could constitutionally prohibit the sexual conduct at issue so long as it applied the prohibition both to same-sex and heterosexual couples. The Court indicated that it wanted to make clear such a law would violate the rights of *all* persons. Do you agree with this reasoning?

2. The Court in *Loving v. Virginia*, 388 U.S. 1 (1967) addressed both the Equal Protection Clause and the Due Process Clause in the context of a state law prohibiting interracial marriage. The *Loving* case appears in Chapter 12. Does the *Loving* case help you to answer question 1?

3. Did the Court rule that the earlier *Bowers* case was incorrectly decided at the time? Or was *Bowers* correctly decided then but later overtaken by changes in society?

4. On what basis does Justice Scalia's dissent oppose the majority's decision? Would he oppose a legislative decision to allow homosexual relations? Do you think it is best to adhere faithfully to the original intention of the drafters of the Bill of Rights, or would you favor an approach that takes into consideration social change?

5. Under what circumstances may the Supreme Court overrule one of its own decisions?

Equal Protection

Generally speaking, equal protection is the theory of choice when a person complains of prohibitions that are applied unequally. The clearest cases, as stated before, involve racial discrimination. But many other persons have found themselves to be the victims of discrimination because of *who* they are. Not all discrimination is unconstitutional of course. The Supreme Court has spoken of "suspect classifications," race being the most obvious. When a plaintiff who shares characteristics with a group can show that the group is (a) a discrete and insular minority; (b) with an immutable characteristic; (c) and a history of suffering discrimination, the Court may consider laws singling the group out for different treatment as suspect too.

"Discrete and insular" means that society actually views the members as part of the same group. For example, Asian-Americans would be considered "discrete and insular." Their physical characteristics cause American society to see them as having something in common even though their ethnic and racial heritage might be quite different in fact. On the other hand, Caucasians are not thought of as having anything that binds them together as members of a group. This reflects the majority status whites have enjoyed in American society, that is to say, they are neither discrete nor insular.

An "immutable characteristic" means something that cannot be changed, or at least not easily changed. The physical appearance of Asian-Americans is not a choice; it is something they are born with. By contrast, people with professional qualifications, such as doctors and lawyers, can be favored for certain jobs because these qualifications are not immutable. Everyone can, at least in theory, go to university and graduate school in order to improve career prospects.

Of all the factors, "history of discrimination" is likely the most important. To what extent have people in a given group or classification been treated unfairly by society? If the reason for the discrimination is because of stereotypical conclusions about the character, abilities and roles of such people, the Court has been willing to protect them from laws passed without proper consideration of the actual facts.

Who are the members of suspect classes? Racial and ethnic minorities certainly are included. Classifications involving race and ethnicity receive strict scrutiny. The same is true for classifications based on religious belief or national origin. The strict scrutiny test asks whether (a) the federal or state government has a compelling interest in treating the class differently, and (b) the law has been "narrowly tailored" to achieve that interest without unfairly intruding on the rights of the members of the suspect class.

Laws operating against women and illegitimate children do not receive strict scrutiny, although such people arguably meet the tests of being discrete and insular, immutable, and victims of historical discrimination. The Supreme Court has determined that laws impacting on these groups are to be judged by what has been called "heightened" or "intermediate" scrutiny. The Court inquires whether the statute is "substantially related" to an important government interest.

Justice O'Connor, the first woman appointed to the Supreme Court, set out the test for gender-based discrimination in *Mississippi University for Women v. Hogan*, 458 U.S. 718 (1982). MUW was a state-supported nursing school that refused to accept men. In declaring the women-only policy of MUW unconstitutional, Justice O'Connor wrote:

> Although the test for determining the validity of a gender-based classification is straightforward, it must be applied free of fixed notions concerning the roles and abilities of males and females. Care must be taken in ascertaining whether the statutory objective itself reflects archaic and stereotypic notions. Thus, if the statutory objective is to exclude or "protect" members of one gender because they are presumed to suffer from an inherent handicap or to be innately inferior, the objective itself is illegitimate.

If the State's objective is legitimate and important, we next determine whether the requisite direct, substantial relationship between objective and means is present. The purpose of requiring that close relationship is to assure that the validity of a classification is determined through reasoned analysis rather than through the mechanical application of traditional, often inaccurate, assumptions about the proper roles of men and women. The need for the requirement is amply revealed by reference to the broad range of statutes already invalidated by this Court, statutes that relied upon the simplistic, outdated assumption that gender could be used as a "proxy for other, more germane bases of classification," to establish a link between objective and classification.

Discrimination against women provides a difficult challenge to the three-part test. Women unquestionably have been discriminated against historically in the United States. They could not even vote until the passage of the Nineteenth Amendment in 1920, fifty years after African-Americans received that right. Their gender is certainly an immutable characteristic, notwithstanding the possibility of sex-change surgery. The question is whether they are a discrete and insular minority. In fact, women are not a minority at all but rather the statistical majority in the United States. Even if that fact could be overcome, proving that women are discrete and insular would be difficult. They do not all act alike, think alike, or congregate together in ways that separate them from the general society.

To overcome this situation, advocates for women's rights supported a constitutional amendment, called the Equal Rights Amendment. The language of the ERA was as follows: "Equality of Rights under the law shall not be denied or abridged by the United States or any state on account of sex." Amending the Constitution, however, is a long and arduous process, and the ERA failed to garner the necessary support. It passed the Congress in 1972, but was ratified by only thirty-five of the required thirty-eight states by the 1982 deadline. Thus, questions involving alleged discrimination against women, and men for that matter, must continue to be decided under the "intermediate scrutiny" test as explained in *Hogan*.

If a suspect classification is not involved, or the law does not unfairly operate against women or illegitimate children, the Court will apply the "rational basis" test. Under this test, the Court asks only if the government has any possible good reason for enacting the law. If the answer is yes, the law must be sustained. Strangely enough, wealth (or lack of wealth) is not a protected classification. Poor people, it turns out, are not able to demand strict or heightened examination of statutes involving them. Laws that discriminate based on wealth are decided by a rational basis analysis. Despite significant evidence to the contrary, the Court apparently feels that poverty in the United States is not immutable.

When fundamental rights are at stake, any person who is treated differently may invoke a strict scrutiny review of the government's action. For example, in cases involving apportionment of representatives, all persons are entitled to an equal chance at electing someone to the legislature. In *Reynolds v. Sims,* 377 U.S. 533 (1964), the Court set forth the principle of one person, one vote. This means that each legislative district must have approximately the same population. Even where there is no reason to suspect discrimination based on race or some other suspect characteristic, the principle is enforced. When fundamental rights, such as voting, are at stake, all persons are entitled to a strict scrutiny review of government action that discriminates against them.

The Equal Protection Clause appears in the Fourteenth Amendment and, therefore, is applicable only to the states. However, the Court has held the right applicable against the federal government by considering it as part of the Fifth Amendment's due process guarantee. Most of the Bill of Rights is enforced against the states by incorporation through the Fourteenth Amendment Due Process Clause, and equal protection is enforced against the federal government by similar process through the Fifth Amendment Due Process Clause. As a result, most of the rights of the people apply equally in cases involving both state and national government action.

Affirmative action programs have raised the question of whether whites, as well as minorities, enjoy constitutional protection against racial discrimination. At first, the premise may seem doubtful. After all, the Fourteenth Amendment was passed for the very purpose of remedying discrimination *by* the white majority. Whites are not discrete and insular, nor have they suffered a history of discrimination. To the contrary, they have enjoyed a position of dominance in American society. Nevertheless, as governments began addressing the effects of discrimination by offering a helping hand to minorities, members of the white majority claimed that "reverse" discrimination was just as invidious and unconstitutional as that imposed on minorities in the past. The Constitution, they argued, should be color blind.

The rationale for affirmative action is that past discrimination has prevented minorities from effectively participating in the benefits of society. The metaphor of a race is often used. Having been held back for so long, minorities cannot be expected to catch up on their own. Whites have too much of a head start. In grappling with this thorny issue, the Supreme Court has decided that persons of all races do, in fact, have a constitutional right to be free of racial discrimination. However, programs favoring minorities can be upheld under certain circumstances, especially if the state can show that the program was enacted to remedy past discriminatory practices unfairly imposed on minorities.

As the country has gained more experience with affirmative action, the rationale for many such programs has changed. Rather than relying only on the benefit to the minority group members (i.e., to make up for past discrimination), the importance of "diversity" is now emphasized as well. In a pluralistic society, the institutions of society will benefit from the insights, opinions and concerns of a broader range of people. Universities have been among those promoting this way of thinking. The Supreme Court was called upon in the *Grutter* case to decide whether affirmative action in the name of diversity is constitutional.

Grutter v. Bollinger
539 U.S. 306 (2003)

O'Connor, J.

This case requires us to decide whether the use of race as a factor in student admissions by the University of Michigan Law School is unlawful.

The Law School ranks among the Nation's top law schools. It receives more than 3,500 applications each year for a class of around 350 students. Seeking to "admit a group of students who individually and collectively are among the most capable," the Law School looks for individuals with "substantial promise for success in law school" and "a strong likelihood of succeeding in the practice of law and contributing in diverse ways to the well-being of others." More broadly, the Law School seeks "a mix of students with varying backgrounds and experiences who will respect and learn from each other." In 1992, the dean of the Law School charged a faculty committee with crafting a written admissions policy to implement these goals.

The hallmark of that policy is its focus on academic ability coupled with a flexible assessment of applicants' talents, experiences, and potential "to contribute to the learning of those around them." The policy requires admissions officials to evaluate each applicant based on all the information in the file, including a personal statement, letters of recommendation, and an essay describing the ways in which the applicant will contribute to the life and diversity of the Law School. In reviewing an applicant's file, admissions officials must consider the applicant's undergraduate grade point average (GPA) and Law School Admissions Test (LSAT) score because they are important tests of academic success in law school.

The policy makes clear, however, that even the highest possible score does not guarantee admission to the Law School. Nor does a low score automatically disqualify an applicant. Rather, the policy requires admissions officials to look beyond grades and test scores to other criteria that are important to the Law School's educational objectives. The policy does, however, reaffirm the Law School's longstanding commitment to "one particular type of diversity," that is, "racial and ethnic diversity with special reference to the inclusion of students from groups which have been historically discriminated against, like African-Americans, Hispanics and Native Americans, who without this commitment might not be represented in our student body in meaningful numbers."

Petitioner Barbara Grutter is a white Michigan resident who applied to the Law School in 1996 with a 3.8 grade point average and 161 LSAT score. The Law School initially placed petitioner on a waiting list, but subsequently rejected her application. In December 1997, petitioner filed suit in the United States District Court. Petitioner alleged that respondents discriminated against her on the basis of race in violation of the Fourteenth Amendment. Petitioner requested compensatory and punitive damages, an order requiring the Law School to offer her admission, and an injunction prohibiting the Law School from continuing to discriminate on the basis of race.

The Equal Protection Clause provides that no State shall "deny to any person within its jurisdiction the equal protection of the laws." We have held that all racial classifications imposed by government "must be analyzed by a reviewing court under strict scrutiny." This means that such classifications are constitutional only if they are narrowly tailored to further compelling governmental interests.

With these principles in mind, we turn to the question whether the Law School's use of race is justified by a compelling state interest. Before this Court, as they have throughout this litigation, respondents assert only one justification for their use of race in the admissions process: obtaining "the educational benefits that flow from a diverse student body." In other words, the Law School asks us to recognize, in the context of higher education, a compelling state interest in student body diversity.

As the District Court emphasized, the Law School's admissions policy promotes "cross-racial understanding," helps to break down racial stereotypes, and "enables [students] to better understand persons of different races." These benefits are "important and laudable," because "classroom discussion is livelier, more spirited, and simply more enlightening and interesting" when the students have "the greatest possible variety of backgrounds."

These benefits are not theoretical but real, as major American businesses have made clear that the skills needed in today's increasingly global marketplace can only be developed through exposure to widely diverse people, cultures, ideas, and viewpoints. Moreover, universities, and in particular, law schools, represent the training ground for a large number of our Nation's leaders. In order to cultivate a set of leaders with legitimacy in the eyes of the citizenry, it is necessary that the path to leadership be visibly open to talented and qualified individuals of every race and ethnicity. All members of our hetero-geneous society must have confidence in the openness and integrity of the educational institutions that provide this training.

Even in the limited circumstance when drawing racial distinctions is permissible to further a compelling state interest, government is still "constrained in how it may pursue that end: the means chosen to accomplish the government's asserted purpose must be specifically and narrowly framed to accomplish that purpose."

We find that the Law School's admissions program is a narrowly tailored plan. There is no policy, of automatic acceptance or rejection based on any single "soft" variable.

We are mindful, however, that "[a] core purpose of the Fourteenth Amendment was to do away with all governmentally imposed discrimination based on race." Accordingly, race-conscious admissions policies must be limited in time. Enshrining a permanent justification for racial preferences would offend this fundamental equal protection principle. We see no reason to exempt race-conscious admissions programs from the requirement that all governmental use of race must have a logical end point.

In summary, the Equal Protection Clause does not prohibit the Law School's narrowly tailored use of race in admissions decisions to further a compelling interest in obtaining the educational benefits that flow from a diverse student body.

* * *

Topics for Further Discussion

1. From the perspective of the rejected non-minority applicant, does the distinction between race as a *factor* and race as a *quota* make any difference? Chief Justice Rehnquist wrote a dissent, joined by three Justices. He concluded: "The Law School has offered no explanation for its actual admissions practices and, unexplained, we are bound to conclude that the Law School has managed its admissions program, not to achieve a 'critical mass,' but to extend offers of admission to members of selected minority groups in proportion to their statistical representation in the applicant pool." In other words, a *de facto* quota was being employed. Would you be inclined to accept the Law School's explanation under these circumstances?

2. In *Gratz v. Bollinger*, 539 U.S. 244 (2003), a companion case decided on the same day as the *Grutter* case, the Supreme Court found that the undergraduate admission policy of the University of Michigan violated the Equal Protection Clause and Title VI of the Civil Rights Act. The undergraduate admissions process automatically assigned twenty extra points to applicants from targeted minority groups based purely on racial identification and without an individual review of each application file. This had the result of virtually insuring a fixed allotment of minority admissions. Chief Justice Rehnquist writing for the Court concluded that "because the University's use of race in its current freshman admissions policy is not narrowly tailored to achieve respondents' asserted compelling interest in diversity, the admissions policy violates the Equal Protection Clause of the Fourteenth Amendment. We further find that the admissions policy also violates Title VI and 42 U. S. C. § 1981." Why does assigning a fixed number of admissions points based solely on race produce a different result from considering race as a factor in admissions as the Law School was permitted to do?

3. For whose benefit did the Law School maintain its affirmative action programs: minorities, their non-minority classmates, society, or all of them? On what basis did the Court find it constitutional? Why is it important to have a "critical mass" of minority students? The Court says race-conscious remedies must have a logical end point. Who de-

cides, and how will they know when, that end point has been reached? Chief Justice Rehnquist's dissent found the absence of a specific end date for race-conscious admissions policies to be problematic. What might be a reasonable length of time?

4. For constitutional analysis, is race different from the other factors the University considered in making admission decisions? Could an academically strong student claim a constitutional violation as a result of the university admitting a less academically accomplished student whose main talent is playing a sport or musical instrument? Many universities also maintain "legacy" programs that give special consideration to the children of alumni. Do such programs present a constitutional issue?

Statutory Protection of Individual Rights

The Bill of Rights and the Fourteenth Amendment limit the power of the federal and state governments. In order for them to be activated, there must be a finding of "state action" in the form of direct or indirect governmental involvement in the deprivation of individual rights. The courts have been quite liberal in holding that state action can exist in a variety of ways, such as by receiving federal funding. In short, the constitutional rights of equal protection and due process involve the relationship of individuals with the government, both state and federal. Many forms of discrimination, however, were created and imposed by non-government, private parties. Businesses refused service to African-Americans; homosexuals and those with AIDS were denied equal housing opportunities; and the elderly faced discrimination in the workplace to cite but a few of the examples of unequal treatment at the hands of non-government entities.

Section five of the Fourteenth Amendment authorizes Congress to pass statutes to further the goals of the Amendment. In addition to the enabling provisions of the Fourteenth Amendment, the Supreme Court has upheld congressionally-created civil rights statutes pursuant to the Commerce Clause power. Congress exercised this power in a sweeping manner when it passed the Civil Rights Act of 1964. This landmark legislation was a culmination of the Civil Rights movement, and was aimed at nothing less than the elimination of all forms of racial discrimination in American society. It was signed into law by President Lyndon Johnson as a tribute to the civil rights efforts of President John Kennedy following his assassination in 1963. The Civil Rights Act, among other things, prohibits discrimination in employment and housing, and requires non-discriminatory access to business establishments otherwise open to the public. Additional civil rights statutes—such as the Voting Rights Act, the Americans with Disabilities Act and the Age Discrimination in Employment Act—have been passed to further extend the protection against discrimination. Because civil rights laws are aimed at private parties, there is no requirement of state action. Congressionally-created civil rights laws have carried the Constitution's theme of equality deep into everyday life in the United States as the following cases show.

McCormick v. School Dist. of Mamaroneck
370 F.3d 275 (2d Cir. 2004)

Straub, J.

Defendants-Appellants the School District of Mamaroneck and the School District of Pelham ("School Districts") appeal from the judgment of the United States District Court for the Southern District of New York, finding that the School Districts' scheduling of girls' high school soccer in the spring and boys' high school soccer in the fall, which deprives girls but not boys of the opportunity to compete in the New York Regional and State Championships in soccer, violated Title IX of the Education Amendments of 1972, 20 U.S.C. § 1681, et seq. ("Title IX"), and its governing regulations, 34 C.F.R. § 106.41(c), and ordering the School Districts to submit compliance plans.

We are unpersuaded by the School Districts' attempt to downplay the significance of the opportunity that they are denying their female athletes but affording their male athletes—the chance to be State champions. We agree with plaintiffs that denying girls at the Pelham and Mamaroneck high schools treatment equal to boys in a matter so fundamental to the experience of sports denies equality of athletic opportunity to the female students. Because the School Districts have failed to show that the disadvantage that girls face is offset by any comparable advantage to girls in their athletics programs, and because they have not adequately justified their denial of opportunity to girls by nondiscriminatory factors, we affirm the District Court's finding that the School Districts are in violation of Title IX.

Title IX of the Education Amendments of 1972 prohibits discrimination on the basis of sex by educational institutions receiving federal financial assistance. Section 901 of Title IX provides with certain exceptions not applicable here that "[n]o person in the United States shall, on the basis of sex, be excluded from participation in, be denied the benefits of, or be subjected to discrimination under any education program or activity receiving Federal financial assistance."

The participation of girls and women in high school and college sports has increased dramatically since Title IX was enacted. In 1971, before Congress enacted the statute, approximately 300,000 girls and 3.67 million boys played competitive high school sports nationwide. In 2002, 2.86 million girls and 3.99 million boys played competitive high school sports nationwide. "Congress enacted Title IX in 1972 with two principal objectives in mind: '[T]o avoid the use of federal resources to support discriminatory practices' and 'to provide individual citizens effective protection against those practices.'" Title IX was enacted in response to evidence of pervasive discrimination against women with respect to educational opportunities, which was documented in hearings held in 1970 by the House Special Subcommittee on Education.

In 1974, HEW proposed regulations which contained provisions specifically addressing Title IX's requirements in the athletics programs of educational institutions. After considering over 9,700 comments regarding its proposed regulations, HEW published a final rule implementing Title IX. After HEW published the regulations, Congress had forty-five days to disapprove them. During this time, Congress held hearings on the regulations over the course of six days. The regulations went into effect after Congress declined to disapprove them.

Particularly relevant for purposes of this case, the regulations state that "[a] recipient which operates or sponsors interscholastic, intercollegiate, club or intramural athletics shall provide equal athletic opportunity for members of both sexes." In determining whether equal opportunities exist, the Department of Education's Office for Civil Rights ("OCR") considers, among other factors:

(1) Whether the selection of sports and levels of competition effectively accommodate the interests and abilities of members of both sexes;

(2) The provision of equipment and supplies;

(3) Scheduling of games and practice time;

(4) Travel and per diem allowance;

(5) Opportunity to receive coaching and academic tutoring;

(6) Assignment and compensation of coaches and tutors;

(7) Provision of locker rooms, practice and competitive facilities;

(8) Provision of medical and training facilities and services;

(9) Provision of housing and dining facilities and services;

(10) Publicity.

Plaintiffs in this case assert that the School Districts do not provide equal opportunities to girls and boys under factor three, "[s]cheduling of games and practice time." Scheduling girls' soccer in the spring clearly creates a disparity—boys can strive to compete in the Regional and State Championships in soccer and girls cannot. Without a doubt, this difference has a negative impact on girls. The School Districts have not pointed to—in their submissions to the District Court or to us—any areas in which female athletes receive comparably better treatment than male athletes at their schools. Thus, the disadvantage that girls face in the scheduling of soccer has not been offset by any advantages given to girls as compared to boys in the Mamaroneck and Pelham athletics programs. Moreover, girls' soccer is the only sport at these schools scheduled in a season that precludes championship game play. Male athletes do not suffer from any comparable disadvantage.

The School Districts offer several reasons for why girls' soccer is scheduled in the spring and why moving it to the fall would be a problem. First, the schools assert that if girls' soccer is moved, there will not be enough field space, they will have to hire another coach, and there might be a shortage of officials. These reasons are not the kind of nondiscriminatory factors that can justify inferior treatment of female athletes. Hiring a new coach and finding more officials may cost money, but the fact that money needs to be spent to comply with Title IX is obviously not a defense to the statute. The schools will have to make some adjustments in order to provide field space to the girls' soccer teams for practices and games. However, the schools have not demonstrated that finding field space for practices will be impossible or will result in significantly shorter or more infrequent practices. In any event, all of these administrative problems could be avoided by moving boys' soccer to the spring. There is no reason that the boys' soccer teams should be entitled to the fields, coaches, and officials in the fall simply because they were in the fall first. The School Districts could comply with Title IX by offering soccer to boys and girls in the fall in alternating years (or every two years)—as long as the girls, who have been thus far denied the fall season, are scheduled in the upcoming 2004 fall season. Because the School Districts could avoid the administrative problems they complain about by alternating boys' and girls' soccer in the fall season, this case does not require us to decide the availability of an "administrative hardship defense," if any, or the threshold that would suffice to justify a significant disparity in equal athletic opportunity on the basis of such a defense.

* * *

Sutton v. United Airlines, Inc.

527 U.S. 471 (1999)

O'Connor, J.

The Americans with Disabilities Act of 1990 (ADA or Act), 42 U.S.C. § 12101 *et seq.*, prohibits certain employers from discriminating against individuals on the basis of their disabilities. Petitioners challenge the dismissal of their ADA action for failure to state a claim upon which relief can be granted. We conclude that the complaint was properly dismissed.

Petitioners are twin sisters, both of whom have severe myopia. Each petitioner's uncorrected visual acuity is 20/200 or worse in her right eye and 20/400 or worse in her left eye, but "[w]ith the use of corrective lenses, each … has vision that is 20/20 or better." Consequently, without corrective lenses, each "effectively cannot see to conduct numerous activities such as driving a vehicle, watching television or shopping in public stores," but with corrective measures, such as glasses or contact lenses, both "function identically to individuals without a similar impairment."

In 1992, petitioners applied to respondent for employment as commercial airline pilots They met respondent's basic age, education, experience, and Federal Aviation Administration certification qualifications. After submitting their applications for employment, both petitioners were invited by respondent to an interview and to flight simulator tests. Both were told during their interviews, however, that a mistake had been made in inviting them to interview because petitioners did not meet respondent's minimum vision requirement, which was uncorrected visual acuity of 20/100 or better. Due to their failure to meet this requirement, petitioners' interviews were terminated, and neither was offered a pilot position.

In light of respondent's proffered reason for rejecting them, petitioners filed suit in the United States District Court for the District of Colorado, alleging that respondent had discriminated against them "on the basis of their disability, or because [respondent] regarded [petitioners] as having a disability" in violation of the ADA. Specifically, petitioners alleged that due to their severe myopia they actually have a substantially limiting impairment or are regarded as having such an impairment, and are thus disabled under the Act.

The ADA provides that no covered employer "shall discriminate against a qualified individual with a disability because of the disability of such individual in regard to job application procedures, the hiring, advancement, or discharge of employees, employee compensation, job training, and other terms, conditions, and privileges of employment." A "qualified individual with a disability" is identified as "an individual with a disability who, with or without reasonable accommodation, can perform the essential functions of the employment position that such individual holds or desires." In turn, a "disability" is defined as:

(A) a physical or mental impairment that substantially limits one or more of the major life activities of such individual;

(B) a record of such an impairment; or

(C) being regarded as having such an impairment."

Because petitioners allege that with corrective measures their vision "is 20/20 or better," they are not actually disabled within the meaning of the Act if the "disability" determination is made with reference to these measures. Respondent maintains that an impairment does not substantially limit a major life activity if it is corrected.

Standing alone, the allegation that respondent has a vision requirement in place does not establish a claim that respondent regards petitioners as substantially limited in the major life activity of working. By its terms, the ADA allows employers to prefer some physical attributes over others and to establish physical criteria. An employer is free to decide that physical characteristics or medical conditions that do not rise to the level of an impairment—such as one's height, build, or singing voice—are preferable to others, just as it is free to decide that some limiting, but not *substantially* limiting, impairments make individuals less than ideally suited for a job.

Because petitioners have not alleged, and cannot demonstrate, that respondent's vision requirement reflects a belief that petitioners' vision substantially limits them, we agree with the decision of the Court of Appeals affirming the dismissal of petitioners' claim that they are regarded as disabled.

Stevens, J., dissenting

When it enacted the Americans with Disabilities Act of 1990, Congress certainly did not intend to require United Airlines to hire unsafe or unqualified pilots. Nor, in all likelihood, did it view every person who wears glasses as a member of a "discrete and insular minority." Indeed, by reason of legislative myopia it may not have foreseen that its definition of "disability" might theoretically encompass, not just "some 43,000,000 Americans," but perhaps two or three times that number. Nevertheless, if we apply customary tools of statutory construction, it is quite clear that the threshold question whether an individual is "disabled" within the meaning of the Act—and, therefore, is entitled to the basic assurances that the Act affords—focuses on her past or present physical condition without regard to mitigation that has resulted from rehabilitation, self-improvement, prosthetic devices, or medication.

If a narrow reading of the term "disability" were necessary in order to avoid the danger that the Act might otherwise force United to hire pilots who might endanger the lives of their passengers, it would make good sense to use the "43,000,000 Americans" finding to confine its coverage. There is, however, no such danger in this case. If a person is "disabled" within the meaning of the Act, she still cannot prevail on a claim of discrimination unless she can prove that the employer took action "because of" that impairment, and that she can, "with or without reasonable accommodation ... perform the essential functions" of the job of a commercial airline pilot. Even then, an employer may avoid liability if it shows that the criteria of having uncorrected visual acuity of at least 20/100 is "job-related and consistent with business necessity" or if such vision (even if correctable to 20/20) would pose a health or safety hazard.

* * *

Topics for Further Discussion

1. The passage of Title IX created considerable concern among athletic directors at major American universities. Many of these schools traditionally provided disproportionally large sums of money to support men's sports programs, especially football and basketball. The justification was that the men's programs produced large profits from the sale of admission tickets and television and radio revenue. Does this justification make sense or is it similar to the arguments advanced by the School Districts in the *McCormick* case? Does emphasizing men's sports over women's sports "reflect archaic and stereotypic notions," as Justice O'Connor wrote in *Hogan*, "concerning the roles and abilities of males and females?

2. Is passing a civil rights law an effective way to force social equality? Is there another way to accomplish the same objective such as education or raising social awareness?

3. In the *Sutton* case, the Court ruled that the applicants were not disabled within the meaning of the Act and, thus, could not complain of discrimination because of their poor eyesight. However, their poor eyesight was the very reason that the airline rejected their application. Is that not proof enough of discrimination based on their physical condition?

4. In 2008, Congress passed an ADA Amendments Act in part "to reject the Supreme Court's reasoning in *Sutton* ... and to reinstate ... a broad view" of a disability that substantially limits a person's ability to work. 42 U.S.C. § 12101.

5. In *PGA Tour, Inc. v. Martin*, 532 U.S. 661 (2001), the Supreme Court ruled that the professional golf tour was required by the Americans with Disabilities Act to accommodate a golfer who suffered from a leg disorder, by allowing him to use a golf cart. Is that accommodation unfair to other competitors who are required to walk?

6. In his *Sutton* dissent, Justice Stevens said the statute should be be given a "generous" construction, in line with its remedial purpose. In that regard, see *Crawford v. Metropolitan Government of Nashville*, 129 S.Ct. 846 (2009), in which the Court held that Title VII's prohibition against firing employees who report race or gender discrimination extends to an employee who answers questions about such matters in an internal investigation.

* * *

Title VII of the Civil Rights Act prohibits not only intentional discrimination in employment but also employment practices that have a disparate impact on minorities, even if not motivated by any intent to discriminate in that way. The City of New Haven discarded the results of a promotion test for firefighters for fear of running afoul of Title VII. The top ten scorers were eligible for promotion to lieutenant. All were white. Nine captain positions were also available. Based on the test results, the promotions would have gone to seven white and two Hispanic candidates. No blacks. Certain white and Hispanic firefighters who would have received the positions sued the city, claiming its decision not to adhere to the test results violated Title VII.

Ricci v. DeStefano
129 S. Ct. 2658 (2009)

Kennedy, J.

The Civil Rights Act of 1964 did not include an express prohibition on policies or practices that produce a disparate impact. But in *Griggs v. Duke Power Co.*, 401 U.S. 424 (1971), the Court interpreted the Act to prohibit, in some cases, employers' facially neutral practices that, in fact, are "discriminatory in operation." The *Griggs* Court stated that the "touchstone" for disparate-impact liability is the lack of "business necessity": "If an employment practice which operates to exclude [minorities] cannot be shown to be related to job performance, the practice is prohibited." [I]f an employer met its burden by showing that its practice was job-related, the plaintiff was required to show a legitimate alternative that would have resulted in less discrimination (allowing complaining party to show "that other tests or selection devices, without a similarly undesirable racial effect, would also serve the employer's legitimate interest").

Twenty years after *Griggs*, the Civil Rights Act of 1991 was enacted. The Act included a provision codifying the prohibition on disparate-impact discrimination. That provision is now in force along with the disparate-treatment section already noted. Under the disparate-impact statute, a plaintiff establishes a prima facie violation by showing that an employer uses "a particular employment practice that causes a disparate impact on the basis of race, color, religion, sex, or national origin." 42 U. S. C. § 2000e-2(k)(1)(A)(i). An employer may defend against liability by demonstrating that the practice is "job related for the position in question and consistent with business necessity." Even if the employer meets that burden, however, a plaintiff may still succeed by showing that the employer refuses to adopt an available alternative employment practice that has less disparate impact and serves the employer's legitimate needs.

Petitioners allege that when the [City] refused to certify the captain and lieutenant exam results based on the race of the successful candidates, it discriminated against them in violation of Title VII's disparate-treatment provision. The City counters that its decision was permissible because the tests "appear[ed] to violate Title VII's disparate-impact provisions."

Our analysis begins with this premise: The City's actions would violate the disparate-treatment prohibition of Title VII absent some valid defense. All the evidence demonstrates that the City chose not to certify the examination results because of the statistical disparity based on race—i.e., how minority candidates had performed when compared to white candidates. As the District Court put it, the City rejected the test results because "too many whites and not enough minorities would be promoted were the lists to be certified." Without some other justification, this express, race-based decisionmaking violates Title VII's command that employers cannot take adverse employment actions because of an individual's race.

The District Court did not adhere to this principle, however. It held that respondents' "motivation to avoid making promotions based on a test with a racially disparate impact ... does not, as a matter of law, constitute discriminatory intent." And the Government makes a similar argument in this Court. It contends that the "structure of Title VII belies any claim that an employer's intent to comply with Title VII's disparate-impact provisions constitutes prohibited discrimination on the basis of race." But both of those statements turn upon the City's objective—avoiding disparate-impact liability—while ignoring the City's conduct in the name of reaching that objective. Whatever the City's ultimate aim—however well intentioned or benevolent it might have seemed—the City made its employment decision because of race. The City rejected the test results solely because the higher scoring candidates were white. The question is not whether that conduct was discriminatory but whether the City had a lawful justification for its race-based action.

We consider, therefore, whether the purpose to avoid disparate-impact liability excuses what otherwise would be prohibited disparate-treatment discrimination. Courts often confront cases in which statutes and principles point in different directions. Our task is to provide guidance to employers and courts for situations when these two prohibitions could be in conflict absent a rule to reconcile them. In providing this guidance our decision must be consistent with the important purpose of Title VII—that the workplace be an environment free of discrimination, where race is not a barrier to opportunity.

In searching for a standard that strikes a more appropriate balance, we note that this Court has considered cases similar to this one, albeit in the context of the Equal Protection Clause of the Fourteenth Amendment. The Court has held that certain government actions to remedy past racial discrimination—actions that are themselves based on race—are constitutional only where there is a "'strong basis in evidence'" that the remedial actions were necessary. This suit does not call on us to consider whether the statutory constraints under Title VII must be parallel in all respects to those under the Constitution. That does not mean the constitutional authorities are irrelevant, however.

Resolving the statutory conflict in this way allows the disparate-impact prohibition to work in a manner that is consistent with other provisions of Title VII, including the prohibition on adjusting employment-related test scores on the basis of race. Examinations like those administered by the City create legitimate expectations on the part of those who took the tests. As is the case with any promotion exam, some of the fire-fighters here invested substantial time, money, and personal commitment in preparing for the tests. Employment tests can be an important part of a neutral selection system that safeguards against the very racial animosities Title VII was intended to prevent. Here, however, the firefighters saw their efforts invalidated by the City in sole reliance upon race-based statistics.

If an employer cannot rescore a test based on the candidates' race, then it follows *a fortiori* that it may not take the greater step of discarding the test altogether to achieve a more desirable racial distribution of promotion-eligible candidates—absent a strong basis in evidence that the test was deficient and that discarding the results is necessary to avoid violating the disparate-impact provision. Restricting an employer's ability to discard test results (and thereby discriminate against qualified candidates on the basis of their race) also is in keeping with Title VII's express protection of bona fide promotional examinations.

For the foregoing reasons, we adopt the strong-basis-in-evidence standard as a matter of statutory construction to resolve any conflict between the disparate-treatment and disparate-impact provisions of Title VII.

Our statutory holding does not address the constitutionality of the measures taken here in purported compliance with Title VII. We also do not hold that meeting the strong-basis-in-evidence standard would satisfy the Equal Protection Clause in a future case. [B]ecause respondents have not met their burden under Title VII, we need not decide whether a legitimate fear of disparate impact is ever sufficient to justify discriminatory treatment under the Constitution.

The City argues that, even under the strong-basis-in-evidence standard, its decision to discard the examination results was permissible under Title VII. That is incorrect. Even if respondents were motivated as a subjective matter by a desire to avoid committing disparate-impact discrimination, the record makes clear there is no support for the conclusion that respondents had an objective, strong basis in evidence to find the tests inadequate, with some consequent disparate-impact liability in violation of Title VII.

On the record before us, there is no evidence—let alone the required strong basis in evidence—that the tests were flawed because they were not job-related or because other, equally valid and less discriminatory tests were available to the City. Fear of litigation alone cannot justify an employer's reliance on race to the detriment of individuals who passed the examinations and qualified for promotions. The City's discarding the test results was impermissible under Title VII, and summary judgment is appropriate for petitioners on their disparate-treatment claim.

Ginsburg, J., dissenting

In assessing claims of race discrimination, "[c]ontext matters." *Grutter v. Bollinger*. In 1972, Congress extended Title VII of the Civil Rights Act of 1964 to cover public employment. At that time, municipal fire departments across the country, including New Haven's, pervasively discriminated against minorities. The extension of Title VII to cover jobs in firefighting effected no overnight change. It took decades of persistent effort, advanced by Title VII litigation, to open firefighting posts to members of racial minorities.

The white firefighters who scored high on New Haven's promotional exams understandably attract this Court's sympathy. But they had no vested right to promotion. Nor have other persons received promotions in preference to them. New Haven maintains that it refused to certify the test results because it believed, for good cause, that it would be vulnerable to a Title VII disparate-impact suit if it relied on those results. The Court today holds that New Haven has not demonstrated "a strong basis in evidence" for its plea. In so holding, the Court pretends that "[t]he City rejected the test results solely because the higher scoring candidates were white." That pretension, essential to the Court's disposition, ignores substantial evidence of multiple flaws in the tests New Haven used. The Court similarly fails to acknowledge the better tests used in other cities, which have yielded less racially skewed outcomes.

By order of this Court, New Haven, a city in which African-Americans and Hispanics account for nearly 60 percent of the population, must today be served — as it was in the days of undisguised discrimination — by a fire department in which members of racial and ethnic minorities are rarely seen in command positions. In arriving at its order, the Court barely acknowledges the pathmarking decision in *Griggs v. Duke Power Co.*, which explained the centrality of the disparate-impact concept to effective enforcement of Title VII. The Court's order and opinion, I anticipate, will not have staying power.

* * *

Topics for Further Discussion

1. What does the Court say is the relationship between the Equal Protection clause of the Constitution and Title VII of the Civil Rights Act? If they are identical, at least insofar as government action is concerned, then what is the purpose of Title VII? On the other hand, if the disparate impact element of Title VII goes beyond the Constitution's standard, might it be unconstitutional? Justice Scalia raised this concern in a concurrence, saying "if the Federal Government is prohibited from discriminating on the basis of race, *Bolling v. Sharpe*, 347 U. S. 497, 500 (1954), then surely it is also prohibited from enacting laws mandating that third parties — e.g., employers, whether private, State, or municipal — discriminate on the basis of race. The Court's resolution of these cases makes it unnecessary to resolve these matters today. But the war between disparate impact and equal protection will be waged sooner or later, and it behooves us to begin thinking about how — and on what terms — to make peace between them."

2. Litigants often sue under both the Equal Protection clause and the Civil Rights Act, as was the case in this lawsuit. Ordinarily, if the Court can resolve a matter on the basis of a statute, it will not proceed to consider the claim under the Constitution. That is what happened here.

3. Justice Ginsburg, in her dissent, doubts the decision will have staying power. It was, in fact, a 5–4 decision, reversing an opinion of the Second Circuit Court of Appeals. One of the members of the Court of Appeals panel was Sonia Sotomayor, who subsequently was confirmed as a member of the Supreme Court, replacing Justice David Souter. Is this change of personnel likely to make Justice Ginsburg's prediction come true?

Freedom of Religion

America was populated, beginning with the fabled Pilgrims' landing on Plymouth Rock in 1620, largely by exiles fleeing Europe in search of greater freedom of conscience and religion. Therefore, it comes as no surprise that the Bill of Rights boldly asserts that: "Congress shall make no law respecting an establishment of religion, or prohibiting the free exercise thereof...." These words were a reaction to the experience in England where state and church were united under a single sovereign. The drafters of the Bill of Rights might well have stopped with enshrining the right to free exercise of religion, but they did not. Recognizing the inherently coercive nature of state religions, they prohibited state support for, or establishment of, religion in any form. Thus, religious freedom in the U.S. takes the form of two separate but related provisions: the Establishment Clause and the Free Exercise Clause.

Establishment Clause

Establishment Clause issues often turn into emotional debates as a result of the tension between the evolving social reality of the United States and the constitutional language. The fact is that a majority of American citizens are Christian, and many of the values underlying the law flow out of Judeo-Christian traditions. It seems quite natural to many Americans that religiously inspired ideology and imagery be included in everyday life, whether that aspect of everyday life is in the private or public sphere. Nativity scenes, crosses, and menorah situated on public property are meant to engender a holiday spirit as much as to represent a belief in their underlying creeds. Religious symbols and exhortations are, to many Americans, largely ceremonial in nature. For example: the words "In God We Trust" appearing on the one dollar bill.

The growing convergence of religion and politics can be seen in the "religious right." This loosely connected federation of churches and Christian fundamentalists sees the expansion of civil liberties (except when they are favorable to their interests) as a threat to what they believe to be the Christian heritage of America. To some fundamentalists, the Supreme Court is a bastion of secular evils, and every religion case is an opportunity to reassert that America is a Christian nation. The Supreme Court decided in *Stone v. Graham*, 449 U.S. 39 (1980) that the posting of the Ten Commandments in public schools was a violation of the Establishment Clause. Under the Court's rulings, laws aiding religion would be struck down unless they had a secular purpose and primary effect, and did not excessively entangle the government with religion. Yet, the Religious Right refuses to accept this and other rulings and, as recently as 2003, the Chief Justice of the Alabama Supreme Court had to be removed from his position for failing to follow an order to remove a stone monument bearing the Ten Commandments from the courthouse.

The leading case in the Establishment Clause area is *Lemon v. Kurtzman*, 403 U.S. 602 (1971). The *Lemon* case involved a challenge to a state aid program for non-public schools. The Court announced a three-part test for assessing whether a government activity can pass constitutional muster under the Establishment Clause. First, the statute must have a secular legislative purpose. Second, its principal or primary effect must be one that neither advances nor inhibits religion. Third, the law must not foster excessive government entanglement with religion.

Questions involving school prayer and the use of school facilities for religious activities remain among the most contentious. Under the *Lemon* test, a variety of state-supported private school programs have survived constitutional scrutiny. In *Zelman v. Simmons-Harris*, 536 U.S. 639 (2002), the Court upheld an Ohio pilot program that provided parents with vouchers from public funds that they could use to help pay for their children's tuition at private religiously-affiliated schools. The majority concluded that the program's purpose and effect was to aid education, and not to assist religion. The following case demonstrates the sensitive position schools often find themselves in when faced with conflicting rights and duties as well as illustrating how the *Lemon* test is applied in the educational context.

Lamb's Chapel v. Center Moriches Union Free School Dist.
508 U.S. 384 (1993)

White, J.

New York Educ. Law 414 authorizes local school boards to adopt reasonable regulations for the use of school property for 10 specified purposes when the property is not in use for school purposes. Among the permitted uses is the holding of "social, civic and recreational meetings and entertainments, and other uses pertaining to the welfare of the community; but such meetings, entertainment and uses shall be nonexclusive and shall be open to the general public." The list of permitted uses does not include meetings for religious purposes, and a New York appellate court, in *Trietley v. Board of Ed. of Buffalo*, 65 A.D.2d (App. Div. 1978), ruled that local boards could not allow student bible clubs to meet on school property because "[r]eligious purposes are not included in the enumerated purposes for which a school may be used under section 414."

Pursuant to 414's empowerment of local school districts, the Board of Center Moriches Union Free School District (District) has issued rules and regulations with respect to the use of school property when not in use for school purposes. The rules allow only 2 of the 10 purposes authorized by 414: social, civic, or recreational uses (Rule 10) and use by political organizations if secured in compliance with 414 (Rule 8). Rule 7, however, consistent with the judicial interpretation of state law, provides that "[t]he school premises shall not be used [by any group for religious purposes."]

The issue in this case is whether, against this background of state law, it violates the Free Speech Clause of the First Amendment, made applicable to the States by the Fourteenth Amendment, to deny a church access to school premises to exhibit for public viewing and for assertedly religious purposes, a film series dealing with family and childrearing issues faced by parents today.

Petitioners (Church) are Lamb's Chapel, an evangelical church in the community of Center Moriches, and its pastor John Steigerwald. Twice the Church applied to the District for permission to use school facilities to show a six-part film series containing lectures by Doctor James Dobson. A brochure provided on request of the District identified Dr. Dobson as a licensed psychologist, former associate clinical professor of pediatrics at the University of Southern California, best-selling author, and radio commentator. The brochure stated that the film series would discuss Dr. Dobson's views on the undermining influences of the media that could only be counterbalanced by returning to traditional Christian family values instilled at an early stage. The brochure went on to describe the contents of each of the six parts of the series. The District denied the first application, saying that "[t]his film does appear to be church-related, and therefore your request must be refused." The second application for permission to use school premises for showing the film series, which described it as a "Family-oriented movie—from a Christian perspective," was denied using identical language.

There is no question that the District, like the private owner of property, may legally preserve the property under its control for the use to which it is dedicated. It is also common ground that the District need not have permitted after-hours use of its property for any of the uses permitted by 414 N.Y. Educ. Law. The District, however, did open its property for 2 of the 10 uses permitted by 414. The Church argued below that, because under Rule 10 of the rules issued by the District, school property could be used for "social, civic, and recreational" purposes, the District had opened its property for such a wide variety of communicative purposes that restrictions on communicative uses of the property were subject to the same constitutional limitations as restrictions in traditional public forums such as parks and sidewalks. Hence, its view was that subject matter or speaker exclusions on District property were required to be justified by a compelling state interest, and to be narrowly drawn to achieve that end.

The District, as a respondent, would save its judgment below on the ground that to permit its property to be used for religious purposes would be an establishment of religion forbidden by the First Amendment. This Court suggested in *Widmar v. Vincent*, 454 U.S. 263 (1981), that the interest of the State in avoiding an Establishment Clause violation "may be [a] compelling" one justifying an abridgment of free speech otherwise protected by the First Amendment; but the Court went on to hold that permitting use of university property for religious purposes under the open access policy involved there would not be incompatible with the Court's Establishment Clause cases.

We have no more trouble than did the *Widmar* Court in disposing of the claimed defense on the ground that the posited fears of an Establishment Clause violation are unfounded. The showing of this film series would not have been during school hours, would not have been sponsored by the school, and would have been open to the public, not just to church members. The District property had repeatedly been used by a wide variety of private organizations. Under these circumstances, as in *Widmar*, there would have been [no realistic danger] that the community would [think that the District was [endorsing religion] or any particular creed,] and any benefit to religion or to the Church would have been no more than incidental. As in *Widmar*, permitting District property to be used to exhibit the film series involved in this case would not have been an establishment of religion under the three-part test articulated in *Lemon v. Kurtzman*: the challenged governmental action has a secular purpose, does not have the principal or primary effect of advancing or inhibiting religion, and does not foster an excessive entanglement with religion.

* * *

Topics for Further Discussion

1. The *Widmar* case involved a university policy that prohibited a student religious group from participating in an open forum on school facilities. As in *Lamb's Chapel*, the Court found that the Free Speech rights of the students to participate equally in a university sponsored activity outweighed the Establishment Clause concern. Do you agree? In *Good News Club v. Milford Central School*, 533 U.S. 98 (2001), the Supreme Court reaffirmed its holding in *Lamb's Chapel* by holding that a school district could not exclude a Christian oriented club for children from using school facilities after school on an equal basis with other activities.

2. Contrast the reasoning of *Lamb's Chapel* with that in the *Santa Fe Independent School Dist.* case which appears later in this chapter. Can you list the distinguishing facts in these two cases?

3. In *Christian Legal Soc. v. Martinez*, 2010 WL 2555187 (2010), the law school of a state university required student organizations to refrain from discrimination based on religion or sexual orientation in order to be "registered." A Christian group excluded persons of different religious convictions and those who engage in "unrepentant homosexual conduct." The Supreme Court ruled that the law school's policy was "viewpoint neutral" and did not violate the religious group's rights to free speech and expressive association. Should a university or a law school have the right to withhold recognition of student groups that advocate positions viewed as being discriminatory?

Free Exercise Clause

Under the Free Exercise Clause, problems arise when religious practices violate secular laws. In *Wisconsin v. Yoder*, 406 U.S. 205 (1972), for example, the right of Amish parents to stop their children's formal school education after eighth grade was upheld. The Court was required to balance the Amish concern for protecting their children from the threats of secular education against a claim by the state that it had a legitimate interest in ensuring that all children attend school until the age of sixteen. In contrast, however, the Court in *United States v. Lee*, 455 U.S. 252 (1982) ruled that Amish workers could be compelled to participate in the national social security system even though it conflicted with their religious tenets. What is the difference? The Court typically inquires into whether the burden on free exercise is significant, and whether that burden is outweighed by the government's interest.

Employment Div., Oregon Dep't of Human Resources v. Smith
494 U.S. 872 (1990)

Scalia, J.

This case requires us to decide whether the Free Exercise Clause of the First Amendment permits the State of Oregon to include religiously inspired peyote use within the reach of its general criminal prohibition on use of that drug, and thus permits the State to deny unemployment benefits to persons dismissed from their jobs because of such religiously inspired use.

I

Oregon law prohibits the knowing or intentional possession of a "controlled substance" unless the substance has been prescribed by a medical practitioner. The law defines "controlled substance" as a drug classified in Schedules I through V of the Federal Controlled Substances Act, as modified by the State Board of Pharmacy. Persons who violate this provision by possessing a controlled substance listed on Schedule I are "guilty of a Class B felony." As compiled by the State Board of Pharmacy under its statutory authority, Schedule I contains the drug peyote, a hallucinogen derived from the plant *Lophophora williamsii Lemaire*.

Respondents Alfred Smith and Galen Black (hereinafter respondents) were fired from their jobs with a private drug rehabilitation organization because they ingested peyote for sacramental purposes at a ceremony of the Native American Church, of which both are members. When respondents applied to petitioner Employment Division (hereinafter petitioner) for unemployment compensation, they were determined to be ineligible for benefits because they had been discharged for work-related "misconduct." The Oregon Court of Appeals reversed that determination, holding that the denial of benefits violated respondents' free exercise rights under the First Amendment.

On appeal to the Oregon Supreme Court, petitioner argued that the denial of benefits was permissible because respondents' consumption of peyote was a crime under Oregon law. The Oregon Supreme Court reasoned, however, that the criminality of respondents' peyote use was irrelevant to resolution of their constitutional claim—since the purpose of the "misconduct" provision under which respondents had been disqualified was not to enforce the State's criminal laws but to preserve the financial integrity of the compensation fund, and since that purpose was inadequate to justify the burden that disqualification imposed on respondents' religious practice. We granted *certiorari*.

Before this Court in 1987, petitioner continued to maintain that the illegality of respondents' peyote consumption was relevant to their constitutional claim. We agreed, concluding that "if a State has prohibited through its criminal laws certain kinds of religiously motivated conduct without violating the First Amendment, it certainly follows that it may impose the lesser burden of denying unemployment compensation benefits to persons who engage in that conduct." *Employment Div., Dept. of Human Resources of Oregon v. Smith*, 485 U.S. 660, 670 (1988) (*Smith I*). We noted, however, that the Oregon Supreme Court had not decided whether respondents' sacramental use of peyote was in fact proscribed by Oregon's controlled substance law, and that this issue was a matter of dispute between the parties. Being "uncertain about the legality of the religious use of peyote in Oregon," we determined that it would not be "appropriate for us to decide whether the practice is protected by the Federal Constitution." Accordingly, we vacated the judgment of the Oregon Supreme Court and remanded for further proceedings.

On remand, the Oregon Supreme Court held that respondents' religiously inspired use of peyote fell within the prohibition of the Oregon statute, which "makes no exception for the sacramental use" of the drug. It then considered whether that prohibition was valid under the Free Exercise Clause, and concluded that it was not. The court therefore reaffirmed its previous ruling that the State could not deny unemployment benefits to respondents for having engaged in that practice.

We again granted *certiorari*.

II

The Free Exercise Clause of the First Amendment, which has been made applicable to the States by incorporation into the Fourteenth Amendment, provides that "Congress shall make no law respecting an establishment of religion, or prohibiting the free exercise thereof...." The free exercise of religion means, first and foremost, the right to believe and profess whatever religious doctrine one desires. Thus, the First Amendment obviously excludes all "governmental regulation of religious beliefs as such." The government may not compel affirmation of religious belief, punish the expression of religious doctrines it believes to be false, impose special disabilities on the basis of religious views or religious status, or lend its power to one or the other side in controversies over religious authority or dogma.

But the "exercise of religion" often involves not only belief and profession but the performance of (or abstention from) physical acts: assembling with others for a worship service, participating in sacramental use of bread and wine, proselytizing, abstaining from certain foods or certain modes of transportation. It would be true, we think (though no case of ours has involved the point), that a State would be "prohibiting the free exercise [of religion]" if it sought to ban such acts or abstentions only when they are engaged in for religious reasons, or only because of the religious belief that they display. It would doubtless be unconstitutional, for example, to ban the casting of "statues that are to be used for worship purposes," or to prohibit bowing down before a golden calf.

Respondents in the present case, however, seek to carry the meaning of "prohibiting the free exercise [of religion]" one large step further. They contend that their religious motivation for using peyote places them beyond the reach of a criminal law that is not specifically directed at their religious practice, and that is concededly constitutional as applied to those who use the drug for other reasons. They assert, in other words, that "prohibiting the free exercise [of religion]" includes requiring any individual to observe a generally applicable law that requires (or forbids) the performance of an act that his religious belief forbids (or requires). As a textual matter, we do not think the words must be given that meaning. It is no more necessary to regard the collection of a general tax, for example, as "prohibiting the free exercise [of religion]" by those citizens who believe support of organized government to be sinful, than it is to regard the same tax as "abridging the freedom ... of the press" of those publishing companies that must pay the tax as a condition of staying in business. It is a permissible reading of the text, in the one case as in the other, to say that if prohibiting the exercise of religion (or burdening the activity of printing) is not the object of the tax but merely the incidental effect of a generally applicable and otherwise valid provision, the First Amendment has not been offended.

Our decisions reveal that the latter reading is the correct one. We have never held that an individual's religious beliefs excuse him from compliance with an otherwise valid law prohibiting conduct that the State is free to regulate. On the contrary, the record of more than a century of our free exercise jurisprudence contradicts that proposition.

Values that are protected against government interference through enshrinement in the Bill of Rights are not thereby banished from the political process. Just as a society that believes in the negative protection accorded to the press by the First Amendment is likely to enact laws that affirmatively foster the dissemination of the printed word, so also a society that believes in the negative protection accorded to religious belief can be expected to be solicitous of that value in its legislation as well. It is therefore not surprising that a number of States have made an exception to their drug laws for sacramental peyote use. But to say that a nondiscriminatory religious-practice exemption is permitted, or even that it is desirable, is not to say that it is constitutionally required, and that the appropriate occasions for its creation can be discerned by the courts. It may fairly be said that leaving accommodation to the political process will place at a relative disadvantage those religious practices that are not widely engaged in; but that unavoidable consequence of democratic government must be preferred to a system in which each conscience is a law unto itself or in which judges weigh the social importance of all laws against the centrality of all religious beliefs.

Because respondents' ingestion of peyote was prohibited under Oregon law, and because that prohibition is constitutional, Oregon may, consistent with the Free Exercise Clause, deny respondents unemployment compensation when their dismissal results from use of the drug. The decision of the Oregon Supreme Court is accordingly reversed.

* * *

Topics for Further Discussion

1. Do you agree that Oregon's interest in prohibiting the use of peyote overrides the importance of the use of the substance in a *bona fide* religious ceremony? Assuming that Oregon has a legitimate interest in outlawing peyote use generally, why doesn't the Court require that interest to be narrowly tailored in a manner to accommodate ceremonial use by Native Americans? Do you see any balancing of interests? Do you think the legal result in this case has only a mere "incidental impact" on free exercise of religion for the Native Americans?

2. The Court notes that a number of states have excluded legitimate religious and ceremonial use of peyote from the reach of their criminal laws. Justice Scalia suggests that this is a proper function of the political process. Do you agree that the exercise of religion should be subject to the democratic political process?

3. In the case of *Church of Lukumi Babalu Aye v. City of Hialeah*, 508 U.S. 520 (1993), the Court was asked to consider a series of local government regulations aimed at prohibiting followers of the Santeria religion from engaging in animal sacrifice. The religion originated in the 19th century when hundreds of thousands of members of the Yoruba people were brought as slaves from western Africa to Cuba. It was clear from the record that the people of Hialeah did not want a voodoo religious center in their community. In an opinion by Justice Kennedy, the Court concluded as follows:

> The Free Exercise Clause commits government itself to religious tolerance, and upon even slight suspicion that proposals for state intervention stem from animosity to religion or distrust of its practices, all officials must pause to remember their own high duty to the Constitution and to the rights it secures. Those in office must be resolute in resisting importunate demands and must ensure that the sole reasons for imposing the burdens of law and regulation are secular. Legislators may not devise mechanisms, overt or disguised, designed to persecute or oppress a religion or its practices. The laws here in question were enacted contrary to these constitutional principles, and they are void.

Can you reconcile the *Church of Lukumi* case with the reasoning of Justice Scalia in the *Smith* case?

4. Congress passed a law to supersede the *Smith* decision and require use of the "compelling interest" test to examine general legislation that impedes religious freedom. The Supreme Court rejected the intervention of Congress, declaring the statute unconstitutional on the grounds that it infringed on the role of the Court. *City of Boerne v. Flores*, 521 U.S. 507 (1997).

Tension between the Free Exercise and Establishment Clauses

The Establishment Clause and the Free Exercise Clause, while intended to be complementary, sometimes lead to direct conflict as seen from the arguments raised by the school district in the *Lamb's Chapel* case. The conflict is sharpest in the area of education where the right of students to exercise their religious beliefs collides head-on with the state's duty to maintain a religion-free environment. The following two cases illustrate the problem.

Santa Fe Indep. School Dist. v. Doe
530 U.S. 290 (2000)

Stevens, J.

Prior to 1995, the Santa Fe High School student who occupied the school's elective office of student council chaplain delivered a prayer over the public address system before each varsity football game for the entire season. This practice, along with others, was challenged in District Court as a violation of the Establishment Clause of the First Amendment. While these proceedings were pending in the District Court, the school district adopted a different policy that permits, but does not require, prayer initiated and led by a student at all home games. The District Court entered an order modifying that policy to permit only nonsectarian, nonproselytizing prayer. The Court of Appeals held that, even as modified by the District Court, the football prayer policy was invalid. We granted the school district's petition for *certiorari* to review that holding.

I

The Santa Fe Independent School District (District) is a political subdivision of the State of Texas, responsible for the education of more than 4,000 students in a small community in the southern part of the State. The District includes the Santa Fe High School, two primary schools, an intermediate school and the junior high school. Respondents are two sets of current or former students and their respective mothers. One family is Mormon and the other is Catholic. The District Court permitted respondents (Does) to litigate anonymously to protect them from intimidation or harassment.

II

In *Lee v. Weisman*, 505 U.S. 577 (1992), we held that a prayer delivered by a rabbi at a middle school graduation ceremony violated [the Establishment] Clause. Although this case involves student prayer at a different type of school function, our analysis is properly guided by the principles that we endorsed in *Lee*.

As we held in that case:

> The principle that government may accommodate the free exercise of religion does not supersede the fundamental limitations imposed by the Establishment Clause. It is beyond dispute that, at a minimum, the Constitution guarantees that government may not coerce anyone to support or participate in religion or its exercise, or otherwise act in a way which "establishes a [state] religion or religious faith, or tends to do so."

In this case the District first argues that this principle is inapplicable to its October policy because the messages are private student speech, not public speech. It reminds us that "there is a crucial difference between government speech endorsing religion, which the Establishment Clause forbids, and private speech endorsing religion, which the Free Speech and Free Exercise Clauses protect." We certainly agree with that distinction, but we are not persuaded that the pregame invocations should be regarded as "private speech."

In *Lee*, the school district made the related argument that its policy of endorsing only "civic or nonsectarian" prayer was acceptable because it minimized the intrusion on the audience as a whole. We rejected that claim by explaining that such a majoritarian policy "does not lessen the offense or isolation to the objectors. At best it narrows their number, at worst increases their sense of isolation and affront." Similarly, while Santa Fe's majoritarian election might ensure that most of the students are represented, it does nothing to protect the minority; indeed, it likely serves to intensify their offense.

Moreover, the District has failed to divorce itself from the religious content in the invocations. It has not succeeded in doing so, either by claiming that its policy is "'one of neutrality rather than endorsement'" or by characterizing the individual student as the "circuit-breaker" in the process. Contrary to the District's repeated assertions that it has adopted a "hands-off" approach to the pregame invocation, the realities of the situation plainly reveal that its policy involves both perceived and actual endorsement of religion. In this case, as we found in *Lee*, the "degree of school involvement" makes it clear that the pregame prayers bear "the imprint of the State and thus put school-age children who objected in an untenable position."

In addition to involving the school in the selection of the speaker, the policy, by its terms, invites and encourages religious messages. The policy itself states that the purpose of the message is "to solemnize the event." A religious message is the most obvious method of solemnizing an event. Moreover, the requirements that the message "promote good citizenship" and "establish the appropriate environment for competition" further narrow the types of message deemed appropriate, suggesting that a solemn, yet nonreligious, message, such as commentary on United States foreign policy, would be prohibited. Indeed, the only type of message that is expressly endorsed in the text is an "invocation"—a term that primarily describes an appeal for divine assistance. In fact, as used in the past at Santa Fe High School, an "invocation" has always entailed a focused religious message. Thus, the expressed purposes of the policy encourage the selection of a religious message, and that is precisely how the students understand the policy. The results of the elections described in the parties' stipulation make it clear that the students understood that the central question before them was whether prayer should be a part of the pregame ceremony. We recognize the important role that public worship plays in many communities, as well as the sincere desire to include public prayer as a part of various occasions so as to mark those occasions' significance. But such religious activity in public schools, as elsewhere, must comport with the First Amendment.

The actual or perceived endorsement of the message, moreover, is established by factors beyond just the text of the policy. Once the student speaker is selected and the message composed, the invocation is then delivered to a large audience assembled as part of a regularly scheduled, school-sponsored function conducted on school property. The message is broadcast over the school's public address system, which remains subject to the control of school officials. It is fair to assume that the pregame ceremony is clothed in the traditional indicia of school sporting events, which generally include not just the team, but also cheerleaders and band members dressed in uniforms sporting the school name and mascot. The school's name is likely written in large print across the field and on banners and flags. The crowd will certainly include many who display the school colors and insignia on their school T-shirts, jackets, or hats and who may also be waving signs displaying the school name. It is in a setting such as this that "[t]he board has chosen to permit" the elected student to rise and give the "statement or invocation."

In this context the members of the listening audience must perceive the pregame message as a public expression of the views of the majority of the student body delivered with the approval of the school administration. In cases involving state participation in a religious activity, one of the relevant questions is "whether an objective observer, acquainted with the text, legislative history, and implementation of the statute, would perceive it as a state endorsement of prayer in public schools." Regardless of the listener's support for, or objection to, the message, an objective Santa Fe High School student will unquestionably perceive the inevitable pregame prayer as stamped with her school's seal of approval.

School sponsorship of a religious message is impermissible because it sends the ancillary message to members of the audience who are nonadherents "that they are outsiders, not full members of the political community, and an accompanying message to adherents that they are insiders, favored members of the political community." The delivery of such a message—over the school's public address system, by a speaker representing the student body, under the supervision of school faculty, and pursuant to a school policy that explicitly and implicitly encourages public prayer—is not properly characterized as "private" speech.

III

The District next argues that its football policy is distinguishable from the graduation prayer in *Lee* because it does not coerce students to participate in religious observances. Its argument has two parts: first, that there is no impermissible government coercion because the pregame messages are the product of student choices; and second, that there is really no coercion at all because attendance at an extracurricular event, unlike a graduation ceremony, is voluntary.

The reasons just discussed explaining why the alleged "circuit-breaker" mechanism of the dual elections and student speaker do not turn public speech into private speech also demonstrate why these mechanisms do not insulate the school from the coercive element of the final message. In fact, this aspect of the District's argument exposes anew the concerns that are created by the majoritarian election system. The parties' stipulation clearly states that the issue resolved in the first election was "whether a student would deliver prayer at varsity football games," and the controversy in this case demonstrates that the views of the students are not unanimous on that issue.

One of the purposes served by the Establishment Clause is to remove debate over this kind of issue from governmental supervision or control. We explained in *Lee* that the "preservation and transmission of religious beliefs and worship is a responsibility and a choice committed to the private sphere." The two student elections authorized by the policy, coupled with the debates that presumably must precede each, impermissibly invade that private sphere. The election mechanism, when considered in light of the history in which the policy in question evolved, reflects a device the District put in place that determines whether religious messages will be delivered at home football games. The mechanism encourages divisiveness along religious lines in a public school setting, a result at odds with the Establishment Clause. Although it is true that the ultimate choice of student speaker is "attributable to the students," the District's decision to hold the constitutionally problematic election is clearly "a choice attributable to the State."

The District further argues that attendance at the commencement ceremonies at issue in *Lee* "differs dramatically" from attendance at high school football games, which it contends "are of no more than passing interest to many students" and are "decidedly extracurricular," thus dissipating any coercion. Attendance at a high school football game, unlike showing up for class, is certainly not required in order to receive a diploma. Moreover, we may assume that the District is correct in arguing that the informal pressure to attend an athletic event is not as strong as a senior's desire to attend her own graduation ceremony.

There are some students, however, such as cheerleaders, members of the band, and, of course, the team members themselves, for whom seasonal commitments mandate their attendance, sometimes for class credit. The District also minimizes the importance to many students of attending and participating in extracurricular activities as part of a complete educational experience. As we noted in *Lee*, "[l]aw reaches past formalism." To assert that high school students do not feel immense social pressure, or have a truly genuine desire, to be involved in the extracurricular event that is American high school football is "formalistic in the extreme." We stressed in *Lee* the obvious observation that "adolescents are often susceptible to pressure from their peers towards conformity, and that the influence is strongest in matters of social convention." High school home football games are traditional gatherings of a school community; they bring together students and faculty as well as friends and family from years present and past to root for a common cause. Undoubtedly, the games are not important to some students, and they voluntarily choose not to attend. For many others, however, the choice between whether to attend these games or to risk facing a personally offensive religious ritual is in no practical sense an easy one. The Constitution, moreover, demands that the school may not force this difficult choice upon these students for "[i]t is a tenet of the First Amendment that the State cannot require one of its citizens to forfeit his or her rights and benefits as the price of resisting conformance to state-sponsored religious practice."

* * *

Topics for Further Discussion

1. In a democratic society, why is a majoritarian election on religion improper? Can the minority prevent the majority from expressing its religious beliefs at the school football game?

2. What is the damage done to the plaintiffs? They, themselves, are Christians. Under the school policy, no one was forced to participate in the prayer. Couldn't those who disagreed with the religious message simply ignore it?

3. Recitation of the "Pledge of Allegiance" to the national flag is a ritual in many school classrooms. In 1954 Congress added the phrase "under God" to the pledge, so that it now reads, "... one nation, under God, indivisible, with liberty and justice for all." Children cannot be required to recite the Pledge. Almost fifty years later, in *Newdow v. United States Congress*, 328 F.3d 466 (9th Cir. 2003), the Ninth Circuit held the "under God" language to violate the Establishment Clause. The case reached the Supreme Court, but the Court declined to address the constitutional question, concluding that the father of the child did not have standing to bring the case to court. Do you think such language in the school environment offends the Establishment Clause?

Locke v. Davey
540 U.S. 712 (2004)

Rehnquist, C.J.

The State of Washington established the Promise Scholarship Program to assist academically gifted students with postsecondary education expenses. In accordance with the State Constitution, students may not use the scholarship at an institution where they are pursuing a degree in devotional theology. We hold that such an exclusion from an otherwise inclusive aid program does not violate the Free Exercise Clause of the First Amendment.

Respondent, Joshua Davey, was awarded a Promise Scholarship, and chose to attend Northwest College. Northwest is a private, Christian college affiliated with the Assemblies of God denomination, and is an eligible institution under the Promise Scholarship Program. Davey had "planned for many years to attend a Bible college and to prepare [himself] through that college training for a lifetime of ministry, specifically as a church pastor." To that end, when he enrolled in Northwest College, he decided to pursue a double major in pastoral ministries and business management/administration. There is no dispute that the pastoral ministries degree is devotional and therefore excluded under the Promise Scholarship Program.

At the beginning of the 1999–2000 academic year, Davey met with Northwest's director of financial aid. He learned for the first time at this meeting that he could not use his scholarship to pursue a devotional theology degree. He was informed that to receive the funds appropriated for his use, he must certify in writing that he was not pursuing such a degree at Northwest. He refused to sign the form and did not receive any scholarship funds.

The Religion Clauses of the First Amendment provide: "Congress shall make no law respecting an establishment of religion, or prohibiting the free exercise thereof." These two Clauses, the Establishment Clause and the Free Exercise Clause, are frequently in tension. Yet we have long said that "there is room for play in the joints" between them. In other words, there are some state actions permitted by the Establishment Clause but not required by the Free Exercise Clause.

This case involves that "play in the joints" described above. Under our Establishment Clause precedent, the link between government funds and religious training is broken by the independent and private choice of recipients. As such, there is no doubt that the State could, consistent with the Federal Constitution, permit Promise Scholars to pursue a degree in devotional theology, and the State does not contend otherwise. The question before us, however, is whether Washington, pursuant to its own constitution, which has been authoritatively interpreted as prohibiting even indirectly funding religious instruction that will prepare students for the ministry, can deny them such funding without violating the Free Exercise Clause.

Far from evincing the hostility toward religion which was manifest in *Lukumi*, we believe that the entirety of the Promise Scholarship Program goes a long way toward including religion in its benefits. The program permits students to attend pervasively religious schools, so long as they are accredited. As Northwest advertises, its "concept of education is distinctly Christian in the evangelical sense." It prepares all of its students, "through instruction, through modeling, [and] through [its] classes, to use ... the Bible as their guide, as the truth," no matter their chosen profession. And under the Promise Scholarship Program's current guidelines, students are still eligible to take devotional theology courses. Davey notes all students at Northwest are required to take at least four devotional courses, "Exploring the Bible," "Principles of Spiritual Development," "Evangelism in the Christian Life," and "Christian Doctrine," and some students may have additional religious requirements as part of their majors. In short, we find neither in the history or text of Article I, § 11 of the Washington Constitution, nor in the operation of the Promise Scholarship Program, anything that suggests animus towards religion. Given the historic and substantial state interest at issue, we therefore cannot conclude that the denial of funding for vocational religious instruction alone is inherently constitutionally suspect.

Without a presumption of unconstitutionality, Davey's claim must fail. The State's interest in not funding the pursuit of devotional degrees is substantial and the exclusion of such funding places a relatively minor burden on Promise Scholars. If any room exists between the two Religion Clauses, it must be here.

Scalia, J., dissenting

In *Church of Lukumi Babalu Aye, Inc. v. Hialeah*, 508 U.S. 520 (1993), the majority opinion held that "[a] law burdening religious practice that is not neutral ... must undergo the most rigorous of scrutiny," and that "the minimum requirement of neutrality is that a law not discriminate on its face." [That is] irreconcilable with today's decision, which sustains a public benefits program that facially discriminates against religion.

We articulated the principle that governs this case more than 50 years ago in *Everson v. Board of Ed. of Ewing*, 330 U.S. 1 (1947):

> New Jersey cannot hamper its citizens in the free exercise of their own religion. Consequently, it cannot exclude individual Catholics, Lutherans, Mohammedans, Baptists, Jews, Methodists, Non-believers, Presbyterians, or the members of any other faith, because of their faith, or lack of it, from receiving the benefits of public welfare legislation.

When the State makes a public benefit generally available, that benefit becomes part of the baseline against which burdens on religion are measured; and when the State withholds that benefit from some individuals solely on the basis of religion, it violates the Free Exercise Clause no less than if it had imposed a special tax.

That is precisely what the State of Washington has done here. It has created a generally available public benefit, whose receipt is conditioned only on academic performance, income, and attendance at an accredited school. It has then carved out a solitary course of study for exclusion: theology. No field of study but religion is singled out for disfavor in this fashion. Davey is not asking for a special benefit to which others are not entitled. He seeks only equal treatment—the right to direct his scholarship to his chosen course of study, a right every other Promise Scholar enjoys.

* * *

Topics for Further Discussion

1. If the State of Washington had provided public scholarships to ministry students, would it have been violating the Establishment Clause? Can you harmonize the holding in the *Davey* case with *Lamb's Chapel*?

2. If a state does allow public scholarships for students training for careers as religious ministers, must it allow them for all religions, even those disliked by a majority in the community? If it may not distinguish among religions, why not?

Freedom of Speech and of the Press

In addition to religious freedom, the early colonists of America desired greater freedom of speech and of the press as well as the related right to protest against the government. They realized that freedom to criticize government and to be exposed to all manner of opinion was the greatest tonic against tyranny. This is expressed in terms of preserving a "free market place of ideas." Even so, the view that the First Amendment provides absolute freedom of speech has never been accepted by a majority of the Supreme Court, despite the fact that the language of the First Amendment is absolute in its injunction that: "Congress shall make *no* law...." Congress has made laws restricting freedom of speech, and these have been upheld by the Supreme Court.

The Sedition Act and the Espionage Act were passed during World War I. In *Schenck v. United States*, 249 U.S. 47 (1919), the Supreme Court found a pamphleteer guilty under the Espionage Act. His crime was sending literature to draft-age men encouraging them to resist military service. Without a doubt, this was restriction of the right of speech and press, but the Court decided that the First Amendment protection was not absolute, especially in the midst of a war. In *Abrams v. United States*, 250 U.S. 616 (1919), the Court also upheld a conviction against defendants whose pamphlets opposed the American government's attempts to stop the Communist government created by the Russian Revolution. In *Gitlow v. New York*, 268 U.S. 652 (1925), the Court allowed a conviction for the crime of distributing literature that urged labor strikes. And in *Whitney v. California*, 274 U.S. 357 (1927) a woman who merely attended a meeting of the Communist Party was convicted of violating a state law criminalizing the teaching or support of unlawful force and violence to bring about change.

The gravity of the First Amendment guarantees of free speech and press, as we know them now, had yet to be recognized in the early part of the 20th century. Even in the 1950s and 1960s, amidst continued fear about Communism, the Court declined to protect unpopular political speech. For example, in *Dennis v. United States*, 340 U.S. 887 (1950), the Supreme Court upheld the conviction of a man for participating in the formation of the Communist Party of the United States.

A more contemporary example of the threat to civil liberties is the Patriot Act, which passed with little debate after the World Trade Center attack of September 11, 2001. The statute gives the government broad powers to investigate the actions of citizens, including, for example, the kind of material they read. To facilitate these investigations, it allows wiretaps and searches that previously would have required more extensive justification. The Act includes a "sunset" provision requiring reconsideration after some time has passed. With the benefit of the passage of time since the attack, the United States will have to decide whether the increased ease in catching potential terrorists is worth the cost of diminished civil liberties. Many civil libertarians feel the Patriot Act is a very dangerous tool in the hands of government. Benjamin Franklin, a signer of the Declaration of Independence, wisely reminded his contemporaries that "people willing to trade their freedom for temporary security deserve neither and will lose both."

The Court has continued to struggle to come up with a formula for deciding which speech would be protected and which would not. Justice Hugo Black, most notably, argued for an absolutist interpretation in the middle part of the 20th century. Instead, however, the Court tried out any number of tests.

One famous version was the "clear and present danger" test proposed by Justice Oliver Wendell Holmes in the *Schenck* case. He gave the example of someone shouting "Fire!" in a crowded theatre, something that would likely set off panic among the patrons. "The question in every case," Holmes said, "is whether the words used are used in such circumstances and are of such a nature as to create a clear and present danger that they will bring about the substantive evils that Congress has a right to prevent."

Justice Louis Brandeis, concurring in *Whitney*, emphasized that the speech should be protected "unless the incidence of the evil apprehended is so imminent that it may befall before there is opportunity for full discussion."

In 1969, the Court embraced a different formula in *Brandenburg v. Ohio*, 395 U.S. 444 (1969). It announced a three part test in cases where lawless conduct might follow from speech. The speech would be protected unless (a) the speaker intended to incite lawless action; (b) it was likely to produce such imminent action; and (c) objectively it did encourage this action. The Supreme Court additionally insists that restrictions on speech be no broader than necessary to achieve the government's legitimate goal. This is often referred to as the "least restrictive means" test. Finally, the law must be neither vague nor overbroad.

The most difficult cases for the government occur when it wishes to stop speech or restrict the press before publication. This is known as "prior restraint," and is viewed very suspiciously by the Supreme Court. In *New York Times Co. v. United States*, 403 U.S. 713 (1971), the government wanted to stop publication of secret government documents concerning the Vietnam War. The war was still underway, but someone (later revealed to be one of the analysts who worked on the project) leaked the documents—7,000 pages in all—to the press. The government asked the Court to restrain publication, arguing that it would do irreparable damage to the national interest. In a *per curiam* opinion, the justices concluded that the Nixon Administration had failed to meet its very heavy burden of proof. Justice Black in a concurring opinion wrote as follows:

> In the First Amendment the Founding Fathers gave the free press the protection it must have to fulfill its essential role in our democracy. The press was to serve the governed, not the governors. The Government's power to censor the press was abolished so that the press would remain forever free to censure the Government. The press was protected so that it could bare the secrets of government and inform the people. Only a free and unrestrained press can effectively expose deception in government. And paramount among the responsibilities of a free press is the duty to prevent any part of the government from deceiving the people and sending them off to distant lands to die of foreign fevers and foreign shot and shell. In my view, far from deserving condemnation for their courageous reporting, the New York Times, the Washington Post, and other newspapers should be commended for serving the purpose that the Founding Fathers saw so clearly. In revealing the workings of government that led to the Vietnam war, the newspapers nobly did precisely that which the Founders hoped and trusted they would do.

Not all forms of expression are included within the guarantees of speech and press freedom. Among the forms of unprotected speech are what the Court has called "fighting words," i.e., insulting or provocative language that incites a physical response. In *Chaplinsky v. New Hampshire*, 315 U.S. 568 (1942), the Court upheld the conviction of a Jehovah's Witness for calling a police officer a racketeer and Fascist on a public street in violation of a state law aimed at maintaining public order. Chaplinsky had been distributing religious literature when a rowdy crowd began to form, causing the police officer to ask Chaplinsky to come to the police station. The Court found the statute to be narrowly drawn and interpreted to prohibit only those words spoken face-to-face in a manner likely to result in a disturbance of the peace.

Likewise, obscenity has also been considered outside the realm of protected speech. Such cases turn on the question of whether the material is, in fact, obscene and, if it is obscene, to whom. The Supreme Court has created tests that attempt to turn this into an objective inquiry, but — no matter what the test may be — obscenity, in the end, is in the eye of the beholder. Justice Potter Stewart became exasperated with the attempt to define obscenity but insisted "I know it when I see it." The Court has also spoken of "contemporary community standards," suggesting that each local community has the right to establish its own benchmarks of decency within certain parameters. That notion is less-than-helpful in a time when publications are distributed nationally and is even less enlightening in the global age of the Internet. Are the standards of the least tolerant community to control what the entire nation may see?

In the *Ashcroft* case, the Court considered whether a law to protect children from online sexual materials (including those that would be suitable and legal for adults to see) was necessary when other means of controlling access were available.

Ashcroft v. American Civil Liberties Union

542 U.S. 656 (2004)

Kennedy, J.

This case presents a challenge to a statute enacted by Congress to protect minors from exposure to sexually explicit materials on the Internet, the Child Online Protection Act

(COPA). We must decide whether the Court of Appeals was correct to affirm a ruling by the District Court that enforcement of COPA should be enjoined because the statute likely violates the First Amendment.

In enacting COPA, Congress gave consideration to our earlier decisions on this subject, in particular the decision in *Reno v. American Civil Liberties Union*, 521 U.S. 824 (1997). For that reason, "the Judiciary must proceed with caution and ... with care before invalidating the Act." The imperative of according respect to the Congress, however, does not permit us to depart from well-established First Amendment principles. Instead, we must hold the Government to its constitutional burden of proof.

Content-based prohibitions, enforced by severe criminal penalties, have the constant potential to be a repressive force in the lives and thoughts of a free people. To guard against that threat the Constitution demands that content-based restrictions on speech be presumed invalid and that the Government bear the burden of showing their constitutionality. This is true even when Congress twice has attempted to find a constitutional means to restrict, and punish, the speech in question.

COPA is the second attempt by Congress to make the Internet safe for minors by criminalizing certain Internet speech. The first attempt was the Communications Decency Act of 1996. The Court held the CDA unconstitutional because it was not narrowly tailored to serve a compelling governmental interest and because less restrictive alternatives were available.

In response to the Court's decision in *Reno*, Congress passed COPA. COPA imposes criminal penalties of a $50,000 fine and six months in prison for the knowing posting, for "commercial purposes," of World Wide Web content that is "harmful to minors." Material that is "harmful to minors" is defined as:

> any communication, picture, image, graphic image file, article, recording, writing, or other matter of any kind that is obscene or that —
>
> (A) the average person, applying contemporary community standards, would find, taking the material as a whole and with respect to minors, is designed to appeal to, or is designed to pander to, the prurient interest;
>
> (B) depicts, describes, or represents, in a manner patently offensive with respect to minors, an actual or simulated sexual act or sexual contact, an actual or simulated normal or perverted sexual act, or a lewd exhibition of the genitals or post-pubescent female breast; and
>
> (C) taken as a whole, lacks serious literary, artistic, political, or scientific value for minors."

"Minors" are defined as "any person under 17 years of age." A person acts for "commercial purposes only if such person is engaged in the business of making such communications." "Engaged in the business," in turn,

> means that the person who makes a communication, or offers to make a communication, by means of the World Wide Web, that includes any material that is harmful to minors, devotes time, attention, or labor to such activities, as a regular course of such person's trade or business, with the objective of earning a profit as a result of such activities (although it is not necessary that the person make a profit or that the making or offering to make such communications be the person's sole or principal business or source of income).

While the statute labels all speech that falls within these definitions as criminal speech, it also provides an affirmative defense to those who employ specified means to prevent minors from gaining access to the prohibited materials on their Web site. A person may escape conviction under the statute by demonstrating that he

has restricted access by minors to material that is harmful to minors—

(A) by requiring use of a credit card, debit account, adult access code, or adult personal identification number;

(B) by accepting a digital certificate that verifies age, or

(C) by any other reasonable measures that are feasible under available technology.

Respondents, Internet content providers and others concerned with protecting the freedom of speech, filed suit in the United States District Court for the Eastern District of Pennsylvania.

The primary alternative considered by the District Court was blocking and filtering software. Blocking and filtering software is an alternative that is less restrictive than COPA, and, in addition, likely more effective as a means of restricting children's access to materials harmful to them. The District Court, in granting the preliminary injunction, did so primarily because the plaintiffs had proposed that filters are a less restrictive alternative to COPA and the Government had not shown it would be likely to disprove the plaintiffs' contention at trial.

Filters are less restrictive than COPA. They impose selective restrictions on speech at the receiving end, not universal restrictions at the source. Under a filtering regime, adults without children may gain access to speech they have a right to see without having to identify themselves or provide their credit card information. Even adults with children may obtain access to the same speech on the same terms simply by turning off the filter on their home computers. Above all, promoting the use of filters does not condemn as criminal any category of speech, and so the potential chilling effect is eliminated, or at least much diminished. All of these things are true, moreover, regardless of how broadly or narrowly the definitions in COPA are construed.

Filters also may well be more effective than COPA. First, a filter can prevent minors from seeing all pornography, not just pornography posted to the Web from America. The District Court noted in its factfindings that one witness estimated that 40% of harmful-to-minors content comes from overseas. COPA does not prevent minors from having access to those foreign harmful materials. That alone makes it possible that filtering software might be more effective in serving Congress' goals. Finally, filters also may be more effective because they can be applied to all forms of Internet communication, including e-mail, not just communications available via the World Wide Web.

On this record, the Government has not shown that the less restrictive alternatives proposed by respondents should be disregarded. Those alternatives, indeed, may be more effective than the provisions of COPA. The District Court did not abuse its discretion when it entered the preliminary injunction.

Breyer, J., dissenting

The Act does not censor the material it covers. Rather, it requires providers of the "harmful to minors" material to restrict minors' access to it by verifying age. They can do so by inserting screens that verify age using a credit card, adult personal identification number, or other similar technology. In this way, the Act requires creation of an internet screen that minors, but not adults, will find difficult to bypass.

I recognize that the screening requirement imposes some burden on adults who seek access to the regulated material, as well as on its providers. In addition to the monetary cost, and despite strict requirements that identifying information be kept confidential, the identification requirements inherent in age-screening may lead some users to fear embarrassment. Both monetary costs and potential embarrassment can deter potential viewers and, in that sense, the statute's requirements may restrict access to a site. But this Court has held that in the context of congressional efforts to protect children, restrictions of this kind do not automatically violate the Constitution. And the Court has approved their use.

In sum, the Act at most imposes a modest additional burden on adult access to legally obscene material, perhaps imposing a similar burden on access to some protected borderline obscene material as well.

* * *

Topics for Further Discussion

1. Does the majority find that the government interest in protecting minors from pornographic materials is not legitimate? Under the statute, adults would have been able to obtain non-obscene sexual material from the Internet by registering. Did that sufficiently protect their rights? Do you agree with the balancing of interests performed by Justice Breyer?

2. Statutes that create a "chilling effect" on the exercise of rights are sometimes struck down, even if they do not deny the right altogether. Did this statute create a chill? If so, was it sufficiently cold to require the statute be struck down?

3. In *United States v. American Library Ass'n*, 539 U.S. 194 (2003), the Supreme Court upheld the Children's Internet Protection Act, which required that libraries receiving federal funds install software that would block access to all obscene data, even that which would be legal for adults to see. Is that decision inconsistent with *Ashcroft*?

Commercial speech, that is—advertising and the like—is considered to be within the realm of the First Amendment, but not at its core. As a result, restrictions on such speech are subjected to somewhat stringent standards, but not so stringent as political speech. The Court has employed the following test in reaching these decisions: first, is the speech truthful and does it concern activity that is lawful? If not, the government may regulate it so long as it does not capture other speech in the process. If the speech is truthful and lawful, then the second stage of the inquiry is reached: does the restriction directly advance a substantial government interest?

The legal profession has been the subject of a number of cases involving restrictions on advertising. The questions have concerned whether the state can regulate lawyers' advertising in view of their special responsibility to the public. Overall, the Court has concluded that a complete ban on advertising would be unconstitutional, but limitations on certain practices (such as sending direct mail solicitations to victims of accidents within thirty days of the event) have been sustained as seen in Chapter 3.

The First Amendment speaks of both speech and press, but the Supreme Court has ruled that these rights are the same. In other words, the press does not enjoy some additional constitutional rights beyond those of the general public. The Court has also tended to take a contradictory view of who qualifies as a member of the "press." For example, regulation of the content of broadcasting, which makes use of public airwaves, has been upheld despite the fact that similar regulations against printed publications would not be allowed. On the other hand, the *Reno* Court concluded that the Internet was unlike broadcasting and, thus, should not be regulated by the same standards.

The following case raises the question of whether freedom of speech and press includes the right to publish information that could lead to the demise of the nation itself.

While you are reading it, note the format used in a District Court opinion, and how it differs from the opinions of the Supreme Court you have read.

United States v. The Progressive, Inc.

467 F. Supp 990 (W.D. Wis. 1979)

Warren, J.

Findings Of Fact

1. Howard Morland is a free-lance writer specializing in energy and nuclear weapons issues.

2. Defendant, The Progressive, Inc., which publishes The Progressive magazine, has its principal place of business in Madison, Wisconsin.

3. While on assignment for The Progressive magazine, defendant Morland completed, at the end of February, an article describing the operation of a hydrogen bomb. The article was entitled, "The H-Bomb Secret: How We Got It, Why We're Telling It."

4. Copies of this article were forwarded for review to John A. Griffin, Director of Classification of the Department of Energy....

7. Based on review of the article, Mr. Griffin determined that a significant portion of the article contained information that the Atomic Energy Act requires to be classified as Restricted Data. The Restricted Data contained in the article has not been declassified and remains classified as Secret Restricted Data.

8. On March 1, 1979, the Department of Energy, telephoned The Progressive magazine and said that, in the opinion of the Department, the article contained Restricted Data, and in the view of the Department of Energy, the Department of State and the Arms Control and Disarmament Agency, publication of the Restricted Data contained in this article would injure the United States and would give an advantage to other nations. He stated that the release of this information would be contrary to the United States' effort to prevent the proliferation of nuclear weapons and requested that The Progressive refrain from publishing the article.

9. On March 2, 1979, the Department of Energy met with representatives of The Progressive and advised them that the Department of Energy had reviewed the Morland manuscript and, based upon that review, had determined that it contains material which is Secret Restricted Data. The Department suggested to The Progressive that they permit the Government to work with them to remove the Secret Restricted Data portions of the manuscript so that they would no longer be classified and publication could go forward.

10. On March 7, 1979, The Progressive, advised the Department of Energy that The Progressive intended to publish the article. He stated that publication would proceed unless the United States promptly obtained a temporary restraining order.

11. On March 8, 1979, the complaint in this action was filed by the plaintiff, United States of America.

12. On March 9, 1979, this Court held a hearing on the Government's request for a temporary restraining order to enjoin the defendants, their employees, and agents from publishing or otherwise disclosing in any manner any of the Restricted Data contained in the Morland article. After hearing from both parties, the Court issued a temporary restrain-

ing order to be in effect for the shortest time possible consistent with the opportunity for the Government to substantiate its claim at a hearing on the request for a preliminary injunction. A preliminary injunction hearing was scheduled for one week later.

Memorandum and Order

From the founding days of this nation, the rights to freedom of speech and of the press have held an honored place in our constitutional scheme. The establishment and nurturing of these rights is one of the true achievements of our form of government. Because of the importance of these rights, any prior restraint on publication comes into court under a heavy presumption against its constitutional validity. However, First Amendment rights are not absolute. They are not boundless. Justice Frankfurter stated it in this fashion: "Free speech is not so absolute or irrational a conception as to imply paralysis of the means for effective protection of all the freedoms secured by the Bill of Rights." In *Near v. Minnesota*, 283 U.S. 697 (1931), the Supreme Court specifically recognized an extremely narrow area, involving national security, in which interference with First Amendment rights might be tolerated and a prior restraint on publication might be appropriate. The Court stated: "When a nation is at war many things that might be said in time of peace are such a hindrance to its effort that their utterance will not be endured so long as men fight and that no Court could regard them as protected by any constitutional right. No one would question but that a government might prevent actual obstruction to its recruiting service or the publication of the sailing dates of transports or the number and location of troops."

The Morland piece could accelerate the membership of a candidate nation in the thermonuclear club. For example, in the late 1930s, physicists in various countries were simultaneously, but independently, working on the idea of a nuclear chain reaction. The French physicists in their equation neglected to take full account of the fact that the neutrons produced by fission could go on to provoke further fissions in a many-step process which is the essence of a chain reaction. Even though this idea seems so elementary, the concept of neutron multiplication was so novel that no nuclear physicists saw through the French team's oversight for about a year. Thus, once basic concepts are learned, the remainder of the process may easily follow.

The point has also been made that it is only a question of time before other countries will have the hydrogen bomb. That may be true. However, there are times in the course of human history when time itself may be very important. This time factor becomes critical when considering mass annihilation weaponry: witness the failure of Hitler to get his V-1 and V-2 bombs operational quickly enough to materially affect the outcome of World War II.

Defendants have stated that publication of the article will alert the people of this country to the false illusion of security created by the government's futile efforts at secrecy. They believe publication will provide the people with needed information to make informed decisions on an urgent issue of public concern. However, this Court can find no plausible reason why the public needs to know the technical details about hydrogen bomb construction to carry on an informed debate on this issue.

The government has met its burden under section 2274 of The Atomic Energy Act. In the Court's opinion, it has also met the test of grave, direct, immediate and irreparable harm to the United States.

The Court will issue a preliminary injunction against The Progressive's use of the Morland article in its current form.

* * *

Topics for Further Discussion

1. The decision in *The Progressive* case was made moot by the printing of the article by other publications. To date, no nuclear device has been traced to the information revealed in the article. Does that prove that the judge ruled incorrectly?

2. Under what circumstances is prior restraint justified, if ever?

3. The trial judge said he expected the case to go to the Supreme Court. Under those circumstances, was it appropriate for him to order the prior restraint and thus maintain the *status quo* until the nation's highest court could decide?

Other cases have dealt with the question of what is included in the concept of speech. Is it only words or can other forms of communication enjoy the same protection? "Symbolic speech" issues deal with ideas that are not spoken but rather expressed through other means. A black armband, for example, has no intrinsic meaning. However, in the context of a particular time and place, the Court ruled it was a protected form of speech opposing the Vietnam conflict. The following case raises the issue of whether such speech can be directed at the symbol of the nation itself.

United States v. Eichman
496 U.S. 310 (1990)

Brennan, J.

We consider whether appellees' prosecution for burning a United States flag in violation of the Flag Protection Act of 1989 is consistent with the First Amendment. The Act provides in relevant part:

(a)(1) Whoever knowingly mutilates, defaces, physically defiles, burns, maintains on the floor or ground, or tramples upon any flag of the United States shall be fined under this title or imprisoned for not more than one year, or both.

(2) This subsection does not prohibit any conduct consisting of the disposal of a flag when it has become worn or soiled.

(b) As used in this section, the term "flag of the United States" means any flag of the United States, or any part thereof, made of any substance, of any size, in a form that is commonly displayed.

The Government concedes in this case, as it must, that appellees' flag-burning constituted expressive conduct, but invites us to reconsider our rejection of the claim that flag-burning as a mode of expression, like obscenity or "fighting words," does not enjoy the full protection of the First Amendment.

The Government contends that the Flag Protection Act is constitutional because the Act does not target expressive conduct on the basis of the content of its message. The Act forbids conduct (other than disposal) that damages or mistreats a flag, without regard to the actor's motive, his intended message, or the likely effects of his conduct on onlookers. The Government's interest in protecting the "physical integrity" of a privately owned flag rests upon a perceived need to preserve the flag's status as a symbol of our Nation and certain national ideals. But the mere destruction or disfigurement of a particular physical manifestation of the symbol, without more, does not diminish or otherwise affect the symbol itself in any way. For example, the secret destruction of a flag in one's own house would not threaten the flag's recognized meaning. Rather, the Government's desire to preserve the flag as a symbol for certain national ideals is implicated "only when a person's treatment of the flag communicates a message" to others that is inconsistent with those ideals.

The Flag Protection Act suffers from the fundamental flaw: it suppresses expression out of concern for its likely communicative impact. The Act therefore must be subjected to "the most exacting scrutiny," and the Government's interest cannot justify its infringement on First Amendment rights.

Government may create national symbols, promote them, and encourage their respectful treatment. But the Flag Protection Act goes well beyond this by criminally proscribing expressive conduct because of its likely communicative impact.

If there is a bedrock principle underlying the First Amendment, it is that the Government may not prohibit the expression of an idea simply because society finds the idea itself offensive or disagreeable. Punishing desecration of the flag dilutes the very freedom that makes this emblem so revered, and worth revering.

* * *

Topics for Further Discussion

1. What standard does the Court use to decide whether the Flag Protection Act is constitutional? How could the Congress and states overcome the Supreme Court's conclusion in this case?

2. To what degree is conduct considered speech? Could the government, for example, require a teacher to sing the national anthem at a school function?

3. In *Citizens United v. Federal Election Comm'n*, 130 S. Ct. 876 (2010), the Supreme Court held that a law restricting election communications spending by corporations unconstitutionally infringed their speech rights. It considered such expenditures to be an exercise of political speech, which is at the core of the First Amendment.

Other Individual Rights

One of the most contentious constitutional claims is that to a right to keep and bear arms under the Second Amendment. The Amendment speaks of such a right within the context of a "well-regulated militia." If, however, the right is construed as belonging to individuals apart from any militia, laws that attempt to reduce gun-based violence by restricting ownership might be considered unconstitutional. That is precisely what happened in *District of Columbia v. Heller*, 128 S. Ct. 2783 (2008). In a 5–4 decision, the Supreme Court struck down a Washington, D.C. prohibition against the ownership of handguns, at least insofar as such guns are kept inside one's home for self-defense. *Heller* involved only the federal government, since the District of Columbia is under federal jurisdiction. The ruling did not apply to the States.

Two years later in *McDonald v. Chicago*, 2010 WL 2555188 (2010), the Court took the opportunity to hold that the right to keep and bear arms is also incorporated against state and local governments. The *McDonald* case concerned municipal gun registration regulations that effectively banned handgun possession by almost all private citizens. The Court wrote as follows:

> [W]e now turn directly to the question whether the Second Amendment right to keep and bear arms is incorporated in the concept of due process. In answering that question, we must decide whether the right to keep and bear arms is fundamental to our scheme of ordered liberty, or as we have said in a related context, whether this right is "deeply rooted in this Nation's history and tradition."

> Our decision in *Heller* points unmistakably to the answer. Self-defense is a basic right, recognized by many legal systems from ancient times to the present day, and in *Heller*, we held that individual self-defense is "the central component" of the Second Amendment right. Explaining that "the need for defense of self, family, and property is most acute" in the home, we found that this right applies to handguns because they are "the most preferred firearm in the nation to 'keep' and use for protection of one's home and family." Thus, we concluded, citizens must be permitted "to use [handguns] for the core lawful purpose of self-defense."

> *Heller* makes it clear that this right is "deeply rooted in this Nation's history and tradition."

Neither the *Heller* case, nor the *McDonald* case, stands for the proposition that the Second Amendment right to keep and bear arms is absolute. Future cases will test what kinds of regulations will survive constitutional scrutiny.

Many other individual rights under the Constitution involve criminal procedure, which is discussed in Chapter 10. Beyond them, the Constitution includes a wealth of language in which rights may find a textual justification. For example, the Court consistently declined to employ Article IV's guarantee of a "republican form of government," but that does not mean some future Court might not make use of it. Similarly, the Court has, in the past, essentially read the Fourteenth Amendment's "privileges or immunities" clause out of existence. ("No State shall make or enforce any law which shall deprive the privileges or immunities of citizens of the United States.") This language too may be waiting to be rediscovered.

The clearest justification for additional constitutional rights, such as privacy, is the Ninth Amendment: "The enumeration in the Constitution of certain rights shall not be construed to deny or disparage others retained by the people." This offers a way of resolving the debate over textual versus non-textual interpretation. The text itself states that the listing of rights is not exhaustive; other rights exist. Professor Charles Black, one of the giants of constitutional scholarship, contended that much of what seems inexplicable under constitutional law is made clear simply by remembering the Ninth Amendment. Black said it "could be the gate to the best kind of decision we can attain according to law."

Key Terms and Concepts

Due Process
Equal Protection
Fundamental Right
Intermediate Scrutiny
Least Restrictive Alternative
Rational Basis
Stare Decisis
Strict Scrutiny
Substantive Due Process
Suspect Classification

Chapter 5

Civil Procedure and the Federal Courts

"The history of American freedom is, in no small measure, the history of procedure."

Frankfurter, J., in *Malinski v. New York*, 324 U.S. 401 (1945)

This chapter looks at the main issues and procedures in a civil lawsuit in the United States. A civil lawsuit includes all trials in court, including lawsuits against governments or about the U.S. Constitution or treaties, which do not involve criminal laws or admiralty (maritime law) and that are not procedures before an administrative agency or military tribunal. Discussions of procedure will focus on the Federal Rules of Civil Procedure ("FRCP"). The FRCP are created by the U.S. Supreme Court with the advice of a committee called the Judicial Conference of the United States, after listening to recommendations by judges, lawyers and professors. There are four reasons for focusing on the FRCP. First, the FRCP are the only centrally-created rules of procedure in American courts and are essentially the same in each federal trial court (U.S. District Court) throughout the country. Second, since the original FRCP were put into effect in 1938, they have been adopted unchanged by many state trial courts and their style and philosophy have influenced every U.S. court. Third, the federal courts handle many major disputes involving treaties, foreign affairs and international trade, so even lawyers outside the United States are likely to be involved with a federal court case during their career. Fourth, the alternative to the FRCP would be to discuss the different rules of procedure in the many jurisdictions of the United States.

Horizontal Federalism

It may come as a shock to learn that there is no uniform body of "American civil procedure." The United States includes over fifty jurisdictions: the federal government, the fifty states, the District of Columbia (Washington, D.C.), the Commonwealth of Puerto Rico, the Territories (U.S. Virgin Islands and Guam) and Saipan. Each jurisdiction has its own system of trial courts (with its own state procedure), appeals courts, and a supreme court. At the same time, and often located next to the state court, there is a federal U.S. District Court (using the FRCP) in each of these jurisdictions. Additionally, there is a U.S. Court of Appeals for the region in which the state is located, and the U.S. Supreme Court. All these federal courts have jurisdiction to hear certain cases based on disputes or parties within the same state. This situation has been called "horizontal federalism." One might reasonably ask why Americans, who are reputed to prefer the efficiency and speed of one-stop shopping at Wal-Mart and one-stop eating at McDonald's, would tolerate a dual track court system.

141

Americans not only tolerate the existing system of dual state and federal jurisdiction, they prefer it. The reasons for the lack of a single national, federal "American law" are historical, practical, and cultural and can be summarized as follows:

1. History. The thirteen original colonies of the United States were in practice self-governing independent states from the time they ceased to be colonies of Great Britain (1781) until they agreed to come together under the Constitution (1789). At the time the federal court system was created by the Constitution, the colonies had recently experienced government authority centralized in a tyrant, King George III of England. During the period immediately after independence from Great Britain, the states came together in a weak confederation without any national executive or judicial authority. The states existed before the federal government, first as colonies and then as states, and they were reluctant to give the federal courts, or the federal government, any more power than was necessary to have effective national government. Even after they granted powers to the federal government, the nervous states quickly limited those powers and took back some of their rights. These rights were contained in the first ten amendments to the Constitution called the "Bill of Rights."

2. Geography. The United States is a vast country of many climates and various cultures. Even after the time of Abraham Lincoln, it might have taken six months for law books and case reports to travel from Washington to San Francisco. It was not practical for frontier courts to wait for direction from the national capital before deciding routine disputes. Americans did not think laws relating to water rights in, for example, New Jersey (a state with a large and concentrated population, agriculture based on small farms, ample rain, and an ocean coastline) should be the same as laws relating to water rights in Wyoming (a state with a small and scattered population, agriculture based on large cattle ranches, little rain and no ocean coastline). Americans did not think laws relating to inheritance should be the same in Connecticut (settled by the British, who allowed the eldest son to inherit everything), Louisiana (settled by the French, who followed the Napoleonic Code in dividing inheritances among children), and California (settled by the Spanish, who allowed wives to manage and pass on their own separate property) should be the same.

3. Culture. Americans still prefer laws that differ among states because that system offers the most chances to match policies and laws locally to present and future issues. Citizens of the United States are concerned about education, health care, family relations, local government services, and many other social and economic issues. Each state has different laws regarding these issues, depending on what the citizens of that state prefer. As Supreme Court Justice Louis Brandeis pointed out in 1932, one of the strengths of the federal system is that "a single courageous state may, if its citizens choose, serve as a laboratory, and try new social and economic experiments without risk to the country as a whole."

Personal Jurisdiction

Under the U.S. Constitution every person in the United States is guaranteed "due process" of law. One aspect of due process is that state or federal courts must have jurisdiction in order to issue a valid judgment against a party. Courts are considered to have automatic jurisdiction to judge a dispute about any property in their jurisdiction (called *in rem* jurisdiction) and to judge a debt dispute where the security for the debt is property within their jurisdiction (called *quasi in rem* jurisdiction). At one time, for a court to have "personal jurisdiction" over a party to a lawsuit, that party had to be located in the court's territory so that a court official could take hold of the person if necessary. With the growth of interstate commerce in the 20th century, cases against parties not present in the territory became common, leading state courts to try to force parties to appear using the "long arm" of the law. In examining a state "long arm statute" allowing jurisdiction over a party outside the state, the Supreme Court concluded, in *International Shoe Co. v. Washington*, 326 U.S. 310 (1945) that "due process requires only that in order to subject a defendant to a judgment, if he is not present within the territory of the forum, he have certain minimum contacts with the forum that the lawsuit does not offend 'traditional notions of fair play and substantial justice.'"

It is not always clear what "fair play" and "justice" are in an era of global commerce and information, even in the English-speaking world, as illustrated by the cases below. In the *Asahi Metal* case, Asahi Metal, a Japanese company, manufactured tire valve parts in Japan and sold them to several tire manufacturers, including a Taiwanese company. The sales to the Taiwanese company, which amounted to at least 100,000 units annually from 1978 to 1982, took place in Taiwan. The Taiwanese company put the parts into its finished tires, which it sold throughout the world, including the United States. Twenty percent of the Taiwanese company's sales were in California. In 1978, in Solano County, California, the driver of a motorcycle lost control of his vehicle and collided with a tractor, as a result of which he was severely injured and his wife was killed. He filed a product liability action in California against the Taiwanese company, among others, claiming that the accident was caused by an explosion in the rear tire of the motorcycle, and that the motorcycle tire, tube, and sealant were defective. The Taiwanese company in turn sued the Japanese valve supplier. The motorcycle driver settled his claims against the Taiwanese company and the other defendants, leaving only the Taiwanese company's lawsuit against the Japanese company. The Japanese company moved to stop the Taiwanese company's service of summons, claiming that California could not exert jurisdiction over it consistent with the due process clause of the Fourteenth Amendment of the Federal Constitution. The Supreme Court granted *certiorari* and, in a plurality decision, agreed with Asahi Metal.

Asahi Metal Industry Co. v. Superior Court
480 U.S. 102 (1987)

O'Connor, J.

Asahi is a Japanese corporation. It manufactures tire valve assemblies in Japan and sells the assemblies to Cheng Shin, and to several other tire manufacturers, for use as components in finished tire tubes. Asahi's sales to Cheng Shin took place in Taiwan. The shipments from Asahi to Cheng Shin were sent from Japan to Taiwan. Cheng Shin bought and put into its tire tubes 150,000 Asahi valve assemblies in 1978; 500,000 in 1979; 500,000 in 1980; 100,000 in 1981; and 100,000 in 1982. Sales to Cheng Shin accounted for 1.24 percent of Asahi's income in 1981 and 0.44 percent in 1982. Cheng Shin alleged that approximately 20 percent of its sales in the United States are in California.

In 1983 an attorney for Cheng Shin conducted an informal examination of the valve stems of the tire tubes sold in one motorcycle store in Solano County. The attorney declared that of the approximately 115 tire tubes in the store, 97 were purportedly manufactured in Japan or Taiwan, and of those 97, 21 valve stems were marked with the circled letter "A," Asahi's trademark. Of the 21 Asahi valve stems, 12 were incorporated into Cheng Shin tire tubes. An affidavit of a manager of Cheng Shin whose duties included the purchasing of component parts stated: "In discussions with Asahi regarding the purchase of valve stem assemblies the fact that my Company sells tubes throughout the world and specifically the United States has been discussed. I believe that Asahi was fully aware that valve stem assemblies sold to my Company and to others would end up throughout the United States and in California." An affidavit of the president of Asahi, on the other hand, declared that Asahi "has never thought that its limited sales of tire valves to Cheng Shin in Taiwan would subject it to lawsuits in California."

The Supreme Court of the State of California found the exercise of jurisdiction over Asahi to be consistent with the Due Process Clause. It concluded that Asahi knew that some of the valve assemblies sold to Cheng Shin would be put into tire tubes sold in California, and that Asahi benefited indirectly from the sale in California of products incorporating its components. The court considered Asahi's intentional act of placing its components into the stream of commerce — that is, by delivering the components to Cheng Shin in Taiwan — coupled with Asahi's awareness that some of the components would eventually find their way into California, sufficient to form the basis for state court jurisdiction under the Due Process Clause.

We granted *certiorari* and now reverse.

The Due Process Clause of the Fourteenth Amendment limits the power of a state court to exert personal jurisdiction over a nonresident defendant. The constitutional standard "remains whether the defendant purposefully established 'minimum contacts' in the forum State." *International Shoe Co. v. Washington.* Most recently we have reaffirmed that minimum contacts must have a basis in "some act by which the defendant purposefully avails itself of the privilege of conducting activities within the forum State, thus invoking the benefits and protections of its laws." When a corporation "purposefully avails itself of the privilege of conducting activities within the forum State," it has clear notice that it is subject to suit there, and can act to reduce the risk of burdensome litigation by procuring insurance, passing the expected costs on to customers, or, if the risks are too great, leaving the State. It is not unreasonable to subject it to suit in one of those States if its allegedly defective merchandise has there been the source of injury to its owners or to others.

The Supreme Court of California held that, because the stream of commerce eventually brought some valves Asahi sold Cheng Shin into California, Asahi's awareness that its valves would be sold in California was sufficient to permit California to exercise jurisdiction over Asahi consistent with the requirements of the Due Process Clause.

In *Humble v. Toyota Motor Co.*, 727 F.2d 709 (8th Cir. 1984), an injured car passenger brought suit against Arakawa Auto Body Company, a Japanese corporation that manufactured car seats for Toyota. Arakawa did no business in the United States; it had no office, affiliate, subsidiary, or agent in the United States; it manufactured its component parts outside the United States and delivered them to Toyota Motor Company in Japan. The Court of Appeals, adopting the reasoning of the District Court in that case, noted that although it "does not doubt that Arakawa could have foreseen that its product would find its way into the United States," it would be "manifestly unjust" to require Arakawa to defend itself in the United States.

We now find this latter position to be consonant with the requirements of due process. The "substantial connection" between the defendant and the forum State necessary for a finding of minimum contacts must come about by an action of the defendant purposefully directed toward the forum State. But a defendant's awareness that the stream of commerce may or will sweep the product into the forum State does not convert the mere act of placing the product into the stream into an act purposefully directed toward the forum State.

Assuming that respondents have established Asahi's awareness that some of the valves sold to Cheng Shin would be incorporated into tire tubes sold in California, respondents have not demonstrated any action by Asahi to purposefully avail itself of the California market. Asahi does not do business in California. It has no office, agents, employees, or property in California. It does not advertise or otherwise solicit business in California. It did not create, control, or employ the distribution system that brought its valves to California. There is no evidence that Asahi designed its product in anticipation of sales in California.

On the basis of these facts, the exertion of personal jurisdiction over Asahi by the Superior Court of California exceeds the limits of due process.

* * *

Topics for Further Discussion

1. Asahi's valves were found on twenty-one tires out of 115 in the motorcycle store. If Asahi's valve were found on forty-two tires out of 115, would that be enough to say that Asahi "purposefully" tried to use the California market? Would your answer be different if Asahi's valves were found on 105 tires out of 115?

2. Imagine that there is a fictional company named Canolta that makes photocopiers in China, which it sells via its own employees in the United States. Twenty percent of the Canolta photocopiers sold in the United States use a part made by Golden Dragon, a Chinese company that does no business in the United States. Mrs. Smith, an American, is burned when a Canolta copier catches fire. Smith sues Canolta. Canolta tries to bring Golden Dragon into the lawsuit. Golden Dragon's lawyers say there is no personal jurisdiction over Golden Dragon, and use the *Asahi Metal* case as precedent. What should happen?

Asahi Metal was decided before Internet technology made possible inexpensive worldwide sales of goods and distribution of ideas. Courts are still struggling with the limits of personal jurisdiction in the Internet age, as the *Pebble Beach* and *Revell v. Lidov* cases illustrate.

Pebble Beach Co. v. Caddy
453 F.3d 1151 (9th Cir. 2006)

Trott, J.

Pebble Beach Company ("Pebble Beach"), a golf course resort in California, appeals the dismissal for lack of jurisdiction of its complaint against Michael Caddy ("Caddy"), a small-business owner located in southern England. Because Caddy did not expressly aim his conduct at California or the United States, we hold that the district court determined correctly that it lacked personal jurisdiction.

Pebble Beach is a well-known golf course and resort located in Monterey County, California. Pebble Beach operates a website located at *www.pebblebeach.com*.

Caddy occupies and runs a three-room bed and breakfast, restaurant, and bar located in southern England on a cliff overlooking the pebbly beaches of England's south shore. The name of Caddy's operation is "Pebble Beach." Caddy advertises his services, which do not include a golf course, at his website, *www.pebblebeach-uk.com*. The website is not interactive. Visitors to the website who have questions about Caddy's services may fill out an on-line inquiry form. The website does not have a reservation system, nor does it allow potential guests to book rooms or pay for services on-line.

Except for a brief time when Caddy worked at a restaurant in Carmel, California, his domicile has been in the United Kingdom.

On October 8, 2003, Pebble Beach sued Caddy for intentional infringement and dilution of its "Pebble Beach" mark. Caddy moved to dismiss the complaint for lack of personal jurisdiction and insufficiency of service of process.

When a defendant moves to dismiss for lack of personal jurisdiction, the plaintiff bears the burden of demonstrating that the court has jurisdiction over the defendant. However, this demonstration requires that the plaintiff "make only a prima facie showing of jurisdictional facts to withstand the motion to dismiss." Moreover, for the purpose of this demonstration, the court resolves all disputed facts in favor of the plaintiff, here, Pebble Beach.

For due process to be satisfied, a defendant, if not present in the forum, must have "minimum contacts" with the forum state such that the assertion of jurisdiction "does not offend traditional notions of fair play and substantial justice."

In this circuit, we employ the following three-part test to analyze whether a party's "minimum contacts" meet the Supreme Court's directive. This "minimum contacts" test is satisfied when, (1) the defendant has performed some act or consummated some transaction within the forum or otherwise purposefully availed himself of the privileges of conducting activities in the forum, (2) the claim arises out of or results from the defendant's forum-related activities, and (3) the exercise of jurisdiction is reasonable. "If any of the three requirements is not satisfied, jurisdiction in the forum would deprive the defendant of due process of law."

Thus, Pebble Beach must establish either that Caddy (1) purposefully availed himself of the privilege of conducting activities in California, or the United States as a whole, or (2) that he purposefully directed its activities toward one of those two forums.

1. Purposeful Availment

Pebble Beach fails to identify any conduct by Caddy that took place in California or in the United States that adequately supports the availment concept. Evidence of availment is typically action taking place in the forum that invokes the benefits and protections of the laws in the forum. All of Caddy's action identified by Pebble Beach is action taking place outside the forum.

2. Purposeful Direction: California

We conclude that Caddy's actions were not expressly aimed at California. The only acts identified by Pebble Beach as being directed at California are the website and the use of the name "Pebble Beach" in the domain name. These acts were not aimed at California and, regardless of foreseeable effect, are insufficient to establish jurisdiction.

The circumstances here are more analogous to *Schwarzenegger v. Fred Martin Motor Co. 374 F.3d 797 (9th Cir. 2004)*. In *Schwarzenegger*, the former movie star and current California governor, brought an action in California alleging that an Ohio car dealership used impermissibly his "Terminator" image in a newspaper advertisement in Akron, Ohio. The federal district court in California dismissed the complaint for lack of personal jurisdiction. We affirmed, concluding that even though the advertisement might lead to eventual harm in California this "foreseeable effect" was not enough because the advertisement was expressly aimed at Ohio rather than California. We held that Schwarzenegger had not established jurisdiction over the car dealership.

3. Purposeful Direction: United States

Even if Pebble Beach is unable to show purposeful direction as to California, Pebble Beach can still establish jurisdiction if Caddy purposefully directed his action at the United

States. This ability to look to the aggregate contacts of a defendant with the United States as a whole instead of a particular state forum is a product of [FRCP] *Rule 4(k)(2)*. Thus, *Rule 4(k)(2)* is commonly referred to as the federal long-arm statute.

The exercise of *Rule 4(k)(2)* as a federal long-arm statute requires the plaintiff to prove three factors. First, the claim against the defendant must arise under federal law. Second, the defendant must not be subject to the personal jurisdiction of any state court of general jurisdiction. Third, the federal court's exercise of personal jurisdiction must comport with due process. Here, the first factor is satisfied because Pebble Beach's claim arises under the Lanham Act [federal trademark law]. And, as established above, the second factor is satisfied as Caddy is not subject to personal jurisdiction of California, or any state court.

That leaves the third factor — due process. The due process analysis is identical to the one discussed above when the forum was California, except here the relevant forum is the entire United States.

We conclude that the selection of a particular domain name is insufficient by itself to confer jurisdiction over a non-resident defendant, even under *Rule 4(k)(2)*, where the forum is the United States. The fact that the name "Pebble Beach" is a famous mark known world-wide is of little practical consequence when deciding whether action is directed at a particular forum via the world-wide web. Also of minimal importance is Caddy's selection of a ".com" domain name instead of a more specific United Kingdom or European Union domain. Neither provides much more than a slight indication of where a website may be located and does not establish to whom the website is directed.

Accordingly, we find no action on the part of Caddy expressly directed at the United States and conclude that an exercise of personal jurisdiction over Caddy would offend due process.

* * *

Topics for Further Discussion

1. Your client comes to you and says "Of course we want to have as many international customers as possible, but how do we avoid being sued in the United States?" What do you tell them?

Revell v. Lidov
317 F.3d 467 (5th Cir. 2002)

Higginbotham, J.

Oliver Revell sued Hart Lidov and Columbia University [in the Northern District of Texas] for defamation arising out of Lidov's authorship of an article that he posted on an Internet bulletin board hosted by Columbia. The district court dismissed Revell's claims for lack of personal jurisdiction over both Lidov and Columbia. We agree.

Lidov wrote a lengthy article on the subject of the Libyan terrorist bombing of Pan Am Flight 103, which exploded over Lockerbie, Scotland, in 1988. The article singles out Oliver Revell, then Associate Deputy Director of the FBI, for severe criticism, accusing him of conspiracy and cover-up. The article further charges that Revell, knowing about the terrorist attack, made certain his son, previously booked on Pan Am 103, took a different flight. At the time he wrote the article, Lidov had never been to Texas and was apparently unaware that Revell then lived in Texas. Lidov has also never been a student or faculty member of Columbia University, but he posted his article on a website maintained by its School of Journalism. In a bulletin board section of the website, users could post their own works and read the works of others. As a result, the article could be viewed by members of the public over the Internet.

Revell, a resident of Texas, sued Columbia University, whose principal offices are in New York City, and Lidov, who is a Massachusetts resident, in the Northern District of Texas. Revell claimed damage to his professional reputation in Texas and emotional distress arising out of the alleged defamation of the defendants, and sought several million dollars in damages.

Our question is whether the district court could properly exercise personal jurisdiction over Hart Lidov and Columbia University, an issue of law we review for the first time.

A federal district court may exercise personal jurisdiction over an out-of-territory defendant if the exercise of personal jurisdiction is consistent with the due process guarantees of the United States Constitution. The Due Process Clause of the Fourteenth Amendment permits a court to exercise personal jurisdiction over a foreign defendant when "(1) that defendant has purposefully availed himself of the benefits and protections of the forum state by establishing 'minimum contacts' with the forum state; and (2) the exercise of jurisdiction over that defendant does not offend 'traditional notions of fair play and substantial justice.'"

Revell first urges that the district court may assert general jurisdiction over Columbia because its website provides Internet users the opportunity to subscribe to the *Columbia Journalism Review*, purchase advertising on the website or in the journal, and submit electronic applications for admission. Though the maintenance of a website is, in a sense, a continuous presence everywhere in the world, the cited contacts of Columbia with Texas are not in any way "substantial." Columbia, since it began keeping records, never received more than twenty Internet subscriptions to the *Columbia Journalism Review* from Texas residents.

The article written by Lidov about Revell contains no reference to Texas, nor does it refer to the Texas activities of Revell, and it was not directed at Texas readers as distinguished from readers in other states. Lidov's article, as it relates to Revell, deals exclusively with his actions as Associate Deputy Director of the FBI — there is no reference to Texas in the article or any reliance on Texas sources. These facts weigh heavily against finding the requisite minimum contacts in this case.

As the Supreme Court has stated, due process requires that "the defendant's conduct and connection with the forum State are such that he should reasonably anticipate being sued in court there." Lidov states that he did not even know that Revell was a resident of Texas when he posted his article. Lidov must have known that the harm of the article would hit home wherever Revell resided. But that is the case with virtually any defamation. A more direct aim is required than we have here. In short, this was not about Texas.

In sum, Revell has failed to make out a case of personal jurisdiction over either Lidov or Columbia University. We find the contacts with Texas insufficient to establish the jurisdiction of its courts, and hence the federal district court in Texas, over Columbia and Lidov. We AFFIRM the dismissal for lack of personal jurisdiction as to both defendants.

* * *

Topics for Further Discussion

1. Should the standard for personal jurisdiction be the same when (a) a company that tried to make good tire valves is sued for accidentally making bad tire valves; (b) a club

owner is appealing for guests worldwide but his club name might infringe on the name of a more famous foreign establishment; or (c) a person who tried to criticize someone is then sued for defamation by that person?

2. Were "traditional notions of 'fair play' and 'substantial justice'" satisfied when Revell's lawsuit was dismissed in his home state?

3. Can you think of any undesirable results if Lidov were required to defend himself in Texas?

4. The majority of the information on the Internet is still generated in the United States, or is transmitted by servers in the United States. How does this affect jurisdiction? The High Court of Australia, in *Dow Jones & Company Inc. v. Gutnick,* (2002) 194 ALR 433, reviewed a case similar to *Revell v. Lidov.* In the *Dow Jones* case, the Dow Jones publishing company placed an article in the online version of *Barron's* financial magazine. The website had about 550,000 subscribers, and at least 1,700 of them paid subscription fees by credit cards whose holders had Australian addresses. The article was called "Unholy Gains" with a headline: "When stock promoters cross paths with religious charities, investors had best be on guard." A large photograph of Joseph Gutnick, an Australian businessman who lived in the State of Victoria, appeared on the first page of the magazine. Gutnick sued for libel and Dow Jones maintained that it should only be sued at the location of its Internet servers in the United States. Justice Kirby, in his concurring opinion that Australian courts had personal jurisdiction over Dow Jones, commented as follows:

> Whatever else is in doubt, it is uncontested that the respondent had suffered damage in Victoria. Once this is shown, the only question to be answered is whether such damage was caused by defendant's wrongful action. The adoption of a rule, expressed in terms of the place of uploading of material on the Internet might, in this case, favour the jurisdiction of the courts and the law of the United States. Because of the vastly disproportionate location of web servers in the United States when compared to virtually all other countries (including Australia) this would necessarily have the result, in many cases, of extending the application of a law of the United States to defamation proceedings brought by Australian and other foreign citizens in respect of local damage to their reputations by publication on the Internet. Because the purpose of a defamation suit is to repair the injury done to a person's reputation, it would be small comfort to the person wronged to subject him or her to the law (and possibly the jurisdiction of the courts) of a place of uploading, when any decision so made would depend upon a law reflecting different values and applied in courts unable to afford assistance in the place where it matters most.

5. The Internet can be accessed by persons all over the world, and anyone who posts on the Internet should know this. Persons all over the world can read a critical article. Should jurisdiction standards be different for the Internet?

Federal Court Subject Matter Jurisdiction

Federal courts are courts of "limited jurisdiction," meaning that, without a special grant of jurisdiction to a federal court, a plaintiff may file a lawsuit only in a state court. A party may agree to waive (not protest against) lack of personal jurisdiction, but a party cannot waive lack of subject matter jurisdiction. If at any time in a case, even after it has started, it appears that the court lacks subject matter jurisdiction, the case must be dismissed. Federal courts have subject matter jurisdiction in only two situations that the Supreme Court has said must in principle exist both when the lawsuit is filed, and at all times during the lawsuit:

1. *Federal question* jurisdiction over *cases* "arising under the Constitution, the laws of the United States, and treaties."

2. *Diversity* jurisdiction over *controversies* "between citizens of different states" where the "amount in controversy" is a substantial amount, currently at least $75,000 in non class-action claims.

Federal Question Jurisdiction

Federal question jurisdiction most commonly comes from the plaintiff's claim for relief under the Constitution or federal statutes (written laws), such as laws relating to areas of federal power like admiralty (maritime law), antitrust, bankruptcy, civil rights, copyright, consumer protection, federal income tax, international trade, labor law, patent law, and securities law. The "federal question" must create the right by which the plaintiff is suing. On the other hand, if a "federal question" is raised as a defense, or is part of a state law claim, the Supreme Court has held that federal question jurisdiction does not exist and only state courts can hear the lawsuit. In fact, except where federal law gives federal courts exclusive jurisdiction, every lawsuit involving a "federal question" can also be heard in state courts. It should be noted, however, that admiralty, bankruptcy, patent matters, and lawsuits against the United States are some areas where federal courts have exclusive jurisdiction and state courts cannot hear the lawsuit.

The Supreme Court has interpreted the Constitutional grant of federal judicial power to "cases ... and controversies" and the Constitutional separation of executive, legislative, and judicial powers to mean:

1. Federal courts cannot issue advisory opinions (because there is no actual case or lawsuit);

2. Federal courts cannot hear plaintiffs who do not have "standing" (because they have an insufficient personal stake in the outcome and therefore no controversy exists);

3. Federal courts cannot hear cases in which neither party has suffered an injury, because the case does not have "ripeness";

4. Federal courts cannot hear cases in which the court's judgment would make no difference because the wrong alleged has been withdrawn, the right to sue has died with one of the parties, or the judgment would otherwise be "moot."

Diversity Jurisdiction

Diversity jurisdiction was created by the Constitution as a way for citizens of different states to have lawsuits involving large amounts of money (currently, more than $75,000 for cases other than class actions) judged in a more neutral venue (location) than if the plaintiff were to have to sue the defendant in the defendant's home state, or if the defendant were to have to defend in the plaintiff's home state, using local judges. Volume 28 of the United States Code of Federal Laws, section 1332 (abbreviated as "28 U.S.C. § 1332"), is the law that defines diversity jurisdiction:

§ 1332. Diversity of citizenship; amount in controversy; costs.

(a) The district courts shall have original jurisdiction of all civil actions where the matter in controversy exceeds the sum or value of $75,000, exclusive of interest and costs, and is between—

(1) citizens of different States;

(2) citizens of a State and citizens or subjects of a foreign state;

(3) citizens of different States and in which citizens or subjects of a foreign state are additional parties; and

(4) a foreign state ... as plaintiff and citizens of a State or of different States....
an alien admitted to the United States for permanent residence shall be deemed a citizen of the State in which such alien is domiciled.

(b) Except when express provision is otherwise made in a statute of the United States, where the plaintiff who files the case originally in the federal courts is finally judged to be entitled to recover less than the sum or value of $75,000, computed without regard to any setoff or counterclaim to which the defendant may be judged to be entitled, and exclusive of interest and costs, the district court may deny costs to the plaintiff and, in addition, may impose costs on the plaintiff.

(c) For the purposes of this section

(1) a corporation shall be deemed to be a citizen of any State by which it has been incorporated and of the State where it has its principal place of business, except that in any direct action against the insurer of a policy or contract of liability insurance ... the insurer shall be deemed a citizen of the State of which the insured is a citizen, as well as of any State by which the insurer has been incorporated and of the State where it has its principal place of business; and

(2) the legal representative of a dead person shall be deemed to be a citizen only of the same State as that person, and the legal representative of an infant or incompetent shall be deemed to be a citizen only of the same State as the infant or incompetent.

(e) The word "States," as used in this section, includes the Territories, the District of Columbia, and the Commonwealth of Puerto Rico.

Even though Americans now share many more common viewpoints than they did in 1789, and frequently live in several states during their lifetime, diversity jurisdiction continues and accounts for an estimated 20% of federal court business and frequently involves parties who are not U.S. citizens.

Federal or State Law

Diversity lawsuits do not necessarily claim relief under federal laws, and typically involve contracts, torts and other disputes between private parties. Plaintiffs in diversity lawsuits have always had the right to sue the defendant in the court of the defendant's home state, where the case would be decided according to state statutory law and state common law using state rules of civil procedure. If the plaintiff satisfies the "amount in controversy" requirement and also has the option of suing the defendant in federal court, should the federal court apply a different law based only on federal judicial opinions (so-called "federal common law"), and different federal procedures, the FRCP?

The principles guiding choice of law and procedure in federal courts hearing diversity claims based on state law were decided in the 1938 Supreme Court case of *Erie R. Co. v. Tompkins,* 304 U.S. 64 (1938). The *Erie* case held that federal courts hearing diversity cases must follow state substantive law, both statutory and common law, but must apply federal procedural law, like the FRCP. In other words, federal courts hearing diversity cases look to state law for the substantive law issues and federal law for the procedural issues. However, defining what is a question of substantive law, requiring the federal court to follow state law, and what is a question of procedure, allowing the federal court to follow federal law, remains a source of continuing controversy. For example, the Supreme Court has decided that all of the following are substantive law issues requiring the use of state law: burden of proof; time limitation for filing a claim (called the "statute of limitations"); choice of law rules; laws prohibiting suit by corporations not licensed in the state; and a requirement that a bond must be posted before shareholders can sue a corporation. In *Shady Grove Orthopedic Associates, PA v. Allstate Ins. Co.,* 559 U.S. ___, 130 S. Ct. 1431 (2010), the Supreme Court permitted a class action lawsuit in a federal diversity case, even though the relevant state law would not permit class treatment. Justice Scalia commented as to whether a rule is a federal procedural issue or a state substantive law issue:

> The framework for our decision is familiar. We must first determine whether [a federal rule] answers the question in dispute. If it does, it governs—[a state's] law notwithstanding—unless it exceeds statutory authorization or Congress's rulemaking power. We do not wade into *Erie's* murky waters unless the federal rule is inapplicable or invalid.

Where to Sue or Defend

A skilled lawyer for a plaintiff with access to a federal trial court will spend time considering whether the plaintiff would gain the greater advantage by filing in state or in federal court. In theory, under the *Erie* case, the law applied in state court and federal court in diversity cases should be the same. However, the plaintiff's lawyer might still feel that the federal court is more neutral, more efficient, that the federal court fees are lower, that the federal procedures are more favorable, that the federal judge is more knowledgeable, or that the federal court's powers to summon parties and enforce judgments is more extensive. For example, the plaintiff may want the jury trial that a federal court is required by the Seventh Amendment of the Constitution to offer him or her in civil cases. The plaintiff would not necessarily be entitled to such a jury trial if the action was brought in a state court. Even if the plaintiff did have such a right in state court, a federal trial court can select members of the jury from a large regional geographic area. On the other hand, a local trial court can only select jury members from its jurisdiction, which may be only one part of a city or county. This means a federal district court jury may have many more kinds of people on the jury than people selected from the same poor section of a city, for example. If the plaintiff also can claim a federal question, the lawyer for the plaintiff has additional considerations. Has the statute of limitations on the state law claim expired, barring a claim in state court, while the federal law statute of limitations still allows a suit in federal court? Does the federal law make it easier for the plaintiff to prove a case than the state law? Does the federal law provide more extensive damages than the state law? There are many other considerations in choosing a forum for a lawsuit, some based on reason and some based on the trial attorney's "feel" for the case. Of course, a skilled lawyer for the defendant will have also to decide whether she wants the case to be heard in state or federal court. The defendant's lawyer may have to think of reasons why the federal court should refuse to hear the case, or why the case should be transferred ("removed") from state court to federal court.

Sovereign Immunity

Even if there is subject matter jurisdiction, the common law doctrine of "sovereign immunity" may be available to the defendant as a defense to personal jurisdiction. Originally the courts in England were created to help the king administer the nation, and so the English courts did not allow persons to sue the king (the "sovereign"). In the United States, the idea of "sovereign immunity" from lawsuits became a doctrine that prevents the United States or any state government from being sued unless that government has consented to being sued. For economic and political reasons, the United States and most states allow themselves to be sued for many claims, just as a corporation may be sued. By allowing itself to be sued, a government shows fairness, reduces the risk to other parties of doing business with that government, and pays for government errors out of public funds rather than having a loss fall entirely on a person or business with no legal recourse.

Although the United States has never had a king, some nations of the world are still governed by royalty or some other leader, such as a military dictator, who does not allow his government to be sued. Since an early U.S. Supreme Court case, *Schooner Exchange v. Mc'Faddon*, 11 U.S. 116 (1812), in which the U.S. declined to exercise jurisdiction over one of Napoleon's warships, U.S. courts have had a tradition of "comity," meaning that they have decided not to claim jurisdiction over foreign governments for certain types of lawsuits. Federal courts are also bound by the separation of powers doctrine that gives authority in foreign affairs to the President and the Congress, not the courts. For many years, each U.S. jurisdiction has decided when a foreign government could be sued in its courts. In 1976, Congress passed the Foreign Sovereign Immunities Act ("FSIA") to create a national standard for jurisdiction over foreign governments. The FSIA allows lawsuits against foreign governments when they act like commercial organizations, when they are disputing property located in the United States, when they intentionally cause personal injury or death in the United States, when they operate ships that are the subject of a lawsuit in the United States, when they are parties to an arbitration agreement to be enforced in the United States, or when they cause personal injury or death due to State-approved terrorism. Foreign governments must appear in court (using their American lawyers) and plead sovereign immunity as a defense if they wish to have the lawsuit dismissed. If a foreign government ignores a U.S. court action, it may suffer a default judgment like any other defendant.

The doctrine of sovereign immunity is not to be confused with the "Act of State" doctrine, which is a substantive defense on the merits. Under the Act of State doctrine, the courts of one state will not question the validity of public acts performed by other sovereigns within their own borders, even when such courts have jurisdiction over a controversy in which one of the litigants has standing to challenge those acts. Under the Act of State doctrine, a foreign government may be able to appear in court, submit to jurisdiction, admit that it performed the action that is the subject of the lawsuit, but escape liability because its action was an Act of State.

Conflict of Laws

Whether the lawsuit is in a federal or a state court, there may be a question whether the proper law governing the construction of a contract (where the parties have not included a choice of law clause) is the law of State A or State B, or whether the nature of a personal injury in tort should be judged by the law of State A or Country C, in other words, a conflict of laws question. Congress has not made any general national rules about conflict of laws, so both federal courts, under the *Erie* doctrine, and state courts, would check the law of the state in which the court was located. However, American doctrines of conflict of laws vary considerably by state. The older doctrine, still used by about 20% of the states, created rules for determining which law applied when the parties failed to agree. These states have rules similar to those in many civil law countries: the construction of a contract is determined by the law of the place where the contract was made; the law concerning a tort is determined by the law where the injury happened, etc. Most other states use an approach to conflicts of laws that seeks to determine the "interests" of States A and B, or State A and Country C, in having its own law used in the case. By balancing these interests, some judges feel they can avoid a "false conflict" when State B or Country C, although important in the traditional legal rule for resolving conflicts, actually has no real interest in requiring that its law be used in the case. Readers from civil law jurisdictions should not assume that conflict of law questions will be judged in a court in the United States according to familiar rules.

Forum Non Conveniens

Even if there is personal and subject matter jurisdiction, a federal court may refuse to hear a lawsuit when there is another more convenient court, or "forum," that could take over. The principle of *forum non conveniens* (Latin for "inconvenient forum") is often applied in international cases where plaintiffs want access to American juries, discovery procedures, or damage awards, and defendants prefer to be sued outside the United States. This may include cases in which one non-American sues another non-American in the United States for actions that happened outside of the United States, such as the *Wiwa* case below.

Wiwa was an opposition leader and President of the Movement for the Survival of the Ogoni People ("MSOP") in Nigeria. The two defendants jointly managed Shell Petroleum Development Company of Nigeria, Ltd. ("Shell Nigeria"), a wholly-owned Nigerian subsidiary of the defendants that engaged in oil exploration and development in the Ogoni Region of Nigeria. According to the plaintiffs, Shell Nigeria took land for oil development without adequate compensation, and caused substantial pollution of the air and water in the homeland of the Ogoni people. The plaintiffs said that Shell Nigeria recruited the Nigerian police and military to attack local villages and the MSOP. The plaintiffs were repeatedly arrested, detained, and tortured by the Nigerian government. The plaintiffs, who were residents of the United States, sued the defendants in the U.S. District Court in New York City under federal law. Defendant Royal Dutch Petroleum was incorporated in the Netherlands. Defendant Shell Transport was incorporated in England. The defendants claimed that the courts of England were a better forum. The District Court judge dismissed the suit as *forum non conveniens*. The plaintiffs appealed to the U.S. Court of Appeals for the Second Circuit. The Court of Appeals reversed the District Court and told it to continue with the lawsuit.

Wiwa v. Royal Dutch Petroleum Co.
226 F. 3d 88 (2d Cir. 2000)

Leval, J.

Plaintiffs appeal from the decision of the district court to dismiss for *forum non conveniens*. The grant or denial of a motion to dismiss for *forum non conveniens* is generally up to the district court's judgment. This assumes that the court used the correct standards and rule of law. We believe that, as a matter of law, in balancing the competing interests, the district court did not give proper significance to a choice of forum by lawful U.S. resident plaintiffs or to the policy interest implicit in our federal statutory law in providing a forum for adjudication of claims of violations of the law of nations.

In 1947, the Supreme Court handed down a pair of decisions laying out the framework for *forum non conveniens* analysis that the federal courts follow to this day: *Gulf Oil Corp. v. Gilbert*, 330 U.S. 501 (1947) and *Koster v. American Lumbermens Mut. Cas. Co.*, 330 U.S. 518 (1947). Under these cases, *forum non conveniens* is a discretionary device permitting a court in rare instances to "dismiss a claim even if the court is a permissible venue with proper jurisdiction over the claim." In assessing whether *forum non conveniens* dismissal is appropriate, courts engage in a two-step process: The first step is to determine if an adequate alternative forum exists. If so, courts must then balance a series of factors involving the private interests of the parties in maintaining the litigation in the competing courts and any public interests at stake. The defendant has the burden to establish that an adequate alternative forum exists and then to show that the other forum is better.

The plaintiffs say that the United States has a policy interest in providing a forum for the adjudication of international human rights abuses. In *Filartiga v. Pena-Irala*, 630 F.2d 876 (2d Cir. 1980), this court held that deliberate torture done by official authority violates universally accepted norms of international human rights law, and that such a violation of international law constitutes a violation of the domestic law of the United States, giving rise to a claim under federal law whenever the torturer is within the borders of the United States.

Dismissal on grounds of *forum non conveniens* can represent a huge setback in a plaintiff's efforts to seek reparations for acts of torture. One of the difficulties that confront victims of torture under color of a nation's law is the enormous difficulty of bringing suits to vindicate such abuses. Most likely, the victims cannot sue in the place where the torture occurred. Indeed, in many instances, the victim would be endangered merely by returning to that place. It is not easy to bring such suits in the courts of another nation. Courts are often inhospitable. Such suits are generally time consuming, burdensome, and difficult to administer. In addition, because they assert outrageous conduct on the part of another nation, such suits may embarrass the government of the nation in whose courts they are brought, courts often regard such suits as "not our business."

We turn to the analysis of the *forum non conveniens* factors in their application to this case. The district court was wrong in the following respects: (a) The district court counted against retention of jurisdiction that the plaintiffs were not residents of the Southern District of New York while failing to count in favor of retention that two of the plaintiffs were residents of the United States, and (b) the court failed to count in favor of retention the interest of the United States in providing a forum for the judgment of claims of torture in violation of the standards of international law. Furthermore, the district court gave no consideration to the very substantial expense and inconvenience (perhaps fatal to the suit) that would be imposed on the poor plaintiffs by dismissal in favor of a British forum, and the inconvenience to the defendants that ultimately justified the dismissal.

In arguing that England is a more appropriate forum, defendants rely upon arguments such as the inconvenience of shipping documents from England to the United States and the additional cost for a Nigerian witness of flying to New York rather than London. These considerations are indeed a legitimate part of the *forum non conveniens* analysis, but (a) the defendants have not demonstrated that these costs are excessively burdensome, especially in view of the defendants' vast resources, and (b) the additional cost and inconvenience to the defendants of being sued in New York is fully counterbalanced by the cost and inconvenience to the plaintiffs of requiring them to reinstitute the litigation in England courts— especially given the plaintiffs' minimal resources in comparison to the huge resources of the defendants. These considerations cannot justify overriding the plaintiffs' choice of forum.

In order to be granted dismissal based on *forum non conveniens*, the defendants bear the burden of establishing that the *Gilbert* factors conclude strongly in favor of trial in the foreign forum. We believe they have failed to meet this burden.

* * *

Topics for Further Discussion

1. Should diversity jurisdiction still apply to corporations? In *Hertz Corp. v. Friend*, 559 U.S. ___, 130 S. Ct. 1181 (2010) the Supreme Court decided that a corporation's "principal place of business" is "the place where a corporation's officers direct, control and coordinate the corporation's activities ... the corporation's 'nerve center.'" The Court commented that the concern of diversity jurisdiction, prejudice against an out-of-state party, will often depend on a corporation's image, its history and its advertising. These are often national attributes, rather than the local factors such as the factory address, sales or employment that some courts had been using to determine "principal place of business."

2. The Supreme Court denied *certiorari* in the *Wiwa* case. Should U.S. courts allow non-Americans to sue each other in the United States for harm done outside of the United States? If yes, in what kinds of cases? What problems do you see?

3. Does the ability of non-Americans to use American courts increase the influence of U.S. law in the world?

Pretrial Procedure

The Complaint and Service of Process

Sample Complaint for Money Lent

1. Jurisdiction is founded on diversity of citizenship and amount. Plaintiff is a citizen of New York. Defendant is a citizen of California. The amount in controversy, exclusive of interest and costs, exceeds the amount specified by 28 U.S.C. § 1332.

2. Defendant owes plaintiff $100,000 for money lent by plaintiff to defendant on January 7, 2010.

3. Plaintiff demands judgment against defendant for the sum of $100,000 interest and costs.

Signed: [Attorney for Plaintiff]   Address:

Under the Federal Rules of Civil Procedure, a civil action begins when the plaintiff files a "complaint" with the clerk of the court. The complaint must state:

1. A short and plain statement of the grounds on which the court's subject matter jurisdiction depends;

2. A short and plain statement of the claim, showing that the pleader is entitled to relief;

3. A demand for judgment for the relief that the pleader seeks.

Under the FRCP, in general, the party does not have to calculate damages or go into detail about all the circumstances that contributed to the lawsuit. These claims will come out during the trial. However, FRCP Rule 9 does require that specific details be pleaded if one party is claiming fraud, mistake, special damages, or that the other party lacks the legal capacity to sue or to be sued. In addition, in *Ashcroft v. Iqbal*, 556 U.S. ___, 129 S. Ct. 1937 (2009), the Supreme Court held that, "in all civil actions and proceedings in the United States district courts," to survive a motion to dismiss by opposing counsel, "a complaint must contain sufficient factual matter, accepted as true, to 'state a claim to relief that is plausible on its face.'"

FRCP Rule 8 allows a party to make statements in a claim that are alternative or mutually exclusive. This means that a party can claim both that "there was no contract" and that "there was a contract but it is no longer in force." A simple complaint is all the FRCP requires, but most lawyers will write much more. FRCP Rule 11 provides that a lawyer must sign every complaint, and that every lawyer filing a complaint certifies that the lawsuit is not being filed just to harass the defendant, that evidence supports the facts claimed and that there is law to support the relief requested. If the party filing the lawsuit is proceeding without an attorney (*pro se*), the party must sign the complaint and the signature of a lawyer is not required.

After the plaintiff files the complaint, the court clerk issues a "summons." The summons is an order from the court to respond to the complaint or lose the lawsuit by default. The plaintiff must arrange to have the summons and a copy of the complaint "served on," or delivered to, the defendant. Service within the United States does not have to be performed by the court. Service of process is usually done by the plaintiff's attorney via certified mail, or by "process servers" hired by the attorney. Process servers are people who specialize in serving legal papers on defendants no matter where the defendant is: in the office or at home, on the golf course, in a television studio, at an airport, or even in the sauna.

The Defendant's Response to the Complaint

Within 21 days, the defendant must respond to the complaint either by "motion to dismiss" or "answer." A motion to dismiss does not argue the facts of the complaint; rather, it states reasons why the court should not go further with the case. The listed reasons are:

1. Lack of jurisdiction over the subject matter. For example, the plaintiff tries to sue the defendant in federal court on a state law claim for $100. The defendant would argue that federal court should dismiss the case because the "amount in controversy" requirement for diversity cases has not been met;

2. Lack of jurisdiction over the person;

3. Improper venue, meaning that the wrong court has been chosen to hear the case;

4. Insufficiency of process. For example, the complaint was delivered with three pages missing;

5. Insufficiency of service of process. For example, the complaint was not delivered directly to the defendant, or a party authorized to accept service on behalf of the defendant;

6. Failure to state a claim upon which relief can be granted. For example, in a diversity case, the plaintiff sues the defendant for a gambling debt, where the federal court is in a state that has laws against enforcing gambling debts;

7. Failure to include a necessary party. For example, A owns a building with fire insurance. B rents a store in the building. The building burns down. Before any insurance has been paid, B sues A with a demand for payment under the fire insurance policy. The defendant would argue that unless the insurance company is also made a party, the case should be dismissed.

The defendant can also file an "answer." The answer is a document that (a) admits, denies or states lack of knowledge about the claims in the complaint; (b) raises affirmative defenses like the expiration of the statute of limitations or duress (being forced to do something); and (c) counterclaims against the plaintiff and cross-claims against third parties. Rather than dismiss a complaint for the reasons stated above, many judges will grant permission to amend the complaint "freely when justice so requires," or to add new parties ("joinder"). The Supreme Court has decided that a complaint should not be dismissed for failure to state a claim "unless it appears beyond doubt that the plaintiff can not prove a set of facts in support of his claim which would entitle him to relief."

Class Actions

The FRCP allow class actions, which are a kind of lawsuit in which damage has been done to many parties, but rather than having many lawsuits it is more efficient or more fair to allow all the plaintiffs to sue, or all the defendants to be sued, in one action via representative parties. If the plaintiff or defendant satisfies certain requirements, they will be named a "representative" of the class. The facts determined in a class action, and a judgment in a class action, will bind all parties in the class (*res judicata*), whether or not they appeared in court. The requirements for a class action are that:

1. There are so many plaintiffs or defendants that bringing them together in one lawsuit is impracticable;

2. There are questions of law or fact common to the class;

3. The claims or defenses of the representative parties are typical of the claims or defenses of the class; and

4. The representative parties will fairly and adequately protect the interests of the class.

Class actions are often filed in consumer protection, mass tort, antitrust or securities cases, where many individuals have suffered a loss but are reluctant to fight big companies using their own money, or in civil rights cases where many persons without much money claim their rights were violated. The advantages of a class action are obvious when the plaintiff is an average person, but the large increase in class actions in the United States in recent years is due to the advantages for defendants' and plaintiffs' lawyers. A defendant such as an asbestos manufacturer may prefer one trial and one judgment in a class action, which all plaintiffs must follow, to the expense and uncertainty of being sued in many states over several generations by persons who suffered lung disease from asbestos. When the law under which the class action is begun allows the court to award attorney's fees to the plaintiffs' lawyers if the plaintiff wins, the plaintiffs' lawyers may obtain attorney's fees multiplied by the number of members of the class, often amounting to tens of millions of dollars, making representation of plaintiffs in class actions very profitable for some lawyers. The Class Action Fairness Act of 2005 sets special requirements for federal diversity class actions.

Discovery

If the plaintiff satisfies the requirements to bring a case in federal court, and the defendant does not show any valid defenses, the judge may conduct a "pre-trial conference." At the pre-trial conference, a judge will typically urge the parties to settle, but will also try to eliminate duplication and poor quality preparation in a trial and establish a schedule for moving ahead.

In the next stage, lawyers investigate the facts of the case for the plaintiffs and defendants in a process called "discovery." Without further action by the court, or even a request, each party must promptly provide:

1. The name (and, if known, the address and telephone number) of any person likely to know about the claim or defenses;

2. A copy of, or description of, all documents and data that each party has that may be used in the case;

3. Materials showing how the plaintiff computed the damages it is claiming;

4. Any contracts showing that an insurance company will pay a party for the judgment; and

5. The names of all witnesses.

Computers as we know them did not exist when the FRCP were adopted in 1934. In contrast, more than 90% of the information generated in the U.S. is now in digital form, according to the Federal Judicial Center. Computer records have become a major object of discovery. Assume that Person A creates one document and stores it on one hard disk drive on A's computer. If Person A's company backs up its records once a month, in a year there are thirteen copies (one on A's hard disk, twelve back up copies). Suppose A sent the document to B, C and D, three other persons in the company, who also have their records backed up monthly. This means there are fifty-two copies of the final document in the company's possession. Suppose that B, C and D looked at two previous drafts, each of which is also backed up. This means there are 104 copies of previous drafts. Suppose that each draft and the final draft were sent with one message via electronic mail: there may be 156 copies of electronic mail dealing with the topic. Suppose that this information exists not only on the hard disks of A, B, C, D and the back up tapes of those disks, but also on the company's servers, the email servers of outside organizations, laptop computers, home computers and PDA devices. This data may include not only saved documents, but system files and deleted files. For any single document, there may be thousands of pieces of information in digital form, perhaps showing key facts or motives in the case.

When paper documents are the subject of discovery, the side holding the documents can usually locate them quickly, and the more documents, the greater cost of the discovery process is on the receiving side, which has to read and copy many boxes of papers. In electronic discovery, however, the greater cost will typically be on the side that has to locate the documents: the side receiving the documents can often use a software program to search and index the electronic documents. Electronic discovery in court cases can cost millions of dollars. To give one example, in *Rowe Entertainment Inc. v. William Morris Agency, 53 Fed. R. Serv. 3d (Callaghan) 296* (S.D.N.Y., May 8, 2002), a group of African-American entertainment agencies sued another agency for alleged antitrust violations in preventing the African-American agencies from booking concerts. The lawsuit involved discovery in the entertainment industry, and not the more heavily computerized electronics or financial services industries. Nevertheless, according to a presentation by the Federal Judicial Center, it cost over $9,500,000 to restore 200 backup tapes, and $247,000 to review the 200,000 email messages that were discovered in the case.

The FRCP have been revised to deal with the costs of electronic discovery. Rule 16(b)(3)(B)(iii) provides for scheduling "disclosure or discovery of electronically stored information." Rule 26(b)(2)(B) limits the general duty to disclose by stating that "a party need not provide discovery of electronically stored information from sources that the party identifies as not reasonably accessible because of undue burden or cost." Rule 34(b)(2)(E)(iii) provides that "a party need not produce the same electronically stored information in more than one form."

In many civil law countries, gathering discovery information would be the work of the judge, but in the United States the lawyers do it under the "adversary system" discussed in other chapters of this book. This is not because federal judges are weak; to the contrary, federal judges are appointed for life. Moreover, federal judges can command armed federal marshals to maintain order and can fine or imprison the parties to a lawsuit. There are many reasons why the American judicial system uses discovery by the parties and not by a judge:

1. Faster Settlement. If each side learns its weak points, settlement is more likely.

2. Fewer Disputed Facts. Discovery may show that the parties agree on certain facts, so they can agree to admit those facts and shorten the time and expense of trial.

3. Fewer Tricks. If all the facts are available to a judge or jury, a fairer judgment is likely to result than if one side suddenly reveals an unknown fact.

4. Better Understanding. Each party already knows what many of the facts in its case means, while a judge would be assembling pieces of information without any background, and therefore is less likely to understand the significance of each fact.

5. Full Effort. Each party has the most motivation to find all the facts and theories that benefit it and argue against all the facts and theories that benefit the other side. Each party only has to do one-half the work of gathering all the facts, and can focus on considering the full meaning of all the facts and theories that benefit it the most. In contrast, a judge would have to guess at the plaintiff's facts and theories part of the time and imagine the defendant's facts and theories part of the time. With multiple plaintiffs or defendants, this becomes impossible.

6. Fairness. Trials in the United States are generally public, and it appears much fairer to Americans to allow each side to do its own work and present its own evidence than to have the discussion limited by what a judge decides is interesting or important.

7. Efficiency. Trials in the United States are usually held in one continuous trial of all the issues and facts, not in a series of short hearings over a long period of time as in many civil law countries. Concentrated trials are viewed as more efficient, easier to follow, more

likely to examine all the facts and issues, and much less likely to interrupt the lives of jurors who must attend every day of a jury trial. In a concentrated trial, each side must be better prepared because they will not have several weeks to investigate new facts before the next hearing. They will also have only one chance to create a factual record, since new evidence is not generally admitted at the appellate level.

8. Cost. Discovery has a reputation of greatly increasing the cost of a trial because people say it encourages expensive and time consuming "fishing expeditions" for facts. However, a study for the Federal Judicial Conference showed that the average cost to an attorney for preparing a civil case was $13,000 and that discovery represented about half of that cost, but that discovery costs were only three percent of the amount at issue in the lawsuit. The same survey found that there was no discovery in 50% of the cases. A different survey found no discovery in 38% of cases, and the average time spent by a lawyer in discovery to be about three hours.

Major Forms of Discovery

Discovery is not done in court. Most often, it is done at a lawyer's office, but, depending on the subject, it can be done at any convenient location or in writing.

Depositions are the most common form of discovery. In a deposition, a party or other witness is "deposed," meaning that the party is placed under oath by a court reporter. The party's lawyer asks questions. The lawyer for the other side asks cross-examination questions. The court reporter creates a full, verbatim written record of all the questions, answers, and objections. A deposition of a party can be used for any purpose by either side. A deposition of a non-party witness can be used if it is different from the witness' testimony at trial, or if the witness is unable to testify. Depositions allow each lawyer to determine how strong the party's case may be, avoid surprises, and determine whether a person would be an effective witness in court.

Interrogatories are written questions, sent only to a party, which must be answered in writing under oath. They are sent directly by the lawyer for one side, without court action and without a court reporter. Usually the party receiving the interrogatory allows a lawyer to draft the answer to the interrogatory so as to answer the question while revealing as little as possible.

"Requests to Produce" can be sent only to an opposing party, and are used to make the other side produce documents or things, or allow inspection of land.

"Orders for Physical or Mental Examination" are used to check on a party's physical or mental health, but, because these orders can be abused, courts will only issue them when physical or mental health is an issue in the lawsuit, and will only issue them against parties and not against general witnesses.

"Requests for Admission" are written requests to the opposing party to admit facts that are not in dispute. Failure to respond is taken as an admission against the party who is silent, but a party may deny a request to admit when there is a good faith dispute about the fact.

Exceptions to Discovery

Persons involved in the U.S. discovery process for the first time are often astonished at its wide range, which extends to "any matter relevant to the claim or defense of any party."

There is no requirement that the information requested in discovery will actually be used in the trial, or even that it would be admissible as evidence. However, discovery does have some limits. Communications between certain categories of professionals and their clients cannot be discovered except with the consent of the client. These communications are called "privileged." Some of the more common privileges are those between an attorney and a client, a doctor and a patient, a husband and a wife, a priest and a penitent, and, in some states, an accountant and a client, or a psychologist or social worker and a patient. Confidential commercial information can be made available to a party under a protective order of the court forbidding the party from using or disclosing the information except in the lawsuit.

Abuses of Discovery

Since a lawsuit in the United States can be an expensive, time consuming, and stressful action for both parties, some readers may find it hard to believe that lawyers all voluntarily cooperate in discovery to show each other facts, documents, and witnesses that could cause the other side to win. It is true that there are some lawyers who try to abuse discovery, but the discovery process succeeds for various reasons:

1. Desire to Avoid Angering the Judge. Judges like to have an efficient courtroom and to hear cases as soon as they are ready. They are impatient with parties who delay or evade discovery or try to gain unfair advantage over the other party. Judges can grant a "motion to compel discovery" forcing the other side to provide information. An angry judge can make decisions that are unfavorable to the party that is seen as uncooperative.

2. Desire to Avoid a Bad Impression on the Jury. In jury trials, a jury will often assume that if a party is uncooperative, that party has something to hide. This may cause a jury to decide against such a party.

3. Limits to Interrogatories. If an individual sues a rich person or corporation, the rich party's lawyers may try to overwhelm the individual ("burying him in paper") with thousands of pages of interrogatories. The FRCP now limit interrogatories to twenty-five unless the court permits more.

4. Penalties. Judges can require the loser in a discovery dispute to pay the other side's attorney fees unless the loser's position was "substantially justified." Judges can order that the other party's facts be taken as established, or that a party be denied the opportunity to present defenses, if the party is uncooperative.

Summary Judgment

A party that was defeated in its earlier motion to dismiss for failure to state a claim may ask for "summary judgment" at the end of discovery. Summary judgment means the judge will decide the case without a full trial. Summary judgment can only be made if "there is no genuine issue as to any material fact and ... the moving party is entitled to judgment as a matter of law." If the other party can show that there is any genuine fact in dispute, summary judgment is not permitted and the case goes to trial.

The Trial

In a jury trial, as discussed in Chapter 2, the jury is selected from a panel of available jurors through a process known as the *voir dire*, placed under oath, and seated to hear the case. First the plaintiff, and then the defendant, in a civil case, has an opportunity to make an "opening statement." The purpose of the opening statement is to explain, as an easy-to-understand story, the party's case by laying out the theory and indicating the evidence that will be produced during the trial, what the other side says, and why what the other side says is wrong. The opening statement is not evidence, but it is a powerful method of persuasion since it lets jurors make sense of the evidence that comes later. Lawyers must be careful to be accurate in their opening statement since, later in the trial, the jurors will remember any changes or omissions in the story and may decide the lawyer failed to prove the case. The lawyer for the other side will certainly point out any statements that were not proven during the trial.

After the opening statements, the plaintiff presents its witnesses and evidence. During "direct examination," the plaintiff asks the witness (1) about the witness' background, such as who the witness is and where the witness works, (2) how the witness came to be involved in the case, and (3) what the witness saw, heard, said, did, etc. After the plaintiff is finished with the "direct examination" of its witness, the defendant can engage in "cross-examination." The purposes of cross-examination are to (1) make the plaintiff's witness less credible or (2) get more information. After the plaintiff has presented its evidence, the defendant conducts direct examination of witnesses for the defense and the plaintiff can cross-examine those witnesses.

When both the plaintiff and the defendant have finished presenting all their evidence, each lawyer makes a "closing argument." This is like the opening statement, but takes account of evidence the other side has presented that could bring a positive or negative result for the lawyer's client. Lawyers are not allowed to refer to facts not in evidence, or make wild remarks that might unfairly prejudice a jury.

The case goes to judgment when the lawyers for each side are finished. If the trial is before a judge rather than a jury, the judge may take several weeks to consider the case and deliver a judgment. In a jury trial, the jurors are ordinary citizens who cannot reasonably be expected to deliberate over an extended period of time. Therefore, the jury is ordered to discuss the case and deliver a judgment, or "verdict," immediately after the trial ends, based on detailed instructions from the judge. The jury's private discussions can take any amount of time, from a few minutes to several weeks.

After the Trial

Appeals in the Federal System

Once the U.S. District Court has recorded a judgment, either side in a civil case may appeal to one of the United States circuit courts of appeals having jurisdiction over the relevant district court. (See the map in Appendix C). Each circuit court of appeals has many judges, usually covering several states, and has its headquarters in a major city. Any circuit court of appeals can hear appeals from district courts in its territory on any subject matter. Cases are typically heard in panels of three judges, but important cases may be heard *en banc* by all of the judges of the circuit court. Some circuits develop expertise in certain areas: the Second Circuit, with jurisdiction over Wall Street, writes many securities law opinions; the Fifth Circuit, with jurisdiction over Texas and Louisiana, is expert in oil and gas law; the Ninth Circuit, with jurisdiction over Silicon Valley and Hollywood, gets many intellectual property questions; and the D.C. Circuit is the primary court of appeals for administrative law cases involving federal government agencies.

The circuit court of appeals can review and change any ruling of law made by a district court within its circuit. However, because circuit courts are not trial courts, do not view witnesses, and base their decisions only on the written record of the lower court and lawyers' arguments, they will almost never change a verdict based on a different interpretation of the facts of any given case. An appeals court cannot ignore the lower court's findings about fact unless those findings are "clearly erroneous." Of course, if an appeals court decides the law differently from the district court, the same facts may cause the other party ultimately to win.

After losing in the court of appeals, a party cannot automatically appeal to the U.S. Supreme Court. Almost all requests for Supreme Court review are via *certiorari*, a procedure in which the Supreme Court decides whether it wants to review a case. The Supreme Court only reviews cases (a) of national importance or (b) when there is a conflict about interpreting federal law between two or more U.S. circuit courts, or two or more state supreme courts on matters involving federal questions. The Supreme Court does not hear cases in small panels of Justices so each case must be heard by the full Court. During the 2007–08 term, for example, the Court considered 8374 petitions and granted review in 95 cases, so it denied review in about 99% of the cases. It takes a vote of four out of the nine justices of the Supreme Court to decide to take a case (the so-called "rule of four"). Thus, for most cases, a U.S. circuit court of appeals is the court of last resort for appeals.

Precedents of a court of appeals are only binding on the circuit court itself, and the district courts contained within the circuit. For example, a decision of the Third Circuit will not be binding on any other circuit court or district court outside of the Third Circuit. The opinion may be cited and followed by other circuit courts for its persuasive reasoning, or rejected entirely. A decision by the Supreme Court to deny *certiorari* does not imply that the Supreme Court agrees with the reasoning of the circuit court. Sometimes, the Supreme Court will deny *certiorari* to give other circuits an opportunity to pass judgment on the same issue, or it will wait until the ideal set of facts presents itself.

Once a party has lost on final appeal, a judgment is entered against the losing party that decides all the claims of fact, issues of law, and defenses that were in dispute, and usually sets an award for damages.

Recognition and Enforcement of Judgments

If the losing party does not pay the damages voluntarily, the winning party may ask the court to enforce the judgment against the loser's property within the court's jurisdiction, using armed force if necessary. The winning party may also seek to enforce the judgment against the loser's property in any state of the United States and possibly foreign nations.

If the losing party is in another part of the United States, Article IV, section 1 of the Constitution requires a court in the losing party's state to give "full faith and credit" to the judgment of the court of another American state. This means that a court in any U.S.

state must treat a judgment from another state as if it had been made in the home state, and cannot refuse to enforce it. What happens when the winning party tries to enforce a judgment from another country?

The United Nations Convention on the Recognition and Enforcement of Foreign Arbitral Awards has been signed by more than 120 countries including the United States. This makes the enforcement of foreign arbitration awards in the United States relatively straightforward, although it can be time-consuming and costly. However, the U.S. is not a party to any international convention on the recognition of foreign court judgments, although the Hague Conference on Private International Law has been circulating a draft treaty for several years. Most treaties between the United States and other countries do not deal with enforcement of foreign judgments. So, a party that has won a lawsuit in Japan against a U.S. company, for example, will have to enforce the judgment according to the laws of each state. Judgments requiring one side to pay a sum of money are much more likely to be enforced by a foreign court than judgments requiring a party to do something, or not to do something, or deciding family or property matters. Most jurisdictions will refuse to enforce a judgment if it is found that the losing party was not provided with due process in the form of adequate notice and an opportunity to be heard, or if the judgment is deemed to violate the public policy of the jurisdiction where it is sought to be enforced.

Since 1962, a group called the National Conference of Commissioners on Uniform State Laws has been trying to have each state pass similar, uniform laws dealing with the recognition of foreign money judgments. The group does this by preparing a "model law" that each state can use as a pattern to enact legislation. The Uniform Foreign Money Judgments Recognition Act (the "UFMJRA") has become law in many states with international contacts. It deals with enforcement of foreign judgments for a sum of money, other than for tax collection, penalty, divorce, or family support purposes.

The UFMJRA provides that, except in certain situations, a foreign money judgment should be given "full faith and credit" like the judgment of another U.S. state. The UFMJRA does not require reciprocity between the state court and the foreign court. Where the UFMJRA has not been made a part of state law, the traditional common law applies. The common law in some states will demand reciprocity, or may refuse to enforce a foreign judgment when the statute of limitations bars a similar action in the state courts, or may apply a different choice of law.

U.S. Civil Procedure Goes Global

Trillions of dollars of trade pass between the United States and its trading partners, and hundreds of thousands of non-Americans are in the United States to work, study or travel. Naturally, there are times when persons in other countries are involved in matters before U.S. courts. Even assuming that a U.S. lawyer can demonstrate personal jurisdiction over the foreign party, problems arise when a U.S. lawyer tries to conduct discovery overseas or a U.S. party tries to "serve" a foreign party or witness.

There may be reasons why the party or witness will voluntarily cooperate in being served and taking a deposition. For example, a foreign corporation might be the plaintiff, or wish to establish a defense, and for that reason wants its managers to be witnesses or experts in the trial. However, there are also times when the foreign person or entity refuses to cooperate.

Service on foreign defendants is simplified if the foreign country is a signatory of the Hague Convention on the Service Abroad of Judicial and Extrajudicial Documents in Civil and Commercial Matters ("Hague Convention"), an international treaty to which the United States is a party. If the Hague Convention does not apply, service by a U.S. party in a foreign country may not be possible, may not be valid if challenged in a U.S. court, or may render the judgment of a U.S. court unenforceable in the foreign country. The lawyer attempting to conduct successful service of process in a foreign country will have to research the law of the particular country and perhaps work with a law firm in the foreign country.

There are several options for conducting discovery in foreign countries. The oldest method is for a U.S. court to ask a foreign court to question a person in the foreign country. This is done by delivering a "letter rogatory" from the U.S. court through the U.S. Department of State and the foreign ministry of the opposing party's nation to the foreign court. This method is unpopular with American lawyers because it relies on a judge unfamiliar with the facts of the case, often does not allow attorneys to add questions as they proceed, does not promote cross-examination, may not require documents to be produced, and may not allow the American attorney to be present when the questions are asked or answered. This method is usually not available for disputes being heard by an officer of an agency, only for lawsuits in court. However, this method can be used to question an uncooperative witness. A second method is for US lawyers to take a American-style deposition inside a U.S. consulate according to a consular convention, if one exists, with the foreign country. This procedure typically can be used for civil, administrative or criminal cases if the witness voluntarily participates. If the foreign country is, like the United States, a signatory to the Hague Convention on the Taking of Evidence Abroad in Civil or Commercial Matters, there may be additional options for international discovery.

Key Terms and Concepts

Certiorari
Deposition
Discovery
Diversity
Federal Question
Forum non conveniens
Interrogatories
Long Arm Statute
Service of Process
Sovereign Immunity

Chapter 6

Contracts

"The [plaintiffs] had a ready escape from their difficulty by insisting upon a contract; and in commercial transactions it does not in the end promote justice to seek strained interpretations in aid of those who do not protect themselves."

Hand, J. in *James Baird Co. v. Gimbel Bros., Inc.,*
64 F.2d 344 (2d Cir. 1933)

The common law, as expressed in the opinions of judges in each state, remains the primary source of contract law in the United States. It is not uncommon to find that hundred-year old cases are still good law. Certain doctrines of contract law, such as the Statute of Frauds, are older than the United States itself. Nevertheless, new sources of contract law have emerged in the 20th century.

Sources of Contract Law

Federal Law

In the area of consumer protection, federal laws have a significant role. The Truth in Lending Act (1968) may regulate the display of annual percentage rates in loan contracts and offers consumers an opportunity to cancel loan contracts during a grace period. The Consumer Credit Protection Act (1968) may offer a consumer protection against charges arising from lost or stolen credit cards and improper requests for payment from creditors. Congress dealt with quality guarantees ("warranties") that deceived consumers by passing the Magnuson-Moss Warranty Act (1975) ("Magnuson-Moss"). Magnuson-Moss provides that, if the seller voluntarily offers a warranty, the seller must offer the warranty to all buyers, make the warranty valid without a registration requirement, and must promptly repair defects or replace a product that cannot be repaired.

The Restatement and the UCC

The American Law Institute, a group of legal scholars, has tried to harmonize the sometimes conflicting opinions of common law judges through the publication of the Restatement (Second) of Contracts (1981) ("Restatement"). Most of the 50 states have also passed model legislation, called the Uniform Commercial Code ("UCC"), creating a common set of commercial laws for merchants. Article 2 of the UCC, relating to the sale of "goods," supersedes many points of common law. Article 2-105 of the UCC defines "goods" as "all things (including specially manufactured goods) which are movable at the time of identification to the contract for sale other than the money in which the price is to be paid." There are, however, many areas of contract law that do not relate to the sale of goods, such as the performance of services, the interpretation of insurance contracts, and the sale of property. These areas continue to be governed by the common law. Sales of "shrink-wrapped" packaged computer software, while resembling the sale of goods off the store shelf, are considered to be licensing of the software and are therefore not subject to the UCC in most jurisdictions.

The United Nations

International contracts for the sale of goods are now common. The United States is a signatory to the United Nations Convention on Contracts for the International Sale of Goods ("CISG") adopted in Vienna in 1980. Since the CISG is a treaty, under Article VI of the Constitution, it is "the supreme law of the land" and therefore preempts state contract law, and gives federal courts subject matter jurisdiction over claims under the CISG. The CISG *automatically* governs the commercial sale of goods (not services) if (i) the parties do not expressly decline to use all or a part of the CISG; and (ii) the headquarters of at least two of the parties are located in two different signatory states, or the rules of private international law lead to the application of the law of a CISG signatory state. The CISG does not determine the validity of a contract or deal with property rights to the goods. However, where the CISG applies, it may alter common law rules (discussed later in this Chapter) regarding offer, acceptance, breach of contract, remedies for breach, calculation of damages, and the "parol evidence rule." Currently, seventy-four nations have signed the CISG, meaning that a contract between a party in the United States and one in seventy-three other countries may be governed automatically by the CISG unless the parties specify otherwise. All of North America, much of South America, most of the EU, the People's Republic of China, Japan and South Korea, for example, are signatories to the CISG. On the other hand, the following major trading countries are not yet CISG signatories: Brazil, India, Ireland, Malaysia, Saudi Arabia, Taiwan, Thailand and the United Kingdom. A detailed discussion of the CISG is beyond the scope of this Chapter, but is available on the Internet web site of the United Nations Commission on International Trade Law ("UNCITRAL").

What Is a Contract?

People often make promises they do not intend to keep, but sometimes another person relies on that promise. The Restatement § 1 defines a contract as "a promise or a set of promises for the breach of which the law gives a remedy, or the performance of which the law in some way recognizes as a duty." In other words, a contract is one kind of promise, a promise that a party can legally enforce. Promises can become enforceable as contracts in a variety of ways.

Classification of Contracts

The major classifications of contracts are as follows:

1. Void Contract. The Restatement defines this as "A promise for breach of which the law neither gives a remedy nor otherwise recognizes a duty of performance." Examples would include situations where the performance of the promise becomes impossible through no fault of the parties, or the promise lacks the basic requirements of "mutual assent" or "consideration."

2. Voidable Contract. A valid contract, but one or both parties to the contract can avoid the legal duties the contract creates. For example, the guardian of a minor (a child) can in most jurisdictions choose whether to enforce a contract made by the minor against the other party, or void the contract by pleading lack of contractual capacity (being too young legally to contract).

3. Unenforceable Contract. A valid contract has been created, and neither party is able to void the contract, but courts will still refuse to enforce the contract. Unenforceable contracts include contracts in oral form where the law requires a written contract (for example, a contract to sell land) and those where performance would be against public policy (such as a contract—sometimes also considered a "void contract"—to pay an illegal gambling debt, or for sexual services, or for the delivery of illegal drugs).

4. Express Contract. Each party shows assent through words. For example, A asks B, "Will you pay me $10 for this hamburger?" and B says "I promise to pay you $10." B has an express contract with A to buy the hamburger for $10.

5. Implied Contract. One or both parties show assent through actions. For example, A asks B, "Will you pay me $10 for this hamburger?" and B says nothing but eats the hamburger. The law will imply a contract binding B to pay A $10 since B's eating of the hamburger will be taken as evidence of B's agreement to A's terms. Contracts can be "implied in fact" based on the course of the parties' dealings, or "implied in law," meaning forced on a party by the court.

6. Bilateral Contract (a promise for a promise). A contract in which each party is both a promisor (person making the promise) and a promisee (person receiving the promise) and each party accepts by making a promise. For example, A says to B "If you will take notes for me during the Contracts lecture, I will pay you $10," and B replies "I promise to take notes for you." A has made a promise to B to pay $10, and has received a promise from B. B has promised A to take notes, and has received a promise to be paid $10.

7. Unilateral Contract (a promise for an action). A contract in which only one party has made a promise and the other party accepts by action. A says to B, C and D that "If you will take notes for me during the Contracts lecture, I will pay you $10." B has not promised to take notes, so B is not under any obligation to do so. However, unless A takes action promptly to revoke the promise, if B does take the notes, A will usually be held to have made a unilateral contract with B and will be required to pay $10.

8. Executed Contract. A contract that has been fully performed by both parties.

9. Executory Contract. A contract that is still unperformed by one or both parties.

10. *Quasi*-Contract. A *quasi*-contract is actually not a contract, but a relationship that is treated "as if" (*quasi*, in Latin) it is a contract to prevent injustice. A *quasi*-contract

usually is found where there is neither an express nor an implied contract, but one party has clearly received something of value that should be paid for. For example, in the *Weichert* case below, Tackaberry was a real estate salesman employed by Weichert. The owner of a large property told Tackaberry in March that he wanted to sell, with the real estate sales commission to be paid by the buyer. Tackaberry notified Ryan, a real estate developer, of the fact that the property was for sale, and Ryan asked for more information. Tackaberry collected and gave Ryan information on the property's current leases, income, expenses, plans for its eventual development, tax and zoning. Tackaberry tried several times to get Ryan to sign a written agreement to pay Tackaberry a 10% sales commission, but Ryan refused to sign the commission agreement. Ryan kept telling Tackaberry that "10% was too much," and that he would discuss the commission later. Ryan never signed any commission agreement with Tackaberry. Tackaberry continued to participate in the sale by carrying documents between the parties and offering negotiating advice. Ryan offered to pay Tackaberry $75,000 in installments as a commission, and later offered $150,000 as a commission, but Tackaberry refused to accept anything other than 10% of the sale price (a commission expected to be $300,000). Ryan bought the property for $3 million. Weichert later sued Ryan for the amount of Tackaberry's sales commission.

Weichert Co. Realtors v. Ryan
608 A. 2d 280 (N.J. 1992)

Stein, J.

We consider two issues: whether Ryan and Tackaberry entered into an enforceable agreement, and, if not, whether Weichert is entitled to recover the reasonable value of Tackaberry's services on a theory of *quantum meruit*. A contract arises from offer and acceptance, and must be sufficiently definite "that the performance to be rendered by each party can be ascertained with reasonable certainty." Thus, if parties agree on essential terms and manifest an intention to be bound by those terms, they have created an enforceable contract. Where the parties do not agree to one or more essential terms, however, courts generally hold that the agreement is unenforceable.

In some circumstances, however, courts will allow recovery even though the parties' words and actions are insufficient to manifest an intention to agree. Recovery based on *quasi*-contract, sometimes referred to as a contract implied-in-law, "is wholly unlike an express or implied-in-fact contract in that it is 'imposed by the law for the purpose of bringing about justice without reference to the intention of the parties.'" Courts generally allow recovery in *quasi*-contract when one party has conferred a benefit on another, and the circumstances are such that to deny recovery would be unjust. *Quasi*-contractual liability "rests on the equitable principle that a person shall not be allowed to enrich himself unjustly at the expense of another."

Applying that principle, courts have allowed *quasi*-contractual recovery for services rendered when a party confers a benefit with a reasonable expectation of payment. That type of *quasi*-contractual recovery is known as *quantum meruit* ("as much as he deserves"), and entitles the performing party to recoup the reasonable value of services rendered.

Accordingly, a broker seeking recovery on a theory of *quantum meruit* must establish that the services were performed with an expectation that the beneficiary would pay for them, and under circumstances that should have put the beneficiary on notice that the plaintiff expected to be paid. Courts have allowed brokers to recover in *quantum meruit* when a principal accepts a broker's services but the contract proves unenforceable for lack of agreement on essential terms—for instance, the amount of the broker's commission. Thus, a broker who makes a sufficient showing can recover fees for services rendered even absent express or implied agreement concerning the amount of the fee.

Application of the foregoing principles to the transaction between Weichert and Ryan demonstrates that the record is insufficient to support a finding that Tackaberry and Ryan mutually manifested assent to the essential terms of the contract. First, Ryan never expressly assented to the terms of Tackaberry's offer. Although Ryan expressed interest in learning more about the Pitt property during the initial March phone call, neither his expression of interest nor his agreement to meet with Tackaberry to learn more about the transaction was sufficient to establish the "unqualified acceptance" necessary to manifest express assent. Moreover, Ryan refused to agree to the ten percent figure during the April 4th meeting, and thereafter consistently rejected that term. Thus, the parties never formed an express contract.

In our view, the circumstances surrounding their negotiations did not justify Tackaberry's belief that Ryan had assented to the terms of his offer.

The record clearly establishes, however, that Tackaberry is entitled to recover in *quantum meruit* for the reasonable value of his services. The trial court's factual finding that Tackaberry was the procuring cause of the sale is supported by substantial evidence. Further, the proofs adduced at trial firmly establish that Tackaberry furnished Ryan with information about the Pitt property with an expectation that Ryan would pay a brokerage fee, and Ryan himself admitted throughout the trial that he had always intended to compensate Tackaberry for his services. Given those circumstances, to deny Tackaberry compensation for services rendered would unjustly enrich Ryan and Saunders.

Accordingly, we remand to determine the reasonable value of Tackaberry's services. By remanding, we do not imply that the reasonable value of Tackaberry's services is less than ten percent of the purchase price, nor do we imply any view concerning the value of such services. The commission amount should be determined on the basis of proofs tending to show the reasonable value of Tackaberry's services, including evidence of customary brokers' fees for similar transactions.

* * *

Topics for Further Discussion

1. What should Tackaberry have done to protect his 10% commission?

2. Why do courts recognize *quasi*-contracts, and what are the policy justifications for the doctrine of *quantum meruit*?

Elements of an Enforceable Contract

American courts do not wish to be involved in the enforcement of every statement made by one person to another, even if that person did not intend to be bound by the statement or did not know what he was saying. As a result, American courts have developed certain tests to determine whether the parties intended to form a legally binding relationship. The

Restatement § 17 summarizes the tests as "… the formation of a contract requires a bargain in which there is a manifestation of mutual assent to the exchange and a consideration." Manifestation of mutual assent is shown through the process of offer and acceptance.

Offer

An offer, according to Restatement § 24, is "the manifestation of willingness to enter into a bargain, so made as to justify another person in understanding that his assent to that bargain is invited and will conclude it." An offer must fulfill certain requirements. It must be communicated to the recipient of the offer ("offeree") by the offer maker ("offeror") or the offeror's authorized agent. If A offers to pay $10 for a translation of a document into the Sanskrit language, and B happens to have made such a translation without having heard of A's offer, B is not entitled to the $10 until such time as A's offer is communicated to B, and B accepts the offer. The offeror must intend to be bound; as Restatement § 2 explains, "[a] promisor manifests an intention if he believes or has reason to believe that the promisee will infer that intention from his words or conduct." If A and B are diamond dealers and on April Fool's Day (April 1st, a day for jokes), A says to B "I will sell you this $1 million diamond for only $10," most courts would not enforce the promise because B should know that A was only joking and had no intention of selling a valuable diamond for $10. However, if A is a diamond dealer and C is an ordinary customer who comes into A's shop on April 1st and says "I need to buy a diamond for a wedding ring and I know nothing about diamonds," and A offered to sell C the diamond for $10, a court might enforce the bargain after concluding that C would not understand the joke and that A should have understood that C would believe the offer to be genuine.

An offer that has terminated no longer creates a contract if accepted. An offer may terminate in a number of ways. The offeror may revoke the offer if the revocation is communicated to the offeree before acceptance. If the offer invites acceptance by performance that necessarily takes time, for example A tells B "I will pay you $10 to keep my car in your garage for thirty days," at common law A could revoke his offer at any time, even if B had kept the car in the garage for twenty-nine days. Normally, B would get nothing because B had not completely performed the contract, but, under the Restatement § 45, the offeree in this situation is given the option of completing the contract as required and holding the offeror to his promise. Offers may also terminate due to a lapse of time, either after a specified period of time or following a "reasonable" period of time after which the offer is no longer valid. The subject of the offer may have been destroyed before the offer is accepted, or if a person is the subject of the offer (as is the case in most Hollywood contracts), that person may die before the offer is accepted. It may also become illegal to perform the action that is the subject of the offer.

An offer must also have definite essential terms, such as price, the time of payment or delivery or performance, the quantity, and when it is not obvious from the circumstances, such terms as the identity of the offeree, the nature and duration of the work, and the subject matter of the contract. At common law, courts refused to enforce as contracts promises between parties where such key terms as price and quantity were unclear because it was felt there was no mutual assent to terms. The UCC, however, is influenced by the way businessmen actually contract: at least among parties that have done business before, or are in the same line of business, price and quantity are sometimes taken for granted based on business usage. The UCC allows certain contracts to be enforced, even if the price term is open or the quantity is not specified, so long as the party seeking enforcement is acting in "good faith." The term "good faith" is defined in UCC § 2-103 to mean, in the case of a person who regularly deals in the type of merchandise at issue (i.e., a "merchant") "honesty in fact and the observance of reasonable commercial standards of fair dealing in the trade." UCC § 2-305 and § 2-306 provide:

2-305. Open Price Term.

(1) The parties if they so intend can conclude a contract for sale even though the price is not settled. In such a case the price is a reasonable price at the time for delivery if

(a) nothing is said as to price; or

(b) the price is left to be agreed by the parties and they fail to agree; or

(c) the price is to be fixed in terms of some agreed market or other standard as set or recorded by a third person or agency and it is not so set or recorded.

(2) A price to be fixed by the seller or by the buyer means a price for him to fix in good faith.

(3) When a price left to be fixed otherwise than by agreement of the parties fails to be fixed through fault of one party, the other may at his option treat the contract as cancelled or himself fix a reasonable price.

(4) Where, however, the parties intend not to be bound unless the price be fixed or agreed and it is not fixed or agreed, there is no contract. In such a case the buyer must return any goods already received or if unable so to do must pay their reasonable value at the time of delivery and the seller must return any portion of the price paid on account.

2-306. Output, Requirements and Exclusive Dealings.

(1) A term which measures the quantity by the output of the seller or the requirements of the buyer means such actual output or requirements as may occur in good faith, except that no quantity unreasonably disproportionate to any stated estimate or in the absence of a stated estimate to any normal or otherwise comparable prior output or requirements may be tendered or demanded.

It often happens that one party tells the other party "I'm interested if we can agree on key terms." For example, A offers to sell his car for "$1,000 or best offer" and B tells A "I'm interested if we can agree on the price and if you will include the spare tire in the price." A more formal version would be the "letter of intent" through which one party tells another party that there is interest in concluding a contract, provided the parties can agree on terms. At common law, these statements would not be considered mutual assent creating a contract, but merely an unenforceable "agreement to agree" in which key terms, such as price and items included, have not been decided. However, in major commercial negotiations, the early "letter of intent" often leads to preparations, negotiations, and decisions that may involve substantial expense. If the "deal" succeeds, the contract may allocate expenses leading up to the contract, but, if the negotiations are not successful, one or both parties may look for some way to get back the wasted expenses. In the case below, when Venture's negotiations with ZDS collapsed, Venture tried to get back the money it had spent developing "an agreement to agree."

Venture Assoc. Corp. v. Zenith Data Sys. Corp.

96 F. 3d 275 (7th Cir. 1996)

Posner, C.J.

One of the most difficult areas of contract law concerns the enforceability of letters of intent and other preliminary agreements, and in particular the subset of such agreements that consists of agreements to negotiate toward a final contract. When if ever are such agreements enforceable as contracts? If they are enforceable, how is a breach to be determined? Is "breach" even the right word? Or is the proper rubric "bad faith"? Could the duty of good faith negotiation that a letter of intent creates be a tort duty rather than a contract duty, even though created by a contract? And can the victim of bad faith ever get more than his reliance damages? These questions lurk on or just beneath the surface of the principal appeal, which is from a judgment by the district court, after a bench trial, finding that the defendant had not acted in bad faith and was not liable for any damages to the plaintiff.

The defendant, Zenith Data Systems Corporation (ZDS), owned Heath Company. Heath was losing money, and in 1990 ZDS decided to sell it. ZDS hired an investment banker to find someone who would buy Heath at ... $11 million.... One of the prospects that the investment banker found was the plaintiff, Venture Associates Corporation. Apparently the investment banker did not conduct a credit check of Venture. Instead he relied on a representation by Venture that its most recent acquisitions had been of companies with revenues of $55 and $97 million.

On May 31, 1991, Venture sent a letter to the investment banker, for forwarding to ZDS, proposing to form a new company to acquire Heath for $5 million in cash, a $4 million promissory note, and $2 million in preferred stock of the new company—a total of $11 million, the price ZDS was seeking. The letter stated that it was "merely a letter of intent subject to the execution by Seller and Buyer of a definitive Purchase Agreement (except for the following paragraph of this letter, which shall be binding ...) and does not constitute a binding obligation on either of us." The following paragraph stated that "this letter is intended to evidence the preliminary understandings which we have reached regarding the proposed transaction and our mutual intent to negotiate in good faith to enter into a definitive Purchase Agreement, and ZDS hereby agrees that, pending execution of a definitive Purchase Agreement and as long as the parties thereto continue to negotiate in good faith," ZDS shall not "solicit, entertain, or encourage" other offers for Heath or "engage in any transaction not in the ordinary course of business which adversely affects" Heath's value.

The letter invited ZDS to sign it. ZDS refused, but did write Venture on June 11 stating that "we are willing to begin negotiations with Venture Associates for the acquisition of the Heath Business based in principle on the terms and conditions outlined in" Venture's May 31 letter. The next day, Venture wrote ZDS accepting the proposal in the June 11 letter.

Let us pause here and ask what if any enforceable obligations were created by this correspondence. The use of the words "in principle" showed that ZDS had *not* agreed to any of the terms in Venture's offer. That construal is reinforced by Venture's statement in its letter that the only binding obligation that ZDS's signing the letter would create would be an obligation of both parties to negotiate in good faith and, on ZDS's part, a further obligation not to entertain other offers or strip Heath of its assets—obligations that might be thought in any event entailed by the concept of good faith but which Venture thought useful to spell out. When last this case was before us, on appeal from an earlier decision, we held that the exchange of letters had established a binding agreement to negotiate in good faith toward the formation of a contract of sale.

We therefore have no occasion to revisit the determination on this appeal, though we are mindful of the powerful argument that the parties' undertakings were too vague to be judicially enforceable … or, if not, that the proper rubric for determining enforceability in such a case is not contract but promissory estoppel. But interpreting Illinois law, we have held that agreements to negotiate toward the formation of a contract are themselves enforceable as contracts if the parties intended to be legally bound.

The process of negotiating multimillion dollar transactions, like the performance of a complex commercial contract, often is costly and time-consuming. The parties may want assurance that their investments in time and money and effort will not be wiped out by the other party's foot dragging or change of heart or taking advantage of a vulnerable position created by the negotiation. Suppose the prospective buyer spends $100,000 on research, planning, and consultants during the negotiation, money that will have bought nothing of value if the negotiation falls through, while the seller has spent nothing and at the end of the negotiation demands an extra $50,000, threatening to cancel the deal unless the buyer consents. This would be an extortionate demand, and … parties to a negotiation would want a contractual remedy. But they might prefer to create one in the form of a deposit or drop fee (what in publishing is called a "kill fee"), rather than rely on a vague duty to bargain in good faith. That is one reason why the notion of a legally enforceable duty to negotiate in good faith toward the formation of a contract rests on somewhat shaky foundations, though some contracts do create such a duty, which shows that some business people want it.

In the prior round of appeals Venture's principal argument, which this court rejected, was that the parties' exchange of nonidentical contract drafts during the negotiation period had created a binding contract on the terms, specifically the $11 million sale price, in Venture's letter of May 31. The argument failed because of the "mirror image" rule; neither party had accepted the terms in the other party's offer. Venture continues to insist that it should be awarded damages equal to the difference between the $11 million price in the letter of May 31 and the current value of Heath … Does this mean that Venture is treating the letter of intent as the contract of sale? It does not. Damages for breach of an agreement to negotiate may be, although they are unlikely to be, the same as the damages for breach of the final contract that the parties would have signed had it not been for the defendant's bad faith. If, quite apart from any bad faith, the negotiations would have broken down, the party led on by the other party's bad faith to persist in futile negotiations can recover only his reliance damages—the expenses he incurred by being misled, in violation of the parties' agreement to negotiate in good faith, into continuing to negotiate futilely. But if the plaintiff can prove that had it not been for the defendant's bad faith the parties would have made a final contract, then the loss of the benefit of the contract is a consequence of the defendant's bad faith, and, provided that it is a foreseeable consequence, the defendant is liable for that loss—liable, that is, for the plaintiff's consequential damages. The difficulty … is that since by hypothesis the parties had not agreed on *any* of the terms of their contract, it may be impossible to determine what those terms would have been and hence what profit the victim of bad faith would have had. Bad faith is deliberate misconduct, whereas many breaches of "final" contracts are involuntary— liability for breach of contract being, in general, strict liability. It would be a paradox to place a lower ceiling on damages for bad faith than on damages for a perfectly innocent breach, though a paradox that the practicalities of proof may require the courts in many or even all cases to accept.

After Venture's confirmatory letter of June 12, the parties negotiated for six months. At the end of that time, with no sale contract signed, ZDS broke off the negotiations on the ground that Venture was refusing to furnish third-party guaranties of its post-closing financial obligations (namely to pay the $4 million promissory note and to honor the terms of the preferred stock) and agree to certain post-closing price adjustments. Early in the negotiations ZDS had asked Venture for financial information, but it had then abandoned the demand, for a time at least, content it seemed with the representations of acquisition prowess that Venture had made to the investment banker. The district judge found that as the negotiations looking to a final sale contract continued, ZDS became anxious about Venture's financial solidity and renewed its request for financial information ...

The price adjustments that ZDS demanded were of two types: adjustments reflecting an increase in the value of Heath's inventory since the onset of negotiations, and adjustments reflecting changes in the estimated size of a debt owed ZDS and that the buyer, Venture, was to pay. This would have entailed, under ZDS's calculations, an increase in the contract price from $11 million to $14 million.

Venture argues that since the letter of intent—its May 31 letter, which ZDS accepted in principle—made no reference to third-party guaranties or contract-price adjustments, ZDS exhibited bad faith by insisting on these terms to the point of impasse. This argument overlooks the difference between an agreement to negotiate a contract and the contract to be thrashed out in those negotiations. The agreement to negotiate does not contain the terms of the final agreement. Otherwise it would *be* the final agreement. A preliminary agreement might contain closed terms (terms as to which a final agreement had been reached) as well as open terms, and thus be preliminary solely by virtue of having some open terms. The parties would be bound by the closed terms. There were no such terms here.

Venture has another argument—that ZDS decided to pull out after the negotiations began because Heath's fortunes began to improve, and to this end imposed new conditions that it knew Venture would not accept. Since ZDS had not agreed on the sale price, it remained free to demand a higher price in order to reflect the market value of the company at the time of actual sale. Self-interest is not bad faith. Not having locked itself into the $11 million price, ZDS was free to demand as high a price as it thought the market would bear, provided that it was not trying to scuttle the deal, or to take advantage of costs sunk by Venture in the negotiating process. The qualification is vital. If the market value of Heath rose, say, to $25 million, ZDS would not be acting in bad faith to demand that amount from Venture even if it knew that Venture would not go so high. ZDS would be acting in bad faith only if its purpose in charging more than Venture would pay was to induce Venture to back out of the deal.

Given that the price term was open, moreover, it is hard to see why ZDS would *want* to bust the deal by insisting on a ridiculously high price or on third-party guaranties that it didn't really want. It could, as we have just pointed out, set a price that reflected Heath's current market value without violating the agreement to negotiate in good faith. Having done so it would presumably be delighted to sell to Venture—because, so far as the record discloses, no other seriously interested prospective purchaser for Heath had appeared during the period of negotiations, and (the district judge could find without committing a clear error) nothing happened during the period of negotiations to make ZDS decide to keep Heath—provided, of course, that Venture was financially responsible. As Venture's financial responsibility was in question, and was an important consideration because this was not a cash purchase, ZDS did not exhibit bad faith in insisting on the protection that a guaranty by a financially responsible third party would provide. Venture argues that since ZDS did not demand a guaranty in its "in principle" letter, it agreed to do without one. But this argument, if accepted, would turn the agreement to negotiate into an agreement with some closed terms (such as, no guaranties) and some open ones. It would no longer be a simple agreement to negotiate; it would be an agreement to the closed terms plus an agreement to negotiate toward a resolution of the open ones.

Cudahy, J., concurring

As a matter of policy, I think it is undesirable to force agreement on parties under threat of a bad faith finding and subsequent imposition of consequential damages, the same sanction as would issue from actual agreement. Freedom not to contract should be protected as stringently as freedom to contract. The present case is an excellent example of how preliminary negotiations may be pyramided into a demand indistinguishable from a claim for breach of contract.

* * *

Topics for Further Discussion

1. Venture and ZDS's advisors were professionals in negotiating the sale of a business. Should "an agreement to agree" have been enforced in this situation? Should an "agreement to agree" ever be enforced as a contract?

2. When might a letter of intent give rise to an enforceable obligation?

Acceptance

The offeree's intent to be bound to a contract is shown by his acceptance of the offer. An offer that requires a promise to be accepted is deemed to be accepted when the offeree communicates acceptance to the offeror. Common law applied the "mailbox rule." When an acceptance or rejection is mailed to the offeror, an acceptance is effective when the acceptance is put in the mailbox and a rejection is effective when it is received by the offeror. The common law required contracts for the performance of an act to be accepted by completing the act. The Restatement § 30(2) provides that "unless otherwise indicated by the language or the circumstances, an offer invites acceptance in any manner and by any medium reasonable in the circumstances."

Silence as Acceptance

Suppose an offeree does not accept or reject an offer, or make a counter-offer, but some time later demands that the offeror perform as promised. Can silence ever be a form of acceptance? The common law rule is that an offeree is not required to reply to an offer, and that silence is not acceptance because it does not communicate acceptance to the offeror. There are several exceptions. If the offeree says nothing but takes the benefit of the item or services offered, the offeree will typically be held to have accepted the offer. To take a previous example, if the menu at A's restaurant offers a hamburger for $10, and B orders the hamburger and eats it, then B will be held to have accepted A's offer of a hamburger for $10. If the offeree and the offeror have had previous dealings, the offeree may accept without notifying the offeror. For example, every week A brings B dirty laundry, and B washes the laundry and hands it to A in return for $10. If A gives some dirty laundry to B, B does not have to tell A "once again I will wash your laundry for $10" or immediately wash the laundry. B can wash the laundry at any time in the next week and demand the usual $10 when A comes to pick up the laundry. Another exception occurs if the offeree does any act inconsistent with the offeror's ownership of the property and the offeror decides to hold the offeree to the bargain. For example, A tells B: "You can have my yellow sports car for $1,000." B does not reply, but when A is away, B paints the sports car red. A may be able to require B to purchase the sports car for $1,000.

Battle of the Forms

An offeree terminates his power of acceptance by rejecting the offer. At common law, an acceptance had to be the "mirror image" of the offer. Any change in the terms was viewed by the courts as a rejection of the offer, terminating the offeree's right to enforce the contract, and a counter-offer to the offeror. Unless the offeror accepted the counter-offer, no contract resulted. A party was free to ask for clarification of the original offer, but not to suggest variations in the terms of the offer. The Restatement § 39(c) continues the common law rule that a counter-offer is a rejection, but allows an offeree to state that he is holding the offer "under advisement" without that statement being seen as a rejection. To illustrate, A offers to sell B his book for $10, with the offer to remain open for thirty days. B replies: "I am keeping your offer under advisement, but if you want to make some money at once, I will give you $8 for the book." A does not reply and does not withdraw the offer. B can still accept A's offer for $10 (or hand over $10 to A) within the original thirty days and enforce a contract to sell the book.

Businesses often deal with their suppliers based on standard printed forms, such as purchase orders and order acceptances. These forms typically have variable terms on one side, such as the delivery date, identity, quantity and price of items ordered, and have preprinted contract terms (sometimes referred to as "boiler plate" because of their broad coverage) on the other side. A business may order a box of pencils on its own standard form, with the preprinted portion of the form specifying payment in ninety days. The pencil supplier may accept the order by confirming on its own standard form, which specifies payment in thirty days. At common law, there was no contract because the pencil supplier seemed to have rejected the ninety day payment term and counter-offered with a thirty day payment term. However, in most business situations, what actually happens is that the customer expects a box of pencils to arrive, the pencil supplier does in fact ship the pencils, the pencil supplier sends a bill to the customer specifying payment in thirty days, and the customer pays the bill in its usual ninety days. In other words, in most cases, the supplier and the customer do not pay too much attention to what their lawyers have put into the printed forms, or the fact that the terms of the forms are different. It is only when there is a major dispute that each side looks to the "fine print" of their forms and tries to determine which party's form can be seen as the last counter-offer that was accepted to win "the battle of the forms." Unlike the common law, the UCC recognizes that at least "between merchants" (dealers or professionals in a certain line of business), the parties intend to conclude a contract even if one side does not reply with a mirror image acceptance of the other's terms. The UCC provides that, for such contracts, the terms will be those on which the parties agree plus those supplied by the general provisions of the UCC:

2-207. Additional Terms in Acceptance or Confirmation.

(1) A definite and seasonable expression of acceptance or a written confirmation which is sent within a reasonable time operates as an acceptance even though it states terms additional to or different from those offered or agreed upon, unless acceptance is expressly made conditional on assent to the additional or different terms.

(2) The additional terms are to be construed as proposals for addition to the contract. Between merchants such terms become part of the contract unless:

(a) the offer expressly limits acceptance to the terms of the offer;

(b) they materially alter it; or

(c) notification of objection to them has already been given or is given within a reasonable time after notice of them is received.

(3) Conduct by both parties which recognizes the existence of a contract is sufficient to establish a contract for sale although the writings of the parties do not otherwise establish a contract. In such case the terms of the particular contract consist of those terms on which the writings of the parties agree, together with any supplementary terms incorporated under any other provisions of this Act.

Defects in Mutual Acceptance

In order to form a contract, mutual acceptance must be (a) voluntary and (b) knowing. Acceptance is not voluntary if it is accompanied by certain improper actions. Acceptance under duress is invalid. Duress is force, and it includes physical duress, such as holding a gun to a person's head, and mental duress, such as threatening economic or emotional harm unless a contract is signed. Contracts concluded under duress are voidable. If one party abuses a confidential relationship with a less experienced or weaker party, there is undue influence. A contract concluded as the result of undue influence is voidable by the weaker party. Confidential relationships that could result in undue influence include those between a parent and a child, an attorney and a client, a doctor and a patient, the clergy and a penitent, a trustee and his or her beneficiary, and a husband and a wife. Fraud is the knowing misstatement of a material fact in order to induce reliance by the other party. In order to commit fraud, a party must know that it is not telling the truth, that its statement concerns a fact and not an opinion, and that the fact is likely to induce the other party to conclude the contract. Fraud "in the execution" means that one party lies about the document being executed, e.g. A tells B to sign a "receipt" and then gives B a contract to sign, which B signs without further inspection. Fraud in the execution is voidable because one party did not intend to contract at all. Fraud "in the inducement" means that one party lies about a factor that motivates the other party to enter into the contract. A, a car dealer, tells B that the Volkswagen in A's showroom was owned by rock singer Elvis Presley, when A knows that Elvis never owned the car and it is worth only $10. B pays A $1,000 for "Elvis Presley's car." Fraud in the inducement is voidable, so B can keep the car for $1,000 or cancel the transaction (and probably receive additional damages for fraud).

Contracts are often used to allocate risks: One party thinks a certain outcome is likely, the other party thinks a different outcome is unlikely, and the two parties bargain to determine who will bear the risk of the outcome. If a dealer at a flea market offers a painting for $10 because he honestly thinks it is only worth $10, and a customer without any duty of disclosure to the dealer buys it thinking the painting is worth $100, the purchase for $10 is enforceable. Each party knew what was being sold and purchased, neither party made a misrepresentation, and the law does not require that each party profit equally from a contract. There are many variations, however, regarding which party makes the mistake and which party understands that the other party is making a mistake. The Restatement § 20 summarizes the effect of various combinations, with the results depending on which party was at fault:

20. Effect of Misunderstanding.

(1) There is no manifestation of mutual assent to an exchange if the parties attach materially different meanings to their manifestations and

(a) neither party knows or has reason to know the meaning attached by the other; or

(b) each party knows or has reason to know the meaning attached by the other.

(2) The manifestations of the parties are operative in accordance with the meaning attached to them by one of parties if

(a) that party does not know of any different meaning attached by the other, and the other knows the meaning attached by the first party; or

(b) that party has no reason to know of any different meaning attached by the other, and the other has reason to know the meaning attached by the first party.

Often it is amateurs that make a mistake, but not always. Experienced merchants in a trade, each of whom is so fixed on his own interests in the contract that he assumes the other party shares his interpretation, can also find themselves in an unfortunate situation as demonstrated by the following case.

Frigaliment Importing Co. v. B.N.S. Int'l Sales Corp.
190 F. Supp. 116 (S.D.N.Y. 1960)

Friendly, J.

The issue is, what is chicken? Plaintiff says 'chicken' means a young chicken, suitable for broiling and frying. Defendant says 'chicken' means any bird of that genus that meets contract specifications on weight and quality, including what it calls 'stewing chicken' and plaintiff pejoratively terms 'fowl'. Dictionaries give both meanings, as well as some others not relevant here. I have concluded that plaintiff has not sustained its burden of persuasion.

Two contracts are in suit. In the first defendant, a New York sales corporation, confirmed the sale to plaintiff, a Swiss corporation, of

U.S. Fresh Frozen Chicken, Grade A, Government Inspected, Eviscerated....

75,000 [pounds] 2½–3 lbs.... @ $33.00

25,000 [pounds] 1½–2 lbs.... @ $36.50

The second contract was identical save that only 50,000 [pounds] of the heavier 'chicken' were called for, the price of the smaller birds was $37 per 100 [pounds], and shipment was scheduled for May 30. When the initial shipment arrived in Switzerland, plaintiff found, on May 28, that the 2½–3 [pound] birds were not young chicken suitable for broiling and frying but stewing chicken or 'fowl'; indeed, many of the cartons and bags plainly so indicated. Protests ensued. Nevertheless, shipment under the second contract was made on May 29, the 2½–3 [pound] birds again being stewing chicken. Defendant stopped the transportation of these at Rotterdam.

Since the word 'chicken' standing alone is ambiguous, I turn first to see whether the contract itself offers any aid to its interpretation. Plaintiff says the 1½–2 [pound] birds necessarily had to be young chicken since the older birds do not come in that size, hence the 2½–3 [pound] birds must likewise be young. This is unpersuasive—a contract for 'apples' of two different sizes could be filled with different kinds of apples even though only one species came in both sizes.

Plaintiff's next contention is that there was a definite trade usage that 'chicken' meant 'young chicken.' Here there was no proof of actual knowledge of the alleged usage; indeed, it is quite plain that defendant's belief was to the contrary. In order to meet the alternative requirement, the law of New York demands a showing that 'the usage is of so long continuance, so well established, so notorious, so universal and so reasonable in itself, as that the presumption is that the parties contracted with reference to it, and made it a part of their agreement.'

When all the evidence is reviewed, it is clear that defendant believed it could comply with the contracts by delivering stewing chicken in the 2½–3 [pound] size. Defendant's subjective intent would not be significant if this did not coincide with an objective meaning of 'chicken.' Here it did coincide with one of the dictionary meanings, with at least some usage in the trade, with the realities of the market, and with what plaintiff's spokesman had said. Plaintiff asserts it to be equally plain that plaintiff's own subjective intent was to obtain broilers and fryers; the only evidence against this is the material as to market prices and this may not have been sufficiently brought home. In any event it is unnecessary to determine that issue. For plaintiff has the burden of showing that 'chicken' was used in the narrower rather than in the broader sense, and this it has not sustained.

* * *

Topics for Further Discussion

1. In contracts for unbranded commodities like frozen chicken, where the quality of items can vary within a commercial term, it is good business practice to require that the commodities conform to a clear standard, or that they be inspected by a third party according to rules determined by the contract parties. What could the plaintiff have done to avoid the problem in the *Frigaliment Chicken* case?

2. What are the rules of interpretation that Judge Friendly reviews in his search for the meaning of the word "chicken"?

Consideration

We have examined one of the two requirements for a bargain to be considered a contract, the requirement of mutual assent. Mutual assent is required in both civil law and common law contracts, but the second requirement, that of "consideration," is unique to Anglo-American common law. Consideration is an indicator that the parties intended to be bound, and is used by common law courts to try to avoid having to guess about the mental state of the parties as they took various actions. It is said that courts will not examine the value of consideration, i.e., consideration is not a doctrine that asks whether or not the parties made a fair deal. The only question is whether there was a mutual exchange of value.

The Restatement § 71 characterizes consideration as a "bargained for performance or return promise." Courts developed the idea of consideration to determine whether to enforce promises in several recurring situations. One situation is the "illusory promise," a promise that in fact promises nothing: A says to B "You may have this $10 until I need it back." B promises to pay C using A's $10, but before B can pay, A takes the $10 back. B is unable to pay C, so C sues B and B sues A for breach of promise. A second situation is the promise to make a gift: A says to B "You are my favorite nephew, and so I will give you $10 on your birthday," but A does not give $10 to B on B's birthday and B sues. A third situation is a promise in exchange for performing a "pre-existing duty." In the classic case, when a ship was in the middle of the ocean, the sailors refused to continue to do the agreed work unless their wages were increased. The captain had no choice but to agree to the sailors' demands at sea, but once the ship returned to port, the employer refused to pay the amount of the increase agreed to at sea. The sailors sued for their extra wages. In the above situations, courts have traditionally refused to enforce illusory promises, gifts and bargains based on pre-existing duty due to lack of consideration. The following two cases illustrate variations on the nature of consideration. In *Hamer v. Sidway*, William E. Story is the uncle, William E. Story 2d is his nephew, Hamer received the right to pursue the nephew's claim, and Sidway administered the uncle's money. In the case of *In re Greene*, a millionaire went bankrupt and was sued by his mistress for the lavish promises of support he made to her during the "Roaring Twenties."

Hamer v. Sidway
27 N.E. 256 (N.Y. 1891)

Parker, J.

The trial court found "on the 20th day of March, 1869, William E. Story agreed to and with William E. Story, 2d, that if he would refrain from drinking liquor, using tobacco, swearing, and playing cards or billiards for money until he should become 21 years of age then he, the said William E. Story, would at that time pay him, the said William E. Story, 2d, the sum of $5,000 for such refraining, to which the said William E. Story, 2d, agreed," and that he "in all things fully performed his part of said agreement."

The defendant contends that the contract was without consideration to support it, and, therefore, invalid. He asserts that the promisee by refraining from the use of liquor and tobacco was not harmed but benefited; that that which he did was best for him to do independently of his uncle's promise, and insists that it follows that unless the promisor was benefited, the contract was without consideration. "A valuable consideration in the sense of the law may consist either in some right, interest, profit or benefit accruing to the one party, or some forbearance, detriment, loss or responsibility given, suffered or undertaken by the other." Courts "will not ask whether the thing which forms the consideration does in fact benefit the promisee or a third party, or is of any substantial value to anyone. It is enough that something is promised, done, forborne or suffered by the party to whom the promise is made as consideration for the promise made to him."

Now, applying this rule to the facts before us, the promisee used tobacco, occasionally drank liquor, and he had a legal right to do so. That right he abandoned for a period of years upon the strength of the promise of [the uncle] that for such forbearance he would give him $5,000. We need not speculate on the effort which may have been required to give up the use of those stimulants. It is sufficient that [the nephew] restricted his lawful freedom of action within certain prescribed limits upon the faith of his uncle's agreement, and now having fully performed the conditions imposed, it is of no moment whether such performance actually proved a benefit to the promisor, and the court will not inquire into it.

* * *

In re Greene
45 F.2d 428 (S.D.N.Y. 1930)

Woolsey, J.

The claimant, a woman, filed in the sum of $375,700, based on an alleged contract, against this bankrupt's estate.

For several years, the bankrupt [Greene], a married man, had apparently lived in adultery with the claimant. He gave her substantial sums of money. He also paid $70,000 for a house on Long Island acquired by her, which she still owns.

Throughout their relations the bankrupt was a married man, and the claimant knew it. The claimant was well over thirty years of age when the connection began. She testified that the bankrupt has promised to marry her as soon as his wife should get a divorce from him; this the bankrupt denied.

The relations between them were discontinued in April 1926, and they then executed a written instrument under seal which is alleged to be a binding contract and which is the foundation of the claim under consideration. The bankrupt undertook (1) to pay to the claimant $1,000 a month during their joint lives; (2) to assign to her a $100,000 life insurance policy on his life and to keep up the premiums on it for life, the bankrupt to pay $100,000 to the claimant in case the policy should lapse for nonpayment of premiums; and (3) to pay the rent for four years on an apartment which she had leased.

It was declared in the instrument that the bankrupt had no interest in the Long Island house or in its contents, and that he should no longer be liable for mortgage interest, taxes, and other charges on this property.

The claimant on her part released the bankrupt from all claims which she had against him.

The preamble to the instrument recites as consideration the payment of $1 by the claimant to the bankrupt, "and other good and valuable considerations."

The bankrupt kept up the several payments called for by the instrument until August 1928, but failed to make payments thereafter.

The law is that a promise to pay a woman on account of cohabitation which has ceased is void, not for illegality, but for want of consideration. The consideration in such a case is past.

Here there was not any offspring as a result of the bankrupt's union with the claimant; there was not any seduction. There was not any past wrong for which the bankrupt owed the claimant.

The question, therefore, is whether there was any consideration for the bankrupt's promises, apart from the past cohabitation. It seems plain that no such consideration can be found, but I will review the following points emphasized by the claimant as showing consideration:

(1) The $1 consideration recited in the paper is nominal. It cannot seriously be urged that $1, recited but not even shown to have been paid, will support an executory promise to pay hundreds of thousands of dollars.

(2) "Other good and valuable considerations" are generalities that sound plausible, but the words cannot serve as consideration where the facts show that nothing good or valuable was actually given at the time the contract was made.

(3) It is said that the release of claims furnishes the necessary consideration. So it would if the claimant had had any claims to release. But the evidence shows no ... lawful claim. Release from imaginary claims is not valuable consideration for a promise. In this connection, apparently, the claimant testified that the bankrupt had promised to marry her as soon as he was divorced. Assuming that he did — though he denies it — the illegality of any such promise, made while the bankrupt was still married, is so obvious that no claim could possibly arise from it, and the release of such claim could not possibly be lawful consideration.

(4) The claimant also urges that by the agreement the bankrupt obtained immunity from liability for taxes and other charges on the Long Island house. The fact is that he was never chargeable for these expenses. It is absurd to suppose that, when a donor gives a valuable house to a donee, the fact that the donor need pay no taxes or upkeep thereafter on the property converts the gift into a contract upon consideration. The present case is even stronger, for the bankrupt had never owned the house and had never been liable for the taxes. He furnished the purchase price, but the conveyance was from the seller direct to the claimant.

(5) Finally, it is said that the parties intended to make a valid agreement.

A man may promise to make a gift to another, and may put the promise in the most solemn and formal document possible; but, barring exceptional cases, such, perhaps, as charitable subscriptions, the promise will not be enforced. The parties may shout consideration to the housetops, yet, unless consideration is actually present, there is not a legally enforceable contract.

What the bankrupt obviously intended in this case was an agreement to make financial contribution to the claimant because of his past cohabitation with her, and, as already pointed out, such an agreement lacks consideration.

The presence of the seal would have been decisive in the claimant's favor a hundred years ago. Then an instrument under seal required no consideration, or, to keep to the language of the cases, the seal was conclusive evidence of consideration. In New York, however, a seal is now only presumptive evidence of consideration ... This presumption was amply rebutted in this case, for the proof clearly shows, I think, that there was not in fact any consideration for the bankrupt's promise contained in the executory instrument signed by him and the claimant.

* * *

Topics for Further Discussion

1. Where there is no fraud or mistake, should courts enforce contracts in which one party has paid too much, or another party gets something valuable with little effort?

2. What if a parent promises to pay his son $5,000 if he refrains from smoking marijuana while away at college? Would this be an enforceable agreement? If not, how is it distinguishable from *Hamer v. Sidway*?

Consideration and the UCC

The UCC recognizes that merchants who deal with each other on a continuing basis often make offers that they hope will become contracts, but which in fact lack consideration. The UCC alters the common law by providing that a merchant may not arbitrarily withdraw an offer to buy or sell goods and claim that lack of consideration prevents the other party from enforcing the offer.

2-205. *Firm Offers.*

An offer by a merchant to buy or sell goods in a signed writing which by its terms gives assurance that it will be held open is not revocable, for lack of consideration, during the time stated or if no time is stated for a reasonable time, but in no event may such period of irrevocability exceed three months; but any such term of assurance on a form supplied by the offeree must be separately signed by the offeror.

Promissory Estoppel

It is one thing to state that consideration is required for a contract to be valid at common law. It is another thing to apply that rule rigidly in situations where one weaker party, thinking a contract had been made, has acted to his detriment, only to find out that lack of consideration prevented a promise from being enforced. To deal with recurring situations in which "injustice" would result from strictly applying the requirement of consideration, American courts have developed the doctrine of "promissory estoppel," meaning that a party is "estopped," or prevented, from arguing that his or her promise, on which the other party justifiably relied, is unenforceable. The following case discusses the requirements for promissory estoppel in a case in which homeowners (the mortgagor) relied on insurance protection from the bank that held their housing loan (the mortgagee), but the house burned down without insurance coverage.

Shoemaker v. Commonwealth Bank
700 A.2d 1003 (Pa. Super. Ct. 1997)

Johnson, J.

We are asked to determine whether a mortgagor who is obligated by a mortgage to maintain insurance on the mortgaged property can establish a cause of action in promissory estoppel based upon an oral promise made by the mortgagee to obtain insurance. We conclude that a mortgagee's promise to obtain insurance can be actionable on a theory of promissory estoppel.

Lorraine and Robert S. Shoemaker obtained a $25,000 mortgage on their home from Commonwealth Bank ("Commonwealth"). The mortgage agreement provided that the Shoemakers were required to "carry insurance" on the property. By January 1994, the Shoemakers had allowed the home-owners' insurance policy covering their home to expire. In 1995, the Shoemakers' home, still uninsured, was destroyed by fire.

The Shoemakers allege that Commonwealth sent a letter to them, dated January 20, 1994, that informed them that their insurance had been cancelled and that if they did not purchase a new insurance policy, Commonwealth might "be forced to purchase [insurance] and add the premium to [their] loan balance." The Shoemakers further allege that Mrs. Shoemaker received a telephone call from a representative of Commonwealth in which the representative informed her that if the Shoemakers did not obtain insurance, Commonwealth would do so and would add the cost of the premium to the balance of the mortgage. The Shoemakers assert that they assumed, based on the letter and phone conversation, that Commonwealth had obtained insurance on their home. They also contend that they received no further contact from Commonwealth regarding the insurance and that they continued to pay premiums as a part of their loan payments. Only after the house burned, the Shoemakers allege, did they learn that the house was uninsured.

Commonwealth, on the other hand, admits that it sent the letter of January 20, but denies the Shoemakers' allegations regarding the contents of the alleged conversation between its representative and Mrs. Shoemaker. Commonwealth also asserts that it elected to allow this coverage to expire on December 1, 1994, and that, by the letter dated October 25, 1994, it informed the Shoemakers of this fact and reminded them of their obligation under the mortgage to carry insurance on the property. The Shoemakers deny receiving any letter from Commonwealth regarding the insurance other than the letter dated January 20, 1994, that informed them that their policy had expired.

Mrs. Shoemaker argues that the trial court erred by granting summary judgment on their promissory estoppel claim. The doctrine of promissory estoppel allows a party, under certain circumstances, to enforce a promise even though that promise is not supported by consideration. To establish a promissory estoppel cause of action, a party must prove that: (1) the promisor made a promise that he should have reasonably expected would induce action or forbearance on the part of the promisee; (2) the promisee actually took action or refrained from taking action in reliance on the promise; and (3) injustice can be avoided only by enforcing the promise.

The first element of a promissory estoppel cause of action is that the promisor made a promise that he should reasonably have expected to induce action or forbearance on the part of the promisee. The Shoemakers have alleged that the bank promised to obtain insurance on their behalf and that it would add this cost to their mortgage payment. Mrs. Shoemaker testified in her deposition and swore in an affidavit that a representative from Commonwealth stated that the bank would acquire insurance if she did not and that she instructed the representative to take that action. Because the Shoemakers claim that Commonwealth's promise to obtain insurance was, essentially, conditioned upon the Shoemakers course of conduct, i.e., that Commonwealth would obtain insurance if they did not, we conclude that this evidence, if believed, would be sufficient to allow a jury to find that Commonwealth made a promise upon which it reasonably should have expected the Shoemakers to rely.

The second element of a promissory estoppel cause of action is that the promisee actually relied upon the promise. The Shoemakers allege that they actually relied upon Commonwealth's promise and, thus, failed to obtain insurance. In support of this allegation, Mrs. Shoemaker testified in her deposition and swore in her affidavit that she instructed Commonwealth's representative to acquire insurance on her behalf. We conclude that this evidence, if believed, would be sufficient to allow a jury to find that the Shoemakers relied upon Commonwealth's promise to obtain insurance.

The final element of a promissory estoppel cause of action is that injustice can be avoided only by enforcement of the promise. One of the factors that a court may consider in determining whether a promisee has satisfied this element is "'the reasonableness of the promisee's reliance.'" Mrs. Shoemaker testified that she and her husband received no communication from Commonwealth regarding their insurance after her conversation with a Commonwealth representative in early 1994. Commonwealth, on the other hand, asserts that it sent the Shoemakers letters informing them that their house would be uninsured after December 1, 1994. We conclude that this evidence is sufficient to create a genuine issue of material fact regarding the reasonableness of the Shoemakers' reliance. Accordingly, we hold that the trial court erred by granting summary judgment on the Shoemakers' promissory estoppel claim.

* * *

Topics for Further Discussion

1. It is said that "hard cases make bad law," meaning that courts sometimes change the law to help a sympathetic party and in so doing create a bad legal precedent that must be followed in later opinions. Is the doctrine of promissory estoppel an illustration of this legal proverb?

2. Who had the greatest interest in maintaining insurance on the house, the Shoemakers or Commonwealth? Can you see any circumstances under which the Shoemakers could have reasonably relied on the statements of Commonwealth?

Evidence of Contractual Terms

In most states of the United States, there are no procedural formalities required (such as placing a seal on the document or swearing to the document before a notary) to conclude a binding contract. This lack of formalities makes it easier for parties to try to regulate their conduct and to allocate risk and reward using contracts, but it often creates problems in determining exactly what the parties agreed to. American law has developed several methods of reviewing conflicting claims about the content of a contract.

In cases in which the parties disagree over the meaning of the contract, the courts first try to construe the contract as a whole, giving words their ordinary meaning unless it is clear the parties had some specialized meaning in mind. The past dealings between the parties, the course of performance, and the general definitions in the trade or industry are all relevant in defining contract terms. Handwritten corrections take precedence over preprinted terms. Ambiguities are construed against the drafter of the contract. As in the *Frigaliment* case above, the party that argues that a term ("chicken") has a narrower meaning ("broiler") than the general term (any type of chicken used in food) has the burden of proving that the contract meant the narrow meaning and not the general meaning. Sometimes contractual interpretation involves public policy questions, as when a consumer misunderstands a contractual term given a specialized meaning by a large company, or one party abuses its bargaining power over another party. Courts will often interpret contract terms so as to have reasonable outcomes rather than participate in enforcing contracts that violate public policy.

The Parol Evidence Rule

The parties often send each other many drafts and proposals before they actually sign a document, and may have said things that influenced their decision to sign. In order to limit the amount of conflicting evidence courts or juries must consider, and in order to encourage parties to be precise in their promises, judges have developed a rule that applies to written contracts that are "integrated." An "integrated" contract is one that expresses the entire agreement of the parties on the subject of the contract. If a written contract expresses the entire agreement of the parties, oral ("parol") or written evidence of agreements prior to or contemporaneous with the written agreement will not be admitted to either clarify or change the meaning of the contract. In other words, if a contract contains the standard "merger clause" that "this contract contains the entire agreement of the parties and supersedes all previous agreements; there are no other agreements on the subject matter herein," courts will not listen to a party's argument that prior to signing the contract there was agreement that a certain term meant something different than stated in the contract, or that an earlier contract on the same subject matter should govern. The parol evidence rule does not prevent evidence about the meaning of a contract term when, as in *Frigaliment,* it is not clear what the parties meant by the contract term "chicken." The parol evidence rule does not prevent the introduction of evidence (written or oral) that the contract was modified *after* signing. The parol evidence rule also does not bar a party's attempt to show that the contract is void or voidable due to duress, lack of consideration, or any other defect of contract formation. Its main purpose is to restrict the agreement of the parties to the "four corners" of their contract when the contract is unambiguous.

The Statute of Frauds

The "Act for the Prevention of Frauds and Perjuries" was a law passed by the English Parliament in 1677, and carried over, with some modification, into every U.S. state except Louisiana (which adopted French law). The purpose of the Statute of Frauds ("Statute") was to prevent cheating on contracts involving large amounts of money or major personal obligations. The Statute requires a "writing" as evidence of certain contracts in order for such contracts to be enforced. The writing does not have to be a formal contract; it can be a memo or a letter, or several documents, or the modification of an existing contract. The writing must identify the person obligated, identify the subject matter of the obligation, and contain some mark of acknowledgment, such as a signature or initials, from the person against whom enforcement is sought. Each state has slight variations on the types of contracts that are covered by the local version of the Statute, but generally include the following:

1. Contracts for the Sale of Goods Valued at $500 or More. Contracts for the sale of expensive "goods" must be evidenced by a writing satisfying the Statute. The UCC modifies the Statute to take account of common business practices, as follows:

2-201. *Formal Requirements; Statute of Frauds.*

(1) Except as otherwise provided in this section a contract for the sale of goods for the price of $500 or more is not enforceable by way of action or defense unless there is some writing sufficient to indicate that a contract of sale has been made between the parties and signed by the party against whom enforcement is sought or by his authorized agent or broker. A writing is not insufficient because it omits or incorrectly states a term agreed upon but the contract is not enforceable under this paragraph beyond the quantity of goods shown in such writing.

(2) Between merchants, if within a reasonable time a writing in confirmation of the contract and sufficient against the sender is received and the party receiving

it has reason to know its contents, it satisfies the requirements of subsection (1) against such party unless written notice of objection to its contents is given within 10 days after it is received.

(3) A contract which does not satisfy the requirements of subsection (1) but which is valid in other respects is enforceable

(a) if the goods are to be specially manufactured for the buyer and are not suitable for sale to others in the ordinary course of the seller's business and the seller, before notice of repudiation is received and under circumstances which reasonably indicate that the goods are for the buyer, has made either a substantial beginning of their manufacture or commitments for their procurement; or

(b) if the party against whom enforcement is sought admits in his pleading, testimony or otherwise in court that a contract for sale was made, but the contract is not enforceable under this provision beyond the quantity of goods admitted; or

(c) with respect to goods for which payment has been made and accepted or which have been received and accepted.

2. Contracts Exceeding One Year. A contract that by its own terms cannot be performed within one year from the date the contract was formed must be in a writing satisfying the Statute. The courts usually construe this requirement to mean that if a contract could conceivably be performed within one year, it is not subject to the Statute. For example, a contract to build a house to start January 1, 2011, and to end January 1, 2013, is subject to the Statute. A contract to build a house, starting January 1, 2011, is not subject to the Statute, even if it normally takes two years to build such a house, because the work could conceivably be finished within one year.

3. Contracts to Sell an Interest in Real Estate. An "interest in real estate" can include leases, mortgages, mineral rights, various other rights to use land, agreements to sell an ongoing business with the real estate it owns, and real estate agent's commission agreements. Since real estate contracts usually involve large amounts of money, and may affect future generations, the Statute requires that they be in a writing acknowledged by the party to be bound.

4. A Promise to Answer for the Debt of Another. Agreements to be a guarantor or a surety, or a co-signer of a debt obligation, must be made in a writing satisfying the Statute.

5. A Promise by an Executor or Administrator to Pay Expenses Out of Personal Funds. An executor or administrator is someone who takes care of the property of another, usually a dead person who has left debts, and who typically pays expenses related to that property out of the funds in their care, not out of their own pocket. The unusual situation in which someone claims that an executor or administrator agreed to pay the expenses of the deceased person's estate out of personal funds must be documented in a writing satisfying the Statute.

6. A Promise in Consideration of Marriage. If a person makes a promise to give someone money or property in return for marrying them, or for a promise to marry them, the promise must be documented in a writing satisfying the Statute to be enforced. Suppose A gives B an engagement ring and does not get a writing from B acknowledging that B received the ring in return for a promise to marry A. If B breaks off the engagement and does not return the ring, A is unlikely successfully to be able to sue B for the return of the ring unless A can somehow overcome the Statute of Frauds. Or, suppose B does marry A, but files to divorce A forty-eight hours later and demands half of A's property as a set-

tlement. A claims that B signed a pre-nuptial ("before the marriage") agreement limiting B's claims to just the engagement ring. A needs to satisfy the Statute in order to have the pre-nuptial agreement considered as evidence.

Remedies for Breach of Contract

Contract Damages vs. Tort Damages

A tortfeasor who injures another person may be liable for a large amount of damages in many different categories. Tort damages are not limited to the victim's actual expenses of medical care or repairing property: damages in tort may include pain and suffering, damage to reputation, loss of business or employment opportunities and other losses that the tortfeasor might not have foreseen. Contractual damages, however, are usually calculated based on the "expectation interest" of the party suffering a breach; that is, the aggrieved party's interest in having the benefit of his bargain by being placed in as good a position as he would have been in had the contract been fully performed. Punitive damages are allowed for torts, but not, at common law, for breach of contract without some accompanying tortious or criminal behavior.

The difference between tort damages and contractual damages is illustrated by what has become known to generations of law students as "The Case of the Hairy Hand," *Hawkins v. McGee*, 146 A. 641 (N.H. 1929). In this case, Dr. McGee promised to fix Hawkins' burned hand by grafting skin from Hawkins' chest onto the burned hand, and leading to "a hundred percent good hand." What Hawkins ended up with was a hand covered with the hair that had formerly grown on his chest. Hawkins sued Dr. McGee. The trial judge's instructions to the jury allowed the jury to consider two elements of damage: (1) pain and suffering due to the operation, and (2) positive ill effects of the operation upon the plaintiff's hand. McGee's lawyer objected to the jury instructions and appealed. The state supreme court ordered a new trial because the trial judge's instructions on damages for breach of contract were wrong. The court declared that "the true measure of the plaintiff's damage in the present case is the difference between the value to him of a perfect hand or a good hand, such as the jury found the defendant promised him, and the value of his hand in its present condition, including any incidental consequences fairly within the contemplation of the parties when they made their contract."

Limits on Contract Damages

Contractual damages are generally awarded as a sum of money equal to the loss in value to the injured party of the other party's failed or deficient performance, plus any other loss caused by the breach. However, damages to the injured party are reduced to the extent of any cost or other loss the injured party avoided by not having to perform his part of the bargain. In addition, the injured party cannot recover damages that he could have avoided without undue risk, burden or humiliation. The law imposes on the injured party the duty of "mitigation," that is, to try to reduce the damages. For example, B owns a restaurant. B thinks he will be able to sell wine to his customers for $10 per bottle on August 1st. On January 1st, B contracts with A to buy 1000 bottles of wine at $1 per bottle to be delivered not later than July 30th. On June 1st, A tells B that A will not be able to deliver any of the wine on time. B cannot just wait until August 1st, sue A for breach of contract, and expect to collect $9,000 (the expected revenue from the sale of 1,000 bottles at $10 minus the cost of 1000 bottles at $1). B must make efforts to "mitigate," e.g. to try to buy the wine elsewhere. If B can buy at least 100 bottles but must pay $5 per bottle to have them delivered on time, B can recover from A the extra profit he would have made had the price been $1 per bottle and the quantity 1000 bottles. B must make some reasonable effort, however, to obtain a substitute product rather than do nothing and try to recover the entire loss from A.

Suppose that on August 1st, an important restaurant critic visits B's restaurant in disguise. Since A has breached the contract to supply wine, there are only 100 bottles available that day, and the wine is gone before the restaurant critic can order some. The restaurant critic writes a negative review of B's restaurant, complaining that a top quality restaurant would never run out of wine. As a result, business at B's restaurant suffers a major decline after potential customers read the negative review. Can B sue A not just for the loss of profits per bottle of wine but also for the damage to the reputation of B's restaurant caused by A's breach of the contract?

The general rule is that A is liable only for damages from the breach that are "foreseeable." Losses are "foreseeable" because they are the probable result of the breach either in terms of common sense or business practice, or because the party in breach knew of special circumstances that would cause the loss. In the above example, if a wine supplier fails to deliver, it is common sense and ordinary business practice for the customer to buy the wine elsewhere, though possibly at a greater cost. Therefore, A would be liable for B's loss in buying the wine from another source. However, A would normally not be liable for the damage caused by the dissatisfied restaurant critic because this loss would normally not be foreseeable to A. On the other hand, if B told A: "You must make sure to deliver that wine not later than July 30th because I have an important restaurant critic coming August 1st and if the wine is not available he will give my restaurant a bad review," and A replied, "Don't worry about the restaurant critic, I'll get the wine to you in plenty of time," then A might be liable for additional losses due to the bad review being "foreseeable" to A as a consequence of late delivery.

Liquidated Damages

Suppose that A, a merchant, contracts with B for B to print an advertisement in the December 24th edition of B's newspaper. A thinks he will increase sales if his advertisement is seen in B's newspaper the day before Christmas. B thinks A's advertisement will be more profitable than others that could be placed in the same space. However, neither A nor B can determine with certainty how much business A would lose if the advertisement was not printed, or whether B could sell the space to another advertiser if A failed to pay the contractual amount. In this situation, the parties can agree at the time of contracting that a stated amount of money will be "liquidated damages," that is, an agreed sum that will compensate either party for breach of contract without the need to prove damages in detail. Liquidated damages will be enforced by a court if the amount set as liquidated appears reasonable given the anticipated loss and the difficulties of proof. However, an unreasonably high amount of liquidated damages may be unenforceable on public policy grounds as a penalty, particularly when one party had greatly superior bargaining power in negotiating the contract.

When Monetary Damages Are Inadequate

While the standard remedy for breach of contract is monetary damages, when money is inadequate to protect the injured party, courts may use other remedies. American courts may order a party to do what the party promised ("specific performance"), or forbid a party from breaching a contract ("injunction"), under pain of massive damages or imprisonment for contempt of court. The most common situation in which monetary damages are inadequate is one involving a unique item. For example, suppose A, an autograph dealer, contracts with B, a poster shop owner, to sell B for $100 the only known example of a poster for the movie *Modern Times* signed by the comedian Charles Chaplin. Later, A discovers that C will pay him $1000 for the same poster, so A tells B: "Sorry, but I have found a better buyer and will not sell you the poster." It would not help B to receive any amount of money, since B could not use the money to buy a similar poster; there is only one known example and A intends to sell it to C. In this situation, a court might order specific performance. A would be ordered to sell the poster to B, or would be enjoined (forbidden) from selling the poster to anyone but B. Specific performance is an equitable remedy, meaning that the party demanding the remedy must have acted "equitably" or in a fair manner. If, in the situation above, B had lied to A by saying, "Don't bother to contact my rival C for a competing offer, C died yesterday," so that A made the offer thinking B was the only immediate buyer, a court might not force a sale based on misrepresentation.

Occasionally neither money nor further performance can bring justice to the relationship between the contracting parties. Particularly when one party has partially performed, and the breaching party would be "unjustly enriched" by the breach, courts may order restitution, the act of restoring each party to their place before the breach. Restitution damages are not limited by the contract price. For example, suppose A is a famous person and B is an architect. B contracts to design and build a new garage for A for only $100. Normally, B would charge $1,000 to design and $1,000 to build a garage, but B wants the opportunity to say that "the new garage on A's property was built by my architecture firm." B thinks this will generate future business from other customers who can be charged the full price. B designs the garage as promised. but before B can begin work building the garage, A says "I've changed my mind. I will keep your design, but I will leave the garage as it is now. Here is $100 for your trouble. At this point, B cannot easily complete his contractual obligation to build the garage over A's opposition, but B has also not received one promised benefit of the contract, the ability to tell people that the new garage on A's property is his work. A has received a design work worth $1,000 in normal circumstances, but since B was paid the contractual amount of $100, B might not receive more in damages in a suit for breach of contract. In this situation, a court might order restitution. A would be ordered to restore to B the benefit of $1,000 worth of design services by paying to B the sum of $1,000 (the $100 already paid plus an additional $900). Restitution damages are another example of courts trying to prevent injustice when a party does not keep his part of the bargain.

Key Terms and Concepts

Consideration
Expectation Interest
Good Faith
Liquidated Damages
Mitigation
Parol Evidence Rule
Promissory Estoppel
*Quantum Merui*t
Restitution
Statute of Frauds

Chapter 7

Tort and Product Liability

*"The Tort Tax adds to the cost of everything we buy because businesses and manu-
facturers have to cover themselves and their employees—just in case they get sued
by a greedy personal injury lawyer."*

John Dennis Hastert (R), Speaker of the House 1999 to 2007

Tort law concerns the issue of when, and to what extent, a private party can be held legally responsible (liable) for injury caused to the person or property of another party by wrongful acts or omissions. It deals, in short, with the allocation of legal responsibility for private wrongs in society. This is the "when" part of the equation. The extent of the defendant's (called the "tortfeasor") liability can best be understood in terms of the remedies, usually in the form of monetary damages, for the harm or damage caused by the wrongful act or omission. Arguably, in tort law more than in any other branch of American law, the potential of receiving a large monetary award serves as a strong motivation for plaintiffs (and their lawyers) to sue. The law of tort is called upon continually to balance the social costs and benefits of preventing, and redressing, private harm. It is an area of law infused with fundamental issues of public policy revolving around the central question of who bears the loss. The "Tort Tax" referred to by former Speaker Hastert is an extreme way of suggesting that business (and, ultimately, the consumer) bears a large portion of the cost of the tort system.

Tort and Criminal Law Compared

The private nature of tort law sets it apart from criminal law, which is concerned with wrongs that are done to both individuals and society. There are three important consequences flowing from this distinction. First, one action or set of behaviors can be both criminal and tortious (i.e., being a tort) at the same time. A person who sets a dangerous trap, such as a gun attached to a trip wire, on his property to prevent intruders may be committing a crime under state law. At the same time, the individual may also be liable in tort for any damages sustained by a person who is injured by the dangerous trap, even if the injured person was trespassing on the tortfeasor's property and the property owner posted warnings. The reason behind this policy is clear. To allow a property owner to place the value of property over human safety would be an unacceptable social result. A child might not appreciate the risk involved even if warnings are posted, or someone might venture onto the property by accident or in response to an emergency. Society simply does not permit individuals to protect property with deadly force, especially when it can be mechanically applied without human thought or judgment.

Second, since criminal law is concerned with the redress of private and public wrongs, the victim does not control the prosecution of the legal action and cannot require the prosecutor to drop the case or to proceed in a certain fashion. The prosecutor represents the state first, which has an independent interest in punishing criminal behavior, and the victim second. A classic example of this is where an individual is arrested for spousal abuse. Even though the abused spouse may not want to press criminal charges against his or her mate, the prosecutor can nevertheless prosecute the abuser. The private nature of tort law, in contrast, would allow the injured party to forgo, settle, or drop a civil lawsuit at any time.

Third, in a criminal prosecution in the United States, the burden of proof remains at all times with the government, which must prove guilt "beyond a reasonable doubt." This is a fundamental rule in all criminal cases because a criminal prosecution brings the entire weight (police, prosecutors, etc.) and resources of the state to bear against the individual. Moreover, a guilty verdict could result in taking the life, liberty, and property of the defendant. In a private lawsuit for tort, the plaintiff and defendant stand on equal footing (although as a practical matter one of the parties may have significantly more money than the other), and the life and liberty of the defendant are not at stake. Thus, the plaintiff bears only the burden of proving the elements of a *prima facie* ("first view") case against the defendant by a "preponderance of the evidence," and the same burden can shift to the defendant with respect to showing the existence of a valid defense excusing, or mitigating, liability.

Elements of a Tort

Every tort has certain basic elements that must be proved by the plaintiff in order to establish the *prima facie* case. The elements will vary for each type of tort. The intentional tort of libel requires, for example, a showing that the defendant published false and defamatory information about the plaintiff causing harm to the good name of the plaintiff. If the party bringing the lawsuit cannot produce sufficient evidence to demonstrate each element of the *prima facie* case, the judge will dismiss the suit without the defendant having to produce any evidence in defense.

In broad terms, there are two classes of private wrongs: Intentional Torts and those based on negligence, known as Unintentional Torts. In addition, certain hazardous activities such as keeping wild animals, blasting, demolition, and transporting dangerous materials are based on strict liability. When reading the cases in this chapter, identify the elements of the tort being alleged keeping in mind that the outcome is highly dependent on the facts and circumstances of each case. The skill of the lawyer in establishing and presenting the facts in a manner favorable to the client is critical. Identify the material facts in each case and consider how the result might be different if one or more material facts were changed.

Intentional Torts

A *prima facie* case of intentional tort requires the plaintiff to show the following three elements: (1) an act; (2) an intention to so act; and (3) harm to the plaintiff that is causally related to the intentional act. The defendant tortfeasor will only be liable for an intentional tort if it is shown that he or she has exercised some measure of "volition" (or positive will) in performing the harmful act. For example, if A were to push B intentionally into C, A would satisfy the requirement of having performed a willful act both as to B and C, but B would not as to C. Person A might be liable to both B and C for damages suffered, whereas B would not be liable to C. On the other hand, if A's action resulted from an uncontrollable seizure because of an unknown medical condition, A would not be liable either to B or C because A's action would lack the necessary volition. If the medical condition is known to A, the situation might be different. For example, A voluntarily driving a car after taking medication known to produce drowsiness.

Intent comes in two varieties: specific and general. Specific intent exists when the tortfeasor intends the result that actually occurred. The case of A pushing B on purpose is an example of specific intent. However, if the tortfeasor does not actually intend the result, but knows with substantial certainty that the result will occur, then general intent is present. It is not necessary that the actor intend the actual harm that was suffered. Under our earlier example, if A intentionally pushes B and B knocks C down as a result, it is not a defense to A's liability that A did not intend for B to cause harm to C. Intent can be transferred when the tortfeasor intends to cause harm to one person but another person is injured instead. The rules of causation are substantially similar to those for unintentional torts taken up later.

Intentional torts can be divided into three broad categories. The first involves intentional torts to persons. These include: Battery (harmful or offensive contact to plaintiff); Assault (a reasonable fear of immediate harmful or offensive contact); False Imprisonment (confining or restraining the plaintiff); and Intentional Infliction of Emotional Distress (extreme or outrageous conduct by defendant intended to cause severe emotional distress).

The second category concerns intentional torts to property. Tort actions in this area include: Trespass to Land (physical invasion of plaintiff's real property); Trespass to Chattels (interference with plaintiff's right to possess movable property); and Conversion (interference with plaintiff's right of possession that deprives the property of use or value; in essence the civil version of the crime of theft).

Finally, there is a category of intentional torts involving harm to reputation and economic interests. This third category of intentional torts, especially those dealing with harm to the reputation of the defendant, often involve complex issues and competing interests relating to freedom of speech and press under the First Amendment. Examples of these kinds of intentional torts are: Defamation (publication of false information damaging the plaintiff's reputation); Invasion of Privacy (prying or intruding on the plaintiff's private matters); Publication of Private Facts (publishing information about plaintiff's private matters); Publication of Facts Putting Plaintiff in a False Light (publication of misleading information); Misrepresentation (using false, fraudulent or deceitful tactics to obtain a benefit from the plaintiff); Wrongful Institution of Legal Proceedings and Malicious Prosecution (bringing a frivolous lawsuit against the plaintiff); and Interference with Business Relations or Contract (inducing a third party to breach or terminate an existing contract with the plaintiff).

A number of defenses are available against an intentional tort claim. These include: Consent (express or implied); Self Defense, Defense of Others or Property; Reentry onto Land and Recapture of Chattels; Privilege (absolute and qualified), Necessity, and Discipline (applicable to parents, guardians, teachers, etc. who administer reasonable discipline to children under their supervision).

Informed Consent

The most commonly asserted defense to an intentional tort is consent. Consent must be informed before it can be a valid defense. "Informed consent" requires that the person be advised (1) in advance (2) of the specific risks being consented to (3) in a manner and to a level of detail that (4) can reasonably be understood by the person asked to give the consent. A general consent that does not provide adequate information about the risk may not be effective. Likewise, consent to one type of risk will not usually be transferred to another type of risk not covered by the consent. To protect themselves against claims based on a lack of informed consent, healthcare providers routinely require patients to sign written informed consent forms. These forms typically list every known risk associated with the medical procedures to be performed and acknowledge that the risks are understood and accepted by the patient. The informed consent form authorizes the physician (or someone under the direction of the physician) to take necessary action should something be discovered during surgery that is best treated while the patient is already under sedation and unable to give consent. After all, few patients would want to wake up in the recovery room of the hospital only to be asked to consent to a second operation.

The medical profession, in order to shield itself from Battery claims whenever lack of informed consent is alleged, has lobbied successfully in many states to have these claims treated as ordinary cases of medical malpractice. The following case provides a good overview of the issues involving informed consent and medical malpractice.

Lugenbuhl v. Dowling
701 So. 2d 447 (La. 1997)

Lemmon, J.

This is an action by a patient against his physician for damages allegedly caused by the doctor's failure to use surgical mesh, as requested by the patient, in repairing an incisional hernia. The principal issues before this court are (1) whether the doctor, in view of the patient's expressed desire that mesh be used in the surgery, properly informed the patient regarding the nature of the proposed procedure and its advisability and attendant risks with and without the use of mesh, and (2) whether plaintiff proved a causal connection between (a) either any lack of informed consent or the doctor's failure to use mesh and (b) the damages awarded for the subsequent additional surgery.

Facts

In November 1987, plaintiff consulted Dr. John Dowling, a general surgeon, to repair an intracostal incisional hernia (hereinafter referred to as the cardiac incisional hernia) that had developed from 1985 coronary bypass surgery.

Plaintiff had a history of hernia problems, having undergone three unsuccessful inguinal hernia repairs by another surgeon between 1963 and 1974 before the surgeon performed a successful procedure in 1975 using surgical mesh. Because of his prior experience, plaintiff expressed to Dr. Dowling in 1987 his desire that the required surgery be performed with mesh.

In preparation for the surgery, plaintiff signed a consent form which stated in pertinent part:

1) I hereby authorize and consent to Dr. Dowling, M.D., and such supervising physicians, surgeons, assistants of his or her choice, to perform upon myself the following surgical, diagnostic, medical procedure Repair incisional hernia with Mesh including any necessary and advisable anesthesia.

2) I understand the nature and purpose of this procedure to be Repair Incisional Hernia with Mersilene Mesh.

During the cardiac incisional hernia repair procedure, Dr. Dowling made the decision not to use mesh based on his intraoperative assessment of plaintiff's condition.

In May 1988, plaintiff developed a large herniated area in his abdominal region. This large herniated area included the site of the small cardiac incisional hernia repair performed by Dr. Dowling. Dr. C. Edward Foti surgically repaired the large herniated area, using mesh primarily because of the size of the hernia. Plaintiff subsequently developed a small incisional hernia at the site of the surgical drain placed in plaintiff's abdomen during the surgery performed by Dr. Foti. This small hernia was repaired by Dr. Foti using mesh.

Plaintiff filed this action against Dr. Dowling, asserting claims based on medical malpractice and on lack of adequate informed consent. Plaintiff alleged that Dr. Dowling's failure to use mesh to repair the cardiac incisional hernia in 1987 caused the subsequent herniation in 1988 and necessitated further surgery.

The jury rendered a verdict in favor of plaintiff for $300,000. Answering special interrogatories, the jury found that Dr. Dowling was liable for damages based both on medical malpractice and on failure to obtain informed consent.

Lack of Informed Consent Generally

The requirement of consent to medical treatment was initially based on the idea that a competent person has the right to make decisions regarding his or her own body. As Justice Cardozo stated in *Schloendorff v. Society of N.Y. Hosp.*, 105 N.E. 92, 93 (1914), "[e]very human being of adult years and sound mind has a right to determine what shall be done with his own body and a surgeon who performs an operation without his patient's consent commits an assault for which he is liable in damages."

After the early cases struggled with the concept of consent that may be implied from the circumstances, including the patient's silence, there was a gradual development of a duty imposed on doctors to disclose information to the patient in order to afford the patient the opportunity of making an informed choice about proposed medical procedures. Significant litigation ensued concerning the scope of the doctor's duty to provide informed consent.

In *Karl J. Pizzalotto, M.D., Ltd. v. Wilson*, 437 So.2d 859 (La.1983), the doctor, after conservatively treating the patient's lower abdominal pain, prescribed exploratory abdominal surgery (*laparotomy*) to determine the cause of the pain. The consent form signed by the patient listed "(1) Pelvic inflammatory disease, marked (2) *endometriosis*" as the diagnosis and "*Laparotomy-Lysis* of adhesions, Fulguration of *endometrioma*" as the recommended procedure. Although the doctor noted "probable *salpingo-oophorectomy*" (the surgical removal of the ovary and its fallopian tube) on the admission chart, he did not inform the patient, who desired to have children, of this probability.

During surgery, the doctor removed the patient's severely damaged reproductive organs, believing that the patient was sterile and that further pain would necessitate additional surgery. This court, concluding that the doctor removed the patient's reproductive organs without obtaining her implied or expressed consent to that operation, held that the doctor committed a battery and remanded the case to the court of appeal to determine the damages due for that tort.

While the early development of liability for failing to obtain informed consent was based on concepts of battery or unconsented touching, the imposition of liability in later cases has been based on breach of a duty imposed on the doctor to disclose material information in obtaining consent. Such a breach of duty by the doctor results in liability based on negligence or other fault. While perhaps the performance of a medical procedure without obtaining any kind of consent, in the absence of an emergency, technically constitutes a battery, liability issues involving inadequate consent are more appropriately analyzed under negligence or other fault concepts.

The Louisiana Legislature has also specified the theory of recovery in lack of informed consent claims as properly based on traditional fault theories, apparently to bring such claims under the Medical Malpractice Act. Pertinent to the present discussion, Subsection 1299.40 E(2)(a) provides:

> In a suit against a physician or other health care provider involving a health care liability or medical malpractice claim which is based on the failure of the physician or other health care provider to disclose or adequately to disclose the risks and hazards involved in the medical care or surgical procedure rendered by the physician or other health care provider, the only theory on which recovery may be obtained is that of negligence in failing to disclose the risks or hazards that could have influenced a reasonable person in making a decision to give or withhold consent.

We therefore reject battery-based liability in lack of informed consent cases (which include no-consent cases) in favor of liability based on breach of the doctor's duty to provide the patient with material information concerning the medical procedure.

Lack of Informed Consent in the Present Case

In support of his contention that Dr. Dowling is liable for damages based on lack of informed consent, plaintiff testified he repeatedly informed Dr. Dowling prior to his cardiac incisional hernia repair that he wanted the doctor to use mesh to close the wound, believing that three of his four prior inguinal hernia repairs had failed because mesh was not used. According to plaintiff, Dr. Dowling promised he would use mesh in the operation and noted the use of mesh on the consent form, and Dr. Dowling never told plaintiff of any risks involved in using mesh or that a decision whether to use mesh would be reserved until during surgery. Had Dr. Dowling told him the decision whether to use mesh would only be made during surgery, plaintiff asserted he would have sought another doctor. This testimony was corroborated by plaintiff's wife.

Dr. Dowling testified that he discussed the use of mesh with plaintiff and that its use was an option during surgery. The doctor stated he never committed to the use of mesh or promised it would be used, and if plaintiff had insisted on such a promise, he would have told plaintiff to find another surgeon. He believed plaintiff understood that mesh was an option and that Dr. Dowling would make the decision whether to use mesh according to the conditions found during the surgery. Dr. Dowling insisted that he included similar language in every consent form for hernia repairs, meaning that he was authorized to use mesh if he determined during the surgery that its use was required.

Plaintiff's wife testified that she asked Dr. Dowling immediately after the operation if he had used mesh, and he told her he had not "because I don't like it." This testimony was corroborated by her daughter. Plaintiff testified that when he asked Dr. Dowling about the decision not to use mesh, Dr. Dowling stated he had sutured the hernia repair in such a way that the sutures would not fail.

Dr. Dowling denied that he said he had used any special sutures or that he said the sutures would not fail. He also denied telling plaintiff's wife that he did not like to use mesh.

The jury apparently accepted plaintiff's testimony, corroborated by that of his wife and daughter, that the doctor agreed to plaintiff's steadfast demand for the use of mesh and simply disregarded that agreement during the surgery. The plain language of the written consent form clearly supports the jury's determination. The term "incisional hernia repair" was sufficient to authorize that surgical repair using normal procedures within the surgeon's judgment; there was no necessity to use the words "with mesh" except to confirm the patient's request.

Causation of Damages

The plaintiff in a lack of informed consent case must prove not only that the physician failed to disclose all material information, but also that there was a causal relationship between the doctor's failure and the damages claimed by the patient. Otherwise, the doctor's conduct, however wrongful, is legally inconsequential.

There are two aspects to the proof of causation in a lack of informed consent case. First, the plaintiff must prove, as in any other tort action, that the defendant's breach of duty was a cause-in-fact of the claimed damages or, viewed conversely, that the defendant's proper performance of his or her duty would have prevented the damages. Second, the plaintiff must further prove that a reasonable patient in the plaintiff's position would not have consented to the treatment or procedure, had the material information and risks been disclosed. Causation is established only if adequate disclosure reasonably would be expected to have caused a reasonable person to decline treatment because of the disclosure of the risk or danger that resulted in the injury. Although the patient has the absolute right, for whatever reason, to prevent unauthorized intrusions and treatments, he or she can only recover damages for those intrusions in which consent would have been reasonably withheld if the patient had been adequately informed.

As to the principal claim for damages in the present case (the subsequent massive herniation in 1988), we need not discuss whether a reasonable person in plaintiff's position would have consented to the cardiac incisional hernia repair if the person had been informed that mesh might not be indicated or used. Based on the complete record, plaintiff has failed to satisfy the threshold element of causation-in-fact. There is no medical evidence from which a rational juror could conclude that Dr. Dowling's failure to use mesh in the cardiac incisional hernia repair caused the plaintiff's subsequent massive herniation.

Inasmuch as plaintiff failed to prove that the use of mesh in the cardiac incisional hernia repair would have prevented any of his subsequent problems, we conclude that Dr. Dowling's failure to use mesh in accordance with plaintiff's request was not a cause-in-fact of the subsequent massive herniation suffered by plaintiff.

Nevertheless, the doctor's breach of duty cannot fairly be said to have resulted in no injury whatsoever. Although we do not base the doctor's liability on a theory of battery, the damages sustained by plaintiff in this case appear to be the type of damages contemplated by the majority of this court in remanding the *Pizzalotto* case to the court of appeal to fix damages based on a battery. While we have herein rejected battery as the basis for analyzing liability in lack of informed consent cases, some of the damages generally awarded in battery cases are applicable in our discussion of damages in this case.

This case is different from the usual lack of informed consent cases where the doctor failed to inform the patient of a material risk and the risk materialized to cause physical damages. Here, the doctor's failure to inform the patient adequately did not cause the patient to undergo a risk that materialized and caused physical damages. Rather, the doctor's breach of duty caused plaintiff to undergo a medical procedure to which the patient expressly objected and for which the doctor failed to provide adequate information in response to the patient's request, thereby causing damages to plaintiff's dignity, privacy and emotional well-being. The doctor, rather than explaining the advantages and disadvantages of the patient's express request, patronized his patient and mentally reserved the right to decide to disregard the patient's expressed wishes.

* * *

Topics for Further Discussion

1. What is the Court's reasoning for rejecting Battery as a cause of action in cases where a lack of informed consent is alleged?

2. How is an action for the absence of informed consent different from a breach of contract action? Can you construct an argument that Dr. Dowling was contractually bound to use mesh? What would the damages be if you were to prevail in contract?

3. Does the Court's decision to reject Battery as the proper cause of action for liability at the same time as referring to the typical measures of damage in Battery cases make sense? If this is a case of "no harm, no foul" as the Court seems to suggest, does an award against Dr. Dowling amount to a new "arrogant practice of medicine" tort? The jury had awarded the patient $300,000 in compensatory damages. The Court reduced this amount to $5,000.

4. In the case of children below the age of majority, the consent of a parent or guardian is typically required before a medical procedure can be performed. Some states have adopted a "mature minor" exception and follow what is known at the Rule of Sevens. Under this rule, children under the age of seven are not able to give consent, the medical service provider must prove that children between the ages of seven and fourteen gave consent, and children over fourteen but not yet adults have a presumption of the ability to give consent that can be rebutted. *See, Cardwell v. Bechtol*, 724 S.W.2d 739 (Tenn. 1987). This issue can be equally critical in the area of refusing medical treatment for religious or other reasons. Can you see how?

The next case demonstrates how the tort of intentional interference with contract can produce devastating consequences in the context of a sophisticated commercial transaction.

Texaco, Inc. v. Pennzoil Co.

729 S.W.2d 768 (Tex. App. 1987)

Warren, J.

This is an appeal from a judgment awarding Pennzoil damages for Texaco's tortious interference with a contract between Pennzoil and the "Getty entities" (Getty Oil Company, the Sarah C. Getty Trust, and the J. Paul Getty Museum). The jury found, among other things, that:

(1) At the end of a board meeting on January 3, 1984, the Getty Entities intended to bind themselves to an agreement providing for the purchase of Getty

Oil stock, whereby the Sarah C. Getty Trust would own 4/7th of the stock and Pennzoil the remaining 3/7th;

(2) Texaco knowingly interfered with the agreement between Pennzoil and the Getty Entities;

(3) As a result of Texaco's interference, Pennzoil suffered damages of $7.53 billion;

(4) Texaco's actions were intentional, willful, and in wanton disregard of Pennzoil's rights; and,

(5) Pennzoil was entitled to punitive damages of $3 billion.

The main question for our determination [is] whether the evidence supports the jury's finding that Texaco knowingly induced a breach of such contract.

The board of Texaco met on January 5, authorizing its officers to make an offer for 100% of Getty Oil and to take any necessary action. Texaco contends that the evidence is legally and factually insufficient to show that Texaco had actual knowledge of any agreement, that it actively induced breach of the alleged contract, and that the alleged contract was valid and capable of being interfered with.

First, Texaco asserts that Pennzoil failed to prove that Texaco had actual knowledge that a contract existed. New York law requires knowledge by a defendant of the existence of contractual rights as an element of the tort of inducing a breach of that contract. However, the defendant need not have full knowledge of all the detailed terms of the contract.

Pennzoil responds that there was legally and factually sufficient evidence to support the jury's finding of knowledge, because the jury could reasonably infer that Texaco knew about the Pennzoil deal from the evidence of how Texaco carefully mapped its strategy to defeat Pennzoil's deal by acting to "stop the train" or "stop the signing"; the notice of a contract given by a January 5 Wall Street Journal article reporting on the Pennzoil agreement—an article that Texaco denied anyone at Texaco had seen; the demands made by the Museum and the Trust for full indemnity from Texaco against any claims by Pennzoil arising out of the Memorandum of Agreement; and the Museum's demand that, even if the Texaco deal fell through, the Museum would be guaranteed the price Pennzoil had agreed to pay for the Museum's shares. Pennzoil contends that these circumstances indicated Texaco's knowledge of Pennzoil's deal too strongly to be overcome by Texaco's "self-serving verbal protestations at trial" that Texaco was told and believed that there was no agreement.

The second major issue Texaco raises is that the evidence was legally and factually insufficient to show that Texaco actively induced breach of the alleged Pennzoil/Getty contract.

A necessary element of the plaintiff's cause of action is a showing that the defendant took an active part in persuading a party to a contract to breach it. Merely entering into a contract with a party with the knowledge of that party's contractual obligations to someone else is not the same as inducing a breach. It is necessary that there be some act of interference or of persuading a party to breach, for example by offering better terms or other incentives, for tort liability to arise. The issue of whether a defendant affirmatively took steps to induce the breach of an existing contract is a question of fact for the jury.

The evidence showed that Texaco knew it had to act quickly, and that it had "24 hours" to "stop the train." This evidence contradicts the contention that Texaco passively accepted a deal proposed by the other parties.

* * *

Topics for Further Discussion

1. If you were advising Texaco in late 1983 and early 1984, what would you advise them regarding the New York law of tortious interference?

2. At the time it was rendered, the *Texaco* award was the largest in U.S. legal history. The punitive damage portion of the award was reduced by $2 billion on appeal. Texaco threatened to seek review by the U.S. Supreme Court and/or to file for bankruptcy if Pennzoil would not agree to settle for a figure reported to be in the $2 billion range. The parties were not able to reach a settlement, and Texaco filed for bankruptcy under Chapter 11 of the Bankruptcy Code. This provision allows a corporation to continue to operate while it negotiates with its creditors. As part of Texaco's reorganization plan, Texaco reportedly agreed to pay Pennzoil $3 billion, and the matter was settled. Eventually, Texaco was merged into Chevron Corporation in 2001, with the new entity being named Chevron Texaco. Should a corporation or an individual be able to escape liability for harm caused by declaring bankruptcy? What are the policy issues inherent in this question?

Unintentional Torts (Negligence)

We now turn to the area of negligence, the category of tort cases making up the bulk of civil lawsuits. The *prima facie* elements of a negligence case are: (1) the existence of a duty owed by the defendant to the plaintiff; (2) a breach of that duty; (3) damage to the person or property of the plaintiff; and (4) a causal relationship between the breach of duty and the resulting harm.

Duty Owed

Every person in society owes a general duty of care to avoid harm to the interests of other persons. This means that we all have an obligation not to engage in activities creating an unreasonable risk of injury to innocent parties or their property. If we fail to meet this duty, then we will be liable for the damage we cause. When we are driving our cars or watering the plants on our balconies for instance, we have a duty to do so in a safe manner so that the car does not crash, or the plant does not fall onto a pedestrian walking below. This duty can be far reaching and can reach actions that induce others to behave recklessly as demonstrated by the following case.

Weirum v. RKO General
539 P.2d 36 (Cal. 1975)

Mosk, J.

A rock radio station with an extensive teenage audience conducted a contest which rewarded the first contestant to locate a disk jockey who moved around in an automobile. Two minors driving in separate automobiles attempted to follow the disc jockey's automobile to its next stop. In the course of their pursuit, one of the minors negligently forced a car off the highway, killing its sole occupant. In a suit filed by the surviving wife and children of the dead person, the jury delivered a verdict against the radio station. We now must determine whether the station owed decedent a duty of due care.

The facts are not disputed. Radio station KHJ is a successful Los Angeles broadcaster with a large teenage following. Among the programs was a contest broadcast on July 16, 1970, the date of the accident. On that day, Donald Steele Revert, known professionally as "The Real Don Steele," a KHJ disc jockey and television personality, traveled in a conspicuous red automobile to a number of locations in the Los Angeles metropolitan area. In Van Nuys, 17-year-old Robert Sentner was listening to KHJ in his car while searching for "The Real Don Steele." Meanwhile in Northridge, 19-year-old Marsha Baime heard and responded to the same information. For the next few miles the Sentner and Baime cars jockeyed for position closest to the Steele car, reaching speeds up to 80 miles an hour. The Steele auto left the freeway at the Westlake off ramp. Either Baime or Sentner, in attempting to follow, forced the dead person's car onto the center divider, where it overturned. Baime stopped to report the accident. Sentner, after pausing momentarily to relate the tragedy to a passing policeman, continued to pursue Steele, successfully located him and collected a cash prize.

Decedent's wife and children brought an action for wrongful death against Sentner, Baime, PKO General, Inc. as owner of KHJ, and the maker of decedent's car. Sentner settled prior to the commencement of trial for the limits of his insurance policy. The jury returned a verdict against Baime and KHJ in the amount of $300,000 and found in favor of the manufacturer of decedent's car. KHJ appeals from the ensuing judgment and from an order denying its motion for judgment notwithstanding the verdict. Baime did not appeal.

The primary question for our determination is whether defendant owed a duty to decedent arising out of its broadcast of the giveaway contest. The determination of duty is primarily a question of law. It is the court's "expression of the sum total of those considerations of policy which lead the law to say that the particular plaintiff is entitled to protection." Any number of considerations may justify the imposition of duty in particular circumstances, including the guidance of history, our continually refined concepts of morals and justice, the convenience of the rule, and social judgment as to where the loss should fall. While the question whether one owes a duty to another must be decided on a case-by-case basis, every case is governed by the rule of general application that all persons are required to use ordinary care to prevent others from being injured as the result of their conduct. However, foreseeability of the risk is a primary consideration in establishing the element of duty. Defendant asserts that the record here does not support a conclusion that a risk of harm to decedent was foreseeable.

While duty is a question of law, foreseeability is a question of fact for the jury. The verdict in plaintiffs' favor here necessarily embraced a finding that decedent was exposed to a foreseeable risk of harm.

We conclude that the record amply supports the finding of foreseeability. These tragic events unfolded in the middle of a Los Angeles summer, a time when young people were free from the constraints of school and responsive to relief from vacation tedium. Seeking to attract new listeners, KHJ devised an "exciting" promotion. Money and a small measure of momentary publicity awaited the swiftest response. It was foreseeable that defendant's youthful listeners, finding the prize had eluded them at one location, would race to arrive first at the next site and in their haste would disregard the demands of highway safety.

It is of no consequence that the harm to decedent was inflicted by third parties acting negligently. Defendant invokes the maxim that "an actor is entitled to assume that others will not act negligently." This concept is valid, however, only to the extent the intervening conduct was not to be anticipated. If the likelihood that a third person may react in a particular manner is a hazard which makes the actor negligent, such reaction whether innocent or negligent does not prevent the actor from being liable for the harm caused thereby. Here, reckless conduct by youthful contestants, stimulated by defendant's broadcast, constituted the hazard to which decedent was exposed. Defendant could have accomplished its objectives of entertaining its listeners and increasing advertising revenues by adopting a contest format which would have avoided danger to the motoring public.

We are not persuaded that the imposition of a duty here will lead to unreasonable extensions of liability. Defendant is fearful that entrepreneurs will henceforth be burdened with an avalanche of obligations: an athletic department will owe a duty to an ardent sports fan injured while hastening to purchase one of a limited number of tickets; a department store will be liable to injuries incurred in response to a "while-they-last" sale. The contest was no commonplace invitation to an attraction available on a limited basis. It was a competitive scramble in which the thrill of the chase to be the one and only victor was intensified by the live broadcasts which accompanied the pursuit. In the situations described by defendant, any haste involved in the purchase of the commodity is an incidental and unavoidable result of the scarcity of the commodity itself. In such situations there is no attempt, as here, to generate a competitive pursuit on public streets.

* * *

Topics for Further Discussion

1. The Court says that: "While duty is a question of law, foreseeability is a question of fact for the jury." What does this statement mean? What is the difference between foreseeability and hindsight, which, as we know, is always 20/20?

2. Are you convinced by the Court's distinguishing of other contest operators and ticket sellers? What if a child is trampled during the grand opening promotion of a new department store offering a mink coat for $1.00 to the first customer to reach the sales counter when the doors open on the first day? What if the injured person was trampled while walking down the street, as opposed to having been in the store?

3. Why did the plaintiffs sue the automobile manufacturer in the *Weirum* case, and why did the court dismiss the claims against the car manufacturer? Would the radio station be liable if, instead of crashing into another car, only the teenage driver was killed after her car ran off the road? How about if the driver of the car was an adult instead of a teenager?

4. What public policy concerns does the Court point to in support of the conclusion that the radio station owed a duty to the victim of the car crash? An innocent person was killed in the car accident in the *Weirum* case and that is a terrible loss to society. Why isn't an award against the reckless driver of the car a sufficient social policy response?

Special and Limited Duties

The particular circumstances of the defendant can also lead to the creation of a special duty or an elevated standard of conduct. Professionals, such as doctors and lawyers, owe their patients and clients a higher level of care than what might be required under the general duty of care. They must act in a manner that is consistent with the level of knowledge, skill and expertise that a member of the same profession would exhibit under similar circumstances. Common carriers (bus operators, taxis, ferries, etc.) and innkeepers are also held to a higher standard of conduct since they hold themselves out as providing these services for hire on an expert basis. Statutes can also increase the standard of care required, such as laws imposing strict liability on parties dealing with hazardous waste or demolition experts. In an opposite manner, courts have sometimes limited the duty owed for policy reasons in order to achieve a higher social objective as shown in the following case. The critical question is whether the beneficiaries merit limited duty protection.

Benejam v. Detroit Tigers, Inc.
635 N.W. 2d 219 (Mich. Ct. App. 2001)

Bandstra, C.J.

In this case, we are asked to determine whether we should adopt, as a matter of Michigan law, the "limited duty" rule that other jurisdictions have applied with respect to spectator injuries at baseball games. Under that rule, a baseball stadium owner is not liable for injuries to spectators that result from projectiles leaving the field during play if safety screening has been provided behind home plate and there are a sufficient number of protected seats to meet ordinary demand. We conclude that the limited duty doctrine should be adopted as a matter of Michigan law and that there was no evidence presented at trial that defendants failed to meet that duty. Further, we conclude that there is no duty to warn spectators at a baseball game of the well-known possibility that a bat or ball might leave the field. We therefore conclude that there is no evidence to support the verdict rendered on behalf of plaintiffs against defendant and we reverse and remand.

Facts

Plaintiff Alyssia M. Benejam, a young girl, attended a Tigers game with a friend and members of the friend's family and was seated quite close to the playing field along the third base line. The stadium was equipped with a net behind home plate, and the net extended part of the way down the first and third base lines. Although Alyssia was behind the net, she was injured when a player's bat broke and a fragment of it curved around the net. There was no evidence, and plaintiffs do not contend, that the fragment of the bat went through the net, that there was a hole in the net, or that the net was otherwise defective. Plaintiffs sued the Tigers, claiming primarily that the net was insufficiently long and that warnings about the possibility of projectiles leaving the field were inadequate. Alyssia suffered crushed fingers as a result of the accident and the jury awarded plaintiffs non-economic damages (past and future) totaling $917,000, lost earning capacity of $56,700 and $35,000 for past and future medical expenses.

Standard of Care/Protective Screening

There is no Michigan case law directly on point. Our review finds that there is an inherent risk of objects leaving the playing field that people know about when they attend baseball games. Also, there is inherent value in having most seats unprotected by a screen because baseball patrons generally want to be involved with the game in an intimate way and are even hoping that they will come in contact with something thrown from the field (in the form of a souvenir baseball that a spectator can keep if they catch it). In other words, spectators know about the risk of being in the stands and, in fact, welcome that risk to a certain extent. On the other hand, the area behind home plate is especially dangerous and spectators who want protected seats should be able to find them in this area. Balancing all of these concerns, courts generally have adopted the limited duty doctrine that prevents liability if there are a sufficient number of protected seats behind home plate to meet the ordinary demand for that kind of seating. If that seating is provided, the baseball stadium owner has fulfilled its duty and there can be no liability for spectators who are injured by a projectile from the field.

The limited duty rule does not ignore or abrogate usual premises liability principles. Instead, it identifies the duty of baseball stadium proprietors with greater specificity than the usual "ordinary care/reasonably safe" standard provides. The limited duty precedents "do not eliminate the stadium owner's duty to exercise reasonable care under the circumstances to protect patrons against injury." Rather, these precedents "define that duty so that once the stadium owner has provided 'adequately screened seats' for all those desiring them, the stadium owner has fulfilled its duty of care as a matter of law." By providing greater detail with regard to the duty imposed on stadium owners, the rule prevents lots of litigation that might signal the end or substantial alteration of the game of baseball as a spectator sport. Applying the limited duty rule here, we conclude that plaintiffs have failed to provide any proof sufficient to find that liability could be imposed. Clearly, there was a screen behind home plate and there was no proof whatsoever that persons wanting seats protected by the screen could not be seated.

* * *

Topics for Further Discussion

1. The Michigan Supreme Court refused to hear the case on appeal. The result in the *Benejam* case was that Alyssia Benejam got no compensation for her injury. In public policy terms, the entire harm resulting from the accident must be borne by her and her family. Do you agree with the Court's balancing of interests in this case? What evidence could she have shown that might have allowed her to prevail?

2. Does the fact that the broken bat curved around the protective netting suggest that the design of the netting was defective? Does the person who designed the net owe a duty to patrons at the game to prevent foreseeable harm, such as that caused by a broken bat curving around the safety net? The court says a person wanting a protected seat can ask for one behind the netting. Isn't that what Alyssia did?

3. How difficult would it have been for the Detroit Tigers to warn patrons about the danger of getting hit by a bat or ball? Parking lot operators routinely warn patrons that they are not responsible for items stolen from parked cars. Do you think that Alyssia would have asked for her money back if her ticket had contained such a warning? Why doesn't the court find that Alyssia assumed the risk of getting hit by the broken bat to avoid establishing a limited liability rule? On the issue of a duty to warn, the court held that there was no duty because the danger of being hit by a flying baseball or bat is well known.

Reasonable Person Standard

The common law does not generally impose an affirmative duty to act for the benefit of others. If there is no duty owed, then there can be no liability in tort. Having decided to act, however, an individual must do so in a reasonable and safe manner. A number of States have adopted "Good Samaritan" laws, named after the story of the same name in the New Testament of the Bible, to exempt people who come to the aid of those in trouble (i.e., with no duty to do so) from liability as a way of encouraging people to assist those in need even when there is no duty to do so.

Whether or not a person has acted negligently is determined by measuring the defendant's behavior against the objective standard of the "reasonable person." The reasonable person is deemed to have the same basic physical characteristics of the defendant, and to possess average intelligence and the same general knowledge of things as the average member of the community. Experts, like doctors and lawyers, are deemed to possess the level of skill of practitioners in their geographical region and area of specialization.

The defendant who owes a duty, whether general or specific, to a plaintiff, will be in breach of that duty when the defendant's actions fall short of the applicable standard of care. This decision is one that can only be made on a case-by-case basis by the judge or jury in light of all of the proven facts and circumstances. The plaintiff bears the burden of showing not only what happened, but also that the actions of the defendant were unreasonable and, therefore, negligent.

Causation

The next element of a negligence claim is for the plaintiff to demonstrate causation. In order to recover, the plaintiff must show that the defendant's conduct was the cause in fact of the injury. This is often decided by using the "but for" test. Under this test, the question is whether the injury would have occurred "but for" the actions of the defendant. If the answer is "No," then causation is satisfied. Courts have modified this test to allow for cases where the defendant's behavior was a joint cause of the harm by asking whether the action was a "substantial factor" in the chain of causation.

The ultimate legal test for causation is whether the conduct complained of is the proximate or legal cause of the injury to the plaintiff. The concept of proximate cause serves to limit liability by cutting off the chain of causation when the injury is deemed to be too remote. This is frequently expressed in terms of the foreseeable nature of the harm as we saw in the *Weirum* case. The general rule is that the wrongdoer is liable for all harm that is reasonably foreseeable as a result of his or her acts or omissions. Hence, a defendant will be liable for all foreseeable damage, even though it results from an intervening force. Such intervening forces are called dependent intervening forces, and include causes such as a subsequent medical malpractice or the negligence of rescuers. For example, assume A is driving recklessly and causes an accident that harms B. If B is picked up in an ambulance driven by C, and C has an accident on the way to the hospital because he failed to put on his siren, C's intervening negligence will not relieve A of liability for the initial injury or the additional injuries caused by the second accident. However, when the plaintiff is unable to produce evidence showing a direct causal relationship to the tort, courts will cut off liability as shown in the following case.

Cyr v. Adamar Assocs.
752 A.2d 603 (Me. 2000)

Rudman, J.

Thelma Cyr, the personal representative for the estate of her daughter, Rachelle Williams, appeals from a summary judgment entered in the Superior Court in favor of Adamar Associates. Cyr contends that she is entitled to recover from Adamar Associates for the wrongful death of Williams. We disagree and affirm the judgment.

On Sunday, November 5, 1995, Rachelle Williams was a registered guest at the Ramada Inn in Lewiston. The Ramada is a facility owned and operated by Adamar Associates. Williams and some of her colleagues from Pizza Hut were in Lewiston for a seminar. That evening, Williams and her co-workers socialized in the Ramada lounge. While in the lounge, Williams noticed that a man, later discovered to be Lloyd Franklin Millett, was staring at her. Around 11:00 P.M., Williams placed a twenty dollar bill on the table and told her colleagues to pay for the beer that she had just ordered because she was going to the ladies' room and would return shortly. Williams also left her cigarettes and lighter at the table in the lounge.

Williams never returned to the lounge. Her corpse was found the next day in a field adjacent to the Ramada parking lot. Ramada did not own the field. Williams had been raped, assaulted and strangled to death; her injuries were consistent with a struggle. Lloyd Franklin Millett later pleaded guilty to murdering Williams.

Cyr asserts that the Ramada breached its duty of care to Williams because Millett's attack was foreseeable and because the Ramada's inadequate security precautions proximately caused Williams' death. Although an innkeeper has a duty to protect its patrons from foreseeable injuries, the innkeeper is not liable for the resulting injuries unless the innkeeper's conduct, or lack thereof, is found to be the proximate cause of the patron's injuries.

Proximate cause is an action occurring in a natural and continuous sequence, uninterrupted by an intervening cause, that produces an injury that would not have occurred but for the action. "A negligent act is the proximate cause of an injury only if the actor's conduct is a substantial factor in bringing about the harm." Although proximate cause is usually a question of fact for the jury, the court has a duty to direct a verdict for the defendant if the jury's determination of proximate cause would be based on speculation or conjecture.

In the present case, no evidence exists to support a conclusion that the Ramada proximately caused Williams' death. Although it would not be unreasonable to assume that Millet abducted Williams from the Ramada' premises, the evidence does not reveal whether Williams voluntarily left the Ramada property with Millet or whether he abducted her. The lack of such evidence and the discovery of Williams' body on property not owned by the Ramada manifest that the relation between the Ramada' security measures and Williams' death is too uncertain and tenuous to hold Adamar liable.

Adamar was entitled to a judgment as a matter of law because without any evidence for the jury to consider regarding the circumstances leading to the assault, the jury would be basing its determination of liability on pure conjecture. There being no genuine issues of material fact and no evidence of proximate cause, the trial court properly entered a summary judgment in favor of Adamar.

* * *

Topics for Further Discussion

1. In *Daniel v. Days Inn of America, Inc.*, 356 S.E. 2d 129 (S.C. Ct. App. 1987), a woman was invited to a hotel room by a guest of the hotel. She was brutally raped and tortured in the room by three men over a five to six hour period. She sued the hotel. The hotel's

motion for summary judgment was granted by the trial judge. The South Carolina Court of Appeals reversed writing that:

> An innkeeper is not automatically exonerated from negligence when a criminal act is the actual cause of the invitee's injuries. The hotel's acts or omissions may be negligent if the hotel realized or should have realized that its conduct involved unreasonable risks of harm through the conduct of a third person, even though such conduct of the third person is criminal. Our Supreme Court has held in an analogous case that while a storeowner is generally not charged with the duty of protecting its customers against criminal acts of third parties, the intervening criminal act of another may not always relieve the storeowner of liability for his negligence. Although a proprietor of a hotel is not an insurer of the safety of his guests against improper acts of other guests or third persons, he is bound to exercise reasonable care in this respect for their safety, and may be held liable on grounds of negligence for failure to do so.

Can you distinguish the facts of *Cyr* from those in *Daniel*?

2. The general rule is that a negligent act or omission is the proximate cause of the harm if the harm is a natural and probable consequence which, in light of the facts and circumstances, is reasonably foreseeable. The court has to determine whether an intervening cause should cut off liability. An intervening cause will relieve the tortfeasor of liability if such intervening cause was not reasonably foreseeable at the time of the tortfeasor's act or omission. Is it reasonably foreseeable that people might be the victims of crime while staying in hotels? If so, what precautions must a hotelkeeper make to prevent this foreseeable harm? What duty does a hotel owe to its patrons while in the bar? How about while they are in their rooms? Should the duty be the same towards visitors as it is to registered guests?

Joint and Several Liability

When there are two or more defendants, and each is found to be responsible for the harm, then each is fully liable for the entire amount of the award. This is called joint and several liability. For example, if defendants A and B cause harm to plaintiff C, and C is awarded a judgment in the amount of $1 million, C can seek recovery of the full amount from either A or B. If C seeks recovery only from A, then A can sue B requiring him to contribute his share of the award. However, if B is deceased or bankrupt, A will still be required to pay the entire amount of the award. Some states, such as Arizona, have abolished joint and several liability in tort cases involving personal injury, property damage, or wrongful death. Other states limit joint and several liability to cases involving noneconomic or exemplary damages.

Defenses

Defenses to a claim of negligence include contributory negligence, comparative negligence, and assumption of risk. Under the traditional common law doctrine of contributory negligence, a plaintiff whose negligence contributed to the harm was completely barred from recovery. This strict and overly harsh rule has given way to the doctrine of comparative negligence. This requires the judge or jury to allocate the percentage of fault between the plaintiff and defendant and to reduce any damage award by the percentage of fault attributed to the plaintiff.

Assumption of risk operates in much the same manner as consent. A plaintiff may be denied recovery if the defendant can show that the plaintiff was aware of the risk of injury and voluntarily assumed it. For example, if A gets into a car driven by B knowing that B is drunk, A will be found to have assumed the risk of a crash. Assumption of risk can be either express or implied. As with informed consent, courts will examine the facts carefully to make sure that the risk assumed was the same as the risk that actually caused the harm. If patient A assumes the risk of open heart surgery, and is then seriously injured when a nurse accidentally bumps the surgeon's arm while he is cutting, patient A will not be deemed to have assumed that risk.

Remedies

In most tort cases the ultimate goal is to recover monetary damages. Since monetary damages are paid to remedy injury, they are not taxed. There are cases where the appropriate remedy will include injunctive relief instead of or along with monetary damages. The basic formula for compensatory damages in tort is that the plaintiff should recover all actual damages suffered as a result of the defendant's negligence. In other words, the plaintiff should be restored to the position he was in before becoming a tort victim.

Damages must be proven with specificity and cannot be speculative. Determining actual damages is not always as straightforward as it might seem. For example, a plaintiff may seek damages for the pain and suffering resulting from an injury. There may also be a claim for lost wages or loss of consortium (intimate relations) if the plaintiff is married. These elements of damage can be proven by direct or expert testimony.

What about a case where a doctor commits malpractice by ineffectively performing a sterilization procedure on a woman who then becomes pregnant? Should actual damages include the reasonable costs of raising the unintended child? The majority trend in the U.S. is to permit full recovery of these expenses in the same manner as any other foreseeable consequence of a doctor's negligence. *Burke v. Rivo*, 551 N.E.2d 1 (Mass. 1990) is a leading "wrongful birth" case. The Massachusetts Supreme Court rejected a number of arguments against damages writing that: "While we firmly reject a universal rule that the birth of an unexpected healthy child is always a net benefit, we also firmly reject any suggestion that the availability of abortion or of adoption furnishes a basis for limiting damages payable by a physician but for whose negligence the child would not have been conceived."

Common law imposes a duty to mitigate on all injured parties. The duty to mitigate requires the injured party to take reasonable steps to stop or reduce the harm caused by defendant's tort. The emphasis is on reasonable steps, and plaintiffs are not required to go to unusual lengths to mitigate. Nevertheless, if the plaintiff fails to act reasonably to reduce the damage, the court will reduce the amount of damages by the amount they could have been reduced had the plaintiff acted prudently to mitigate them.

Punitive Damages

American law recognizes the social utility of punitive (sometimes called exemplary) damages as a highly effective method of discouraging grossly negligent behavior. Some countries do not permit them at all on the theory that the power to "punish" wrongdoers resides exclusively with the government under the criminal law. Japan is one such country, and Japanese courts refuse to enforce foreign judicial awards for punitive damages on the grounds that they violate Japanese public policy.

Punitive damages require more than mere negligence, but if a successful plaintiff can make a case for punitive damages, the potential recovery can be huge. Juries are not free to award any amount they want however. In *BMW v. Gore*, 517 U.S. 559 (1996), the U.S. Supreme Court struck down an award of punitive damages for being "grossly excessive" under the Due Process Clause of the Fourteenth Amendment. The Court has consistently refused to mandate a mathematical formula for determining when an award is grossly excessive opting instead for a three-pronged analysis. For a punitive damage award to be sustained, the Court will look at "(1) the degree of reprehensibility of the defendant's misconduct; (2) the disparity between the actual or potential harm suffered by the plaintiff and the punitive damages award; and (3) the difference between the punitive damages awarded by the jury and the civil penalties authorized or imposed in comparable cases." Of the three factors, the first is clearly the most significant.

The following case deals with punitive damages resulting from a defective automobile design. Ford designed, manufactured, and sold a car in the 1970s called the Pinto. The gas tank of the Pinto was located in the rear of the car and was not properly reinforced against a rear end impact. When the car was struck from behind, even at relatively slow speeds, the gas tank would frequently burst into flames turning the car into an inferno. A similar gas tank design was used in Ford's Mustang II. As you read the case, ask whether you think the punitive damage award would pass the *BMW v. Gore* test if it were to come up today.

Ford Motor Co. v. Stubblefield
319 S.E.2d 470 (Ga. Ct. App. 1984)

Sognier, J.

This wrongful death action arising out of an automobile collision was brought by William O. Stubblefield, individually and as administrator of the estate of his minor child, and by Linda P. Standley, individually and as natural mother of the deceased minor child. The sole theory of liability against Ford was its alleged negligence in the design of the automobile in which 15-year-old Terri Stubblefield was a passenger when she was fatally injured. William O. Stubblefield prayed for recovery in his individual capacity for medical, hospital and funeral expenses, and in his capacity as administrator sought damages for personal injury, pain and suffering and an award of punitive damages and expenses of litigation. Linda P. Standley sought damages for the wrongful death of her daughter. The death resulted from injuries sustained in a collision occurring July 10, 1977, when the 1975 Ford Mustang II in which Terri Stubblefield was riding was struck from behind while stopped in traffic by another car traveling at an estimated speed of 56 to 65 m.p.h. A "ball of fire" engulfed the rear of the Mustang II at impact and Terri, who was sitting in the back seat, was severely burned.

The question presented to the jury was whether Ford, through the negligent design and placement of its fuel system in the 1975 Mustang II, exposed the occupants of this automobile to unreasonable risk of injury and, insofar as punitive damages were concerned, whether Ford's management acted with that entire want of care which would give rise to conscious indifference to the consequences in marketing the automobile. The jury found in favor of appellees on all counts. Ford appeals the judgment entered on the verdict, enumerating as error the failure of the trial court to direct a verdict in its favor on the issues of negligence and causation, liability for punitive damages, and expenses of litigation including attorney fees; and in refusing to grant a motion for judgment notwithstanding the verdict, or in the alternative a new trial, on these issues.

Appellees presented copious documentary exhibits, internal memoranda and confidential corporate reports reflecting the course of Ford's research and development of the Mustang II, which were explained and interpreted to the jury by two expert witnesses. The negligence issue in this case turned on an evaluation of mass production engineering design and policy objectives.

Ford urges that the award of $8 million as punitive damages to William O. Stubblefield as administrator of the estate of Terri J. Stubblefield was so shockingly excessive and so resulted from the bias and prejudice of the jury that the trial court abused its discretion by denying Ford's motion for a new trial on this ground. Ford argues that no appellate court in any jurisdiction has ever approved an award of this magnitude in any personal injury suit arising out of a manufacturer's negligence.

The evidence here was sufficient to authorize the jury to find that the sum of $8 million was an amount necessary to deter Ford from repeating its conduct; that is, its conscious decisions to defer implementation of safety devices in order to protect its profits. One internal memo estimated that "the total financial effect of the Fuel System Integrity program [would] reduce Company profits over the 1973–1976 cycle by $(109) million," and recommended that Ford "defer adoption of the [safety measures] on all affected cars until 1976 to realize a design cost savings of $20.9 million compared to 1974." Another Ford document referred to a $2 million cost differential as "marginal." "Unless a jury verdict is palpably unreasonable or excessive, or the product of bias, it will not be disturbed on appeal." "In discussing when a verdict may be found so excessive as to infer undue bias or prejudice, courts have said such a verdict must 'carry its death warrant upon its face,' be 'monstrous indeed,' 'must shock,' or 'appear exorbitant.'" It is also true in considering excessiveness that an appellate court "... does not have the broad discretionary powers invested in trial courts to set aside verdicts, and where the trial court before whom the witnesses appeared had the opportunity of personally observing the witnesses ... has approved the verdict, this court is without power to interfere unless it is clear from the record that the verdict of the jury was prejudiced or biased or was procured by corrupt means." The excessiveness of the verdict was raised below on motion for new trial and overruled by the judge who had presided over the trial. Considering all of the circumstances in this case, we do not find the trial court erred in declining to find the verdict excessive.

* * *

Topics for Further Discussion

1. The appellate court defers almost entirely to the decision of the trial court judge on the issue of whether the amount of punitive damages was excessive. Is this a question of fact or law or both?

2. Ford made a very tragic business judgment when it decided, in essence, that the cost of paying product liability judgments was less than recalling all Ford vehicles with the defectively designed gas tank. The Ford memos are classic examples of "smoking gun" evidence. They reveal the precise kind of "profit over safety" decision that punitive damages are intended to discourage. Would relying solely on the criminal law have the same

impact in terms of assuring the safety of products? What are the problems with relying on the criminal law to correct this kind of behavior?

3. At the time of this writing, the U.S. Supreme Court has continued to grapple with the Constitutional limits on punitive damages as illustrated in *State Farm Mut. Auto. Ins. Co. v. Campbell*, 538 U.S. 408 (2003), excerpted in Chapter 2. In *Exxon Shipping v. Baker*, 128 S. Ct. 2605 (2008) a case arising from the negligent operation of a oil tanker resulting in an environmentally disastrous spill off of Alaska, the Supreme Court stated as follows: "... given the need to protect against the possibility (and the disruptive cost to the legal system) of awards that are unpredictable and unnecessary, either for deterrence or for measured retribution, we consider that a 1:1 ratio, which is above the median award, is a fair upper limit in such maritime cases." The *Baker* case involved concerns of maritime common law not present in the typical tort case, but, arguably, the Court is moving towards a numerical ratio for testing the constitutionality of punitive damage awards.

Contingency Fee System

Personal injury lawyers do not generally work for free. In fact, they almost always work on a "contingency fee" basis, which means their fee is paid out of the judgment, if any, against the defendant. If the plaintiff does not win a verdict and recover damages, the lawyer gets nothing. A contingency fee is usually a percentage of the award in the range of 33.3% to 50%. Some legal systems, such as in the United Kingdom, do not allow lawyers to work on a contingency fee basis because of a public policy concern against encouraging frivolous lawsuits.

In the U.S., contingency fees are seen as giving even the poorest plaintiffs an opportunity to be represented and to get their proverbial "day in court." One clear benefit of the system is that lawyers act as a first check on the validity of a claim to the extent they screen out cases with little or no chance of winning or which are against "judgment proof" (i.e., a person with no assets from which to satisfy the judgment) defendants. Plaintiffs' lawyers are always on the lookout for so-called "deep pocket" defendants, that is, those capable of paying large monetary judgments if the plaintiff wins. Insurance companies are the most frequently sought after deep pocket defendants for obvious reasons. The risk of prejudice against insurance companies is so high that evidence rules prohibit mentioning insurance coverage in a tort trial.

The plaintiffs sued the two teenage drivers, the parent company of the radio station and the maker of the automobile (a deep pocket defendant) in which the deceased was driving in *Weirum*. The action against the car manufacturer was dismissed, but not before it had to pay its lawyers to respond to the complaint and to move for the dismissal. The tendency of personal injury lawyers to sue everybody in sight is part of the growing argument for tort law reform.

Mass Torts

Actions arising from mass torts became highly popular, and controversial, in the 1970s and 1980s. Major deep pocket corporations (asbestos makers, tobacco companies, gun manufacturers, and drug companies to name just a few) were sued by personal injury lawyers representing large numbers of plaintiffs, assembled as a class under the Federal Rules of Civil Procedure. The claims are based on common facts, such as injuries resulting from use of a particular drug or product. Mass tort lawyers work on a contingency fee basis in the same way as ordinary personal injury attorneys. By grouping thousands or sometimes even tens of thousands of individual plaintiffs into a single class, the bargaining power of the plaintiffs becomes large as do the potential fees for the lawyers.

Mass torts (called "toxic torts" when the damage results from use or exposure to poisonous substances) share two distinct features. First, multiple plaintiffs bring their lawsuit against one or more defendants, usually in the same industry, based on virtually identical factual and legal claims. For example, that the defendants all sold a product including the same chemical or drug that resulted in harm to each plaintiff individually. The severity of the harm and the amount of damages claimed may differ, but the underlying cause of action does not. Second, there is a commonality of factual and legal issues in all of the cases even though they may have occurred at different times and places. In such cases, judicial efficiency and overall fairness are best served by trying all of these cases together at one time. Efficiency must be balanced against the fact that a class action deprives each plaintiff of the right to control her own case.

The certification of a class, and the subsequent finding of liability, can have devastating economic effects on the defendants. The potential damages can be so large that a defendant might be willing to settle rather than face the uncertainty of a huge damage award after losing a class action lawsuit. Dow Corning, for example, was sued by thousands of women who claimed they suffered injury as a result of using Dow Corning's silicone breast implants. It was alleged, among other things, that the breast implants ruptured and/or leaked silicone. Dow Corning was ultimately forced into Chapter 11 Bankruptcy proceedings as a result of these cases. The company set aside $3 billion to satisfy individual claims ranging from $1,000 to $200,000 per person. Targets of these suits often complain that they are the victims of "junk" science promoted by experts who are lucratively paid by plaintiff lawyers.

Asbestos, a natural substance that was used throughout America as an insulator in buildings, was found to cause serious illness when it was inhaled. In addition to compensation for the harm resulting to the health of persons living and working in asbestos infested buildings, the government ordered asbestos-bearing materials to be removed from every building in the U.S. The following *In re School Asbestos Litigation* case is an example of a court's analysis of the pros and cons of class certification.

In re School Asbestos Litigation, School Dist. of Lancaster v. Lake Asbestos of Quebec, Ltd.
789 F.2d 996 (3rd Cir. 1986)

Weis, J.

In an effort to reach an equitable result in these asbestos property damage cases brought by school authorities, the district court certified a nationwide mandatory class for punitive damages and an opt-out class for compensatory damages. We conclude that the Federal Rules of Civil Procedure 23(b)(1) mandatory class cannot be approved because of a lack of necessary findings and for the additional reason that the class, being under-inclusive, cannot in the circumstances here accomplish the objectives for which it was created. We will, however, affirm the denial of a FRCP 23(b)(2) class and will affirm the district court's conditional certification of a FRCP 23(b)(3) opt-out class on compensatory damages.

This lawsuit began with the filing of class action complaints in the Eastern District of Pennsylvania by several Pennsylvania school districts and the Barnwell, South Carolina School District. The cases were consolidated soon after filing. Defendants, numbering approximately fifty, are associated with the asbestos industry as miners, bulk suppliers, brokers, assemblers, manufacturers, distributors, and at least one contractor.

As a result of federal legislation and regulation, plaintiffs are required to test for the presence of asbestos in schools. The complaints seek compensatory and punitive damages as well as injunctive relief stemming from compliance with the federal legislation and the alleged need to remove or treat materials containing asbestos. The claims are based on theories of negligence, strict liability, intentional tort, breach of warranty, concert of action, and civil conspiracy.

This appeal must be decided against the background of the asbestos scene, an unparalleled situation in American tort law. To date, more than 30,000 personal injury claims have been filed against asbestos manufacturers and producers. An estimated 180,000 additional claims of this type will be on court dockets by the year 2010. Added to those monumental figures are the claims for property damage—the cost of removing or treating asbestos-based materials used in building construction. Some indication of the magnitude of that potential liability may be gleaned from the fact that the property damage claims filed in the Johns-Manville bankruptcy proceedings stood at $69 billion as of June 1985. The procedures of the traditional tort system proved effective in unearthing the hazards of asbestos to workers and the failure of its producers to reduce the risk. However, the undeniable limitations of the "one-on-one" approach in coping with the massive onset of claims now in the courts have caused serious and justified concern.

A report compiled by the Rand Corporation, entitled Asbestos in the Court (1985), points out the high cost and inefficiencies in handling these individual claims as well as the uneven, inconsistent, and unjust results often achieved. Perhaps the least flattering statistic is the high cost of processing these claims: "On the average, the total cost to plaintiffs and defendants of litigating a claim was considerably greater than the amount paid in compensation." Inefficiency results primarily from relitigation of the same basic issues in case after case. Since a different jury is selected in each action, it must hear the same evidence that was presented in previous trials. A clearer example of reinventing the wheel thousands of times is hard to imagine.

A certain prejudice exists when a litigant is forced to participate in an undesired mandatory class action. That result may be acceptable where the class device will serve the worthwhile goal of protecting the interests of all litigants to a potentially limited fund, but is hard to justify where only a small number of potential claimants can be included in the mandatory action. A class action may promote efficiency by reducing repetitive testimony and evidence that otherwise would be required in individual trials. Those advantages, however, are secured at the price of delaying the disposition of individual cases that might be tried to conclusion in a number of state and district courts in the interim. In effect, a mandatory class action creates a bottleneck by concentrating the litigation, at least for a period, before one judge instead of spreading the individual cases out among many trial forums.

The advisory committee notes to (b)(3) state that a "mass accident" causing injuries to numerous persons is generally not appropriate for class action treatment because "significant questions, not only of damages but of liability and defenses of liability, would be present, affecting the individuals in different ways." If such an action were conducted as a class action, it "would degenerate in practice into multiple lawsuits separately tried." Although that statement continues to be repeated in case law, there is growing acceptance of the notion that some mass accident situations may be good candidates for class action treatment. An airplane crash, for instance, would present the same liability questions for each passenger, although the damages would depend on individual circumstances. Determination of the liability issues in one suit may represent a substantial savings in time and resources. Even if the action thereafter "degenerates" into a series of individual damage suits, the result nevertheless is an improvement over the situation in which the same separate suits require adjudication on liability using the same evidence over and over again.

Settlements of class actions often result in savings for all concerned. Part of the reluctance to apply the class action to mass torts is rooted in the notion that individual plaintiffs have the right to select their own counsel and forum, particularly in personal injury actions. That factor has little, if any, relevance in this case because the claims are limited to property damage, and school districts are unlikely to have strong emotional ties to the litigation.

Experience shows that in case after case, the health issues, the question of injury causation, and the knowledge of the defendants are explored, often by the same witnesses. The use of the class action device appears to offer some hope of reducing the expenditure of time and money needed to resolve the common issues which are of substantial importance.

* * *

Topics for Further Discussion

1. The Court discusses the pros and cons of mandatory versus opt-out class certification. Why do you think the district court certified a nationwide mandatory class for punitive damages and an opt-out class for compensatory damages? In a mandatory certification, all plaintiffs in the class will be bound by the results of the class action trial. In an opt-out certification, plaintiffs are given a period of time to join or withdraw from the class. If they opt out, they are free to take their chances against the defendant in a separate lawsuit.

2. Class action lawsuits are not restricted to tort cases. They are frequently employed in antitrust and securities law cases. It was reported in the press that the attorneys who brought an antitrust case against Microsoft, which was ultimately settled, sought $258 million in attorneys' fees. This worked out to $3,019 per hour for the lead counsel for the plaintiffs. What limits, if any, should courts place on attorneys' fees? Should there be a mandatory scaling of fees so that the plaintiffs receiving smaller awards can keep a larger percentage of the recovery?

3. Johns-Manville was a major manufacturer of insulation materials, including asbestos. As a result of the large number of lawsuits and judgments rendered against it, it filed for bankruptcy under Chapter 11. It is now a part of the Berkshire Hathaway group.

Product Liability

Negligence remains the predominant standard for liability in tort law. In recent times, however, there has been an explosion of cases in the area of product liability. These cases rest on the theory that liability should be imposed on a defendant without strict proof of negligence when a consumer is injured by a defective product. The development of product liability law has been evolutionary. Courts have long been concerned with cases where negligence is obvious from the resulting damage, but proof is difficult. The classic example is an individual hit on the head by an object falling out of a second story window of a warehouse. The plaintiff will have a difficult time knowing exactly how the object came to fall on his head if there are no witnesses. To avoid an inequitable result, the courts used the doctrine of *res ipsa loquitur* ("the thing speaks for itself"). The doctrine is available to overcome the burden of proving negligence whenever an accident occurs that would not ordinarily occur without negligence and the defendant is the only party that reasonably could have committed the negligent act.

While *res ipsa loquitur* was useful to the courts in avoiding injustices, many judges and lawyers were dissatisfied with the artificiality of the doctrine, especially in the era of rapid industrialization. Critics called for product manufacturers to bear liability whenever the products caused harm as a result of a defect in design or manufacture. This is a form of strict liability because the plaintiff no longer has to prove negligence. Under modern product liability law, a manufacturer is liable for harm whenever it puts a product on the market and harm is caused as a result of a defect. Defects come in many varieties. One of the principle defenses available to manufacturers is the product was used in a manner other than for its intended purpose. The following two cases illustrate the evolution from *res ipsa loquitur* to product liability. Note that Justice Traynor wrote the concurring opinion in *Escola* and the majority opinion in *Yuba Power* nearly twenty years later.

Escola v. Coca Cola Bottling Co. of Fresno
150 P.2d 436 (Cal. 1944)

Gibson, C.J.

Plaintiff, a waitress in a restaurant, was injured when a bottle of Coca Cola broke in her hand. She alleged that defendant company, which had bottled and delivered the alleged defective bottle to her employer, was negligent in selling "bottles containing said beverage which on account of excessive pressure of gas or by reason of some defect in the bottle was dangerous ... and likely to explode." This appeal is from a judgment upon a jury verdict in favor of plaintiff.

Defendant's driver delivered several cases of Coca Cola to the restaurant, placing them on the floor, one on top of the other, under and behind the counter, where they remained at least thirty-six hours. Immediately before the accident, plaintiff picked up the top case and set it upon a near-by ice cream cabinet in front of and about three feet from the refrigerator. She then proceeded to take the bottles from the case with her right hand, one at a time, and put them into the refrigerator. One of defendant's drivers, called as a witness by plaintiff, testified that he had seen other bottles of Coca Cola in the past explode and had found broken bottles in the warehouse when he took the cases out, but that he did not know what made them blow up.

Plaintiff then rested her case, having announced to the court that being unable to show any specific acts of negligence she relied completely on the doctrine of *res ipsa loquitur.* Defendant contends that the doctrine of *res ipsa loquitur* does not apply in this case, and that the evidence is insufficient to support the judgment. Many jurisdictions have applied the doctrine in cases involving exploding bottles of carbonated beverages. Other courts for varying reasons have refused to apply the doctrine in such cases. It would serve no useful purpose to discuss the reasoning of the foregoing cases in detail, since the problem is whether under the facts shown in the instant case the conditions warranting application of the doctrine have been satisfied. *Res ipsa loquitur* does not apply unless (1) defendant had exclusive control of the thing causing the injury and (2) the accident is of such a nature that it ordinarily would not occur in the absence of negligence by the defendant.

Many authorities state that the happening of the accident does not speak for itself where it took place some time after defendant had relinquished control of the instrumentality causing the injury. Under the more logical view, however, the doctrine may be applied upon the theory that defendant had control at the time of the alleged negligent act, although not at the time of the accident, provided plaintiff first proves that the condition of the instrumentality had not been changed after it left the defendant's possession.

Upon an examination of the record, the evidence appears sufficient to support a reasonable inference that the bottle here involved was not damaged by any outside force after delivery to the restaurant by defendant. It follows, therefore, that the bottle was in some manner defective at the time defendant relinquished control, because sound and properly prepared bottles of carbonated liquids do not ordinarily explode when carefully handled. The next question, then, is whether plaintiff may rely upon the doctrine of *res ipsa loquitur* to supply an inference that defendant's negligence was responsible for the defective condition of the bottle at the time it was delivered to the restaurant. Under the general rules pertaining to the doctrine, as set forth above, it must appear that bottles of carbonated liquid are not ordinarily defective without negligence by the bottling company.

An explosion such as took place here might have been caused by an excessive internal pressure in a sound bottle, by a defect in the glass of a bottle containing a safe pressure, or by a combination of these two possible causes. The question is whether under the evidence there was a probability that defendant was negligent in any of these respects. If so, the doctrine of *res ipsa loquitur* applies.

The bottle was admittedly charged with gas under pressure, and the charging of the bottle was within the exclusive control of defendant. As it is a matter of common knowledge that an overcharge would not ordinarily result without negligence, it follows under the doctrine of *res ipsa loquitur* that if the bottle was in fact excessively charged an inference of defendant's negligence would arise. If the explosion resulted from a defective bottle containing a safe pressure, the defendant would be liable if it negligently failed to discover such flaw.

[T]here is available to the industry a commonly-used method of testing bottles for defects not apparent to the eye, which is almost infallible. Since Coca Cola bottles are subjected to these tests by the manufacturer, it is not likely that they contain defects when delivered to the bottler which are not discoverable by visual inspection. Both new and used bottles are filled and distributed by defendant. The used bottles are not again subjected to the tests referred to above, and it may be inferred that defects not discoverable by visual inspection do not develop in bottles after they are manufactured. Although it is not clear in this case whether the explosion was caused by an excessive charge or a defect in the glass, there is a sufficient showing that neither cause would ordinarily have been present if due care had been used. Further, defendant had exclusive control over both the charging and inspection of the bottles. Accordingly, all the requirements necessary to entitle plaintiff to rely on the doctrine of *res ipsa loquitur* to supply an inference of negligence are present.

It is true that defendant presented evidence tending to show that it exercised considerable precaution by carefully regulating and checking the pressure in the bottles and by making visual inspections for defects in the glass at several stages during the bottling process. It is well settled, however, that when a defendant produces evidence to oppose the idea of negligence which arises upon application of the doctrine of *res ipsa loquitur,* it is ordinarily a question of fact for the jury to determine whether defendant has been successful.

The judgment is affirmed.

Traynor, J., concurring

I concur in the judgment, but I believe the manufacturer's negligence should no longer be singled out as the basis of a plaintiff's right to recover in cases like the present one. In my opinion it should now be recognized that a manufacturer incurs an absolute liability when an article that he has placed on the market, knowing that it is to be used without inspection, proves to have a defect that causes injury to human beings. Even if there is no negligence, however, public policy demands that responsibility be fixed wherever it will most effectively reduce the hazards to life and health inherent in defective products that reach the market. It is evident that the manufacturer can anticipate some hazards and guard against the recurrence of others, as the public cannot. Those who suffer injury from defective products are unprepared to meet its consequences. The cost of an injury and the loss of time or health may be an overwhelming misfortune to the person injured, and a needless one, for the risk of injury can be insured by the manufacturer and distributed among the public as a cost of doing business. It is to the public interest to discourage the marketing of products having defects that are a menace to the public. If such products nevertheless find their way into the market it is to the public interest to place the responsibility for whatever injury they may cause upon the manufacturer, who, even if he is not negligent in the manufacture of the product, is responsible for its reaching the market. However intermittently such injuries may occur and however haphazardly they may strike, the risk of their occurrence is a constant risk and a general one. Against such a risk there should be general and constant protection and the manufacturer is best situated to afford such protection.

As handicrafts have been replaced by mass production with its great markets and transportation facilities, the close relationship between the producer and consumer of a product has been altered. Manufacturing processes, frequently valuable secrets, are ordinarily either inaccessible to or beyond the ken of the general public. The consumer no longer has means or skill enough to investigate for himself the soundness of a product, even when it is not contained in a sealed package. The manufacturer's obligation to the consumer must keep pace with the changing relationship between them; it cannot be escaped because the marketing of a product has become so complicated as to require one or more intermediaries. Certainly there is greater reason to impose liability on the manufacturer than on the retailer who is but a conduit of a product that he is not himself able to test.

* * *

Greenman v. Yuba Power Products, Inc.
377 P. 2d 897 (Cal. 1963)

Traynor, J.

Plaintiff brought this action for damages against the retailer and the manufacturer of a Shopsmith, a combination power tool that could be used as a saw, drill, and wood lathe. He saw a Shopsmith demonstrated by the retailer and studied a brochure prepared by the manufacturer. He decided he wanted a Shopsmith for his home workshop, and his wife bought and gave him one for Christmas in 1955. In 1957 he bought the necessary attachments to use the Shopsmith as a lathe for turning a large piece of wood he wished to make into a chalice. After he had worked on the piece of wood several times without difficulty, it suddenly flew out of the machine and struck him on the forehead, inflicting serious injuries. About ten and a half months later, he gave the manufacturer written notice of claimed breaches of warranties and filed a complaint alleging such breaches and negligence.

After a trial before a jury, the court ruled that there was no evidence that the retailer was negligent. Accordingly, it submitted to the jury only the causes of action alleging negligence and breach of express warranties against the manufacturer. The jury returned a verdict for plaintiff against the manufacturer in the amount of $65,000. The manufacturer seeks a reversal.

Plaintiff introduced substantial evidence that his injuries were caused by defective design and construction of the Shopsmith. His expert witnesses testified that inadequate screws were used to hold parts of the machine together so that normal vibration caused the piece of wood being turned to fly out of the lathe. They also testified that there were other more positive ways of fastening the parts of the machine together, the use of which would have prevented the accident. The jury could therefore reasonably have concluded that the manufacturer negligently constructed the Shopsmith. The jury could also reasonably have concluded that statements in the manufacturer's brochure were untrue, that they constituted express warranties, and that plaintiff's injuries were caused by their breach.

Although strict liability has usually been based on the theory of an express or implied warranty running from the manufacturer to the plaintiff, the abandonment of the requirement of a contract between them, the recognition that the liability is not assumed by agreement but imposed by law, and the refusal to permit the manufacturer to define the scope of its own responsibility for defective products make clear that the liability is not one governed by the law of contract warranties but by the law of strict liability in tort. Accordingly, rules defining and governing warranties that were developed to meet the needs of commercial transactions cannot properly be invoked to govern the manufacturer's liability to those injured by their defective products unless those rules also serve the purposes for which such liability is imposed.

The purpose of such liability is to insure that the costs of injuries resulting from defective products are borne by the manufacturers that put such products on the market rather than by the injured persons who are powerless to protect themselves. Implicit in the machine's presence on the market, however, was a representation that it would safely do the jobs for which it was built. Under these circumstances, it should not be controlling whether plaintiff selected the machine because of the statements in the brochure, or because of the machine's own appearance of excellence that belied the defect lurking beneath the surface, or because he merely assumed that it would safely do the jobs it was built to do. It should not be controlling whether the details of the sales from manufacturer to retailer and from retailer to plaintiff's wife were such that one or more of the implied warranties of the sales act arose. To establish the manufacturer's liability it was sufficient that plaintiff proved that he was injured while using the Shopsmith in a way it was intended to be used as a result of a defect in design and manufacture of which plaintiff was not aware that made the Shopsmith unsafe for its intended use.

* * *

Topics for Further Discussion

1. Was there anything the defendant could have done to escape liability in the *Escola* case? What if, for example, the defendant was able to show that, in ten years of bottling Coke, it had never had a single instance of a defective bottle or one that was over-pressurized? Would that evidence be relevant to the case at hand?

2. Do you think it is natural for the plaintiff to throw away the broken pieces of glass after the bottle exploded or would a reasonable person save them as evidence? It could be argued that *res ipsa loquitur* shifts the traditional burden of proof from the plaintiff to the defendant. Is this fair and reasonable?

3. The *Yuba Power* case does not do away with the doctrine of *res ipsa loquitur*. It still remains as a viable theory to assist plaintiffs in cases where the doctrine of product liability does not apply. Can you think of a case where this doctrine might be useful in establishing liability?

4. As can be seen from the *Yuba Power* case, principles of contract and tort law intersect in many product liability cases. What is the relationship between a warranty supplied with a product and a claim of product liability? What would be the effect of a disclaimer in the warranty that sought to exclude damages for personal injury?

5. Justice Traynor, when summarizing the reason for the adoption of a strict liability standard at the end of his opinion, wrote: "The purpose of such liability is to insure that the costs of injuries resulting from defective products are borne by the manufacturers that put such products on the market rather than by the injured persons who are powerless to protect themselves. Sales warranties serve this purpose fitfully at best." Why is contract law insufficient to address the social policy concerns identified by the court? What are the practical results of imposing a form of strict liability on manufacturers? Is it possible that some manufacturers may choose to withdraw from specific markets, thereby depriving society of the benefit of their products, out of concern for product liability? To what extent do you think that the price of products reflects the product liability insurance premiums and damage awards paid by manufacturers? Do you agree that this social cost should be borne by, or spread among, consumers at-large? If so, why didn't the court in the *Benejam* baseball injury case adopt similar reasoning?

Tort Reform

Tort litigation in the U.S. has been labeled a "liability crisis." The argument is that litigation creates waste and abuse and seriously damages the competitiveness of American industries. Industry groups have been particularly vocal in calling for tort reform to stem this problem. The main reform initiatives are aimed at curbing huge damage awards from "runaway" juries. The underlying source of the problem is frequently identified as greedy personal injury lawyers, who bring ill-founded lawsuits in the hope of extracting a settlement from the defendants or, if the case goes to trial before a jury, a large monetary award. For their part, trial lawyers fire back that the courts are often the last resort for otherwise helpless victims who have suffered at the hands of greedy corporations or incompetent professionals. They further argue that government is unable or unwilling to efficiently regulate corporations and powerful interests, like doctors, lawyers and hospitals. There is truth in both sides of this debate. It is ironic though that the main villains are the trial lawyers. Corporations do not seem to have the same distaste for the hordes of corporate, tax, labor, and criminal lawyers that are hired to do the bidding of big business. Nor, are the lawyer-lobbyists so prevalent in Washington and every state capital high on the "hit list" of evils plaguing America and impeding productivity.

Of the many proposed reforms, the most controversial have been those aimed at capping punitive (exemplary) and other non-economic damages. For example, the Texas Civil Procedure and Remedies Code caps punitive damages "at the greater of: (1)(A) two times the amount of economic damages; plus (B) an amount equal to any noneconomic damages found by the jury, not to exceed $750,000; or (2) $200,000." The plaintiff must prove fraud, malice, or gross negligence by clear and convincing evidence (ordinary negligence, bad faith, or deceptive trade practices cannot be used to shift the burden), and compensatory damages other than nominal damages must be awarded. A jury must unanimously agree to award punitive damage in a separate proceeding.

Other states have attempted to solve this problem by requiring that punitive damage awards be paid to a public interest entity or a fund other than the plaintiff. The tort law of Georgia, for example, permits punitive damages "when it is proven by clear and convincing evidence that the defendant's actions showed willful misconduct, malice, fraud, wantonness, oppression, or that entire want of care which would raise the presumption of conscious indifference to consequences." There is no limit on the amount of punitive damages in product liability cases, but, as a way of removing the litigation lottery effect, 75% of the punitive damages must be paid to the State treasury.

Key Terms and Concepts

Assumption of Risk
Contingency Fee
Duty to Mitigate
Duty to Warn
Foreseeability
Informed Consent
Joint and Several Liability
Proximate Cause
Reasonable Expert Standard
Reasonable Person Standard

Chapter 8

Property

"But not all economic interests are 'property rights'; only those economic advantages are 'rights' which have the law back of them, and only when they are so recognized may courts compel others to forbear from interfering with them or to compensate for their invasion."

Jackson, J., in *United States v. Willow River Power Co.*, 324 U.S. 499 (1945)

Property law is first and foremost about ownership, possession, and the rights springing therefrom. It is among the oldest and slowest-changing areas of law. Vestiges of its ancient lineage can still be seen in modern property law, especially regarding the operation of principles of law and equity. There are three basic types of property: real, movable, and intellectual. Property can also be either private or public. The focus in this chapter will be on rights relating to private ownership and use of real property, namely, land and structures appurtenant to land. The issues relating to intellectual property (sometimes referred to as intangible property) are taken up in Chapter 9. Rights relating to movable property (sometimes referred to as tangible property or chattel) will be discussed briefly in connection with the discussion of creating and perfecting security interests, but will not be dealt with in detail.

Another topic that lies beyond the scope of this chapter is the area of trusts, although they are taken up briefly in Chapter 11. A trust comes into being when a person or entity (the grantor) transfers legal ownership to property (real, movable or intellectual; the *res* or substance of the trust) in trust for the benefit and use of others known as beneficiaries. A trustee is appointed to operate and manage the trust in accordance with its terms, and is treated as the legal owner of the property in trust. The beneficiaries have only a beneficial interest or a future interest in the trust. Trust law has many modern day applications, particularly in the financial investment field and in estate and tax planning. One frequent use of trusts occurs when parents or grandparents establish a current trust fund for the future education of their children or grandchildren. Trusts are creatures of contract, and the grantor can, with a few exceptions, freely establish the terms of the trust.

Ownership of Property

The private ownership of property is a central principle of the American legal system. Private property rights are strongly protected by both civil and criminal remedies. A person who enters the land of another without permission can be convicted of the crime of trespass. In a similar manner, a person who takes the property of another can be convicted of theft. A person who occupies another's property unlawfully, such as a squatter or a renter who fails to pay rent, can be ejected. An action for ejectment is a relatively streamlined procedure for allowing the owner of land to regain possession against a wrongful occupier. Its analog for movable property is an action for *replevin*.

Owners of property enjoy wide freedom to use, lease, or sell their property in a manner that they feel is appropriate. Ownership does not, however, amount to absolute freedom. Zoning and environmental laws restrict what an owner can do with its property. For example, city zoning ordinances rightly forbid an owner from keeping livestock in residential neighborhoods. In a similar fashion, owners are not permitted to use their property in a manner that creates a nuisance (a form of tort) or disturbs the quiet enjoyment of others to own and use their own property. An owner is also prohibited from entering into arrangements that attempt to forbid forever the sale of land. Restraints on alienation are prohibited as a way of preventing "dead hand" control of land for all time. It is not socially acceptable to allow the living to tie up land in perpetuity to satisfy a selfish desire to control the destiny of property (or people) after death. Finally, the courts have struck down restrictive covenants attempting to forbid owners from discriminating against potential buyers based on impermissible factors such as race.

One attribute of ownership is the right to create multiple interests in property. These interests consist of "bundles of rights" that can be conveyed separately from the right to own, possess, or use the entire property. A building owner may, for example, elect to rent a part of the building and retain a portion. Tall commercial buildings frequently grant cell phone operating companies the right to place transmission towers on the tops of their buildings. An owner can grant sign or naming rights to a building. Selling naming rights is popular among owners of professional sports facilities. Property can also be the subject of easements, licenses, and rights of way. An easement is a right to use some part of the property for a specified purpose. Easements can be voluntary or by operation of law. An example of a voluntary easement is an office building permitting the public to enter and walk around the lobby. An easement by operation of law is granted in favor of water, gas, sewage, and electricity utilities.

Estates in Land and Deeds

Common law recognizes a number of estates in land. The strongest and most common form of legal ownership is a fee simple. An owner in fee simple has absolute ownership and a superior right to land against the world. This ownership includes the rights to minerals under the ground and the air above it. Lesser types of estates are the estate for years and the life estate. In the former, ownership is granted for a fixed time after which it reverts back to the original owner, while in the latter ownership reverts upon the death of the life estate holder. Joint or shared ownership of land is possible. A married couple can own their property as tenants by the entirety. In such a case, each spouse is deemed to own an undivided interest in the total property. When one spouse dies, the property interest of the deceased spouse is extinguished, leaving the surviving spouse with sole ownership. The "transfer" occurs automatically upon death, and no probate or other proceedings are required. Unmarried persons might opt for ownership as tenants in common or joint tenants with the right of survivorship. This latter form of ownership operates in the same manner as the tenants by the entirety form available to married couples.

Unlike civil law countries, common law jurisdictions prohibit the separate sale of land and buildings. A purchaser of a piece of land automatically acquires all buildings (including fixtures permanently attached to buildings) located on the property.

The legal document manifesting ownership of land is called a title. The document used to transfer ownership of land is known as a deed. The deed is critical for determining a variety of legal rights, such as who can sell the property and whether and how much of the value of the land is available to creditors, whether there are restrictive covenants (a contractual condition limiting what the owner can do with the property), and whether the property will be subject to probate upon the death of a co-owner. A valid deed is almost always required to transfer an interest in land.

The three most common types of deed are the warranty deed, the grant deed, and the quitclaim deed. In a warranty deed, the seller gives the buyer an express promise that the seller's title to the property is good. A grant deed is very similar insofar as the seller states in the deed that the property has not been transferred to a third party. A quitclaim deed is the least reliable for a buyer. The seller represents only that he is transferring whatever ownership interest he has in the property without warranting the validity of the interest. The quitclaim is effective against the person who gives it, but it provides little or no protection against third party claims. Quitclaim deeds are frequently used to resolve property disputes between adjacent land owners and in divorce proceedings.

To avoid ownership disputes and to reduce the chance for fraud, every American jurisdiction maintains a registration system for recording the ownership of real property. A recorded deed constitutes notice to the world of the ownership status and restrictions (restrictive covenants, mortgages, liens, etc.) relating to the property. It is advisable for a buyer to hire a title search company before completing a purchase in order to determine whether there are any problems with the property that have to be resolved before the seller can deliver a clean and marketable title. The title company will also issue, for a one-time fee, title insurance to protect the buyer against any title challenges arising after the purchase. The title insurance policy lists the exceptions to the title insurance company's duty to pay, and these must be carefully reviewed by the buyer. Standard exceptions to title are easements and rights of way for utilities. Immediately after the sale is closed, it is prudent for a buyer to record the deed transferring ownership. Recording is a simple process done at the Recorder of Deeds office, usually located in the local courthouse.

There is no requirement that there be only one deed for a single piece of property, and a *bona fide* purchaser who buys without notice of another's unrecorded ownership could prevail. Suppose A sells his home to B, and B neglects to record the deed. Thereafter, A sells the same home to C, and C promptly records the deed. C will take ownership of the home, provided C did not know of the prior transfer between A and B. B can sue A, but there is no guarantee that A can be located or that A will have the resources to satisfy the judgment.

A trust deed is another form of deed, but it is not used to transfer ownership of property between the seller and the buyer. Its sole function is to perform like a mortgage. The buyer places the property in trust for the benefit of the lender as security against repayment of the loan. The trustee has no rights to the property unless the buyer defaults on the loan. If a default occurs, the trustee can sell the property and repay the lender from the proceeds of the sale without having to go to court to foreclose on the property. Trust deeds are commonly used in California and in international finance transactions.

Acquisition of Property

The Contract of Sale

When an owner of property desires to sell to a willing buyer, the first step in the process is to enter into a Contract of Sale. All of the general rules applicable to contracts apply. The process begins with offer and acceptance (and often multiple counter-offers leading to agreement on price), and ends with a written agreement (the Statute of Frauds requires all contracts regarding interests in real property to be in writing) that must be supported by consideration and sufficiently definite in its terms and conditions. Real estate brokers are often hired by one or both of the parties and are paid a percentage of the final purchase price. There is an inherent conflict of interest in this arrangement in that the broker will not receive any compensation unless a deal is consummated. Nevertheless, the broker presumably is an expert in local market conditions and can provide the client with relevant information on comparable prices and customary conditions.

The Contract of Sale will establish other important terms, such as any conditions that must be fulfilled by the seller or the buyer prior to the Closing, and the time and date on which the Closing will take place. The period between the signing of the Contract of Sale and the Closing is used for conducting due diligence and satisfying conditions. The general rule of the common law is *caveat emptor* ("let the buyer beware"), and the buyer has the duty to check the property carefully. It is also important to determine who has the risk of loss during this period so that insurance can be purchased. A seller may require the buyer to pay "earnest" money or make a down payment at the time of the Contract of Sale. The seller will normally be required to deliver a deed representing clean and marketable title. This means the seller is obligated to pay off and remove all mortgages or liens on the property prior to the Closing. The buyer in a residential transaction will ask for the right to have an independent inspector check the home for termites and other structural problems. Local regulations may require the seller to disclose and/or repair known defects in the property before selling the property. If the buyer currently owns a home, he or she may want a condition that obligates him or her to proceed to the Closing only after the existing home has been sold. In a similar manner, buyers will ask for a mortgage contingency that allows them to escape from the contract if they cannot arrange suitable financing to buy the property.

Mortgages

Most real estate transactions involve a third party lender, usually a bank or a savings and loan company. Borrowers can approach lenders in advance of the Contract of Sale to determine whether the lender is willing to lend money for the proposed transaction. If the lender is willing to do so, it will issue a commitment letter setting forth the principal amount of the loan, the interest rate, the term of the loan (typically anywhere from 10 to 30 years), the period of validity of the commitment, and other relevant terms and conditions. Truth in Lending laws require the lender to disclose the full amount of interest the borrower will be paying as well as any other fees, costs, or expenses.

The lender will agree to lend a certain percentage of the purchase price to the buyer provided that the buyer comes up with a suitable down payment. This amount and all subsequent amounts the owner pays towards the principal of the loan make up the owner's equity in the property. The amount of down payment required by the lender depends on the creditworthiness of the borrower and the estimated value of the property. The lender will want to know that the property has sufficient market value so it can be sold for at least what it is owed in the event the lender has to foreclose on the property. In return for lending the buyer the balance of the purchase price over the amount of the down payment, the buyer must agree to a mortgage over the property as collateral for the loan.

The lender is called the mortgagee and the borrower is the mortgagor. A mortgage is a registered priority over the property that allows the lender to satisfy the debt from the value of the property before other creditors of the buyer can look to the property to satisfy the amounts they are owed. Mortgages are ranked by their priority. Second mortgages, sometimes called home owner; home improvement; or home equity loans, are not uncommon. The loan agreement will contain many important terms and conditions, such as upfront payments (called "points" representing from one percent to three percent of the principal amount of the loan), the interest rate, the term of the loan, whether it can be repaid early, and other standard "boilerplate" conditions. The loan agreement may also determine whether the lender has the right to seek repayment from the borrower beyond the value of the property sold in foreclosure. Lenders usually require the buyer to purchase relatively inexpensive mortgage insurance that will pay off the mortgage in the event the mortgagor dies before repaying the loan.

The Uniform Commercial Code has a similar registration process for securing debt using movable property. This is critical for business because it allows borrowers to borrow money using their assets (accounts receivable, equipment, raw materials, vehicles, machinery, etc.) as collateral. Lenders are more willing to lend because they can place a lien over the pledged assets and then register that lien in what is known as a UCC 1 filing. A duly registered filing gives notice to the world that the assets described in the filing have been pledged to a lender. The lender has a first priority interest if the assets must be sold to repay the obligations of the borrower.

The Closing

Assuming all of the terms and conditions to the Contract of Sale have been satisfied or waived, the parties will proceed to the Closing. The Closing is usually held at the office of a title company, which acts as an escrow agent. An escrow agent is a third party that agrees to hold documents or property pending the fulfillment of contractually created conditions. If the conditions are satisfied, the documents or property is released. If not, it is returned to the person who placed it with the escrow agent. The seller presents the buyer with a deed showing clean and marketable title, or some lesser level of title if agreed, and the buyer presents the seller with a check. The seller is referred to as the grantor and the buyer as the grantee in the deed.

Real estate practice is governed by state law and local practice. In most jurisdictions, most of the paperwork for residential property sales transactions is done by real estate agents or the title company without either the seller or buyer being represented by an attorney. Real estate associations produce standard form contracts that are often used by both sides. In complicated transactions, or when commercial property is involved, the parties usually hire a lawyer to ensure that their rights are adequately protected. As indicated above, the deed is recorded immediately following the Closing.

Foreclosure Proceedings

The loan agreement specifies certain Events of Default. These are events that allow the lender to foreclose on the property if one or more of them occur. The most frequent event of default is failure by the borrower to make monthly mortgage payments of principal and interest when due. There are two types of foreclosures: judicial sale and power of sale. In a judicial sale, the property is placed on the market and sold under the supervision of the court. The proceeds of the foreclosure sale will be used first to pay court costs and the amount owed to any secured mortgage or lien holders. The balance, if any, left over after the debts of the property have been satisfied will be paid to the borrower. This method is available throughout the U.S., and is the only method of foreclosure permitted in many states. A power of sale foreclosure operates like a judicial sale except that the lender can sell the property by following detailed notice and sale procedures without court supervision. The purchaser of property in foreclosure takes a clean title against the original owner and the lenders.

If the property is sold and the value received is not enough to pay off the debt, the lender can sue the borrower personally for the balance owed. Some states, however, require an election of remedies so that, if the lender forecloses on the property, it must look exclusively to the proceeds from the sale to satisfy the obligation, i.e., the lender is barred from suing the borrower for any deficiency.

Options over Property

The owner of property is permitted to grant an option over it. The option must be supported by independent consideration. It cannot rely on the underlying consideration for its validity. For example, if law firm A rents ten floors from owner B in building X for an agreed monthly rental, with an option to take five more floors at any time after the third year of the lease, A must give B something of value (even a nominal amount of one dollar will be enough) to secure the option.

One form of option is the right of first refusal. The following case explores the rights and duties flowing from the grant of a right of first refusal over real property in a relatively complicated factual context.

Cipriano v. Glen Cove Lodge
801 N.E.2d 388 (N.Y. 2003)

Rosenblatt, J.

In this real property case, we are called upon to adjudicate the rights and remedies of the three parties before us: the holder of a right of first refusal, the buyer of the property and the seller.

I.

In June 1955, five trustees of the Benevolent and Protective Order of Elks, Glen Cove Lodge # 1458 (Lodge) entered into a stipulation with Gasper Buffa—who was selling a parcel of land to the Lodge—that promised Buffa a "first option to repurchase" the property at fair market value in the event the Lodge offered the premises for sale. For the first three decades following the grant of this right, the Lodge scrupulously honored its obligations to Buffa. In October 1995, after it had received a *bona fide* offer to purchase the property, the Lodge extended Buffa the opportunity to exercise his right. In a letter of October 28, 1995 (inadvertently dated 1996), Buffa declined, but said he wanted to keep his "options open" should the Lodge's deal fall through. Again, in May 1996 and December 1996, the Lodge advised Buffa that it had received *bona fide* offers for the property and extended him the right of first refusal. In both instances, Buffa declined.

In 1997, the Lodge entered into negotiations with Michael Cipriano for the sale of the property, and on February 10, 1998, the Lodge sent Cipriano a proposed agreement. After substantial delay, the Lodge and Cipriano entered into a contract of sale on July 2, 1999. The agreement, however, was not made contingent on Buffa waiving his right of first refusal, nor did it disclose the existence of that right. Cipriano agreed to pay $550,000 for the property, with $55,000 down. The contract set August 2, 1999, as the closing date. A rider to the contract further provided that: "In the event title is unmarketable, the sole remedy of the Purchaser will be to accept such title as the Seller shall be able to deliver without abatement in the purchase price, or in the alternative, to cancel this Agreement and receive a refund of the Contract down payment, together with the net charges actually charged to the Purchaser for the examination of title, without insurance ... and cost of a survey. Upon such refund ... the Seller shall not be liable for any other costs or damages whatsoever."

When Cipriano and the Lodge entered into the contract, Cipriano evidently had notice of Buffa's outstanding right of first refusal. Indeed, Buffa and Cipriano, as long-time members of the Lodge, were well acquainted with one another. Nevertheless, based on the Lodge's representations, Cipriano was led to believe that Buffa had waived his right. In an August 3, 1999, letter, Cipriano asked the Lodge to confirm that it had Buffa's written waiver, and to produce it. The Lodge, however, ignored the request. Two days later, Cipriano informed the Lodge that Buffa had not waived his right of first refusal, and, indeed, wanted a price for the waiver. On August 9, Cipriano wrote the Lodge, demanding "immediate clarification" concerning the status of Buffa's right of first refusal.

Contrary to the Lodge's representations to Cipriano, Buffa had never waived his right of first refusal. Indeed, the Lodge never extended Buffa the opportunity to exercise his right before or after it entered into its contract with Cipriano, even though Buffa advised the Lodge of his claim. In a September 2, 1999, letter to the Lodge, Buffa expressed his "sincere interest in exercising his 're-purchase right'" and asked for a copy of the executed contract for his review. The Lodge ignored this request as well. Instead, it demanded proof of Buffa's right of first refusal. On September 20, Buffa forwarded the Lodge a copy of the 1955 agreement creating the right. He again asked the Lodge for a copy of the Lodge's contract with Cipriano, and again the Lodge ignored the request.

On September 15, 1999, the Lodge wrote Cipriano to inform him that Buffa had not effected a waiver, and it furnished Cipriano a copy of Buffa's "purported right of first refusal." The Lodge also reminded Cipriano that it was "unwilling to bring any action or proceeding or to expend any money or expense with respect to this title issue" and asked him if he was willing to take title, subject to Buffa's right. On September 24, 1999, Cipriano wrote the Lodge, asking it to clarify its position regarding the status of Buffa's right of first refusal. When the Lodge failed to reply, Cipriano, by a letter dated October 4, 1999, again asked the Lodge to explain its position with respect to Buffa's rights. On October 5, in a letter to Cipriano, the Lodge reaffirmed the position it assumed in its September 15 letter: that Cipriano could take title, subject to Buffa's right of first refusal, but without abatement of the purchase price.

Meanwhile, Cipriano initiated negotiations with Buffa, with the goal of buying out Buffa's preemptive right. These discussions proved unavailing and delayed Cipriano's closing with the Lodge. Finally, in a letter to Cipriano dated December 28, 1999, the Lodge attempted to cancel its contract and returned Cipriano's down payment of $55,000. On January 3, 2000, Cipriano sent the check back, rebuking the Lodge for its attempt at unilateral cancellation. The Lodge responded on January 13, instructing Cipriano to close on January 28. It warned that time was of the essence and that it would count Cipriano's failure to appear as a default entitling it to keep the down payment. On January 26, 2000, Cipriano informed the Lodge that he was initiating litigation to quiet title and that he did not intend to close on January 28. On January 27, the Lodge informed Cipriano that he had committed an anticipatory breach and that it would keep the down payment.

Cipriano brought this action against the Lodge and Buffa. He alleged that the Lodge could not and did not deliver marketable title to the property, and that the Lodge had interfered with his contractual right to the property. Cipriano sought specific performance and damages for breach of contract. In its answer, the Lodge denied Cipriano's allegations and argued that when Cipriano signed the contract he had notice of Buffa's claims to the property. The Lodge also counterclaimed against Cipriano for failing to attend the scheduled January 28, 2000, closing. This default, the Lodge asserted, entitled it to keep the down payment. In his answer, Buffa claimed that he held a valid right of first refusal, that the Lodge violated that right by contracting with Cipriano and that it had failed to extend him an offer to purchase the property or even furnish him with a copy of the contract. Buffa moved for dismissal of Cipriano's claim and filed a cross claim against the Lodge for damages or specific performance of his right of first refusal.

II. Buffa's Right of First Refusal

This Court last addressed the enforceability of a right of first refusal in *LIN Broadcasting Corp. v. Metromedia, Inc.*, 542 N.E.2d 629 (N.Y. 1989). All the parties claim that *LIN* supports their position. In *LIN* we settled the question of "whether a contractual right of first refusal, which has been triggered by a contract to sell to a third party, may be exercised during the specified duration of the right but after the third-party transaction has been abandoned." Stressing the difference between an option and a right of first refusal, we held that the grantor of a right of first refusal is obligated to give the holder of the right only an opportunity to buy the property. The grantor is not obligated to "render more than its promised performance ... by keeping the offer open for the period specified in the first refusal clause." The holder of a right of first refusal must be given the opportunity to exercise the preemptive right, but the right is extinguished when the contract with the third party expires or is abandoned.

In *Yudell Trust I v. API Westchester Assoc.*, 643 N.Y.S.2d 161 (N.Y. App. 1996), the Appellate Division elaborated on our holding in *LIN* by concluding that someone who holds a right of first refusal may create a "binding contract" with the grantor by exercising the right before the third-party contract expires. The validity of this contract is not affected by "the subsequent expiration of the triggering event."

Had Buffa been given the opportunity to exercise his right of first refusal, this case would fall squarely under the settled authority of *LIN* or *Yudell Trust I*. One of two scenarios would result, assuming Buffa did not decline his right to buy the property: either (1) Buffa would have exercised his right of first refusal before the breakdown of the Lodge-Cipriano transaction, or (2) he would have attempted to do so after its abandonment. In the first scenario, Buffa's exercise would have created a binding offer and acceptance between him and the Lodge. In the second scenario, *LIN* would govern, and Buffa's ability to exercise his right would have evaporated.

The Lodge, however, never gave Buffa the opportunity to exercise his right of first refusal. In its earlier attempts to sell its property in 1995 and 1996, the Lodge honored an obligation to advise Buffa of any bona fide offers it received and to extend him the opportunity to buy the property on the same terms. Here, the Lodge took no steps to inform Buffa of its impending sale to Cipriano and did not make the contract subject to Buffa's right. Indeed, it ignored Buffa's repeated requests for a copy of its contract with Cipriano, as well as his written expressions of interest in exercising his right. The Lodge argues that its failure to respond to Buffa did not deny him a meaningful opportunity to exercise his right of first refusal because Buffa already knew that the Lodge had contracted to sell the property to Cipriano. Inasmuch as Buffa was apprised of the transaction, the argument goes, the Lodge was under no duty to answer his letters or inform him of the terms of its contract with Cipriano. We find this argument wholly unpersuasive.

A right of first refusal is a right to receive an offer, and the grantor's failure or refusal to extend the holder the opportunity to exercise the right constitutes a breach. As we stated in *LIN* "[t]he effect of a right of first refusal ... is to bind the party who desires to sell not to sell without first giving the other party the opportunity to purchase the property at the price specified." Thus, an owner of land subject to a right of first refusal is obligated contractually to make an offer to the rightholder. A rightholder may be familiar with the broad contours of the grantor's transaction with a third party, but may nevertheless be handicapped in exercising the right when there is no specific offer from the grantor.

Rather than extending an offer to Buffa, the Lodge ignored his repeated requests for a copy of its contract with Cipriano, as well as his written affirmations of interest in exercising his right. Through its failure to act, the Lodge denied Buffa his bargained-for performance, that is, an opportunity to exercise his preemptive right to buy the property.

Although the Lodge breached its contractual obligations to Buffa, on the unique facts before us, neither specific performance nor damages provides a satisfactory remedy for the Lodge's default. Specific performance—the principal remedy which Buffa has sought—is inapt when the relations between two parties as to the transfer of an interest in land have yet to ripen into a binding contractual agreement. Specific performance may be granted only where the holder of the right of first refusal is shown to be "ready, willing, and able to purchase the property, not only when the right ripens, but also when specific performance is ordered." Notwithstanding Buffa's letters to the Lodge or his effort to vindicate his right of first refusal through litigation, there is little in the record to support his assertion that he was ready, willing, and able to buy the property. If anything, his readiness to negotiate with Cipriano and waive his right of first refusal suggests that Buffa was less interested in buying the property than he was in selling his right. Given the haze of uncertainty surrounding Buffa's actual intent in the summer and fall of 1999, as well as the likely appreciation of the Lodge's property over the past four years, a grant of specific performance enabling Buffa to purchase the Lodge's property at the 1999 contract price could yield him a potential windfall.

As an alternative to specific performance, Buffa seeks damages against the Lodge for breach of his right of first refusal. We conclude that an award of damages is not warranted under the unusual facts before us. Although the Lodge wrongfully deprived Buffa of an opportunity to exercise his right, Buffa suffered no injury as a result of the Lodge's breach. Buffa continues to hold the same right he held at the outset of the Lodge's initial

1998 negotiations with Cipriano. As in the past, Buffa can still invoke his right of first refusal against the offer of any future prospective purchaser. Moreover, he will still cast a cloud over the Lodge's title, and may seek compensation from potential buyers who want him to waive his right. Because the Lodge caused no appreciable injury to Buffa, no damages can flow from its breach.

III. Cipriano's Down Payment

[T]he Appellate Division found that the Lodge had fulfilled its contractual obligations to Cipriano and that Cipriano could have cancelled the contract and retained his down payment. The Court concluded that Cipriano had been "given more than a reasonable opportunity to perform under the contract of sale" but had failed to do so. The Lodge, the Court reasoned, was therefore entitled to hold Cipriano in default and keep the down payment.

Cipriano maintains that the courts below erred in granting the Lodge summary judgment on its counterclaim. The Lodge's failure to produce marketable title, he argues, barred it from holding him in default and retaining his down payment. Under the circumstances of this case, we agree with Cipriano.

In *Maxton Bldrs. v. Lo Galbo*, 502 N.E.2d 184 (N.Y. 1986), we reaffirmed a rule that has become axiomatic: a "vendee who defaults on a real estate contract without lawful excuse, cannot recover the down payment." Cipriano had such a lawful excuse. Although Cipriano did not appear at the January 28, 2000, closing, his failure is at least matched by the Lodge's recalcitrant behavior. To the extent the Appellate Division found that the Lodge acted in good faith in its efforts to convey title, there is no evidence in the record to support this determination. First, the Lodge contracted with Cipriano while misrepresenting Buffa's readiness to waive his right of first refusal. It then handicapped Cipriano's efforts to clear title by ignoring Buffa's repeated entreaties for a copy of the contract. After that, the Lodge tried to effect a unilateral cancellation of its contract with Cipriano. The Lodge maintains that Cipriano's refusal to accept this cancellation should, in effect, estop him from attacking its failure to deliver marketable title. We are not persuaded.

We acknowledge that a rider to the Cipriano-Lodge contract relieved the Lodge of any obligation "to bring any action or proceeding or to expend any sums of money or to incur any expense in order to render title marketable." Nevertheless, this clause does not excuse the Lodge's dereliction. Where a seller draws a prospective buyer into a transaction when it cannot possibly convey marketable title and then itself stymies the efforts of the buyer to remove the encumbrance, the seller may not rely on the language of the rider to keep the buyer's down payment. Because the Lodge was in material breach of its contractual obligations to Cipriano, we conclude that Cipriano had a lawful excuse for his failure to appear on the January 28 closing date. The Appellate Division's holding that the Lodge was entitled to retain Cipriano's down payment was therefore in error.

* * *

Topics for Further Discussion

1. Why do you think that Buffa requested a right of first refusal from the Lodge? It is not clear from the case, but we can surmise that he was only willing to sell the property if it were going to be used by the Lodge in which he was a member. Perhaps, he sold the property at a favorable price to assist the Lodge. If the Lodge wanted or needed to sell the property, then Buffa wanted the right, but not the obligation, to buy back the property. Do you think that Buffa was successful with his strategy?

2. Cipriano refused the Lodge's offer to give the down payment back and to terminate the contract. Why did Cipriano refuse this offer and why doesn't it bar him from later claiming that the Lodge would not return his down payment?

3. Why did the Court say that Buffa was not entitled to the remedy of specific performance? Why would granting him that right constitute a "windfall" and why is that a bad thing?

4. When all is said and done, what was the status of each of the parties after the *Cipriano* decision?

Remedies

Remedies are of critical importance to parties in real estate transactions. The common law has a general preference for monetary damages. There are many reasons for this, among them, the court's reluctance to remain involved in disputes beyond determining liability and damages. The normal measure of damages for breach of contract is the amount required to put the non-breaching party into the same position it would have been had there been no breach. This is called "benefit of the bargain" damages. However, it has long been recognized that there are cases in which monetary damages are not adequate. One such case is where the object of the sale is considered unique. For example, if A agrees to sell B a rare, one-of-a-kind postal stamp and then reneges on the deal, no amount of monetary damages will be able to give B what he bargained for, i.e., the stamp. A court will order A to deliver the stamp to B if it determines that A did, in fact, breach the obligation to sell the stamp. Real estate is always considered unique because no two pieces of property are the same. They may have identical monetary values, and they may even be located next to each other, but plot X can never be the same as plot Y.

Condominiums and Cooperatives

Urban development has led to new forms of collective property ownership. The most common form of collective ownership is the condominium, or condo. A condo property is a building or complex of apartment-style buildings containing multiple units that are specifically owned by separate owners, each of whom owns an undivided fractional interest in the building and its common areas. It is different from an apartment complex in that each unit is owned rather than rented. The condo building may be located on land owned by the condo association or on rented land. The owners enjoy the benefits and risks of home ownership, such as appreciation or loss in market value, without having to come up with the large sums of money required to purchase land and a house. Condos are governed by associations under the direction of elected boards consisting of unit holders, which operate pursuant to Articles; By-laws; and/or regulations. These charters and regulations determine how each unit can be used, what restrictions apply (for example, a ban on keeping pets, or on renting to third parties without the approval of the board), and how common areas and expenses will be managed and funded. Condo units can be sold and subjected to mortgages by their owners. In addition to financing the purchase of their own units, owners pay a monthly or quarterly condo fee that goes towards paying a management company or staff and to the funding an account for common expenses. Every state in the U.S. has laws governing condos, and some have strict rules limiting the ability of apartment building owners to convert to condos out of a concern for ensuring access to affordable rental properties for people with limited financial resources.

A less popular form of collective ownership is the cooperative. In a cooperative, the building and all of the units are owned by the cooperative, which is usually formed as a corporation. The owners have stock in the corporation and do not directly own the unit in which they reside. Each unit is leased on a long-term basis to the shareholder/owners. The economic effect is much the same as with a condominium, but the control of transferability is much stricter. It is very common for the co-op to provide in its rules that sales of shares and any sub-rental agreement must be approved by the board. Co-ops are popular in New York City, and there have been many cases where transfers to famous people, such as former Beatles member John Lennon and former President Richard Nixon, have been rejected because the other shareholders did not want to suffer the nuisance of *paparrazi*, fans, or reporters stalking the building.

Acquisition by Adverse Possession and Prescription

Adverse possession is a judicially created doctrine, closely related to a statute of limitations, which allows a person to obtain ownership over land involuntarily against the legal owner. The basis of adverse possession is the unlawful occupancy of land for a specified period of time, typically twenty years. In this sense, adverse possession is one of the few legal doctrines where wrongdoers are rewarded for their bad behavior. Prescription is like adverse possession except that the party obtains an easement (a right to use) over property instead of ownership. The terms "adverse possession" and "prescription" are frequently used interchangeably.

In *Pierz v. Gorski*, 276 N.W.2d 352 (Wis. Ct. App. 1979), the Wisconsin Court of Appeals articulated the conditions for adverse possession as follows: "To constitute adverse possession, the use of the land must be open, notorious, visible, exclusive, hostile and continuous, such as would apprise a reasonably diligent landowner and the public that the possessor claims the land as his own." The possessor has the burden of proving each of the elements in support of the claim to ownership. If the legal owner can demonstrate that the possession was with permission, then the action for adverse possession will be defeated.

While the doctrine of adverse possession is not a favored or encouraged method of acquiring ownership, it is useful in avoiding social waste. If the legal owner has abandoned the land, or cares so little about it that he does not bother to take legal action to eject a squatter or to keep trespassers out, then society benefits by stripping ownership from the legal owner and transferring it to someone who is willing to own or use the property productively. It is a doctrine, as one court expressed it, enforced to "stimulate activity and punish negligence."

Landlord and Tenant

A lease creates an interest in land and/or the premises located on the land (a leasehold) allowing a party (the tenant) to occupy and use property in accordance with the terms and conditions of the lease. The owner of the land (the landlord) maintains ownership of the land and premises. A lease is, in essence, a contract permitting the landlord and tenant to negotiate freely, with a few notable exceptions, the terms and conditions of the tenant's right to use the property. Examples of restrictions on the freedom of contract are Fair Housing laws and local rent control regulations. These rules prohibit the landlord from discriminating against certain classes of renters and raising rents unreasonably. It is believed that, without rent control, the gentrification process will result in the poor being driven out of their neighborhoods. One of the negative aspects of rent control is a strong disincentive for landlords to make improvements to their properties. Rent control is not widely practiced in the U.S., and many jurisdictions that once had it have repealed or severely curtailed it. Other restrictions on the freedom of contract can be also found in state law. California, for example, prohibits landlords from charging "key money" to enter or renew a lease unless the amount is clearly specified in the rental agreement.

Leases differ from other estates in land in that they are limited by time. A lease can be for a fixed period of years or "at will," i.e., it can be terminated at any time by the landlord. Leases involve a right to possession of the property. This is what separates a lease from licenses, easements, and other interests in land that allow use of property, such as the right to walk across another's land, to put up a billboard, or to stay in a hotel room.

Under traditional property law, the duty of the tenant to pay rent and the obligation of the landlord to make the premises habitable were separate covenants. This meant that the tenant was required to continue to pay rent regardless of the condition of the premises. Set-off was not permitted. If the tenant refused to pay the rent because of poor conditions, the tenant could be evicted. The only available remedy was to sue the landlord for breach of the lease. This proved very disadvantageous to tenants for obvious reasons, and the modern trend is now to allow the tenant to withhold rent payments while the unsatisfactory conditions exist. This motivates landlords to make repairs promptly.

The remedies for breach of a lease are substantially the same as in contract and include the duty to mitigate. Landlords have one major remedy that is peculiar to property law, namely, the right to evict the tenant from the premises. Landlords require security deposits to reduce the risk of a tenant not paying rent. The following case discusses the issue of constructive eviction while the notes that follow consider issues relating to the appropriate remedy.

Wade v. Jobe
818 P.2d 1006 (Utah 1991)

Durham, J.

In June 1988, defendant Lynda Jobe (the tenant) rented a house in Ogden, Utah, from plaintiff Clyde Wade (the landlord). Jobe had three young children. Shortly after she took occupancy, the tenant discovered numerous defects in the dwelling, and within a few days, she had no hot water. Investigation revealed that the flame of the water heater had been extinguished by accumulated sewage and water in the basement which also produced a foul odor throughout the house. The tenant notified the landlord, who came to the premises a number of times, each time pumping the sewage and water from the basement onto the sidewalk and relighting the water heater. These and other problems persisted from July through October 1988.

In November 1988, the tenant notified the landlord that she would withhold rent until the sewage problem was solved permanently. The situation did not improve, and an inspection by the Ogden City Inspection Division (the division) in December 1988 revealed that the premises were unsafe for human occupancy due to the lack of a sewer connection and other problems. Within a few weeks, the division made another inspection, finding numerous code violations which were a substantial hazard to the health and safety of the occupants. The division issued a notice that the property would be condemned if the violations were not remedied.

After the tenant moved out of the house, the landlord brought suit in the second circuit court to recover the unpaid rent. The tenant filed a counterclaim, seeking an offset against rent owed because of the uninhabitable condition of the premises and seeking damages, attorney fees, and declaratory relief under the Utah Consumer Sales Practices Act.

At trial, the landlord was awarded judgment of unpaid rent of $770, the full rent due under the parties' original agreement. The tenant was denied any offsets, and her counterclaim was dismissed. This appeal followed, raising [the issue]: [M]ay a tenant recover at common law for breach of a warranty of habitability?

At common law, the leasing of real property was viewed primarily as a conveyance of land for a term, and the law of property was applied to landlord/tenant transactions. At a time when the typical lease was for agricultural purposes, it was assumed that the land, rather than any improvements, was the most important part of the leasehold. Under the rule of *caveat emptor*, a tenant had a duty to inspect the premises to determine their safety and suitability for the purposes for which they were leased before entering a lease. Moreover, absent deceit or fraud on the part of the landlord or an express warranty to the contrary, the landlord had no duty to make repairs during the course of the tenancy. Under the law of waste, it was the tenant's implied duty to make most repairs.

Unlike tenants in feudal England, most modern tenants bargain for the use of structures on the land rather than the land itself. Modern tenants generally lack the necessary skills or means to inspect the property effectively or to make repairs. Moreover, the rule of *caveat emptor* assumes an equal bargaining position between landlord and tenant. Modern tenants, like consumers of goods, however, frequently have no choice but to rely on the landlord to provide a habitable dwelling. Where they exist, housing shortages, standardized leases, and racial and class discrimination place today's tenants, as consumers of housing, in a poor position to bargain effectively for express warranties and covenants requiring landlords to lease and maintain safe and sanitary housing.

In consumer law, implied warranties are designed to protect ordinary consumers who do not have the knowledge, capacity, or opportunity to ensure that goods which they are buying are in safe condition. The implied warranty of habitability has been adopted in other jurisdictions to protect the tenant as the party in the less advantageous bargaining position.

The concept of a warranty of habitability is in harmony with the widespread enactment of housing and building codes which reflect a legislative desire to ensure decent housing. It is based on the theory that the residential landlord warrants that the leased premises are habitable at the outset of the lease term and will remain so during the course of the tenancy. The warranty applies to written and oral leases, and to single-family as well as to multiple-unit dwellings. The warranty of habitability has been adopted, either legislatively or judicially, in over forty states and the District of Columbia.

In recent years, this court has conformed the common law in this state to contemporary conditions by rejecting the strict application of traditional property law to residential leases, recognizing that it is often more appropriate to apply contract law. Similarly, we have expanded landlord liability in tort. Consistent with prevailing trends in consumer law, products liability law, and the law of torts, we reject the rule of *caveat emptor* and recognize the common law implied warranty of habitability in residential leases.

The determination of whether a dwelling is habitable depends on the individual facts of each case. To guide the trial court in determining whether there is a breach of the warranty of habitability, we describe some general standards that the landlord is required to satisfy. We note initially that the warranty of habitability does not require the landlord to maintain the premises in perfect condition at all times, nor does it preclude minor housing code violations or other defects. Moreover, the landlord will not be liable for defects caused by the tenant. Further, the landlord must have a reasonable time to repair material defects before a breach can be established.

As a general rule, the warranty of habitability requires that the landlord maintain "bare living requirements," and that the premises are fit for human occupation. Failure to supply heat or hot water, for example, breaches the warranty. A breach is not shown, however, by evidence of minor deficiencies such as the malfunction of venetian blinds, minor water leaks or wall cracks, or a need for paint.

Substantial compliance with building and housing code standards will generally serve as evidence of the fulfillment of a landlord's duty to provide habitable premises. Evidence of violations involving health or safety, by contrast, will often sustain a tenant's claim for relief. At the same time, just because the housing code provides a basis for implication of the warranty, a code violation is not necessary to establish a breach so long as the claimed defect has an impact on the health or safety of the tenant.

In the instant case, in support of her claim that the premises were not in habitable condition, the tenant presented two city housing inspection reports detailing numerous code violations which were, in the words of the trial judge, "a substantial hazard to the health and safety of the occupants." Those violations included the presence of raw sewage on the sidewalks and stagnant water in the basement, creating a foul odor. At trial, the tenant testified that she had repeatedly informed the landlord of the problem with the sewer connection and the resulting lack of hot water, but the landlord never did any more than temporarily alleviate the problem. The landlord did not controvert the evidence of substantial problems. At trial, the court granted judgment for the landlord, concluding that Utah law did not recognize an implied warranty of habitability for residential rental premises. As discussed above, we have now recognized the warranty. We therefore remand this case to the trial court to determine whether the landlord has breached the implied warranty of habitability as defined in this opinion. If the trial court finds a breach of the warranty of habitability, it must then determine damages.

* * *

Topics for Further Discussion

1. What factors did the Court point to for treating landlord/tenant disputes under contract instead of traditional property law? What reasons are given for recognizing the implied warranty of habitability? What if the premises are only partially uninhabitable?

2. What is the proper measure of damages? Courts have generally applied general contract remedies, including ordinary and special damages when foreseeable. Rent abatement or reimbursement can also be awarded. This is based on the difference in fair market value of the property repaired and unrepaired. How is fair market value determined? To avoid the problem of proof, some jurisdictions use a formula whereby the trier of fact determines the percentage of diminution of use and then reduces the rent by that percentage.

Fair Housing

An owner of land has broad freedom to sell or rent (or to refuse to do so) property as the owner sees fit. There are major restrictions on this freedom however. For example, the Fair Housing Act embodied in Title VIII of the Civil Rights Act of 1968 establishes a federal policy of providing fair housing throughout the U.S. Section 3604 makes it illegal to "refuse to sell or rent after the making of a *bona fide* offer, or to refuse to negotiate for the sale or rental of, or otherwise make unavailable or deny, a dwelling to any person because of race, color, religion, sex, familial status, or national origin." It is similarly illegal to discriminate in conditions or services based on the same factors. Other laws prohibit discrimination based on other impermissible factors, such as handicap. In addition to the federal fair housing law, states and municipalities have similar regulatory regimes.

The U.S. Department of Housing and Urban Development (HUD) is the agency charged with policing the federal antidiscrimination regime. HUD maintains an extensive network of branch offices throughout the U.S. Its grievance procedures are available on line, and HUD has jurisdiction to take enforcement action against parties accused of violating Title VIII and its related regulations.

Eminent Domain and the Takings Clause

Government has the power to take private property for public purposes through eminent domain or condemnation proceedings. The Takings Clause of the Fifth Amendment mandates that compensation be paid for property taken for public use. The language of the Takings Clause is straightforward. It does not prohibit the government from taking private property; it only requires that the taking be for a public use and the owner be paid just compensation. The public use standard has been broadly interpreted, and government officials are given wide discretion in deciding when a taking is necessary and appropriate. Public use does not, for example, have to result in public access so long as there is a public benefit deriving from the condemnation. Eminent domain cases typically involve the taking of property for the building of roads, airports, military bases, schools, fire and police stations, parks, and other government facilities.

The government is required to provide the owner of property with due process of law under the Fifth and Fourteenth Amendments. The process begins with a government agency contacting the landowner in an effort to purchase the property voluntarily. The taking of property against the owner's will, no matter how justified, is heavy with emotion and the potential for dispute. If the landowner is not willing to sell, the agency will give notice of its intention to take the property and engage an independent appraiser to determine the value of the property. The appraisal forms the basis of an offer to purchase the property and a public hearing is then scheduled to determine the necessity of the taking. The owner is permitted to have a lawyer and to participate in the hearing. If the result of the public hearing is a resolution confirming the necessity of the taking, an eminent domain case will be filed in court.

Once a case has been filed in court, the proceedings are much the same as in any civil lawsuit. The landowner will be served and given an opportunity to challenge the necessity determination by the agency. The agency is required to post a bond with the court in the amount the agency believes is just compensation. The parties are free to engage in discovery and settlement discussions in an effort to resolve the matter by mutual agreement. If they cannot so agree, a judge or jury will render a verdict deciding (1) whether eminent domain is appropriate, and (2) if so, the amount of compensation to be paid to the property owner. Following judgment in favor of the agency, the government can avail itself of the power of the court to evict the owner and take possession of the property. There are very few defenses to an action for eminent domain, and property owners rarely prevail as can be seen from the following case.

Kelo v. City of New London, Conn.
545 U.S. 469 (2005)

Stevens, J.

In 2000, the city of New London approved a development plan that, in the words of the Supreme Court of Connecticut, was "projected to create in excess of 1,000 jobs, to increase tax and other revenues, and to revitalize an economically distressed city, including its downtown and waterfront areas." In assembling the land needed for this project, the city's development agent has purchased property from willing sellers and proposes to use the power of eminent domain to acquire the remainder of the property from unwilling owners in exchange for just compensation. The question presented is whether the city's proposed disposition of this property qualifies as a "public use" within the meaning of the Takings Clause of the Fifth Amendment to the Constitution.

I

The city of New London (hereinafter City) sits at the junction of the Thames River and the Long Island Sound in southeastern Connecticut. Decades of economic decline led a state agency in 1990 to designate the City a "distressed municipality." In 1996, the Federal Government closed the Naval Undersea Warfare Center, which had been located in the Fort Trumbull area of the City and had employed over 1,500 people. In 1998, the City's unemployment rate was nearly double that of the State, and its population of just under 24,000 residents was at its lowest since 1920.

These conditions prompted state and local officials to target New London, and particularly its Fort Trumbull area, for economic revitalization. To this end, respondent New London Development Corporation (NLDC), a private nonprofit entity established some years earlier to assist the City in planning economic development, was reactivated. In January 1998, the State authorized a $5.35 million bond issue to support the NLDC's planning activities and a $10 million bond issue toward the creation of a Fort Trumbull State Park. After receiving initial approval from the city council, the NLDC continued its planning activities and held a series of neighborhood meetings to educate the public about the process. In May, the city council authorized the NLDC to formally submit its plans to the relevant state agencies for review. Upon obtaining state-level approval, the NLDC finalized an integrated development plan focused on 90 acres of the Fort Trumbull area.

The city council approved the plan in January 2000, and designated the NLDC as its development agent in charge of implementation. The city council also authorized the NLDC to purchase property or to acquire property by exercising eminent domain in the City's name. The NLDC successfully negotiated the purchase of most of the real estate in the 90-acre area, but its negotiations with petitioners failed. As a consequence, in November 2000, the NLDC initiated the condemnation proceedings that gave rise to this case.

II

Petitioner Susette Kelo has lived in the Fort Trumbull area since 1997. She has made extensive improvements to her house, which she prizes for its water view. Petitioner Wilhelmina Dery was born in her Fort Trumbull house in 1918 and has lived there her entire life. Her husband Charles (also a petitioner) has lived in the house since they married some 60 years ago. In all, the nine petitioners own 15 properties in Fort Trumbull—4 in parcel 3 of the development plan and 11 in parcel 4A. Ten of the parcels are occupied by the owner or a family member; the other five are held as investment properties. There is no allegation that any of these properties is blighted or otherwise in poor condition; rather, they were condemned only because they happen to be located in the development area.

III

Two polar propositions are perfectly clear. On the one hand, it has long been accepted that the sovereign may not take the property of A for the sole purpose of transferring it to another private party B, even though A is paid just compensation. On the other hand, it is equally clear that a State may transfer property from one private party to another if future "use by the public" is the purpose of the taking; the condemnation of land for a railroad with common-carrier duties is a familiar example. Neither of these propositions, however, determines the disposition of this case.

As for the first proposition, the City would no doubt be forbidden from taking petitioners' land for the purpose of conferring a private benefit on a particular private party. Nor would the City be allowed to take property under the mere pretext of a public purpose, when its actual purpose was to bestow a private benefit. The takings before us, however, would be executed pursuant to a "carefully considered" development plan. The trial judge and all the members of the Supreme Court of Connecticut agreed that there was no evidence of an illegitimate purpose in this case. Therefore, the City's development plan was not adopted "to benefit a particular class of identifiable individuals."

On the other hand, this is not a case in which the City is planning to open the condemned land—at least not in its entirety—to use by the general public. Nor will the private lessees of the land in any sense be required to operate like common carriers, making their services available to all comers. But although such a projected use would be sufficient to satisfy the public use requirement, this "Court long ago rejected any literal requirement that condemned property be put into use for the general public." Indeed, while many state courts in the mid-19th century endorsed "use by the public" as the proper definition of public use, that narrow view steadily eroded over time. Not only was the "use by the public" test difficult to administer (e.g., what proportion of the public need have access to the property? at what price?), but it proved to be impractical given the diverse and always evolving needs of society. Accordingly, when this Court began applying the Fifth Amendment to the States at the close of the 19th century, it embraced the broader and more natural interpretation of public use as "public purpose." Thus, in a case upholding a mining company's use of an aerial bucket line to transport ore over property it did not own, Justice Holmes' opinion for the Court stressed "the inadequacy of use by the general public as a universal test." We have repeatedly and consistently rejected that narrow test ever since.

The disposition of this case therefore turns on the question whether the City's development plan serves a "public purpose." Without exception, our cases have defined that concept broadly, reflecting our longstanding policy of deference to legislative judgments in this field.

Viewed as a whole, our jurisprudence has recognized that the needs of society have varied between different parts of the Nation, just as they have evolved over time in response to changed circumstances. Our earliest cases in particular embodied a strong theme of federalism, emphasizing the "great respect" that we owe to state legislatures and state courts in discerning local public needs. For more than a century, our public use jurisprudence has wisely eschewed rigid formulas and intrusive scrutiny in favor of affording legislatures broad latitude in determining what public needs justify the use of the takings power.

IV

Those who govern the City were not confronted with the need to remove blight in the Fort Trumbull area, but their determination that the area was sufficiently distressed to justify a program of economic rejuvenation is entitled to our deference. The City has carefully formulated an economic development plan that it believes will provide appreciable benefits to the community, including—but by no means limited to—new jobs and increased tax revenue. As with other exercises in urban planning and development, the City is endeavoring to coordinate a variety of commercial, residential, and recreational uses of land, with the hope that they will form a whole greater than the sum of its parts. To effectuate this plan, the City has invoked a state statute that specifically authorizes the use of eminent domain to promote economic development. Given the comprehensive character of the plan, the thorough deliberation that preceded its adoption, and the limited scope of our review, it is appropriate for us to resolve the challenges of the individual owners, not on a piecemeal basis, but rather in light of the entire plan. Because that plan unquestionably serves a public purpose, the takings challenged here satisfy the public use requirement of the Fifth Amendment.

To avoid this result, petitioners urge us to adopt a new bright-line rule that economic development does not qualify as a public use. Putting aside the unpersuasive suggestion that the City's plan will provide only purely economic benefits, neither precedent nor logic supports petitioners' proposal. Promoting economic development is a traditional and long-accepted function of government. There is, moreover, no principled way of distinguishing economic development from the other public purposes that we have recognized. Clearly, there is no basis for exempting economic development from our traditionally broad understanding of public purpose.

Petitioners contend that using eminent domain for economic development impermissibly blurs the boundary between public and private takings. Again, our cases foreclose this objection. Quite simply, the government's pursuit of a public purpose will often benefit individual private parties.

It is further argued that without a bright-line rule nothing would stop a city from transferring citizen A's property to citizen B for the sole reason that citizen B will put the property to a more productive use and thus pay more taxes. Such a one-to-one transfer of property, executed outside the confines of an integrated development plan, is not presented in this case. While such an unusual exercise of government power would certainly raise a suspicion that a private purpose was afoot, the hypothetical cases posited by petitioners can be confronted if and when they arise. They do not warrant the crafting of an artificial restriction on the concept of public use.

Just as we decline to second-guess the City's considered judgments about the efficacy of its development plan, we also decline to second-guess the City's determinations as to what lands it needs to acquire in order to effectuate the project.

In affirming the City's authority to take petitioners' properties, we do not minimize the hardship that condemnations may entail, notwithstanding the payment of just compensation. We emphasize that nothing in our opinion precludes any State from placing further restrictions on its exercise of the takings power. Indeed, many States already impose "public use" requirements that are stricter than the federal baseline. Some of these requirements have been established as a matter of state constitutional law, while others are expressed in state eminent domain statutes that carefully limit the grounds upon which takings may be exercised. As the submissions of the parties and their *amici* make clear, the necessity and wisdom of using eminent domain to promote economic development are certainly matters of legitimate public debate. This Court's authority, however, extends only to determining whether the City's proposed condemnations are for a "public use" within the meaning of the Fifth Amendment to the Federal Constitution. Because over a century of our case law interpreting that provision dictates an affirmative answer to that question, we may not grant petitioners the relief that they seek.

O'Connor, J., dissenting

Over two centuries ago, just after the Bill of Rights was ratified, Justice Chase wrote: "An Act of the Legislature (for I cannot call it a law) contrary to the great first principles of the social compact, cannot be considered a rightful exercise of legislative authority.... A few instances will suffice to explain what I mean.... [A] law that takes property from A. and gives it to B: It is against all reason and justice, for a people to entrust a Legislature with such powers; and, therefore, it cannot be presumed that they have done it."

Today the Court abandons this long-held, basic limitation on government power. Under the banner of economic development, all private property is now vulnerable to being taken and transferred to another private owner, so long as it might be upgraded— i.e., given to an owner who will use it in a way that the legislature deems more beneficial to the public—in the process. To reason, as the Court does, that the incidental public benefits resulting from the subsequent ordinary use of private property render economic development takings "for public use" is to wash out any distinction between private and public use of property—and thereby effectively to delete the words "for public use" from the Takings Clause of the Fifth Amendment. Accordingly I respectfully dissent.

* * *

Topics for Further Discussion

1. Do you agree with the majority's deference to the City's determination that taking the petitioners' homes was justified for public use? What test did the Court apply to judge the constitutionality of the taking? Why did the Court reject the bright-line test proposed by the petitioners? Why would a one-to-one transfer cause greater suspicion than the compulsory transfers of ownership in this case?

2. The *Kelo* case was extremely controversial, and it met with a barrage of criticism. As a result, forty-three states revised their eminent domain laws to prohibit similar takings. A number of state supreme courts have also ruled that takings similar to those in *Kelo* are unconstitutional under state constitutions.

3. As a final irony, the City of New London's redevelopment project proved to be a failure. Nothing has been built on the property as of this writing at the start of 2010. The company that was to be the primary beneficiary of the redevelopment plan, Pfizer, announced in 2009 that it was abandoning its plan to build a research facility on the property and would move its operations to Groton, Connecticut, taking with it approximately 1,400 jobs.

4. Occasionally, private property owners do prevail. In the *City of Oakland v. Oakland Raiders*, 174 Cal. App. 3d 414 (Cal. Ct. App. 1985), the City attempted to take by eminent domain the franchise rights of the Oakland Raiders as a member of the National Football League (NFL) in an effort to block the team's move from Oakland to Los Angeles. The owners of the Raiders and the City were locked in a battle over the use of a municipal stadium where the Raiders played their home games. The City's argument amounted to a claim that the departure of the Raiders from the region would have a devastating economic impact and, therefore, taking the property was a public use. The case bounced back and forth between the trial court and the appellate courts a number of times before a final decision by the California Court of Appeal in 1985 in favor of the Oakland Raiders. The court held that the use of eminent domain by the City to force the Raiders to remain in Oakland was a violation of the Commerce Clause of the U.S. Constitution. The court explained:

> Plaintiff's proposed action would more than indirectly or incidentally regulate interstate commerce: plaintiff claims authority—pursuant to authorization found in state eminent domain statutes—to bar indefinitely defendant's business from relocating out of Oakland. This is the precise brand of parochial meddling with the national economy that the commerce clause was designed to prohibit. As shown above, relocation of the Raiders would implicate the welfare not only of the individual team franchise, but of the entire League. The spectre of such local action throughout the state or across the country demonstrates the need for uniform, national regulation. In these circumstances (and apart from other potential bases of commerce clause violation), if relocation threatens disproportionate harm to a local entity, regulation—if necessary—should come from Congress; only then can the consequences to interstate commerce be assessed and a proper balance struck to consider and serve the various interests involved in a uniform manner.

The Oakland Raiders moved to Los Angeles, but eventually returned to Oakland.

Regulation of Land Use

Zoning

It is a well-established principle of American property law that state and local governments have the authority to use their regulatory powers to prohibit "harmful and noxious" uses of private property. They also have the power to require that land use be in accordance with duly promulgated zoning regulations intended to preserve the character and nature of their communities. Most Americans, unlike residents in some other countries of the world, would find it extremely undesirable to have neighborhoods consisting of a hodgepodge of residential dwellings, small farms, and manufacturing facilities. Zoning prevents this by restricting the private use and development of property in accordance with a local municipal plan.

The broad categories of zoning are agriculture, residential (frequently subdivided into sub-sections such as single family dwelling homes, apartments, townhouses, condominiums, etc.), recreational, industrial, and commercial. Zoning regulations are administered by a local Zoning Board vested with authority to prescribe permitted and prohibited uses in certain areas or specific pieces of land under the Board's jurisdiction. For example, an area might be zoned for single family dwellings, thereby making the building of apartments illegal. Another area or property might be zoned as commercial, which would allow the owner to build and operate a store on the land. In order to obtain a commercial zone permit, the owner might be required to demonstrate that there will be ample parking available on site and that the local access roads are capable of handling the anticipated level of traffic.

Land use is not stagnant, and local communities find it in their best interests to remain flexible. Zoning regulations usually contain a process for changing the zoning of properties, or for seeking a variance for a specific purpose.

The power to zone is not without limits. The regulations must be within the legitimate range of the police power of the government, and they must not be used in a manner that unduly infringes on constitutional rights. Courts have regularly upheld reasonable time, place, and manner restrictions, as well as content-neutral permit requirements on the exercise of free speech. But, in *Metromedia v. City of San Diego*, 453 U.S. 490 (1981), the Court struck down a city ordinance prohibiting the erection of all outdoor advertising displays within the city.

Likewise, the Court has had no difficulty striking down zoning regulations that were found to be intentional efforts to exclude the handicapped, poor, or minorities from certain residential areas. In *City of Cleburne, Tex. v. Cleburne Living Center*, 473 U.S. 432 (1985), the City refused to issue a permit for a group home for the mentally retarded under a zoning ordinance. The Supreme Court declined to give "suspect or quasi-suspect class" status to the mentally handicapped but, nevertheless, invalidated the zoning ordinance because "requiring the permit in this case appears to us to rest on an irrational prejudice against the mentally retarded." However, in *Village of Arlington Heights v. Metropolitan Housing Development*, 429 U.S. 252 (1977), the Court declined to hold a non-racially motivated zoning ordinance unconstitutional even though it had the effect of prohibiting the construction of low income housing that would have permitted more African-Americans to move to Arlington Heights.

Finally, recollect the discussion of *Church of Lukumi Babalu Aye v. City of Hialeah*, 508 U.S. 520 (1993) in Chapter 4, where the Supreme Court struck down zoning ordinances because they infringed on the Free Exercise Clause rights of members of the Santeria religion to practice animal sacrifice. The Court held that: "Legislators may not devise mechanisms, overt or disguised, designed to persecute or oppress a religion or its practices. The laws here in question were enacted contrary to these constitutional principles, and they are void."

Regulatory Taking

The Supreme Court has struggled, in a long line of cases, with the question of when a regulatory imposition on property use constitutes a taking for constitutional purposes. In *Mugler v. Kansas*, 123 U.S. 623 (1887), the Court held that a state-wide ban on the manufacture of alcoholic beverages did not amount to a taking even though the owner of a brewery had operated his facility in a perfectly lawful manner before the passage of the law. Nearly twenty-five years later in *Pennsylvania Coal v. Mahon*, 260 U. S. 393 (1922), Justice Holmes recognized the principle that government regulation of land could amount to a taking if the government were found to have gone "too far." The *Mahon* court unfortunately did not set a clear standard for what would constitute going too far.

The Supreme Court took up the issue again in *Penn Central Transp. v. New York City*, 438 U. S. 104 (1978). This case presented the question of "whether the application of New York City's Landmarks Preservation Law to the parcel of land occupied by Grand Central Terminal has 'taken' its owners' property in violation of the Fifth and Fourteenth Amendments." Under the Landmarks Preservation Law, the city was authorized to designate certain buildings as important landmarks, thereby obligating their owners to keep them in good order and preventing material changes without first obtaining permission from the Commission. Grand Central Station was so designated, and Penn Central sued after its plan to build a multistory high rise office building over top of it was rejected. The Court endorsed an *ad hoc* standard requiring an examination of the particular facts of each case. In particular, the Court said the economic impact has to be examined along with the interference to the investment expectation of the land owner. It concluded that: "A 'taking' may more readily be found when the interference with property can be characterized as a physical invasion by government, than when interference arises from some public program adjusting the benefits and burdens of economic life to promote the common good."

The notion of a regulatory taking was called into question by the Court's decision in *Keystone Bituminous Coal v. DeBenedictis*, 480 U.S. 470 (1987) when Justice Stevens labeled the "too far" comment of Justice Holmes as *dictum*. The *DeBenedictis* case was followed by *First English Evangelical Lutheran Church v. County of Los Angeles*, 482 U.S. 304 (1987). In *First English*, the church had purchased a large parcel of land in a canyon along the banks of a river. The site was used as a recreational facility, campground, and retreat. After a flood destroyed the buildings on the site, the County passed an ordinance prohibiting construction in certain parts of the canyon, including part of the church's property, in order to protect the public health and safety. The California courts limited the remedy to an action to have the ordinance declared invalid, and the U.S. Supreme Court took the case to determine if the church should be able to recover monetary damages for the "temporary" taking period between the issuance of the ordinance and its invalidation. The Court concluded that "invalidation of the ordinance without payment of fair value for the use of the property during this period of time would be a constitutionally insufficient remedy."

The next major case was *Lucas v. South Carolina Coastal Council*, 505 U.S. 1003 (1992), where the Supreme Court considered a case of a developer who had purchased two lots on the Isle of Palms for $975,000 with the intention of building a single family home. The state passed a coastal management law after Lucas purchased his lots and before he had time to build, effectively banning the construction of permanent habitable structures. Justice Scalia, writing for the Court, balanced the legitimate interests of the state in managing its coastline against the interest of the landowner who was deprived of the economic value and reasonable use of his land. The Court concluded that "when the owner of real property has been called upon to sacrifice *all* economically beneficial uses in the name of the common good, that is, to leave property economically idle, he has suffered a taking."

The following case presents the issue of whether a moratorium on development, which effectively denied land owners the use of their property, constituted a taking under the Fifth Amendment. Lake Tahoe is a magnificent natural resource located on the border between California and Nevada. Environmental jurisdiction is maintained by both states and the federal government largely through the Tahoe Regional Planning Agency. Growing increasingly concerned that rapid development around Lake Tahoe would lead to the destruction of Lake Tahoe, the TRPA imposed two separate moratoria on all construction while it designed a strategy to cope with the problem. Landowners challenged the moratoria arguing that the moratoria constituted a taking of property without compensation.

Tahoe-Sierra Pres. Council v. Tahoe Reg'l Planning Agency
535 U.S. 302 (2002)

Stevens, J.

The question presented is whether a moratorium on development imposed during the process of devising a comprehensive land-use plan constitutes a *per se* taking of property requiring compensation under the Takings Clause of the United States Constitution. This case actually involves two moratoria ordered by respondent Tahoe Regional Planning Agency (TRPA) to maintain the status quo while studying the impact of development on Lake Tahoe and designing a strategy for environmentally sound growth. As a result of these two directives, virtually all development on a substantial portion of the property subject to TRPA's jurisdiction was prohibited for a period of 32 months.

Petitioners make only a facial attack on Ordinance 81-5 and Resolution 83-21. They contend that the mere enactment of a temporary regulation that, while in effect, denies a property owner all viable economic use of her property gives rise to an unqualified constitutional obligation to compensate her for the value of its use during that period. Hence, they "face an uphill battle," that is made especially steep by their desire for a categorical rule requiring compensation whenever the government imposes such a moratorium on development. Under their proposed rule, there is no need to evaluate the landowners' investment-backed expectations, the actual impact of the regulation on any individual, the importance of the public interest served by the regulation, or the reasons for imposing the temporary restriction. For petitioners, it is enough that a regulation imposes a temporary deprivation—no matter how brief—of all economically viable use to trigger a *per se* rule that a taking has occurred.

In our view the answer to the abstract question whether a temporary moratorium effects a taking is neither "yes, always" nor "no, never"; the answer depends upon the particular circumstances of the case. Resisting "[t]he temptation to adopt what amount to *per se* rules in either direction," we conclude that the circumstances in this case are best analyzed within the *Penn Central Transp. Co. v. New York City*, 438 U. S. 104 (1978) framework.

The text of the Fifth Amendment itself provides a basis for drawing a distinction between physical takings and regulatory takings. Its plain language requires the payment of compensation whenever the government acquires private property for a public purpose, whether the acquisition is the result of a condemnation proceeding or a physical appropriation. But the Constitution contains no comparable reference to regulations that prohibit a property owner from making certain uses of her private property. Our jurisprudence involving condemnations and physical takings is as old as the Republic and, for the most part, involves the straightforward application of *per se* rules. Our regulatory takings jurisprudence, in contrast, is of more recent vintage and is characterized by "essentially *ad hoc*, factual inquiries," designed to allow "careful examination and weighing of all the relevant circumstances."

When the government physically takes possession of an interest in property for some public purpose, it has a categorical duty to compensate the former owner, regardless of whether the interest that is taken constitutes an entire parcel or merely a part thereof. Thus, compensation is mandated when a leasehold is taken and the government occupies the property for its own purposes, even though that use is temporary. Similarly, when the government appropriates part of a rooftop in order to provide cable TV access for apartment tenants; or when its planes use private airspace to approach a government airport, it is required to pay for that share no matter how small. But a government regulation that merely prohibits landlords from evicting tenants unwilling to pay a higher rent; that bans certain private uses of a portion of an owner's property; or that forbids the private use of certain airspace, does not constitute a categorical taking. "The first category of cases requires courts to apply a clear rule; the second necessarily entails complex factual assessments of the purposes and economic effects of government actions."

This longstanding distinction between acquisitions of property for public use, on the one hand, and regulations prohibiting private uses, on the other, makes it inappropriate to treat cases involving physical takings as controlling precedents for the evaluation of a claim that there has been a "regulatory taking," and vice versa. For the same reason that we do not ask whether a physical appropriation advances a substantial government interest or whether it deprives the owner of all economically valuable use, we do not apply our precedent from the physical takings context to regulatory takings claims. Land-use regulations are ubiquitous and most of them impact property values in some tangential way—often in completely unanticipated ways. Treating them all as *per se* takings would transform government regulation into a luxury few governments could afford. By contrast, physical appropriations are relatively rare, easily identified, and usually represent a greater affront to individual property rights.

Perhaps recognizing this fundamental distinction, petitioners wisely do not place all their emphasis on analogies to physical takings cases. Instead, they rely principally on our decision in *Lucas v. South Carolina Coastal Council*, 505 U. S. 1003 (1992)—a regulatory takings case that, nevertheless, applied a categorical rule—to argue that the *Penn Central* framework is inapplicable here.

Considerations of "fairness and justice" arguably could support the conclusion that TRPA's moratoria were takings of petitioners' property based on any of seven different theories. First, even though we have not previously done so, we might now announce a categorical rule that, in the interest of fairness and justice, compensation is required whenever government temporarily deprives an owner of all economically viable use of her property. Second, we could craft a narrower rule that would cover all temporary land-use restrictions except those "normal delays in obtaining building permits, changes in zoning ordinances, variances, and the like" which were put to one side in our opinion in *First English*. Third, we could adopt a rule like the one suggested by an *amicus* supporting petitioners that would "allow a short fixed period for deliberations to take place without compensation—say maximum one year—after which the just compensation requirements" would "kick in." Fourth, with the benefit of hindsight, we might characterize the successive actions of TRPA as a "series of rolling moratoria" that were the functional equivalent of a permanent taking. Fifth, were it not for the findings of the District Court that TRPA acted diligently and in good faith, we might have concluded that the agency was stalling in order to avoid promulgating the environmental threshold carrying capacities and regional plan mandated by the 1980 Compact. Sixth, apart from the District Court's finding that TRPA's actions represented a proportional response to a serious risk of harm to the lake, petitioners might have argued that the moratoria did not substantially advance a legitimate state interest. Finally, if petitioners had challenged the application of the moratoria to their individual parcels, instead of making a facial challenge, some of them might have prevailed under a *Penn Central* analysis.

With respect to these theories, the ultimate constitutional question is whether the concepts of "fairness and justice" that underlie the Takings Clause will be better served by one of these categorical rules or by a *Penn Central* inquiry into all of the relevant circumstances in particular cases. From that perspective, the extreme categorical rule that any deprivation of all economic use, no matter how brief, constitutes a compensable taking surely cannot be sustained. Petitioners' broad submission would apply to numerous "normal delays in obtaining building permits, changes in zoning ordinances, variances, and the like," as well as to orders temporarily prohibiting access to crime scenes, businesses that violate health codes, fire-damaged buildings, or other areas that we cannot now foresee. Such a rule would undoubtedly require changes in numerous practices that have long been considered permissible exercises of the police power. As Justice Holmes warned in *Mahon*, "[g]overnment hardly could go on if to some extent values incident to property could not be diminished without paying for every such change in the general law." A rule that required compensation for every delay in the use of property would render routine government processes prohibitively expensive or encourage hasty decision-making. Such an important change in the law should be the product of legislative rulemaking rather than adjudication.

In rejecting petitioners' *per se* rule, we do not hold that the temporary nature of a land-use restriction precludes finding that it effects a taking; we simply recognize that it should not be given exclusive significance one way or the other.

We would create a perverse system of incentives were we to hold that landowners must wait for a taking claim to ripen so that planners can make well-reasoned decisions while, at the same time, holding that those planners must compensate landowners for the delay.

Indeed, the interest in protecting the decisional process is even stronger when an agency is developing a regional plan than when it is considering a permit for a single parcel. In the proceedings involving the Lake Tahoe Basin, for example, the moratoria enabled TRPA to obtain the benefit of comments and criticisms from interested parties, such as the petitioners, during its deliberations. Since a categorical rule tied to the length of deliberations would likely create added pressure on decisionmakers to reach a quick resolution of land-use questions, it would only serve to disadvantage those landowners and interest groups who are not as organized or familiar with the planning process. Moreover, with a temporary ban on development there is a lesser risk that individual landowners will be "singled out" to bear a special burden that should be shared by the public as a whole. At least with a moratorium there is a clear "reciprocity of advantage," because it protects the interests of all affected landowners against immediate construction that might be inconsistent with the provisions of the plan that is ultimately adopted. "While each of us is burdened somewhat by such restrictions, we, in turn, benefit greatly from the restrictions that are placed on others." In fact, there is reason to believe property values often will continue to increase despite a moratorium. Such an increase makes sense in this context because property values throughout the Basin can be expected to reflect the added assurance that Lake Tahoe will remain in its pristine state. Since in some cases a 1-year moratorium may not impose a burden at all, we should not adopt a rule that assumes moratoria always force individuals to bear a special burden that should be shared by the public as a whole.

It may well be true that any moratorium that lasts for more than one year should be viewed with special skepticism. But given the fact that the District Court found that the 32 months required by TRPA to formulate the 1984 Regional Plan was not unreasonable, we could not possibly conclude that every delay of over one year is constitutionally unacceptable. Formulating a general rule of this kind is a suitable task for state legislatures. In our view, the duration of the restriction is one of the important factors that a court must consider in the appraisal of a regulatory takings claim, but with respect to that factor as with respect to other factors, the "temptation to adopt what amount to *per se* rules in either direction must be resisted." There may be moratoria that last longer than one year which interfere with reasonable investment-backed expectations, but as the District Court's opinion illustrates, petitioners' proposed rule is simply "too blunt an instrument," for identifying those cases. We conclude, therefore, that the interest in "fairness and justice" will be best served by relying on the familiar *Penn Central* approach when deciding cases like this, rather than by attempting to craft a new categorical rule.

* * *

Topics for Further Discussion

1. Why does the Court reject the *per se* rule in regulatory taking cases? If the courts must examine each case on an *ad hoc* basis, won't this lead to a drastic increase in litigation? Does the majority say that a temporary moratorium can never constitute a taking?

2. The Court expresses a concern for protecting government from having to pay compensation every time a regulation impacts an owner's use of property. What is the proper balance between private ownership and government regulation? Courts have held, for example, that the imposition of rent control regulations can constitute a taking when the controls do not support a valid governmental purpose.

Key Terms and Concepts

Caveat Emptor (buyer beware)
Chattel
Deed
Easement
Eminent Domain
Escrow Agent
Implied Warranty of Habitability
Intangible and Tangible Property
Public Use
Restrictive Covenant
Right of Way
Title

Chapter 9

Intellectual Property

"Discovery consists of seeing what everybody has seen and thinking what nobody else has thought."

Jonathan Swift, *Gulliver's Travels*
(pt. III, ch. V, Voyage to Laputa)

Mickey Mouse is no laughing matter. The humble rodent who made his movie debut in 1928 as Steamboat Willie is the origin of what has become the Walt Disney Co. communication empire. In 2009, revenue of that empire exceeded $36 billion, money earned from film and television production, broadcasting, sales of programs in video and audio formats, publishing, licensing of the image of characters for toys, music, theme parks, and a large number of related activities. To be sure, many of the company's assets are in traditional forms of property—real and personal. But those assets exist to serve the main asset of the company: intellectual property. The company's ability to make money depends on its legal right to control the use of its products, which are primarily images and sounds such as Mickey.

For this, it has the United States Constitution to thank. One of the powers given to Congress in Article I of the Constitution is the power "[t]o promote the progress of science and useful arts, by securing for limited times to authors and inventors the exclusive right to their respective writings and discoveries."

Bill Gates can be grateful for the same section of the Constitution. He became the richest man in the world through the founding of a computer software company whose products are also protected by copyright. Microsoft makes money because it has the legal right to control its software products, which are primarily arrangements of computer code designed to achieve particular results.

For Disney and Microsoft, copyright is the principal form of protection, but hardly the only one. Both companies make use of trademarks to distinguish them from competitors, and both companies have trade secrets that allow them to maintain what they believe to be continuing advantages in the marketplace.

Companies that make the machinery on which Disney and Microsoft products are used also are indebted to the same section of the Constitution. In their case, it is patent protection that allows them to reap a profit from inventions that produce improved ways of watching and listening to various media. Since the time Steamboat Willie debuted, inventors have developed new ways for him to be perceived, year after year. In 1928, "talking pictures" (movies with sound) had only just begun. Television was unknown. After television came videotape recorders, laser discs, digital video discs, and streaming online video over the Internet. Television screens have evolved from big and bulky picture tubes to flat liquid crystal and plasma displays. For their part, computers (and computer chips) have become smaller and more powerful by the month. Each incarnation creates new sales both of the hardware and the software it supports (or often fails to support, thus requiring users to buy new software too).

In 18th century America, when the Constitution was written, land was the principal measure of property. In 21st century America, intellectual property reigns supreme. According to 2009 data in Forbes magazine, after Bill Gates, the third-richest person in America is Lawrence Ellison, founder of the Oracle software company. Michael Bloomberg, of the Bloomberg information conglomerate (and mayor of New York) is eighth. The top 20 also include the founders of Google and Dell, as well as two other individuals from Microsoft.

The primacy of intellectual property is due to its nature. The same item of copyrighted or patented intellectual property can be reproduced and sold millions of times over. By contrast, land—no matter how valuable and how many ways it may be used—remains immovable and fixed in size. The ease of duplication, however, makes intellectual property easily subject to theft. Land, on the other hand, is fixed and, quite hard to steal. Thus, different forms of law have grown up around intellectual property, reflecting its distinctive strengths and weaknesses.

Overview

In this chapter, we will examine four principal forms of intellectual property law: copyright, patent, trade secret, and trademark law. As you read the chapter, try to determine which kind of law is best suited to the various types of creations, and how several of the laws might be used together to provide protection that no one of them could supply by itself. At the same time, keep in mind the balance between the rights of intellectual property owners ("authors and inventors") and those of the public. Who should be entitled to exclusive rights? For what kind of things? For how long? As consumers of intellectual property, we all have a stake in the answers to these questions.

To begin, consider the following case in which the interests of owners of long-standing copyrights were contested by those who wished to make use of those materials freely. Congress passed a law extending the term of copyright, allowing copyright owners to maintain control of their intellectual property for a longer period of time. When a copyright term expires, the material falls into the "public domain," which means that anyone can use it freely. A well-known law professor attempted to convince the Court that the extension was unconstitutional, but the majority rejected his argument. He has since helped found an organization called "Creative Commons," dedicated to trying to achieve a balance between the exclusive control that copyright gives to authors and the polar opposite of complete public access without compensation.

At this juncture, do not be concerned about the details of copyright. Rather, you should focus on the social balance between giving exclusive rights to intellectual property versus free access.

Eldred v. Ashcroft

537 U.S. 186 (2003)

Ginsburg, J.

This case concerns the authority the Constitution assigns to Congress to prescribe the duration of copyrights. The Copyright and Patent Clause of the Constitution, Art. I, §8, cl. 8, provides as to copyrights: "Congress shall have Power ... [t]o promote the Progress of Science ... by securing [to Authors] for limited Times ... the exclusive Right to their ... Writings." In 1998, in the measure here under inspection, Congress enlarged the duration of copyrights by 20 years. Copyright Term Extension Act (CTEA) (amending 17 U.S.C. § 302, 304). As in the case of prior extensions, principally in 1831, 1909, and 1976, Congress provided for application of the enlarged terms to existing and future copyrights alike.

Petitioners are individuals and businesses whose products or services build on copyrighted works that have gone into the public domain. They seek a determination that the CTEA fails constitutional review under both the Copyright Clause's "limited Times" prescription and the First Amendment's free speech guarantee. Under the 1976 Copyright Act, copyright protection generally lasted from the work's creation until 50 years after the author's death. Under the CTEA, most copyrights now run from creation until 70 years after the author's death. Petitioners do not challenge the "life-plus-70-years" time span itself. "Whether 50 years is enough, or 70 years too much," they acknowledge, "is not a judgment for this Court." Congress went awry, petitioners maintain, not with respect to newly created works, but in enlarging the term for published works with existing copyrights. The "limited Tim[e]" in effect when a copyright is secured, petitioners urge, becomes the constitutional boundary, a clear line beyond the power of Congress to extend.

In accord with the District Court and the Court of Appeals, we reject petitioners' challenges to the CTEA. In that 1998 legislation, as in all previous copyright term extensions, Congress placed existing and future copyrights in parity. In prescribing that alignment, we hold, Congress acted within its authority and did not transgress constitutional limitations.

We address first the determination of the courts below that Congress has authority under the Copyright Clause to extend the terms of existing copyrights. Text, history, and precedent, we conclude, confirm that the Copyright Clause empowers Congress to prescribe "limited Times" for copyright protection and to secure the same level and duration of protection for all copyright holders, present and future.

The CTEA's baseline term of life plus 70 years, petitioners concede, qualifies as a "limited Tim[e]" as applied to future copyrights. Petitioners contend, however, that existing copyrights extended to endure for that same term are not "limited." Petitioners' argument essentially reads into the text of the Copyright Clause the command that a time prescription, once set, becomes forever "fixed" or "inalterable." The word "limited," however, does not convey a meaning so constricted. At the time of the Framing, that word meant what it means today: "confine[d] within certain bounds," "restrain[ed]," or "circumscribe[d]." Thus understood, a time span appropriately "limited" as applied to future copyrights does not automatically cease to be "limited" when applied to existing copyrights.

To comprehend the scope of Congress' power under the Copyright Clause, "a page of history is worth a volume of logic." History reveals an unbroken congressional practice of granting to authors of works with existing copyrights the benefit of term extensions so that all under copyright protection will be governed evenhandedly under the same regime. The First Congress accorded the protections of the Nation's first federal copyright statute to existing and future works alike. Since then, Congress has regularly applied duration extensions to both existing and future copyrights.

Because the Clause empowering Congress to confer copyrights also authorizes patents, congressional practice with respect to patents informs our inquiry. We count it significant that early Congresses extended the duration of numerous individual patents as well as copyrights.

Further, although prior to the instant case this Court did not have occasion to decide whether extending the duration of existing copyrights complies with the "limited Times" prescription, the Court has found no constitutional barrier to the legislative expansion of existing patents. *McClurg v. Kingsland*, 1 How. 202 (1843), is the pathsetting precedent. The patentee in that case was unprotected under the law in force when the patent issued because he had allowed his employer briefly to practice the invention before he obtained the patent. Only upon enactment, two years later, of an exemption for such allowances did the patent become valid, retroactive to the time it issued. *McClurg* upheld retroactive application of the new law. The Court explained that the legal regime governing a particular patent "depend[s] on the law as it stood at the emanation of the patent, together with such changes as have been since made; for though they may be retrospective in their operation, that is not a sound objection to their validity." Neither is it a sound objection to the validity of a copyright term extension, enacted pursuant to the same constitutional grant of authority, that the enlarged term covers existing copyrights.

Congress' consistent historical practice of applying newly enacted copyright terms to future and existing copyrights reflects a judgment stated concisely by Representative Huntington at the time of the 1831 Act: "[J]ustice, policy, and equity alike forb[id]" that an "author who had sold his [work] a week ago, be placed in a worse situation than the author who should sell his work the day after the passing of [the] act." The CTEA follows this historical practice by keeping the duration provisions of the 1976 Act largely in place and simply adding 20 years to each of them. Guided by text, history, and precedent, we cannot agree with petitioners' submission that extending the duration of existing copyrights is categorically beyond Congress' authority under the Copyright Clause.

The CTEA reflects judgments of a kind Congress typically makes, judgments we cannot dismiss as outside the Legislature's domain. As respondent describes, a key factor in the CTEA's passage was a 1993 European Union (EU) directive instructing EU members to establish a copyright term of life plus 70 years. Consistent with the Berne Convention, the EU directed its members to deny this longer term to the works of any non-EU country whose laws did not secure the same extended term. By extending the baseline United States copyright term to life plus 70 years, Congress sought to ensure that American authors would receive the same copyright protection in Europe as their European counterparts.

In addition to international concerns, Congress passed the CTEA in light of demographic, economic, and technological changes, and rationally credited projections that longer terms would encourage copyright holders to invest in the restoration and public distribution of their works.

In sum, we find that the CTEA is a rational enactment; we are not at liberty to second-guess congressional determinations and policy judgments of this order, however debatable or arguably unwise they may be. Accordingly, we cannot conclude that the CTEA—which continues the unbroken congressional practice of treating future and existing copyrights in parity for term extension purposes—is an impermissible exercise of Congress' power under the Copyright Clause.

As we read the Framers' instruction, the Copyright Clause empowers Congress to determine the intellectual property regimes that, overall, in that body's judgment, will serve the ends of the Clause. Beneath the facade of their inventive constitutional interpretation, petitioners forcefully urge that Congress pursued very bad policy in prescribing the CTEA's long terms. The wisdom of Congress' action, however, is not within our province to second guess. Satisfied that the legislation before us remains inside the domain the Constitution assigns to the First Branch, we affirm the judgment of the Court of Appeals.

Stevens, J., dissenting

The express grant of a perpetual copyright would unquestionably violate the textual requirement that the authors' exclusive rights be only "for limited Times." Whether the extraordinary length of the grants authorized by the 1998 Act are invalid because they are the functional equivalent of perpetual copyrights is a question that need not be answered in this case because the question presented by the *certiorari* petition merely challenges Congress' power to extend retroactively the terms of existing copyrights. Accordingly, there is no need to determine whether the deference that is normally given to congressional policy judgments may save from judicial review its decision respecting the appropriate length of the term. It is important to note, however, that a categorical rule prohibiting retroactive extensions would effectively preclude perpetual copyrights. More importantly, as the House of Lords recognized when it refused to amend the Statute of Anne in 1735, unless the Clause is construed to embody such a categorical rule, Congress may extend existing monopoly privileges *ad infinitum* under the majority's analysis.

By failing to protect the public interest in free access to the products of inventive and artistic genius—indeed, by virtually ignoring the central purpose of the Copyright/ Patent Clause—the Court has quitclaimed to Congress its principal responsibility in this area of the law. Fairly read, the Court has stated that Congress' actions under the Copyright/Patent Clause are, for all intents and purposes, judicially unreviewable. That result cannot be squared with the basic tenets of our constitutional structure. It is not hyperbole to recall the trenchant words of Chief Justice John Marshall: "It is emphatically the province and duty of the judicial department to say what the law is." *Marbury v. Madison*, 1 Cranch 137, 177 (1803). We should discharge that responsibility.

Breyer, J., dissenting

This statute will cause serious expression-related harm. It will likely restrict traditional dissemination of copyrighted works. It will likely inhibit new forms of dissemination through the use of new technology. It threatens to interfere with efforts to preserve our Nation's historical and cultural heritage and efforts to use that heritage, say, to educate our Nation's children. It is easy to understand how the statute might benefit the private financial interests of corporations or heirs who own existing copyrights. But I cannot find any constitutionally legitimate, copyright-related way in which the statute will benefit the public. Indeed, in respect to existing works, the serious public harm and the virtually nonexistent public benefit could not be more clear.

* * *

Topics for Further Discussion

1. The statute at issue in the case is called the "Sonny Bono Copyright Term Extension Act." Sonny Bono was the Congressman who introduced the bill. Before entering politics, he was the husband of singer/actress Cher, and half of the team called "Sonny & Cher." The bill was passed after his death in a skiing accident. What do you imagine were some of the reasons that led Congress to extend the term of copyright?

2. Justice Breyer, in his dissent, worries that the majority decision may inhibit new forms of communication. In what way might that happen?

3. The Statute of Anne, mentioned in Justice Stevens' dissent, was a British law of 1710 that granted copyright in books for fourteen years from publication.

Copyright

Copyright law concerns exactly what its name suggests, the right to copy. The details, however, are far less simple. Modern American copyright law has gone through three major periods. The first was the passage of the 1909 copyright statute. That law governed the area until a major revision enacted in 1976. The next major revision was the Digital Millennium Copyright Act, signed into law in 1998.

With both the 1976 and 1998 statutes, changes in technology prompted Congress to review the balance between content producers and consumers. In 1909, for example, phonograph records were in their infancy. The first commercial radio station was still more than ten years in the future. The first major silent film, "Birth of a Nation," appeared in 1915. "Talkies" did not debut until 1927, with "The Jazz Singer." In the intervening years, television, audio and video tape, photocopy machines, and numerous other methods of communication and copying all came into existence. The 1976 Act was designed to prevent copyright law from falling behind the technology.

Technology, however, refused to remain still. Digital-based methods, arising out of the computer industry, brought the ability to send, receive, and copy content directly to the desktop. The Internet made it possible for anyone to download text, audio, and video; and for unknown people to share their files with one another. All this gave rise to the 1998 Act.

Despite the advances in technology, the basic tenets of copyright law remain the same. What has changed is the ease with which consumers can copy. Before the advent of the printing press, copying was a process that could only be accomplished by hand. The effort itself was a deterrent. Printing technology made copying somewhat less laborious but still far from easy. With the invention of the photocopy machine, however, copying became easier than simply purchasing an authorized edition. Digitalization now has turned copying (whether authorized or not) into a matter of the push of a button and a few seconds.

As copying has become easier, consumers have—quite predictably—done more of it. Some also argue that, because it is so easy, it should be legal. Copyright owners, on the other hand, have become more aggressive in pursuing copyright violators. They fear that technology may erode and perhaps extinguish their ability to profit from their own creative acts.

The Copyright Act of 1976 remains the fundamental law, with supplements and revisions from time to time. Its opening chapter addresses the question of what is copyrightable. Section 102 states:

> (a) Copyright protection subsists ... in original works of authorship, fixed in any tangible medium of expression, now know or later developed, from which they can be perceived, reproduced, or otherwise communicated, either directly or with the aid of a machine or device. Works of authorship include the following categories:
>
> (1) literary works;
>
> (2) musical works, including any accompanying words
>
> (3) dramatic works, including any accompanying music
>
> (4) pantomimes and choreographic works;
>
> (5) pictorial, graphic, and sculptural works;
>
> (6) motion pictures and other audiovisual works;

(7) sound recordings; and

(8) architectural works

(b) In no case does copyright protection for an original work of authorship extend to any idea, procedure, process, system, method of operation, concept, principle, or discovery, regardless of the form in which it is described, explained, illustrated, or embodied in such work.

A quick glance at Section 102 reveals the general scope of copyright protection. It extends primarily to the world of the arts. Those who enrich the public's lives through their creative works are given the legal right to control them and, thus, benefit from them financially. The key phrase of Section 102 is "original works of authorship, fixed in any tangible medium of expression." Those few words include a number of the following important points.

1. Original. The work in question must have been created by the person claiming copyright (or someone who purchased the right from him). It cannot be a copy of someone else's creation. Originality, however, is not the same thing as "novelty," a concept we will study later in patent law. Novelty means "new." Originality is often new, but—strictly speaking—only requires that the creator has done it himself. Thus, in copyright law, two writers may independently come up with the same song. In theory, both of them have valid copyrights. By contrast, in patent law, only the first inventor is entitled to legal protection.

2. Authorship. The work must involve at least a modicum of creative activity. Some early cases, for example, questioned whether photographs involved authorship because the camera mechanically captured what was right in front of it. Courts eventually, and wisely, concluded that the decisions of where to point the camera, how to arrange the subject (in some instances), what exposure to select (including aperture—the size of the opening of the lens, and shutter speed), and how to develop the negatives all indicated that more than enough authorship was involved to qualify for copyright protection.

3. Fixed. The work must somehow be capable of being perceived repeatedly. In other words, a live performance of an opera is not "fixed." A recording of a performance of a live opera is.

4. Tangible medium. "Tangible" means having some form. A movie, for example, has tangible form in the physical film. Even though what we watch is the non-tangible images produced when light passes through the film, the content is copyrightable because it is fixed in the film itself.

5. Expression. Ideas, by themselves, are not copyrightable. In order to benefit under the copyright law, the person who comes up with an idea must express it in some way. Thus, the idea for a screenplay is not copyrightable, but a written proposal outlining the screenplay would give rise to protection.

6. Now known or later developed. With this language, the Act remains up to date regardless of changes in technology.

Keeping the concepts of section 102 in mind, consider the following case, in which a member of the Beatles was sued for copyright infringement.

Bright Tunes Music Corp. v. Harrisongs Music, Ltd.
420 F. Supp. 177 (S.D.N.Y. 1976)

Owen, J.

This is an action in which it is claimed that a successful song, My Sweet Lord, listing George Harrison as the composer, is plagiarized from an earlier successful song, He's So

Fine, composed by Ronald Mack, recorded by a singing group called the "Chiffons," the copyright of which is owned by plaintiff, Bright Tunes Music Corp.

He's So Fine, recorded in 1962, is a catchy tune consisting essentially of four repetitions of a very short basic musical phrase, "sol-mi-re," (hereinafter motif A), altered as necessary to fit the words, followed by four repetitions of another short basic musical phrase, "sol-la-do-la-do," (hereinafter motif B). While neither motif is novel, the four repetitions of A, followed by four repetitions of B, is a highly unique pattern. In addition, in the second use of the motif B series, there is a grace note inserted making the phrase go "sol-la-do-la-re-do."

My Sweet Lord, recorded first in 1970, also uses the same motif A (modified to suit the words) four times, followed by motif B, repeated three times, not four. In place of He's So Fine's fourth repetition of motif B, My Sweet Lord has a transitional passage of musical attractiveness of the same approximate length, with the identical grace note in the identical second repetition. The harmonies of both songs are identical.

George Harrison, a former member of The Beatles, was aware of He's So Fine. In the United States, it was No. 1 on the billboard charts for five weeks; in England, Harrison's home country, it was No. 12 on the charts on June 1, 1963, a date upon which one of the Beatle songs was, in fact, in first position. For seven weeks in 1963, He's So Fine was one of the top hits in England.

According to Harrison, the circumstances of the composition of My Sweet Lord were as follows. Harrison and his group, which include an American black gospel singer named Billy Preston, were in Copenhagen, Denmark, on a singing engagement. There was a press conference involving the group going on backstage. Harrison slipped away from the press conference and went to a room upstairs and began "vamping" some guitar chords, fitting on to the chords he was playing the words, "Hallelujah" and "Hare Krishna" in various ways. During the course of this vamping, he was alternating between what musicians call a Minor II chord and a Major V chord.

At some point, germinating started and he went down to meet with others of the group, asking them to listen, which they did, and everyone began to join in, taking first "Hallelujah" and then "Hare Krishna" and putting them into four part harmony. Harrison obviously started using the "Hallelujah," etc., as repeated sounds, and from there developed the lyrics, to wit, "My Sweet Lord," "Dear, Dear Lord," etc. In any event, from this very free-flowing exchange of ideas, with Harrison playing his two chords and everybody singing "Hallelujah" and "Hare Krishna," there began to emerge the My Sweet Lord text idea, which Harrison sought to develop a little bit further during the following week as he was playing it on his guitar. Thus developed motif A and its words interspersed with "Hallelujah" and "Hare Krishna."

Approximately one week after the idea first began to germinate, the entire group flew back to London because they had earlier booked time to go to a recording studio with Billy Preston to make an album. In the studio, Preston was the principal musician. Harrison did not play in the session. He had given Preston his basic motif A with the idea that it be turned into a song, and was back and forth from the studio to the engineer's recording booth, supervising the recording "takes." Under circumstances that Harrison was utterly unable to recall, while everybody was working toward a finished song, in the recording studio, somehow or other the essential three notes of motif A reached polished form.

The Billy Preston recording, listing George Harrison as the composer, was thereafter issued by Apple Records. The music was then reduced to paper by someone who prepared a "lead sheet" containing the melody, the words and the harmony for the United States copyright application.

Seeking the wellsprings of musical composition—why a composer chooses the succession of notes and the harmonies he does—whether it be George Harrison or Richard Wagner—is a fascinating inquiry. It is apparent from the extensive colloquy between the Court and Harrison covering forty pages in the transcript that neither Harrison nor Preston were conscious of the fact that they were utilizing the He's So Fine theme. However, they in fact were, for it is perfectly obvious to the listener that in musical terms, the two songs are virtually identical except for one phrase. There is motif A used four times, followed by motif B, four times in one case, and three times in the other, with the same grace note in the second repetition of motif B.

What happened? I conclude that the composer, in seeking musical materials to clothe his thoughts, was working with various possibilities. As he tried this possibility and that, there came to the surface of his mind a particular combination that pleased him as being one he felt would be appealing to a prospective listener; in other words, that this combination of sounds would work. Why? Because his subconscious knew it already had worked in a song his conscious mind did not remember. Having arrived at this pleasing combination of sounds, the recording was made, the lead sheet prepared for copyright and the song became an enormous success. Did Harrison deliberately use the music of He's So Fine? I do not believe he did so deliberately. Nevertheless, it is clear that My Sweet Lord is the very same song as He's So Fine with different words, and Harrison had access to He's So Fine. This is, under the law, infringement of copyright, and is no less so even though subconsciously accomplished.

* * *

Topics for Further Discussion

1. What is the problem in the *Bright Tunes* case? Is the issue one of originality or authorship?

2. In theory, two authors can legally come up with the same expression. What is the proof that led the court to conclude that is not what happened in this case?

3. Composer John Cage wrote several works sometimes called "chance music." In them, he included parts that would be determined by chance, relying on, for example, the flipping of coins to decide what notes would be played. One composition entitled 4'33" consisted of sitting at the piano, opening and closing the lid several times, and then leaving without playing a note. What authorship is involved in these works? What originality? How do you imagine they are "fixed"?

* * *

Section 106 of the Copyright Act sets forth the rights to which creators are entitled. The rights are exclusive, meaning that no one else can do these things without the owner's permission:

(1) to reproduce the copyrighted work in copies or phonorecords;

(2) to prepare derivative works based upon the copyrighted work;

(3) to distribute copies or phonorecords of the copyrighted work to the public by sale or other transfer of ownership, or by rental, lease, or lending;

(4) in the case of literary, musical, dramatic, and choreographic works, pantomimes, and motion pictures and other audiovisual works, to perform the copyrighted work publicly;

(5) in the case of literary, musical, dramatic, and choreographic works, pantomimes, and pictorial, graphic, or sculptural works, including the individual images of a motion picture or other audiovisual work, to display the copyrighted work publicly; and

(6) in the case of sound recordings, to perform the copyrighted work publicly by means of a digital audio transmission.

The essential elements of Section 106 are as follows:

1. Reproduce. This means, in simple terms, to copy the work. In other words, after the action, does at least one more copy of the work exist?

2. Derivative works. These are creations that depend on a pre-existing work. For example, a movie based on a novel is a derivative work. The movie may include many additional original elements of authorship, but the movie producer must obtain the permission of the owner of the copyright in the novel in order to use the story.

3. Perform. This means to show the work in some way. A musical composition is copyrighted through the sheet music. In other words, the sheet music is the "tangible medium of expression" through which it is "fixed." The sheet music itself, however, does not make any sounds. Someone who plays the music on an instrument is "performing" it. A radio station broadcasting the event also is "performing" the music.

4. Publicly. Performing a work for oneself is not a copyright violation. Section 101 of the statute defines "publicly" as "at a place open to the public or at any place where a substantial number of persons outside of a normal circle of a family and its social acquaintances is gathered."

For works created after January 1, 1978, copyright protection lasts for seventy years after the death of the author. If more than one author is involved, the term is seventy years after the last of them dies. Works for hire, that is, those made under contract for an employer, endure for ninety-five years after their publication or 120 years from their creation, whichever is shorter. The copyright in such works, by the way, belongs to the employer and not the creator. The work of a staff writer for a magazine, for example, is usually work for hire. On the other hand, articles contributed by freelance writers are not. The freelance writers hold the copyrights themselves, and merely grant the magazine or newspaper permission to publish it. In *New York Times Co. v. Tasini*, 533 U.S. 483 (2001), the Supreme Court ruled that a newspaper that had purchased the right to publish an article did not have the right to allow the article to be included in a computer data base. The data base, the Court ruled, was different from the original newspaper and, thus, a violation of the writer's copyright.

As discussed at the beginning of the chapter, copyright is not a one-sided bargain. Authors receive economic protections in order to encourage them to continue to create works that the public can enjoy. Even before a copyright expires, the public is entitled to certain rights to what is called "fair use." The Copyright Act does not define fair use, but Section 107 does give some examples. It says that copying "for purposes such as criticism, comment, news reporting, teaching (including multiple copies for classroom use), scholarship, or research, is not an infringement of copyright." From that language, it would appear that mere convenience for enjoying entertainment would not be included in fair use. The fair use categories listed all involve adding some value. Nevertheless, some fair use advocates contend that ordinary ease of use should be included, as if preventing them from taking advantage of convenience would be unfair.

Even for those activities that are within the meaning of fair use, the Act does not permit unlimited use. It says that a judgment must be made based on factors such as (1) the purpose of the use (for example, commercial or nonprofit educational); (2) the nature of the work itself; (3) the amount used as compared to the entire work (for example, the number of pages from a book); and (4) the effect the use will have on the work's potential market.

Under these standards, making copies of a complete textbook for all members of a class would not be a fair use. Although the use is educational, the copying involves the entire product and prevents the publisher from selling the textbook. Keep the fair use criteria in mind as you consider the following cases.

Sony Corp. v. Universal City Studios
464 U.S. 417 (1984)

Stevens, J.

Petitioners manufacture and sell home video tape recorders. Respondents own the copyrights on some of the television programs that are broadcast on the public airwaves. Some members of the general public use video tape recorders sold by petitioners to record some of these broadcasts, as well as a large number of other broadcasts. The question presented is whether the sale of petitioners' copying equipment to the general public violates any of the rights conferred upon respondents by the Copyright Act.

The two respondents in this action, Universal City Studios, Inc., and Walt Disney Productions, produce and hold the copyrights on a substantial number of motion pictures and other audiovisual works. In the current marketplace, they can exploit their rights in these works in a number of ways: by authorizing theatrical exhibitions, by licensing limited showings on cable and network television, by selling syndication rights for repeated airings on local television stations, and by marketing programs on prerecorded videotapes or videodiscs. Some works are suitable for exploitation through all of these avenues, while the market for other works is more limited.

Petitioner Sony manufactures millions of Betamax video tape recorders and markets these devices through numerous retail establishments.

The separate tuner in the Betamax enables it to record a broadcast off one station while the television set is tuned to another channel, permitting the viewer, for example, to watch two simultaneous news broadcasts by watching one "live" and recording the other for later viewing. Tapes may be reused, and programs that have been recorded may be erased either before or after viewing. A timer in the Betamax can be used to activate and deactivate the equipment at predetermined times, enabling an intended viewer to record programs that are transmitted when he or she is not at home. Thus a person may watch a program at home in the evening even though it was broadcast while the viewer was at work during the afternoon.

In a case like this, in which Congress has not plainly marked our course, we must be circumspect in construing the scope of rights created by a legislative enactment which never contemplated such a calculus of interests. In doing so, we are guided by Justice Stewart's exposition of the correct approach to ambiguities in the law of copyright:

> The limited scope of the copyright holder's statutory monopoly, like the limited copyright duration required by the Constitution, reflects a balance of competing claims upon the public interest: Creative work is to be encouraged and rewarded, but private motivation must ultimately serve the cause of promoting broad public availability of literature, music, and the other arts. The immediate

effect of our copyright law is to secure a fair return for an author's creative labor. But the ultimate aim is, by this incentive, to stimulate artistic creativity for the general public good.

The question is thus whether the Betamax is capable of commercially significant non-infringing uses. Even unauthorized uses of a copyrighted work are not necessarily infringing. An unlicensed use of the copyright is not an infringement unless it conflicts with one of the specific exclusive rights conferred by the copyright statute. Moreover, the definition of exclusive rights in 106 of the present Act is prefaced by the words "subject to sections 107 through 118." Those sections describe a variety of uses of copyrighted material that "are not infringements of copyright" "notwithstanding the provisions of section 106." The most pertinent in this case is 107, the legislative endorsement of the doctrine of "fair use."

That section identifies various factors that enable a court to apply an "equitable rule of reason" analysis to particular claims of infringement. Although not conclusive, the first factor requires that "the commercial or nonprofit character of an activity" be weighed in any fair use decision. If the Betamax were used to make copies for a commercial or profitmaking purpose, such use would presumptively be unfair. The contrary presumption is appropriate here, however, because the District Court's findings plainly establish that time-shifting for private home use must be characterized as a noncommercial, nonprofit activity.

This is not, however, the end of the inquiry because Congress has also directed us to consider "the effect of the use upon the potential market for or value of the copyrighted work." The purpose of copyright is to create incentives for creative effort. Even copying for noncommercial purposes may impair the copyright holder's ability to obtain the rewards that Congress intended him to have. But a use that has no demonstrable effect upon the potential market for, or the value of, the copyrighted work need not be prohibited in order to protect the author's incentive to create. The prohibition of such noncommercial uses would merely inhibit access to ideas without any countervailing benefit.

One may search the Copyright Act in vain for any sign that the elected representatives of the millions of people who watch television every day have made it unlawful to copy a program for later viewing at home, or have enacted a flat prohibition against the sale of machines that make such copying possible.

It may well be that Congress will take a fresh look at this new technology, just as it so often has examined other innovations in the past. But it is not our job to apply laws that have not yet been written. Applying the copyright statute, as it now reads, to the facts as they have been developed in this case, the judgment of the Court of Appeals must be reversed.

Blackmun, J., dissenting

The introduction of the home videotape recorder (VTR) upon the market has enabled millions of Americans to make recordings of television programs in their homes, for future and repeated viewing at their own convenience. While this practice has proved highly popular with owners of television sets and VTR's, it understandably has been a matter of concern for the holders of copyrights in the recorded programs.

It is fairly clear from the legislative history of the 1976 Act that Congress meant to change the old pattern and enact a statute that would cover new technologies, as well as old.

Sony's advertisements, at various times, have suggested that Betamax users "record favorite shows" or "build a library." Sony's Betamax advertising has never contained warnings about copyright infringement, although a warning does appear in the Betamax operating instructions.

The Studios produce copyrighted "movies" and other works that they release to theaters and license for television broadcast. They also rent and sell their works on film and on prerecorded videotapes and videodiscs. License fees for television broadcasts are set according to audience ratings, compiled by rating services that do not measure any playbacks of videotapes. The Studios make the serious claim that VTR recording may result in a decrease in their revenue from licensing their works to television and from marketing them in other ways.

The doctrine of fair use has been called, with some justification, "the most troublesome in the whole law of copyright." Although courts have constructed lists of factors to be considered in determining whether a particular use is fair, no fixed criteria have emerged by which that determination can be made.

Nor did Congress provide definitive rules when it codified the fair use doctrine in the 1976 Act; it simply incorporated a list of factors "to be considered." No particular weight, however, was assigned to any of these, and the list was not intended to be exclusive.

The monopoly created by copyright thus rewards the individual author in order to benefit the public. There are situations, nevertheless, in which strict enforcement of this monopoly would inhibit the very "Progress of Science and useful Arts" that copyright is intended to promote. An obvious example is the researcher or scholar whose own work depends on the ability to refer to and to quote the work of prior scholars. Obviously, no author could create a new work if he were first required to repeat the research of every author who had gone before him. But there is a crucial difference between the scholar and the ordinary user. When the ordinary user decides that the owner's price is too high, and forgoes use of the work, only the individual is the loser. When the scholar forgoes the use of a prior work, not only does his own work suffer, but the public is deprived of his contribution to knowledge. I am aware of no case in which the reproduction of a copyrighted work for the sole benefit of the user has been held to be fair use.

The making of a videotape recording for home viewing is an ordinary rather than a productive use of the Studios' copyrighted works. A VTR recording creates no public benefit sufficient to justify limiting this right. Although a television broadcast may be free to the viewer, this fact is equally irrelevant; a book borrowed from the public library may not be copied any more freely than a book that is purchased.

Having bypassed the initial hurdle for establishing that a use is fair, the Court then purports to apply to time-shifting the four factors explicitly stated in the statute. The first is "the purpose and character of the use, including whether such use is of a commercial nature or is for nonprofit educational purposes." The Court confidently describes time-shifting as a noncommercial, nonprofit activity. It is clear, however, that personal use of programs that have been copied without permission is not what 107(1) protects. The intent of the section is to encourage users to engage in activities the primary benefit of which accrues to others. Time-shifting involves no such humanitarian impulse.

The second factor — "the nature of the copyrighted work" — strongly supports the view that time-shifting is an infringing use. Informational works, such as news reports, that readily lend themselves to productive use by others, are less protected than creative works of entertainment. Sony's own surveys indicate that entertainment shows account for more than 80% of the programs recorded by Betamax owners.

The third statutory factor — "the amount and substantiality of the portion used" — is even more devastating to the Courts interpretation. It is undisputed that virtually all VTR owners record entire works, thereby creating an exact substitute for the copyrighted original. Fair use is intended to allow individuals engaged in productive uses to copy small portions of original works that will facilitate their own productive endeavors.

The fourth factor requires an evaluation of "the effect of the use upon the potential market for or value of the copyrighted work." The development of the VTR has created a new market for the works produced by the Studios. That market consists of those persons who desire to view television programs at times other than when they are broadcast, and who therefore purchase VTR recorders to enable them to time-shift. Because time-shifting of the Studios' copyrighted works involves the copying of them, however, the Studios are entitled to share in the benefits of that new market.

Like so many other problems created by the interaction of copyright law with a new technology, "[t]here can be no really satisfactory solution to the problem presented here, until Congress acts." But in the absence of a congressional solution, courts cannot avoid difficult problems by refusing to apply the law. We must "take the Copyright Act ... as we find it," and "do as little damage as possible to traditional copyright principles ... until the Congress legislates."

Metro-Goldwyn-Mayer Studios v. Grokster, Ltd.
545 U.S. 913 (2005)

Souter, J.

Respondents, Grokster, Ltd., and StreamCast Networks, Inc., defendants in the trial court, distribute free software products that allow computer users to share electronic files through peer-to-peer networks, so called because users' computers communicate directly with each other, not through central servers.

Other users of peer-to-peer networks include individual recipients of Grokster's and StreamCast's software, and although the networks that they enjoy through using the software can be used to share any type of digital file, they have prominently employed those networks in sharing copyrighted music and video files without authorization. A group of copyright holders sued Grokster and StreamCast for their users' copyright infringements, alleging that they knowingly and intentionally distributed their software to enable users to reproduce and distribute the copyrighted works in violation of the Copyright Act.

Although Grokster and StreamCast do not therefore know when particular files are copied, a few searches using their software would show what is available on the networks the software reaches. MGM commissioned a statistician to conduct a systematic search, and his study showed that nearly 90% of the files available for download on the FastTrack system were copyrighted works. Grokster and StreamCast dispute this figure, raising methodological problems and arguing that free copying even of copyrighted works may be authorized by the rightholders. They also argue that potential noninfringing uses of their software are significant in kind, even if infrequent in practice. Some musical performers, for example, have gained new audiences by distributing their copyrighted works for free across peer-to-peer networks, and some distributors of unprotected content have used peer-to-peer networks to disseminate files, Shakespeare being an example.

MGM's evidence gives reason to think that the vast majority of users' downloads are acts of infringement, and because well over 100 million copies of the software in question are known to have been downloaded, and billions of files are shared across the Fast-

Track and Gnutella networks each month, the probable scope of copyright infringement is staggering.

After the notorious file-sharing service, Napster, was sued by copyright holders for facilitation of copyright infringement, StreamCast gave away a software program of a kind known as OpenNap, designed as compatible with the Napster program and open to Napster users for downloading files from other Napster and OpenNap users' computers. StreamCast developed promotional materials to market its service as the best Napster alternative. One proposed advertisement read: "Napster Inc. has announced that it will soon begin charging you a fee. That's if the courts don't order it shut down first. What will you do to get around it?"

The evidence that Grokster sought to capture the market of former Napster users is sparser but revealing, for Grokster launched its own OpenNap system called Swaptor and inserted digital codes into its Web site so that computer users using Web search engines to look for "Napster" or "[f]ree filesharing" would be directed to the Grokster Web site, where they could download the Grokster software. And Grokster's name is an apparent derivative of Napster.

[N]othing in *Sony* requires courts to ignore evidence of intent if there is such evidence, and the case was never meant to foreclose rules of fault-based liability derived from the common law. Thus, where evidence goes beyond a product's characteristics or the knowledge that it may be put to infringing uses, and shows statements or actions directed to promoting infringement, *Sony*'s staple-article rule will not preclude liability.

Three features of this evidence of intent are particularly notable. First, each company showed itself to be aiming to satisfy a known source of demand for copyright infringement, the market comprising former Napster users. Second ... neither company attempted to develop filtering tools or other mechanisms to diminish the infringing activity using their software. Third ... StreamCast and Grokster make money by selling advertising space, by directing ads to the screens of computers employing their software.

In sum, this case is significantly different from *Sony*. *Sony* dealt with a claim of liability based solely on distributing a product with alternative lawful and unlawful uses, with knowledge that some users would follow the unlawful course. The case struck a balance between the interests of protection and innovation.

MGM's evidence in this case most obviously addresses a different basis of liability for distributing a product open to alternative uses. Here, evidence of the distributors' words and deeds going beyond distribution as such shows a purpose to cause and profit from third-party acts of copyright infringement. If liability for inducing infringement is ultimately found, it will not be on the basis of presuming or imputing fault, but from inferring a patently illegal objective from statements and actions showing what that objective was.

The unlawful objective is unmistakable.

* * *

Topics for Further Discussion

1. In the *Sony* decision, the majority did not believe that movie production companies would suffer any economic harm from home videotaping. Has that proved to be correct? What other methods of movie distribution have developed since then?

2. The *Sony* majority concluded that Congress did not indicate home videotaping was a violation of copyright law. On the other hand, Justice Blackmun, in dissent, noted that the 1976 Copyright Act refers to "any tangible medium of expression, now known or later developed." Having written that open-ended language, would Congress have been expected to address the issue of one particular medium specifically?

3. The *Grokster* Court attempted to distinguish the *Sony* case, but were the facts really all that different? Did Sony not benefit from users' copying of copyrighted material? On the other hand, if the copyrighted materials involved in *Grokster* were of the same type as those in the *Sony* case, didn't individuals have a fair use right to copy them? If so, then what illegal act did Grokster facilitate?

4. The Napster service, referred to in the opinion, was an earlier form of file-sharing in which some information flowed through Napster's servers. *Grokster* involved a more pure form of peer-to-peer file exchange. Its software did not route the exchange, but rather served as an introduction service that told users where to find what they wanted. Does that technological distinction make a difference? *See A & M Records v. Napster, Inc.*, 239 F.3d 1004 (9th Cir. 2001).

Patent and Trade Secret

While copyright generally concerns artistic creations, patent and trade secret law typically involve industrial inventions. To give a simple example, copyrighted movies are played on DVD machines that include patented technology. In reality, however, many matters are not so simple. Computer systems in particular operate through an interaction between the software often embedded in the hardware. The software contains processes to reach particular results, but the different ways of reaching those results (as well as the face they show to the users) may well contain forms of expression.

Like copyright, patent law is federal law based on the section of the Constitution we studied at the beginning of this chapter. Trade secret law, on the other hand, comes from the states. Inventors must choose one form of protection or the other since using both at the same time is not possible. The reason is that patent law requires public disclosure of the details of the invention, while trade secret law requires that the details be kept secret. The dilemma is choosing between certain protection for a limited time and uncertain protection for an unlimited period of time.

Those who succeed in receiving a patent are granted 20 years of exclusivity. During that time, they may keep the technology to themselves or grant licenses to others to use it (in return for the payment of royalties to the patent owner). Many companies make DVD machines, but all must pay royalties to those who invented and patented the technology. In the case of patent, the inventor "lays open" the technology. This means that he tells the patent office how it works and allows the patent office to publish the information. When the 20 years are up, anyone is free to make use of what was disclosed. Generic medicines reflect this tradeoff. The company that invents the medicine markets it under its brand name during the term of the patent. The brand name may become well-known in that time, and some physicians and consumers will continue to select it even after the patent has expired. However, once the patent has expired, other companies can market medicine with the same formula, but not under the same name. A savvy company will trademark the name of its medicine, as we will see later in this chapter.

For those who choose to follow the trade secret approach, the exclusive period may last many years longer than any patent. In rough terms, a trade secret lasts as long as the owner is able to keep it secret. Trade secret law will protect owners from aggressive attempts to steal the secret, but it will not protect them from their own carelessness. Coca-Cola has kept the formula of its soft drink a secret for longer than 100 years. At any one time, only a handful of people is said to have access to the complete information. If the company were inadvertently to publish the formula in a document that was sent outside its offices, the trade secret status of the formula could be undermined.

The Patent Act, 35 U.S.C. § 1, sets out the basic structure of patent protection. The language of section 101 is a model of clarity and simplicity: "Whoever invents or discovers any new and useful process, machine, manufacture, or composition of matter, or any new and useful improvement thereof, may obtain a patent therefore, subject to the conditions and requirements of this title." A patentable process, however, cannot be an abstract concept or an abstract concept that is reduced to a mathematical formula. For this reason, in *Bilski v. Kappos*, 2010 WL 2555192 (2010), the Supreme Court rejected a patent application for a business method for hedging against price fluctuations in a commodities market. The Court did indicate, though, that some other types of business methods might be eligible for patent protection.

Section 101 includes the following key terms:

1. New. This is called the "novelty" requirement. Unlike copyright law, patent law requires that something be the first of its kind. Even if an inventor independently arrived at the same result as another person, only the first of them receives protection. In the United States, the first person to invent wins; in most other countries it is the first to file a patent application who wins.

2. Useful. The "utility" requirement also distinguishes patent from copyright. While copyright protects any form of "expression," patent law demands that the thing be useful in some way. In other words, the "art" (as patent professionals often call it) must accomplish something and not simply exist for itself. A piece of music need not make people work faster when they listen to it in order to be copyrighted, but a system using music to make people work faster must actually accomplish that goal in order to receive a patent.

Section 103 of the Act sets forth the other major requirement for patentability: non-obviousness. A patent will not be granted to an invention, even if it is new, "if the differences between the subject matter sought to be patented and the prior art are such that the subject matter as a whole would have been obvious at the time the invention was made to a person having ordinary skill in the art to which the subject matter pertains." To paraphrase, an inventor who just improves a previous invention, in a way that other inventors would find obvious, receives no patent. Consider the following excerpts from a patent application:

U.S. Patent No. 5,960,411 (filed Sept. 28, 1999)
*Method and system for placing a purchase order
via a communications network*

Abstract

A method and system for placing an order to purchase an item via the Internet. The order is placed by a purchaser at a client system and received by a server system. The server system receives purchaser information including identification of the purchaser, payment information, and shipment information from the client system. The server system then assigns a client identifier to the client system and associates the assigned client identifier with the received purchaser information. The server system sends to the client system the assigned client identifier and an HTML document identifying the item and including an order button. The client system receives and stores the assigned client identifier and receives and displays the HTML document. In response to the selection of the order button, the client system sends to the server system a request to purchase the identified item. The server system receives the request and combines the purchaser information associated with the client identifier of the client system to generate an order to purchase the item in accordance with the billing and shipment information whereby the purchaser effects the ordering of the product by selection of the order button.

Inventors: Hartman; Peri (Seattle, WA); Bezos; Jeffrey P. (Seattle, WA); Kaphan; Shel (Seattle WA); Spiegel, Joel (Seattle, WA)

Assignee: Amazon.com, Inc. (Seattle, WA)

Appl. No: 928951

Filed: Sept. 12, 1997

We claim:

1. A method of placing an order for an item comprising:

under control of a client system, displaying information identifying the item; and in response to only a single action being performed, sending a request to order the item along with an identifier of a purchaser of the item to a server system;

under control of a single-action ordering component of the server system, receiving the request;

retrieving additional information previously stored for the purchaser identified by the identifier in the received request; and

generating an order to purchase the requested item for the purchaser identified by the identifier in the received request using the retrieved additional information; and

fulfilling the generated order to complete purchase of the item whereby the item is ordered without using a shopping cart ordering model.

2. The method of claim 1 wherein the displaying of information includes displaying information indicating the single action.

3. The method of claim 1 wherein the single action is clicking a button.

4. The method of claim 1 wherein the single action is speaking of a sound.

5. The method of claim 1 wherein a user of the client system does not need to explicitly identify themselves when placing an order.

* * *

The application describes Amazon.com's one-click ordering system. Its basic claim involves a computer system that allows a customer to place an order by minimizing the number of actions on the screen. Amazon later sued another large online bookstore, Barnesandnoble.com, for infringing its patent, and asked for a temporary injunction from the Court of Appeals for the Federal Circuit, the court that specializes in patent matters. Barnes & Noble had argued that the one-click system was just an "obvious" form of previous approaches to online ordering, which had existed before Amazon's patent. The following excerpt from the court's opinion describes the technology at issue.

Amazon.com v. Barnesandnoble.com
239 F.3d 1343 (Fed. Cir. 2001)

Clevenger, J.

This is a patent infringement suit brought by Amazon.com, Inc. ("Amazon") against barnesandnoble.com, inc., and barnesandnoble.com. llc (together, "BN"). Amazon moved for a preliminary injunction to prohibit BN's use of a feature of its website called "Express Lane." BN resisted the preliminary injunction on several grounds, including that its Express Lane feature did not infringe the claims of Amazon's patent, and that substantial questions exist as to the validity of Amazon's patent. The United States District Court for the Western District of Washington rejected BN's contentions. Instead, the district court held that Amazon had presented a case showing a likelihood of infringement by BN, and that BN's challenges to the validity of the patent in suit lacked sufficient merit to avoid awarding extraordinary preliminary injunctive relief to Amazon. The district court granted Amazon's motion, and now BN brings its timely appeal from the order entering the preliminary injunction.

After careful review of the district court's opinion, the record, and the arguments advanced by the parties, we conclude that BN has mounted a substantial challenge to the validity of the patent in suit. Because Amazon is not entitled to preliminary injunctive relief under these circumstances, we vacate the order of the district court that set the preliminary injunction in place and remand the case for further proceedings.

This case involves United States Patent No. 5,960,411 ("the '411 patent"), which issued on September 28, 1999, and is assigned to Amazon. On October 21, 1999, Amazon brought suit against BN alleging infringement of the patent and seeking a preliminary injunction.

Amazon's patent is directed to a method and system for "single action" ordering of items in a client/server environment such as the Internet. Typically, the client computer system and the server computer system are located remotely from each other and communicate via a data communication network.

The '411 patent describes a method and system in which a consumer can complete a purchase order for an item via an electronic network using only a "single action," such as the click of a computer mouse button on the client computer system. Amazon developed the patent to cope with what it considered to be frustrations presented by what is known as the "shopping cart model" purchase system for electronic commerce purchasing events. In previous incarnations of the shopping cart model, a purchaser using a client computer system (such as a personal computer executing a web browser program) could select an item from an electronic catalog, typically by clicking on an "Add to Shopping Cart" icon, thereby placing the item in the "virtual" shopping cart. Other items from the catalog could be added to the shopping cart in the same manner. When the shopper completed the selecting process, the electronic commercial event would move to the check-out counter, so to speak. Then, information regarding the purchaser's identity, billing and shipping addresses, and credit payment method would be inserted into the transactional information base by the soon-to-be purchaser. Finally, the purchaser would "click" on a button displayed on the screen or somehow issue a command to execute the completed order, and the server computer system would verify and store the information concerning the transaction.

As is evident from the foregoing, an electronic commerce purchaser using the shopping cart model is required to perform several actions before achieving the ultimate goal of the placed order. The '411 patent sought to reduce the number of actions required from a consumer to effect a placed order. In the words of the written description of the '411 patent:

> How, one may ask, is the number of purchaser interactions reduced? The answer is that the number of purchaser interactions is reduced because the purchaser has previously visited the seller's web site and has previously entered into the database of the seller all of the required billing and shipping information that is needed to effect a sales transaction. Thereafter, when the purchaser visits the seller's web site and wishes to purchase a product from that site, the patent specifies that only a single action is necessary to place the order for the item. In the words of the written description, "once the description of an item is displayed, the purchaser need only take a single action to place the order to purchase that item."

Conclusion

While it appears on the record before us that Amazon has carried its burden with respect to demonstrating the likelihood of success on infringement, it is also true that BN has raised substantial questions as to the validity of the '411 patent. For that reason, we must conclude that the necessary prerequisites for entry of a preliminary injunction are presently lacking. We therefore vacate the preliminary injunction and remand the case for further proceedings.

* * *

Topics for Further Discussion

1. Playing the role of Amazon's attorney, describe how its system meets the test of patentability (i.e. novelty, utility, and non-obviousness).

2. Now, playing the role of Barnes and Noble's attorney, make an argument disputing those points.

3. Since Amazon held a patent at the time of the decision, why didn't the court of appeals stop Barnes and Noble from continuing to use the technology in question, at least until the district court could reconsider the case?

4. In the end, the two companies reached an out-of-court settlement, with no public disclosure of the terms.

5. In *Quanta Computer v. LG Electronics*, 128 S. Ct. 2109 (2008), the Supreme Court ruled that patent holders are entitled to only one bite of the apple. LG licensed its technology to Intel, which made use of it in computer microprocessors and chipsets. Intel then sold these components to computer manufacturers for inclusion in the final product. Notwithstanding the license to Intel, LG insisted the manufacturers could not use the technology without obtaining licenses of their own. The Court, however, disagreed, relying on the doctrine of "patent exhaustion."

* * *

Trade secret law, unlike patent law, is state law rather than federal law. As a result, the details may differ from state to state. Nevertheless, the basic understanding is that a trade secret may be almost anything that gives the owner a business advantage. So long as the "owner" maintains the secret, the law will protect him from anyone who obtains it improperly. Many cases involve a breach of a confidential relationship. In these instances, the "owner" discloses the secret to another for a particular purpose, with the understanding that the secret will not be misused or communicated further. Employees using information on the job is the most common example. When they change jobs, questions often arise as to what part of their knowledge is general information and what part is trade secret.

American Derringer Corp. v. Bond
924 S.W.2d 773 (Tex. App. — Waco 1996)

Vance, J.

Upon the formation of an employment relationship, certain duties arise apart from any written contract. One of those duties forbids an employee from using confidential or proprietary information acquired during the relationship in a manner adverse to the employer. This obligation survives termination of employment. Although this duty does not bar use of general knowledge, skill, and experience, it prevents the former employee's use of confidential information or trade secrets acquired during the course of employment.

Elizabeth Saunders testified that she was the president of ADC, having succeeded her husband, Robert Saunders (Bob), when he died in 1993. She said that ADC's customers fall into one of three categories: distributors who purchase one hundred or more guns within a twelve month period, jobbers who purchase five or more guns, and individuals who buy just one gun. Distributors and jobbers are required to hold a federal firearms license. She described the various models of the guns that ADC manufactured. Two-thirds of all guns sold by ADC were "Model 1" derringers, about 40,000 of which had been manufactured since 1988.

Part of her duties with ADC involved the handling of customer complaints and comments about the product. These communications were directed, first, to Bob Saunders, then to the appropriate department within the company. They were considered confidential. A large number of complaints about the Model 1 had been made to the company, many about safety aspects of the gun. Elizabeth said that the company "had several lawsuits pending because of that."

In 1991, because of the safety complaints, the company sought an engineer to work on those and other problems. ADC hired [Greg] Bond to "find out what the problems were." During the first six or seven months, Bond set up a "gun drill," a machine designed to drill a hole with the perfection needed to make a gun barrel. When the gun drill was "up and running," it helped increase production. He also created a "flow chart" to track the process of assembling guns. Elizabeth said that Bond was acting as the plant manager and had access to everything that ADC had, including all drawings developed for the company for the manufacture of its guns. He also worked with companies that produced the components for ADC and had full access to complaints and comments made by customers about the products.

Elizabeth said that various employees of the company discussed solutions to the safety problems, such as "a retractable firing pin," "a rebounding hammer," and "a cross-bolt safety," in Bond's presence. Cosmetic changes, such as "an octagonal barrel," which the company wanted to offer as a customer option, were also discussed with him.

In July of 1992, Bob Saunders fired Bond because of a disagreement over allowing employees time-off.

In January of 1993, Bob Saunders learned that Bond was displaying "a gun that looked similar to ours" at a "Shot Show," a large trade show for the firearms industry. ADC obtained Bond's literature describing his gun as the "Defender." She said that some of the features that the Defender's brochure described were features that ADC had sought to get Bond to produce for its guns.

Elizabeth said that she had seen Bond "doing a lot of drawing" while employed at the company. She further said that the frame of the Defender "looked a lot like our frame"; that the Defender was offered with interchangeable barrels which ADC had offered in the past; that "the calibers he was offering it in was similar to our calibers"; and that "he incorporated all the things that-on this gun that we had basically discussed while he was employed ... that needed to be on for safety purposes." When the directory for the 1994 Shot Show came out and she knew that Bond was going to be there, Elizabeth made the decision on behalf of ADC to take legal action.

Bond testified that he "toyed with" the idea of designing a gun before he was fired by ADC. It never went beyond the "concept" stage and he had committed nothing to paper. He said he had spoken to Don Pilant, the owner of Custom Molds and Tools in Waco. He told Pilant that "things were getting kind of flaky down at American Derringer, and I really didn't know what was going to happen, but if-if I was asked to leave, fired, laid off, whatever, I thought I might want to come up with a different gun." He decided to design and build a gun "the day I was fired." His initial concept included having a trigger guard; a longer grip that would accommodate at least two fingers, a feature that was an option on ADC guns; and interchangeable barrels, an idea that Bob Saunders rejected before Bond went to work at ADC, but which was discussed while he worked there.

Bond maintained that knowledge of the design of derringers is in the public domain, available in books and parts lists. He said that the design of the Defender was "totally different" from that of the Model 1.

Bond's employment by ADC gave rise to a duty not to use ADC's proprietary information and trade secrets in a manner adverse to it. Although the information was not patented, it need not be. That Bond might have learned about derringers through other means, such as inspection, books, parts lists, and the like, does not necessarily mean that ADC knew that he did so. "The question is not, 'How could he have secured the knowledge?' but 'How did he?'"

Bond admits that he gained full knowledge of the details of the design, the manufacturing process, and customer comments and complaints while he was an employee of ADC. Indeed, ADC employed Bond to learn all about and improve its product. Within six months of his being fired, ADC learned that Bond was offering a similar gun for sale.

We find that ADC had a legitimate interest in protecting confidential information relating to the design and manufacture of its derringer. Viewing the remaining evidence from the standpoint of a reasonable, prudent person under the circumstances with which ADC was faced, we find no evidence that the motives, grounds, beliefs, and other evidence upon which ADC acted were not probable cause to institute the proceeding.

* * *

Topics for Further Discussion

1. As a matter of fact, a jury had found that Bond did not convert any trade secrets. Bond filed a counterclaim alleging malicious prosecution against ADC for suing him. The jury ruled in his favor, and awarded him $131,500 in damages. The excerpts above are from the company's appeal of that malicious prosecution award. The court of appeals ruled that, even though the jury found Bond had done nothing wrong, his former employer had sufficient cause to sue him. The damage award was voided, and Bond was required to pay all costs of the appeal.

2. Although trade secret law is within the control of each state, attempts have been made to achieve a level of uniformity. The most notable is the Uniform Trade Secret Act, which has been adopted in 45 states.

Trademark Law

Trademark law in the United States is primarily governed by what is known as the Lanham Act, codified at 15 U.S.C. § 1051. It allows for the registration of trademarks, service marks, and trade names, as well as several other categories. In order to qualify for protection, a mark must be or have become "distinctive." When a mark that was not originally distinctive has acquired distinctiveness, the process is referred to as having acquired "secondary meaning." In other words, the mark must have become associated with a particular producer or source. By demonstrating distinctiveness, and maintaining the registration, a trademark owner can enjoy protection continuously. Remedies for infringement include both money damages and injunctive relief.

In trademark litigation, a key question is often whether another company's use of the mark "is likely to cause confusion." The inquiry, thus, depends on how the public sees the situation. For example, would prospective buyers of LEXUS cars be confused and mistakenly believe that the producer of the LEXIS legal database was somehow involved? As the example suggests, trademark protection is not restricted to marks that are exactly alike. Names that are somewhat different may be restrained, if the public is likely to be confused by them.

The link between the product and the producer is crucial. When filing a trademark application, one must specify the area of business within which the mark is used. A claim that is too broad will be rejected by the trademark examiner. One that is too narrow may limit the company's ability to expand its business on the strength of its trademark. For example, Apple Records Co. (officially Applecorps, the firm founded by the Beatles) moved to block Apple Computer Co. from using the name once the latter used sound on its computers. The case ended in a settlement, widely believed to have included a payment to refrain from further action, and an agreement that the computer company would not use the name in the music business. The trademark once again turned into a dispute when the Apple Computer began its iTunes online music service.

Even the design or shape of a product can be protected, but only if it is distinctive and not just functional. A particular section of the Lanham Act protects what is known as "trade dress." In the following case, the Supreme Court considered the extent of that protection.

Wal-Mart Stores v. Samara Bros.

529 U.S. 205 (2000)

Scalia, J.

In this case, we decide under what circumstances a product's design is distinctive, and therefore protectible, in an action for infringement of unregistered trade dress under § 43(a) of the Trademark Act of 1946 (Lanham Act).

Respondent Samara Brothers, Inc., designs and manufactures children's clothing. Its primary product is a line of spring/summer one-piece seersucker outfits decorated with appliques of hearts, flowers, fruits, and the like. A number of chain stores, including JCPenney, sell this line of clothing under contract with Samara.

Petitioner Wal-Mart Stores, Inc., is one of the Nation's best known retailers, selling among other things children's clothing. In 1995, Wal-Mart contracted with one of its suppliers, Judy-Philippine, Inc., to manufacture a line of children's outfits for sale in the 1996 spring/summer season. Wal-Mart sent Judy-Philippine photographs of a number of garments from Samara's line, on which Judy-Philippine's garments were to be based; Judy-Philippine duly copied, with only minor modifications, 16 of Samara's garments, many of which contained copyrighted elements. In 1996, Wal-Mart briskly sold the so-called knockoffs, generating more than $1.15 million in gross profits.

In June 1996, a buyer for JCPenney called a representative at Samara to complain that she had seen Samara garments on sale at Wal-Mart for a lower price than JCPenney was allowed to charge under its contract with Samara. The Samara representative told the buyer that Samara did not supply its clothing to Wal-Mart. Their suspicions aroused, however, Samara officials launched an investigation, which disclosed that Wal-Mart and several other major retailers — Kmart, Caldor, Hills, and Goody's — were selling the knockoffs of Samara's outfits produced by Judy-Philippine.

After sending cease-and-desist letters, Samara brought this action in the United States District Court for the Southern District of New York against Wal-Mart, Judy-Philippine, Kmart, Caldor, Hills, and Goody's for copyright infringement under federal law, consumer fraud and unfair competition under New York law, and — most relevant for our purposes — infringement of unregistered trade dress under § 43(a) of the Lanham Act, 15 U.S.C. § 1125(a). All of the defendants except Wal-Mart settled before trial. After a weeklong trial, the jury found in favor of Samara on all of its claims.

The Lanham Act provides for the registration of trademarks, which it defines in § 45 to include "any word, name, symbol, or device, or any combination thereof [used or intended to be used] to identify and distinguish [a producer's] goods ... from those manufactured or sold by others and to indicate the source of the goods...."

In addition to protecting registered marks, the Lanham Act, in § 43(a), gives a producer a cause of action for the use by any person of "any word, term, name, symbol, or device, or any combination thereof ... which ... is likely to cause confusion ... as to the origin, sponsorship, or approval of his or her goods...." It is the latter provision that is at issue in this case.

The breadth of the definition of marks registrable under § 2, and of the confusion-producing elements recited as actionable by § 43(a), has been held to embrace not just word marks, such as "Nike" and symbol marks, such as Nike's "swoosh" symbol, but also "trade dress" — a category that originally included only the packaging, or "dressing," of a product, but in recent years has been expanded by many Courts of Appeals to encompass the design of a product.

The text of §43(a) provides little guidance as to the circumstances under which unregistered trade dress may be protected. It does require that a producer show that the allegedly infringing feature is not "functional," and is likely to cause confusion with the product for which protection is sought.

In evaluating the distinctiveness of a mark under §2 (and therefore, by analogy, under §43(a)), courts have held that a mark can be distinctive in one of two ways. First, a mark is inherently distinctive if "[its] intrinsic nature serves to identify a particular source." Second, a mark has acquired distinctiveness, even if it is not inherently distinctive, if it has developed secondary meaning, which occurs when, "in the minds of the public, the primary significance of a [mark] is to identify the source of the product rather than the product itself."

It seems to us that design, like color, is not inherently distinctive. Consumers are aware of the reality that, almost invariably, even the most unusual of product designs—such as a cocktail shaker shaped like a penguin—is intended not to identify the source, but to render the product itself more useful or more appealing. The fact that product design almost invariably serves purposes other than source identification not only renders inherent distinctiveness problematic; it also renders application of an inherent-distinctiveness principle more harmful to other consumer interests. Consumers should not be deprived of the benefits of competition with regard to the utilitarian and esthetic purposes that product design ordinarily serves by a rule of law that facilitates plausible threats of suit against new entrants based upon alleged inherent distinctiveness.

To the extent there are close cases, we believe that courts should err on the side of caution and classify ambiguous trade dress as product design, thereby requiring secondary meaning. The very closeness will suggest the existence of relatively small utility in adopting an inherent-distinctiveness principle, and relatively great consumer benefit in requiring a demonstration of secondary meaning.

We hold that, in an action for infringement of unregistered trade dress under §43(a) of the Lanham Act, a product's design is distinctive, and therefore protectible, only upon a showing of secondary meaning.

* * *

Another feature of the Lanham Act is protecting owners of trademarks from what is called "dilution" of the mark. Dilution involves a competing mark that does not confuse consumers about the ownership, but which tends to diminish the power of the original trademark. In the following case, the Supreme Court considered what kind of proof of dilution is necessary.

Moseley v. V Secret Catalogue
537 U.S. 418 (2003)

Stevens, J.

In 1995 Congress amended §43 of the Trademark Act of 1946, 15 U.S.C. §1125, to provide a remedy for the "dilution of famous marks." That amendment, known as the Federal Trademark Dilution Act (FTDA), describes the factors that determine whether a mark is "distinctive and famous," and defines the term "dilution" as "the lessening of the capacity of a famous mark to identify and distinguish goods or services." The question we granted *certiorari* to decide is whether objective proof of actual injury to the economic value of a famous mark (as opposed to a presumption of harm arising from a subjective "likelihood of dilution" standard) is a requisite for relief under the FTDA.

Petitioners, Victor and Cathy Moseley, own and operate a retail store named "Victor's Little Secret" in a strip mall in Elizabethtown, Kentucky. They have no employees. Respondents are affiliated corporations that own the VICTORIA'S SECRET trademark and operate over 750 Victoria's Secret stores, two of which are in Louisville, Kentucky, a short drive from Elizabethtown. In 1998 they spent over $55 million advertising "the VICTORIA'S SECRET brand—one of moderately priced, high quality, attractively designed lingerie sold in a store setting designed to look like a wom[a]n's bedroom." They distribute 400 million copies of the Victoria's Secret catalog each year, including 39,000 in Elizabethtown. In 1998 their sales exceeded $1.5 billion.

In the February 12, 1998, edition of a weekly publication distributed to residents of the military installation at Fort Knox, Kentucky, petitioners advertised the "GRAND OPENING Just in time for Valentine's Day!" of their store "VICTOR'S SECRET" in nearby Elizabethtown. The ad featured "Intimate Lingerie for every woman"; "Romantic Lighting"; "Lycra Dresses"; "Pagers"; and "Adult Novelties/Gifts." An army colonel, who saw the ad and was offended by what he perceived to be an attempt to use a reputable company's trademark to promote the sale of "unwholesome, tawdry merchandise," sent a copy to respondents. Their counsel then wrote to petitioners stating that their choice of the name "Victor's Secret" for a store selling lingerie was likely to cause confusion with the well-known VICTORIA'S SECRET mark and, in addition, was likely to "dilute the distinctiveness" of the mark. They requested the immediate discontinuance of the use of the name "and any variations thereof." In response, petitioners changed the name of their store to "Victor's Little Secret." Because that change did not satisfy respondents, they promptly filed this action in Federal District Court.

The record in this case establishes that an army officer who saw the advertisement of the opening of a store named "Victor's Secret" did make the mental association with "Victoria's Secret," but it also shows that he did not therefore form any different impression of the store that his wife and daughter had patronized. There is a complete absence of evidence of any lessening of the capacity of the VICTORIA'S SECRET mark to identify and distinguish goods or services sold in Victoria's Secret stores or advertised in its catalogs. The officer was offended by the ad, but it did not change his conception of Victoria's Secret. His offense was directed entirely at petitioners, not at respondents. Moreover, the expert retained by respondents had nothing to say about the impact of petitioners' name on the strength of respondents' mark.

Noting that consumer surveys and other means of demonstrating actual dilution are expensive and often unreliable, respondents argue that evidence of an actual "lessening of the capacity of a famous mark to identify and distinguish goods or services," may be difficult to obtain. It may well be, however, that direct evidence of dilution such as consumer surveys will not be necessary if actual dilution can reliably be proved through circumstantial evidence—the obvious case is one where the junior and senior marks are identical. Whatever difficulties of proof may be entailed, they are not an acceptable reason for dispensing with proof of an essential element of a statutory violation. The evidence in the present record is not sufficient to support the summary judgment on the dilution count. The judgment is therefore reversed, and the case is remanded for further proceedings consistent with this opinion.

* * *

Topics for Further Discussion

1. Following the *Moseley* decision, Congress passed the Trademark Dilution Revision Act of 2006. Section 1125(c)(1) of the Act authorizes courts to enjoin the use of any mark that is likely to cause dilution by blurring or dilution by tarnishment of a famous mark. It permits the owner of a famous mark to obtain injunctive relief against anyone commencing use of the mark *after* it has become famous when such use is likely to cause dilution by blurring or tarnishment. The District Court on remand issued an injunction under the Act against the use of the names "Victor's Little Secret" and "Victor's Secret." The basis of the District Court's ruling was that the sex-related nature of the shop disparaged and tended to reduce the positive associations and the "selling power" of the "Victoria's Secret" mark, thereby harming the reputation of the famous mark. The opinion of the District Court was affirmed by the Sixth Circuit Court of Appeals in *V Secret Catalogue, Inc. et al. v. Moseley, et al.*, 605 F.3d 382 (6th Cir. 2010). The owners of the shop changed the name to "Cathy's Little Secret."

2. As the *Wal-Mart* case reflects, federal law is not the only theory upon which plaintiffs may sue. In particular, state unfair competition law may protect against claimed "passing off" of products. Unfair competition is another area for which a Restatement has been written. The Restatement (Third) of Unfair Competition includes not only passing off issues, but also other forms of deceptive trade practices such as false advertising.

3. Now that you have read this chapter, imagine that you are a lawyer whose client is in business. As part of your overall review of the client's legal matters, what sorts of intellectual property "checks" would you provide? If a lawyer who represented a business on an ongoing basis did not provide such checks, would that be professional malpractice?

* * *

Trademarks often are among the most valuable assets held by entertainers, especially bands. However, when relations among the band members break down, as they often do, the ownership of the asset can be cast into confusion. The following case deals with the question of legal rights to the name of one of the most famous American pop-rock groups of all time.

Brother Records v. Jardine
318 F. 3d 939 (9th Cir. 2003)

Tashima, J.

In 1961, Al Jardine, Mike Love, Brian Wilson, Carl Wilson, and Dennis Wilson formed The Beach Boys. The band shortly thereafter achieved huge commercial success, producing numerous hit songs and touring to huge audiences throughout the country. In 1967, the members of the Beach Boys incorporated BRI to hold and administer the intellectual property rights for The Beach Boys. Currently, BRI is equally owned by four shareholders, who are also its directors: Al Jardine, Mike Love, Brian Wilson, and the estate of Carl Wilson. BRI is the registered owner of "The Beach Boys" trademark.

Over the years, personal difficulties arose between some of the members, and some members of the band decided to not tour full time, or at all. In 1991, the members of the Beach Boys incorporated Brother Tours, Inc., which handled their touring and distributed their touring income. In 1993, the directors of BRI agreed to devote a certain percentage of the touring income to the corporation for use of the trademark and designated a larger percentage of the income to those members who actually toured. By 1998, Carl

Wilson had died, Love and Jardine no longer wanted to tour together, and Brian Wilson did not want to tour at all. Love began negotiating with BRI the terms of a license to use "The Beach Boys" trademark in connection with his own band.

BRI's directors met on July 14, 1998, to discuss how the trademark should be used. The representative of Carl Wilson's estate suggested that BRI issue non-exclusive licenses to each shareholder on the same terms and conditions as the license that was being negotiated with Love, thus giving each member an equal right to tour. Three of the four board members, including Jardine, voted to grant each Beach Boy a non-exclusive license.

After the July 1998 BRI board meeting, Jardine began touring with his own band, using a booking agent and manager that were not included in the list approved by the Love license. On October 25, 1998, Jardine's attorney sent BRI a letter saying that Jardine would be performing as "Beach Boys Family and Friends," and that therefore, "a license from BRI [was] unnecessary." On October 28, 1998, BRI told Jardine that his unlicensed use of the trademark would be an infringement.

Jardine and his band continued to perform using names that included "The Beach Boys" trademark. The performances were promoted under names such as: Al Jardine of the Beach Boys and Family & Friends; The Beach Boys "Family and Friends"; Beach Boys Family & Friends; The Beach Boys, Family & Friends; Beach Boys and Family; as well as, simply, The Beach Boys. Jardine and his band performed in locations and on dates close to Love's "The Beach Boys" shows. With two bands touring as The Beach Boys or as a similar-sounding combination, show organizers sometimes were confused about what exactly they were getting when they booked Jardine's band. A number of show organizers booked Jardine's band thinking they would get The Beach Boys along with special added guests, but subsequently canceled the booking when they discovered that Jardine's band was not what they thought it was. Numerous people who attended one of Jardine's shows said that they had been confused about who was performing. During this time period, BRI sent Jardine cease and desist letters objecting to Jardine's use of the trademark.

Jardine contends that his use of BRI's trademark is protected by either the classic fair use doctrine or the nominative fair use doctrine. In *New Kids on the Block v. News Am. Publ'g Inc.*, 971 F.2d 302 (9th Cir.1992), we noted that the classic fair use defense could not be applied in that case because "this is not the classic fair use case where the defendant has used the plaintiff's mark to describe the defendant's own product." We then held that, "where the defendant uses a trademark to describe the plaintiff's product, rather than its own ... a commercial user is entitled to a nominative fair use defense." In *Cairns v. Franklin Mint Co.*, 292 F.3d 1139, 1150–52 (9th Cir.2002), we reiterated the distinction between the classic fair use and nominative fair use doctrines.

The nominative fair use analysis is appropriate where a defendant has used the plaintiff's mark to describe the plaintiff's product, even if the defendant's ultimate goal is to describe his own product. Conversely, the classic fair use analysis is appropriate where a defendant has used the plaintiff's mark only to describe his own product, and not at all to describe the plaintiff's product.

Here, as in *New Kids*, Jardine does not use the trademark in any primary, descriptive sense. That is, Jardine does not use "The Beach Boys" trademark to denote its primary, descriptive meaning of "boys who frequent a stretch of sand beside the sea." Instead, Jardine uses "The Beach Boys" trademark in its secondary, trademark sense, which denotes the music band—and its members—that popularized California surfing culture. The classic fair use defense does not apply.

Where the defendant uses the trademark not in its primary, descriptive sense, but rather in its secondary, trademark sense, the nominative fair use analysis applies.

In *New Kids,* we articulated the three requirements of the nominative fair use defense:

First, the product or service in question must be one not readily identifiable without use of the trademark; second, only so much of the mark or marks may be used as is reasonably necessary to identify the product or service; and third, the user must do nothing that would, in conjunction with the mark, suggest sponsorship or endorsement by the trademark holder.

Just as it is virtually impossible to refer to the New Kids on the Block, the Chicago Bulls, Volkswagens, or the Boston Marathon without using the trademarked names, so too is it virtually impossible to refer to the Beach Boys without using the trademark, and Jardine therefore meets the first requirement. Also, BRI does not allege that Jardine uses any distinctive logo "or anything else that isn't needed" to identify the Beach Boys, and Jardine therefore satisfies the second requirement.

Jardine fails, however, to meet the third requirement. Jardine's promotional materials display "The Beach Boys" more prominently and boldly than "Family and Friends," suggesting sponsorship by the Beach Boys. Also, there is evidence that Jardine uses "The Beach Boys" trademark to suggest that his band is in fact sponsored by the Beach Boys. Finally, Jardine's use of the trademark caused actual consumer confusion, as both event organizers that booked Jardine's band and people who attended Jardine's shows submitted declarations expressing confusion about who was performing.

We therefore affirm the district court's grant of summary judgment in favor of BRI on BRI's trademark infringement claim.

* * *

Topics for Further Discussion

1. What does "The Beach Boys" mean legally? What does "The Beach Boys" mean artistically?

2. Litigation concerning The Beach Boys continued over a number of years. In 2008, the members/directors reportedly reached an amicable settlement.

Key Terms and Concepts

Confidential Relationship
Downloading
Fair Use
Patent Claim
Prior Art
Public Domain
Secondary Meaning
Trade Dress
Trademark Dilution
Uploading

Chapter 10

Criminal Law and Procedure

"Laws are partly formed for the sake of good men, in order to instruct them how they may live on friendly terms with one another, and partly for the sake of those who refuse to be instructed, whose spirit cannot be subdued, or softened, or hindered from plunging into evil."

Plato, Law, Book IX (360 B.C.)

Criminal law represents the power to deprive an individual of life, liberty, or property for committing specified acts prohibited by society. In a democratic society, it is through the authority of the criminal law, as enacted by elected representatives, that the majority determines the full range of unacceptable and, thus, punishable behavior. The Constitution establishes limits on the power of the majority to criminalize behavior by providing various substantive limits on state power and institutionalizing procedural protections intended to preserve important principles to a free society. These principles include the presumption of innocence, the right to be free from unwarranted governmental intrusion, and due process.

The Founding Fathers had a high degree of concern for the potential for abuse inherent in the criminal law. The Fourth, Fifth, Sixth, and Eighth Amendments of the Bill of Rights are devoted almost entirely to limiting the power of the state to use the criminal law to suppress individual rights. Criminal law is, at once, a frontline defense essential for a peaceful and well ordered society, and a potential tool of tyranny capable of trampling freedom. The major features of the Bill of Rights dealing with criminal law and procedure will be examined in this chapter. Clearly, one of the major functions of a written constitution is to protect the individual from what has been called the "tyranny of the majority," and nowhere is this tyranny more evident and oppressive than when the majority uses the criminal law to ban dissent and stifle minority rights. Of equal concern is the problem of selective enforcement regarding whom society chooses to prosecute and punish.

There are many different stakeholders in the criminal justice system, among them society at large. Society is represented by the legislators who make the laws, the police (or the FBI in the case of federal crimes) who enforce the laws, the prosecutors who decide whether and to what degree to prosecute a case, the defense lawyers who protect the rights of the defendant, judges and jurors who determine a defendant's guilt or innocence and set the punishment, and a myriad of court and prison officials who have custody over defendants passing through the system. The frequently forgotten party in the criminal justice system is the victim of the crime. Victims have little say in whether or how a case is prosecuted, or in determining the penalty a convicted offender receives. Sometimes, it seems that these victims are twice victimized; once by the criminal and then again by a system that too often treats them as just another cog in the wheel.

Basic Principles of Criminal Law

A crime is any behavior for which an individual can be imprisoned, fined, or both. The common law recognized eight core crimes as follows: (1) Murder (killing a person with malice); (2) Manslaughter (killing a person without malice); (3) Mayhem (mutilating a person); (4) Rape (sexual intercourse without consent); (5) Larceny (taking and carrying away another's property with the intent to steal); (6) Robbery (larceny using force); (7) Burglary (breaking and entering a building with intent to commit a crime); and (8) Arson (intentionally and maliciously setting a building on fire).

Modern criminal law is largely statutory. The various state and federal lawmakers are charged with creating a system of laws that reflect the values of society. In the U.S. system, the federal government and the state legislatures have authority to pass criminal laws. Congress, however, can only pass a law when it does so under an enumerated power in the Constitution. Federal jurisdiction is often found in the power to regulate commerce between states under Article I, section 8, and in the inherent power to pass laws protecting and preserving institutions in which there is a federal interest (e.g. the posts, banks, and securities markets). *Ex post facto* laws (those making an action illegal retroactively) are prohibited by Article I, section 9 of the Constitution.

Since states and the federal government can pass laws making essentially the same behavior criminal, a defendant committing a single act can violate both federal and state law at the same time. Therefore, the defendant can, in theory, be prosecuted by both sovereigns. The fact that there are two authorities empowered to pass and prosecute criminal laws has a direct impact on the Fifth Amendment prohibition against placing an individual in double jeopardy. In general, federal criminal law is restricted to behaviors committed against federal employees or institutions, or involving interstate activities. It is, for example, a federal crime to assault, rob, or murder a postman. Income tax evasion is a federal crime because the Internal Revenue Code is a federal statute. It is also a federal crime to rob a bank because banks are insured by the federal government. In a similar manner, crimes using the postal system or other means of interstate commerce, such as wire fraud or internet crime, are subject to federal jurisdiction. Finally, an individual who commits a crime in one state and flees across the state border into another state commits a federal crime of fleeing across state lines to avoid prosecution. The FBI can investigate and arrest the individual for the offense of fleeing, and the U.S. Attorney can prosecute in federal court, even though the underlying crime is not federal.

Criminal law begins with the passage of a law making some behavior unlawful, and fixing the range and degree of punishments available to judge or jury for anyone convicted. This is not always a completely rational or consistent process. The law books are littered with outdated prohibitions that have not been repealed. Moreover, the laws in different states can, and do, differ. One state may make it a crime for people to drink alcohol under the age of 21, while a neighboring state may set the age at eighteen. It is legal to buy, sell, and use tobacco, but not marijuana. This is despite the fact that both are substances commonly found in nature and tobacco is thought by some to be more dangerous to the individual user and more costly to society. Also, the law does not always keep up with changes in society. In *Bowers v. Hardwick*, 478 U.S. 186 (1986), the Supreme Court declined to make it unconstitutional for Georgia to criminalize homosexual behavior conducted by consenting adults in the privacy of their home. Twenty years later, in *Lawrence v. Texas*, 539 U.S. 558 (2003), the Supreme Court changed course by recognizing that new lifestyles had emerged. The point is simply that times change, and what society considers acceptable changes with it, albeit sometimes slowly.

The majority of criminal statutes governing social behavior are passed by state legislatures. While society has become increasingly complex, and the making of new laws that deal with advances in technology is certainly necessary, the basic principles of criminal law trace their roots much farther back in history. The common law required two factors for most crimes. First, there had to be a criminal act (*actus reus*), and, second, the actor had to have an intention to commit the crime (*mens rea*, or a guilty mind). An act was required so that an individual would not be convicted merely for thinking of committing a crime. While it may be morally wrong to think of stealing property, or wishing you could kill an enemy, the thought alone is not criminal. Even the crime of conspiracy requires that two or more parties agree to commit a crime *and* then take some step in furtherance of their plan.

The guilty mind requirement prevents an honest mistake from being treated as a crime. A person who walks out of a store with a piece of merchandise that he honestly believes his spouse had already paid for should not be convicted of shoplifting. Ignorance of the law is not, however, a defense. Indeed, all members of society are deemed to know what is prohibited by the law. There is also a relatively small class of crimes based on strict liability. For example, a person can be convicted of statutory rape for having sex with a person under a certain age (determined state-by-state), regardless of whether the minor consented or the adult reasonably believed the other person was of age. Finally, the Constitution prohibits what are called "status" offenses, for example, a state law cannot make it a crime to be a drug addict. The state can certainly make possessing, using, transporting, buying, or selling drugs a crime, but it cannot punish a person for the mere fact that he is addicted to an illegal substance.

Crimes can be divided into a number of different categories. Naturally, crimes of violence against persons are treated more harshly than property crimes. Moreover, certain crimes are considered to be *malum in se*, meaning that the behavior is inherently evil. We do not need a law to tell us that murder, rape, or robbery are wrong. Crimes that are *malum in se* attract the most severe punishment precisely because they are morally wrong on a very base level. Other crimes can be called *malum prohibitum*, meaning the behavior is criminal because society has deemed it so. Returning to the example of marijuana possession, it can be argued that there is nothing inherently immoral about smoking pot, although a state clearly has the authority to make it a crime. Crimes can be further separated into felonies (serious crimes) or misdemeanors (minor crimes). Felonies are a class of crimes for which the offender can potentially receive a punishment in excess of one year in prison. Misdemeanors, on the other hand, are those crimes where the maximum prison term is one year or less. Behavior punishable only by the payment of a fine (such as parking tickets, most traffic offenses, failures to file required documents, or other minor misdeeds) are typically not considered criminal in nature. Rather, they are what is known as administrative offenses.

White Collar and Organized Crime

It is a commonly held belief in the United States that business people who commit crimes such as stock fraud, tax evasion, or corporate corruption receive lighter punishments than most "common criminals." Clearly, this was true in the past and it may still be true to a certain degree in the present. There have certainly been many justifications offered for why white collar crime is different from the everyday criminal offense. First, it has been posited that, because wealthy individuals have (i) the resources to hire the best private investigators, (ii) jury consultants, and (iii) defense attorneys to represent them, that such white collar criminals have an inherent advantage when defending themselves against criminal prosecution. Second, it has been vigorously argued that, as established members of the community, white collar criminals can call upon other influential people to support leniency from any given judicial body that may levy any criminal sanction against them. Third, it has been argued that the likelihood of recidivism (returning to crime after conviction) is low among these so called "white collar criminals." Fourth, most white collar crime is non-violent and economic in nature. Therefore, as the argument goes, such crime does not cause fear on the streets or threaten our sense of security at home and, therefore, is not worthy of severe punishment. And, finally, public disgrace and the fall from a high position in society is argued as a great enough punishment in and of itself.

White collar criminals, when they are convicted, frequently avoid doing hard time in the worst prisons. Instead, they are ordered to perform public service or are sent to minimum security facilities (the so-called "Club Feds") where they are isolated from the worst elements of the penal system. The arguments for treating white collar criminals differently from common criminals are gradually eroding. This trend has been hastened by the many corporate scandals that have plagued the economy. One large scale financial scandal can destroy the futures of far more hard working and honest people than any crime spree.

A more invidious threat to society and the national economy is the infiltration by organized crime into the world of legitimate business. The roots of organized crime lie in the immigrant communities of the United States where access to mainstream institutions was often denied. The mob, in its many forms, ran an underground economy centered on loan sharking, numbers running, extortion, protection, black marketing, and other rackets. The success of organized crime required an outlet for money laundering so that their influence could spread into legitimate banks and business enterprises.

In 1970, as the Congress became increasingly concerned about this creeping infiltration, it passed the Racketeer Influenced and Corrupt Organization Act (RICO). RICO makes it "unlawful for any person who has received any income derived, directly or indirectly, from a pattern of racketeering activity or through collection of an unlawful debt in which such person has participated as a principal within the meaning of section 2, title 18, United States Code, to use or invest, directly or indirectly, any part of such income, or the proceeds of such income, in acquisition of any interest in, or the establishment or operation of, any enterprise which is engaged in, or the activities of which affect, interstate or foreign commerce." A pattern of racketeering activity exists whenever two or more racketeering activities occur within a ten year period. The maximum penalty for violating RICO is twenty years (or life if the underlying racketeering behavior allows for life imprisonment) in jail. The law also calls for the forfeiture of all property and assets acquired through the pattern of racketeering activity or through any gains from the proceeds of such activities.

RICO has both civil and criminal implications that are far-reaching. The National Organization for Women (NOW) used RICO to bring an action against a syndicate of anti-abortion groups to allege a conspiricy to shut-down abortion clinics. The Supreme Court, in *National Organization of Women v. Scheidler*, 510 U.S. 249 (1994), held that RICO does not require proof that either the racketeering enterprise or the predicate acts of racketeering were motivated by an economic purpose.

Due Process of Law

The Due Process Clause of the Fifth Amendment requires that criminal statutes be specific in describing prohibited behavior. Vague or overbroad criminal laws are inherently unfair because no one can be sure what behavior is prohibited. This can have a chilling effect on perfectly lawful activities. In *City of Chicago v. Morales*, 527 U.S. 41 (1999), the Supreme Court considered the constitutionality of an Illinois law that targeted gangs by making it a crime for them not to disperse when the police so ordered. The Supreme Court struck down the law writing that: "Vagueness may invalidate a criminal law for either of two independent reasons. First, it may fail to provide the kind of notice that will enable ordinary people to understand what conduct it prohibits; second, it may authorize and even encourage arbitrary and discriminatory enforcement." Any given state clearly has an interest in breaking up gangs that loiter on street corners, but this interest cannot be satisfied by a vague prohibition that could easily be interpreted to capture other lawful activities.

Most recently, in *Holder v. Humanitarian Law Project*, 561 U.S. __ (2010), the Supreme Court upheld, in a 6 to 3 decision, a federal criminal statute (18 U.S.C. §2339B) that makes it a crime to provide "material support or resources to a foreign terrorist organization." The Secretary of State is empowered by the law to designate any entity as a foreign terrorist organization. The plaintiffs were two U.S. citizens and six domestic organizations that desired "to facilitate only the lawful, nonviolent purposes" of two designated groups by providing "monetary contributions, other tangible aid, legal training, and political advocacy." They contended they could not do so out of fear (a chilling effect on behavior) of being prosecuted under a statute that "is too vague, in violation of the Fifth Amendment, and that infringes their rights to freedom of speech and association, in violation of the First Amendment."

The dissent, written by Justice Breyer, accepted the majority view that the statute is not unconstitutionally vague, but rejected the conclusion that the Government could "prosecute the plaintiffs criminally for engaging in coordinated teaching and advocacy furthering the designated organizations' lawful activities." The dissenters explained their objection the majority's holding as follows:

> the Government has not made the strong showing necessary to justify under the First Amendment the criminal prosecution of those who engage in these activities. All the activities involve the communication and advocacy of political ideas and lawful means of achieving political ends. Even the subjects the plaintiffs wish to teach—using international law to resolve disputes peacefully or petitioning the United Nations, for instance—concern political speech. We cannot avoid the constitutional significance of these facts on the basis that some of this speech takes place outside the United States and is directed at foreign governments, for the activities also involve advocacy in this country directed to our government and its policies. The plaintiffs, for example, wish to write and distribute publications and to speak before the United States Congress.

> That this speech and association for political purposes is the kind of activity to which the First Amendment ordinarily offers its strongest protection is elementary.

What is the real problem with vague laws, or laws that potentially capture lawful behavior within their ambit? The fight against terrorism is of particular concern because of the unsettled political nature of the underlying issues. It is often said that one person's terrorist is another's freedom fighter. Could the Government constitutionally criminalize all forms of support to groups designated as foreign terrorist organizations? Would this include an editorial in a newspaper commenting favorably on a designated organization?

Another example of a crime that is difficult to define with precision is stalking. Section 646.9 of the California Penal Code states, in relevant part, that: "Any person who willfully, maliciously, and repeatedly follows or harasses another person and who makes a credible threat with the intent to place that person in reasonable fear for his or her safety, or the safety of his or her immediate family, is guilty of the crime of stalking." The subjective elements of this offense are obvious, as is the potential for catching lawful behavior in the net. Nevertheless, while there is potential under the California stalking law for interpretation, the basic elements of the prohibited behavior are reasonably defined and detailed.

The Presumption of Innocence and the Burden of Proof

The criminal justice process begins with the alleged commission of a crime. Not all crimes are discovered, nor do they all end up in arrest, prosecution, or conviction. Sometimes an investigation reveals that no crime has been committed. However, in other cases, while there is no question that a crime has occurred, the perpetrator (doer) cannot be identified or apprehended. Because of such ambiguity, the criminal justice system provides a multitude of procedural protections at every stage of the process to protect the accused. This is necessary to balance the overwhelming power and resources of the state with the societal values that dictate that it is better for some guilty people to go free than to convict an innocent person.

Constitutional rules, such as the exclusionary rule, require the suppression of improperly obtained evidence. A major criticism of such exclusion is that guilty people are set free on technicalities. This, in turn, leads to a public outcry against giving so many "rights" to criminals. These rights afforded to people accused of crimes in America, however, are not the rights of criminals. They protect the freedoms of all members of society. It is important to remember the historical origins of the Bill of Rights when considering this issue. The rights enjoyed in American society are a direct effort to avoid the abuses of power enumerated in the Declaration of Independence. The Founding Fathers desired that their new nation would be free and fair, so that people could live in peace without fear of unjust persecution, arrest, or conviction. Protecting the individual against the police power of the state will occasionally result in bad people, who have done bad things, going free. That is, however, a small price to pay in light of the alternatives.

The cornerstone of American justice is the presumption of innocence, which is protected by the Due Process Clause of the Fifth Amendment. Every defendant is presumed to be innocent unless and until the state proves, beyond a reasonable doubt, that the accused is guilty of a crime. The burden of proving guilt beyond such a reasonable doubt remains exclusively with the prosecution throughout the trial. The defendant has no obligation to present evidence of innocence, and, moreover, has an affirmative right under the Fifth Amendment to remain silent throughout the proceedings. The defendant's silence, at least in theory, cannot be used against him.

The reasonable doubt standard does not mean that the judge or jury must be 100% certain of guilt. Such a standard would be almost impossible absent the defendant's voluntary confession, or, at the very least, an unimpeachable witnesses. The Supreme Court in *Cage v. Louisiana*, 498 U.S. 39 (1990) addressed the reasonable doubt standard in the context of jury instructions. That Court held that:

> In construing the instruction, we consider how reasonable jurors could have understood the charge as a whole. The charge did at one point instruct that, to convict, guilt must be found beyond a reasonable doubt; but it then equated a reasonable doubt with a "grave uncertainty" and an "actual substantial doubt, and stated that what was required was a "moral certainty" that the defendant was guilty. It is plain to us that the words "substantial" and "grave," as they are commonly understood, suggest a higher degree of doubt than is required for acquittal under the reasonable doubt standard. When those statements are then considered with the reference to "moral certainty," rather than evidentiary certainty, it becomes clear that a reasonable juror could have interpreted the instruction to allow a finding of guilt based on a degree of proof below that required by the Due Process Clause.

The Supreme Court in *Boyde v. California*, 494 U.S. 370 (1990), and again in *Estelle v. McGuire*, 502 U.S. 62 (1991), rejected the "could have understood" standard of *Cage* in favor of a jury instruction review standard that asked whether there was "a reasonable likelihood" of misunderstanding the appropriate legal test.

States have adopted standard form jury instructions to assist judges in the preparation of appropriate jury charges. It has not proven easy to define the "reasonable doubt" standard in terms that are clear. California Jury Instructions-Criminal, Section 2.90 defines a "reasonable doubt" as follows: "It is not a mere possible doubt; because everything relating to human affairs is open to some possible or imaginary doubt. It is that state of the case which, after the entire comparison and consideration of all the evidence, leaves the minds of the jurors in that condition that they cannot say they feel an abiding conviction of the truth of the charge." Does this definition help?

Search and Seizure

The Fourth Amendment provides that: "The right of the people to be secure in their persons, houses, papers, and effects, against unreasonable searches and seizures, shall not be violated, and no warrants shall issue, but upon probable cause, supported by oath or affirmation, and particularly describing the place to be searched, and the persons or things to be seized." The threshold question under the Fourth Amendment is what is "unreasonable," followed closely by the issue of what constitutes a search and seizure. Clearly, a police officer who has probable cause to believe that a crime has been committed can go before a judge to either obtain a warrant to search for evidence or to arrest a suspect. Probable cause means only that there is sufficient evidence to support the suspicion of the police. In the case of a search, the warrant must describe, with reasonable specificity, the area to be searched and the objects to be seized. A search warrant is not a license for the police to go on a "fishing expedition" to find evidence.

Just as clearly, an officer who witnesses the commission of a crime has a right to search the perpetrator and to seize any criminal evidence in her possession. In a similar fashion, a police officer in "hot pursuit" of a fleeing suspect can enter a place that would otherwise be "private" to make an arrest. The immediately surrounding environs can be searched to make sure no weapons or other dangerous articles are in easy reach. Similar rules have been adopted in cases where the police have stopped a motor vehicle for a traffic violation and have observed contraband in plain view. What then of searches and seizures where the police do not have probable cause? What if they search beyond the scope of what is necessary to protect their safety?

The Exclusionary Rule

When a court finds that evidence has been seized as a result of an unreasonable search, the remedy is to prohibit the government from using such improperly seized evidence in the trial against the defendant. This is known as the "exclusionary rule," and it is a doctrine of constitutional law rather than a rule of evidence. The exclusionary rule was first adopted in the federal system in *Weeks v. United States*, 232 U.S. 383 (1914). The rule was later extended to the states in the case of *Mapp v. Ohio*, 367 U.S. 643 (1961). In the *Mapp* case, the police arrived at the home of Ms. Mapp believing that an individual implicated in a recent bombing, would be found there along with political materials supporting insurrection. Mapp demanded to see a search warrant before admitting the police into her home. The police did not possess a warrant, and so they withdrew and placed her home under surveillance. Some time thereafter, the police forcibly entered the home and showed Mapp a piece of paper that they claimed to be a warrant. This "warrant" was not produced at trial, nor was the failure to produce it adequately explained by the prosecution. This led the lower court to express considerable doubt as to whether it ever existed. The Supreme Court concluded that:

> The ignoble shortcut to conviction left open to the State tends to destroy the entire system of constitutional restraints on which the liberties of the people rest. Having once recognized that the right to privacy embodied in the Fourth Amendment is enforceable against the States, and that the right to be secure against rude invasions of privacy by state officers is, therefore, constitutional in origin, we can no longer permit that right to remain an empty promise. Because it is enforceable in the same manner and to like effect as other basic rights secured by the Due Process Clause, we can no longer permit it to be revocable at the whim of any police officer who, in the name of law enforcement itself, chooses to suspend its enjoyment. Our decision, founded on reason and truth, gives to the individual no more than that which the Constitution guarantees him, to the police officer no less than that to which honest law enforcement is entitled, and, to the courts, that judicial integrity so necessary in the true administration of justice.

Many scholars and social critics have argued that the exclusionary rule is wrong since, as Justice Cardozo said, "the criminal is to go free because the constable has blundered." However, the courts continue to adhere to this rule as the only effective bulwark against police abuse. Alternatives such as sanctioning police officers for violating constitutional rights are not likely to be effective deterrents. Moreover, it would be unacceptable to have the police engage in any premeditated violation of the Constitution by weighing the risk of sanctions against getting the evidence necessary for conviction. The exclusionary rule has been extended to cover leads to additional evidence through what is called the "Fruit of the Poisonous Tree" doctrine.

The Expectation of Privacy

Many search and seizure cases turn on whether the defendant has a legitimate expectation of privacy. Clearly, we can expect that the government will not open our mail or tap our phone lines absent a warrant approved by a judicial officer based on probable cause. But what about "searches" conducted by dogs trained to sniff for bags of contraband or drugs in public locations? Or the use of directional microphones to listen in on conversations in public places? And what of the interception of cellular phone calls through the use of innovative technology? What of the search of a suspect's discarded trash bags? The following case demonstrates how the concept of a search can be expanded by advances in technology.

Kyllo v. United States
533 U.S. 27 (2001)

Scalia, J.

This case presents the question whether the use of a thermal-imaging device aimed at a private home from a public street to detect relative amounts of heat within the home constitutes a search within the meaning of the Fourth Amendment.

I

In 1991 Agent William Elliott of the United States Department of the Interior came to suspect that marijuana was being grown in the home belonging to petitioner Danny Kyllo, part of a triplex on Rhododendron Drive in Florence, Oregon. Indoor marijuana growth typically requires high-intensity lamps. In order to determine whether an amount of heat was emanating from petitioner's home consistent with the use of such lamps, at 3:20 a.m. on January 16, 1992, Agent Elliott and Dan Haas used an Agema Thermovision 210 thermal imager to scan the triplex. Thermal imagers detect infrared radiation, which virtually all objects emit but which is not visible to the naked eye. The imager converts radiation into images based on relative warmth black is cool, white is hot, shades of gray connote relative differences; in that respect, it operates somewhat like a video camera showing heat images. The scan of Kyllos home took only a few minutes and was performed from the passenger seat of Agent Elliotts vehicle across the street from the front of the house and also from the street in back of the house. The scan showed that the roof over the garage and a side wall of petitioners home were relatively hot compared to the rest of the home and substantially warmer than neighboring homes in the triplex. Agent Elliott concluded that petitioner was using halide lights to grow marijuana in his house, which indeed he was. Based on tips from informants, utility bills, and the thermal imaging, a Federal Magistrate Judge issued a warrant authorizing a search of petitioner's home, and the agents found an indoor growing operation involving more than 100 plants. Petitioner was indicted on one count of manufacturing marijuana, in violation of 21 U.S.C. 841(a)(1). He unsuccessfully moved to suppress the evidence seized from his home and then entered a conditional guilty plea.

II

The Fourth Amendment provides that "[t]he right of the people to be secure in their persons, houses, papers, and effects, against unreasonable searches and seizures, shall not be violated." At the very core of the Fourth Amendment stands the right of a man to retreat into his own home and there be free from unreasonable governmental intrusion. With few exceptions, the question whether a warrantless search of a home is reasonable and hence constitutional must be answered no.

On the other hand, the antecedent question of whether or not a Fourth Amendment search has occurred is not so simple under our precedent. The permissibility of ordinary visual surveillance of a home used to be clear because, well into the 20th century, our Fourth Amendment jurisprudence was tied to common-law trespass. Visual surveillance was unquestionably lawful because the eye cannot by the laws of England be guilty of a trespass. We have since decoupled violation of a person's Fourth Amendment rights from trespassory violation of his property, but the lawfulness of warrantless visual surveillance of a home has still been preserved. As we observed in *California v. Ciraolo*, 476 U.S. 207, 213 (1986), "[t]he Fourth Amendment protection of the home has never been extended to require law enforcement officers to shield their eyes when passing by a home on public thoroughfares."

One might think that the new validating rationale would be that examining the portion of a house that is in plain public view, while it is a search despite the absence of trespass, is not an unreasonable one under the Fourth Amendment. But in fact we have held that visual observation is no search at all perhaps in order to preserve somewhat more intact our doctrine that warrantless searches are presumptively unconstitutional. In assessing when a search is not a search, we have applied somewhat in reverse the principle first enunciated in *Katz v. United States*, 389 U.S. 347 (1967). *Katz* involved eavesdropping by means of an electronic listening device placed on the outside of a telephone booth a location not within the catalog (persons, houses, papers, and effects) that the Fourth Amendment protects against unreasonable searches. We held that the Fourth Amendment nonetheless protected *Katz* from the warrantless eavesdropping because he "justifiably relied" upon the privacy of the telephone booth. As Justice Harlan's oft-quoted concurrence described it, a Fourth Amendment search occurs when the government violates a subjective expectation of privacy that society recognizes as reasonable. We have subsequently applied this principle to hold that a Fourth Amendment search does *not* occur even when the explicitly protected location of a *house* is concerned unless "the individual manifested a subjective expectation of privacy in the object of the challenged search," and "society [is] willing to recognize that expectation as reasonable." We have applied this test in holding that it is not a search for the police to use a pen register at the phone company to determine what numbers were dialed in a private home, and we have applied the test on two different occasions in holding that aerial surveillance of private homes and surrounding areas does not constitute a search.

The present case involves officers on a public street engaged in more than naked-eye surveillance of a home. We have previously reserved judgment as to how much technological enhancement of ordinary perception from such a vantage point, if any, is too much. While we upheld enhanced aerial photography of an industrial complex in *Dow Chemical*, we noted that we found "it important that this is *not* an area immediately adjacent to a private home, where privacy expectations are most heightened."

III

It would be foolish to contend that the degree of privacy secured to citizens by the Fourth Amendment has been entirely unaffected by the advance of technology. For example, as the cases discussed above make clear, the technology enabling human flight has exposed to public view (and hence, we have said, to official observation) uncovered portions of the house and its curtilage that once were private. The question we confront today is what limits there are upon this power of technology to shrink the realm of guaranteed privacy.

The *Katz* test—whether the individual has an expectation of privacy that society is prepared to recognize as reasonable—has often been criticized as circular, and hence subjective and unpredictable. While it may be difficult to refine *Katz* when the search of areas such as telephone booths, automobiles, or even the curtilage and uncovered portions of residences are at issue, in the case of the search of the interior of homes—the prototypical and hence most commonly litigated area of protected privacy—there is a ready criterion, with roots deep in the common law, of the minimal expectation of privacy that exists, and that is acknowledged to be *reasonable*. To withdraw protection of this minimum expectation would be to permit police technology to erode the privacy guaranteed by the Fourth Amendment. We think that obtaining by sense-enhancing technology any information regarding the interior of the home that could not otherwise have been obtained without physical "intrusion into a constitutionally protected area," constitutes a search at least where (as here) the technology in question is not in general public use. This assures preservation of that degree of privacy against government that existed when the Fourth Amendment was adopted. On the basis of this criterion, the information obtained by the thermal imager in this case was the product of a search.

The Government maintains, however, that the thermal imaging must be upheld because it detected "only heat radiating from the external surface of the house." The dissent makes this its leading point, contending that there is a fundamental difference between what it calls "off-the-wall" observations and "through-the-wall surveillance." But just as a thermal imager captures only heat emanating from a house, so also a powerful directional microphone picks up only sound emanating from a house—and a satellite capable of scanning from many miles away would pick up only visible light emanating from a house. We rejected such a mechanical interpretation of the Fourth Amendment in *Katz*, where the eavesdropping device picked up only sound waves that reached the exterior of the phone booth. Reversing that approach would leave the homeowner at the mercy of advancing technology including imaging technology that could discern all human activity in the home. While the technology used in the present case was relatively crude, the rule we adopt must take account of more sophisticated systems that are already in use or in development.

The Government also contends that the thermal imaging was constitutional because it did not "detect private activities occurring in private areas." It points out that in *Dow Chemical v. United States*, 476 U.S. 227 (1986) we observed that the enhanced aerial photography did not reveal any intimate details. *Dow Chemical*, however, involved enhanced aerial photography of an industrial complex, which does not share the Fourth Amendment sanctity of the home. The Fourth Amendments protection of the home has never been tied to measurement of the quality or quantity of information obtained.

Limiting the prohibition of thermal imaging to "intimate details" would not only be wrong in principle; it would be impractical in application, failing to provide "a workable accommodation between the needs of law enforcement and the interests protected by the Fourth Amendment." To begin with, there is no necessary connection between the sophistication of the surveillance equipment and the "intimacy" of the details that it observes—which means that one cannot say (and the police cannot be assured) that use of the relatively crude equipment at issue here will always be lawful. The Agema Thermovision 210 might disclose, for example, at what hour each night the lady of the house takes her daily sauna and bath—a detail that many would consider "intimate;" and a much more sophisticated system might detect nothing more intimate than the fact that someone left a closet light on. We could not, in other words, develop a rule approving only that through-the-wall surveillance which identifies objects no smaller than 36 by 36 inches, but would have to develop a jurisprudence specifying which home activities are "intimate" and which are not. And even when (if ever) that jurisprudence were fully developed, no police officer would be able to know *in advance* whether his through-the-wall surveillance picks up "intimate" details — and thus would be unable to know in advance whether it is constitutional.

We have said that the Fourth Amendment draws "a firm line at the entrance to the house." That line, we think, must be not only firm but also bright — which requires clear specification of those methods of surveillance that require a warrant. While it is certainly possible to conclude from the videotape of the thermal imaging that occurred in this case that no "significant" compromise of the homeowner's privacy has occurred, we must take the long view, from the original meaning of the Fourth Amendment forward. The Fourth Amendment is to be construed in the light of what was deemed an unreasonable search and seizure when it was adopted, and in a manner which will conserve public interests as well as the interests and rights of individual citizens.

Where, as here, the Government uses a device that is not in general public use, to explore details of the home that would previously have been unknowable without physical intrusion, the surveillance is a "search" and is presumptively unreasonable without a warrant.

Stevens, J., dissenting

There is, in my judgment, a distinction of constitutional magnitude between "through-the-wall surveillance" that gives the observer or listener direct access to information in a private area, on the one hand, and the thought processes used to draw inferences from information in the public domain, on the other hand. The Court has crafted a rule that purports to deal with direct observations of the inside of the home, but the case before us merely involves indirect deductions from "off-the-wall" surveillance, that is, observations of the exterior of the home. Those observations were made with a fairly primitive thermal imager that gathered data exposed on the outside of petitioners home but did not invade any constitutionally protected interest in privacy. Moreover, I believe that the supposedly "bright-line" rule the Court has created in response to its concerns about future technological developments is unnecessary, unwise, and inconsistent with the Fourth Amendment.

* * *

Topics for Further Discussion

1. Agent Elliot used the infrared reading to support his application for a search warrant. The majority said, however, that the imaging itself constituted a search that should have been conducted pursuant to a validly issued warrant. Do you agree? What is the distinction between a "search" and the collection of information on which to conclude that there is probable cause?

2. Justice Scalia suggests that the general unavailability of infrared sensor technology means its use "constitutes a search at least where (as here) the technology in question is not in general public use." What if Kyllo lived in a house set far back from the road, beyond the vision of the naked eye, and the police officer observed the marijuana plants through an open window using high powered binoculars? What if he used night vision goggles? How did the Court distinguish the *Kyllo* case from the *Dow Chemical* case mentioned in the majority opinion?

3. Why does the dissent believe that the majority was wrong in attempting to enunciate a clear bright line test in this area? Do you agree with the dissent that Kyllo's expectation of privacy was not violated because the heat had already escaped from the house?

4. In *Illinois v. Caballes*, 125 S. Ct. 834 (2005), a motorist was lawfully stopped for speeding. While the first police officer was in the process of writing a ticket, a second officer arrived on the scene with a narcotic sniffing dog. The dog was led around the car and began barking when it smelled drugs. The Supreme Court ruled that the use of the dog to sniff the exterior of the car during an otherwise lawful stop, even though there was no probable cause to suspect the motorist of transporting drugs, did not violate the defendant's legitimate expectation of privacy. Do you agree?

5. As a general rule, the police are permitted to search a premise without a warrant if consent is given. Permission can be given by any person with authority over the area. But, what about a situation where one party with authority gives consent and another with equal authority refuses consent? The Supreme Court faced this question in *Georgia v. Randolph*, 547 U.S. 103 (2006). The police were called to a house to quell a domestic dispute between an irate wife and her estranged husband. When the police arrived, the wife accused her husband of drug possession and use. The wife gave consent to search the house, which the police did, over the objection of the husband. Drugs were found and the husband was arrested. The Court held that the search was not reasonable as to the husband because he had not given his consent writing as follows:

> Since the co-tenant wishing to open the door to a third party has no recognized authority in law or social practice to prevail over a present and objecting co-tenant, his disputed invitation, without more, gives a police officer no better claim to reasonableness in entering than the officer would have in the absence of any consent at all. Accordingly, in the balancing of competing individual and governmental interests entailed by the bar to unreasonable searches, the cooperative occupant's invitation adds nothing to the government's side to counter the force of an objecting individual's claim to security against the government's intrusion into his dwelling place. What is it about a person's house that requires heightened protection against government intrusion?

Indictment and Arrest

An indictment is a legal document that both accuses an individual of committing one or more crimes and authorizes his or her arrest. In the federal system, as well as in many state systems, the prosecutor must obtain a grand jury indictment before ordering an arrest. The Fifth Amendment provides, in relevant part, that "[n]o person shall be held to answer for capital, or otherwise infamous crime, unless on presentment or indictment of a Grand Jury." In some state systems, the arrest can be ordered directly by the prosecutor in a charging document called an "information." Grand juries are also discussed in Chapter 2.

Grand juries are empanelled by either U.S. Attorneys or state prosecutors to hear the evidence of crime. Such a grand jury is usually selected from the same pool of available persons (typically voter registration lists) as regular juries. They sit for extended periods of time (up to thirty-six months in the federal system), but, usually, meet either once a week or as convened by the prosecutor. The role of the grand jury is to decide whether there is probable cause, and not to determine guilt or innocence. The grand jury has the power to issue subpoenas requiring persons to appear before the grand jury to answer questions the prosecutor poses. An individual called to testify before a grand jury has the right, under the Fifth Amendment, to remain silent, but does not have a Sixth Amendment right to be accompanied by a lawyer. Testimony before the grand jury is taken under oath, and, therefore, failure to tell the truth can result in being charged with the crime of perjury. Because grand juries hear only the prosecutor's side of the story, such "objective panels of due process" have been criticized for being little more than "rubber stamps" for the government.

The federal system also allows for the convening of a special grand jury to investigate organized crime, political corruption, and the like. President Clinton, for example, was investigated and impeached (but not indicted for perjury) as a result of evidence produced by a special grand jury that Independent Counsel Kenneth Star convened in the Monica Lewinsky affair. It is estimated that that grand jury investigations of President Clinton, including the one in which Monica Lewinsky actually gave testimony, cost the U.S. taxpayers in excess of $40 million.

Miranda **Rights**

Certain constitutional rights attach to an individual at the moment of arrest. The Supreme Court enunciated these rights in the landmark decision of *Miranda v. Arizona*, 384 U.S. 436 (1966). In *Miranda*, the Court considered the admissibility of a confession obtained from a suspect while in police custody. In ruling that the statement was improperly obtained, Chief Justice Warren wrote as follows:

> [T]he prosecution may not use statements, whether exculpatory or inculpatory, stemming from custodial interrogation of the defendant unless it demonstrates the use of procedural safeguards effective to secure the privilege against self-incrimination. By custodial interrogation, we mean questioning initiated by law enforcement officers after a person has been taken into custody or otherwise deprived of his freedom of action in any significant way. As for the procedural safeguards to be employed, unless other fully effective means are devised to inform accused persons of their right of silence and to assure a continuous opportunity to exercise it, the following measures are required. Prior to any questioning, the person must be warned that he has a right to remain silent, that any statement he does make may be used as evidence against him, and that he has a right to the presence of an attorney, either retained or appointed. The defendant may waive effectuation of these rights, provided the waiver is made voluntarily, knowingly and intelligently. If, however, he indicates in any manner and at any stage of the process that he wishes to consult with an attorney before speaking there can be no questioning. Likewise, if the individual is alone and indicates in any manner that he does not wish to be interrogated, the police may not question him. The mere fact that he may have answered some questions or volunteered some statements on his own does not deprive him of the right to refrain from answering any further inquiries until he has consulted with an attorney and thereafter consents to be questioned.

As a result of the *Miranda* case, police officers and FBI agents all across the U.S. carry a card containing the "*Miranda* Rights," which they read to suspects at the time of arrest. It is not uncommon for the police to videotape interrogations so that there is an accurate record of the defendant waiving his rights and agreeing to talk to the police. The *Miranda* case is also important for clarifying that the rights attach at the point when the individual is placed in custody. Custody occurs when the individual is no longer free to leave or to move about. It is not necessary that the police bring the individual to the police station. Custody starts when freedom to move away from the police is restricted. A number of cases have sought to limit the reach of the *Miranda* ruling.

The Supreme Court in *United States v. Patane*, 542 U.S. 630 (2004) declared that the fruits of a voluntary confession given without the benefit of the *Miranda* rights are admissible at trial. And, in *Hiibel v. Sixth Judicial Dist. Court of Nevada, Humboldt County*, 542 U.S. 177 (2004), the Court was asked to decide whether the right to remain silent when questioned by the police should be extended to a police officer's request to produce identification. The defendant met the description of an individual involved in an assault. The police approached him by standing next to his car, and asked him for identification, which he refused to give. Hiibel was arrested and convicted under Nevada's "stop and identify" law. The Court concluded that Hiibel's conviction did not violate the Constitution because his "refusal to disclose his name was not based on any articulated real and appreciable fear that his name would be used to incriminate him, or that it 'would furnish a link in the chain of evidence needed to prosecute' him. As best we can tell, petitioner refused to identify himself only because he thought his name was none of the officer's business." Can the *Hiibel* case be squared with *Miranda*? Was Hiibel in custody when he was asked to provide his name?

The most recent case is *Berghuis v. Thompkins*, 560 U.S. ___ (2010). This case involved a fatal shooting outside of a shopping mall in Michigan. The defendant, Thompkins, fled the scene of the crime and was arrested one year later in Ohio. Two police officers from Michigan traveled to Ohio to interrogate Thompkins, which they did for approximately three hours, while he was waiting to be transported back to Michigan. Thompkins was duly *Mirandized* before the interrogation began. Thompkins did not affirmatively say that he wanted to remain silent, or to have a lawyer present. He remained largely silent throughout the questioning. There is no evidence that he was coerced beyond being locked in a room and subjected to three hours of questioning. About 15 minutes before the questioning ended, one of the police officers asked Thompkins if he believed in God and if he prayed to God. When Tompkins said that he did, the officer asked "Do you pray to God to forgive you for shooting the boy down?" According to the transcript, Thompkins answered "Yes" and looked away.

The prosecutor sought to introduce these statements at trial as a confession of guilt and Thompkins moved to suppress them as having been obtained in violation of his Fifth Amendment right to remain silent. The trial court denied the motion to suppress and the Michigan Court of Appeals rejected Thompkins *Miranda* claim on the grounds that he had not invoked his right to remain silent and had waived it. When Thompkins had exhausted all of his appeals at the state level, he filed a writ of *habeas corpus* in the federal court.

The case eventually reached the Supreme Court, which found by a vote of 5 to 4 that "[t]here is good reason to require an accused who wants to invoke his or her right to remain silent to do so unambiguously." The Court argued that if remaining silent constituted the exercise of *Miranda* rights the "police would be required to make difficult decisions about an accused's unclear intent and face the consequences of suppression 'if they guessed wrong.'" The Court concluded under the circumstances "a suspect who has received and understood the *Miranda* warnings, and has not invoked his *Miranda* rights, waives the right to remain silent by making an uncoerced statement to the police."

Justice Sotomayer, writing for the four dissenting Justices, concluded as follows:

> Today's decision turns *Miranda* upside down. Criminal suspects must now unambiguously invoke their rights to remain silent — which, counterintuitively, requires them to speak. At the same time, suspects will be legally presumed to have waived their rights even if they have given no clear expression of their intent to do so.

Given *Miranda's* purpose of ensuring that statements are given voluntarily after a knowing waiver of the rights to remain silent and to have counsel present, do you think the majority is correct in requiring accused individuals unambiguously to say they want to remain silent and to have a lawyer? Isn't sitting without speaking for nearly three hours of interrogation an unambiguous indication of the defendant's intention to remain silent? What if the interrogation had lasted for twelve hours? What do you think of the dissent's argument that it is the waiver of the right that should be unambiguous, not the assertion of the right?

Arraignment and Probable Cause

The next step following arrest and interrogation is for the suspect to be brought before the court for an arraignment. The main purpose of the arraignment is to advise the suspect of the criminal charges being leveled against him, and to allow such a suspect to enter a plea of guilty or not guilty. The Sixth Amendment requires that all suspects have the right "to be informed of the nature and cause of the accusation" brought against them. If the arrest was made without a warrant, the judge will also determine if probable cause exists. Finally, the judge will decide whether bail should be set.

In *Draper v. United States*, 358 U.S. 307 (1959) the Supreme Court discussed the meaning of "probable cause":

> In dealing with probable cause, as the very name implies, we deal with probabilities. These are not technical; they are the factual and practical considerations of everyday life on which reasonable and prudent men, not legal technicians, act.' Probable cause exists where 'the facts and circumstances within [the arresting officers'] knowledge and of which they had reasonably trustworthy information [are] sufficient in themselves to warrant a man of reasonable caution in the belief that' an offense has been or is being committed.

Probable cause can, therefore, be derived from direct observation by experienced police officers, circumstantial evidence, or reliable reports by citizens and informants.

Courts recognize the inherently coercive nature of police custody, and have excluded even voluntary confessions when there has been an improper delay in bringing the defendant before the court for arraignment. Rule 5(a) of the Federal Rules of Criminal Procedure requires that suspects be brought before a magistrate without "unnecessary delay." The Supreme Court decided in *Gerstein v. Pugh*, 420 U.S. 103 (1975), that the Fourth Amendment also mandates a "prompt judicial determination of probable cause" when the arrest is made without a warrant. In *County of Riverside v. McLaughlin*, 500 U.S. 44 (1991), the Supreme Court declined to provide a bright line time test and, instead, opted to create a safe harbor by indicating that "a jurisdiction that provides judicial determinations of probable cause within 48 hours of arrest will, as a general matter, comply with the promptness requirement of *Gerstein*."

Plea Bargaining

American courts are overloaded with criminal cases. In an effort to reduce and manage the backlog, defendants and prosecutors are permitted to negotiate plea bargains. It is estimated that as many as 90% of all criminal cases are resolved in this manner. The typical plea bargain results in the defendant agreeing to plead guilty to a single (rather than multiple) or a lesser charge in return for the prosecutor's agreement to either drop the more serious charges or to recommend a more lenient sentence. Negotiated pleas can cause public outrage when it either appears that a heinous crime has gone unpunished or that a notorious figure will "beat the system." For this reason, all plea agreements must be submitted to and approved by the trial judge—who is obligated to question the defendant to make sure the plea is voluntary and the defendant has knowingly waived the right to trial—and prosecutors are not permitted to promise any specific result from the court. In the federal system, judges are prohibited by the Federal Rules of Criminal Procedure from participating in plea bargain negotiations. Trial judges must reject plea bargains when they feel they do not adequately serve the interests of justice. Pleas of *nolo contendere* (no contest) are particularly contentious because they allow a defendant to accept a punishment without formally admitting guilt.

Prosecution and Trial

The Constitution provides a number of critical procedural rights during any given criminal trial. Among these are the Fifth Amendment right against self-incrimination and the Sixth Amendment rights to a "speedy and public trial, by an impartial jury" and "to have the Assistance of Counsel for his defense." The defendant also has the right, under the Sixth Amendment, to confront all of the witnesses against him or her as well as to compel the testimony of favorable witnesses. Constitutional rights can be waived, but only if the waiver is knowing and intelligent. As stated in *United States v. Ruiz*, 536 U.S. 622 (2002), "the law ordinarily considers a waiver knowing, intelligent, and sufficiently aware if the defendant fully understands the nature of the right and how it would likely apply *in general* in the circumstances—even though the defendant may not know the *specific detailed* consequences of invoking it."

The Right against Self-Incrimination

The right against self-incrimination means that a defendant cannot be forced to either give testimony or to provide any evidence in support of the prosecution's case. As we saw in the discussion of the *Miranda* case above, a defendant has the right to remain silent at every stage of the criminal proceedings. The fact that a defendant chooses to remain silent cannot be used to infer guilt, or to lessen the burden of the prosecutor to prove guilt beyond a reasonable doubt. The right against self-incrimination also extends to certain confidants of the defendant such as his or her spouse, doctor, lawyer, or clergy member.

The issue of self-incrimination arises whenever the voluntariness of a confession is challenged. Before a confession is considered to be "voluntary," the defendant must first have been "Mirandized." Second, he or she must knowingly and intelligently waive his or her rights to remain silent and to be represented by counsel. The Supreme Court in *Townsend v. Sain*, 372 U.S. 293 (1963) reconfirmed the voluntariness standard by writing that, if "the individual's 'will was overborne' or if his confession was not 'the product of a rational intellect and a free will,' his confession is inadmissible because coerced. These standards are applicable whether a confession is the product of physical intimidation or psychological pressure and, of course, are equally applicable to a drug induced statement."

The Right to Counsel and to Confront Hostile Witnesses

Of equal importance to the right to remain silent is the right to counsel. The federal system was the first to establish the right to counsel for all defendants in any criminal case. This right was extended to the states in the case of *Gideon v. Wainwright*, 372 U.S. 335 (1963). There, an indigent defendant in a non-capital (a case not involving the death penalty) felony case requested the assistance of counsel. The state court judge denied his request under a law that required the appointment of counsel for poor defendants only in capital cases. The Supreme Court concluded:

> [I]n our adversary system of criminal justice, any person haled into court, who is too poor to hire a lawyer, cannot be assured a fair trial unless counsel is provided for him. This seems to us to be an obvious truth. Governments, both state and federal, quite properly spend vast sums of money to establish machinery to try defendants accused of crime. Lawyers to prosecute are everywhere deemed essential to protect the public's interest in an orderly society. Similarly, there are few defendants charged with crime, few indeed, who fail to hire the best lawyers they can get to prepare and present their defenses. That government hires lawyers to prosecute and defendants who have the money hire lawyers to defend are the strongest indications of the widespread belief that lawyers in criminal courts are necessities, not luxuries. The right of one charged with crime to counsel may not be deemed fundamental and essential to fair trials in some countries, but it is in ours. From the very beginning, our state and national constitutions and laws have laid great emphasis on procedural and substantive safeguards designed to assure fair trials before impartial tribunals in which every defendant stands equal before the law. This noble ideal cannot be realized if the poor man charged with crime has to face his accusers without a lawyer to assist him.

Such a right to counsel is also a waivable right, provided that the waiver is "knowing and intelligent." In *Iowa v. Tovar*, 541 U.S. 77 (2004), the Supreme Court held that a waiver at the plea stage meets this standard if the trial judge informs the accused of the nature of the charges, the right to have counsel advise on the plea, and the range of punishments possible if the plea is accepted. It is not necessary to advise the defendant that counsel may be able to mount a viable defense to the charges.

States and the federal government maintain public defender offices with full-time staff attorneys available to represent defendants (but not those facing the death penalty) who are unable to pay for a lawyer. These offices are funded by the state, and are usually understaffed and overworked. Public defenders have a reputation for aggressively representing the rights of indigent defendants, and their almost daily appearances in court make them among the most knowledgeable and experienced of criminal lawyers. Courts also maintain a list of available lawyers who are willing to accept criminal appointments from the court. The payment for court appointments comes from the government, and is generally low when compared with what private clients will pay. In death penalty cases, the court will appoint an experienced lawyer and the rates are somewhat higher. A defendant is not required to have a lawyer, and is free to represent himself in court (*pro se*), provided that the defense is conducted in a non-disruptive manner. Disruptive defendants can be bound and gagged or even removed from the courtroom and counsel can be appointed to continue their defense.

The right to counsel includes not only the right to a lawyer, but also a right to "competent" counsel. However, courts will not overturn a conviction based on incompetent counsel if the challenge is based on tactical decisions made by the lawyer before or during the trial. Something far more egregious is required. The aggrieved party must demonstrate that the lawyer was so incompetent that the defendant was effectively deprived of the benefit of having counsel.

Criminal defendants also have the right to confront the witnesses against them at trial. This is accomplished through the cross-examination of each witness following the witness' direct testimony. The cardinal rule of cross-examination is that a question should only be asked if the answer to it is already known. A difficult issue arises in cases of alleged child abuse where forcing the victim to appear in the same room as the accused may result in further trauma to the child. Courts have permitted the child to sit in a separate room and to testify via video-conferencing technology in such cases.

The defendant can apply to the court to have a subpoena issued for friendly witnesses (for example, a witness who could support the defendant's alibi but who might not want to admit having been with the defendant at the time of the crime) who might be reluctant or unwilling to appear on behalf of the defendant. Limited discovery is also available to the defendant. The prosecutor is basically obligated to disclose all potentially exculpatory evidence in its possession and to provide a list of witnesses to the defense before the trial commences.

The Right to a Speedy and Public Trial

Every defendant has the right to a speedy and public trial under the Sixth Amendment. This is crucial so that the accused is not forced to linger under the threat of prosecution for an extended period of time. Being arrested and charged with a crime causes considerable hardship to the accused. The accused should have the right to clear his name as promptly as possible. The right to a speedy trial attaches after the issuance of an indictment. It does not matter how much time has expired from the date of the crime until indictment, although most crimes except murder have a statute of limitation. In *Barker v. Wingo*, 407 U.S. 514 (1972), the Supreme Court set out a four-factor test for determining whether a delay between the initiation of criminal proceedings and the beginning of trial violates a defendant's Sixth Amendment right to a speedy trial. The court must weigh the length of the delay, the cause of the delay, the defendant's assertion of his right to a speedy trial, and the presence or absence of prejudice resulting from the delay before determining that the Sixth Amendment has been violated. The remedy for a violation of the right to a speedy trial is dismissal of the charges.

Congress passed the Speedy Trial Act of 1974, in response to the *Barker v. Wingo* case. It applies only in federal cases and provides that "the trial of a defendant charged in an information or indictment with the commission of an offense shall commence within seventy days from the filing date (and making public) of the information or indictment, or from the date the defendant has appeared before a judicial officer of the court in which such charge is pending, whichever date last occurs." Many states have adopted similar rules to ensure that defendants are brought to trial without undue delay. In Pennsylvania, for example, a defendant must be tried within 180 days if incarcerated pending trial and within 365 days if out on bail.

Coupled with the right to a speedy trial is the right to a public trial. A public trial serves a number of important social functions. It helps to ensure that the defendant is treated fairly and not "railroaded" by government proceedings conducted behind closed doors. It encourages judges, prosecutors and defense attorneys to act professionally and transparently. Opening courtrooms supports the public interest in the criminal justice system and enhances public confidence. The right to a public trial, however, raises a number of thorny issues. Who possesses the right, the public or the defendant? If the defendant, can it be waived? How do we balance the right of the defendant to a fair trial against the freedom of the press? Should cameras be permitted in the courtroom? The Supreme Court has held that the right belongs to the public and cannot be waived by the defendant. Trial judges are given wide discretion to control the trial and to balance competing interests. There is a presumption that trials will be open to the public unless doing so will result in prejudice to the defendant's right to a fair trial or threaten the integrity or good order of the proceedings. Judges are inclined to close proceedings in cases involving (1) organized crime where there is a risk that witnesses and jurors might be intimidated, (2) juveniles where society places the privacy and welfare of the child over the public interest, and (3) sex offenders where the victim might suffer public humiliation.

The Right to Trial by Jury

The right to trial by jury in criminal cases is so fundamental to the American system that it is contained in both the main body of the Constitution and in the Bill of Rights. Article III, section 2 provides that: "The trial of all crimes, except in cases of impeachment, shall be by jury; and such trial shall be held in the state where the said crimes shall have been committed" while the Sixth Amendment guarantees the right to "an impartial jury of the state and district wherein the crime shall have been committed." The right to trial by jury was extended to the states by *Duncan v. Louisiana*, 391 U.S. 145 (1968). The Court explained that:

> [I]n the American States, as in the federal judicial system, a general grant of jury trial for serious offenses is a fundamental right, essential for preventing miscarriages of justice and for assuring that fair trials are provided for all defendants. We would not assert, however, that every criminal trial—or any particular trial— held before a judge alone is unfair or that a defendant may never be as fairly treated by a judge as he would be by a jury. Thus we hold no constitutional doubts about the practices, common in both federal and state courts, of accepting waivers of jury trial and prosecuting petty crimes without extending a right to jury trial. However, the fact is that in most places more trials for serious crimes are to juries than to a court alone; a great many defendants prefer the judgment of a jury to that of a court. Even where defendants are satisfied with bench trials, the right to a jury trial very likely serves its intended purpose of making judicial or prosecutorial unfairness less likely.

The court did not expressly decide the line between petty and serious crimes. It did conclude, however, that a prosecution for a crime carrying a possible two-year jail term was serious enough to require trial by jury if requested by the defendant. In a similar vein, there is no right to a jury in juvenile or administrative law cases even though they may have a disciplinary and punitive nature.

Defenses

As already explained, the defendant does not have a legal obligation to testify or to present an affirmative defense. The prosecutor bears the burden of proving guilt beyond a reasonable doubt, and a skillful lawyer can often get her client acquitted by demonstrating nothing more than the weaknesses in the prosecution's case. Defense counsel may cross-examine the prosecution's witnesses to show that they are not telling the truth, or that they are not credible because of a deal offered to them by the prosecutor in return for their testimony against the defendant. This latter tactic is frequently employed in organized crime prosecutions where the prosecution has granted immunity from prosecution to a lower ranked member of the syndicate in order to get evidence to convict the higher ups. Defense counsel might also try to deflect attention from the defendant's guilt by focusing on mistakes made by, or the biases of, the police.

Defendants may choose to present affirmative defenses in an effort to get off. These defenses have subjective (the defendant believes it) and objective (there must be reasonable support beyond what the defendant believes) elements. Ultimately, whether the defense is successful in creating a reasonable doubt is for the jury to decide. Even when the defense fails to result in an acquittal, an affirmative defense can be helpful in mitigating the punishment. Some of the more common defenses are explained below.

Justification, Necessity, and Duress

Justification and necessity exist as valid defenses when the action of the defendant is supported by a higher purpose or good. Breaking down a door to enter private property in response to an urgent cry for help is an example of a valid excuse to the crime of breaking and entering. For this reason, the defenses of justification and necessity are often referred to as the "lesser of two evils" defense. The harm or evil sought to be avoided must be greater than the harm or evil resulting from the defendant's actions.

Duress requires proof that the defendant acted under the threat of unlawful coercion. A mother who assists an individual to elude arrest in the face of a genuine threat to her child will be cleared. The cause of duress must be objective and specific. If the defendant could have sought help from the police because the wrongdoer was not present all of the time, the defense will be less likely to succeed. In any event, duress is not available as a defense to a charge of homicide.

Defense of Property or Persons

The law recognizes the right to use force for self-defense, the defense of others, and the defense of property. The right to use force begins and ends with necessity. In other words, it must be necessary to use force in order for there to be a valid defense, and the right ends when the threat stops. The use of force must be commensurate with the risk to the defendant. Deadly force is never permitted to defend property because society values life over property. A defendant is permitted, however, to use deadly force when he has a reasonable belief that his, or some other person's, life is in danger. Retreat is required if it can be done safely, except that people are not required to retreat when they are in their own home. In 1992, a young Japanese exchange student, Yoshi Hattori, was shot to death in Louisiana when he entered the wrong house in a Halloween costume. The owner of the house yelled "Freeze!" and shot Hattori dead when he continued to move forward, apparently not understanding the meaning of the command. The owner was found not guilty, although he was found liable for monetary damages in a subsequent civil action. Other controversial cases have involved battered women killing their husbands and claiming self-defense, even though there was a lapse of time, or the husband was drunk or asleep when the killing occurred. These self-defense cases meet with uneven results depending on how sympathetic the battered spouse appears to be to the jury.

Alibi

An alibi exists when the defendant can show he could not have committed the crime because he was at some other place at the time of the crime. The strength of an alibi usually comes down to whether the alibi can be corroborated by a credible witness. A defendant who says that he could not have robbed the bank because he was home alone taking a nap is not likely to get far with his alibi defense. On the other hand, a defendant who can show he was in a public location with many people who can identify him will be successful. Organized crime leaders often arrange to be in highly public settings when crimes they have ordered are being committed.

Entrapment

A defendant can assert that she was entrapped by the police. This defense requires the defendant to show she had no intention of committing a crime and was induced by the police to do so. If the police supplied the necessary intent for the crime, as a matter of public policy, the defendant should be acquitted. The defense will fail if the prosecution can show the defendant was a ready and willing party to the crime. Factors that tend to suggest entrapment are when the idea for the crime is supplied by the police, or when the police strongly urge the defendant to commit the crime and the defendant resisted before giving in to pressure. When the defendant argues entrapment, the government must prove beyond a reasonable doubt that the defendant was not entrapped.

In *Jacobson v. United States*, 503 U.S. 540 (1992), a child pornography conviction under the Child Protection Act of 1984 was challenged on entrapment grounds. Keith Jacobson, a fifty-six year old farmer in Nebraska, had ordered two magazines ("Bare Boys I" and "Bare Boys II") and a brochure from an adult store in California. Ordering and receiving these materials was legal under both state and federal law. A postal inspector decided to tempt Jacobson into committing a crime. He sent a series of letters to Jacobson purporting to be from fictitious groups such as the American Hedonist Society, Midlands Data Research, and the Heartland Institute for a New Tomorrow. These mailings all urged Jacobson, in one way or the other, to support free speech and resist efforts by the government to restrict sexual freedom in the U.S. The efforts of the government extended over a thirty-two month period, and finally culminated in Jacobson's placing an order for "Boys Who Love Boys," a pornographic magazine showing young boys engaged in sexual acts. He was arrested and convicted. The Supreme Court overturned the conviction writing that: "In their zeal to enforce the law, however, Government agents may not originate a criminal design, implant in an innocent person's mind the disposition to commit a criminal act, and then induce commission of the crime so that the Government may prosecute."

Insanity and Diminished Capacity

As we have seen, criminal law requires a subjective awareness or intent to commit a crime. Certain individuals, such as children, those with diminished mental capacity, and the insane, are not capable of forming the degree of intent necessary to justify criminal sanctions. The problem of juvenile crime is particularly controversial. We know from experience that underage kids are frequently used by gangs and crime syndicates to commit the most heinous of crimes. Most states have provisions in the criminal law to allow the prosecutor to certify a juvenile for trial as an adult in more egregious cases. The Supreme Court has been asked to consider a series of cases challenging the death penalty for minors and people with severe mental retardation. Another controversial issue is the insanity defense. In the mid-19th century, the English House of Lords in the famous *M'Naughton* case announced the common law standard for insanity. M'Naughton was a deranged Scot who tried to kill Prime Minister Sir Robert Peel because he believed that the Prime Minister was plotting against him. Instead of killing the Prime Minister, M'Naughton killed his secretary. His lawyers argued that he was insane. The House of Lords proclaimed that "to establish a defense on the ground of insanity, it must clearly be proved that, at the time of the committing of the act, the party accused was laboring under such a defect of reason, from disease of the mind, as not to know the nature and quality of the act he was doing; or if he did know it, that he did not know he was doing was wrong." The standard applied by courts today is similar in that it focuses on whether the defendant knew the difference between right and wrong.

If an individual is found to be insane, a special verdict of innocent by reason of insanity will be entered. The defendant cannot be convicted of the crime because he lacked the necessary mental capacity to form a guilty mind. This does not mean that the individual will go free. The judge can, and almost always does, order the individual committed to a mental institution for treatment for so long as he remains a threat to himself or to society. When the individual is cured, however, he can no longer be involuntarily held and must be released back into society. Consider the following case dealing with the civil commitment of a repeat sexual offender and re-interpreting the earlier Supreme Court decision of *Kansas v. Hendricks*, 521 U.S. 346 (1997).

Kansas v. Crane
534 U.S. 407 (2002)

Breyer, J.

This case concerns the constitutional requirements substantively limiting the civil commitment of a dangerous sexual offender a matter that this Court considered in *Kansas v. Hendricks*. The State of Kansas argues that the Kansas Supreme Court has interpreted our decision in *Hendricks* in an overly restrictive manner. We agree and vacate the Kansas court's judgment.

I

In *Hendricks*, this Court upheld the Kansas Sexually Violent Predator Act against constitutional challenge. In doing so, the Court characterized the confinement at issue as civil, not criminal, confinement. And it held that the statutory criterion for confinement embodied in the statutes words mental abnormality or personality disorder satisfied substantive due process requirements.

In reaching its conclusion, the Court's opinion pointed out that States have in certain narrow circumstances provided for the forcible civil detainment of people who are unable to control their behavior and who thereby pose a danger to the public health and safety. It said that we have consistently upheld such involuntary commitment statutes when (1) the confinement takes place pursuant to proper procedures and evidentiary standards, (2) there is a finding of dangerousness either to ones self or to others, and (3) proof of dangerousness is coupled with the proof of some additional factor, such as a mental illness or mental abnormality. It noted that the Kansas Act unambiguously requires a finding of dangerousness either to ones self or to others, and then links that finding to the existence of a mental abnormality or personality disorder that makes it difficult, if not impossible, for the person to control his dangerous behavior. And the Court ultimately determined that the statutes requirement of a mental abnormality or personality disorder is consistent with the requirements of other statutes that we have upheld in that it narrows the class of persons eligible for confinement to those who are unable to control their dangerousness.

II

In the present case the State of Kansas asks us to review the Kansas Supreme Courts application of *Hendricks*. The State here seeks the civil commitment of Michael Crane, a previously convicted sexual offender who, according to at least one of the States psychiatric witnesses, suffers from both exhibitionism and antisocial personality disorder. After a jury trial, the Kansas District Court ordered Cranes civil commitment. In that court's view, the Federal Constitution as interpreted in *Hendricks* insists upon a finding that the defendant cannot control his dangerous behavior even if (as provided by Kansas law) problems of emotional capacity and not volitional capacity prove the source of bad behavior warranting commitment. And the trial court had made no such finding.

Kansas now argues that the Kansas Supreme Court wrongly read *Hendricks* as requiring the State always to prove that a dangerous individual is completely unable to control his behavior. That reading, says Kansas, is far too rigid.

III

We agree with Kansas insofar as it argues that *Hendricks* set forth no requirement of total or complete lack of control. *Hendricks* referred to the Kansas Act as requiring a mental abnormality or personality disorder that makes it difficult, if not impossible, for the [dangerous] person to control his dangerous behavior. The word difficult indicates that the lack of control to which this Court referred was not absolute. Indeed, as different *amici* on opposite sides of this case agree, an absolutist approach is unworkable. Insistence upon absolute lack of control would risk barring the civil commitment of highly dangerous persons suffering severe mental abnormalities.

We do not agree with the State, however, insofar as it seeks to claim that the Constitution permits commitment of the type of dangerous sexual offender considered in *Hendricks* without any lack-of-control determination. *Hendricks* underscored the constitutional importance of distinguishing a dangerous sexual offender subject to civil commitment from other dangerous persons who are perhaps more properly dealt with exclusively through criminal proceedings. That distinction is necessary lest civil commitment become a mechanism for retribution or general deterrence functions properly those of criminal law, not civil commitment. The presence of what the psychiatric profession itself classifie[d] as a serious mental disorder helped to make that distinction in *Hendricks*. And a critical distinguishing feature of that serious disorder there consisted of a special and serious lack of ability to control behavior.

In recognizing that fact, we did not give to the phrase lack of control a particularly narrow or technical meaning. And we recognize that in cases where lack of control is at issue, inability to control behavior will not be demonstrable with mathematical precision. It is enough to say that there must be proof of serious difficulty in controlling behavior. And this, when viewed in light of such features of the case as the nature of the psychiatric diagnosis, and the severity of the mental abnormality itself, must be sufficient to distinguish the dangerous sexual offender whose serious mental illness, abnormality, or disorder subjects him to civil commitment from the dangerous but typical recidivist convicted in an ordinary criminal case.

Scalia, J., dissenting

Today the Court holds that the Kansas Sexually Violent Predator Act (SVPA) cannot, consistent with so-called substantive due process, be applied as written. It does so even though, less than five years ago, we upheld the very same statute against the very same contention in an appeal by the very same petitioner (the State of Kansas) from the judgment of the very same court. Not only is the new law that the Court announces today wrong, but the Court's manner of promulgating it snatching back from the State of Kansas a victory so recently awarded cheapens the currency of our judgments. I would reverse, rather than vacate, the judgment of the Kansas Supreme Court.

I not only disagree with the Courts gutting of our holding in *Hendricks*; I also doubt the desirability, and indeed even the coherence, of the new constitutional test which (on the basis of no analysis except a misreading of *Hendricks*) it substitutes. Under our holding in *Hendricks*, a jury in an SVPA commitment case would be required to find, beyond a reasonable doubt, (1) that the person previously convicted of one of the enumerated sexual offenses is suffering from a mental abnormality or personality disorder, and (2) that this condition renders him likely to commit future acts of sexual violence. Both of these findings are coherent, and (with the assistance of expert testimony) well within the capacity of a normal jury. Today's opinion says that the Constitution requires the addition of a third finding: (3) that the subject suffers from an inability to control behavior not utter inability, and not even inability in a particular constant degree, but rather inability in a degree that will vary in light of such features of the case as the nature of the psychiatric diagnosis, and the severity of the mental abnormality itself.

This formulation of the new requirement certainly displays an elegant subtlety of mind. Unfortunately, it gives trial courts, in future cases under the many commitment statutes similar to Kansas' SVPA, not a clue as to how they are supposed to charge the jury!

I suspect that the reason the Court avoids any elaboration is that elaboration which passes the laugh test is impossible. How is one to frame for a jury the degree of inability to control which, in the particular case, the nature of the psychiatric diagnosis, and the severity of the mental abnormality require? Will it be a percentage (Ladies and gentlemen of the jury, you may commit Mr. Crane under the SVPA only if you find, beyond a reasonable doubt, that he is 42% unable to control his penchant for sexual violence)? Or a frequency ratio (Ladies and gentlemen of the jury, you may commit Mr. Crane under the SVPA only if you find, beyond a reasonable doubt, that he is unable to control his penchant for sexual violence 3 times out of 10)? Or merely an adverb (Ladies and gentlemen of the jury, you may commit Mr. Crane under the SVPA only if you find, beyond a reasonable doubt, that he is appreciably or moderately, or substantially, or almost totally unable to control his penchant for sexual violence)? None of these seems to me satisfactory.

A jury determined beyond a reasonable doubt that respondent suffers from antisocial personality disorder combined with exhibitionism, and that this is either a mental abnormality or a personality disorder making it likely he will commit repeat acts of sexual violence. That is all the SVPA requires, and all the Constitution demands. Since we have already held precisely that in another case (which, by a remarkable feat of jurisprudential jujitsu the Court relies upon as the only authority for its decision), I would reverse the judgment below.

* * *

Topics for Further Discussion

1. The *Hendricks* and *Crane* cases address the constitutionality of civil commitments, i.e., when the person being committed has not been convicted of a crime. As mentioned above, individuals cannot be imprisoned for so-called status crimes. How should society deal with a sexual predator likely to repeat his offense soon after being returned to society? Some states require sexual predators to register with the local police in the area where they live upon release. They further require that the registry be open for public inspection. Does this violate the rights of the offender?

2. The majority finds the arguments of Kansas unpersuasive because there was no determination that the sexual offender lacked control of his behavior. The dissent objects that the addition of this new standard will result in considerable uncertainty among judges and juries. Do you agree?

Bail

Consistent with the presumption of innocence, a person who has been arrested has the right to request the judge to set bail so he can remain free pending trial. After bail is set, the accused can pay the full amount or post a bond with the court (frequently via a licensed bail bondsman who posts the money on behalf of the defendant for a fee) and obtain his release from detention. If the defendant fails to show up in court on the date set for the trial, the bond money is forfeited and a bench warrant is issued for the immediate arrest of the defendant on the original charges plus the additional charge of failing to appear in court. Bail allows the accused to more effectively mount a defense than might be possible from a pre-trial detention center. It also permits the accused to continue as normally as possible with his life. He can continue to work and provide for his family while out on bail. Finally, it is consistent with the presumption of innocence.

The Eighth Amendment prohibits excessive bail, but does not provide an absolute right to bail. Judges can refuse bail when they believe that the defendant represents a serious danger to the community or a high risk of flight. People accused of murder, known members of organized crime syndicates, drug lords and others accused of violent crimes are likely to be denied bail, or to at least have bail set at a very high level. Bail should be granted to any defendant who presents neither a risk to the community nor a risk of flight. An accused who is a low risk of flight and who has roots in the community, will often be released on his own recognizance (called ROR) without the need to post a bond. People who do not qualify for ROR, or who cannot afford to make bail, will be held in a detention center until their trial. It is not uncommon for the poor and disenfranchised to spend months in detention before being brought to court for trial.

Habeas Corpus

Article I, section 9 of the Constitution provides that: "The privilege of the writ of *habeas corpus* shall not be suspended, unless when in cases of rebellion or invasion the public safety may require it." The essence of a petition for a writ of *habeas corpus* (to produce the body) is that an individual is being held in custody in violation of the law. A federal *habeas* petition is filed in the federal district court and can be used to challenge the lawfulness of incarcerating a person in the state or federal penitentiary. The Supreme Court in *Harris v. Nelson*, 394 U.S. 286 (1969) wrote that the writ is "the fundamental instrument for safeguarding individual freedom against arbitrary and lawless state action." The standard for granting *habeas* relief is high, however, and the courts will not grant the petition unless all appeals have been exhausted and it can be concluded that the fundamental right to due process has been violated. *Habeas corpus* is discussed further in the *Hamdi v. Rumsfeld* case in Chapter 1.

Crime and Punishment

One of the great social debates is whether the aim of the criminal justice system is to seek retribution against wrongdoers, to deter the offender and others from committing crimes, or to rehabilitate offenders so they can be reintroduced into society as productive members. These disparate values are not necessarily at odds with each other, and elements of each can be found in the system. At various times in American history one or the other has taken precedence. The death penalty debate and mandatory sentencing guidelines, represented in their most extreme form by the "Three Strikes" legislation discussed below, indicate a trend in public mood towards punishment and a policy of "locking them up and throwing away the key." This is a debate that is as much philosophical as it is legal. The focus of the remaining sections of this chapter will be on the legal and constitutional aspects of crime and punishment.

The Prohibition against Cruel and Unusual Punishment

The Eighth Amendment prohibits the infliction of "cruel and unusual punishment." The Supreme Court in *Gregg v. Georgia*, 428 U.S. 153 (1976), a case involving the constitutionality of the death penalty, reviewed the history of the Cruel and Unusual Clause:

In the earliest cases raising Eighth Amendment claims, the Court focused on particular methods of execution to determine whether they were too cruel to pass constitutional muster. The constitutionality of the sentence of death itself was not at issue, and the criterion used to evaluate the mode of execution was its similarity to "torture" and other "barbarous" methods.

But the Court has not confined the prohibition embodied in the Eighth Amendment to "barbarous" methods that were generally outlawed in the 18th century. Instead, the Amendment has been interpreted in a flexible and dynamic manner. The Court early recognized that "a principle to be vital must be capable of wider application than the mischief which gave it birth." Thus the Clause forbidding "cruel and unusual" punishments "is not fastened to the obsolete but may acquire meaning as public opinion becomes enlightened by a humane justice."

It is clear from the foregoing precedents that the Eighth Amendment has not been regarded as a static concept. As Mr. Chief Justice Warren said, in an oftquoted phrase, "[t]he Amendment must draw its meaning from the evolving standards of decency that mark the progress of a maturing society." Thus, an assessment of contemporary values concerning the infliction of a challenged sanction is relevant to the application of the Eighth Amendment. As we develop below more fully, this assessment does not call for a subjective judgment. It requires, rather, that we look to objective indicia that reflect the public attitude toward a given sanction.

But our cases also make clear that public perceptions of standards of decency with respect to criminal sanctions are not conclusive. A penalty also must accord with "the dignity of man," which is the "basic concept underlying the Eighth Amendment." This means, at least, that the punishment not be "excessive." When a form of punishment in the abstract (in this case, whether capital punishment may ever be imposed as a sanction for murder) rather than in the particular (the propriety of death as a penalty to be applied to a specific defendant for a specific crime) is under consideration, the inquiry into "excessiveness" has two aspects. First, the punishment must not involve the unnecessary and wanton infliction of pain. Second, the punishment must not be grossly out of proportion to the severity of the crime.

The two standards enumerated by the Court in *Gregg*, namely that the punishment must not cause "unnecessary and wanton" pain and must not be "grossly out of proportion to the severity of the crime," continue to be tested in the area of capital punishment.

The Death Penalty

The ultimate punishment society can inflict on a convict is death. Historically, the death penalty was applicable to a wide range of crimes, including minor ones involving crimes such as petty theft. As society evolves, awareness and concern has continued to grow over the propriety of executing even those convicted of heinous crimes. The global trend has clearly been to abolish the death penalty. The European Community abolished it as have many other nations, leaving the U.S. and Japan among the only developed nations that continue to impose the death penalty. Over 100 countries voted in December of 2008 for a United Nations resolution calling for a moratorium on the death penalty.

Despite such developments, Amnesty International reported that there were at least 2,390 people executed in 25 countries in 2008.

There is no question that the death penalty is popular among a large segment of Americans. Polls regularly confirm that a majority favors it. The Death Penalty Information Center reports that as of March 2010, thirty-five states retain the death penalty and only fifteen states plus the District of Columbia have abolished it. The federal government and the military also maintain a death penalty. Many of the jurisdictions that retain the death penalty on the books do not use it often while others like Florida and Texas do. As of July 1, 2009, 3279 people were on death row. The Governor of Illinois declared a moratorium on executions in his state in 2000, when it was learned that more convictions of death row inmates had been overturned (thirteen) than people had been executed (twelve). One death row inmate was two days away from dying by lethal injection when journalism students uncovered evidence of his innocence.

In *Furman v. Georgia*, 408 U.S. 238 (1972), a Supreme Court plurality struck down a Georgia statute authorizing the death penalty as applied on the grounds that it constituted cruel and unusual punishment. In response to the *Furman* decision, the Georgia legislature revised its death penalty statute in an effort to eliminate the concerns of the Justices who declared it unconstitutional as applied. The new statute narrowed and clearly specified the serious crimes for which death could be imposed, and required a determination of whether there were mitigating factors. It also enumerated ten aggravating factors that, if one or more were present, might justify the death penalty. Finally, it provided for an expedited appeal process to the Georgia Supreme Court. The new statute was soon tested in *Gregg*, cited above, a case involving the imposition of the death penalty on a defendant in a felony murder case. A felony murder occurs when a person is killed during the commission of a crime. Under the felony murder rule, all defendants involved in the crime can be convicted of murder even if their participation was only minimal and they did not take part in the murder. The Supreme Court held that the death penalty was not inherently unconstitutional, and it could be used by states if certain procedural (bifurcation of the guilt and penalty stages) trial and statutory (listing aggravating and mitigating factors) safeguards were available. As the next case shows, the *Gregg* case did not end the debate.

Coker v. Georgia
433 U.S. 584 (1977)

White, J.

Georgia Code Ann. 26-2001 provides that "[a] person convicted of rape shall be punished by death or by imprisonment for life, or by imprisonment for not less than one nor more than 20 years." Punishment is determined by a jury in a separate sentencing proceeding in which at least one of the statutory aggravating circumstances must be found before the death penalty may be imposed. Petitioner Coker was convicted of rape and sentenced to death. Both the conviction and the sentence were affirmed by the Georgia Supreme Court. Coker was granted a writ of *certiorari*, limited to the single claim, rejected by the Georgia court, that the punishment of death for rape violates the Eighth Amendment, which proscribes "cruel and unusual punishments" and which must be observed by the States as well as the Federal Government.

I

While serving various sentences for murder, rape, kidnapping, and aggravated assault, petitioner escaped from the Ware Correctional Institution near Waycross, Ga., on September

2, 1974. At approximately 11 o'clock that night, petitioner entered the house of Allen and Elnita Carver through an unlocked kitchen door. Threatening the couple with a "board," he tied up Mr. Carver in the bathroom, obtained a knife from the kitchen, and took Mr. Carver's money and the keys to the family car. Brandishing the knife and saying "you know what's going to happen to you if you try anything, don't you," Coker then raped Mrs. Carver. Soon thereafter, petitioner drove away in the Carver car, taking Mrs. Carver with him. Mr. Carver, freeing himself, notified the police; and not long thereafter petitioner was apprehended. Mrs. Carver was unharmed.

Petitioner was charged with escape, armed robbery, motor vehicle theft, kidnapping, and rape. Counsel was appointed to represent him. Having been found competent to stand trial, he was tried. The jury returned a verdict of guilty, rejecting his general plea of insanity. A sentencing hearing was then conducted in accordance with the procedures dealt with at length in *Gregg v. Georgia*, where this Court sustained the death penalty for murder when imposed pursuant to the statutory procedures. The jury was instructed that it could consider as aggravating circumstances whether the rape had been committed by a person with a prior record of conviction for a capital felony and whether the rape had been committed in the course of committing another capital felony, namely, the armed robbery of Allen Carver. The court also instructed, pursuant to statute, that even if aggravating circumstances were present, the death penalty need not be imposed if the jury found they were outweighed by mitigating circumstances, that is, circumstances not constituting justification or excuse for the offense in question, "but which, in fairness and mercy, may be considered as extenuating or reducing the degree" of moral culpability or punishment. The jury's verdict on the rape count was death by electrocution. Both aggravating circumstances on which the court instructed were found to be present by the jury.

II

It is now settled that the death penalty is not invariably cruel and unusual punishment within the meaning of the Eighth Amendment; it is not inherently barbaric or an unacceptable mode of punishment for crime; neither is it always disproportionate to the crime for which it is imposed. It is also established that imposing capital punishment, at least for murder, in accordance with the procedures provided under the Georgia statutes saves the sentence from the infirmities which led the Court to invalidate the prior Georgia capital punishment statute in *Furman v. Georgia*.

In sustaining the imposition of the death penalty in *Gregg*, however, the Court firmly embraced the holdings and *dicta* from prior cases to the effect that the Eighth Amendment bars not only those punishments that are "barbaric" but also those that are "excessive" in relation to the crime committed. Under *Gregg*, a punishment is "excessive" and unconstitutional if it (1) makes no measurable contribution to acceptable goals of punishment and hence is nothing more than the purposeless and needless imposition of pain and suffering; or (2) is grossly out of proportion to the severity of the crime. A punishment might fail the test on either ground. Furthermore, these Eighth Amendment judgments should not be, or appear to be, merely the subjective views of individual Justices; judgment should be informed by objective factors to the maximum possible extent. To this end, attention must be given to the public attitudes concerning a particular sentence-history and precedent, legislative attitudes, and the response of juries reflected in their sentencing decisions are to be consulted. In *Gregg*, after giving due regard to such sources, the Court's judgment was that the death penalty for deliberate murder was neither the purposeless imposition of severe punishment nor a punishment grossly disproportionate to the crime. But the Court reserved the question of the constitutionality of the death penalty when imposed for other crimes.

III

That question, with respect to rape of an adult woman, is now before us. We have concluded that a sentence of death is grossly disproportionate and excessive punishment for the crime of rape and is therefore forbidden by the Eighth Amendment as cruel and unusual punishment.

As advised by recent cases, we seek guidance in history and from the objective evidence of the country's present judgment concerning the acceptability of death as a penalty for rape of an adult woman. At no time in the last 50 years have a majority of the States authorized death as a punishment for rape. In 1925, 18 States, the District of Columbia, and the Federal Government authorized capital punishment for the rape of an adult female. By 1971 just prior to the decision in *Furman v. Georgia*, that number had declined, but not substantially, to 16 States plus the Federal Government. *Furman* then invalidated most of the capital punishment statutes in this country, including the rape statutes, because, among other reasons, of the manner in which the death penalty was imposed and utilized under those laws.

With their death penalty statutes for the most part invalidated, the States were faced with the choice of enacting modified capital punishment laws in an attempt to satisfy the requirements of *Furman* or of being satisfied with life imprisonment as the ultimate punishment for any offense. Thirty-five States immediately reinstituted the death penalty for at least limited kinds of crime. This public judgment as to the acceptability of capital punishment, evidenced by the immediate, post-*Furman* legislative reaction in a large majority of the States, heavily influenced the Court to sustain the death penalty for murder in *Gregg v. Georgia*.

But if the "most marked indication of society's endorsement of the death penalty for murder is the legislative response to *Furman*," it should also be a telling *datum* that the public judgment with respect to rape, as reflected in the statutes providing the punishment for that crime, has been dramatically different. In reviving death penalty laws to satisfy *Furman's* mandate, none of the States that had not previously authorized death for rape chose to include rape among capital felonies.

The current judgment with respect to the death penalty for rape is not wholly unanimous among state legislatures, but it obviously weighs very heavily on the side of rejecting capital punishment as a suitable penalty for raping an adult woman.

IV

These recent events evidencing the attitude of state legislatures and sentencing juries do not wholly determine this controversy, for the Constitution contemplates that in the end our own judgment will be brought to bear on the question of the acceptability of the death penalty under the Eighth Amendment. Nevertheless, the legislative rejection of capital punishment for rape strongly confirms our own judgment, which is that death is indeed a disproportionate penalty for the crime of raping an adult woman.

We do not discount the seriousness of rape as a crime. It is highly reprehensible, both in a moral sense and in its almost total contempt for the personal integrity and autonomy of the female victim and for the latter's privilege of choosing those with whom intimate relationships are to be established. Short of homicide, it is the "ultimate violation of self." It is also a violent crime because it normally involves force, or the threat of force or intimidation, to overcome the will and the capacity of the victim to resist. Rape is very often accompanied by physical injury to the female and can also inflict mental and psychological damage. Because it undermines the community's sense of security, there is public injury as well.

Rape is without doubt deserving of serious punishment; but in terms of moral depravity and of the injury to the person and to the public, it does not compare with murder, which does involve the unjustified taking of human life. Although it may be accompanied by another crime, rape by definition does not include the death of or even the serious injury to another person. The murderer kills; the rapist, if no more than that, does not. Life is over for the victim of the murderer; for the rape victim, life may not be nearly so happy as it was, but it is not over and normally is not beyond repair. We have the abiding conviction that the death penalty, which "is unique in its severity and irrevocability," is an excessive penalty for the rapist who, as such, does not take human life.

Powell, J., concurring in the judgment in part and dissenting in part

I concur in the judgment of the Court on the facts of this case, and also in the plurality's reasoning supporting the view that ordinarily death is disproportionate punishment for the crime of raping an adult woman. Although rape invariably is a reprehensible crime, there is no indication that petitioner's offense was committed with excessive brutality or that the victim sustained serious or lasting injury. The plurality, however, does not limit its holding to the case before us or to similar cases. Rather, in an opinion that ranges well beyond what is necessary, it holds that capital punishment always — regardless of the circumstances — is a disproportionate penalty for the crime of rape.

Today, in a case that does not require such an expansive pronouncement, the plurality draws a bright line between murder and all rapes — regardless of the degree of brutality of the rape or the effect upon the victim. I dissent because I am not persuaded that such a bright line is appropriate.

Burger, C.J., dissenting

In a case such as this, confusion often arises as to the Court's proper role in reaching a decision. Our task is not to give effect to our individual views on capital punishment; rather, we must determine what the Constitution permits a State to do under its reserved powers. In striking down the death penalty imposed upon the petitioner in this case, the Court has overstepped the bounds of proper constitutional adjudication by substituting its policy judgment for that of the state legislature. I accept that the Eighth Amendment's concept of disproportionality bars the death penalty for minor crimes. But rape is not a minor crime; hence the Cruel and Unusual Punishments Clause does not give the Members of this Court license to engraft their conceptions of proper public policy onto the considered legislative judgments of the States. Since I cannot agree that Georgia lacked the constitutional power to impose the penalty of death for rape, I dissent from the Court's judgment.

* * *

Topics for Further Discussion

1. *Coker* was a plurality decision. Justices Brennan and Marshall joined in the holding that Georgia's imposition of the death penalty for rape was unconstitutional. They believed the death penalty to be unconstitutional in all circumstances, even in cases of murder. Do you think that the death penalty constitutes cruel and unusual punishment such that it should be banned? If not, do you favor the bright line test indicated by Justice White, or the case-by-case standard advocated by Justice Powell?

2. What was the basis for Chief Justice Burger's dissent?

3. If you think that the death penalty is constitutional in principle, where would you draw the line on its use? For example, can a state execute an individual who rapes a young child? What if the defendant is mentally retarded? The Supreme Court answered this question in *Atkins v. Virginia*, 536 U.S. 304 (2002) holding that:

> Our independent evaluation of the issue reveals no reason to disagree with the judgment of "the legislatures that have recently addressed the matter" and concluded that death is not a suitable punishment for a mentally retarded criminal. We are not persuaded that the execution of mentally retarded criminals will measurably advance the deterrent or the retributive purpose of the death penalty. Construing and applying the Eighth Amendment in the light of our "evolving standards of decency," we therefore conclude that such punishment is excessive and that the Constitution "places a substantive restriction on the State's power to take the life' of a mentally retarded offender."

Chief Justice Rehnquist and Justices Scalia and Thomas dissented, arguing, in essence, that the decision should be left to the judge and jury. Are you persuaded by the Court's use of an "evolving standards of decency" analysis?

Parole, Probation, and Mandatory Sentencing (Three Strikes Law)

A convicted felon sentenced to jail is usually eligible for parole after serving a fixed minimum portion of his sentence. Parole is discretionary, and the inmate has no right to receive it. Decisions are made by a parole board typically appointed by the Governor of each state. In the federal system, parole is administered by the United States Parole Commission under the Department of Justice.

Parole is granted to inmates who have both demonstrated good behavior while incarcerated, and whose release does not jeopardize society. Parole boards give consideration to the seriousness of the offense committed and whether an early release would denigrate society's interest in condemning heinous crimes. Parole benefits the government by reducing prison overcrowding, a serious problem in the U.S. It is estimated that more than two million people are incarcerated in federal, state, and local prisons. Finally, parole supports rehabilitation by recognizing that there is little to be gained by continuing to imprison a person who has made progress in reforming his behavior, especially when the original crime is one that is not likely to be recommitted upon release.

A paroled inmate is released on probation and serves the balance of his sentence in the community under the supervision of a probation officer. The parolee's freedom and rights may be restricted during the period of probation. For example, the parolee may be required to hold a job, report at regular intervals to his probation officer, avoid the company of known felons, or even to remain in his own home after dark and on weekends. Violating the conditions of probation will result in the parolee being returned to prison to finish his jail term.

The problem of recidivism has led some states to crack down on early release programs in the face of outcries from the public. Newspapers rarely miss a chance to highlight crimes committed by repeat offenders, or light prison terms handed out by lenient judges. This has led many states to pass laws requiring mandatory sentencing, often without the chance of parole. The following case presents the issue of whether California's "three strikes" law violates the Eighth Amendment.

Ewing v. California
538 U.S. 11 (2003)

O'Connor, J.

In this case, we decide whether the Eighth Amendment prohibits the State of California from sentencing a repeat felon to a prison term of 25 years to life under the State's "Three Strikes and You're Out" law.

I
A

California's three strikes law reflects a shift in the State's sentencing policies toward incapacitating and deterring repeat offenders who threaten the public safety. The law was designed "to ensure longer prison sentences and greater punishment for those who commit a felony and have been previously convicted of serious and/or violent felony offenses." On March 3, 1993, California Assemblymen Bill Jones and Jim Costa introduced Assembly Bill 971, the legislative version of what would later become the three strikes law. The Assembly Committee on Public Safety defeated the bill only weeks later. Public outrage over the defeat sparked a voter initiative to add Proposition 184, based loosely on the bill, to the ballot in the November 1994 general election.

On October 1, 1993, while Proposition 184 was circulating, 12-year-old Polly Klaas was kidnaped from her home in Petaluma, California. Her admitted killer, Richard Allen Davis, had a long criminal history that included two prior kidnaping convictions. Davis had served only half of his most recent sentence (16 years for kidnaping, assault, and burglary). Had Davis served his entire sentence, he would still have been in prison on the day that Polly Klaas was kidnaped.

Polly Klaas' murder galvanized support for the three strikes initiative. Within days, Proposition 184 was on its way to becoming the fastest qualifying initiative in California history. On January 3, 1994, the sponsors of Assembly Bill 971 resubmitted an amended version of the bill that conformed to Proposition 184. On January 31, 1994, Assembly Bill 971 passed the Assembly by a 63 to 9 margin. The Senate passed it by a 29 to 7 margin on March 3, 1994. Governor Pete Wilson signed the bill into law on March 7, 1994. California voters approved Proposition 184 by a margin of 72 to 28 percent on November 8, 1994.

California thus became the second State to enact a three strikes law. In November 1993, the voters of Washington State approved their own three strikes law, Initiative 593, by a margin of 3 to 1. Between 1993 and 1995, 24 States and the Federal Government enacted three strikes laws. Though the three strikes laws vary from State to State, they share a common goal of protecting the public safety by providing lengthy prison terms for habitual felons.

B

California's current three strikes law consists of two virtually identical statutory schemes "designed to increase the prison terms of repeat felons." When a defendant is convicted of a felony, and he has previously been convicted of one or more prior felonies defined as "serious" or "violent" in Cal. Penal Code Ann. §§ 667.5 and 1192.7, sentencing is conducted pursuant to the three strikes law. Prior convictions must be alleged in the charging document, and the defendant has a right to a jury determination that the prosecution has proved the prior convictions beyond a reasonable doubt.

If the defendant has one prior "serious" or "violent" felony conviction, he must be sentenced to "twice the term otherwise provided as punishment for the current felony conviction." If the defendant has two or more prior "serious" or "violent" felony convictions, he must receive "an indeterminate term of life imprisonment." Defendants sentenced to life under the three strikes law become eligible for parole on a date calculated by reference to a "minimum term," which is the greater of (a) three times the term otherwise provided for the current conviction, (b) 25 years, or (c) the term determined by the court pursuant to § 1170 for the underlying conviction, including any enhancements.

Under California law, certain offenses may be classified as either felonies or misdemeanors. These crimes are known as "wobblers." Some crimes that would otherwise be misdemeanors become "wobblers" because of the defendant's prior record. For example, petty theft, a misdemeanor, becomes a "wobbler" when the defendant has previously served a prison term for committing specified theft-related crimes. Other crimes, such as grand theft, are "wobblers" regardless of the defendant's prior record. Both types of "wobblers" are triggering offenses under the three strikes law only when they are treated as felonies. Under California law, a "wobbler" is presumptively a felony and "remains a felony except when the discretion is actually exercised" to make the crime a misdemeanor.

In California, prosecutors may exercise their discretion to charge a "wobbler" as either a felony or a misdemeanor. Likewise, California trial courts have discretion to reduce a "wobbler" charged as a felony to a misdemeanor either before preliminary examination or at sentencing to avoid imposing a three strikes sentence.

California trial courts can also vacate allegations of prior "serious" or "violent" felony convictions, either on motion by the prosecution or *sua sponte*. In ruling whether to vacate allegations of prior felony convictions, courts consider whether, "in light of the nature and circumstances of [the defendant's] present felonies and prior serious and/or violent felony convictions, and the particulars of his background, character, and prospects, the defendant may be deemed outside the [three strikes'] scheme's spirit, in whole or in part." Thus, trial courts may avoid imposing a three strikes sentence in two ways: first, by reducing "wobblers" to misdemeanors (which do not qualify as triggering offenses), and second, by vacating allegations of prior "serious" or "violent" felony convictions.

C

On parole from a 9-year prison term, petitioner Gary Ewing walked into the pro shop of the El Segundo Golf Course in Los Angeles County on March 12, 2000. He walked out with three golf clubs, priced at $399 apiece, concealed in his pants leg. A shop employee, whose suspicions were aroused when he observed Ewing limp out of the pro shop, telephoned the police. The police apprehended Ewing in the parking lot.

Ewing is no stranger to the criminal justice system. In 1984, at the age of 22, he pleaded guilty to theft. The court sentenced him to six months in jail (suspended), three years' probation, and a $300 fine. In 1988, he was convicted of felony grand theft auto and sentenced to one year in jail and three years' probation. After Ewing completed probation, however, the sentencing court reduced the crime to a misdemeanor, permitted Ewing to withdraw his guilty plea, and dismissed the case. In 1990, he was convicted of petty theft with a prior and sentenced to 60 days in the county jail and three years' probation. In 1992, Ewing was convicted of battery and sentenced to 30 days in the county jail and two years' summary probation. One month later, he was convicted of theft and sentenced to 10 days in the county jail and 12 months' probation. In January 1993, Ewing was convicted of burglary and sentenced to 60 days in the county jail and one year's summary probation. In February 1993, he was convicted of possessing drug paraphernalia and sentenced to six months in the county jail and three years' probation. In July 1993, he was convicted of appropriating lost property and sentenced to 10 days in the county jail and two years' summary probation. In September 1993, he was convicted of unlawfully possessing a firearm and trespassing and sentenced to 30 days in the county jail and one year's probation.

In October and November 1993, Ewing committed three burglaries and one robbery at a Long Beach, California, apartment complex over a 5-week period. He awakened one of his victims, asleep on her living room sofa, as he tried to disconnect her video cassette recorder from the television in that room. When she screamed, Ewing ran out the front door. On another occasion, Ewing accosted a victim in the mailroom of the apartment complex. Ewing claimed to have a gun and ordered the victim to hand over his wallet. When the victim resisted, Ewing produced a knife and forced the victim back to the apartment itself. While Ewing rifled through the bedroom, the victim fled the apartment screaming for help. Ewing absconded with the victim's money and credit cards.

On December 9, 1993, Ewing was arrested on the premises of the apartment complex for trespassing and lying to a police officer. The knife used in the robbery and a glass cocaine pipe were later found in the back seat of the patrol car used to transport Ewing to the police station. A jury convicted Ewing of first-degree robbery and three counts of residential burglary. Sentenced to nine years and eight months in prison, Ewing was paroled in 1999.

Only 10 months later, Ewing stole the golf clubs at issue in this case. He was charged with, and ultimately convicted of, one count of felony grand theft of personal property in excess of $400. As required by the three strikes law, the prosecutor formally alleged, and the trial court later found, that Ewing had been convicted previously of four serious or violent felonies for the three burglaries and the robbery in the Long Beach apartment complex.

At the sentencing hearing, Ewing asked the court to reduce the conviction for grand theft, a "wobbler" under California law, to a misdemeanor so as to avoid a three strikes sentence. Ewing also asked the trial court to exercise its discretion to dismiss the allegations of some or all of his prior serious or violent felony convictions, again for purposes of avoiding a three strikes sentence. Before sentencing Ewing, the trial court took note of his entire criminal history, including the fact that he was on parole when he committed his latest offense. The court also heard arguments from defense counsel and a plea from Ewing himself.

In the end, the trial judge determined that the grand theft should remain a felony. The court also ruled that the four prior strikes for the three burglaries and the robbery in Long Beach should stand. As a newly convicted felon with two or more "serious" or "violent" felony convictions in his past, Ewing was sentenced under the three strikes law to 25 years to life.

II

A

The Eighth Amendment, which forbids cruel and unusual punishments, contains a "narrow proportionality principle" that "applies to noncapital sentences." We have most recently addressed the proportionality principle as applied to terms of years in a series of cases beginning with *Rummel v. Estelle*, 445 U.S. 263 (1980).

In *Rummel*, we held that it did not violate the Eighth Amendment for a State to sentence a three-time offender to life in prison with the possibility of parole. Like Ewing, Rummel was sentenced to a lengthy prison term under a recidivism statute. Rummel's two prior offenses were a 1964 felony for "fraudulent use of a credit card to obtain $80 worth of goods or services," and a 1969 felony conviction for "passing a forged check in the amount of $28.36." His triggering offense was a conviction for felony theft—"obtaining $120.75 by false pretenses."

This Court ruled that "[h]aving twice imprisoned him for felonies, Texas was entitled to place upon Rummel the onus of one who is simply unable to bring his conduct within the social norms prescribed by the criminal law of the State." The recidivism statute "is nothing more than a societal decision that when such a person commits yet another felony, he should be subjected to the admittedly serious penalty of incarceration for life, subject only to the State's judgment as to whether to grant him parole." We noted that this Court "has on occasion stated that the Eighth Amendment prohibits imposition of a sentence that is grossly disproportionate to the severity of the crime." But "[o]utside the context of capital punishment, successful challenges to the proportionality of particular sentences have been exceedingly rare." Although we stated that the proportionality principle "would ... come into play in the extreme example ... if a legislature made overtime parking a felony punishable by life imprisonment," we held that "the mandatory life sentence imposed upon this petitioner does not constitute cruel and unusual punishment under the Eighth and Fourteenth Amendments."

Three years after *Rummel*, in *Solem v. Helm*, 463 U. S. 277, 279 (1983), we held that the Eighth Amendment prohibited "a life sentence without possibility of parole for a seventh nonviolent felony." The triggering offense in *Solem* was "uttering a 'no account' check for $100." We specifically stated that the Eighth Amendment's ban on cruel and unusual punishments "prohibits ... sentences that are disproportionate to the crime committed," and that the "constitutional principle of proportionality has been recognized explicitly in this Court for almost a century." The *Solem* Court then explained that three factors may be relevant to a determination of whether a sentence is so disproportionate that it violates the Eighth Amendment: "(i) the gravity of the offense and the harshness of the penalty; (ii) the sentences imposed on other criminals in the same jurisdiction; and (iii) the sentences imposed for commission of the same crime in other jurisdictions."

B

When the California Legislature enacted the three strikes law, it made a judgment that protecting the public safety requires incapacitating criminals who have already been convicted of at least one serious or violent crime. Nothing in the Eighth Amendment prohibits California from making that choice. To the contrary, our cases establish that "States have a valid interest in deterring and segregating habitual criminals." Recidivism has long been recognized as a legitimate basis for increased punishment.

California's justification is no pretext. Recidivism is a serious public safety concern in California and throughout the Nation. According to a recent report, approximately 67 percent of former inmates released from state prisons were charged with at least one "serious" new crime within three years of their release.

To be sure, California's three strikes law has sparked controversy. Critics have doubted the law's wisdom, cost-efficiency, and effectiveness in reaching its goals. This criticism is appropriately directed at the legislature, which has primary responsibility for making the difficult policy choices that underlie any criminal sentencing scheme. We do not sit as a "superlegislature" to second-guess these policy choices. It is enough that the State of California has a reasonable basis for believing that dramatically enhanced sentences for habitual felons "advance[s] the goals of [its] criminal justice system in any substantial way."

III

Against this backdrop, we consider Ewing's claim that his three strikes sentence of 25 years to life is unconstitutionally disproportionate to his offense of "shoplifting three golf clubs." We first address the gravity of the offense compared to the harshness of the penalty. At the threshold, we note that Ewing incorrectly frames the issue. The gravity of his offense was not merely "shoplifting three golf clubs." Rather, Ewing was convicted of felony grand theft for stealing nearly $1,200 worth of merchandise after previously having been convicted of at least two "violent" or "serious" felonies. Even standing alone, Ewing's theft should not be taken lightly. His crime was certainly not "one of the most passive felonies a person could commit." To the contrary, the Supreme Court of California has noted the "seriousness" of grand theft in the context of proportionality review. Theft of $1,200 in property is a felony under federal law, and in the vast majority of States.

In weighing the gravity of Ewing's offense, we must place on the scales not only his current felony, but also his long history of felony recidivism. Any other approach would fail to accord proper deference to the policy judgments that find expression in the legislature's choice of sanctions. In imposing a three strikes sentence, the State's interest is not merely punishing the offense of conviction, or the "triggering" offense: "[I]t is in addition the interest ... in dealing in a harsher manner with those who by repeated criminal acts have shown that they are simply incapable of conforming to the norms of society as established by its criminal law."

We hold that Ewing's sentence of 25 years to life in prison, imposed for the offense of felony grand theft under the three strikes law, is not grossly disproportionate and therefore does not violate the Eighth Amendment's prohibition on cruel and unusual punishments.

Stevens, J., dissenting

Throughout most of the Nation's history—before guideline sentencing became so prevalent—federal and state trial judges imposed specific sentences pursuant to grants of authority that gave them uncabined discretion within broad ranges. It was not unheard of for a statute to authorize a sentence ranging from one year to life, for example. In exercising their discretion, sentencing judges wisely employed a proportionality principle that took into account all of the justifications for punishment—namely, deterrence, incapacitation, retribution and rehabilitation. Likewise, I think it clear that the Eighth Amendment's prohibition of "cruel and unusual punishments" expresses a broad and basic proportionality principle that takes into account all of the justifications for penal sanctions. It is this broad proportionality principle that would preclude reliance on any of the justifications for punishment to support, for example, a life sentence for overtime parking.

* * *

Topics for Further Discussion

1. What are the main arguments of the plurality opinion? Justice Scalia joined in the judgment of the Court but filed a concurring opinion expressing his view that the pro-

hibition of the Eighth Amendment is aimed only at modes of punishment. In his view, it has no applicability in a claim challenging the length of a prison sentence.

2. Justice Breyer's dissent in *Ewing* noted that, under the Federal Sentencing Guidelines, a recidivist like Mr. Ewing would have received a maximum sentence of eighteen months. What does the plurality have to say about proportionality as a basis for challenging a punishment? If you do not favor the Three Strikes law, how would you deal with the serious problem of recidivism noted in the opinion?

3. The Supreme Court in *Harmelin v. Michigan*, 501 U.S. 957 (1991) held that mandatory sentencing provisions do not violate the Eighth Amendment by eliminating discretion on the part of the judge or jury to fix a sentence in light of the facts and circumstances of each case. In *Blakely v. Washington*, 124 S. Ct. 2531 (2004), the defendant pled guilty to kidnapping his estranged wife. Washington's sentencing guidelines supported a maximum sentence of fifty-three months. The trial judge imposed a ninety month sentence after determining that the actions of the defendant were done with deliberate cruelty. The Supreme Court found that the prison term violated the defendant's Sixth Amendment right because he had not admitted to cruelty in his plea, nor was cruelty determined beyond a reasonable doubt in a trial.

4. *Blakely* called into question the validity of the Federal Sentencing Guidelines, which appeared to suffer from the same constitutional infirmities as the Washington guidelines. This was confirmed in *United States v. Booker*, 125 S. Ct. 738 (2005). The Supreme Court issued two opinions in this case. In the first by Justice Stevens, the Court concluded that "[a]ny fact (other than a prior conviction) which is necessary to support a sentence exceeding the maximum authorized by the facts established by a plea of guilty or a jury verdict must be admitted by the defendant or proved to a jury beyond a reasonable doubt." In a second opinion of the Court by Justice Breyer, the Court addressed the appropriate remedy, concluding as follows:

> We answer the question of remedy by finding the provision of the federal sentencing statute that makes the Guidelines mandatory incompatible with today's constitutional holding. We conclude that this provision must be severed and excised, as must one other statutory section, which depends upon the Guidelines' mandatory nature. So modified, the Federal Sentencing Act makes the Guidelines effectively advisory. It requires a sentencing court to consider Guidelines ranges, but it permits the court to tailor the sentence in light of other statutory concerns as well.

Key Terms and Concepts

Arrest Warrant
Cruel and Unusual Punishment
Indictment
Information
Mens Rea
Miranda Rights
Parole and Probation
RICO
Search Warrant
Three Strikes Legislation

Chapter 11

Business Law

"A corporation, it has been said, has no body to kick and no soul to damn"

Blue, J. in *Thermatool Corp. v. Dep't of Revenue Services,*
651 A.2d 763 (Conn. Super Ct. 1994)

This chapter surveys the major forms of business organization in the United States, and highlights some of the major laws regulating their operations. Many of these topics are studied by American lawyers for their entire careers, so the reader will not be an expert after reading this chapter. Rather, this chapter will introduce aspects of regulatory philosophy and key concepts that will alert the reader to the need for further study.

Forms of Business Organization

Sole Proprietorship

A sole proprietorship is the simplest and most common form of business organization. The owner of a business starts buying or selling a product, or supplying a service, in his own name or after filing a notice that he will be doing business under a "fictitious name" such as "John Smith, d/b/a (doing business as) Julius Caesar's Pizza Shop." Perhaps the business may require a business license from local regulators, but, in general, sole proprietorships are set up without significant legal expense or paper work. The profits, losses, assets, and liabilities of a sole proprietor are legally the same as those of the proprietor's business: the proprietor puts the profits into his pocket, bears the losses out of his personal funds, and pays personal income taxes on the taxable income of the business. The proprietor may lose his business, house, and life savings if the proprietorship fails to pay a large debt or court judgment. Sole proprietorships are popular because they can be run without much administrative expense or legal knowledge. The sole proprietor is personally liable for all the debts of the business, and so sole proprietorships are a major risk for the owner. Since the assets of the business are the same as the assets of the proprietor, sole proprietorships find it hard to obtain investment funds and must usually rely on loans.

Fiduciary Duty

A sole proprietor handles only his own assets, but partners, trustees, and corporate directors manage the property and rights of others. American law imposes upon partners, trustees, and corporate directors a "fiduciary" duty of total honesty and disclosure

323

concerning any dealings that might profit them personally, and a duty to put the interests of the partnership, trust or corporation before and above their own interests. A person who fails in his fiduciary duty must make up losses, or give up a share of the profits, out of his personal assets. The standard of fiduciary duty is idealistic and rigid, as famously stated by Benjamin Cardozo, later a Justice of the U.S. Supreme Court, in *Meinhard v. Salmon*, 164 N.E. 545 (N.Y. 1928):

> Many forms of conduct permissible in a workaday world for those acting at arm's length, are forbidden to those bound by fiduciary ties. A trustee is held to something stricter than the morals of the market place. Not honesty alone, but the punctilio of an honor the most sensitive, is then the standard of behavior. Uncompromising rigidity has been the attitude of courts when petitioned to undermine the rule of undivided loyalty by the "disintegrating erosion" of particular exceptions. Only thus has the level of conduct for fiduciaries been kept at a level higher than that trodden by the crowd.

In *Meinhard,* a partner in a real estate venture made profitable secret deals on the side without telling his other partner. The court required the partner who profited to share the proceeds with his other partner. A fiduciary is not allowed to defend himself by arguing, for example, that "everyone in the real estate industry cheats, so I was just doing what was common in the business." Moreover, the courts state that they will not make exceptions to the rigid duty of a fiduciary to account for all of his business actions.

General Partnership and Limited Partnership

Section 6 of the Uniform Partnership Act defines a partnership as "an association of two or more persons to carry on as co-owners of a business for profit." A general partnership can be created by operation of law, but usually is created when people sign a partnership agreement among themselves. Unless the partnership agreement changes the terms, (a) a partnership is dissolved by the death, bankruptcy or withdrawal of any partner; (b) each partner shares equally in profits and losses; (c) a majority vote is needed to decide ordinary partnership matters and a unanimous vote is needed to propose changes to the partnership agreement; and (d) a partner cannot transfer his partnership interest without the unanimous approval of the other partners. By law, each general partner is an agent of all other partners and can bind the partnership. Each general partner also owes the other partners a fiduciary duty in handling the partnerships affairs. And, each general partner has unlimited liability to third parties for the partnership's obligations, which can reach to the personal assets of each partner. For U.S. federal income tax purposes, a partnership is not a separate legal person, and the profits and losses of the partnership appear on the personal income tax return of each partner.

Many famous U.S. law, accounting, consulting, and financial firms remained classic partnerships until the end of the last century. Recently, however, most large professional firms have converted to limited liability corporations or regular corporations (each discussed below). Since each partner is liable for the mistakes of every other partner, a partner must know at all times what his fellow partners are doing, but with partnerships of thousands of members being created, many firms found it hard to monitor what too many other partners were doing. In addition, some professional firms found they lacked the funds to compete in a global market since partnerships, like sole proprietorships, cannot offer investors meaningful ownership of the partnership and therefore typically have to rely on loans.

In contrast to general partnerships, limited partnerships remain popular. A limited partnership is created only by a written agreement that is filed with the state and available for public view. A limited partnership requires at least one general partner, with authority to bind the partnership and unlimited liability, but it also requires one or more limited partners. Limited partners are "limited" in their liability and power; i.e. they cannot be held liable for more than their investment in the partnership, they typically have no control over the daily operations of the partnership, and are not agents that can bind the partnership. Limited partners typically can transfer both their partnership interest and their right to profits. The share of profits and losses each limited partner receives is determined by the limited partnership agreement, and may differ among partners and among limited partners. The limited partnership is created, governed, modified, and dissolved according to the limited partnership agreement.

The popularity of limited partnerships is due to their status under U.S. tax laws as a "pass through" vehicle for profits and losses to the limited partners. Typically, a wealthy individual without business experience (such as a dentist or a professional golf player) will invest in a type of business with very favorable federal tax treatment, like oil drilling or horse breeding. The wealthy limited partner relies on the general partner, who is supposed to be an expert in the business, to actually run the oil drilling or horse breeding business. What the wealthy limited partner desires is the large tax losses that are often generated in the early years of the limited partnership, and which will "pass through" the limited partnership to offset the other taxable income of the investor. If the limited partnership actually strikes oil or breeds a famous racehorse, the limited partner will receive his contractual share of the profits, but in most cases limited partnerships are usually more attractive as a source of tax-reducing losses.

Trust

A trust is a legal relationship created by a person (called the "trustor" or "settlor"), either during that person's life or upon his death, by which that person's assets have been placed under the control of a "trustee" for the benefit of a beneficiary or for a specified purpose. Legal title to the trust assets is in the name of the trustee, but the assets of the trust constitute a separate fund that are not part of the trustee's property. The trustee has a fiduciary duty to manage or dispose of the assets as directed by the trust document, and must account for his actions. A trust can manage property, hire and fire employees, contract in its own name, and behave like a business. A trust continues until the happening of events specified in the trust document or until the trust purpose or assets no longer exist. Trusts that are hundreds of years old continue in the United States, with the human trustees being replaced while the trust remains immortal.

A trust document does not have to be filed with the state or be made available to the public, and can remain hidden in a lawyer's desk drawer. As a result, trusts remain widely used in the United States to lower taxes, shelter assets, or to manage assets after the trustor has died. Before the 20th century, it was very difficult to create a corporation, so many businesses were organized as trusts. For example, John D. Rockefeller's Standard Oil Company was a trust that monopolized the petroleum industry in late 19th century. It was, in fact, this infamous trust that led to the creation of laws against such monopolies in that period which are still known as the "antitrust" laws. A business run by a trust in this century is likely to be either very old, the result of an attempt by the founder to reduce taxes or to make his dealings more secret, or to control the disposition of the enterprise after his death.

Limited Liability Company

Professional firms, particularly law firms, increasingly form limited liability companies (abbreviated "LLC") so that they can use attractive features of both partnership and corporation law. Like a partnership, a LLC lets the partners or shareholders (called "members") manage their affairs according to an agreement (which must be in writing and filed with the state), and allows partners to forbid the transfer of interests in the LLC. Like a corporation, the LLC limits the liability of each shareholder to his investment in the LLC, and members are *not* personally liable for the debts of the LLC. The LLC agreement may provide for voting power to be determined by amount invested in the LLC or may give each member an equal vote, and may provide that every member can bind the LLC or that only certain members—or professional managers—can bind the LLC. Federal income tax laws allow the LLC to choose whether it will be taxed as a partnership (profits and losses passed through to the partners), or as a corporation (profits and losses stop at the LLC and are not taxable to the members). Readers familiar with corporation law in other countries should note that, in the United States, the term "limited liability company" refers only to this kind of partnership-corporation hybrid and not to any corporation in general.

Corporation

Corporations have always been attractive because they (a) can contract in their own name; (b) have perpetual life; (c) can sell shares to obtain investment; and (d) protect their shareholders from personal liability beyond the value of the shares held. In the 20th century, simplified incorporation laws, the creation of a professional managerial class, and the rise of national and international financial markets made the corporation the most common form of business organization in the United States. With the exception of a few public corporations (like "Amtrak," the National Passenger Railroad Corporation) and historic companies (like Citibank, N.A., "National Association"), corporations are created under the laws of each state. In practice, there is no "United States Corporation Law."

Most state laws make it very simple to incorporate. Sitting at one's computer, one can determine whether a certain corporate name is available, download standard articles of incorporation, mail the articles of incorporation to a state official with a "rush processing" fee, and expect to receive a certificate of incorporation in a few days. A lawyer is not required, nor is a visit to a notary or a government office. So long as one does not want to set up a regulated business (like a bank, insurance company, public utility, etc.), one does not need a special license to incorporate. Most state laws automatically empower corporations to conduct "any lawful activity," so one does not have to worry about carefully listing the purposes and powers of the corporation. Initial filings usually require some contact address and an address at which the corporation may receive service of process, but many states do not require public disclosure of directors or even officers. Most states have a filing fee of less than $400 and there is no minimum investment requirement because the wide availability of credit reports in the United States means that investors need not rely on the initial capital ("stated capital") of the corporation to determine creditworthiness. Most states do not require registration of a corporate seal or officer's signature. Shares can have a stated minimum value of "one cent per share," or even no minimum value (called "no par value" shares).

Once a state official certifies that the company has been incorporated, the corporation holds a private organizational meeting. At this meeting, initial directors are elected; the directors set an internal, non-public set of rules called the "Bylaws"; the directors appoint officers of the corporation starting with the president; the directors authorize the issuance of shares; and the directors designate a bank for depositing corporate funds. In the United States, there is no "Managing Director" system, and, while a manager may be appointed to the board of directors, it is legally the president and other officers who run the daily business of the company rather than the board of directors. The board of directors is responsible for setting general strategy and policies for the corporation, for dealing with extraordinary purchases and sales by the corporation, and for supervising the actions of corporate officers to make sure they follow both company policies and legal requirements.

All fifty states have corporation laws, but a majority of publicly traded corporations are currently incorporated in Delaware, though this small Eastern state is not the principal place of business of even five percent of those companies. Delaware runs its incorporation services as a key local business, with state officials working to satisfy customers, and the state legislature busily modifying Delaware corporation law to meet the needs of publicly traded corporations. Lawyers working for corporations often prefer Delaware because most routine questions of corporate law have already been decided in the 200 years or so of Delaware case law.

Duties of Majority Shareholders, Directors and Officers

Majority Shareholders

Officers and directors of publicly traded corporations owe their shareholders a wide variety of state and federal fiduciary duties. However, in the United States, even owners of privately-held "close corporations" owe the company and their co-owners a fiduciary duty. In *Sugarman v. Sugarman*, the four Sugarman brothers started a paper company in 1906. By 1986, the company had become the Statler Corporation and was owned 61% by defendant Leonard Sugarman. Leonard was the son of one of the four founding brothers, and served as President and Chairman of the Board of Statler. The plaintiffs were children or grandchildren of the other three Sugarman brothers, and owned 21.78% of the stock in Statler. The plaintiffs alleged that the defendant tried to cut them off from the profits of the company by refusing to pay them dividends as shareholders, refusing to hire them as employees, and paying himself an excessive salary and expenses in an attempt to take all the company profits for himself. After denying plaintiffs a way to make money from Statler, Leonard Sugarman offered to buy the plaintiffs' stock in 1980 for $3.33 per share. In 1980, the company's accountant, Price Waterhouse, had informed the defendant that the book value of the company's stock was $16.30 per share.

Sugarman v. Sugarman
797 F.2d 3 (1st Cir. 1986)

Coffin, J.

Plaintiff-appellees brought suit, alleging that Leonard had abused his fiduciary duty to Statler and to appellees. The district court ... also found that Leonard had received excessive compensation from Statler and that this overcompensation "was effected in bad faith, as part of an attempt to freeze out minority interests." The court concluded that this combination of factors was proof of Leonard's effort to improperly freeze appellees out of the company.

We first examine the legal standard that must be met to establish a "freeze-out" of minority shareholders. The Massachusetts Supreme Judicial Court held that shareholders in a close corporation owe one another a fiduciary duty of "utmost good faith and loyalty." According to the court, stockholders in a close corporation "may not act out of avarice, expediency or self-interest in derogation of their duty of loyalty to the other stockholders and to the corporation."

The court's decision was premised on the rationale that the corporate form of a close corporation "supplies an opportunity for the majority stockholders to oppress or disadvantage minority stockholders."

When these types of "freeze-outs" are attempted by the majority, "the minority stockholders, cut off from all corporation-related revenues, must either suffer their losses or seek a buyer for their shares." This, according to the court, is often "the capstone of the majority plan." Because minority shareholders cannot sell their stock on the open market, as can shareholders in public corporations, the minority shareholders may be compelled to deal with the majority. As the court explained, "when the minority stockholder agrees to sell out at less than fair value, the majority has won."

Majority shareholders have an independent duty to exercise complete candor with minority shareholders, when they negotiate stock transactions; they must fully disclose all the material facts and circumstances surrounding or affecting a proposed transaction. If a majority shareholder breaches this duty, and a minority shareholder sells stock at an inadequate price, the minority shareholder can seek damages based on the difference between the offered price and the fair value of the stock.

* * *

Topics for Further Discussion

1. Should family-run corporations be subject to a less strict set of rules about the fiduciary duty of majority shareholders?

2. Why does the Court conclude that majority shareholders in a close corporation "have an independent duty to exercise complete candor with minority shareholders"? If Leonard had just received an offer from a much larger company to merge and acquire Statler, would he have to disclose it?

The Business Judgment Rule

Directors of a corporation have a fiduciary duty to care for the affairs of the corporation. This means that directors must make their decisions with (1) reasonable care, (2) honesty, and (3) an absence of conflict of interest.

Reasonable care means that a director must inform himself of facts he needs to know to make decisions. A director may rely on information he receives from other directors, company employees, or outside experts so long as the director has no reason to suspect that the information is unreliable or subject to a conflict of interest. A director, through a committee or the board as a whole, must make adequate efforts to supervise the president and other key employees, and make sure that systems are in place to supervise the activities of all employees regardless of rank. The duty of honesty requires directors to use their independent judgment. They must not mislead other directors, and must not allow the company to violate the law. Finally, the absence of conflict of interest dictates that directors fully disclose any conflict or interest to the board and not participate in votes on matters in which they have a conflict of interest.

If a director maintains the above standards of "reasonable care," "honesty," and "absence of conflict of interest," courts will generally refuse to review board decisions that are based on almost any rational purpose. This doctrine, called "the business judgment rule," means that courts will not try to review every decision of a corporate board or try to second-guess the board when a corporation tries a new idea and fails. Courts understand that even the most intelligent and honest directors cannot predict the future, and sometimes authorize money-losing ventures or fail to prevent corporate mistakes. Typically, unless a party questioning the board's judgment provides adequate proof of such factors as fraud, self-dealing, or failure to gather all material information prior to making a decision, the board's judgment will not be questioned by a court. When a board of directors does fail in its duties, however, the members may be held personally liable, and actions approved by the board may be enjoined by a court.

The poison pill a spy swallows when captured makes him useless to an enemy. Should a board of directors be protected by the business judgment rule when it makes a "poison pill" decision to defend itself from an unwelcome acquisition by making the company much harder to acquire or much less attractive? In *Moran v. Household International*, the board adopted a rights plan "poison pill" that would issue new rights to additional stock to every shareholder except a hostile potential buyer. Moran, a director of Household International, sued to invalidate the poison pill. Some common-law jurisdictions outside of the United States have held poison pills invalid as a matter of corporate law or public policy, but the Delaware Supreme Court has allowed them subject to restrictions.

Moran v. Household International, Inc.
500 A.2d 1346 (Del. 1985)

McNeilly, J.

On August 14, 1984, the Board of Directors of Household International, Inc. adopted the Rights Plan by a fourteen to two vote. Basically, the Plan provides that Household common stockholders are entitled to the issuance of one Right per common share under certain triggering conditions. There are two triggering events that can activate the Rights. The first is the announcement of a tender offer for 30 percent of Household's shares ("30% trigger") and the second is the acquisition of 20 percent of Household's shares by any single entity or group ("20% trigger").

[H]ere we have a defensive mechanism adopted to ward off possible future advances and not a mechanism adopted in reaction to a specific threat. This distinguishing factor does not result in the Directors losing the protection of the business judgment rule. To the contrary, pre-planning for the contingency of a hostile takeover might reduce the risk that, under the pressure of a takeover bid, management will fail to exercise reasonable judgment. Therefore, in reviewing a pre-planned defensive mechanism it seems even more appropriate to apply the business judgment rule. Of course, the business judgment rule can only sustain corporate decision making or transactions that are within the power or authority of the Board.

Appellants contend that the Board is unauthorized to usurp stockholders' rights to receive tender offers by changing Household's fundamental structure. We conclude that the Rights Plan does not prevent stockholders from receiving tender offers, and that the change of Household's structure was less than that which results from the implementation of other defensive mechanisms upheld by various courts.

The evidence at trial evidenced many methods around the Plan. One could also form a group of up to 19.9% and solicit proxies for consents to remove the Board and redeem the Rights. These are but a few of the methods by which Household can still be acquired by a hostile tender offer.

The Rights Plan does not destroy the assets of the corporation. The Plan neither results in any outflow of money from the corporation nor impairs its financial flexibility. It does not dilute earnings per share and does not have any adverse tax consequences for the corporation or its stockholders. The Plan has not adversely affected the market price of Household's stock.

There is little change in the governance structure as a result of the adoption of the Rights Plan. The Board does not now have unfettered discretion in refusing to redeem the Rights. The Board has no more discretion in refusing to redeem the Rights than it does in enacting any defensive mechanism.

Appellants contend that the "20% trigger" effectively prevents any stockholder from first acquiring 20% or more shares before conducting a proxy contest and further, it prevents stockholders from banding together into a group to solicit proxies if, collectively, they own 20% or more of the stock.

We conclude that there was sufficient evidence at trial to support the finding that the effect upon proxy contests will be minimal. Evidence at trial established that many proxy contests are won with an insurgent ownership of less than 20%, and that very large holdings are no guarantee of success. There was also testimony that the key variable in proxy contest success is the merit of an insurgent's issues, not the size of his holdings.

Having concluded that the adoption of the Rights Plan was within the authority of the Directors, we now look to whether the Directors have met their burden under the business judgment rule.

The "directors must show that they had reasonable grounds for believing that a danger to corporate policy and effectiveness existed. They satisfy that burden 'by showing good faith and reasonable investigation.'" In addition, the directors must show that the defensive mechanism was "reasonable in relation to the threat posed." Moreover, that proof is materially enhanced, where, as here, a majority of the board favoring the proposal consisted of outside independent directors who have acted in accordance with the foregoing standards. Then, the burden shifts back to the plaintiffs who have the ultimate burden of persuasion to show a breach of the directors' fiduciary duties.

There are no allegations here of any bad faith on the part of the Directors' action in the adoption of the Rights Plan. There is no allegation that the Directors' action was taken for entrenchment purposes. Household has adequately demonstrated, as explained above, that the adoption of the Rights Plan was in reaction to what it perceived to be the threat in the market place of coercive two-tier tender offers.

To determine whether a business judgment reached by a board of directors was an informed one, we determine whether the directors were grossly negligent. Upon a review of this record, we conclude the Directors were not grossly negligent. The information supplied to the Board on August 14 provided the essentials of the Plan. The Directors were given beforehand a notebook which included a three-page summary of the Plan along with articles on the current takeover environment.

In addition, to meet their burden, the Directors must show that the defensive mechanism was "reasonable in relation to the threat posed". The record reflects a concern on the part of the Directors over the increasing frequency of takeovers. In sum, the Directors reasonably believed Household was vulnerable to coercive acquisition techniques and adopted a reasonable defensive mechanism to protect itself.

In conclusion, the Household Directors receive the benefit of the business judgment rule in their adoption of the Rights Plan.

While we conclude for present purposes that the Household Directors are protected by the business judgment rule, that does not end the matter. The ultimate response to an actual takeover bid must be judged by the Directors' actions at that time, and nothing we say here relieves them of their basic fundamental duties to the corporation and its stockholders.

* * *

Topics for Further Discussion

1. Is the business judgment rule a reasonable compromise between the interests of shareholders and the need for a board of directors to make decisions in rapidly-changing business environments?

2. What policy reasons support the business judgment rule? Do you think deference to corporate directors remains a good thing in light of the many corporate scandals?

Prohibition on Self-Dealing

Officers and directors of a corporation are not allowed to use corporate assets for their personal benefit, to contract with the corporation for personal benefit (beyond their compensation as employee or director), or to take a business opportunity from the corporation and use it for their personal benefit. If an officer or director has been involved in self-dealing, the corporation may either void the transaction or sue the individual for damages. However, most states allow self-dealing if (a) the terms are fair to both sides, and, either, (b) the terms are honestly disclosed to and approved by a majority of disinterested directors, or (c) the terms are honestly disclosed to and approved by a majority of disinterested shareholders.

In a case involving self-dealing by a majority shareholder, *Sinclair Oil Corp. v. Levien*, 280 A.2d 717 (Del. 1971), Sinclair owned 97% of a subsidiary, Sinclair Venezuelan Oil Company ("Sinven"), and Levien owned a few thousand shares. All of the members of the Sinven board and its officers were appointed by Sinclair. Sinven was required by Sinclair to pay out most of its profits as dividends to shareholders instead of reinvesting the profits in company expansion. Sinclair Oil executed a contract with Sinven but was late in making payments to Sinven. Levien sued on behalf of Sinven, arguing that Sinclair, as majority shareholder, had violated a fiduciary duty to the minority shareholders of Sinven. The Delaware court ruled that merely paying out dividends did not violate a fiduciary duty so long as Levien received the same dividend per share as Sinclair, but that the self-dealing involved when Sinclair did not allow Sinven to enforce its contract with Sinclair did violate Sinclair's duty as majority shareholder.

Remedies Available to Shareholders

Shareholder's Derivative Suit

A shareholder's derivative suit is one in which a corporate shareholder sues the corporation to force it to enforce its own corporate rights. If the plaintiff wins, the corporation receives the award and the plaintiff's court costs and attorney fees are paid by the corporation. A derivative suit is different from a direct lawsuit to require the company to pay dividends or to hold a shareholders' meeting, because a derivative action does not try to enforce the rights of a shareholder, only the rights of the corporation. For example, a typical derivative action tries to make the company recover damages for a breach of duty by its executives or directors. Most state laws require that a derivative suit plaintiff first demand that the board of directors resolve the problem and give the board a reasonable period of time to act. In addition, most state rules of civil procedure require that the plaintiff in a derivative suit be able to represent the corporation's best interests without personal conflict.

Cumulative Voting

Suppose a corporation has four directors and two shareholders, one shareholder who owns fifty-one shares and one who owns forty-nine shares. Normally, the majority shareholder could elect every one of the directors. However, if the state or the articles of incorporation require cumulative voting, minority shareholders may have the opportunity to elect directors. Under cumulative voting, a shareholder may multiply the number of votes it is entitled to cast for all directors by the number of directors to be elected, and then cast the total multiplied amount for one director, or distribute the vote among several directors. The formula is

$$S = \frac{ac}{b+1} + 1$$

Where:

S = the number of shares needed to elect the desired number of directors

a = the total number of shares voting

c = the desired number of directors

b = the total number of directors to be elected

So, in the above example, if the minority shareholder wished to elect one director under cumulative voting, the calculation would be,

$$S = \frac{100x1}{4+1} + 1$$

meaning that the 49% shareholder could elect one director with only twenty-one shares, but the majority shareholder will not have enough shares to elect all four of the directors. In this example, the majority shareholder may be able to elect two directors, the minority shareholder one director, and neither shareholder can force the election of the remaining one director without the consent of the other.

Right to Dissent

Most states give shareholders the right to dissent, meaning the right to obtain separate payment for their shares, if they disagree with major changes in the corporation's organization and the organization is not listed on an established stock market. Typically rights of dissent arise when (a) the corporation has decided to sell or lease substantially all of its assets not in the usual course of business; (b) the corporation has decided to merge; (c) the corporation has decided to consolidate with another corporation; or (d) there is a major change to the articles of incorporation. Corporations must inform their shareholders of the right to dissent, and the shareholder must comply with deadlines for making demands for an appraisal of the fair value of the corporation's shares and payment of that fair value. Since stock market prices are believed to reflect the fair value of a listed corporation, many states do not offer additional appraisal rights for publicly traded corporations.

Shareholder Proposals

Securities and Exchange Commission Rule 14 under the Securities Exchange Act of 1934 requires that any shareholder in a publicly traded corporation who has continuously held at least $2,000 in market value or one percent of the company's securities be entitled to be voted on the proposal, for a period of at least one year by the date of submission of the proposal, be entitled to submit a proposal directly to other shareholders at company expense. There are some exceptions, for example, if (1) the proposal is not a proper subject for shareholder action under state law; (2) the proposal is illegal; (3) the proposal is beyond the company's power to achieve; or (4) the proposal does not relate to a significant portion of the company's business.

Securities Regulation

Scope of the Securities Act of 1933

Many investors who lost their life savings in the stock market crash of 1929 felt that they had been cheated into buying stock in weak companies at inflated prices. In response, Congress created the Securities and Exchange Commission ("SEC") and passed the Securities Act of 1933 and the Securities Exchange Act of 1934. Many states also have their own securities laws (called "blue sky" laws), and their own agency to monitor securities sold in that state. Securities law is a complicated and highly technical area of law. The summary below should help the reader to understand some of the issues.

The SEC is an independent agency with the primary mission of protecting investors. It has the power to seek civil injunctions in federal court against violators and to recommend that the Justice Department bring criminal prosecutions. The SEC directly regulates through its power to make binding rules, to issue warnings to and suspensions of broker-dealers; investment companies; and investment advisors, and to ban from the securities industry major individual and corporate violators.

The Securities Act of 1933 has two primary goals (1) to provide investors with "material" information about securities offered for sale to the public, and (2) to prohibit misrepresentation and fraud in the sale of securities. "Material" information is any information that might cause a reasonable investor to make a decision about buying, selling, holding or trading the security. The 1933 Act subjects issuers to strict and absolute civil liability for losses caused by sales of securities to the public unless (a) a registration statement has been filed with the SEC and investors have been given a "prospectus," a formal document including information from the registration statement and describing any risks in investing in the security, or (b) the securities or the investors are subject to an exemption from registration. The 1933 Act provides penalties for any fraud or misrepresentation in the sale of securities, even exempt securities, including fines and imprisonment of individuals for up to five years.

The scope of the Securities Act of 1933 is so broad that almost any investment is subject to the Act. Section 2(a)(1) of the 1933 Act states defines a "security" as:

> any note, stock, treasury stock, security future, bond, debenture, evidence of indebtedness, certificate of interest or participation in any profit-sharing agreement, collateral-trust certificate, preorganization certificate or subscription, transferable share, investment contract, voting-trust certificate, certificate of deposit for a security, fractional undivided interest in oil, gas, or other mineral rights, any put, call, straddle, option, or privilege on any security, certificate of deposit, or group or index of securities (including any interest therein or based on the value thereof), or any put, call, straddle, option, or privilege entered into on a national securities exchange relating to foreign currency, or, in general, any interest or instrument commonly known as a "security," or any certificate of interest or participation in, temporary or interim certificate for, receipt for, guarantee of, or warrant or right to subscribe to or purchase, any of the foregoing.

Most of the terms in the definition refer to well-known stock trading contracts or legal certificates, but what is an "investment contract"? In *SEC v. W. J. Howey Co.,* 328 U.S. 293 (1946), the Supreme Court ruled that "an investment contract for purposes of the Securities Act means a contract, transaction or scheme whereby a person invests his money in a common enterprise and is led to expect profits solely from the efforts of the promoter or a third party." Since almost any investment qualifies as an "investment contract," lawyers need to pay attention to the various exemptions from the Securities Act of 1933 to determine if their clients can avoid the costly process of preparing a registration statement and prospectus.

Exemptions from the Securities Act of 1933

The Securities Act of 1933 exempts certain kinds of securities, certain kinds of issuers, and certain kinds of transactions from the requirement of filing a registration statement before sales begin and giving each potential investor a prospectus. Securities that are exempt may be sold without registration regardless of amount or the nature of the investor, and can be resold without restriction. Exempted securities include:

1. Commercial Paper. Any note, draft or banker's acceptance issued for working capital that has a maturity of not more than nine months when issued, provided the funds are only used for temporary financing.

2. Municipal Bonds. Securities guaranteed by domestic government organizations, like U.S. cities.

3. Nonprofit Securities. Securities of nonprofit or charitable organizations.

4. Common Carrier Securities. Certain securities issued by federally-regulated common carriers, like railroads.

5. Insurance Policies. Insurance policies and annuities issued by state-regulated insurance companies. An annuity is a contract to pay the policy holder a certain amount of money per year for the life of the policy holder, in return for a lump-sum payment to the insurance company at the start of the contract.

The issuers exempted from registration under the Securities Act of 1933 include companies in reorganization or debtors in bankruptcy that issue or exchange securities as part of a reorganization plan under court supervision, as well as to many exchanges of securities between an issuer and its pre-existing security holders. In these situations, it is felt that investors are less likely to be cheated due to bankruptcy court supervision or pre-existing experience with the issuer. Resales of these securities, however, require registration.

The most common exemptions from the registration requirements of the Securities Act of 1933 involve either sales under $5 million or sales to sophisticated investors. Such sophisticated investors are called "accredited investors" and include:

1. Financial Institutions. Banks, investment companies, insurance companies, savings and loan associations, employee pension plans with assets exceeding $5 million, and the executive management and directors of the issuing company.

2. Stock Brokers and Dealers. Securities trading professionals registered with the SEC.

3. High Net Worth Individuals. Persons whose net worth (assets minus liabilities) exceeds $1 million or who had an income in excess of $200,000 for the past two years and expect to have an income in excess of $200,000 this year also.

The details of each exemption are set out in a number of SEC Rules. The exemptions only apply to the first issuance of the security, and resales of the security must either be registered or benefit from another exemption. Securities issued using an exemption generally must carry a warning (usually printed in red) that they have not been registered and cannot be resold without registration or via another exemption. The SEC must be informed of securities issued under exemptions provided by SEC Rules.

Scope of the Securities Exchange Act of 1934

The Securities Exchange Act of 1934 focuses on the resale or trading of securities on stock exchanges. In addition to preventing fraud and manipulation of unsophisticated investors, the 1934 Act creates disclosure requirements that publicly-held companies must meet. The 1934 Act also regulates proxy solicitations, tender offers and communications with shareholders so that investors receive information from all sides of an issue affecting the corporation.

An "insider" is someone inside an issuer of securities who has access to information about the issuer or the securities that is not available to the general public. The Securities Exchange Act authorizes the SEC and the courts to punish insiders who take certain actions in regard to the issuer or its securities. Depending on the violation, civil penalties can include the insider being forced to pay back all profits on a trade, and, in addition, being fined up to three times the profit gained or loss avoided as a result of the unlawful trade. The Securities Exchange Act authorizes criminal penalties for most violations. For example, individuals can be fined up to $5 million and/or be imprisoned for up to twenty years. Moreover, juristic persons (such as corporations that have an existence under the law apart from the natural persons that own and/or manage them) may be fined up to $25 million.

Section 16(b) of the Securities Exchange Act makes directors, officers and shareholders owning more than ten percent of the stock of an issuer liable for "short swing" trades. A "short swing" trade is a purchase of the issuer's stock followed by a sale within six months from the date of purchase, or a sale of the issuer's stock followed by a purchase within six months from the date of sale.

Section 10(b) of the Securities Exchange Act makes it illegal to use any manipulation or fraud, or to make any untrue statement or omit any material fact, in the purchase or sale of any security. Rule 10b-5 makes insiders who have nonpublic material information and who trade on that information subject to being sued and/or prosecuted for violation of the Securities Exchange Act. Insiders, who must keep material nonpublic information confidential without trading on that information, include not only directors, officers and shareholders, but also persons who gain confidential information while assisting the issuer. Such extended insiders include agents of the corporation, professional advisors (lawyers, accountants, investment bankers, underwriters and consultants), and, in some cases, a person outside the corporation ("tippees") who receive confidential information from insiders.

In *United States v. O'Hagan,* 521 U.S. 642 (1997), O'Hagan was a partner in a law firm. Grand Metropolitan ("Grand Met"), a company based in England, retained O'Hagan's law firm as local counsel to represent Grand Met regarding a potential tender offer for the common stock of the Pillsbury Company. Both Grand Met and the law firm took precautions to protect the confidentiality of Grand Met's tender offer plans. O'Hagan did no work on the Grand Met case. In August, while other partners at his law firm were representing Grand Met, O'Hagan began trading Pillsbury options and stock. When Grand Met announced its tender offer, O'Hagan then sold his Pillsbury options and common stock, making a profit of more than $4.3 million. The SEC had a criminal indictment brought against O'Hagan, and a jury sentenced him to forty-one months in prison. However, the federal appeals court reversed O'Hagan's conviction for violating Rule 10b-5 on the ground that O'Hagan was not an "insider" at Pillsbury and, therefore, did not have any relationship of trust with Pillsbury. The Supreme Court ruled that O'Hagan's conviction should remain in place because it is possible to justify Rule 10b-5 both under a "classic" theory of breach of duty by an insider, and under a theory of "misappropriation" of property that belonged to the issuer, Pillsbury. In addition to his criminal conviction, O'Hagan was disbarred (disqualified) as an attorney in Minnesota.

The Sarbanes-Oxley Act

The general regulatory philosophy of the past thirty years in the United States has been to allow companies considerable freedom of action, but to enact tough laws when scandals seem to demonstrate that companies have abused their freedom. One widely-reported scandal involved the Enron Corporation. Although Enron was a public corporation, its accountants and lawyers allowed it to hide corporate funds in secret overseas subsidiaries. In another set of scandals, Wall Street stock analysts publicly recommended financially weak companies while privately calling the companies "garbage stock" and helping the investment banking portion of their company make money dumping the stock on unsuspecting individual investors. In response to these abuses, Congress passed as a supplement to the Securities Exchange Act known as the Sarbanes-Oxley Act of 2002 ("SOX").

SOX applies to any company that issues public securities in the United States and files reports with the SEC. This includes companies headquartered outside of the United States. SOX also applies to any public accounting firm, including firms located outside the United States, that prepares an audit report for any issuer of stock subject to the SEC, and to any lawyer anywhere who advises an issuer subject to SOX. SOX exempts foreign companies that only engage in private placements in the United States and lawyers who practice outside the United States and confine their work to local law not including U.S. securities law. Violations of SOX are punished strictly, and the law provides for up to twenty-five years in prison for securities fraud. For a company subject to SOX, there are many layers of corporate responsibility:

1. Board of Directors. The Board must create an audit committee. If the company fails to create a qualified audit committee, it can be removed from trading on public stock exchanges. Every member of the audit committee must be independent (not affiliated with the company) and can only earn fees as a member of the audit committee rather than as a consultant to the company. The audit committee must have at least one "financial expert," a person with experience in preparing and understanding financial statements prepared according to generally accepted accounting principles ("GAAP") in the United States. The "financial expert" must also understand internal audit controls, and so experience as a Chief Financial Officer or Certified Public Accountant is effectively required. The audit committee has the power to hire, at the company's cost, lawyers, accountants, and professional advisors without prior approval of the Board. Since SOX was partially a reaction to scandals involving accounting firms that disregarded audit violations in order to retain profitable consulting contracts, the audit committee must approve in advance any permitted services other than auditing (such as tax preparation) by any accounting firm. The directors must also create and maintain a code of ethics for senior financial officers that prevents conflicts of interest and that requires full and fair disclosure of personal transactions.

Senior officers must also inform the audit committee of any problems with the internal controls or of any fraud that has been discovered. The board must also establish procedures that allow employees at any level to report illegal acts by the company in confidence and without fear of losing their jobs as a result of "blowing the whistle" and alerting the board to wrongdoing. SOX provides that a company cannot fire, demote, suspend, threaten or discriminate against an employee who reports illegal acts, and allows employees to sue the company for damages and attorney fees if they suffer retaliation for "whistle blowing." Officers who retaliate against a "whistle blower" are also subject to criminal penalties of up to twenty years in prison.

2. Chief Executive Officer (CEO) and Chief Financial Officer (CFO). The CEO and the CFO must certify (1) that the annual and quarterly reports are accurate and not misleading; (2) that internal controls are in place to make material information available during the time when financial reports are being prepared; and (3) that the internal con-

trols have been tested in the past ninety days and are either satisfactory or have been improved as stated. If there is any misconduct by the corporation happening within twelve months of the company's initial public offering, or within twelve months of the CEO's or CFO's receiving a bonus, the CEO and/or the CFO must return the bonus and any profits from trading in company stock during that period. Publicly traded companies no longer can make personal loans to directors or officers, except on market terms and at market interest.

3. Accounting Firms. SOX makes corporate auditors subject to the supervision of a government regulatory board for the accounting profession. Auditors are disqualified if the CEO or CFO worked for the auditor within the year before joining the client corporation. Auditors cannot provide non-audit services like bookkeeping, financial information systems, appraisals, fairness opinions, actuarial services, management consulting, investment advice or legal services, but they may provide tax services. The corporation's auditors must independently assess internal controls every year.

4. Lawyers. Both in-house lawyers and outside counsel for the issuer are required by SOX to report to the CEO or to the top in-house lawyer any material violations of securities laws or fiduciary breaches they discover. If corporate officers do not take prompt action, lawyers must report the problem to the audit committee or the board as a whole. A "noisy withdrawal" obligation now requires a lawyer whose report on violations or breaches has been ignored to notify the SEC that the lawyer is withdrawing from representing the company "for professional considerations," and that he or she does not take any responsibility for filings with the SEC that contain false or misleading information. This obligation conflicts with duties under the traditional attorney-client privilege, whereby ethical rules in most states require attorneys to preserve client confidences (discussed in Chapter 3). Such a "noisy withdrawal" would almost certainly invite an SEC investigation of the client.

5. Stock Analysts. Brokerage houses and investment banks are required by SOX to separate the part of their business that gives advice to traders (the stock analysts) from the part of their business that trades the stock for its own account (the investment bank or brokerage house). Analysts must disclose any compensation received from the company being analyzed. This new requirement makes it less likely that investors in the future will be misled by a supposedly "independent" analyst who was in fact paid by a company to recommend purchase of that company's stock.

The Foreign Corrupt Practices Act

According to a 2009 survey by the nonprofit organization Transparency International, there are only eighteen foreign countries with business practices at least as honest as those of the United States, and over 160 countries that are more corrupt. In much of the world, it is difficult or impossible to do business without bribes to the ruling family, secret commissions to the generals in charge, or hidden "grease payments" to local government officials to issue documents or approve shipments. Although the United States is not rated as the least corrupt country in the world (that honor, in the 2009 survey, went to New Zealand), it has long been perhaps the most vigorous in exporting its own ethics. The United States passed the Foreign Corrupt Practices Act (FCPA) in 1977 as a supplement to the Securities and Exchange Act. The FCPA makes it illegal for a U.S. corporation, its officers, directors, employees, or agents to give anything of value to a foreign official to cause the foreign official to do something, refrain from doing something, or to use his influence to help the U.S. company get business. A promise to pay the foreign official is a violation of the FCPA even if the payment is not accepted or the foreign official does not help the U.S. company. In 1988, the FCPA was amended to state that it was not illegal to make (1) routine payments of small amounts for actions that do not involve discretion on the part of the foreign official ("grease payments" for taking actions that the official is actually required by local law to take), or (2) payments that are not illegal under the law of the foreign country.

In 1997, the United States signed the Organization for Economic Cooperation and Development (OECD) Convention on Combating Bribery of Foreign Public Officials in International Business Transactions along with thirty-seven other advanced industrial nations. As a result, most of the major commercial competitors of U.S. companies are now bound by some kind of legislation against bribery in their own countries. In 1998, Congress amended the FCPA again with the International Anti-Bribery and Fair Competition Act, which subjects to the FCPA's penalties certain foreign persons and officials of public international organizations.

Antitrust Laws

The Sherman Act and the Clayton Antitrust Act

In 1890, Congress decided to outlaw the "robber baron" business tactics of Rockefeller and other monopoly makers. Congress declared in the first two sections of the Sherman Antitrust Act that:

> Section 1. Every contract, combination in the form of trust or otherwise, or conspiracy, in restraint of trade or commerce among the several States, or with foreign nations, is declared to be illegal. Every person who shall make any contract or engage in any combination or conspiracy hereby declared to be illegal shall be deemed guilty of a felony ...

> Section 2. Every person who shall monopolize, or attempt to monopolize, or combine or conspire with any other person or persons, to monopolize any part of the trade or commerce among the several States, or with foreign nations, shall be deemed guilty of a felony.

In 1914, Congress passed the Clayton Antitrust Act, which deals with price discrimination, tying, market allocation and mergers. The Clayton Act provides that

> ... any person who shall be injured in his business or property by reason of anything forbidden in the antitrust laws may sue therefor in any district court of the United States in the district in which the defendant resides or is found or has an agent, without respect to the amount in controversy, and shall recover threefold the damages by him sustained, and the cost of suit, including a reasonable attorney's fee.

The result of the Sherman and Clayton Acts, and later antitrust laws, has been to create a huge amount of litigation as individuals and corporations act as "private attorneys general" to sue for three times the damage they have suffered due to unfair competition. In contrast to most other nations, the United States authorizes private parties to sue for antitrust violations, thereby providing more protection for fair competition than would occur if antitrust lawsuits could only be started by slow-moving, resource-limited, central government bureaucrats. U.S. courts, however, recognizing that every business seeks to limit competition from its rivals, have struggled to determine the limits of fair competition short of following the text of the Sherman Act and declaring that "every contract" that limits competition is illegal. Antitrust law has become a complicated blend of economic and business theory, government regulation, and case law that requires hundreds of pages to explain in detail. Therefore, the discussion that follows just presents the highlights.

Exemptions from the Antitrust Laws

There are a number of statutory exemptions from the antitrust laws. The holder of certain intellectual property rights, like patent; copyright; or trademark rights, may stop competitors from using that intellectual property. The Webb-Pomerene Act allows industries to obtain permission to form export cooperatives to develop commerce outside of the United States. The National Cooperative Research and Production Act encourages competitors to apply for clearance to operate joint research programs in areas that require cooperative efforts to yield major new technology. Labor unions, agricultural cooperatives, the insurance business, export cartels, airlines operating under orders from aviation control authorities, and professional sports teams all have special exemptions from the antitrust laws.

Interpretation of the Antitrust Laws

The Sherman Act does not automatically make a monopoly illegal. To violate the Sherman Act, one must engage in some "combination" or "conspiracy" to reduce competition. For example, if a software company has 95% of a given market because customers feel it has a clearly superior product, the existence of a near-monopoly would not necessarily be an antitrust law violation. However, if testimony showed that the software company, in order to preserve its 95% share, pressured its suppliers and customers to "cut off the oxygen" to a rival company, the software company might well be found to have violated the Sherman Act or other antitrust laws. Would the software company be seen as violating the antitrust laws if it petitioned state or national government for laws making it much harder for competitors to enter the market? Under the "Noerr-Pennington Doctrine," named after the two leading cases on the topic, the courts have decided that a genuine attempt to petition one's government for action does not constitute illegal action even if the purpose is to reduce competition.

After a short period in the late 1800s when courts interpreted the Sherman Act literally to find "every combination" in restraint of trade to be illegal, the courts came to distinguish between practices that are *per se* (meaning "by itself") violations and "rule of reason" practices. *Per se* violations are business practices that the courts believe are so unlikely to promote competition, and so likely to promote monopoly, that courts do not have to conduct an additional competitive analysis of the market to determine guilt. *Per se* violations are by themselves instant violations of the antitrust laws. Rule of Reason practices, however, are business practices that may or may not have an anticompetitive effect, and the court must examine in detail the market and the reasonableness of the practice when balanced against its effects on competition. Courts further distinguish between practices that affect "vertical" chains of commerce (for example, from manufacturer to wholesale distributor to retail store) and "horizontal" layers of commerce (for example, among competing manufacturers of a product or competing wholesale distributors of a product).

Price fixing is an attempt by one party to a contract to specify the price at which a product is sold or resold. For example, all of the competing manufacturers of a product agree not to sell that product to any wholesale distributor for less than a specified minimum price. An agreement among competitors to fix prices remains a per se violation of US antitrust laws. However, it often happens that a manufacturer tries to control the end price of a product by telling its wholesalers and retailers that they will not be given any more product if they sell the product below a specified minimum price (known as "resale price maintenance"). The Supreme Court decided in 1911 that resale price maintenance was a *per se* violation, but, in *Leegin Creative Leather Prods. v. PSKS, Inc.*, 551 U.S. 877 (2007), this nearly century-old decision was overruled. The Court concluded in *Leegin* that, since price restraints in a vertical chain of commerce are likely to promote competition between brands that deliver high service at a high price and brands that offer less service at a lower price, vertical price restraints are subject to a Rule of Reason analysis.

The major categories of *per se* violations remaining are:

1. Concerted Refusal To Deal. An organization can refuse to deal with any supplier or customer without violating the antitrust laws so long as the refusal is independent of an agreement with other organizations in the business. However, when a group of businesses decide to "shut out" or "boycott" another member of the industry, a *per se* violation is likely to be found. The classic cases are those in which existing members of an industry decide together to refuse to deal with a newcomer to the industry, or with a member that wants to sell at a lower price or via new distribution channels.

2. Market Allocation Agreements. Market allocation agreements are illegal at the horizontal level, for example if two competing automobile manufacturers agree that one will market only in states west of the Mississippi River and the other will market only in states east of the Mississippi River. However, it is very common for manufacturers and other top-level suppliers to try to create a rational supply system by allocating territories to distributors or retail stores. Territories can promote competitive goals, such as making sure that customers in all areas of the country have access to the product, or in making sure that distributors or retailers have enough of a customer base that they can maintain certain quality or service levels. For example, if a maker of luxury cars did not allocate territories, and did not require distributors and retailers to sell only in the allocated territories, it is possible that, even with totally free competition, all the distributors would end up in a few major cities with lots of rich people. Within the major cities, competition might be so severe that car distributors might try to save money by not performing adequate quality checks, and car retailers might try to save money by hiring poorly-trained mechanics because they were cheaper. Outside the major cities, a possible result would be that customers would not be able to either buy cars or have them properly serviced. Therefore, in recent years courts have applied a "Rule of Reason" test to vertical market allocation agreements, which may benefit competition or other public policies, while continuing to view most horizontal market allocation agreements as *per se* illegal.

3. Tying. Tying is the practice of forcing a customer to buy a second product or service if the customer wants to buy the first product or service. Common situations are those of requiring a customer who wants to buy a machine to also buy a maintenance contract from the manufacturer of the machine, to buy spare parts exclusively from the manufacturer of the machine, or to buy a machine the customer does not want in order

to be able to buy the machine the customer desires. Tying is generally still seen as a *per se* violation of the antitrust laws.

What Is the Market?

When a company is accused by a competitor or the U.S. government of monopolizing a market, there is often a battle between the parties to define the market. In *U.S. v. E.I. du Pont*, the government accused the du Pont chemical company of creating a monopoly in violation of section 2 of the Sherman Act because du Pont had 75% of the market for cellophane tape, a transparent adhesive tape. Du Pont lost in the district court, but won in the appeals court with the argument that the proper market was that of "flexible packaging materials." Du Pont had only 20% of the flexible packaging materials market, too small a share, it argued, to be guilty of monopolizing the market.

United States v. E.I. du Pont de Nemours & Co.
351 U.S. 377 (1956)

Reed, J.

The Government contends that, by dominating cellophane production, du Pont monopolized a "part of the trade or commerce." The court below found that the "relevant market for determining the extent of du Pont's market control is the market for flexible packaging materials," and that competition from those other materials prevented du Pont from possessing monopoly powers in its sales of cellophane.

This Court must determine whether the trial court erred in its estimate of the competition afforded cellophane by other materials. The burden of proof, of course, was upon the Government to establish monopoly.

The Government makes no challenge ... that cellophane furnishes less than 7% of wrappings for bakery products, 25% for candy, 32% for snacks, 35% for meats and poultry, 27% for crackers and biscuits, 47% for fresh produce, and 34% for frozen foods. Thus, cellophane shares the packaging market with others. The over-all result is that cellophane accounts for 17.9% of flexible wrapping materials, measured by the wrapping surface.

An element for consideration as to cross-elasticity of demand between products is the responsiveness of the sales of one product to price changes of the other. If a slight decrease in the price of cellophane causes a considerable number of customers of other flexible wrappings to switch to cellophane, it would be an indication that a high cross-elasticity of demand exists between them; that the products compete in the same market. The court below held that the "great sensitivity of customers in the flexible packaging markets to price or quality changes" prevented du Pont from possessing monopoly control over price.... We conclude that cellophane's interchangeability with the other materials mentioned suffices to make it a part of this flexible packaging material market.

The "market" which one must study to determine when a producer has monopoly power will vary with the part of commerce under consideration. The tests are constant. That market is composed of products that have reasonable interchangeability for the purposes for which they are produced—price, use and qualities considered. While the application of the tests remains uncertain, it seems to us that du Pont should not be found to monopolize cellophane when that product has the competition and interchangeability with other wrappings that this record shows.

* * *

Topics for Further Discussion

1. Is the "market" test of competitive effect too complicated?
2. What does the Court say is the relationship between cross-elasticity and price?

Conscious Parallelism

Just as the antitrust laws are not always violated when a competitor like du Pont has a large share of the market, monopolization is not demonstrated merely because every competitor in the industry adopts similar prices. Companies will often meet the price of their competitors without engaging in a conspiracy to fix prices or restrain trade. This business practice, called "conscious parallelism," can be a sign of vigorous competition in a market where no single competitor can control prices. A classic example is when several gasoline stations at an intersection post the same price. While it is true that none of the gasoline station operators can control the price or where their customers choose to buy gas, when the operators look at the station next door they may see a lower price. Such owners will often believe that customers will ignore their stations and go to the least expensive seller unless they meet the lowest price. In most cases the gasoline station operators sell different brands of gasoline and are unlikely even to talk to their neighboring competitors, let alone try to conspire with that competitor.

Mergers and Acquisitions

Section 7 of the Clayton Act makes it a violation of the antitrust laws to acquire stock or assets of another company "where in any line of commerce or in any activity affecting commerce in any section of the country, the effect of such acquisition may be substantially to lessen competition, or to tend to create a monopoly." For many years, mergers between large corporations would proceed and then be attacked in the courts as antitrust violations. In 1976, the Hart-Scott-Rodino Act created a system of prior screening by the U.S. Department of Justice and the Fair Trade Commission that allows companies to know before they complete a merger whether the government will attack the merger as an antitrust violation. Companies hoping to receive a favorable review often file hundreds of pages of business and economic analysis arguing that the proposed merger is between competitors in completely different markets and their merger will not reduce competition.

Other Antitrust Laws

The Federal Trade Commission Act of 1914 created an independent agency, the Federal Trade Commission (FTC), and gives it the power to prevent competitors "from using unfair methods of competition in or affecting commerce and unfair or deceptive acts or practices in or affecting commerce." The FTC is active in preventing consumer fraud, but also has jurisdiction over any "unfair" method of competition. The Robinson-Patman

Act of 1936 makes it unlawful "to discriminate in price between different purchasers of commodities of like grade and quality." The intent of the Robinson-Patman Act was to prevent large, national buyers or sellers from squeezing small local or regional competitors out of business through price discrimination. Two defenses are set up in the Robinson-Patman Act. First, that the price discrimination is the result of differences in the cost of manufacture, sale or delivery resulting from different methods or quantities of sale or delivery. The second defense is that the seller thought in good faith that it had to lower prices for, or furnish services to, one customer but not the other in order to meet competition. As one might expect, businesses that must purchase the same product or service at a higher price than their competitors are quick to claim antitrust law violations, and the broad language of the Robinson-Patman Act keeps courts busy writing clarifying opinions.

The International Reach of U.S. Antitrust Laws

Actions outside the United States that reduce competition in the United States have been subject to U.S. antitrust laws since the Sherman Act extended itself to "restraints of trade or commerce" involving "foreign nations." The two chief antitrust enforcement agencies, the Department of Justice and the Federal Trade Commission, issue "Antitrust Guidelines for International Operations" that outline situations in which international activities might be investigated as antitrust violations. Almost as old as the Sherman Act is the judicial conclusion that U.S. antitrust law does not extend to actions that are entirely outside of the United States and do not produce any domestic effects.

Since foreign competitors caught in U.S. antitrust enforcement actions and fined treble damages regularly complain loudly to their own governments, Congress has occasionally tried to clarify when foreign companies should be subject to U.S. antitrust enforcement. Unfortunately, the complexity and constantly changing nature of international trade means that no law can completely clarify every situation. In 2004, the Supreme Court had to decide whether an Ecuadorian buyer of vitamins could sue in U.S courts under U.S. antitrust laws because anticompetitive actions in the United States and other countries had raised the price of vitamins to the buyer in Ecuador.

F. Hoffman-La Roche Ltd. v. Empagran S.A.
542 U.S. 155 (2004)

Breyer, J.

The Foreign Trade Antitrust Improvements Act of 1982 (FTAIA) excludes from the Sherman Act's reach much anticompetitive conduct that causes only foreign injury. It does so by setting forth a general rule stating that the Sherman Act "shall not apply to conduct involving trade or commerce ... with foreign nations." It then creates exceptions to the general rule, applicable where (roughly speaking) that conduct significantly harms imports, domestic commerce, or American exporters.

We here focus upon anticompetitive price-fixing activity that is in significant part foreign, that causes some domestic antitrust injury, and that independently causes separate foreign injury. We ask two questions about the price-fixing conduct and the foreign injury that it causes. First, does that conduct fall within the FTAIA's general rule excluding the Sherman Act's application? That is to say, does the price-fixing activity constitute "conduct involving trade or commerce ... with foreign nations"? We conclude that it does.

Second, we ask whether the conduct nonetheless falls within a domestic-injury exception to the general rule, an exception that applies (and makes the Sherman Act nonetheless applicable) where the conduct (1) has a "direct, substantial, and reasonably foreseeable effect" on domestic commerce, and (2) "such effect gives rise to a [Sherman Act] claim." We conclude that the exception does not apply where the plaintiff's claim rests solely on the independent foreign harm.

To clarify: The issue before us concerns (1) significant foreign anticompetitive conduct with (2) an adverse domestic effect and (3) an independent foreign effect giving rise to the claim. In more concrete terms, this case involves vitamin sellers around the world that agreed to fix prices, leading to higher vitamin prices in the United States and independently leading to higher vitamin prices in other countries such as Ecuador. We conclude that, in this scenario, a purchaser in the United States could bring a Sherman Act claim under the FTAIA based on domestic injury, but a purchaser in Ecuador could not bring a Sherman Act claim based on foreign harm.

The plaintiffs in this case originally filed a class-action suit on behalf of foreign and domestic purchasers of vitamins under the Sherman Act. Their complaint alleged that petitioners, foreign and domestic vitamin manufacturers and distributors, had engaged in a price-fixing conspiracy, raising the price of vitamin products to customers in the United States and to customers in foreign countries.

The FTAIA ... initially lays down a general rule placing all (non-import) activity involving foreign commerce outside the Sherman Act's reach. It then brings such conduct back within the Sherman Act's reach provided that the conduct both (1) sufficiently affects American commerce, i.e., it has a "direct, substantial, and reasonably foreseeable effect" on American domestic, import, or (certain) export commerce, and (2) has an effect of a kind that antitrust law considers harmful.

No one denies that America's antitrust laws, when applied to foreign conduct, can interfere with a foreign nation's ability independently to regulate its own commercial affairs. But our courts have long held that application of our antitrust laws to foreign anticompetitive conduct is nonetheless reasonable, and hence consistent with principles of prescriptive comity, insofar as they reflect a legislative effort to redress domestic antitrust injury that foreign anticompetitive conduct has caused.

But why is it reasonable to apply those laws to foreign conduct insofar as that conduct causes independent foreign harm and that foreign harm alone gives rise to the plaintiff's claim?... Why should American law supplant, for example, Canada's or Great Britain's or Japan's own determination about how best to protect Canadian or British or Japanese customers from anticompetitive conduct engaged in significant part by Canadian or British or Japanese or other foreign companies?... We can find no good answer to the question.

Regardless, even where nations agree about primary conduct, say price fixing, they disagree dramatically about appropriate remedies. The application, for example, of American private treble-damages remedies to anticompetitive conduct taking place abroad has generated considerable controversy. And several foreign nations have filed briefs here arguing that to apply our remedies would unjustifiably permit their citizens to bypass their own less generous remedial schemes, thereby upsetting a balance of competing considerations that their own domestic antitrust laws embody.

Where foreign anticompetitive conduct plays a significant role and where foreign injury is independent of domestic effects, Congress might have hoped that America's antitrust

laws, so fundamental a component of our own economic system, would commend themselves to other nations as well. But, if America's antitrust policies could not win their own
way in the international marketplace for such ideas, Congress, we must assume, would
not have tried to impose them, in an act of legal imperialism, through legislative fiat.

* * *

Topics for Further Discussion

1. Suppose Empagran had used its U.S. subsidiary to buy the over-priced vitamins in
the U.S. and then ship them to Ecuador. Could Empagran sue under U.S. antitrust laws?
How about Empagran's U.S. subsidiary?

2. Would the U.S. have jurisdiction if the top three Japanese automakers were to conspire in Tokyo to fix the price of their new cars in the U.S.?

Bankruptcy

Cultural Philosophy

The United States has long been a country of fresh starts. In the beginning, immigrants leaving the Old World could start with a clean record in America. Later on, merchants who failed on the East Coast could start again in the frontier towns of the West.
Bankruptcy laws have been a part of U.S. culture since Congress was given the exclusive
power to create such laws by the Constitution. Unlike many other industrialized countries, the United States has historically tried to make it relatively easy for debtors to pay
off their creditors fairly, erase their debts, and attempt to recreate their fortunes without
further persecution by creditors or lasting damage to the debtor's social relations. For
much of U.S. history, creditors were located in the major cities while debtors were farmers and ranchers located in the Midwest and West. Many of the frontier states strongly dis-
trusted creditors in far-away cities; some states have provisions in their state constitution
requiring debtors to be allowed to keep their homestead, their horse (or automobile),
their tools of trade, professional books, clothing, disability and pension payments, etc.
State exemptions from seizure by creditors remain to this day, even if the "homestead" is
not a wooden hut without running water but a $25 million estate along the Florida
seashore. U.S. bankruptcy laws still generally forbid involuntary bankruptcy petitions
against individual farmers.

In addition, the American economy believes in risk taking, and the ability to fail is a
necessary part of risk taking. An entrepreneur can create a start-up corporation, solicit
funding, try to grow rich, and, if the entrepreneur fails, have the corporation declare
bankruptcy. An honest entrepreneur can walk away to start another corporation and try
again, perhaps with better luck. In contrast, other cultures require the entrepreneur to take
social responsibility for business failures. In some other countries, the corporate executive whose company goes bankrupt must hide from society, or, in extreme cases, may feel
compelled to commit suicide to make up for failing to pay his debts. Social exiles and
dead entrepreneurs do not found new companies.

Finally, in the United States there exist financial services companies willing to lend to
recently bankrupt debtors after compensating themselves for the higher risk by taking

more security and charging higher interest rates. Although a record of bankruptcy remains on a debtor's credit file for ten years, it is rare that an individual or corporate debtor has to wait that long for new credit.

A traditional definition of "insolvent" is "being unable to pay one's debts in the usual course of business." However, the U.S. Bankruptcy Code definition of "insolvent" for a person or private corporation is "a financial condition such that the sum of ... debts is greater than all ... property." In recent years, however, businesses in the United States have used bankruptcy proceedings to rid themselves of liabilities without necessarily being short of cash. For example, corporations have declared bankruptcy to rid themselves of huge potential tort liabilities (discussed in Chapter 7), such as claims by victims of asbestos inhalation from the company's products. Airlines have filed for bankruptcy to get rid of expensive contracts with union-wage employees. The United States allows these and other companies to "restructure" using the Bankruptcy Code on the theory that it is better for the economy to allow a company to reduce its liabilities and stay in business than to go out of business completely.

Bankruptcy Petitions

The Bankruptcy Code contains special provisions for certain types of businesses and municipal governments, but the discussion that follows applies generally (unless indicated) to corporations. A bankruptcy case begins with the filing of a petition in the federal district court with jurisdiction over the debtor. The Bankruptcy Code provides that federal district courts have original and exclusive jurisdiction over bankruptcy cases, and original, but not exclusive, jurisdiction over civil cases related to the bankruptcy proceedings. Federal district courts also have exclusive jurisdiction over the debtor's property, and the exclusive right to issue a final order or judgment in the bankruptcy case. The actual hearing of bankruptcy cases is handled by a "bankruptcy court" staffed by federal bankruptcy judges under the jurisdiction of the federal district court. Bankruptcy cases can be appealed like any other judgment to the circuit court that hears appeals from the district court.

The great majority of bankruptcy cases are voluntary, meaning that they are started by the debtor. Any debtor, whether insolvent or not, may file a voluntary petition for bankruptcy. The petition must list all creditors, all property the debtor owns, all property that the debtor claims is exempt from being divided up among creditors, and a statement of the debtor's financial situation.

An involuntary bankruptcy petition may be filed if there are eleven or fewer creditors, or where the total unsecured claims of one or more creditors are $14,425 or more. (The dollar amount reflects a process by which the claim amounts were set in 1998 at $10,000 and have been adjusted upward for inflation on April 1 every three years since 1998). If the debtor accepts the involuntary petition, the bankruptcy court will order bankruptcy relief for the debtor. If the debtor opposes the involuntary petition, the court may order bankruptcy relief against the debtor only (a) if the debtor is generally not paying debts as they become due or (b) within 120 days before the filing of the petition, a third party took possession of substantially all of the debtor's property to enforce a debt against the property.

An involuntary bankruptcy petition can only be filed under Chapter 7 or Chapter 11 of the Bankruptcy Code. "Chapter 7" bankruptcies are liquidations, i.e. the debtor's assets are liquidated, the proceeds are divided among creditors, and the debtor is discharged. A Chapter 7 bankruptcy usually means the end of a corporation. A "Chapter 11" bankruptcy, on the other hand, allows the corporation to be reorganized and continue if that is acceptable to creditors.

The Bankruptcy Trustee

The filing of a bankruptcy petition, whether voluntary or involuntary, operates as an "automatic stay" against creditors. This means that, from the moment the bankruptcy petition is accepted, a creditor cannot recover property from the debtor, enforce judgments against the debtor, or otherwise try to get payment or security for the debt except through bankruptcy proceedings. Any creditor that violates the stay can be ordered by the bankruptcy court to undo its action. This automatic stay procedure stops a race by creditors to grab the debtor's assets and forces all creditors into working out their claims at the bankruptcy court.

The property of the debtor is called the bankruptcy "estate." It includes all property, assets, and valuable rights of the debtor that are not subject to exemption. It also includes property the debtor receives within 180 days after filing the petition as a result of inheritance, property settlement, a divorce settlement, or property the debtor gains as the beneficiary of a life insurance policy. As discussed below, it also includes any assets or valuable rights that the trustee can bring into the estate. The bankruptcy court will select a trustee by vote of creditors in a Chapter 7 proceeding, and may in certain cases name a trustee in a Chapter 11 proceeding.

The bankruptcy trustee has a variety of duties and broad powers to carry out those duties. Trustees are, on the one hand, supervised by the bankruptcy judge and ultimately the federal district court. On the other hand, trustees are usually compensated based on a percentage of the value of the bankruptcy estate. Expenses of administration of the debtor's estate are paid before the claims of creditors without security (collateral) for their debts. With the stick of federal court supervision on one side, and the carrot of a percentage of asset value on the other side, trustees are usually motivated vigorously to increase the bankruptcy estate. The trustee must make a list of the property of the estate without including property subject to exemptions. The trustee must also receive a proof of claim from each creditor, or file such proof on behalf of a creditor, because only creditor claims that have been proven to a bankruptcy court can be satisfied and discharged in bankruptcy.

One of the characteristics of U.S. bankruptcy law is the ability of the trustee to accept or reject transfers of property away from the estate. The trustee can pull the property, or its value, back into the estate to be shared by all creditors. In order for the trustee to cancel a "voidable preference" of one creditor over another, the transfer must have been made: (1) to or for the benefit of a creditor; (2) for a debt owed by the debtor before the transfer was made; (3) while the debtor was insolvent; (4) within ninety days before the filing of the bankruptcy petition and not subject to an exemption; or (5) in such a manner as to allow the creditor to receive more than the creditor would receive under the Bankruptcy Code. If the transfer was to an insider, such as a relative or general partner of an individual debtor or a director or officer of a corporate debtor, the trustee can void preferences made up to one year before the filing of the bankruptcy petition. The trustee can also bring back property transferred due to "fraudulent transfers" within one year before the date of the filing of the bankruptcy petition. Transferring property to hide it from creditors is one kind of fraudulent transfer. Selling property at far less than fair value while insolvent is another common type of fraudulent transfer. Finally, the trustee has all of the powers of a hypothetical creditor with a judicial lien against the debtor that has not been satisfied. This means the trustee has superior rights to many creditors who did not complete all the steps needed to protect themselves before the bankruptcy petition was filed.

The trustee has the power to manage the estate. This includes using, selling, or renting property in the estate; employing professional advisors and agents; and investing or depositing money for the estate. The trustee also has the power to accept or reject any contract made by the debtor that has not been fully performed, and any lease signed by the debtor that has not expired. The trustee is also "subrogated" to the debtor's rights under any existing contract. This means that the trustee can use any rights the debtor had to collect payment. For example, if the debtor was a guarantor of A's debt to B and the debtor had to pay B because A failed to pay, the trustee can use the debtor's right of subrogation to sue A for repayment.

A Chapter 7 trustee will make a final report of the administration of the estate and a proposed plan for paying creditors at least some of the money they are owed, according to the order for distribution of assets specified by the Bankruptcy Code. The creditors may accept the trustee's recommendation, work as a committee of creditors to have the recommendation modified, or appeal to the bankruptcy court or, ultimately, to the federal court system to have the plan modified. If the plan is accepted, the bankruptcy court will order the debtor discharged, meaning legally relieved of all debts before the date of the bankruptcy discharge. A few kinds of debts cannot be discharged in bankruptcy. The major categories of debts that cannot be discharged in bankruptcy are taxes and fines due to the government; unlisted debts; debts due to criminal activity; and, for individuals, student loans, child support, and certain consumer loans made within sixty days of discharge.

Chapter 11 Bankruptcies

One often hears that a business is "in Chapter 11," meaning that it is reorganizing under Chapter 11 of the Bankruptcy Code. Once a bankruptcy petition requesting Chapter 11 status has been filed by an eligible debtor, a committee of unsecured creditors, and possibly other creditors, is appointed by the court. The committee may investigate the debtor's finances and participate in creating a plan of reorganization.

Chapter 11 is often called "debtor in possession" bankruptcy because normally a trustee is not required. The debtor corporation continues to manage its assets, often with the same management team that was in place when the debtor went bankrupt. In fact, corporations often file for bankruptcy under Chapter 11 because the management knows it will not be terminated, whereas a trustee in a Chapter 7 liquidation may work to replace managers who caused the problem. If the bankruptcy court is convinced that the debtor is being mismanaged, or is dishonest, or the appointment of a trustee is in the interest of creditors or shareholders, the court will appoint a trustee elected by the creditors.

For the first 120 days after a Chapter 11 petition is filed, only the debtor (meaning the management of a corporation) has the right to file a plan of reorganization. The plan of reorganization lists the debts, divides the claims into creditors' and shareholders' interests, classifies the debts, explains how each class will be treated, demonstrates that within each class each debtor is treated equally, and shows how the debtor has the ability to carry out the plan as stated. After 120 days, the creditors' committee or the trustee can propose a plan of reorganization in addition to the debtor.

The plan of reorganization binds all classes of creditors, shareholders, and the debtor. When the plan is confirmed by the court, and a final bankruptcy decree is made, the debtor is discharged. In order for a bankruptcy court to confirm a plan of reorganization, the court must agree that the plan has been proposed in good faith and can be carried out as stated. Next, the court must find either that an adequate number of classes of creditors and shareholders have accepted the plan of reorganization, or a reason exists to force creditors to accept the plan. Creditors and shareholders who do not have their legal rights changed under a plan are not "impaired" (damaged) and automatically accept the plan. A class of creditors or shareholders that has its legal rights adjusted or "impaired" under the plan accepts the plan if more than half of the members of that class, who also represent at least two-thirds of the value of the class in amount, accept the plan. What happens if creditors from various classes cannot agree on whether to approve the plan of reorganization? The bankruptcy court can "cram down" the plan, i.e., force it down the throats of all creditors and interests. The court can do so if the parties cannot agree, the court finds the plan of reorganization to be fair, and at least one "impaired" class has approved the plan.

Recent Trends in Bankruptcy Law

Since the 1980s, the consumer credit industry has used its political power to make it harder for individuals to be discharged in bankruptcy when they have borrowed too much. Congress remains reluctant, however, to make bankruptcy protection unavailable to individuals who are insolvent due to disaster or honest business failures. Chapter 11, originally used almost exclusively by publicly traded corporations, was expressly made available to small businesses in 1994. As a result, it is increasingly common to find oneself dealing with a corporation that, while technically bankrupt, appears to do "business as usual." The struggle is likely to continue between special interest groups that use their political power to limit the benefits of the Bankruptcy Code and those who wish to maintain the availability of bankruptcy as a complete new start for the financially exhausted.

Key Terms and Concepts

Business Judgment Rule
Fiduciary Duty
General Partnership
Horizontal Commerce
Insider Trading
Limited Partnership
Rule of Reason
Shareholder's Derivative Suit
Trustee
Vertical Commerce

Chapter 12

Marriage and the Family

"Since the common nature of all living creatures is to wish to continue their line, the first relationship is between husband and wife; the next, between parent and child; and then comes the household belonging to all. This is the origin of the city and the nursery of civil society."

Cicero, *De Officiis*, Book I (78 B.C.)

The institution of marriage is inextricably linked to the family and reproductive rights. These most basic human rights reside at the core of every society, and few areas of law generate more heated debate over fundamental social values. Whether the issue is the validity of same-sex marriage, abortion, the appropriateness of utilizing cutting edge technologies for cloning, stem cell research, or the birth of "test tube" babies, you can be sure that the opinions for and against each side will be heard loud and clear. In these debates, some see the changing patterns and lifestyles of American life as a threat to traditional values forming the bedrock of an orderly society. Others look at the same changes and proclaim that liberation is finally at hand and the long march of social progress is ready to provide all members of society with freedom of self-expression and self-actualization.

The one thing certain in this area is that values change with time. Not long ago women were considered to be property, and the notion they should have the right to enter into contracts, to choose their mates freely, or to vote was considered a serious threat to the social order. In the 1970s, some states made it illegal even to provide information about contraceptive devices and now some of those very devices are readily available over the counter and in vending machines.

The materials in this chapter are intended to explore some of these conflicts. When reading the materials, there are two underlying points you should bear in mind. First, the line between state and federal government jurisdiction is becoming increasingly blurred. Traditionally, marriage, family and reproduction were matters thought best left to local (and even individual), as opposed to national, regulation. The recent trend in litigation has been to ask courts to find fundamental rights in the Constitution to support emerging realities and alternative lifestyles. This trend has led to a conservative backlash against "activist" judges and has resulted in a regressive national and state legislative response as represented by the proposed Federal Marriage Amendment, the Defense of Marriage Act, and a plethora of state initiatives to protect "sacred" institutions. Second, as courts find constitutional protections, the ability of the majority to determine the parameters of acceptable social behavior through the democratic process erodes. This is not necessarily bad, as one of the most critical roles of the courts is to protect individual rights. Each reader should consider these issues while reading through the materials in this chapter, but you will have to draw your own conclusions as to what is right and moral in society.

Marriage

The formalities of marriage are a matter of state law, and states are given wide latitude to regulate this social institution. The law historically recognized two forms of marriage: ceremonial and common law. The first is accomplished when two people (traditionally, a man and a woman) officially take their marriage vows before an authorized official (usually a judge) or a member of the clergy authorized by law to perform marriages. Unlike civil law countries, the United States does not have a comprehensive family registration system. States do, however, require that the individuals be of a certain age (usually sixteen or over without parental consent), and have a valid marriage license before getting married. Marriage licenses are usually issued by the office of records located in the local city or town hall after the payment of a small administrative fee. The only requirements, apart from meeting the minimum age requirement, are that the parties submit to a blood test and not be in a prohibited range of blood relationship (degree of consanguinity), such as first cousins.

Judges, justices of the peace, clergy members, certain elected officials, and ship captains are legally qualified to marry people. The common law recognized that it was not always possible to conduct a wedding ceremony. Hence, the second form of marriage, the so-called common law marriage, came into effect. In order for there to be a valid common law marriage, the respective spouses need only utter words of a present intention to be married followed by behavior consistent with living in wedlock. The *Staudenmayer* case, and the notes that follow it, explain the roots of common law marriage and why it is gradually being eliminated by the states.

Traditional Values

For most of the existence of the U.S., people thought of marriage as a union between one man and one woman for life. Divorce was rare, and tolerance for other traditions even rarer. Bigamy (having two spouses at the same time) and polygamy (having multiple spouses at the same time) were considered crimes from the very beginning of the common law. In *Reynolds v. United States*, 98 U.S. 145 (1878), the Supreme Court was called upon to decide whether a *bona fide* religious belief in polygamy should outweigh the Territory of Utah's criminal laws preventing it. Utah desired to be admitted as a state and, as a condition of statehood, the elders of the Mormon Church agreed to revise the tenets of their religion to prohibit polygamy. George Reynolds, a practicing Mormon who rejected the decision of the elders, was charged with bigamy, in violation of Section 5352 of the Utah Revised Statutes, which provided, in relevant part, as follows: "Every person having a husband or wife living, who marries another, whether married or single, in a Territory, or other place over which the United States have exclusive jurisdiction, is guilty of bigamy, and shall be punished by a fine of not more than $500, and by imprisonment for a term of not more than five years."

At trial, Reynolds asserted that his First Amendment rights under the Free Exercise Clause should prevail over Utah's right to criminalize polygamy. Chief Justice Waite, writing for the Court, rejected the defense asserted by Reynolds and concluded as follows:

> Polygamy has always been odious among the northern and western nations of Europe, and, until the establishment of the Mormon Church, was almost exclusively a feature of the life of Asiatic and of African people. At common law, the second marriage was always void, and from the earliest history of England polygamy has been treated as an offence against society.

Marriage, while from its very nature a sacred obligation, is nevertheless, in most civilized nations, a civil contract, and usually regulated by law. Upon it society may be said to be built, and out of its fruits spring social relations and social obligations and duties, with which government is necessarily required to deal. In fact, according as monogamous or polygamous marriages are allowed, do we find the principles on which the government of the people, to a greater or less extent, rests.

In our opinion, the statute immediately under consideration is within the legislative power of Congress. It is constitutional and valid as prescribing a rule of action for all those residing in the Territories, and in places over which the United States have exclusive control. This being so, the only question which remains is, whether those who make polygamy a part of their religion are excepted from the operation of the statute. If they are, then those who do not make polygamy a part of their religious belief may be found guilty and punished, while those who do, must be acquitted and go free. This would be introducing a new element into criminal law. Laws are made for the government of actions, and while they cannot interfere with mere religious belief and opinions, they may with practices. Suppose one believed that human sacrifices were a necessary part of religious worship, would it be seriously contended that the civil government under which he lived could not interfere to prevent a sacrifice? Or if a wife religiously believed it was her duty to burn herself upon the funeral pile of her dead husband, would it be beyond the power of the civil government to prevent her carrying her belief into practice?

So here, as a law of the organization of society under the exclusive dominion of the United States, it is provided that plural marriages shall not be allowed. Can a man excuse his practices to the contrary because of his religious belief? To permit this would be to make the professed doctrines of religious belief superior to the law of the land, and in effect to permit every citizen to become a law unto himself. Government could exist only in name under such circumstances.

The *Loving* case, decided nearly 100 years after *Reynolds*, and the passage of the Fourteenth Amendment arose out of efforts by segregationists to prevent interracial marriages through miscegenation laws. In 1958, two residents of Virginia, Richard Loving, a white man, and Mildred Jeter, an African-American woman, were married in the District of Columbia. They moved back to Virginia and were arrested for violating the Virginia's ban on interracial marriages. The Lovings pleaded guilty, and were given a twenty-five year suspended sentence on the condition that they leave Virginia and not return for twenty-five years. The trial judge remarked that: "Almighty God created the races white, black, yellow, malay and red, and he placed them on separate continents. And but for the interference with his arrangement there would be no cause for such marriages. The fact that he separated the races shows that he did not intend for the races to mix." In 1963, they filed a motion in state court to throw out the earlier judgment and sentence as being in violation of the Fourteenth Amendment, eventually ending up before the Supreme Court.

Loving v. Virginia
388 U.S. 1 (1967)

Warren, C.J.

This case presents a constitutional question never addressed by this Court: whether a statutory scheme adopted by the State of Virginia to prevent marriages between persons solely on the basis of racial classifications violates the Equal Protection and Due Process Clauses of the Fourteenth Amendment. For reasons which seem to us to reflect the central meaning of those constitutional commands, we conclude that these statutes cannot stand consistently with the Fourteenth Amendment.

Virginia is now one of 16 States which prohibit and punish marriages on the basis of racial classifications. Penalties for miscegenation arose as an incident to slavery and have been common in Virginia since the colonial period. The central features of this Act, and current Virginia law, are the absolute prohibition of a "white person" marrying other than another "white person," a prohibition against issuing marriage licenses until the issuing official is satisfied that the applicants' statements as to their race are correct, certificates of "racial composition" to be kept by both local and state registrars, and the carrying forward of earlier prohibitions against racial intermarriage.

I

While the state court is no doubt correct in asserting that marriage is a social relation subject to the State's police power, the State does not contend in its argument before this Court that its powers to regulate marriage are unlimited notwithstanding the commands of the Fourteenth Amendment. Instead, the State argues that the meaning of the Equal Protection Clause, as illuminated by the statements of the Framers, is only that state penal laws containing an interracial element as part of the definition of the offense must apply equally to whites and Negroes in the sense that members of each race are punished to the same degree. Thus, the State contends that, because its miscegenation statutes punish equally both the white and the Negro participants in an interracial marriage, these statutes, despite their reliance on racial classifications, do not constitute an invidious discrimination based upon race. The second argument advanced by the State assumes the validity of its equal application theory. The argument is that, if the Equal Protection Clause does not outlaw miscegenation statutes because of their reliance on racial classifications, the question of constitutionality would thus become whether there was any rational basis for a State to treat interracial marriages differently from other marriages. On this question, the State argues, the scientific evidence is substantially in doubt and, consequently, this Court should defer to the wisdom of the state legislature in adopting its policy of discouraging interracial marriages.

Because we reject the notion that the mere "equal application" of a statute containing racial classifications is enough to remove the classifications from the Fourteenth Amendment's proscription of all invidious racial discriminations, we do not accept the State's contention that these statutes should be upheld if there is any possible basis for concluding that they serve a rational purpose.

There is patently no legitimate overriding purpose independent of invidious racial discrimination which justifies this classification. The fact that Virginia prohibits only interracial marriages involving white persons demonstrates that the racial classifications must stand on their own justification, as measures designed to maintain White Supremacy. We have consistently denied the constitutionality of measures which restrict the rights of citizens on account of race. There can be no doubt that restricting the freedom to marry solely because of racial classifications violates the central meaning of the Equal Protection Clause.

II

These statutes also deprive the Lovings of liberty without due process of law in violation of the Due Process Clause of the Fourteenth Amendment. The freedom to marry has long been recognized as one of the vital personal rights essential to the orderly pursuit of happiness by free men.

Marriage is one of the "basic civil rights of man," fundamental to our very existence and survival. To deny this fundamental freedom on so unsupportable a basis as the racial classifications embodied in these statutes, classifications so directly subversive of the principle of equality at the heart of the Fourteenth Amendment, is surely to deprive all the State's citizens of liberty without due process of law. The Fourteenth Amendment requires that the freedom of choice to marry not be restricted by invidious racial discriminations. Under our Constitution, the freedom to marry, or not marry, a person of another race resides with the individual and cannot be infringed by the State.

* * *

Topics for Further Discussion

1. The *Reynolds* case clearly rejected the practice of polygamy in the United States, even when it was supported by a *bona fide* religious belief, because it was the will of the majority to make monogamy the law of Utah. Is that a fair statement when Utah was required to change its laws, and the Mormons their religious beliefs, in order to obtain statehood? Is it convincing to compare polygamy with human sacrifice? What social harm would follow from allowing people with a *bona fide* religious belief in polygamy to practice their religion? A review of the Free Exercise Clause section in Chapter 4 may help to answer these questions.

2. The Court in *Loving* made it clear that miscegenation laws are unconstitutional under both the Equal Protection Clause and the Due Process Clause. Recollect that the *Loving* case was cited in *Lawrence v. Texas* for the proposition that mere equality of treatment among two or more disparate groups will not always save a statute. Do you think that the *Reynolds* opinion continues to represent good law in light of *Lawrence*?

Common Law Marriage

A small number of states recognize what are known as common law or de facto marriages. A common law marriage is one that comes into being without a ceremony of any kind, and simply by two parties declaring themselves to be husband and wife before acting in a manner consistent with being married. Few formalities are required to create a common law marriage beyond having the legal capacity to marry followed by the uttering words of present intention to be married and cohabitation. Words that indicate only a future intention to marry are not sufficient. Common law marriages are inherently suspect because they can lead to fraud, especially in cases where one of the alleged spouses dies and the other seeks rights, privileges, and benefits as a legal spouse.

The *Staudenmayer* case arose in the context of a property settlement following divorce. The Staudenmayers lived together for a number of years before getting married in a civil ceremony. During the time they were living together, but before getting married, Theodore Staudenmayer was injured at work and received a structured tort settlement. When the Staudenmayers got divorced, Linda Staudenmayer claimed that Theodore's structured tort settlement should be the subject of equitable distribution in the divorce proceedings since it occurred during the period the couple lived together in a common law marriage.

Staudenmayer v. Staudenmayer
714 A.2d 1016 (Pa. 1998)

Newman, J.

This case presents the issue of whether the Superior Court erred when it reversed the trial court and found the existence of a common law marriage prior to a ceremonial marriage between the parties. We reverse and reinstate the trial court's conclusion that the parties were not married prior to their ceremonial marriage.

Marriage in Pennsylvania is a civil contract by which a man and a woman take each other for husband and wife. There are two kinds of marriage: (1) ceremonial; and (2) common law. A ceremonial marriage is a wedding or marriage performed by a religious or civil authority with the usual or customary ceremony or formalities.

Because claims for the existence of a marriage in the absence of a certified ceremonial marriage present a "fruitful source of perjury and fraud," Pennsylvania courts have long viewed such claims with hostility. Common law marriages are tolerated, but not encouraged. While we do not today abolish common law marriages in Pennsylvania, we reaffirm that claims for this type of marriage are disfavored.

A common law marriage can only be created by an exchange of words in the present tense [*verba in praesenti*], spoken with the specific purpose that the legal relationship of husband and wife is created by that.

The burden to prove the marriage is on the party alleging a marriage, and we have described this as a "heavy" burden where there is an allegation of a common law marriage. When an attempt is made to establish a marriage without the usual formalities, the claim must be reviewed with "great scrutiny."

Generally, words in the present tense are required to prove common law marriage. Because common law marriage cases arose most frequently because of claims for a putative surviving spouse's share of an estate, however, we developed a rebuttable presumption in favor of a common law marriage where there is an absence of testimony regarding the exchange of *verba in praesenti*. When applicable, the party claiming a common law marriage who proves: (1) constant cohabitation; and, (2) a reputation of marriage "which is not partial or divided but is broad and general," raises the rebuttable presumption of marriage. Constant cohabitation, however, "even when conjoined with general reputation are not marriage, they are merely circumstances which give rise to a rebuttable presumption of marriage."

Here, we are mindful that the trial court in equitable distribution proceedings, as factfinder, makes determinations concerning the credibility of witnesses and that its conclusions of law based on those determinations will not be disturbed absent an abuse of discretion. We cannot conclude, based on a review of the record that the trial court abused its discretion when it determined that Linda failed to prove clearly and convincingly, the existence of the common law marriage contract between her and Theodore. She was unable to recall the specific instance of when she and Theodore said to each other, "we are husband and wife." She admitted that she and Theodore were married in a civil ceremony in 1984, and offered no explanation as to why she thought this civil ceremony necessary. Theodore's counsel sufficiently impeached her on cross-examination regarding the timing of her assertion of a common law marriage, suggesting that she did not raise the issue until it became apparent that Theodore claimed that the structured tort settlement was non-marital property. Her claim of common law marital status in 1978 contradicts her admission that, in the support papers filed in 1993, she indicated that she was "not married" at the time of her daughter's birth. The record as a whole, therefore, supports the trial court's conclusion that Linda's testimony on this issue lacked credibility, and that she failed to prove, by clear and convincing evidence, the establishment of a common law marriage through the exchange of *verba in praesenti* between her and Theodore.

* * *

Topics for Further Discussion

1. What conditions are required for a valid common law marriage in Pennsylvania? Why does the court say that this form of marriage is disfavored? Why should any government approval be required?

2. The majority opinion in *Staudenmayer* noted that there are only twelve states plus the District of Columbia that continue to recognize common law marriage. The pioneer conditions (the absence of preachers and civil servants, the fragile nature of life on the frontier, etc.) making common law marriage necessary no longer exist in contemporary society. Do you see any reason to continue to recognize common law marriages? The term "significant other" is often used to describe an intimate relationship avoiding the need to confirm marital status or gender.

3. While there are still states that recognize common law marriage, it should be noted that there is no such thing as common law divorce. Why not?

Same-Sex Marriage and Civil Union

The debate over same-sex marriage was kicked off in earnest by *Baehr v. Lewin*, 852 P.2d 44 (Haw. 1993), a Hawaii Supreme Court decision holding that a ban on same-sex marriage violated the Constitution of Hawaii. The ruling was based in large part on the findings of the trial court that the "sexual orientation of parents is not in and of itself an indicator of the overall adjustment and development of children." Hawaii amended its Constitution in 1998 in response to *Baehr*, giving the legislature the power "to reserve marriage to opposite-sex couples."

In the same year that *Lawrence v. Texas* was decided, the Supreme Court of Massachusetts in *Goodridge v. Department of Pub. Health*, 798 N.E.2d 941 (Mass. 2003) ruled that the state ban on same-sex marriages violated the Constitution of Massachusetts. The state Senate responded by asking the state Supreme Court whether a state law permitting civil unions, while reserving marriage as an exclusive institution for a man and woman, would be constitutional. The Massachusetts Supreme Court answered the question in the following advisory opinion.

In re Opinions of the Justices to the Senate
802 N.E.2d 565 (Mass. 2004)

To the Honorable the Senate of the Commonwealth of Massachusetts:

The order indicates that there is pending before the General Court a bill, Senate No. 2175, entitled "An Act relative to civil unions." The order indicates that grave doubt exists as to the constitutionality of the bill if enacted into law and requests the opinions of the Justices on the following "important question of law": "Does Senate, No. 2175, which prohibits same-sex couples from entering into marriage but allows them to form civil unions with all 'benefits, protections, rights and responsibilities' of marriage, comply with the equal protection and due process requirements of the Constitution of the Commonwealth and articles 1, 6, 7, 10, 12 and 16 of the Declaration of Rights?"

We have now been asked to render an advisory opinion on Senate No. 2175, which creates a new legal status, "civil union," that is purportedly equal to "marriage," yet separate from it. The constitutional difficulty of the proposed civil union bill is evident in its stated purpose to "preserv[e] the traditional, historic nature and meaning of the institution of civil marriage." Preserving the institution of civil marriage is of course a legislative priority of the highest order, and one to which the Justices accord the General Court the greatest deference. We recognize the efforts of the Senate to draft a bill in conformity with the *Goodridge* opinion. Yet the bill, as we read it, does nothing to "preserve" the civil marriage law, only its constitutional infirmity. This is not a matter of social policy but of constitutional interpretation. As the court concluded in *Goodridge*, the traditional, historic nature and meaning of civil marriage in Massachusetts is as a wholly secular and dynamic legal institution, the governmental aim of which is to encourage stable adult relationships for the good of the individual and of the community, especially its children. The very nature and purpose of civil marriage, the court concluded, renders unconstitutional any attempt to ban all same-sex couples, as same-sex couples, from entering into civil marriage.

The same defects of rationality evident in the marriage ban considered in *Goodridge* are evident in, if not exaggerated by, Senate No. 2175. Segregating same-sex unions from opposite-sex unions cannot possibly be held rationally to advance or "preserve" what we stated in *Goodridge* were the Commonwealth's legitimate interests in procreation, child rearing, and the conservation of resources. Because the proposed law by its express terms forbids same-sex couples entry into civil marriage, it continues to relegate same-sex couples to a different status. The holding in *Goodridge*, by which we are bound, is that group classifications based on unsupportable distinctions, such as that embodied in the proposed bill, are invalid under the Massachusetts Constitution. The history of our nation has demonstrated that separate is seldom, if ever, equal.

In *Goodridge*, the court acknowledged, as we do here, that "[m]any people hold deep-seated religious, moral, and ethical convictions that marriage should be limited to the union of one man and one woman, and that homosexual conduct is immoral. Many hold equally strong religious, moral, and ethical convictions that same-sex couples are entitled to be married, and that homosexual persons should be treated no differently than their heterosexual neighbors." The court stated then, and we reaffirm, that the State may not interfere with these convictions, or with the decision of any religion to refuse to perform religious marriages of same-sex couples. These matters of belief and conviction are properly outside the reach of judicial review or government interference. But neither may the government, under the guise of protecting "traditional" values, even if they be the traditional values of the majority, enshrine in law an invidious discrimination that our Constitution, "as a charter of governance for every person properly within its reach," forbids.

The bill's absolute prohibition of the use of the word "marriage" by "spouses" who are the same sex is more than semantic. The dissimilitude between the terms "civil marriage" and "civil union" is not innocuous; it is a considered choice of language that reflects a demonstrable assigning of same-sex, largely homosexual, couples to second-class status. The denomination of this difference by the separate opinion of Justice Sosman (separate opinion) as merely a "squabble over the name to be used" so clearly misses the point that further discussion appears to be useless. If, as the separate opinion posits, the proponents of the bill believe that no message is conveyed by eschewing the word "marriage" and replacing it with "civil union" for same-sex "spouses," we doubt that the attempt to circumvent the court's decision in *Goodridge* would be so purposeful. For no rational reason the marriage laws of the Commonwealth discriminate against a defined class; no amount of tinkering with language will eradicate that stain. The bill would have the effect of maintaining and fostering a stigma of exclusion that the Constitution prohibits. It would deny to same-sex "spouses" only a status that is specially recognized in society and has significant social and other advantages. The Massachusetts Constitution, as was explained in the *Goodridge* opinion, does not permit such invidious discrimination, no matter how well intentioned.

We recognize that the pending bill palliates some of the financial and other concrete manifestations of the discrimination at issue in *Goodridge*. But the question the court considered in *Goodridge* was not only whether it was proper to withhold tangible benefits from same-sex couples, but also whether it was constitutional to create a separate class of citizens by status discrimination, and withhold from that class the right to participate in the institution of civil marriage, along with its concomitant tangible and intangible protections, benefits, rights, and responsibilities. Maintaining a second-class citizen status for same-sex couples by excluding them from the institution of civil marriage is the constitutional infirmity at issue.

Conclusion. We are of the opinion that Senate No. 2175 violates the equal protection and due process requirements of the Constitution of the Commonwealth and the Massachusetts Declaration of Rights. The bill maintains an unconstitutional, inferior, and discriminatory status for same-sex couples, and the bill's remaining provisions are too entwined with this purpose to stand independently.

The answer to the question is "No."

* * *

Topics for Further Discussion

1. The first *Goodridge* opinion was sweeping in its scope. Nevertheless, the Court did say that religious authorities could not be required to perform same-sex wedding ceremonies in contravention of their beliefs. Is this an appropriate balance of interests between proponents of same-sex marriage and those who believe that homosexuality is a sin against divine law and the law of nature?

2. Why did the Court in the advisory opinion excerpted above reject the proposed bill allowing civil unions? What did the court mean when it wrote that the "history of our nation has demonstrated that separate is seldom, if ever, equal?" Is this a matter that should be decided by judges or the legislature? What does the Court have to say about the roles of each branch of government? If you think it is an appropriate matter for the legislature, what is the proper role of the court in protecting the rights of the minority in a democratic society?

3. President George W. Bush, with strong support from the "religious right" (including the Christian Coalition organization) and supporters of traditional family values, pushed for the so-called Federal Marriage Amendment to the Constitution. The FMA is composed of the following two clauses:

1. Marriage in the United States shall consist only of the union of a man and a woman.

2. Neither this constitution or the constitution of any state, nor state or federal law, shall be construed to require that marital status or the legal incidents thereof be conferred upon unmarried couples or groups.

In a public address on February 24, 2004, calling for passage of the FMA, President Bush remarked as follows:

> Marriage cannot be severed from its cultural, religious and natural roots without weakening the good influence of society. Government, by recognizing and protecting marriage, serves the interests of all. Today I call upon the Congress to promptly pass, and to send to the states for ratification, an amendment to our Constitution defining and protecting marriage as a union of man and woman as husband and wife. The amendment should fully protect marriage, while leaving the state legislatures free to make their own choices in defining legal arrangements other than marriage.
>
> America is a free society, which limits the role of government in the lives of our citizens. This commitment of freedom, however, does not require the redefinition of one of our most basic social institutions. Our government should respect every person, and protect the institution of marriage.

The FMA failed to obtain the required two-thirds vote in the Senate, and appears to be stalled for the time being. Do you think permitting same-sex marriages would weaken "the good influence of society?" How can the government respect every person and protect the institution of marriage at the same time? Do you agree that a free society has no obligation to redefine even the most basic of social institutions when it appears to be out of touch with the lifestyle patterns of a growing number of citizens?

4. Notwithstanding President Bush's statement that states should remain "free to make their own choices in defining legal arrangements other than marriage," federal law excludes partners to a civil union from the benefits afforded to married couples. Taking their lead from the President, 11 states had ballot initiatives during the 2004 presidential election seeking to ban same-sex marriage, with all 11 passing. It should also be remembered that homosexual relationships remain illegal in some countries.

5. Article 24 of the Constitution of Japan provides, in relevant part, as follows: "Marriage shall be based only on the mutual consent of both sexes and it shall be maintained through mutual cooperation with the equal rights of husband and wife as a basis." The Japanese Constitution was drafted in English by the Allies during the Occupation Period following World War II, and was translated into Japanese before adoption. It is relatively clear that the thrust was to end the system of arranged marriages and to give women a measure of equal rights. Does Article 24 deprive the people of Japan of the social evolution represented by the *Lawrence* and *Goodridge* decisions?

6. In *Baker v. Vermont*, 744 A.2d 864 (Vt. 1999), the Vermont Supreme Court held that the Vermont Constitution prohibited the exclusion of same-sex couples from the benefits and protections provided to married couples, finding that:

> While many have noted the symbolic or spiritual significance of the marital relation, it is plaintiffs' claim to the secular benefits and protections of a singularly human relationship that, in our view, characterizes this case. The State's interest in extending official recognition and legal protection to the professed commitment of two individuals to a lasting relationship of mutual affection is predicated on the belief that legal support of a couple's commitment provides stability for the individuals, their family, and the broader community.... Vermonters

who seek nothing more, nor less, than legal protection and security for their avowed commitment to an intimate and lasting human relationship is simply, when all is said and done, a recognition of our common humanity.

Following the *Baker* decision, Vermont enacted An Act Relating to Civil Unions. The Civil Union Act requires that the partners "[be] of the same sex and therefore excluded from the marriage laws of this state." It gives to persons in a civil union all of the benefits, protections and responsibilities enjoyed by spouses in a marriage. Civil unions are subject to the same rules as govern prenuptial contracts and to the same divorce proceedings in the family court. Does this law address all of the needs of the homosexual community, or does discrimination continue to exist in the refusal to permit same-sex couples to marry as the Massachusetts Supreme Court believes?

7. In 2004, the Mayor of San Francisco ordered the County Clerk to prepare new marriage license applications to allow same-sex couples to apply. The County Clerk did so, and approximately 18,000 same-sex couples were married. In *Lockyer v. City and County of San Francisco*, 95 P.3d 459 (Cal. 2004), the California Supreme Court held that government officials did not have authority to change state law regarding marriage without a judicial determination of invalidity under the California Constitution. The same-sex marriages already performed were "grandfathered" and remained valid, although no new ones could be registered. This did not end the issue. The California Supreme Court took on the issue again in six consolidated cases known as *In re Marriage Cases*, 183 P.3d 384 (Cal. 2008). These cases considered whether the prohibition on same-sex marriage violated the state constitution when same-sex couples were given the right to enter into civil unions. The court, like the Massachusetts Supreme Court before it, held that allowing civil unions did not cure the discrimination suffered by same-sex couples denied access to the institution of marriage. The Court pointed to four reasons: (1) allowing same-sex marriage causes no harm to the rights and benefits of opposite sex marriages; (2) relegating same-sex couples to civil unions deprives them of equal dignity; (3) denying gays access to "the institution of marriage is likely to be viewed as reflecting an official view that their committed relationships are of lesser stature ..."; and (4) retaining marriage for only heterosexual couples may perpetuate a stereotype that homosexuals are second-class citizens. Do you find these reasons persuasive?

8. The people of California reacted by passing Proposition 8, which added the following language to the California Constitution: "Only marriage between a man and woman is valid and recognized in California." In the case of *Strauss v. Horton*, 207 P.3d 48 (Cal. 2009), the California Supreme Court held that Proposition 8 was a valid expression of the will of the people. In a strongly worded dissent, Justice Moreno contended that "Proposition 8 represents an unprecedented instance of a majority of voters altering the meaning of the equal protection clause ... to require deprivation of a fundamental right on the basis of a suspect classification." How would you explain the tension between the right of the majority to alter the state constitution through the ballot box and the duty of the court to protect the fundamental rights of minorities? Revisit the U.S. Supreme Court's opinion in *Lawrence v. Texas* excerpted in Chapter 4, especially the dissenting opinion of Justice Scalia. Could the U.S. Constitution be amended to eliminate the First Amendment protections of freedom of speech and freedom of religion?

9. As this second edition is being prepared, a case challenging the constitutionality of Proposition 8 under the U.S. Constitution (Equal Protection and Due Process), and 42 U.S.C. 1983, is proceeding in the United States District Court for the Northern District of California. It seems that the issue of same-sex marriage is bound for decision by the U.S. Supreme Court.

The Full Faith and Credit Clause and the Defense of Marriage Act

Article IV of the United States Constitution provides that: "Full faith and credit shall be given in each state to the public acts, records, and judicial proceedings of every other state." Arguably, the Full Faith and Credit Clause means a same-sex marriage in Massachusetts or California or a civil union in Vermont must be recognized in any other state of the union where the same-sex couple resides. The Supreme Court, however, has long recognized a public policy exception to the Full Faith and Credit Clause.

Congress passed the Defense of Marriage Act (DOMA) in 1996, in anticipation of the Full Faith and Credit Clause issue. DOMA does two things. First, it provides that:

> No State, territory, or possession of the United States, or Indian tribe, shall be required to give effect to any public act, record, or judicial proceeding of any other State, territory, possession, or tribe respecting a relationship between persons of the same sex that is treated as a marriage under the laws of such other State, territory, possession, or tribe, or a right or claim arising from such relationship.

Second, it defines, for federal law purposes, "marriage" to mean only a legal union between one man and one woman as husband and wife, and "spouse" to mean only a person of the opposite sex who is a husband or a wife. The Supreme Court has yet to rule on the constitutionality of DOMA, and it is arguable whether it will be able to withstand constitutional scrutiny after *Lawrence*. Indeed, the potential impact of the Supreme Court's opinion in *Lawrence* led Justice Scalia to remark in his dissenting opinion that:

> Today's opinion dismantles the structure of constitutional law that has permitted a distinction to be made between heterosexual and homosexual unions, insofar as formal recognition in marriage is concerned. If moral disapproval of homosexual conduct is 'no legitimate state interest' for purposes of proscribing that conduct; and if, as the Court coos (casting aside all pretense of neutrality), '[w]hen sexuality finds overt expression in intimate conduct with another person, the conduct can be but one element in a personal bond that is more enduring;' what justification could there possibly be for denying the benefits of marriage to homosexual couples exercising '[t]he liberty protected by the Constitution'?

Same-sex marriages and civil unions are still in their infancy, and we may eventually see the day when the idea of denying same-sex couples the same protections as heterosexual couples in marriage seems as alien to us as prohibiting interracial marriage in *Loving*.

Divorce

"What God hath joined together, let no man put asunder" are the solemn words spoken at the end of a traditional religious wedding ceremony. The reality is, however, that marriages fail, and they seem to be doing so at an increasing rate in virtually every society. The U.S. Census Bureau estimates that as many as 50% of all first time marriages in America will end in divorce. The reasons for the increasing divorce rate are many. At one time, it was virtually impossible for a person to get a divorce without the consent of the other party, or at least a judicial finding that one of a limited number of statutorily recognized grounds for divorce existed. These grounds were all based on the principle of fault. The fault standard required the party seeking the divorce to allege and prove that the other party had engaged in bad or immoral behavior, such as abandonment, adultery, spousal abuse or the like.

The modern trend is to grant "No Fault" divorces when neither party contests dissolution. If one or both of the parties no longer desires to be married, and there is no reasonable expectation they can or will reconcile their differences, the divorce will be granted. Most states require only that the couple have lived apart for a minimum period of time, usually one year. Divorce has become routine, and "Do It Yourself" divorce packages can be purchased for under $250.

Marriages can be annulled by court order. Annulment requires a finding that some factor (impaired judgment due to alcohol or drugs, an underage party, duress, fraud, the failure to dissolve an earlier marriage before entering into the second marriage, etc.) existed making the marriage void from the outset.

Judges are protective of the rights of both spouses in an action for divorce. While divorce has become easier, it is still an equitable action requiring judicial sanction. Judges are particularly careful to protect the weaker spouse in long-term marriages. The dissolution of the marital relationship (and the civil union) presents many difficult issues concerning the division of property, spousal and child support, child custody, and visitation rights.

Division of Property, Alimony, and Prenuptial Agreements

Parties to a divorce are free to negotiate a mutually acceptable property settlement, and most divorce settlements are achieved in this way. There are two main systems of property distribution in use in the U.S. when the parties cannot reach agreement on property distribution: Equitable Distribution and Community Property. In equitable distribution jurisdictions, all assets acquired during the marriage are divided by the judge (juries are not used in these proceedings) between the two spouses in a manner that is fair under all of the facts and circumstances. Judges are free to consider a wide range of factors in reaching their decisions, such as the relative contributions of the spouses, the length of the marriage, and the likely economic condition of the spouse after the divorce. Separate property of the spouses, such as property acquired before the marriage, compensation for personal injury, and property the spouse agrees to be so, is not subject to equitable distribution.

In the following case, the Supreme Court of South Dakota was asked to consider whether a professional degree should be considered marital property.

Wehrkamp v. Wehrkamp
357 N.W.2d 264 (S.D. 1984)

Henderson, J.

A divorce was granted to both of these parties by the Second Judicial Circuit Court on June 21, 1983. Appellant, Audrey R. Wehrkamp, appeals the property award provided in the judgment of divorce. We affirm.

At the time of their marriage on August 2, 1975, appellee Scott R. Wehrkamp held a Bachelor of Science degree from South Dakota State University, Brookings and appellant had completed one year of college. During the first years of the marriage, appellee attended dental school at Loyola University in Chicago, Illinois, where he received a D.D.S. degree. Appellant, during this same period, completed five years of college and obtained a dental hygiene certification.

While in Chicago attending school, both parties received educational loans, grants, and gifts from relatives. Both parties also maintained part-time employment during these years.

Under the decision of the trial court, it was found that both parties had saleable skills as licensed professionals. Both parties were in good health and both had a trade or skill sufficient to maintain their accustomed station in life without financial contribution from the other party. The personal property and real estate acquired during marriage were divided equitably between the parties, each receiving roughly one-half. Appellant did not ask for alimony and it was not awarded.

The trial court further found that the future earnings of the parties, being too speculative, were not to be considered part of the property award. Also, the court did not consider appellee's education and professional license a marital asset for property division purposes. Considering the respective educational benefits, degree, certification and the contributions of both parties in obtaining these, the trial court held that neither party had established they were individually entitled to a contribution award.

Appellant contests the trial court's failure to take into consideration appellee's increased earning capacity resulting from his D.D.S. degree. Appellant claims this is the most valuable asset acquired by the parties during the term of their marriage and that it is an asset subject to appraisal. She contends it was an abuse of discretion not to consider this in dividing the marital property.

We are faced with this question: Is an individual's future earning capacity resulting from an advanced degree "property" in divorce cases? There is a growing body of case law on this subject throughout the various jurisdictions. The majority view is that an advanced degree or professional license is not "property" as that term is used in divorce settlement cases. An early leading case in this area was *In re Marriage of Graham*, 574 P.2d 75 (Colo. 1978), wherein it was stated: "An educational degree ... is simply not encompassed even by the broad views of the concept of 'property.' It does not have an exchange value or any objective transferable value on an open market. It is personal to the holder. It terminates on death of the holder and is not inheritable. It cannot be assigned, sold, transferred, conveyed, or pledged. An advanced degree is a cumulative product of many years of previous education, combined with diligence and hard work. It may not be acquired by the mere expenditure of money. It is simply an intellectual achievement that may potentially assist in the future acquisition of property ... it has none of the attributes of property in the usual sense of that term."

Whether a professional education is and will be of future value to its recipient is a matter resting on factors which are at best difficult to anticipate or measure. A person qualified by education for a given profession may choose not to practice it, may fail at it, or may practice in a speciality, location or manner which generates less than the average income enjoyed by fellow professionals. The potential worth of the education may never be realized for these or many other reasons. An award based upon the prediction of the degree holder's success at the chosen field may bear no relationship to the reality he or she faces after the divorce. Unlike an award of alimony, which can be adjusted after divorce to reflect unanticipated changes in the parties' circumstances, a property division may not. The potential for inequity to the failed professional or one who changes careers is at once apparent; his or her spouse will have been awarded a share of something which never existed in any real sense.

We note that not all courts have rejected the concept that potential earning capacity made possible by an advanced degree may be considered an asset for distribution by the court. See *In re Marriage of Horstmann*, 263 N.W.2d 885 (Iowa 1978); *Inman v. Inman*, 578 S.W.2d 266 (Ky.App.1979). However, it was the particular circumstances of each case which motivated these decisions. In *Horstmann*, wife did not complete her formal education and provided the major source of support through employment with a bank while husband attended law school. The court found husband's law degree was conferred upon him with the aid of his wife's efforts, and thus, she should share in the potential for increase in earning capacity made possible by the degree.

Despite strong reservations to the contrary, similar circumstances prompted the holding in *Inman* that under "certain instances ... treating a professional license as marital property is the only way in which a court can achieve an equitable result." The court cited the most common instance as being a situation where one spouse supports the other through school, only to have the marriage dissolve immediately upon graduation.

We concede the equities to be adjusted between the parties will vary with the facts and circumstances of each particular case. Thus, the parties seeking divorce may be from a marriage that lasted many years in which substantial property was accumulated. An equitable division of that property should result in each party realizing the benefits of the college degree. On the other hand, where the working spouse supports the family while the other attends college, obtains an advanced professional degree, and promptly seeks a divorce, there is no property accumulated to divide. The inequity of a divorce with no award to the working spouse is obvious. In this situation, an award to that spouse which would afford an opportunity to obtain the same degree under the same circumstances, or in the alternative, a sum of money equal to that benefit seems equitable; and cases falling between these two extremes should be adjusted accordingly. Some authorities dub this "rehabilitative alimony." However, these issues are not pertinent to this case. Appellant did not request alimony, nor is she in need of some sort of rehabilitative contribution. She has already pursued a career of her choice, one that should provide adequate support in the manner to which she is accustomed.

* * *

Topics for Further Discussion

1. Why did the Supreme Court of South Dakota decide that the economic value of the husband's dental license should not be considered marital property subject to equitable distribution? How were the *Horstmann* and *Inman* decisions distinguished? Can you articulate a principle of governing law in this area?

2. In *Mahoney v. Mahoney*, 453 A.2d 527 (N.J. 1982), the Supreme Court of New Jersey rejected a wife's claim that her husband's Wharton School MBA degree should be considered property for purposes of equitable distribution. The Court did, however, find that fairness required that the husband pay back the support he received from his wife while pursuing his MBA. The Court explained that:

> In this case, the supporting spouse made financial contributions towards her husband's professional education with the expectation that both parties would enjoy material benefits flowing from the professional license or degree. It is therefore patently unfair that the supporting spouse be denied the mutually anticipated benefit while the supported spouse keeps not only the degree, but also all of the financial and material awards flowing from it.

The Court introduced what it called a concept of "Reimbursement Alimony" in divorce proceedings where the spouse has sacrificed his or her own career in order to allow the other spouse to pursue a career. How do rehabilitation alimony and reimbursement alimony differ?

The other major system for property distribution is community property. There are nine community property states (Arizona, California, Idaho, Louisiana, Nevada, New Mexico, Texas, Washington, and Wisconsin). In community property jurisdictions, all property acquired during the marriage, other than by a gift or inheritance, is considered to be the result of the equal efforts of both spouses. It does not matter that one spouse earned substantially more income than the other. Thus, community property is owned 50-50 and is split equally at the time of divorce. Do you think community property is more just than equitable distribution?

Alimony

The traditional view of marriage held that a husband had a duty to support his wife regardless of her wealth. Marriage was a lifetime commitment and, thus, this obligation continued after divorce in the form of an alimony order requiring the husband to support his wife financially in the manner to which she has become accustomed. The law no longer assumes that all men are the "bread winners" in the family, and that all women are dependent. Indeed, the Supreme Court in *Orr v. Orr*, 440 U.S. 268 (1979) invalidated an Alabama statute requiring men to pay alimony, but not women.

The duty to pay alimony, whether by the husband or the wife, remains a central part of divorce law. Courts have the power to award either temporary or permanent alimony to a spouse during a period of separation or following divorce. Alimony is intended to preserve the lifestyle of the weaker party. This can be a staggering sum when one of the spouses is an extremely wealthy individual such as Ted Turner, Donald Trump or Jack Welch. It was widely reported in the newspapers that the wife of the former CEO of General Electric, Jack Welch, detailed approximately $125,000 per month for living expenses after a nine year marriage before considering the value of corporate perks, such as use of a corporate jet and Manhattan condo, that her husband received as part of his retirement package from GE.

In awarding alimony, courts historically considered three principles: (1) the standard of living to which the receiving spouse had become accustomed, (2) the ability of the paying spouse to pay, and (3) the fault, if any, of the receiving spouse in the divorce. The modern trend is to disregard fault altogether, and to award maintenance payments sufficient to support a receiving spouse who is incapable of returning to the workplace, or to provide sufficient funds for the spouse to obtain the education and training necessary to obtain the skills to return to work. The last element is, as we have seen, referred to as "rehabilitation alimony." Judges have wide latitude to decide the structure, amount and duration of alimony payments, and they maintain continuing jurisdiction to consider changed circumstances.

Prenuptial Agreements

Prenuptial (sometimes called antenuptial) agreements are special contracts made in advance of marriage that limit the property one spouse will receive upon divorce. They are used predominately to protect the rich and famous from "gold diggers" who marry them only for their money. Prenuptial agreements were historically disfavored by American courts as being against public policy. Largely as a result of the emerging equality between men and women, the modern trend is to enforce them in accordance with their terms if they are validly procured and fair in result. The West Virginia Supreme Court of Appeals, representing the modern view, wrote in *Gant v. Gant*, 329 S.E.2d 106 (W.Va. 1985) that: "In order for the procurement to be valid there must be an absence of fraud, duress, or misrepresentation, and the agreement must have been executed voluntarily, with knowledge of its content and legal effect."

There is no general requirement that the parties to a prenuptial agreement be represented by counsel, although having counsel for each party will certainly increase the likelihood that the contract will be upheld. Fairness presents a more difficult question. Should the fairness of the prenuptial contract be examined at the time of its making, at the time of divorce, or both? How should a disparity in bargaining power be evaluated? The *Gant* court addressed the bargaining power issue and concluded:

> Throughout all of contract law there is the recurring problem of disparity of bargaining power; thus if mere disparate bargaining power alone is grounds for invalidating contracts, contracts between rich and poor or between strong and weak will always be of questionable validity. Such, however, is not the rule elsewhere in contract law, and we see no policy reasons to make it so in the law of prenuptial agreements.

The following case was the first to recognize the principle of palimony, a form of alimony based on contract theory instead of marriage. Lee Marvin was a highly successful Hollywood movie star famous for playing tough guys and outlaws. While separated from his wife, Marvin began to live with Michelle Triola. Their cohabitation continued after Marvin's divorce was finalized, but all of his property remained in his own name. Seven years after taking up residence together, the couple split, and Triola sued Marvin seeking support and a share of his property acquired during their period of cohabitation. She alleged in her complaint that she had an oral agreement with Marvin whereby she would give up her career as a singer and take care of him on a full-time basis "as a companion, homemaker, housekeeper and cook" in return for his agreeing to "provide for all of [Triola's] financial support and needs for the rest of her life."

Marvin v. Marvin
557 P.2d 106 (Cal. 1976)

Tobriner, J.

During the past 15 years, there has been a substantial increase in the number of couples living together without marrying. Such nonmarital relationships lead to legal controversy when one partner dies or the couple separates. We take this opportunity to resolve that controversy and to declare the principles which should govern distribution of property acquired in a nonmarital relationship.

We conclude: (1) The provisions of the Family Law Act do not govern the distribution of property acquired during a nonmarital relationship; such a relationship remains subject solely to judicial decision. (2) The courts should enforce express contracts between nonmarital partners except to the extent that the contract is explicitly founded on the consideration of meretricious sexual services. (3) In the absence of an express contract, the courts should inquire into the conduct of the parties to determine whether that conduct demonstrates an implied contract, agreement of partnership or joint venture, or some other tacit understanding between the parties. The courts may also employ the doctrine of *quantum meruit*, or equitable remedies such as constructive or resulting trusts, when warranted by the facts of the case.

In the instant case plaintiff and defendant lived together for seven years without marrying; all property acquired during this period was taken in defendant's name. When plaintiff sued to enforce a contract under which she was entitled to half the property and to support payments, the trial court granted judgment on the pleadings for defendant, thus leaving him with all property accumulated by the couple during their relationship. Since the trial court denied plaintiff a trial on the merits of her claim, its decision conflicts with the principles stated above, and must be reversed.

Although that court did not specify the ground for its conclusion that plaintiff's contractual allegations stated no cause of action, defendant offers some four theories to sustain the ruling; we proceed to examine them.

Defendant first and principally relies on the contention that the alleged contract is so closely related to the supposed "immoral" character of the relationship between plaintiff and himself that the enforcement of the contract would violate public policy.

Although the past decisions hover over the issue in the somewhat wispy form of the figures of a Chagall painting, we can abstract from those decisions a clear and simple rule. The fact that a man and woman live together without marriage, and engage in a sexual relationship, does not in itself invalidate agreements between them relating to their earnings, property, or expenses. Neither is such an agreement invalid merely because the parties may have contemplated the creation or continuation of a nonmarital relationship when they entered into it. Agreements between nonmarital partners fail only to the extent that they rest upon a consideration of meretricious sexual services. Thus the rule asserted by defendant, that a contract fails if it is "involved in" or made "in contemplation" of a nonmarital relationship, cannot be reconciled with the decisions.

Defendant secondly relies upon the ground suggested by the trial court: that the 1964 contract violated public policy because it impaired the community property rights of Betty Marvin, defendant's lawful wife. But whether or not defendant's contract with plaintiff exceeded his authority as manager of the community property, defendant's argument fails for the reason that an improper transfer of community property is not void *ab initio*, but merely voidable at the instance of the aggrieved spouse.

In the present case Betty Marvin, the aggrieved spouse, had the opportunity to assert her community property rights in the divorce action. The interlocutory and final decrees in that action fix and limit her interest. Enforcement of the contract between plaintiff and defendant against property awarded to defendant by the divorce decree will not impair any right of Betty's, and thus is not on that account violative of public policy.

Defendant's third contention is noteworthy for the lack of authority advanced in its support. He contends that enforcement of the oral agreement between plaintiff and himself is barred by Civil Code section 5134, which provides that "All contracts for marriage settlements must be in writing...." A marriage settlement, however, is an agreement in contemplation of marriage in which each party agrees to release or modify the property rights which would otherwise arise from the marriage. The contract at issue here does not conceivably fall within that definition, and thus is beyond the compass of section 5134.

Defendant finally argues that enforcement of the contract is barred by Civil Code section 43.5, subdivision (d), which provides that "No cause of action arises for ... breach of promise of marriage." This rather strained contention proceeds from the premise that a promise of marriage impliedly includes a promise to support and to pool property acquired after marriage to the conclusion that pooling and support agreements not part of or accompanied by promise of marriage are barred by the section.

In summary, we believe that the prevalence of nonmarital relationships in modern society and the social acceptance of them, marks this as a time when our courts should by no means apply the doctrine of the unlawfulness of the so-called meretricious relationship to the instant case. As we have explained, the nonenforceability of agreements expressly providing for meretricious conduct rested upon the fact that such conduct, as the word suggests, pertained to and encompassed prostitution. To equate the nonmarital relationship of today to such a subject matter is to do violence to an accepted and wholly different practice.

We are aware that many young couples live together without the solemnization of marriage, in order to make sure that they can successfully later undertake marriage. This trial period, preliminary to marriage, serves as some assurance that the marriage will not subsequently end in dissolution to the harm of both parties. We are aware, as we have stated, of the pervasiveness of nonmarital relationships in other situations.

The mores of the society have indeed changed so radically in regard to cohabitation that we cannot impose a standard based on alleged moral considerations that have apparently been so widely abandoned by so many. Lest we be misunderstood, however, we take this occasion to point out that the structure of society itself largely depends upon the institution of marriage, and nothing we have said in this opinion should be taken to derogate from that institution. The joining of the man and woman in marriage is at once the most socially productive and individually fulfilling relationship that one can enjoy in the course of a lifetime.

We conclude that the judicial barriers that may stand in the way of a policy based upon the fulfillment of the reasonable expectations of the parties to a nonmarital relationship should be removed. As we have explained, the courts now hold that express agreements will be enforced unless they rest on an unlawful meretricious consideration. We add that in the absence of an express agreement, the courts may look to a variety of other remedies in order to protect the parties' lawful expectations.

The courts may inquire into the conduct of the parties to determine whether that conduct demonstrates an implied contract or implied agreement of partnership or joint venture, or some other tacit understanding between the parties. The courts may, when appropriate, employ principles of constructive trust or resulting trust. Finally, a nonmarital partner may recover in *quantum meruit* for the reasonable value of household services rendered less the reasonable value of support received if he can show that he rendered services with the expectation of monetary reward.

Since we have determined that plaintiff's complaint states a cause of action for breach of an express contract, and, as we have explained, can be amended to state a cause of action independent of allegations of express contract, we must conclude that the trial court erred in granting defendant a judgment on the pleadings.

* * *

Topics for Further Discussion

1. The *Marvin* decision caused a big stir when it was announced. A number of other states have declined to follow its reasoning. Do you agree with the Court's use of contract theory in a cohabitation case? How does this contract differ from the rights that ordinarily flow from marriage? After reading the *Marvin* opinion, can you explain the line between a contract resting "upon immoral and illicit consideration or meretricious sexual services" and an enforceable cohabitation agreement?

2. How does the rule in *Marvin* differ from what the Pennsylvania Supreme Court said about common law marriage in the *Staudenmayer* case? Consider the implications of the reasoning in both *Marvin* and *Staudenmayer* in the context of same-sex relationships.

3. The *Marvin* case was remanded for trial to determine whether there was an express or an implied contract between Lee Marvin and Michelle Triola, and whether equitable remedies should be permitted. The trial court judge concluded, after hearing extensive testimony lasting nearly three months, that "no express contract was negotiated between the parties. Neither party entertained any expectations that the property was to be divided between them." The judge also rejected the plaintiff's argument that there was an implied contract. The court did, however, find that plaintiff was entitled to an equitable award of $104,000 so that she could rehabilitate herself and find a new career. The equitable award portion of the trial court's decision was reversed on appeal because "it is clear that no basis whatsoever, either in equity or in law, exists for the challenged rehabilitative award."

Child Custody and Support

The parent-child relationship enjoys a special status in American law. For many purposes, such as contracting, children are not deemed to have legal capacity and can only act with and through the consent of their legal guardians. Guardian status is usually, but not always, vested in the parents and carries with it a general duty to act in the best interest of the child. Parents and guardians have a specific duty to provide for the education, support and welfare of their children. Great deference is given to the child rearing decisions of parents and legal guardians. For example, in *Wisconsin v. Yoder*, 406 U.S. 205 (1972), the Supreme Court backed the right of the Amish not to send their children to school beyond the eighth grade out of a fear they would be corrupted by a secular education and exposure to the temptations and freedoms of American teenage school life. Courts have split over whether medical procedures should be ordered for children over the religious objections of the parents.

The historical deference to parental control has given way to a growing social awareness of the tragedy of child abuse. Now, when parents fail to meet the standards of care required by law for any reason, either through inability or abuse, social service workers and the courts are empowered and encouraged to intervene to protect the child. Police and medical personnel are required by law to report suspected instances of abuse and to remove the child immediately from the risk of harm until a court can make an appropriate finding of what is in the best interest of the child.

Child custody typically arises in the context of divorce. Custody carries with it the legal right to make decisions concerning the well being of the child. It can be shared or awarded to only one party. Separating a child temporarily or permanently from a parent, or from siblings, remains one of the hardest decisions a judge must make as seen in the following case.

Painter v. Bannister
140 N.W.2d 152 (Iowa 1966)

Stuart, J.

We are here setting the course for Mark Wendell Painter's future. Our decision on the custody of this 7 year old boy will have a marked influence on his whole life. The fact that we are called upon many times a year to determine custody matters does not make the exercising of this awesome responsibility any less difficult. Legal training and experience are of little practical help in solving the complex problems of human relations. However, these problems do arise and under our system of government, the burden of rendering a final decision rests upon us. It is frustrating to know we can only resolve, not solve, these unfortunate situations.

The custody dispute before us in this *habeas corpus* action is between the father, Harold Painter, and the maternal grandparents, Dwight and Margaret Bannister. Mark's mother and younger sister were killed in an automobile accident on December 6, 1962 near Pullman, Washington. The father, after other arrangements for Mark's care had proved unsatisfactory, asked the Bannisters, to take care of Mark. They went to California and brought Mark to their farm home near Ames in July, 1963. Mr. Painter remarried in November, 1964 and about that time indicated he wanted to take Mark back. The Bannisters refused to let him leave and this action was filed in June, 1965. Since July 1965 he has continued to remain in the Bannister home under an order of this court staying execution of the judgment of the trial court awarding custody to the father until the matter could be determined on appeal. For reasons hereinafter stated, we conclude Mark's better interests will be served if he remains with the Bannisters.

We are not confronted with a situation where one of the contesting parties is not a fit or proper person. There is no criticism of either the Bannisters or their home. There is no suggestion in the record that Mr. Painter is morally unfit. It is obvious the Bannisters did not approve of their daughter's marriage to Harold Painter and do not want their grandchild raised under his guidance. The philosophies of life are entirely different.

It is not our prerogative to determine custody upon our choice of one of two ways of life within normal and proper limits and we will not do so. However, the philosophies are important as they relate to Mark and his particular needs.

The Bannister home provides Mark with a stable, dependable, conventional, middle-class, middlewest background and an opportunity for a college education and profession, if he desires it. It provides a solid foundation and secure atmosphere. In the Painter home, Mark would have more freedom of conduct and thought with an opportunity to develop his individual talents. It would be more exciting and challenging in many respects, but romantic, impractical and unstable.

Our conclusion as to the type of home Mr. Painter would offer is based upon his Bohemian approach to finances and life in general. We feel there is much evidence which supports this conclusion. His main ambition is to be a free lance writer and photographer. He has had some articles and picture stories published, but the income from these efforts has been negligible. At the time of the accident, Jeanne was willingly working to support the family so Harold could devote more time to his writing and photography. In the 10 years since he left college, he has changed jobs seven times. He was asked to leave two of them; two he quit because he didn't like the work; two because he wanted to devote more time to writing and the rest for better pay. He was contemplating a move to Berkeley at the time of trial.

Mr. Painter is either an agnostic or atheist and has no concern for formal religious training. He has read a lot of Zen Buddhism and "has been very much influenced by it." Mrs. Painter is Roman Catholic. They plan to send Mark to a Congregational Church near the Catholic Church, on an irregular schedule.

He is a political liberal and got into difficulty in a job at the University of Washington for his support of the activities of the American Civil Liberties Union in the university news bulletin.

There were "two funerals" for his wife. One in the basement of his home in which he alone was present. He conducted the service and wrote her a long letter. The second at a church in Pullman was for the gratification of her friends. He attended in a sport shirt and sweater.

These matters are not related as a criticism of Mr. Painter's conduct, way of life or sense of values. An individual is free to choose his own values, within bounds, which are not exceeded here. They do serve however to support our conclusion as to the kind of life Mark would be exposed to in the Painter household. We believe it would be unstable, unconventional, arty, Bohemian, and probably intellectually stimulating.

Were the question simply which household would be the most suitable in which to raise a child, we would have unhesitatingly chosen the Bannister home. We believe security and stability in the home are more important than intellectual stimulation in the proper development of a child. There are, however, several factors which have made us pause.

First, there is the presumption of parental preference, which though weakened in the past several years, exists by statute. We have a great deal of sympathy for a father, who in the difficult period of adjustment following his wife's death, turns to the maternal grandparents for their help and then finds them unwilling to return the child. There is no merit in the Bannister claim that Mr. Painter permanently relinquished custody. It was intended to be a temporary arrangement. A father should be encouraged to look for help with the children, from those who love them without the risk of thereby losing the custody of the children permanently. This fact must receive consideration in cases of this kind. However, as always, the primary consideration is the best interest of the child and if the return of custody to the father is likely to have a seriously disrupting and disturbing effect upon the child's development, this fact must prevail.

Second, Jeanne's will named her husband guardian of the children and if he failed to qualify or ceased to act, named her mother. The parent's wishes are entitled to consideration.

Third, the Bannister's are 60 years old. By the time Mark graduates from high school they will be over 70 years old. Care of young children is a strain on grandparents and Mrs. Bannister's letters indicate as much.

We have considered all of these factors and have concluded that Mark's best interest demands that his custody remain with the Bannisters. Mark was five when he came to their home. The evidence clearly shows he was not well adjusted at that time. He did not distinguish fact from fiction and was inclined to tell 'tall tales' emphasizing the big "I." He was very aggressive toward smaller children, cruel to animals, not liked by his classmates and did not seem to know what was acceptable conduct. As stated by one witness: "Mark knew where his freedom was and he didn't know where his boundaries were." In two years he made a great deal of improvement. He now appears to be well disciplined, happy, relatively secure and popular with his classmates, although still subject to more than normal anxiety.

We place a great deal of reliance on the testimony of Dr. Glenn R. Hawks, a child psychologist. The trial court, in effect, disregarded Dr. Hawks' opinions stating: "The court has given full consideration to the good doctor's testimony, but cannot accept it at full face value because of exaggerated statement and the witness' attitude on the stand." We, of course, do not have the advantage of viewing the witness' conduct on the stand, but we have carefully reviewed his testimony and find nothing in the written record to justify such a summary dismissal of the opinions of this eminent child psychologist.

Dr. Hawks concluded that it was not for Mark's best interest to be removed from the Bannister home. He is criticized for reaching this conclusion without investigating the Painter home or finding out more about Mr. Painter's character. He answered: "I was most concerned about the welfare of the child, not the welfare of Mr. Painter, not about the welfare of the Bannisters. In as much as Mark has already made an adjustment and sees the Bannisters as his parental figures in his psychological makeup, to me this is the most critical factor. Disruption at this point, I think, would be detrimental to the child even tho Mr. Painter might well be a paragon of virtue. I think this would be a kind of thing which would not be in the best interest of the child. I think knowing something about where the child is at the present time is vital. I think something about where he might go, in my way of thinking is essentially untenable to me, and relatively unimportant. It isn't even helpful. The thing I was most concerned about was Mark's view of his own reality in which he presently lives. If this is destroyed I think it will have rather bad effects on Mark. I think then if one were to make a determination whether it would be to the parents' household, or the McNelly household, or X-household, then I think the further study would be appropriate."

We know more of Mr. Painter's way of life than Dr. Hawks. We have concluded that it does not offer as great a stability or security as the Bannister home. Throughout his testimony he emphasized Mark's need at this critical time is stability. He has it in the Bannister home.

Mark has established a father-son relationship with Mr. Bannister, which he apparently had never had with his natural father. He is happy, well adjusted and progressing nicely in his development. We do not believe it is for Mark's best interest to take him out of this stable atmosphere in the face of warnings of dire consequences from an eminent child psychologist and send him to an uncertain future in his father's home. Regardless of our appreciation of the father's love for his child and his desire to have him with him, we do not believe we have the moral right to gamble with this child's future. He should be encouraged in every way possible to know his father. We are sure there are many ways in which Mr. Painter can enrich Mark's life.

For the reasons stated, we reverse the trial court and remand the case for judgment in accordance herewith.

* * *

Topics for Further Discussion

1. Justice Stuart spends a large portion of his opinion discussing the lifestyle and beliefs of Mr. Painter, but then says these matters are not related by way of criticism. Do you find this statement plausible in light of the decision to take Mark away from his natural father? On what basis does the Court rely on the expert opinion of Dr. Hawks, after conceding that the justices knew more about Mr. Painter than did the doctor? Why didn't the Court defer to the judgment of the trial judge who heard the doctor testify?

2. What does it mean to say there is a statutory presumption in favor of awarding custody to a natural parent? Why didn't that presumption trump the right of elderly grandparents in a case where the Court admits the natural father is healthy, non-abusive and financially able to provide for his son? Mark was with his grandparents for approximately two years. Is this long enough to form so strong a bond that his natural father should lose custody? *See, Hulbert v. Hines,* 178 N.W.2d 354 (Iowa 1970), where the Iowa Supreme Court ordered the return of a child to her natural mother after liv-

ing her entire life from birth to age six with an aunt and uncle. The mother and father of the child asked the child's aunt and uncle right after the child's birth to take care of the child because the mother had a relapse of mental illness requiring institutionalization and the natural father was required to devote his energies to caring for his wife and the couple's older children. When the mother recovered her health enough to be released from the mental institution, the natural parents requested that the child be returned to them. The girl's aunt and uncle refused, and the parents filed a *habeas corpus* suit. The Iowa Supreme Court held that "[n]o doubt she will experience some upset by being returned to her parents but we conclude her best interest now and in the future will be served thereby."

3. In *Troxel v. Granville*, 530 U.S. 57 (2000), the Supreme Court was asked to consider the constitutionality of a Washington State statute that permitted "any person" to petition the court for visitation rights and authorized the state court to grant the right whenever it was in the best interests of the child. Paternal grandparents petitioned for the right to visit the children of their deceased son after the mother of the children, who had never married the son, decided to limit the right of the grandparents to see the kids. The Supreme Court, in an opinion by Justice O'Connor, found the Washington statute to be a violation of substantive due process. The Court held that, in the absence of a finding by a judge that a parent is unfit, it is a fundamental right of a parent to determine what is in the best interest of the children. Justice O'Connor observed as follows:

> In an ideal world, parents might always seek to cultivate the bonds between grandparents and their grandchildren. Needless to say, however, our world is far from perfect, and in it the decision whether such an intergenerational relationship would be beneficial in any specific case is for the parent to make in the first instance. And, if a fit parent's decision of the kind at issue here becomes subject to judicial review, the court must accord at least some special weight to the parent's own determination.

Can the *Painter* case be squared with *Troxel*?

In divorce proceedings where children are involved, the judge must decide three critical issues. Which parent will get custody of the children? How much money must the non-custodial parent pay for the support of the children? What are the rights and conditions under which the non-custodial parent can visit the children? These issues can be resolved by mutual agreement, but they often become a major point of dispute in divorce proceedings. The overriding standard for answering each of these questions is what is in the best interests of the children. Unfortunately, this is a legal standard that is far easier to state than it is to apply in real cases as demonstrated by the *Painter* case. Judges used to assume in custody matters that the best interests of the children would be served by their remaining with their mother. As gender based stereotypes have eroded, this presumption has begun to fade from the case law.

The duty to pay child support applies equally to legitimate and illegitimate children. Judges look to a variety of factors in determining the proper level of child support to be paid by the non-custodial parent. The Uniform Marriage and Divorce Act lists the following five factors: "(1) the financial resources of the child; (2) the financial resources of the custodial parent; (3) the standard of living the child would have enjoyed had the marriage not been dissolved; (4) the physical and emotional conditions of the child and his educational needs; and (5) the financial resources and needs of the noncustodial parent." Support orders can be modified to reflect changes in circumstances. The obligation to pay child support usually ends when the child reaches the age of majority or leaves the home of the custodial parent, but some courts and legislatures have extended the duty to include paying for the costs of a college education.

As difficult as it may be to determine the proper amount or duration of the support obligation, the larger problem has proven to be in the area of enforcement. It is one thing for a court to order support, and quite another altogether for the custodial parent to collect it. People move to distant locations, or simply cannot be located in the large and anonymous cities of America. The federal government became vitally interested in this issue as the number of children being supported under the provisions of the Aid to Families with Dependent Children (AFDC) program escalated. This interest led to the creation of the Office of Child Support Enforcement under the auspices of the U.S. Department of Health and Human Services. The federal government now funds the Child Support Enforcement Program in cooperation with state and local governments, allowing the local officials to find and prosecute, civilly or criminally, persons who willfully fail to make support payments as obligated. The State Department has also entered in a number of international agreements with foreign countries to locate support scofflaws who have moved from the U.S.

Visitation

Once a judge has granted a divorce and has decided custody and support, the final issue will be the rights, if any, of the non-custodial spouse to visit the children. A typical arrangement is for the non-custodial spouse to have the children on one or more weekends a month and then for a more extended period during the summer school holidays. This kind of arrangement presents the least amount of disruption to the school routine of the children. The visitation order can contain conditions, such as the exact place where the visitation is to occur; the time of pick-up and return; and whether it must be supervised. The custodial parent can be ordered by the court not to move to a distant location if it would effectively result in the inability of the non-custodial parent to visit the children. The next case takes the custody issue to the extreme, but students should be aware of the growing field of animal rights law that might one day shift the focus to the rights and interests of "parties" such as Zach.

Nuzzaci v. Nuzzaci
1995 Del. Fam. Ct. LEXIS 30 (April 19, 1995)

Crompton, J.

The Court has been asked to sign a Stipulation and Order concerning personal property, signed by both parties and their counsel. The gist of the Stipulation and Order concerns the visitation of a Golden Retriever (hereinafter "Zach") with Gail A. Nuzacci (hereinafter "Wife"). Because Wife's rental lease agreement does not permit Zach to stay with her more than one weekend per month and one afternoon per week, both Wife and Edward A. Nuzacci (hereinafter "Husband") have asked the Court to place its blessing on what is described as a "personal property division arrangement."

The Stipulation and Order is quite detailed as to when Wife shall have visitation and even goes so far as to say that, the specific weeknight to be chosen for visitation is flexible, taking into account the business engagements, vacations, and other social events of the "parents."

13 *Del.C.* §1507(f) gives this Court jurisdiction to determine, in addition to decrees of divorce or annulment, other matters where appropriate under the facts and law. Those

other matters include prayers for interim relief, alimony, property disposition, resumption of prior name, costs and attorneys fees, support for a child and custody and/or child visitation.

It is true that 13 Del.C. § 1513 gives the Court the right to dispose of marital property by equitably dividing it, distributing it or assigning it between the parties in such proportions as the Court deems just, after considering eleven relevant factors. The term "marital property" is defined as "all property acquired by either party subsequent to the marriage" with certain exceptions. Black's Law Dictionary, 1095 (5th ed. 1979) describes property as being "that which is peculiar or proper to any person; that which belongs exclusively to one.... The term is said to extend to every species of valuable right and interest." Thus, there is little doubt but that Zach is marital property to be distributed in some fashion by this Court, but I decline to sign an order which is in essence a visitation order in every respect, except as to the biological classification of the "*object d'etre*."

Carrying this argument even further, how could the Court possibly be able to make a decision in the event that the parties were unable to come to an agreement as to Zach's visitation? Chapter 5 of Title 13 speaks of the Duty to Support children, spouses, poor persons, and women with child conceived out of wedlock. Nowhere does it mention any duty to support a canine, bovine, ovine or even a guppy. Chapter 6 speaks of the uniform reciprocal enforcement of support, but before this Chapter can be placed into action, there must be a duty of support, which is found in Chapter 5 previously discussed. Chapter 7 speaks of parents and children in regard to such issues as custody and visitation. While it goes into great detail as to the factors which this Court must consider prior to determining the best interest of the *child*, nowhere does it mention what factors would have to be considered in the best interests of a non-human genus, should the parties not be able to agree on visitation. And, quite truthfully, the prospect of applying the seven factors of § 722(a) to a Zach, a Tabitha or even a fish called Wanda for that matter, would be an impossible task. For example, would it be abusive to forget to clean the fish bowl or have Tabitha declawed? If the door were opened on this type of litigation, the Court would next be forced to decide such issues as which dog training school, if any, is better for Zach's personality type and whether he should be clipped during the summer solstice or allowed to romp "*au naturel.*"

I do not in any way intend to offend Husband and Wife in the present action. While their dilemma is certainly a viable one, particularly in a marriage where there have been no children, the fact is that this Court is simply not going to get into the flora or fauna visitation business. The Court only has jurisdiction to award the dog to one spouse or the other.

On the other hand, these parties should be mature enough to realize that Zach means a great deal to each of them and that even though their marriage may not have succeeded, at one point or other they did presumably respect and care about each other. I would hope that they could resolve this issue peacefully and with regard for each other's positions, but if they cannot, the Court is powerless to come to their aid, except to award the entire dog to one spouse or the other.

* * *

Adoption

Not all parents are fit or able to take care of their children. Sometimes the parents are deceased, and sometimes the children are simply abandoned. In these cases, the state will arrange for the care and support of the children. This is done by placing the children in an institution or a foster home. Foster parents are paid a monthly sum to provide for one or more children in a home setting. There are many cases of abuse in the foster care system, but it is still seen as being better for children than growing up in an institution.

The ideal solution is to find adoptive parents who will provide the children with a loving and nurturing home. Adoption is a judicial process that permanently severs the legal rights and relationship of the natural parents to the child and transfers it to the adoptive parents. The general rule is that the decision to put a child up for adoption must be voluntarily made and be free from fraud or duress. The consent of both natural parents is required unless the biological parent is unknown or has abandoned the mother and child.

Adoption records used to be sealed so that neither the natural parents nor the adoptive child could find each other in the future. It was thought a clean break was in the best interests of all of the parties. The compelling need of some children to know their biological parents, combined with the growing importance of DNA and medical history information, has led to a cottage industry for private investigators. The amount of information to provide to adopted children remains a difficult and unanswered question.

There are two additional issues of interest in the area of adoption. The first relates to the huge growth in international adoptions. This presents a myriad of concerns regarding the best interests of the child (including the thorny issue of interracial adoption) and the horrors of an underground market in babies, where poor women are induced to sell their infants in order to survive. The Hague Adoption Convention, which entered into force in 1995, is a multilateral treaty setting internationally acceptable standards for adoption and procedures.

The second issue relates to whether same-sex couples are suitable candidates as adoptive parents. While the general trend in the state courts has been to permit adoption (*see*, e.g., *Adoptions of B.L.V.B. and E.L.V.B.* 628 A.2d 1271 (Vt. 1993) holding that "when the family unit is comprised of the natural mother and her partner, and the adoption is in the best interests of the children, terminating the natural mother's rights is unreasonable and unnecessary"), the court of appeals in *Lofton v. Secretary of Dept. of Children and Family Services*, 358 F.3d 804 (11th Cir. 2004), *cert denied*, 543 U.S. 1081 (2005) held that a Florida statute prohibiting adoption by actively practicing homosexuals was constitutional. The reasoning of the Court was as follows:

> In short, a person who seeks to adopt is asking the state to conduct an examination into his or her background and to make a determination as to the best interests of a child in need of adoption. In doing so, the state's overriding interest is not providing individuals the opportunity to become parents, but rather identifying those individuals whom it deems most capable of parenting adoptive children and providing them with a secure family environment. Indicative of the strength of the state's interest — indeed duty — in this context is the fact that appellants have not cited to us, nor have we found, a single precedent in which the Supreme Court or one of our sister circuits has sustained a constitutional challenge to an adoption scheme or practice by any individual other than a natural parent, and even many challenges by natural parents have failed.

Surrogate Mother Contracts

A surrogate mother is a woman who agrees, usually for a fee, to be impregnated for the purpose of giving birth to a child on behalf of a couple who are not able to have a child of their own. Such arrangements typically provide that the birth mother will give the baby up for adoption to the other party as soon as the baby is born. The issue presented is one deeply rooted in public policy as can be seen from the following case.

In the Matter of Baby M
537 A.2d 1227 (N.J. 1988)

Wilentz, C.J.

In this matter the Court is asked to determine the validity of a contract that purports to provide a new way of bringing children into a family. For a fee of $10,000, a woman agrees to be artificially inseminated with the semen of another woman's husband; she is to conceive a child, carry it to term, and after its birth surrender it to the natural father and his wife. The intent of the contract is that the child's natural mother will thereafter be forever separated from her child. The wife is to adopt the child, and she and the natural father are to be regarded as its parents for all purposes. The contract providing for this is called a "surrogacy contract," the natural mother inappropriately called the "surrogate mother."

We invalidate the surrogacy contract because it conflicts with the law and public policy of this State. While we recognize the depth of the yearning of infertile couples to have their own children, we find the payment of money to a "surrogate" mother illegal, perhaps criminal, and potentially degrading to women. Although in this case we grant custody to the natural father, the evidence having clearly proved such custody to be in the best interests of the infant, we void both the termination of the surrogate mother's parental rights and the adoption of the child by the wife/stepparent. We thus restore the "surrogate" as the mother of the child. We remand the issue of the natural mother's visitation rights to the trial court, since that issue was not reached below and the record before us is not sufficient to permit us to decide it *de novo*.

We find no offense to our present laws where a woman voluntarily and without payment agrees to act as a "surrogate" mother, provided that she is not subject to a binding agreement to surrender her child. Moreover, our holding today does not preclude the Legislature from altering the current statutory scheme, within constitutional limits, so as to permit surrogacy contracts. Under current law, however, the surrogacy agreement before us is illegal and invalid.

* * *

Topics for Further Discussion

1. The *Baby M* case made news around the world when the surrogate mother changed her mind after Baby M was born and refused to turn her over to the natural father as provided in the contract. Instead, she fled to Florida where the baby was eventually found and returned to New Jersey. What are the public policy grounds against surrogacy contracts? Do you agree with the Court's conclusions?

2. On remand to the trial court, the natural mother was granted liberal visitation rights with Baby M. Do you think either of the parties to the agreement should be satisfied with the result? How about Baby M? When Baby M turned eighteen in 2004, she terminated the parental relationship with her surrogate mother and was adopted by her natural father's wife.

3. In *Johnson v. Calvert*, 851 P.2d 776 (Cal. 1993), the California Supreme Court was called upon to decide who was the "mother" of a child born by a surrogate mother under California law. It held as follows:

Because two women each have presented acceptable proof of maternity, we do not believe this case can be decided without enquiring into the parties' intentions as manifested in the surrogacy agreement. Mark and Crispina are a couple who desired to have a child of their own genes but are physically unable to do so without the help of reproductive technology. They affirmatively intended the birth of the child, and took the steps necessary to effect in vitro fertilization. But for their acted-on intention, the child would not exist. Anna agreed to facilitate the procreation of Mark's and Crispina's child. The parties' aim was to bring Mark's and Crispina's child into the world, not for Mark and Crispina to donate a zygote to Anna. Crispina from the outset intended to be the child's mother. Although the gestative function Anna performed was necessary to bring about the child's birth, it is safe to say that Anna would not have been given the opportunity to gestate or deliver the child had she, prior to implantation of the zygote, manifested her own intent to be the child's mother. No reason appears why Anna's later change of heart should vitiate the determination that Crispina is the child's natural mother.

We conclude that although the Act recognizes both genetic consanguinity and giving birth as means of establishing a mother and child relationship, when the two means do not coincide in one woman, she who intended to procreate the child—that is, she who intended to bring about the birth of a child that she intended to raise as her own—is the natural mother under California law.

The court also addressed the public policy issue (one that had split feminists in the Baby M case) deciding as follows:

The argument that a woman cannot knowingly and intelligently agree to gestate and deliver a baby for intending parents carries overtones of the reasoning that for centuries prevented women from attaining equal economic rights and professional status under the law. To resurrect this view is both to foreclose a personal and economic choice on the part of the surrogate mother, and to deny intending parents what may be their only means of procreating a child of their own genes. Certainly in the present case it cannot seriously be argued that Anna, a licensed vocational nurse who had done well in school and who had previously borne a child, lacked the intellectual wherewithal or life experience necessary to make an informed decision to enter into the surrogacy contract.

Illegitimacy

For centuries, law and society denied virtually all rights (inheritance for example) to children born out of wedlock. Courts and legislatures alike have erased most, if not all, of these forms of discrimination from the law. So important was the determination of legitimacy, that states long ago enacted statutes providing a presumption of legitimacy to any child born to a married woman living together with her husband. In *Michael H. v. Gerald D.*, 491 U.S. 110 (1989), the Supreme Court was called upon to rule on the constitutionality of a California statute containing a presumption of legitimacy and providing that it could only be rebutted by the mother or father, and then only in limited circumstances. Michael H. sought to challenge the paternity of a child born to Carole D. at the time when she was married to Gerald D. Carole and Michael had an affair, and blood tests revealed that Michael was 98% certain to be the father of the child. He sought to challenge the legitimacy presumption in order to get visitation rights with the child.

Justice Scalia, in a plurality opinion, reaffirmed the validity of statutory presumptions in favor of legitimacy, and rejected the constitutional arguments saying "[w]hat counts is whether the States in fact award substantive parental rights to the natural father of a child conceived within, and born into, an extant marital union that wishes to embrace the child. We are not aware of a single case, old or new, that has done so. This is not the stuff of which fundamental rights qualifying as liberty interests are made."

Reproductive Rights

The right to procreate is one of the most fundamental of rights under the Constitution. In *Griswold v. Connecticut*, 381 U.S. 479 (1965), the Court struck down a state statute making it a crime to use contraceptive devices, or to aid and abet their use. A doctor and the Executive Director of Planned Parenthood were convicted for giving birth control information to married women. The Court stated that the relations between a husband and wife, including the decision whether to have children, were "intimate to the degree of being sacred" and within the zone of privacy; a right "older than the Bill of Rights— older than our political parties, older than our school system."

The *Griswold* decision was followed by *Eisenstadt v. Baird*, 405 U.S. 438 (1972). In *Eisenstadt*, an individual was convicted in Massachusetts after giving a lecture to a group of college students on contraception and providing one woman in the audience with a contraceptive device. Massachusetts argued that this case could be distinguished from *Griswold* because the women in the audience were single and, hence, no right of marital privacy was implicated. The Supreme Court rejected this argument writing that:

> It is true that in *Griswold* the right of privacy in question inhered in the marital relationship. Yet the marital couple is not an independent entity with a mind and heart of its own, but an association of two individuals each with a separate intellectual and emotional makeup. If the right of privacy means anything, it is the right of the *individual*, married or single, to be free from unwarranted government intrusion into matters so fundamentally affecting a person as the decision whether to bear or beget a child.

Soon after *Eisenstadt*, the Supreme Court rendered its landmark decision in *Roe v. Wade*, 410 U.S. 113 (1973). This has arguably been the single most controversial decision in the history of the Supreme Court. In an opinion by Justice Blackmun, the Supreme Court extended the right of privacy to include the absolute right of a pregnant woman to obtain an abortion during the first trimester of pregnancy. The Court declared that the state's legitimate interest in protecting the life of the unborn fetus grows progressively as the pregnancy evolves. In her second trimester, the state can place restrictions on abortion and during the third trimester, when the fetus is capable of living outside of the womb, it can be banned altogether.

It is unlikely that anyone could have predicted the firestorm of protest the *Roe* decision would set off in America. It has pitted the "Right to Life" camp squarely against the "Pro-Choice" movement. Anti-abortion extremists have set up websites encouraging the murder of doctors who perform abortions, women entering abortion clinics have been splattered with blood and had pictures of aborted fetuses thrust into their faces. In the 2004 presidential election, some elements of the Catholic Church urged its members to vote against Senator John Kerry, a devout Catholic, based on the single issue of his support of choice. Multiple attempts have been made in state legislatures and by the federal government to overturn or roll back the import of *Roe* by requiring mandatory waiting periods, consent requirements and other obstacles as explained in the following case.

Planned Parenthood of S.E. Pennsylvania v. Casey

505 U.S. 833 (1992)

O'Connor, Kennedy, and Souter, JJ.

Liberty finds no refuge in a jurisprudence of doubt. Yet, 19 years after our holding that the Constitution protects a woman's right to terminate her pregnancy in its early stages, that definition of liberty is still questioned. Joining the respondents as *amicus curiae*, the United States, as it has done in five other cases in the last decade, again asks us to overrule *Roe v. Wade*.

At issue in these cases are five provisions of the Pennsylvania Abortion Control Act of 1982, as amended in 1988 and 1989. The Act requires that a woman seeking an abortion give her informed consent prior to the abortion procedure, and specifies that she be provided with certain information at least 24 hours before the abortion is performed. For a minor to obtain an abortion, the Act requires the informed consent of one of her parents, but provides for a judicial bypass option if the minor does not wish to or cannot obtain a parent's consent. Another provision of the Act requires that, unless certain exceptions apply, a married woman seeking an abortion must sign a statement indicating that she has notified her husband of her intended abortion. The Act exempts compliance with these three requirements in the event of a "medical emergency," which is defined in 3203 of the Act. In addition to the above provisions regulating the performance of abortions, the Act imposes certain reporting requirements on facilities that provide abortion services.

Before any of these provisions took effect, the petitioners, who are five abortion clinics and one physician representing himself as well as a class of physicians who provide abortion services, brought this suit seeking declaratory and injunctive relief. Each provision was challenged as unconstitutional on its face.

It must be stated at the outset and with clarity that Roe's essential holding, the holding we reaffirm, has three parts. First is a recognition of the right of the woman to choose to have an abortion before viability and to obtain it without undue interference from the State. Before viability, the State's interests are not strong enough to support a prohibition of abortion or the imposition of a substantial obstacle to the woman's effective right to elect the procedure. Second is a confirmation of the State's power to restrict abortions after fetal viability if the law contains exceptions for pregnancies which endanger the woman's life or health. And third is the principle that the State has legitimate interests from the outset of the pregnancy in protecting the health of the woman and the life of the fetus that may become a child. These principles do not contradict one another; and we adhere to each.

Men and women of good conscience can disagree, and we suppose some always shall disagree, about the profound moral and spiritual implications of terminating a pregnancy, even in its earliest stage. Some of us as individuals find abortion offensive to our most basic principles of morality, but that cannot control our decision. Our obligation is to define the liberty of all, not to mandate our own moral code. The underlying constitutional issue is whether the State can resolve these philosophic questions in such a definitive way that a woman lacks all choice in the matter, except perhaps in those rare circumstances in which the pregnancy is itself a danger to her own life or health, or is the result of rape or incest.

Some guiding principles should emerge. What is at stake is the woman's right to make the ultimate decision, not a right to be insulated from all others in doing so. Regulations which do no more than create a structural mechanism by which the State, or the parent or guardian of a minor, may express profound respect for the life of the unborn are permitted, if they are not a substantial obstacle to the woman's exercise of the right to choose. Unless it has that effect on her right of choice, a state measure designed to persuade her to choose childbirth over abortion will be upheld if reasonably related to that goal. Regulations designed to foster the health of a woman seeking an abortion are valid if they do not constitute an undue burden.

Even when jurists reason from shared premises, some disagreement is inevitable. That is to be expected in the application of any legal standard which must accommodate life's complexity. We do not expect it to be otherwise with respect to the undue burden standard. We give this summary:

(a) To protect the central right recognized by *Roe v. Wade* while at the same time accommodating the State's profound interest in potential life, we will employ the undue burden analysis as explained in this opinion. An undue burden exists, and therefore a provision of law is invalid, if its purpose or effect is to place a substantial obstacle in the path of a woman seeking an abortion before the fetus attains viability.

(b) We reject the rigid trimester framework of *Roe v. Wade*. To promote the State's profound interest in potential life, throughout pregnancy, the State may take measures to ensure that the woman's choice is informed, and measures designed to advance this interest will not be invalidated as long as their purpose is to persuade the woman to choose childbirth over abortion. These measures must not be an undue burden on the right.

(c) As with any medical procedure, the State may enact regulations to further the health or safety of a woman seeking an abortion. Unnecessary health regulations that have the purpose or effect of presenting a substantial obstacle to a woman seeking an abortion impose an undue burden on the right.

(d) Our adoption of the undue burden analysis does not disturb the central holding of *Roe v. Wade*, and we reaffirm that holding. Regardless of whether exceptions are made for particular circumstances, a State may not prohibit any woman from making the ultimate decision to terminate her pregnancy before viability.

(e) We also reaffirm *Roe's* holding that, subsequent to viability, the State, in promoting its interest in the potentiality of human life, may, if it chooses, regulate, and even proscribe, abortion except where it is necessary, in appropriate medical judgment, for the preservation of the life or health of the mother.

Scalia, J., concurring in the judgment in part and dissenting in part

My views on this matter are unchanged from those I set forth in my separate opinions in *Webster v. Reproductive Health Services*, 492 U.S. 490, 532 (1989) (opinion concurring in part and concurring in judgment), and *Ohio v. Akron Center for Reproductive Health*, 497 U.S. 502, 520 (1990) (Akron II) (concurring opinion). The States may, if they wish, permit abortion on demand, but the Constitution does not require them to do so. The permissibility of abortion, and the limitations upon it, are to be resolved like most important questions in our democracy: by citizens trying to persuade one another and then voting. As the Court acknowledges, "where reasonable people disagree, the government can adopt one position or the other." The Court is correct in adding the qualification that this "assumes a state of affairs in which the choice does not intrude upon a protected liberty," — but the crucial part of that qualification is the penultimate word. A

State's choice between two positions on which reasonable people can disagree is constitutional even when (as is often the case) it intrudes upon a "liberty" in the absolute sense. Laws against bigamy, for example—with which entire societies of reasonable people disagree—intrude upon men and women's liberty to marry and live with one another. But bigamy happens not to be a liberty specially "protected" by the Constitution.

That is, quite simply, the issue in this case: not whether the power of a woman to abort her unborn child is a "liberty" in the absolute sense; or even whether it is a liberty of great importance to many women. Of course it is both. The issue is whether it is a liberty protected by the Constitution of the United States. I am sure it is not. I reach that conclusion not because of anything so exalted as my views concerning the "concept of existence, of meaning, of the universe, and of the mystery of human life." Rather, I reach it for the same reason I reach the conclusion that bigamy is not constitutionally protected—because of two simple facts: (1) the Constitution says absolutely nothing about it, and (2) the longstanding traditions of American society have permitted it to be legally proscribed.

* * *

Topics for Further Discussion

1. The Court was badly fractured in its reasoning, with multiple concurrences and dissents being filed. The basic holding was that a state cannot ban abortion but can place restrictions on it so long as the restrictions are not an "undue burden." Is this a workable standard for such an important matter?

2. Is it possible to reconcile the statement that the Liberty interest in abortion overrides any personal moral objection against abortion with Justice Scalia's argument?

3. In *Stenberg v. Carhart*, 530 U.S. 914 (2000), the Supreme Court in an opinion by Justice Breyer invalidated a Nebraska statute making partial birth abortions illegal. The reasons for striking down the law were its failure to provide an exception for the health of the mother and the undue burden it placed on the woman's right to an abortion.

Key Terms and Concepts

Alimony
Civil Union
Legitimacy and Illegitimacy
"No Fault" Divorce
Palimony
Rebuttable Presumption
Rehabilitation Alimony
Reimbursement Alimony
Same-Sex Marriage
Wedlock

Chapter 13

Administrative Law

"Most of the problems that we now face are technical problems, are administrative problems. They are very sophisticated judgments, which do not lend themselves to the great sort of passionate movements which have stirred this country so often in the past. [They] deal with questions which are now beyond the comprehension of most men."

John F. Kennedy, Remarks to Members of the White House Conference on National Economic Issues, 1962 Pub. Papers 420 (May 21, 1962)

While the image of American lawyers is based on the courtroom, much of their work in fact concerns administrative agencies. These are the entities that oversee most of the day-to-day regulations covering innumerable facets of American life. At the federal level, one can begin to understand the breadth of administrative law just by looking to the positions in the President's cabinet. Each of the cabinet members heads an agency: the Departments of Agriculture, Commerce, Defense, Education, Energy, Health and Human Services, Homeland Security, Housing and Urban Development, Interior, Justice, Labor, State, Transportation, Treasury, and Veterans Affairs. Numerous sub-agencies reside within those departments. The Patent and Trademark Office, for example, is part of the Department of Commerce. Similarly, the Internal Revenue Service (the tax agency) is part of the Department of the Treasury. These are all part of the Executive branch of the government. Some freestanding, purely executive agencies, such as the Environmental Protection Agency, or the Small Business Administration, also exist. Most of these are run by a single agency head.

Some federal agencies within the Executive Branch are called "independent agencies" because—unlike the others—their leaders cannot be fired by the President once they have been confirmed for a term of specific years. Most of these are multi-member regulatory boards and commissions, such as the Federal Communications Commission and the National Labor Relations Board.

Administrative agencies also exist in every state. In Texas, for example, the Department of Public Safety is responsible for issuing driver's licenses, the Parks and Wildlife Department handles hunting and fishing licenses, the Board of Barber Examiners sets qualifications for barbers and manicurists, and the Department of State Health Services regulates body piercing studios.

What is obvious from even this short list is that administrative law reaches deep into the daily activities of people all over the country. Rules and regulations made by administrative agencies affect not only those directly involved in the activities but also those they act upon. One who wants to engage in the business of body piercing in Texas must meet certain standards. Consumers then are restricted to choosing from among those licensed. The agency balances the value of free and open competition against the importance of ensuring safe practices.

No Administrative Law book can explain every aspect of administrative activity throughout the United States, let alone just one chapter in an overall study of American law. In this chapter, we will look to federal administrative practice as representative of the area. The general themes are the same in the states, but like the federal government, which enacted an Administrative Procedure Act (APA) in 1946, each state has its own administrative procedure act. A lawyer whose work involves such matters must consult the law of the particular state. The APA covers four major aspects of government—administrative adjudication, administrative rulemaking, judicial review of agency action, and openness (transparency) of government operations. Each of these aspects will be discussed in this chapter.

Delegation

The first issue in any administrative law matter is whether the agency has the power (i.e., jurisdiction) to act. Administrative agencies are a concession to the complexity of life, but, in a democratic society such as the United States, ultimate decision-making power rests with elected representatives. What this means is that agencies exist to do the bidding of Congress (or in a state setting, the legislature). Not only do elected representatives have the power to make the ultimate decisions, they have the duty to do so.

To what extent must elected officials tell agencies what to do? The "non-delegation" doctrine holds that legislators must at least give agencies some direction as to how to proceed. The agency members, who are not elected, can fill in the details, but Congress must provide sufficient standards. The Constitution gives lawmaking power to the Congress, and it does not mention administrative agencies by name.

In considering the following case, try to determine just what kind of standards were required.

A.L.A. Schechter Poultry v. United States
295 U.S. 495 (1935)

Hughes, C.J.

Petitioners were convicted in the District Court of the United States for the Eastern District of New York on eighteen counts of an indictment charging violations of what is known as the "Live Poultry Code," and on an additional count for conspiracy to commit such violations. [T]he defendants contended that the code had been adopted pursuant to an unconstitutional delegation by Congress of legislative power.

The defendants are slaughterhouse operators. A.L.A. Schechter Poultry Corporation and Schechter Live Poultry Market are corporations conducting wholesale poultry slaughterhouse markets in Brooklyn, New York City. Defendants ordinarily purchase their live poultry from commission men at the West Washington Market in New York City or at the railroad terminals serving the city, but occasionally they purchase from commission men in Philadelphia. They buy the poultry for slaughter and resale. After the poultry is trucked to their slaughterhouse markets in Brooklyn, it is there sold, usually within twenty-four hours, to retail poultry dealers and butchers who sell directly to consumers. The poultry purchased from defendants is immediately slaughtered, prior to delivery, by [persons] in defendants' employ.

The "Live Poultry Code" was promulgated under section 3 of the National Industrial Recovery Act. That section authorizes the President to approve "codes of fair competition." Such a code may be approved for a trade or industry, upon application by one or more trade or industrial associations or groups, if the President finds (1) that such associations or groups "impose no inequitable restrictions on admission to membership therein and are truly representative," and (2) that such codes are not designed "to promote monopolies or to eliminate or oppress small enterprises and will not operate to discriminate against them, and will tend to effectuate the policy" of title 1 of the act. Such codes "shall not permit monopolies or monopolistic practices." As a condition of his approval, the President may provide such exceptions to and exemptions as the President in his discretion deems necessary to effectuate the policy herein declared." Where such a code has not been approved, the President may prescribe one, either on his own motion or on complaint.

The "Live Poultry Code" was approved by the President on April 13, 1934. The declared purpose is "To effect the policies of title I of the National Industrial Recovery Act." The code is established as "a code for fair competition for the live poultry industry of the metropolitan area in and about the City of New York." The code fixes the number of hours for workdays. It provides that no employee, with certain exceptions, shall be permitted to work in excess of forty hours in any one week, and that no employees, save as stated, "shall be paid in any pay period less than at the rate of fifty (50) cents per hour." The article containing "general labor provisions" prohibits the employment of any person under 16 years of age, and declares that employees shall have the right of "collective bargaining" and freedom of choice with respect to labor organizations.

Of the eighteen counts of the indictment upon which the defendants were convicted, aside from the count for conspiracy, two counts charged violation of the minimum wage and maximum hour provisions of the code.

The Question of the Delegation of Legislative Power. We recently had occasion to review the pertinent decisions and the general principles which govern the determination of this question. *Panama Refining Co. v. Ryan*, 293 U.S. 388 (1935). The Constitution provides that "All legislative powers herein granted shall be vested in a Congress of the United States, which shall consist of a Senate and House of Representatives." Article 1, § 1. And the Congress is authorized 'To make all Laws which shall be necessary and proper for carrying into Execution' its general powers. The Congress is not permitted to abdicate or to transfer to others the essential legislative functions with which it is thus vested. We have repeatedly recognized the necessity of adapting legislation to complex conditions involving a host of details with which the national Legislature cannot deal directly. We pointed out in the *Panama Refining Co.* case that the Constitution has never been regarded as denying to Congress the necessary resources of flexibility and practicality, which will enable it to perform its function in laying down policies and establishing standards, while leaving to selected instrumentalities the making of subordinate rules within prescribed limits and the determination of facts to which the policy as declared by the Legislature is to apply. But we said that the constant recognition of the necessity and validity of such provisions, and the wide range of administrative authority which has been developed by means of them, cannot be allowed to obscure the limitations of the authority to delegate, if our constitutional system is to be maintained.

Accordingly, we look to the statute to see whether Congress has overstepped these limitations—whether Congress in authorizing "codes of fair competition" has itself established the standards of legal obligation, thus performing its essential legislative function, or, by the failure to enact such standards, has attempted to transfer that function to others.

The act does not define "fair competition." "Unfair competition," as known to the common law, is a limited concept. Primarily, and strictly, it relates to the palming off of one's goods as those of a rival trader. Unfairness in competition has been predicated on acts which lie outside the ordinary course of business and are tainted by fraud or coercion or conduct otherwise prohibited by law. But it is evident that in its widest range, "unfair competition," as it has been understood in the law, does not reach the objectives of the codes which are authorized by the National Industrial Recovery Act.

The government urges that the codes will "consist of rules of competition deemed fair for each industry by representative members of that industry—by the persons most vitally concerned and most familiar with its problems." But would it be seriously contended that Congress could delegate its legislative authority to trade or industrial associations or groups so as to empower them to enact the laws they deem to be wise and beneficent for the rehabilitation and expansion of their trade or industries? Such a delegation of legislative power is unknown to our law, and is utterly inconsistent with the constitutional prerogatives and duties of Congress.

Section 3 of the Recovery Act is without precedent. It supplies no standards for any trade, industry, or activity. It does not undertake to prescribe rules of conduct to be applied to particular states of fact determined by appropriate administrative procedure. Instead of prescribing rules of conduct, it authorizes the making of codes to prescribe them. For that legislative undertaking, section 3 sets up no standards, aside from the statement of the general aims of rehabilitation, correction, and expansion described in section 1. In view of the scope of that broad declaration and of the nature of the few restrictions that are imposed, the discretion of the President in approving or prescribing codes, and thus enacting laws for the government of trade and industry throughout the country, is virtually unfettered. We think that the code-making authority thus conferred is an unconstitutional delegation of legislative power.

* * *

National Cable Television Assoc. v. United States
415 U.S. 336 (1974)

Marshall, J., concurring

The notion that the Constitution narrowly confines the power of Congress to delegate authority to administrative agencies, which was briefly in vogue in the 1930s, has been virtually abandoned by the Court for all practical purposes, at least in the absence of a delegation creating "the danger of overbroad, unauthorized, and arbitrary application of criminal sanctions in an area of (constitutionally) protected freedoms." It is hardly surprising that, until today's decision, the Court had not relied upon *Schechter Poultry Corp. v. United States*, almost since the day it was decided.

> In only two cases in all American history have congressional delegations to public authorities been held invalid. Neither delegation was to a regularly constituted administrative agency which followed an established procedure designed to afford the customary safeguards to affected parties. The *Panama* case was influenced by exceptional executive disorganization and in absence of such a special factor would not be followed today. The *Schechter* case involved excessive delegation of the kind that Congress is not likely again to make.

In absence of palpable abuse or true congressional abdication, the non-delegation doctrine to which the Supreme Court has in the past often paid lip service is without practical force. 1 K. Davis, Administrative Law Treatise § 2.01 (1958).

* * *

The following case involved the Clean Air Act, in which Congress required the Environmental Protection Agency to set air quality standards based on a rather broad standard of "requisite to protect the public health." The D.C. Circuit Court of Appeals ruled that the agency's interpretation of the delegated power, but not the statute itself, lacked an "intelligible principle." It remanded the standards to the agency to allow it to adopt a more limited interpretation of the Act. That provided the Supreme Court an opportunity to take up the non-delegation doctrine yet again.

Whitman v. American Trucking Assn.
531 U.S. 457 (2001)

Scalia, J.

The idea that an agency can cure an unconstitutionally standardless delegation of power by declining to exercise some of that power seems to us internally contradictory. The very choice of which portion of the power to exercise — that is to say, the prescription of the standard that Congress had omitted — would *itself* be an exercise of the forbidden legislative authority. Whether the statute delegates legislative power is a question for the courts, and an agency's voluntary self-denial has no bearing upon the answer.

The scope of discretion § 109(b)(1) allows is in fact well within the outer limits of our nondelegation precedents. In the history of the Court we have found the requisite "intelligible principle" lacking in only two statutes, one of which provided literally no guidance for the exercise of discretion, and the other of which conferred authority to regulate the entire economy on the basis of no more precise a standard than stimulating the economy by assuring "fair competition." We have, on the other hand, upheld the validity of the Public Utility Holding Company Act of 1935, which gave the Securities and Exchange Commission authority to modify the structure of holding company systems so as to ensure that they are not "unduly or unnecessarily complicate[d]" and do not "unfairly or inequitably distribute voting power among security holders." We have approved the wartime conferral of agency power to fix the prices of commodities at a level that "'will be generally fair and equitable and will effectuate the [in some respects conflicting] purposes of th[e] Act.'" And we have found an "intelligible principle" in various statutes authorizing regulation in the "public interest." In short, we have "almost never felt qualified to second-guess Congress regarding the permissible degree of policy judgment that can be left to those executing or applying the law." *Mistretta v. United States* (1989) (Scalia, J., dissenting).

[E]ven in sweeping regulatory schemes we have never demanded, as the Court of Appeals did here, that statutes provide a "determinate criterion" for saying "how much [of the regulated harm] is too much." Section 109(b)(1) of the CAA, which to repeat we interpret as requiring the EPA to set air quality standards at the level that is "requisite" that is, not lower or higher than is necessary — to protect the public health with an adequate margin of safety, fits comfortably within the scope of discretion permitted by our precedent.

We therefore reverse the judgment of the Court of Appeals remanding for reinterpretation that would avoid a supposed delegation of legislative power.

* * *

Topics for Further Discussion

1. Is anything left of the non-delegation doctrine after *Whitman*?

2. If you were a staff member of the Environmental Protection Agency, would you understand what Congress wanted you to do in calling for "requisite" standards? Did the Congress itself understand what it meant?

* * *

If elected officials must maintain ultimate authority because of democratic principles, may the legislature overturn the decision of an administrative agency? This approach has been called a "legislative veto." In the case of *INS v. Chadha*, an alien who had been in the United States legally overstayed his student visa. He could have been deported, but the Attorney General decided to suspend deportation per his authority set forth in Section 244(c)(2) of the Immigration and Nationality Act (Act). The same section of the Act, however, allowed for a "legislative veto." It said that either the House of Representatives or the Senate could invalidate such a suspension because Congress holds ultimate responsibility for setting immigration policy, which is then implemented by the Immigration and Naturalization Service. The House passed such a resolution, and Chadha challenged it as unconstitutional.

INS v. Chadha
462 U.S. 919 (1983)

Burger, C.J.

The Constitution sought to divide the delegated powers of the new federal government into three defined categories, legislative, executive and judicial, to assure, as nearly as possible, that each Branch of government would confine itself to its assigned responsibility. The hydraulic pressure inherent within each of the separate Branches to exceed the outer limits of its power, even to accomplish desirable objectives, must be resisted.

In purporting to exercise power defined in Art. I, § 8, cl. 4, to "establish an uniform Rule of Naturalization," the House took action that had the purpose and effect of altering the legal rights, duties and relations of persons, including the Attorney General, Executive Branch officials and Chadha, all outside the legislative branch. Section 244(c)(2) purports to authorize one House of Congress to require the Attorney General to deport an individual alien whose deportation otherwise would be cancelled under § 244. The one-House veto operated in this case to overrule the Attorney General and mandate Chadha's deportation; absent the House action, Chadha would remain in the United States. Congress has *acted* and its action has altered Chadha's status.

The nature of the decision implemented by the one-House veto in this case further manifests its legislative character. After long experience with the clumsy, time consuming private bill procedure, Congress made a deliberate choice to delegate to the Executive Branch, and specifically to the Attorney General, the authority to allow deportable aliens to remain in this country in certain specified circumstances. It is not disputed that this choice to delegate authority is precisely the kind of decision that can be implemented only in accordance with the procedures set out in Art. I. Disagreement with the Attorney

General's decision on Chadha's deportation — that is, Congress' decision to deport Chadha — no less than Congress' original choice to delegate to the Attorney General the authority to make that decision, involves determinations of policy that Congress can implement in only one way; bicameral passage followed by presentment to the President. Congress must abide by its delegation of authority until that delegation is legislatively altered or revoked.

Since it is clear that the action by the House under § 244(c)(2) was not within any of the express constitutional exceptions authorizing one House to act alone, and equally clear that it was an exercise of legislative power, that action was subject to the standards prescribed in Article I. The bicameral requirement, the Presentment Clauses, the President's veto, and Congress' power to override a veto were intended to erect enduring checks on each Branch and to protect the people from the improvident exercise of power by mandating certain prescribed steps. To preserve those checks, and maintain the separation of powers, the carefully defined limits on the power of each Branch must not be eroded. To accomplish what has been attempted by one House of Congress in this case requires action in conformity with the express procedures of the Constitution's prescription for legislative action: passage by a majority of both Houses and presentment to the President.

In purely practical terms, it is obviously easier for action to be taken by one House without submission to the President; but it is crystal clear from the records of the Convention, contemporaneous writings and debates, that the Framers ranked other values higher than efficiency.

There is unmistakable expression of a determination that legislation by the national Congress be a step-by-step, deliberate and deliberative process.

The choices we discern as having been made in the Constitutional Convention impose burdens on governmental processes that often seem clumsy, inefficient, even unworkable, but those hard choices were consciously made by men who had lived under a form of government that permitted arbitrary governmental acts to go unchecked. There is no support in the Constitution or decisions of this Court for the proposition that the cumbersomeness and delays often encountered in complying with explicit Constitutional standards may be avoided, either by the Congress or by the President. With all the obvious flaws of delay, untidiness, and potential for abuse, we have not yet found a better way to preserve freedom than by making the exercise of power subject to the carefully crafted restraints spelled out in the Constitution.

We hold that the Congressional veto provision in § 244(c)(2) is unconstitutional.

White, J., dissenting

Today the Court not only invalidates § 244(c)(2) of the Immigration and Nationality Act, but also sounds the death knell for nearly 200 other statutory provisions in which Congress has reserved a "legislative veto." The prominence of the legislative veto mechanism in our contemporary political system and its importance to Congress can hardly be overstated. It has become a central means by which Congress secures the accountability of executive and independent agencies. Without the legislative veto, Congress is faced with a Hobson's choice: either to refrain from delegating the necessary authority, leaving itself with a hopeless task of writing laws with the requisite specificity to cover endless special circumstances across the entire policy landscape, or in the alternative, to abdicate its lawmaking function to the executive branch and independent agencies. To choose the former leaves major national problems unresolved; to opt for the latter risks unaccountable policymaking by those not elected to fill that role. Accordingly, over the past five decades, the legislative veto has been placed in nearly 200 statutes. The device is known in every field of governmental concern: reorganization, budgets, foreign affairs, war powers, and regulation of trade, safety, energy, the environment and the economy.

The history of the legislative veto also makes clear that it has not been a sword with which Congress has struck out to aggrandize itself at the expense of the other branches—the concerns of Madison and Hamilton. Rather, the veto has been a means of defense, a reservation of ultimate authority necessary if Congress is to fulfill its designated role under Article I as the nation's lawmaker. While the President has often objected to particular legislative vetoes, generally those left in the hands of congressional committees, the Executive has more often agreed to legislative review as the price for a broad delegation of authority. To be sure, the President may have preferred unrestricted power, but that could be precisely why Congress thought it essential to retain a check on the exercise of delegated authority.

If Congress may delegate lawmaking power to independent and executive agencies, it is most difficult to understand Article I as forbidding Congress from also reserving a check on legislative power for itself. Absent the veto, the agencies receiving delegations of legislative or quasi-legislative power may issue regulations having the force of law without bicameral approval and without the President's signature. It is thus not apparent why the reservation of a veto over the exercise of that legislative power must be subject to a more exacting test. In both cases, it is enough that the initial statutory authorizations comply with the Article I requirements.

I do not suggest that all legislative vetoes are necessarily consistent with separation of powers principles. A legislative check on an inherently executive function, for example that of initiating prosecutions, poses an entirely different question. But the legislative veto device here—and in many other settings—is far from an instance of legislative tyranny over the Executive. It is a necessary check on the unavoidably expanding power of the agencies, both executive and independent, as they engage in exercising authority delegated by Congress.

I regret that I am in disagreement with my colleagues on the fundamental questions that this case presents. But even more I regret the destructive scope of the Court's holding. It reflects a profoundly different conception of the Constitution than that held by the Courts which sanctioned the modern administrative state. Today's decision strikes down in one fell swoop provisions in more laws enacted by Congress than the Court has cumulatively invalidated in its history. I fear it will now be more difficult "to insure that the fundamental policy decisions in our society will be made not by an appointed official but by the body immediately responsible to the people." I must dissent.

* * *

Topics for Further Discussion

1. Does the majority's decision in *Chadha* lead to more democratic consideration of administrative issues?

2. Justice White, in his dissent, noted than some 200 statutes containing a legislative veto would be invalidated by *Chadha*. What do you suppose that Congress has done since *Chadha*: delegated less power to agencies, become more specific in its delegation, or simply allowed the agencies (and thus the President) wider authority?

3. In *Mistretta v. United States*, 488 U.S. 361 (1989), the Court upheld the delegation of power to set sentencing guidelines in federal criminal cases to an independent commission

in the Judicial branch. The Court acknowledged that the Commission, which is not a court, is "a particular institution within the framework of our Government." Nevertheless, it held that, "[o]ur constitutional principles of separated powers are not violated by mere anomaly or innovation." Is this reasoning consistent with *Chadha*?

4. Congress belatedly reacted to the *Chadha* decision by passing, in 1996, the Congressional Review Act, 5 U.S.C. §§ 801–808. It requires a joint resolution of Congress (in other words, both the House and the Senate) to disapprove of an agency rule. However, in the first twelve years of the Act's existence, it only was used once, and even then with the assent of the President.

Rulemaking: Informal and Formal

Much of the work done by administrative agencies is in the form of what is called "rulemaking." Rulemaking is exactly what its name states, making rules. *How* rules are made is defined by the Administrative Procedure Act (APA), 5 U.S.C. §§ 551, *et seq*. Section 551 (4) of the APA defines a rule as "an agency statement of general or particular applicability and future effect...." Rules affect matters in the future; they do not resolve disputes from the past. Thus, the safety standards for seatbelts can be set in a rule, but the rule cannot retroactively define what the standards should have been in the past.

Although the definition speaks of both "general and particular applicability," in fact rulemaking today is almost completely concerned with general matters. That is to say, decisions about policies that apply to everyone in the field are the proper subject of rulemaking. Decisions about the rights and actions of particular individuals are matters for "adjudication."

Rulemaking is divided into two categories: informal and formal. Although these terms are not in the statute, they are the words used to describe the procedures. Informal rulemaking is governed by section 553 of the APA. It requires only that the agency publish a notice of its proposal to make a rule on a subject in the Federal Register (a government publication for that purpose) and provide an opportunity for people to file written comments on the proposal. The comment is in written form. The agency may allow for oral presentation too, but the APA does not require it to do so, and most agencies do not. The agency then must publish its rule at least thirty days before it takes effect.

What does the agency do with the comments that come in? In theory, it should consider them in making its rule. In fact, all the statute requires is that "after consideration ... the agency shall incorporate in the rules adopted a concise general statement of their basis and purpose." In other words, it is not required to document how and to what extent it made use of the comments it received. In practice, agencies generally provide a "preamble" to their final rule, setting forth a summary of the comments received, the agency's response, an explanation of the rule, and changes made from the proposed rule. The following is an excerpt from a notice of proposed rulemaking:

Proposed Rules
Federal Communications Commission
69 Federal Register 16873-01
47 CFR Part 64

[CG Docket Nos. 04-53 and 02-278; FCC 04-52]

Rules and Regulations Implementing the Controlling the Assault of Non-Solicited Pornography and Marketing Act of 2003

Rules and Regulations Implementing the Telephone Consumer Protection Act of 1991

Wednesday, March 31, 2004

AGENCY: Federal Communications Commission.

ACTION: Proposed rule.

SUMMARY: This document seeks comment on how best to implement regulations to protect consumers from unwanted mobile service commercial messages.

DATES: Comments in CG Docket No. 04-53, concerning unwanted mobile service commercial messages and the CAN-SPAM Act, are due on or before April 30, 2004 and reply comments are due on or before May 17, 2004.

ADDRESSES: Parties who choose to file comments by paper must file an original and four copies to the Office of the Secretary, Federal Communications Commission, 445 12th Street, SW., Room TW-A325, Washington, DC 20554. Comments may also be filed using the Commission's Electronic Filing System, which can be accessed via the Internet at http://www.fcc.gov/e-file/ecfs.html.

Synopsis

Section 14(b)(1) of the Controlling the Assault of Non-Solicited Pornography and Marketing Act of 2003 (CAN-SPAM Act or the Act) states that the Commission shall adopt rules to provide subscribers with the ability to avoid receiving a "mobile service commercial message" (MSCM) unless the subscriber has expressly authorized such messages beforehand. The Act defines an MSCM as a "commercial electronic mail message that is transmitted directly to a wireless device that is utilized by a subscriber of commercial mobile service" as defined in 47 U.S.C. § 332(d) "in connection with that service." For purposes of this discussion, we shall refer to mobile service messaging as MSM.

We seek comment on ways in which we can implement Congress's directive to protect consumers from "unwanted mobile service commercial messages." As explained above, section 14(b)(1) of the CAN-SPAM Act states that the Commission shall adopt rules to provide subscribers with the "ability to avoid receiving [MSCMs] unless the subscriber has provided express prior authorization to the sender." The legislative history of the Act suggests that section 14 was included so that wireless subscribers would have greater protections from commercial electronic mail messages than those protections provided elsewhere in the Act. As explained below, we believe that section 14(b)(1) is intended to provide consumers the opportunity to generally bar receipt of all MSCMs (except those from senders who have obtained the consumer's prior express consent). However, we believe that in order to do so, the consumer must take affirmative action to bar the MSCMs in the first instance. Although it appears that Congress intended to afford wireless subscribers greater protection from unwanted commercial electronic mail messages than those protections provided elsewhere in the Act, it is not clear that Congress necessarily sought to impose a flat prohibition against such messages in the first instance. However, as set forth below, we seek comment on both of these different interpretations of section 14(b)(1).

The language of the CAN-SPAM Act requires the Commission to "protect consumers from unwanted mobile service commercial messages." The protections extend to unwanted MSCMs from senders who may ignore the provisions of the CAN-SPAM Act. As a practical matter, the particular protections for wireless subscribers required by the Act may require comprehensive solutions. Therefore, in addition to those considerations directed by the CAN-SPAM Act discussed below, we seek comment generally on technical mechanisms that could be made available to wireless subscribers so that they may voluntarily, and at the subscriber's discretion, protect themselves against unwanted mobile service commercial messages. We seek comment on means by which wireless providers might protect consumers from MSCMs transmitted by senders who may willfully violate the wireless provisions of the CAN-SPAM Act addressed in this proceeding. We seek comment on how, in particular, small businesses would be affected by the various proposals we consider.

We are aware that a number of other countries have taken a variety of technical and regulatory steps to protect their consumers from unwanted electronic mail messages in general. In doing so, some countries such as Japan and South Korea have adopted an opt-out approach; while others such as the United Kingdom, France, and Germany had adopted an opt-in approach. Still others have a mixed approach. Also, different countries have taken a variety of positions on whether labeling and identification of commercial messages is required, whether a Do-Not-E-Mail registry can be developed, and whether the use of "spamware" is prohibited. We seek comment on any of these approaches, consistent with section 14, applicable to unwanted mobile service commercial messages, with particular emphasis on their effectiveness, associated costs and burdens, if any, on carriers, subscribers or other relevant entities. Commenters should not only focus on the present, but also on the foreseeable future.

Accordingly, it is ordered that, pursuant to the authority contained in sections 1–4, 227 and 303(r) of the Communications Act of 1934, as amended; the Controlling the Assault of Non-Solicited Pornography and Marketing Act of 2003; and the Do-Not-Call Implementation Act,; 47 U.S.C. 151–154, 227, and 303(r), the Notice of Proposed Rulemaking and Further Notice of Proposed Rulemaking are Adopted.

* * *

Topics for Further Discussion

1. Who is likely to file comments in this proposed rulemaking? Could a member of the public file comments? APA section 553(c) says, "the agency shall give interested persons an opportunity to participate." What kind of information do you imagine would be included in a comment?

2. Why did the agency devote so much of its notice to a discussion of the legislation passed by Congress?

The other kind of rulemaking, formal, requires both the compilation of a more complete record and a greater explanation of the basis for the decision. It comes about through the language of the same part of the APA that governs informal rulemaking. Section 553(c) states that the procedures of sections 556 and 557 (which also apply to adjudication) are necessary for rulemaking as well "[w]hen rules are required by statute to be made on the record after opportunity for an agency hearing."

If Congress always made its intent clear on which kind of rulemaking it wished, it could simply write the same words into the statute authorizing the particular action: "on the record after opportunity for an agency hearing." Unfortunately, it frequently does not do so, leaving the situation ambiguous. From the standpoint of both the agency and those who wish to influence the agency's decision, this is a matter of crucial importance. The requirements of section 556 resemble those of a court, with oral and documentary evidence as well as transcripts. Section 557(c) imposes a duty on the agency to produce a statement of "findings and conclusions, and the reasons or basis thereof, on all the material issues of fact, law, or discretion presented on the record." Thus, the use of formal rulemaking creates a great amount of extra work for the agency, a greater opportunity for others to be heard, and the duty for the agency to justify its decision in terms of the record created. Adjudicative procedures are not well-suited for the legislative-like process of rulemaking. For this reason, the courts have asserted that if Congress wants formal proceedings it can explicitly require them. However, Congress rarely does.

United States v. Florida East Coast Ry.
410 U.S. 224 (1973)

Rehnquist, J.

Appellees, two railroad companies, brought this action in the District Court for the Middle District of Florida to set aside the incentive *per diem* rates established by appellant Interstate Commerce Commission in a rule-making proceeding. The District Court sustained appellees' position that the Commission had failed to comply with the applicable provisions of the Administrative Procedure Act.

The District Court held that the language of § 1(14)(a) of the Interstate Commerce Act, as amended, required the Commission in a proceeding such as this to act in accordance with the Administrative Procedure Act, and that the Commission's determination to receive submissions from the appellees only in written form was a violation of that section because the respondents were "prejudiced" by that determination within the meaning of that section.

Section 1(14)(a) provides: "The Commission may, after hearing, on a complaint or upon its own initiative without complaint, establish reasonable rules, regulations, and practices with respect to car service by common carriers by railroad subject to this chapter."

We here decide that the Commission's proceeding was governed only by § 553 of that Act, and that appellees received the "hearing" required by § 1(14)(a) of the Interstate Commerce Act. We, therefore, reverse the judgment of the District Court.

The term "hearing" in its legal context undoubtedly has a host of meanings. Its meaning undoubtedly will vary, depending on whether it is used in the context of a rulemaking-type proceeding or in the context of a proceeding devoted to the adjudication of particular disputed facts. It is by no means apparent what the drafters of the Esch Car Service Act of 1917, which became the first part of § 1(14)(a) of the Interstate Commerce Act, meant by the term. Such an intent would surely be an ephemeral one if, indeed, Congress in 1917 had in mind anything more specific than the language it actually used, for none of the parties refer to any legislative history that would shed light on the intended meaning of the words "after hearings." What is apparent, though, is that the term was used in granting authority to the Commission to make rules and regulations of a prospective nature.

We think this treatment of the term "hearing" in the Administrative Procedure Act affords sufficient basis for concluding that the requirement of a "hearing" contained in § 1(14)(a); in a situation where the Commission was acting under the 1966 statutory rulemaking authority that Congress had conferred upon it, did not by its own force require the Commission either to hear oral testimony, to permit cross-examination of Commission witnesses, or to hear oral argument. Here, the Commission promulgated a tentative draft of an order, and accorded all interested parties 60 days in which to file statements of position, submissions of evidence, and other relevant observations. The parties had fair notice of exactly what the Commission proposed to do, and were given an opportunity to comment, to object, or to make some other form of written submission. The final order of the Commission indicates that it gave consideration to the statements of the two appellees here. Given the "open-ended" nature of the proceedings, and the Commission's announced willingness to consider proposals for modification after operating experience had been acquired, we think the hearing requirement of § 1(14)(a) of the Act was met.

The basic distinction between rulemaking and adjudication is illustrated by this Court's treatment of two related cases under the Due Process Clause of the Fourteenth Amendment. In *Londoner v. Denver*, cited in oral argument by appellees, 210 U.S. 373 (1908), the Court held that due process had not been accorded a landowner who objected to the amount assessed against his land as its share of the benefit resulting from the paving of a street. Local procedure had accorded him the right to file a written complaint and objection, but not to be heard orally. This Court held that due process of law required that he "have the right to support his allegations by argument, however brief; and, if need be, by proof, however informal." But in the later case of *Bi-Metallic Investment Co. v. State Board of Equalization*, 239 U.S. 441 (1915), the Court held that no hearing at all was constitutionally required prior to a decision by state tax officers in Colorado to increase the valuation of all taxable property in Denver by a substantial percentage. The Court distinguished *Londoner* by stating that there a small number of persons "were exceptionally affected, in each case upon individual grounds."

Here, the incentive payments proposed by the Commission in its tentative order, and later adopted in its final order, were applicable across the board to all of the common carriers by railroad subject to the Interstate Commerce Act. No effort was made to single out any particular railroad for special consideration based on its own peculiar circumstances. Indeed, one of the objections of appellee Florida East Coast was that it and other terminating carriers should have been treated differently from the generality of the railroads. But the fact that the order may in its effects have been thought more disadvantageous by some railroads than by others does not change its generalized nature. Though the Commission obviously relied on factual inferences as a basis for its order, the source of these factual inferences was apparent to anyone who read the order of December 1969. The factual inferences were used in the formulation of a basically legislative-type judgment, for prospective application only, rather than in adjudicating a particular set of disputed facts.

The Commission's procedure satisfied both the provisions of § 1(14)(a) of the Interstate Commerce Act and of the Administrative Procedure Act, and were not inconsistent with prior decisions of this Court. We, therefore, reverse the judgment of the District Court.

* * *

National Rifle Ass'n v. Brady
914 F.2d 475 (4th Cir. 1990)

Wilkinson, J.

In this case, we must determine the validity of certain firearms regulations promulgated by the Secretary of the Treasury pursuant to the Gun Control Act of 1968, as amended by the Firearm Owners Protection Act of 1986, presently codified at 18 U.S.C. §§ 921. The National Rifle Association, along with several other groups and individuals involved with the use and promotion of firearms, challenges the regulations as inconsistent with the Firearm Owners Protection Act.

The NRA contends that all of the regulations must be invalidated because the Secretary failed to follow the procedures mandated in FOPA by refusing to afford interested parties an opportunity for an oral hearing.

FOPA contains no provision guaranteeing interested parties the right to an oral hearing. Instead, it provides: "The Secretary shall give not less than ninety days public notice, and shall afford interested parties opportunity for hearing, before prescribing such rules and regulations." It is well-settled that the requirement of a hearing does not necessitate that the hearing be oral. Here, the Secretary, pursuant to regulation, reserved for himself the right to determine whether an oral hearing should be held. He ultimately determined that an oral hearing was unwarranted, but did provide interested parties with the opportunity to submit written comments. This is all the hearing requirement in § 926(b) demands.

The NRA points to the fact that the Secretary conducted a public oral hearing in 1968 soon after enactment of the Gun Control Act, and argues that this demonstrates that the Secretary believed that an oral hearing was mandated by the Act. We are not persuaded. That the Secretary may once have chosen to accord parties additional procedural rights by holding an oral hearing "does not carry the necessary implication that [he] felt [he] was required to do so." The choice to provide an oral hearing on one occasion does not bind the Secretary to continue to do so in the future. Thus, we hold that the Secretary complied with the hearing requirement of § 926(b) by permitting interested parties to submit written comments on the proposed regulations.

* * *

Topics for Further Discussion

1. Why would Congress not clearly indicate in its legislation whether rulemaking proceedings are to be formal or informal? If Congress wished to require oral hearings in specific legislation, could it do so? Would the *Chadha* case present any difficulties in this regard? Do you think the word "hearing" means an actual oral hearing, or only the opportunity to be heard via a written submission?

2. The Supreme Court has held that the categories of administrative action are fixed by the Administrative Procedure Act, i.e. formal and informal rulemaking and adjudication. Courts have no power to require additional procedure by the agency, even when they believe the information produced would assist them in reviewing the agency's decision.

Vermont Yankee Nuclear Power v. Natural Res. Def. Council
435 U.S. 519 (1978)

Rehnquist, J.

In 1946, Congress enacted the Administrative Procedure Act, which as we have noted elsewhere was not only "a new, basic and comprehensive regulation of procedures in many agencies," but was also a legislative enactment which settled "long-continued and hard-fought contentions, and enacts a formula upon which opposing social and political forces have come to rest." Section 4 of the Act, dealing with rulemaking, requires in subsection (b) that "notice of proposed rule making shall be published in the Federal Register ..." describes the contents of that notice, and goes on to require in subsection (c) that after the notice the agency "shall give interested persons an opportunity to participate in the rule making through submission of written data, views, or arguments with or without opportunity for oral presentation. After consideration of the relevant matter presented, the agency shall incorporate in the rules adopted a concise general statement of their basis and purpose." Interpreting this provision of the Act in *United States v. Allegheny-Ludlum Steel Corp.*, 406 U.S. 742 (1972), and *United States v. Florida East Coast R. Co,* 410 U.S. 224 (1973) we held that generally speaking this section of the Act established the maximum procedural requirements which Congress was willing to have the courts impose upon agencies in conducting rulemaking procedures. Agencies are free to grant additional procedural rights in the exercise of their discretion, but reviewing courts are generally not free to impose them if the agencies have not chosen to grant them. This is not to say necessarily that there are no circumstances which would ever justify a court in overturning agency action because of a failure to employ procedures beyond those required by the statute. But such circumstances, if they exist, are extremely rare.

Even apart from the Administrative Procedure Act this Court has for more than four decades emphasized that the formulation of procedures was basically to be left within the discretion of the agencies to which Congress had confided the responsibility for substantive judgments. In *FCC v. Schreiber,* 381 U.S. 279 (1965), the Court explicated this principle, describing it as "an outgrowth of the congressional determination that administrative agencies and administrators will be familiar with the industries which they regulate and will be in a better position than federal courts or Congress itself to design procedural rules adapted to the peculiarities of the industry and the tasks of the agency involved."

It is in the light of this background of statutory and decisional law that we granted *certiorari* to review two judgments of the Court of Appeals for the District of Columbia Circuit because of our concern that they had seriously misread or misapplied this statutory and decisional law cautioning reviewing courts against engrafting their own notions of proper procedures upon agencies entrusted with substantive functions by Congress. We conclude that the Court of Appeals has done just that in these cases, and we therefore remand them to it for further proceedings.

Absent constitutional constraints or extremely compelling circumstances, the "administrative agencies 'should be free to fashion their own rules of procedure and to pursue methods of inquiry capable of permitting them to discharge their multitudinous duties.'" Indeed, our cases could hardly be more explicit in this regard.

In the first place, if courts continually review agency proceedings to determine whether the agency employed procedures which were, in the court's opinion, perfectly tailored to reach what the court perceives to be the "best" or "correct" result, judicial review would be totally unpredictable. And the agencies, operating under this vague injunction to employ the "best" procedures and facing the threat of reversal if they did not, would undoubtedly adopt full adjudicatory procedures in every instance. Not only would this totally disrupt the statutory scheme, through which Congress enacted "a formula upon which opposing social and political forces have come to rest," but all the inherent advantages of informal rulemaking would be totally lost.

Finally, and perhaps most importantly, this sort of review fundamentally misconceives the nature of the standard for judicial review of an agency rule. The court below uncritically assumed that additional procedures will automatically result in a more adequate record because it will give interested parties more of an opportunity to participate in and contribute to the proceedings. But informal rulemaking need not be based solely on the transcript of a hearing held before an agency. Indeed, the agency need not even hold a formal hearing. See 5 U.S.C. § 553(c). Thus, the adequacy of the "record" in this type of proceeding is not correlated directly to the type of procedural devices employed, but rather turns on whether the agency has followed the statutory mandate of the Administrative Procedure Act or other relevant statutes. If the agency is compelled to support the rule which it ultimately adopts with the type of record produced only after a full adjudicatory hearing, it simply will have no choice but to conduct a full adjudicatory hearing prior to promulgating every rule. In sum, this sort of unwarranted judicial examination of perceived procedural shortcomings of a rulemaking proceeding can do nothing but seriously interfere with that process prescribed by Congress.

* * *

Adjudication

As formal adjudication, like formal rulemaking, is governed by sections 556–557 of the APA, one might well ask, what is the difference? One difference is adjudication also has a section of its own, 554, which requires information about hearings be given to "persons entitled to notice" and the opportunity to present evidence and arguments to "all interested parties." The implication is that adjudication is focusing on particular individuals (which may, of course, be companies or organizations). Those individuals then have specific procedural rights, which are similar to those in a court trial. By contrast, in rulemaking the agency is normally promulgating a more generally applicable requirement.

Section 554(a) applies to "every case of adjudication required by statute to be determined on the record after opportunity for an agency hearing." So, as decided in the *Florida East Coast Ry.* case, a formal adjudication is only triggered when another statute requires a "hearing on the record." In such cases, an administrative law judge (ALJ) normally presides. ALJs are not federal judges in the same sense as those who preside in federal district and appellate courts (known as Article III judges because their power is defined in that section of the Constitution). Rather, they are federal employees with judge-like functions. ALJs do not have lifetime appointments; however, the APA does guarantee them a large measure of independence from the rest of the agency within which they may be adjudicating. An ALJ will hand down a decision after the taking of evidence has finished. In some cases, the decision will take effect automatically unless the agency leadership reconsiders it ("initial decision"). In other cases, the decision takes effect only after the agency leadership approves it ("recommended decision"). In still other cases, primarily involving licenses granted (or not granted) for the first time, an agency employee rather than an ALJ may make the initial decision.

As of September 2008, the federal government employed nearly 1,500 administrative law judges, in 30 agencies. The great majority, more than 1,200 of them, are assigned to the Social Security Administration. The Department of Health and Human Services' Medicare program has 65. The Department of Labor has 43, and the National Labor Relations Board has 40. Like trial judges, ALJs are supposed to make their decisions based on what happens in the hearings, and refrain from "out-of-court" (*ex parte*) contact with those involved.

Agencies also make numerous adjudicative decisions using more informal procedures. Examples include the granting of campground permits, immigration rulings, and decisions to award grant funds to projects. This is known as informal adjudication. The APA does not spell out a set of procedures for such actions. Even so, agencies have to be concerned that the procedures comport with the general principles of due process.

The following case is an example of adjudication conducted by the National Labor Relations Board (NLRB). As you read it, consider how the decision of the ALJ differs in style and tone from decisions of other cases you have read in this book.

National Labor Relations Board
San Francisco Branch Office
Vae Nortrak North America, Inc. and
United Steelworkers of America, Local 3405
2004 NLRB LEXIS 475

Rose, A.L.J.

This matter was tried before me at Pueblo, Colorado, on July 20, 2004, upon the General Counsel's [of the NLRB] complaint which alleged that January 14, the Respondent refused to hire Sam Pantello in violation of Section 8(a)(3) of the National Labor Relations Act.

The Respondent generally denied that it committed any violations of the Act and affirmatively contends that it did not hire Pantello for good cause and not in violation of the Act.

Upon the record as a whole, including my observation of the witnesses, briefs and arguments of counsel, I hereby make the following findings of fact, conclusions of law and recommended order:

The Facts

In 2003 Nortrak began the process of acquiring the assets of Meridian Rail Corporation of Pueblo, Colorado. Preliminary to the acquisition, in early to mid-November, three members of Nortrak management made an inspection trip to Pueblo, one of whom was Jeffery Clay Johnson, the Respondent's human resources manager. Johnson's job was to inspect, check serial numbers and photograph the equipment, to insure that in fact Meridian's machines were as stated. He was not to have any interchange with Meridian employees nor was he to tell them what he was about (though this would seem to have been obvious).

Craig Fetty, Meridian's plant manager (who was subsequently hired by the Respondent in that position) took Johnston on an orientation walk through the plant, and then Johnston was on his own to do his inspection. While doing this, according to Johnson, Pantello, whom he did not know, approached him in a confrontational manner and said, "Who the hell are you?" "What are you doing?" "What are the pictures for?" While Pantello agrees that he had a discussion with Johnson, he denied that he was in any way rude or confrontational. In fact Pantello testified that he offered to help get a serial number off his machine and had been introduced to Johnston and the other two Nortrak managers by Fetty. Pantello testified that he even suggested an Italian restaurant to them for dinner that evening which, assertions were denied by Johnston and Fetty.

In December 2003 the Respondent was about to acquire Meridian and thus began the process of interviewing applicants (off premises) and making decisions as to whom to send offer letters. At some point, Johnson told Robert Dillard, the director of human resources for Pueblo (and two other plants), about his perception of the incident with Pantello and suggested that Pantello was not the sort of person the Respondent wanted as an employee. Though Dillard interviewed Pantello, he had predetermined not to offer him a job and did not.

Dillard had received applications from 80 plus individuals who had not worked for Meridian but he interviewed only 15. Dillard testified that a couple of Meridian employees he interviewed were hostile and he declined to offer them jobs. He did agree that Pantello was not hostile during the interview.

Pantello had worked for Meridian and its predecessors 29 years and, as far as the Respondent knew, was a competent employee. He was also the Union's president, and had been for 12 years. It was because of his position, the General Counsel alleges, that he was not hired. The Respondent contends that the only reason he was not hired was its evaluation of him based on the confrontation with Johnson.

Analysis and Concluding Findings

As a general proposition, when one company acquires the assets of another, it is not required to hire the predecessor's employees. However, the successor company may not lawfully deny a job offer because of the employee's activity on behalf of a labor organization. And, whether the refusal to hire and individual is unlawful is controlled by *Wright Line, a Division of Wright Line, Inc.*, 251 NLRB 1083 (1980), enfd. 662 F.2d 899 (1st Cir. 1981), cert. denied 455 U.S. 989 (1982) which requires the General Counsel to establish a *prima facie* case of discrimination based on the employer's knowledge of union activity and evidence of union animus. Then the burden of going forward shifts to employer to show that the same hiring decision would have been made even in the absence of union activity.

The refusal to offer Pantello a job is alleged to have been because of his union activity—specifically, that he was the Union's president. The General Counsel argues that the Respondent's stated reason for not hiring Pantello must necessarily have been a pretext, since the critical event relied on by the Respondent did not happen as testified to by Johnson, or, at any event, it was too trivial to deny employment to an experienced, competent employee. Therefore, the true reason must have been the fact that Pantello is the Union's president.

In arguing that the Respondent had animus against Panello's known and extensive union activity, the General Counsel offered the testimony of two witnesses: Pantello's uncle and Pantello's wife. The uncle testified that at a regular poker game in January, he asked Fetty if Pantello would be hired and Fetty told him no, because Pantello was a "troublemaker." Fetty denied the comment to Pantello's uncle.

And in 2001 (or early 2002), at the time Meridian acquired the plant, following which Pantello was not hired, Fetty (who was then the production manager) told Pantello's wife (though they were not married at the time) "he had finally gotten the union out of the plant, which he had wanted to do for the last two years...." Somewhat before that, Fetty, according to Pantello's wife, said that Pantello had said things to make people mad. Fetty was not asked about these statements to Pantello's wife, which tends to suggest that he made them. However, it is difficult to credit the alleged statement that Fetty said he had finally gotten the union out of the plant since in fact the Union continued to represent the production employees. Further, the witness testified about an alleged event occurring two years before the Respondent acquired the plant and has an obvious stake in the outcome of this proceeding. While I do not credit her testimony, I conclude that even if true, the facts she testified to are irrelevant.

There is no evidence tending to disprove the testimony of Fetty and Dillard that Fetty was not involved in the decision not to offer Pantello a job or that this decision was made prior to Fetty himself being offered the position of plant manager. Thus it is difficult to accept the General Counsel's argument that whatever animus Fetty had toward Pantello (whether or not because of Pantello's union activity) could be imputed to the Respondent.

Though there are credibility conflicts, particularly concerning the November incident, which I tend to resolve in favor of the Respondent's witnesses, even accepting Pantello's version I cannot conclude that he was not hired because of his union presidency.

First, there is no contention that when Pantello confronted Johnson (or talked to him in Pantello's version) that he was acting on behalf of the Union, in his capacity as president or otherwise in concert with other employees. Most importantly, there is no evidence of union animus. The Union had represented employees of the plant since about 1944 and there is no suggestion that the relationship between the Respondent's various predecessors and Union was anything other than harmonious.

The Respondent has recognized the Union and is negotiating for a collective-bargaining agreement. There is no evidence that Pantello's activity as the Union president (for instance in processing grievances) was a matter of concern to Meridian, the plant manager or, more importantly, to the Respondent.

Assuming Pantello was considered a "troublemaker" and said things to make people mad, such does not imply that these evaluations were based on Pantello's union or other protected concerted activity. While "troublemaker" is sometimes a code word for "union activist" it can also be literal. In short, the General Counsel has offered no persuasive rationale for why the Respondent would single out Pantello to discriminate against because he was an officer of the Union. Finally, Pantello was not the only employee of Meridian not to be offered a job with the Respondent, yet he is the only one alleged to have been discriminated against.

In effect, the General Counsel argues that because Pantello was the Union's president, *prima facie* the Respondent's failure to hire him was unlawful. I do not agree that simply refusing to hire the president of the union representing a predecessor's employees makes out a *prima facie* case. The Charging Party cites *Champion Rivet Co.,* 314 NLRB 1097 (1994) wherein a successor company's failure to hire the union president and two other union activists was found unlawful. In that case, however, there was substantial evidence of union animus including the company's stated desire to operate nonunion as it did at other facilities. Such facts are simply not present here.

I conclude that the evidence is insufficient to support a finding that the Respondent did not hire Pantello because of his union activity. Accordingly, I shall recommend that the complaint be dismissed.

* * *

Topics for Further Discussion

1. In this case, the General Counsel of the NLRB brought the complaint. The General Counsel is appointed to a four-year term by the President, subject to approval by the Sen-

ate. The Office of the General Counsel, among other things, investigates allegations of unfair labor practices and prosecutes those cases deemed worthy. The General Counsel is not a board member of the NLRB, and is independent of the Board.

2. What was the basis of the ALJ's conclusion? Was it that Pantello was a "troublemaker"? Or that the General Counsel could not provide enough proof that the company was anti-union? Or some other reason?

3. In this kind of proceeding, is the ALJ functioning like a judge, jury, or both?

4. The title of the case does not use the word "versus" ("v") as is customary in ordinary court decisions. Rather, it uses "and." Who is the plaintiff? Who is the defendant? Why is Mr. Pantello's name not mentioned in the title?

Judicial Review

One of the main purposes of administrative law is to provide a relatively swift and flexible decision about matters that are often detailed and involve a great deal of specialized knowledge. If courts were to review every decision of agencies in a *de novo* fashion (meaning, as though the issue were being presented for the first time), the benefits of administration would be lost and the judiciary would be overburdened. On the other hand, to not provide any judicial review at all would be unduly harsh to persons involved and unreasonably deferential to the government.

The Administrative Procedure Act takes a liberal approach to who can seek review, that is any "person suffering legal wrong because of agency action, or adversely affected by agency action within the meaning of a relevant statute." However, the Supreme Court has decided numerous cases interpreting the constitutional requirement that a challenger must demonstrate an "injury in fact" before he has standing to bring a claim. In *Lujan v. Def. of Wildlife*, 504 U.S. 555 (1992), Justice Scalia, writing for the majority, denied standing to members of an environmental group. The opinion said the injury must be "an invasion of a legally protected interest which is concrete and particularized and actual or imminent rather than conjectural or hypothetical; that there be a causal connection between the injury and conduct complained of so that the injury is fairly traceable to the challenged action of the defendant and not the result of the independent action of some third party who is not before the court; and that it be likely, as opposed to merely speculative, that injury will be redressed by a favorable decision." In 2007, however, the Court distinguished *Lujan*, over the protests of Justice Scalia and three other dissenters, in allowing the State of Massachusetts to challenge the failure of the Environmental Protection Agency to adopt rules restricting greenhouse gas emissions from motor vehicles.

Massachusetts v. E.P.A.
549 U.S. 497 (2007)

Stevens, J.

If sea levels continue to rise as predicted, one Massachusetts official believes that a significant fraction of coastal property will be "either permanently lost through inundation or temporarily lost through periodic storm surge and flooding events." Remediation costs alone, petitioners allege, could run well into the hundreds of millions of dollars.

Causation

EPA does not dispute the existence of a causal connection between man-made green-house gas emissions and global warming. At a minimum, therefore, EPA's refusal to regulate such emissions "contributes" to Massachusetts' injuries.

EPA nevertheless maintains that its decision not to regulate greenhouse gas emissions from new motor vehicles contributes so insignificantly to petitioners' injuries that the agency cannot be haled into federal court to answer for them. For the same reason, EPA does not believe that any realistic possibility exists that the relief petitioners seek would mitigate global climate change and remedy their injuries. That is especially so because predicted increases in greenhouse gas emissions from developing nations, particularly China and India, are likely to offset any marginal domestic decrease.

But EPA overstates its case. Its argument rests on the erroneous assumption that a small incremental step, because it is incremental, can never be attacked in a federal judicial forum. Yet accepting that premise would doom most challenges to regulatory action. Agencies, like legislatures, do not generally resolve massive problems in one fell regulatory swoop.

That a first step might be tentative does not by itself support the notion that federal courts lack jurisdiction to determine whether that step conforms to law.

Judged by any standard, U.S. motor-vehicle emissions make a meaningful contribution to greenhouse gas concentrations and hence, according to petitioners, to global warming.

The Remedy

While it may be true that regulating motor-vehicle emissions will not by itself reverse global warming, it by no means follows that we lack jurisdiction to decide whether EPA has a duty to take steps to slow or reduce it. Because of the enormity of the potential consequences associated with man-made climate change, the fact that the effectiveness of a remedy might be delayed during the (relatively short) time it takes for a new motor-vehicle fleet to replace an older one is essentially irrelevant. Nor is it dispositive that developing countries such as China and India are poised to increase greenhouse gas emissions substantially over the next century: A reduction in domestic emissions would slow the pace of global emissions increases, no matter what happens elsewhere.

In sum—at least according to petitioners' uncontested affidavits—the rise in sea levels associated with global warming has already harmed and will continue to harm Massachusetts. The risk of catastrophic harm, though remote, is nevertheless real. That risk would be reduced to some extent if petitioners received the relief they seek. We therefore hold that petitioners have standing to challenge the EPA's denial of their rulemaking petition.

* * *

Judicial review is for the most part restricted to "final agency action." This is related to an "exhaustion of remedies" requirement, meaning that an aggrieved person must first use all opportunities to achieve a favorable decision within the agency itself before going to court. The following case probes the boundaries of finality and exhaustion.

Darby v. Cisneros
509 U.S. 137 (1993)

Blackmun, J.

This case presents the question whether federal courts have the authority to require that a plaintiff exhaust available administrative remedies before seeking judicial review under the Administrative Procedure Act (APA), where neither the statute nor agency rules specifically mandate exhaustion as a prerequisite to judicial review. At issue is the relationship between the judicially created doctrine of exhaustion of administrative remedies and the statutory requirements of § 704 of the APA.

Petitioner R. Gordon Darby is a self employed South Carolina real estate developer who specializes in the development and management of multifamily rental projects. In the early 1980s, he began working with Lonnie Garvin, Jr., a mortgage banker, who had developed a plan to enable multifamily developers to obtain single family mortgage insurance from respondent Department of Housing and Urban Development (HUD). Respondent Secretary of HUD (Secretary) is authorized to provide single family mortgage insurance under § 203(b) of the National Housing Act. Although HUD also provides mortgage insurance for multifamily projects under § 207 of the National Housing Act, the greater degree of oversight and control over such projects makes it less attractive for investors than the single family mortgage insurance option. Under Garvin's plan, a person seeking financing would use straw purchasers as mortgage insurance applicants. Once the loans were closed, the straw purchasers would transfer title back to the development company.

HUD had become suspicious of Garvin's financing plan as far back as 1983. In 1986, HUD initiated an audit but concluded that neither Darby nor Garvin had done anything wrong or misled HUD personnel. Nevertheless, in June 1989, HUD issued a limited denial of participation (LDP) that prohibited petitioners for one year from participating in any program in South Carolina administered by respondent Assistant Secretary of Housing. Two months later, the Assistant Secretary notified petitioners that HUD was also proposing to debar them from further participation in all HUD procurement contracts and in any nonprocurement transaction with any federal agency.

Petitioners' appeals of the LDP and of the proposed debarment were consolidated, and an Administrative Law Judge (ALJ) conducted a hearing on the consolidated appeals in December 1989. The judge issued an "Initial Decision and Order" in April 1990, finding that the financing method used by petitioners was "a sham...." The ALJ concluded, however, that most of the relevant facts had been disclosed to local HUD employees, that petitioners lacked criminal intent, and that Darby himself "genuinely cooperated with HUD to try [to] work out his financial dilemma and avoid foreclosure." In light of these mitigating factors, the ALJ concluded that an indefinite debarment would be punitive and that it would serve no legitimate purpose; good cause existed, however, to debar petitioners for a period of 18 months.

Under HUD regulations,

> [t]he hearing officer's determination shall be final unless, pursuant to 24 CFR part 26, the Secretary or the Secretary's designee, within 30 days of receipt of a request decides as a matter of discretion to review the finding of the hearing officer. The 30 day period for deciding whether to review a determination may be extended upon written notice of such extension by the Secretary or his designee. Any party may request such a review in writing within 15 days of receipt of the hearing officer's determination.

Neither petitioners nor respondents sought further administrative review of the ALJ's "Initial Decision and Order." On May 31, 1990, petitioners filed suit in the United States District Court for the District of South Carolina. They sought an injunction and a declaration that the administrative sanctions were imposed for purposes of punishment, in violation of HUD's own debarment regulations, and therefore were "not in accordance with law" within the meaning of § 10(e)(B)(1) of the APA.

Respondents moved to dismiss the complaint on the ground that petitioners, by forgoing the option to seek review by the Secretary, had failed to exhaust administrative remedies.

We have recognized that the judicial doctrine of exhaustion of administrative remedies is conceptually distinct from the doctrine of finality:

> [T]he finality requirement is concerned with whether the initial decisionmaker has arrived at a definitive position on the issue that inflicts an actual, concrete injury; the exhaustion requirement generally refers to administrative and judicial procedures by which an injured party may seek review of an adverse decision and obtain a remedy if the decision is found to be unlawful or otherwise inappropriate.

The purpose of § 10(c) was to permit agencies to require an appeal to "superior agency authority" before an examiner's initial decision became final. This was necessary because, under § 8(a), initial decisions could become final agency decisions in the absence of an agency appeal. Agencies may avoid the finality of an initial decision, first, by adopting a rule that an agency appeal be taken before judicial review is available, and, second, by providing that the initial decision would be "inoperative" pending appeal. Otherwise, the initial decision becomes final and the aggrieved party is entitled to judicial review.

Appropriate deference in this case requires the recognition that, with respect to actions brought under the APA, Congress effectively codified the doctrine of exhaustion of administrative remedies in § 10(c). Of course, the exhaustion doctrine continues to apply as a matter of judicial discretion in cases not governed by the APA. But where the APA applies, an appeal to "superior agency authority" is a prerequisite to judicial review only when expressly required by statute or when an agency rule requires appeal before review and the administrative action is made inoperative pending that review. Courts are not free to impose an exhaustion requirement as a rule of judicial administration where the agency action has already become "final" under § 10(c).

* * *

Topics for Further Discussion

1. What do you think the reaction of HUD and other agencies would be to this decision?

2. Is there a distinction between exhaustion and finality? If you were a dissenting justice in this case, what would you write in your opinion?

3. Even if a person obtains judicial review, convincing a court to overturn an agency's decision is no easy thing. Section 706 of the APA sets forth two main standards for overturning an agency decision based on its fact finding:

> *Informal rulemaking*: "hold unlawful and set aside agency action, findings, and conclusions found to be arbitrary, capricious, an abuse of discretion, or otherwise not in accordance with law."

> *Formal rulemaking and adjudication*: "unsupported by substantial evidence."

The "arbitrary and capricious" standard is broadly tolerant of agency action. What this means is that rules made in the least formal way are the most likely to be upheld by the courts. The "substantial evidence" standard imposes a greater duty on the agency to justify its conclusion; however, even here courts often give great deference to an agency's interpretation of both the facts and the law because it is the agency that deals with such matters every day. Broadly speaking, both require courts to affirm agency rules or adjudications when the findings and conclusions are reasonably based on the factual record.

Judicial Review of Agency Interpretations of Law

Courts are empowered to hear challenges to the constitutionality of agency action. In such cases, the courts use a *de novo* review standard. What about when an agency is interpreting its own statute? APA section 706(2)(C) requires a reviewing court to set aside an agency action that is "in excess of statutory jurisdiction, authority, or limitations, or short of statutory right." This formulation leaves it to the courts to decide how much deference to give to the agency when it makes a statutory interpretation.

Barnhart v. Thomas
540 U.S. 20 (2003)

Scalia, J.

Under the Social Security Act, the Social Security Administration (SSA) is authorized to pay disability insurance benefits and Supplemental Security Income to persons who have a "disability." A person qualifies as disabled, and thereby eligible for such benefits, "only if his physical or mental impairment or impairments are of such severity that he is not only unable to do his previous work but cannot, considering his age, education, and work experience, engage in any other kind of substantial gainful work which exists in the national economy." The issue we must decide is whether the SSA may determine that a claimant is not disabled because she remains physically and mentally able to do her previous work, without investigating whether that previous work exists in significant numbers in the national economy.

Pauline Thomas worked as an elevator operator for six years until her job was eliminated in August 1995. In June 1996, at age 53, Thomas applied for disability insurance benefits under Title II and Supplemental Security Income under Title XVI of the Social Security Act. She claimed that she suffered from, and was disabled by, heart disease and cervical and lumbar radiculopathy.

After the SSA denied Thomas's application initially and on reconsideration, she requested a hearing before an Administrative Law Judge (ALJ). The ALJ found that Thomas had "hypertension, cardiac arrythmia, [and] cervical and lumbar strain/sprain." He concluded, however, that Thomas was not under a "disability" because her "impairments do not prevent [her] from performing her past relevant work as an elevator operator." He rejected Thomas's argument that she is unable to do her previous work because that work no longer exists in significant numbers in the national economy. The SSA's Appeals Council denied Thomas's request for review.

Thomas then challenged the ALJ's ruling in the United States District Court for the District of New Jersey, renewing her argument that she is unable to do her previous work due to its scarcity. The District Court affirmed the ALJ, concluding that whether Thomas's old job exists is irrelevant under the SSA's regulations. The Court of Appeals for the Third Circuit, sitting en banc, reversed and remanded. Over the dissent of three of its members, it held that the statute unambiguously provides that the ability to perform prior work disqualifies from benefits only if it is "substantial gainful work which exists in the national economy." That holding conflicts with the decisions of four other Courts of Appeals.

As relevant to the present case, Title II of the Act defines "disability" as the "inability to engage in any substantial gainful activity by reason of any medically determinable physical or mental impairment which can be expected to result in death or which has lasted or can be expected to last for a continuous period of not less than 12 months."

Acting pursuant to its statutory rulemaking authority, the agency has promulgated regulations establishing a five-step sequential evaluation process to determine disability. If at any step a finding of disability or non-disability can be made, the SSA will not review the claim further. At the first step, the agency will find non-disability unless the claimant shows that he is not working at a "substantial gainful activity." At step two, the SSA will find non-disability unless the claimant shows that he has a "severe impairment," defined as "any impairment or combination of impairments which significantly limits [the claimant's] physical or mental ability to do basic work activities." At step three, the agency determines whether the impairment which enabled the claimant to survive step two is on the list of impairments presumed severe enough to render one disabled; if so, the claimant qualifies. If the claimant's impairment is not on the list, the inquiry proceeds to step four, at which the SSA assesses whether the claimant can do his previous work; unless he shows that he cannot, he is determined not to be disabled. If the claimant survives the fourth stage, the fifth, and final, step requires the SSA to consider so-called "vocational factors" (the claimant's age, education, and past work experience), and to determine whether the claimant is capable of performing other jobs existing in significant numbers in the national economy.

As the above description shows, step four can result in a determination of no disability without inquiry into whether the claimant's previous work exists in the national economy; the regulations explicitly reserve inquiry into the national economy for step five. Thus, the SSA has made it perfectly clear that it does not interpret the clause "which exists in the national economy" in § 423(d)(2)(A) as applying to "previous work." The issue presented is whether this agency interpretation must be accorded deference.

As we held in *Chevron U.S.A. Inc. v. Natural Resources Defense Council, Inc.*, 467 U.S. 837 (1984), when a statute speaks clearly to the issue at hand we "must give effect to the unambiguously expressed intent of Congress," but when the statute "is silent or ambiguous" we must defer to a reasonable construction by the agency charged with its implementation. The Third Circuit held that, by referring first to "previous work" and then to "*any other* kind of substantial gainful work which exists in the national economy," the statute unambiguously indicates that the former is a species of the latter. "When," it said, "a sentence sets out one or more specific items followed by 'any other' and a description, the specific items must fall within the description." We disagree. For the reasons discussed below the interpretation adopted by SSA is at least a reasonable construction of the text and must therefore be given effect.

The proper *Chevron* inquiry is not whether the agency construction can give rise to undesirable results in some instances (as here *both* constructions can), but rather whether, in light of the alternatives, the agency construction is reasonable. In the present case, the SSA's authoritative interpretation certainly satisfies that test.

We need not decide today whether § 423(d)(2)(A) compels the interpretation given it by the SSA. It suffices to conclude, as we do, that § 423(d)(2)(A) does not unambiguously require a different interpretation, and that the SSA's regulation is an entirely reasonable interpretation of the text. The judgment of the Court of Appeals is reversed.

* * *

Topics for Further Discussion

1. On questions of fact, giving deference to the findings of an agency is similar to an appellate court deferring to a district court or jury on such matters. However, an appellate court will consider questions of law for itself. In *Barnhart* and in *Chevron,* the Supreme Court takes a different approach with respect to administrative interpretation of law. Why?

2. What precisely did the Supreme Court decide in *Barnhart?* In other words, can you identify the issue in the case and the holding?

3. In *FDA v. Brown & Williamson Tobacco Corp.,* 529 U.S. 120 (2000), the Court ruled that the Food and Drug Administration did not have authority under the Food, Drug, and Cosmetic Act to regulate tobacco products. The Court held that, under *Chevron,* the first question for a reviewing court is whether Congress has spoken directly to the question. It concluded that Congress had, in fact, clearly spoken directly and had not given the FDA authority in this area.

Freedom of Information

Although passed separately and amended extensively in 2007, the Freedom of Information Act (FOIA) has been merged into the coverage of the Administrative Procedure Act in section 552. It requires agencies to publish their final rules and make their adjudicative opinions available to the public. Agencies, however, possess a great deal of information in their files, and the FOIA is the tool that is used to dig the data out.

The basic assumption behind the law is that information possessed by the government belongs to the people and, absent special circumstances, the people have a right to see it. In fact, the right is not even restricted to citizens. The FOIA affords the right to "any person." As a result, foreign entities, and even prison inmates, have been among the most vigorous users. Section 52 (a)(3) commands, "each agency, upon any request for records which (A) reasonably describes such records and (B) is made in accordance with public rules ... shall make the records promptly available to any person." The term "records" refers to documents, including electronic documents.

Of course, not every piece of information is available. No government would permit access to details of national security briefings or deliberations about foreign policy. Beyond that, the government holds much information that affects the privacy of individuals and trade secrets of businesses. To deal with such matters, the FOIA lists nine exceptions to its general principle of open access. The fact that they are listed as exceptions, however, underscores the point that access is the norm. The exceptions involve: (i) properly classified secret material on national defense and foreign policy; (ii) internal personnel rules and practices; (iii) matters that other statutes specifically exempt from disclosure; (iv) trade secrets, and privileged and confidential business information; (v) inter-agency and intra-agency memos; (vi) personnel and medical files that would be a clearly unwarranted invasion of personal privacy if disclosed; (vii) certain law enforcement records; (viii) certain information regarding regulation of financial institutions; and (ix) geological information.

If some part of a document falls within these exceptions, the government cannot refuse to disclose the entire document. It must give up all portions of the information that is not

If some part of a document falls within these exceptions, the government cannot refuse to disclose the entire document. It must give up all portions of the information that is not subject to an exception. Also, it is required to respond to requests promptly and to not charge inordinate fees for copying. Disputes about refusal to turn over information can be heard in federal district court, and the court itself may examine the records privately to determine if they fit within any of the exemptions.

Nat'l Archives and Records Admin. v. Favish
541 U.S. 157 (2004)

Kennedy, J.

This case requires us to interpret the Freedom of Information Act (FOIA). FOIA does not apply if the requested data fall within one or more exemptions. Exemption 7(C) excuses from disclosure "records or information compiled for law enforcement purposes" if their production "could reasonably be expected to constitute an unwarranted invasion of personal privacy."

In *Department of Justice v. Reporters Comm. for Freedom of Press*, 489 U.S. 749 (1989), we considered the scope of Exemption 7(C) and held that release of the document at issue would be a prohibited invasion of the personal privacy of the person to whom the document referred. The principal document involved was the criminal record, or rap sheet, of the person who himself objected to the disclosure. Here, the information pertains to an official investigation into the circumstances surrounding an apparent suicide. The initial question is whether the exemption extends to the decedent's family when the family objects to the release of photographs showing the condition of the body at the scene of death. If we find the decedent's family does have a personal privacy interest recognized by the statute, we must then consider whether that privacy claim is outweighed by the public interest in disclosure.

Vincent Foster, Jr., deputy counsel to President Clinton, was found dead in Fort Marcy Park, located just outside Washington, D. C. The United States Park Police conducted the initial investigation and took color photographs of the death scene, including 10 pictures of Foster's body. The investigation concluded that Foster committed suicide by shooting himself with a revolver. Subsequent investigations by the Federal Bureau of Investigation, committees of the Senate and the House of Representatives, and independent counsels Robert Fiske and Kenneth Starr reached the same conclusion. Despite the unanimous finding of these five investigations, a citizen interested in the matter, Allan Favish, remained skeptical. Favish is now a respondent in this proceeding.

Favish filed the present FOIA request in his own name, seeking, among other things, 11 pictures, 1 showing Foster's eyeglasses and 10 depicting various parts of Foster's body. Like the National Park Service, the Office of Independent Counsel (OIC) refused the request under Exemption 7(C).

It is common ground among the parties that the death-scene photographs in OIC's possession are "records or information compiled for law enforcement purposes" as that phrase is used in Exemption 7(C). This leads to the question whether disclosure of the four photographs "could reasonably be expected to constitute an unwarranted invasion of personal privacy."

Favish contends the family has no personal privacy interest covered by Exemption 7(C). His argument rests on the proposition that the information is only about the decedent, not his family. FOIA's right to personal privacy, in his view, means only "the right to control information about oneself." We disagree. The right to personal privacy is not confined, as Favish argues, to the "right to control information about oneself." To say that the concept of personal privacy must "encompass" the individual's control of information about himself does not mean it cannot encompass other personal privacy interests as well.

Law enforcement documents obtained by Government investigators often contain information about persons interviewed as witnesses or initial suspects but whose link to the official inquiry may be the result of mere happenstance. There is special reason, therefore, to give protection to this intimate personal data, to which the public does not have a general right of access in the ordinary course. In this class of cases where the subject of the documents "is a private citizen," "the privacy interest … is at its apex."

Certain *amici* in support of Favish rely on the modifier "personal" before the word "privacy" to bolster their view that the family has no privacy interest in the pictures of the decedent. This, too, misapprehends the family's position and the scope of protection the exemption provides. The family does not invoke Exemption 7(C) on behalf of Vincent Foster in its capacity as his next friend for fear that the pictures may reveal private information about Foster to the detriment of his own posthumous reputation or some other interest personal to him. If that were the case, a different set of considerations would control. Foster's relatives instead invoke their own right and interest to personal privacy. They seek to be shielded by the exemption to secure their own refuge from a sensation-seeking culture for their own peace of mind and tranquility, not for the sake of the deceased.

The statutory scheme must be understood, moreover, in light of the consequences that would follow were we to adopt Favish's position. As a general rule, withholding information under FOIA cannot be predicated on the identity of the requester. We are advised by the Government that child molesters, rapists, murderers, and other violent criminals often make FOIA requests for autopsies, photographs, and records of their deceased victims. Our holding ensures that the privacy interests of surviving family members would allow the Government to deny these gruesome requests in appropriate cases. We find it inconceivable that Congress could have intended a definition of "personal privacy" so narrow that it would allow convicted felons to obtain these materials without limitations at the expense of surviving family members' personal privacy.

We hold that FOIA recognizes surviving family members' right to personal privacy with respect to their close relative's death-scene images. Our holding is consistent with the unanimous view of the Courts of Appeals and other lower courts that have addressed the question. Neither the deceased's former status as a public official, nor the fact that other pictures had been made public, detracts from the weighty privacy interests involved.

Our ruling that the personal privacy protected by Exemption 7(C) extends to family members who object to the disclosure of graphic details surrounding their relative's death does not end the case. Although this privacy interest is within the terms of the exemption, the statute directs nondisclosure only where the information "could reasonably be expected to constitute an unwarranted invasion" of the family's personal privacy. The term "unwarranted" requires us to balance the family's privacy interest against the public interest in disclosure.

We hold that, where there is a privacy interest protected by Exemption 7(C) and the public interest being asserted is to show that responsible officials acted negligently or otherwise improperly in the performance of their duties, the requester must establish more than a bare suspicion in order to obtain disclosure. Rather, the requester must produce evidence that would warrant a belief by a reasonable person that the alleged Government impropriety might have occurred. Favish has not produced any evidence that would warrant a belief by a reasonable person that the alleged Government impropriety might have occurred to put the balance into play.

* * *

United States Dep't of Justice v. Landano
508 U.S. 165 (1993)

O'Connor, J.

Exemption 7(D) of the Freedom of Information Act exempts from disclosure agency records "compiled for law enforcement purposes ... by criminal law enforcement authority in the course of a criminal investigation" if release of those records "could reasonably be expected to disclose" the identity of, or information provided by, a "confidential source." This case concerns the evidentiary showing that the Government must make to establish that a source is "confidential" within the meaning of Exemption 7(D). We are asked to decide whether the Government is entitled to a presumption that all sources supplying information to the Federal Bureau of Investigation (FBI or Bureau) in the course of a criminal investigation are confidential sources.

Respondent Vincent Landano was convicted in New Jersey state court for murdering Newark, New Jersey, police officer John Snow in the course of a robbery. The crime received considerable media attention. Evidence at trial showed that the robbery had been orchestrated by Victor Forni and a motorcycle gang known as "the Breed." There was testimony that Landano, though not a Breed member, had been recruited for the job. Landano always has maintained that he did not participate in the robbery and that Forni, not he, killed Officer Snow. He contends that the prosecution withheld material exculpatory evidence in violation of *Brady v. Maryland,* 373 U.S. 83 (1963).

Although his efforts to obtain state postconviction and federal *habeas* relief thus far have proved unsuccessful, Landano apparently is currently pursuing a *Brady* claim in the state courts. Seeking evidence to support that claim, Landano filed FOIA requests with the FBI for information that the Bureau had compiled in the course of its involvement in the investigation of Officer Snow's murder. Landano sought release of the Bureau's files on both Officer Snow and Forni. The FBI released several hundred pages of documents. The Bureau redacted some of these, however, and withheld several hundred other pages altogether.

Landano filed an action in the United States District Court for the District of New Jersey seeking disclosure of the entire contents of the requested files. In response, the Government submitted a declaration of FBI Special Agent Regina Superneau explaining the Bureau's reasons for withholding portions of the files. The information withheld under Exemption 7(D) included information provided by five types of sources: regular FBI informants; individual witnesses who were not regular informants; state and local law enforcement agencies; other local agencies; and private financial or commercial institutions. Agent Superneau explained why, in the Government's view, all such sources should be presumed confidential. The deleted portions of the files were coded to indicate which type of source each involved. The Bureau provided no other information about the withheld materials.

Exemption 7(D) permits the Government to withhold

records or information compiled for law enforcement purposes, but only to the extent that the production of such law enforcement records or information ... could reasonably be expected to disclose the identity of a confidential source, including a State, local, or foreign agency or authority or any private institution which furnished information on a confidential basis, and, in the case of a record or information compiled by criminal law enforcement authority in the course of a criminal investigation ... information furnished by a confidential source.

The Government bears the burden of establishing that the exemption applies.

Under Exemption 7(D), the question is not whether the requested *document* is of the type that the agency usually treats as confidential, but whether the particular *source* spoke with an understanding that the communication would remain confidential. In this case, the Government has not attempted to demonstrate that the FBI made explicit promises of confidentiality to particular sources. That sort of proof apparently often is not possible: The FBI does not have a policy of discussing confidentiality with every source, and when such discussions do occur, agents do not always document them. The precise question before us, then, is how the Government can meet its burden of showing that a source provided information on an implied assurance of confidentiality.

FOIA does not define the word "confidential." In common usage, confidentiality is not limited to complete anonymity or secrecy. A statement can be made "in confidence" even if the speaker knows the communication will be shared with limited others, as long as the speaker expects that the information will not be published indiscriminately. The Government maintains that an assurance of confidentiality can be inferred whenever an individual source communicates with the FBI because of the risk of reprisal or other negative attention inherent in criminal investigations. It acknowledges, however, that reprisal may not be threatened or even likely in any given case. It may be true that many, or even most, individual sources will expect confidentiality. But the Government offers no explanation, other than ease of administration, why that expectation always should be presumed.

The Government has argued forcefully that its ability to maintain the confidentiality of all of its sources is vital to effective law enforcement. A prophylactic rule protecting the identities of all FBI criminal investigative sources undoubtedly would serve the Government's objectives and would be simple for the Bureau and the courts to administer. But we are not free to engraft that policy choice onto the statute that Congress passed. For the reasons we have discussed, and consistent with our obligation to construe FOIA exemptions narrowly in favor of disclosure, we hold that the Government is not entitled to a presumption that a source is confidential within the meaning of Exemption 7(D) whenever the source provides information to the FBI in the course of a criminal investigation.

* * *

Topics for Further Discussion

1. *Brady* material, as mentioned in the case above, is information that a prosecutor has which would tend to support a criminal defendant's claim of innocence. Under the Court's decision in that case, a prosecutor is required to turn over all such information to a defendant.

2. After the decision in this case, what should the FBI do in order to prevent disclosure of investigatory records? Should it routinely enter into confidentiality agreements with all sources? If so, would a court be able to inquire into whether confidentiality truly was required?

3. The *Favish* case mentions *amici*. *Amici* is the plural of *amicus*, as used in the phrase *amicus curiae*. It means "friend of the court." Many cases that reach the Supreme Court affect interests far beyond the actual parties in the case. Such interests can petition the Supreme Court for permission to file briefs in the case. These briefs are then said to come from "friends of the court" because they will assist the justices in reaching the best decision in the case.

Open Meetings

Section 552b of the APA is what is known as the "Government in the Sunshine Act." As with the Freedom of Information Act, it expresses a strong preference for openness. The times and places of meetings of multi-member federal government boards, commissions, and agencies are to be provided in advance. The meetings themselves are to be open to the public, if attended by at least the number of members who could take action. It is subject to ten exceptions, roughly similar to those found in the FOIA. Of course, members may talk to one another during the course of their daily work activities. The requirements of the Act apply to a "meeting," which section 552(a)(2) defines as "deliberations ... where such deliberations determine or result in the joint conduct or disposition of official agency business." When one of the exemptions is invoked, a meeting may be closed if a majority of the members vote to do so, but those voting must make the decision to close a matter of public record, including the reasons for doing so and who voted for and against.

A similar statute, known as the Federal Advisory Committee Act (FACA), imposes open meeting requirements when the President or an agency meets with an outside group to receive advice or recommendations. It was designed to prevent secret lobbying by influential persons and groups. Alleged FACA violations have been raised in some high-profile cases, including the following one involving the Vice President of the United States. Because the case involved the White House, it also raised separation-of-powers concerns, which the Court found persuasive. Finally, the case was also widely reported because of the attack on the impartiality of Justice Scalia as discussed in Chapter 3.

Cheney v. U.S. Dist. Court
542 U.S. 367 (2004)

Kennedy, J.

A few days after assuming office, President George W. Bush issued a memorandum establishing the National Energy Policy Development Group (NEPDG or Group). The Group was directed to "develo[p] ... a national energy policy designed to help the private sector, and government at all levels, promote dependable, affordable, and environmentally sound production and distribution of energy for the future." The President assigned a number of agency heads and assistants—all employees of the Federal Government— to serve as members of the committee. He authorized the Vice President, as chairman of the Group, to invite "other officers of the Federal Government" to participate "as appropriate." Five months later, the NEPDG issued a final report and, according to the Government, terminated all operations.

Following publication of the report, respondents Judicial Watch and the Sierra Club filed these separate actions, which were later consolidated in the District Court. Respondents alleged the NEPDG had failed to comply with the procedural and disclosure requirements of the Federal Advisory Committee Act (FACA or Act).

FACA was enacted to monitor the "numerous committees, boards, commissions, councils, and similar groups [that] have been established to advise officers and agencies in the executive branch of the Federal Government," and to prevent the "wasteful expenditure of public funds" that may result from their proliferation, *Public Citizen v. Department of Justice*, 491 U.S. 440 (1989). Subject to specific exemptions, FACA imposes a variety of open-meeting and disclosure requirements on groups that meet the definition of an "advisory committee."

> As relevant here, an "advisory committee" means "any committee, board, commission, council, conference, panel, task force, or other similar group, or any subcommittee or other subgroup thereof ... which is—"

> (B) established or utilized by the President ... except that [the definition] excludes (i) any committee that is composed wholly of full-time, or permanent part-time, officers or employees of the Federal Government."

Respondents do not dispute the President appointed only Federal Government officials to the NEPDG. They agree that the NEPDG, as established by the President in his memorandum, was "composed wholly of full-time, or permanent part-time, officers or employees of the Federal Government." The complaint alleges, however, that "non-federal employees," including "private lobbyists," "regularly attended and fully participated in non-public meetings." Relying on *Association of Physicians & Surgeons, Inc. v. Clinton*, 997 F.2d 898 (C.A.D.C. 1993), respondents contend that the regular participation of the non-Government individuals made them *de facto* members of the committee. According to the complaint, their "involvement and role are functionally indistinguishable from those of the other [formal] members." As a result, respondents argue, the NEPDG cannot benefit from the Act's exemption under subsection B and is subject to FACA's requirements.

Vice President Cheney, the NEPDG, the Government officials who served on the committee, and the alleged *de facto* members were named as defendants. The suit seeks declaratory relief and an injunction requiring them to produce all materials allegedly subject to FACA's requirements.

The District Court held that FACA's substantive requirements could be enforced against the Vice President and other Government participants on the NEPDG under the Mandamus Act, and against the agency defendants under the Administrative Procedure Act (APA). The District Court recognized the disclosure duty must be clear and nondiscretionary for *mandamus* to issue, and there must be, among other things, "final agency actions" for the APA to apply. According to the District Court, it was premature to decide these questions. It held only that respondents had alleged sufficient facts to keep the Vice President and the other defendants in the case. In due course the District Court approved respondents' discovery plan, entered a series of orders allowing discovery to proceed. Petitioners sought a writ of *mandamus* in the Court of Appeals to vacate the discovery orders, to direct the District Court to rule on the basis of the administrative record, and to dismiss the Vice President from the suit. A divided panel of the Court of Appeals dismissed the petition for a writ of *mandamus* and the Vice President's attempted interlocutory appeal.

We now come to the central issue in the case—whether the Court of Appeals was correct to conclude it "ha[d] no authority to exercise the extraordinary remedy of *mandamus*," on the ground that the Government could protect its rights by asserting executive privilege in the District Court.

It is well established that "a President's communications and activities encompass a vastly wider range of sensitive material than would be true of any '"ordinary individual."'" Chief Justice Marshall, sitting as a trial judge, recognized the unique position of the Executive Branch when he stated that "[i]n no case ... would a court be required to proceed against the president as against an ordinary individual." *United States v. Burr,* 25 F. Cas. 187, 192 (No. 14,694) (CC Va. 1807). These principles do not mean that the "President is above the law." Rather, they simply acknowledge that the public interest requires that a coequal branch of Government "afford Presidential confidentiality the greatest protection consistent with the fair administration of justice," and give recognition to the paramount necessity of protecting the Executive Branch from vexatious litigation that might distract it from the energetic performance of its constitutional duties.

These separation-of-powers considerations should inform a court of appeals' evaluation of a *mandamus* petition involving the President or the Vice President. Accepted *mandamus* standards are broad enough to allow a court of appeals to prevent a lower court from interfering with a coequal branch's ability to discharge its constitutional responsibilities.

We note only that all courts should be mindful of the burdens imposed on the Executive Branch in any future proceedings. Special considerations applicable to the President and the Vice President suggest that the courts should be sensitive to requests by the Government for interlocutory appeals to reexamine, for example, whether the statute embodies the *de facto* membership doctrine.

The judgment of the Court of Appeals for the District of Columbia is vacated, and the case is remanded for further proceedings consistent with this opinion.

* * *

Topics for Further Discussion

1. A writ of *mandamus* is an order from a court to a public official to do his duty. This case involved two *mandamus* actions. In the first one, the plaintiffs wanted the court to order the Vice President and other defendants to turn over information. The plaintiffs believed the defendants had a duty to do so under the open meetings provisions of the Federal Advisory Committee Act. The district court granted some of their requests. Then, the government asked the court of appeals to issue a writ of *mandamus* against the district court's decision. The court of appeals declined to do so. The Supreme Court ruled that whether by *mandamus* or some other means, the court of appeals should have taken into consideration the special role of executive privilege. Thus, the government won.

Key Terms and Concepts

Adjudication
Arbitrary, Capricious, or an Abuse of Discretion
Executive Privilege
Exhaustion of Administrative Remedies
Finality
Formal Rulemaking
Informal Rulemaking
Legislative Veto
Non-delegation Doctrine
Substantial Evidence

Appendix A

The Declaration of Independence of the Thirteen Colonies

In CONGRESS, July 4, 1776

The unanimous Declaration of the thirteen united States of America,

When in the Course of human events, it becomes necessary for one people to dissolve the political bands which have connected them with another, and to assume among the powers of the earth, the separate and equal station to which the Laws of Nature and of Nature's God entitle them, a decent respect to the opinions of mankind requires that they should declare the causes which impel them to the separation.

We hold these truths to be self-evident, that all men are created equal, that they are endowed by their Creator with certain unalienable Rights, that among these are Life, Liberty and the pursuit of Happiness.—That to secure these rights, Governments are instituted among Men, deriving their just powers from the consent of the governed,—That whenever any Form of Government becomes destructive of these ends, it is the Right of the People to alter or to abolish it, and to institute new Government, laying its foundation on such principles and organizing its powers in such form, as to them shall seem most likely to effect their Safety and Happiness. Prudence, indeed, will dictate that Governments long established should not be changed for light and transient causes; and accordingly all experience hath shewn, that mankind are more disposed to suffer, while evils are sufferable, than to right themselves by abolishing the forms to which they are accustomed. But when a long train of abuses and usurpations, pursuing invariably the same Object evinces a design to reduce them under absolute Despotism, it is their right, it is their duty, to throw off such Government, and to provide new Guards for their future security.—Such has been the patient sufferance of these Colonies; and such is now the necessity which constrains them to alter their former Systems of Government. The history of the present King of Great Britain [George III] is a history of repeated injuries and usurpations, all having in direct object the establishment of an absolute Tyranny over these States. To prove this, let Facts be submitted to a candid world.

He has refused his Assent to Laws, the most wholesome and necessary for the public good.

He has forbidden his Governors to pass Laws of immediate and pressing importance, unless suspended in their operation till his Assent should be obtained; and when so suspended, he has utterly neglected to attend to them.

He has refused to pass other Laws for the accommodation of large districts of people, unless those people would relinquish the right of Representation in the Legislature, a right inestimable to them and formidable to tyrants only.

He has called together legislative bodies at places unusual, uncomfortable, and distant from the depository of their public Records, for the sole purpose of fatiguing them into compliance with his measures.

He has dissolved Representative Houses repeatedly, for opposing with manly firmness his invasions on the rights of the people.

He has refused for a long time, after such dissolutions, to cause others to be elected; whereby the Legislative powers, incapable of Annihilation, have returned to the People at large for their exercise; the State remaining in the mean time exposed to all the dangers of invasion from without, and convulsions within.

He has endeavoured to prevent the population of these States; for that purpose obstructing the Laws for Naturalization of Foreigners; refusing to pass others to encourage their migrations hither, and raising the conditions of new Appropriations of Lands.

He has obstructed the Administration of Justice, by refusing his Assent to Laws for establishing Judiciary powers.

He has made Judges dependent on his Will alone, for the tenure of their offices, and the amount and payment of their salaries.

He has erected a multitude of New Offices, and sent hither swarms of Officers to harass our people, and eat out their substance.

He has kept among us, in times of peace, Standing Armies without the consent of our legislatures.

He has affected to render the Military independent of and superior to the Civil power.

He has combined with others to subject us to a jurisdiction foreign to our constitution and unacknowledged by our laws; giving his Assent to their Acts of pretended Legislation:

For Quartering large bodies of armed troops among us:

For protecting them, by a mock Trial, from punishment for any Murders which they should commit on the Inhabitants of these States:

For cutting off our Trade with all parts of the world:

For imposing Taxes on us without our Consent:

For depriving us, in many cases, of the benefits of Trial by Jury:

For transporting us beyond Seas to be tried for pretended offences:

For abolishing the free System of English Laws in a neighbouring Province, establishing therein an Arbitrary government, and enlarging its Boundaries so as to render it at once an example and fit instrument for introducing the same absolute rule into these Colonies:

For taking away our Charters, abolishing our most valuable Laws, and altering fundamentally the Forms of our Governments:

For suspending our own Legislatures, and declaring themselves invested with power to legislate for us in all cases whatsoever.

He has abdicated Government here, by declaring us out of his Protection and waging War against us.

He has plundered our seas, ravaged our Coasts, burnt our towns, and destroyed the lives of our people.

He is at this time transporting large Armies of foreign Mercenaries to compleat the works of death, desolation and tyranny, already begun with circumstances of Cruelty and perfidy scarcely paralleled in the most barbarous ages, and totally unworthy the Head of a civilized nation.

He has constrained our fellow Citizens taken Captive on the high Seas to bear Arms against their Country, to become the executioners of their friends and Brethren, or to fall themselves by their Hands.

He has excited domestic insurrections amongst us, and has endeavoured to bring on the inhabitants of our frontiers, the merciless Indian Savages, whose known rule of warfare, is an undistinguished destruction of all ages, sexes and conditions.

In every stage of these Oppressions We have Petitioned for Redress in the most humble terms: Our repeated Petitions have been answered only by repeated injury. A Prince whose character is thus marked by every act which may define a Tyrant, is unfit to be the ruler of a free people.

Nor have We been wanting in attentions to our British brethren. We have warned them from time to time of attempts by their legislature to extend an unwarrantable jurisdiction over us. We have reminded them of the circumstances of our emigration and settlement here. We have appealed to their native justice and magnanimity, and we have conjured them by the ties of our common kindred to disavow these usurpations, which, would inevitably interrupt our connections and correspondence. They too have been deaf to the voice of justice and of consanguinity. We must, therefore, acquiesce in the necessity, which denounces our Separation, and hold them, as we hold the rest of mankind, Enemies in War, in Peace Friends.

We, therefore, the Representatives of the united States of America, in General Congress, Assembled, appealing to the Supreme Judge of the world for the rectitude of our intentions, do, in the Name, and by the Authority of the good People of these Colonies, solemnly publish and declare, That these United Colonies are, and of Right ought to be Free and Independent States; that they are Absolved from all Allegiance to the British Crown, and that all political connection between them and the State of Great Britain, is and ought to be totally dissolved; and that as Free and Independent States, they have full Power to levy War, conclude Peace, contract Alliances, establish Commerce, and to do all other Acts and Things which Independent States may of right do. And for the support of this Declaration, with a firm reliance on the protection of divine Providence, we mutually pledge to each other our Lives, our Fortunes and our sacred Honor.

The signers of the Declaration represented the new states as follows:

New Hampshire
Josiah Bartlett, William Whipple, Matthew Thornton

Massachusetts
John Hancock, Samual Adams, John Adams, Robert Treat Paine, Elbridge Gerry

Rhode Island
Stephen Hopkins, William Ellery

Connecticut
Roger Sherman, Samuel Huntington, William Williams, Oliver Wolcott

New York
William Floyd, Philip Livingston, Francis Lewis, Lewis Morris

New Jersey
Richard Stockton, John Witherspoon, Francis Hopkinson, John Hart, Abraham Clark

Pennsylvania
Robert Morris, Benjamin Rush, Benjamin Franklin, John Morton, George Clymer, James Smith, George Taylor, James Wilson, George Ross

Delaware
Caesar Rodney, George Read, Thomas McKean

Maryland
Samuel Chase, William Paca, Thomas Stone, Charles Carroll of Carrollton

Virginia
George Wythe, Richard Henry Lee, Thomas Jefferson, Benjamin Harrison, Thomas Nelson, Jr., Francis Lightfoot Lee, Carter Braxton

North Carolina
William Hooper, Joseph Hewes, John Penn

South Carolina
Edward Rutledge, Thomas Heyward, Jr., Thomas Lynch, Jr., Arthur Middleton

Georgia
Button Gwinnett, Lyman Hall, George Walton

Appendix B

The Constitution of the United States

We the people of the United States, in order to form a more perfect union, establish justice, insure domestic tranquility, provide for the common defense, promote the general welfare, and secure the blessings of liberty to ourselves and our posterity, do ordain and establish this Constitution for the United States of America.

Article I

Section 1. All legislative powers herein granted shall be vested in a Congress of the United States, which shall consist of a Senate and House of Representatives.

Section 2. The House of Representatives shall be composed of members chosen every second year by the people of the several states, and the electors in each state shall have the qualifications requisite for electors of the most numerous branch of the state legislature.

No person shall be a Representative who shall not have attained to the age of twenty five years, and been seven years a citizen of the United States, and who shall not, when elected, be an inhabitant of that state in which he shall be chosen.

Representatives and direct taxes shall be apportioned among the several states which may be included within this union, according to their respective numbers, which shall be determined by adding to the whole number of free persons, including those bound to service for a term of years, and excluding Indians not taxed, three fifths of all other Persons. The actual Enumeration shall be made within three years after the first meeting of the Congress of the United States, and within every subsequent term of ten years, in such manner as they shall by law direct. The number of Representatives shall not exceed one for every thirty thousand, but each state shall have at least one Representative; and until such enumeration shall be made, the state of New Hampshire shall be entitled to chuse three, Massachusetts eight, Rhode Island and Providence Plantations one, Connecticut five, New York six, New Jersey four, Pennsylvania eight, Delaware one, Maryland six, Virginia ten, North Carolina five, South Carolina five, and Georgia three.

When vacancies happen in the Representation from any state, the executive authority thereof shall issue writs of election to fill such vacancies.

The House of Representatives shall choose their speaker and other officers; and shall have the sole power of impeachment.

Section 3. The Senate of the United States shall be composed of two Senators from each state, chosen by the legislature thereof, for six years; and each Senator shall have one vote.

Immediately after they shall be assembled in consequence of the first election, they shall be divided as equally as may be into three classes. The seats of the Senators of the first class shall be vacated at the expiration of the second year, of the second class at the expiration of the fourth year, and the third class at the expiration of the sixth year, so that one third may be chosen every second year; and if vacancies happen by resignation, or otherwise, during the recess of the legislature of any state, the executive thereof may make temporary appointments until the next meeting of the legislature, which shall then fill such vacancies.

No person shall be a Senator who shall not have attained to the age of thirty years, and been nine years a citizen of the United States and who shall not, when elected, be an inhabitant of that state for which he shall be chosen.

The Vice President of the United States shall be President of the Senate, but shall have no vote, unless they be equally divided.

The Senate shall choose their other officers, and also a President pro tempore, in the absence of the Vice President, or when he shall exercise the office of President of the United States.

The Senate shall have the sole power to try all impeachments. When sitting for that purpose, they shall be on oath or affirmation. When the President of the United States is tried, the Chief Justice shall preside: And no person shall be convicted without the concurrence of two thirds of the members present.

Judgment in cases of impeachment shall not extend further than to removal from office, and disqualification to hold and enjoy any office of honor, trust or profit under the United States: but the party convicted shall nevertheless be liable and subject to indictment, trial, judgment and punishment, according to law.

Section 4. The times, places and manner of holding elections for Senators and Representatives, shall be prescribed in each state by the legislature thereof; but the Congress may at any time by law make or alter such regulations, except as to the places of choosing Senators.

The Congress shall assemble at least once in every year, and such meeting shall be on the first Monday in December, unless they shall by law appoint a different day.

Section 5. Each House shall be the judge of the elections, returns and qualifications of its own members, and a majority of each shall constitute a quorum to do business; but a smaller number may adjourn from day to day, and may be authorized to compel the attendance of absent members, in such manner, and under such penalties as each House may provide.

Each House may determine the rules of its proceedings, punish its members for disorderly behavior, and, with the concurrence of two thirds, expel a member.

Each House shall keep a journal of its proceedings, and from time to time publish the same, excepting such parts as may in their judgment require secrecy; and the yeas and nays of the members of either House on any question shall, at the desire of one fifth of those present, be entered on the journal.

Neither House, during the session of Congress, shall, without the consent of the other, adjourn for more than three days, nor to any other place than that in which the two Houses shall be sitting.

Section 6. The Senators and Representatives shall receive a compensation for their services, to be ascertained by law, and paid out of the treasury of the United States. They shall in all cases, except treason, felony and breach of the peace, be privileged from arrest during their attendance at the session of their respective Houses, and in going to and returning from the same; and for any speech or debate in either House, they shall not be questioned in any other place.

No Senator or Representative shall, during the time for which he was elected, be appointed to any civil office under the authority of the United States, which shall have been created, or the emoluments whereof shall have been increased during such time: and no person holding any office under the United States, shall be a member of either House during his continuance in office.

Section 7. All bills for raising revenue shall originate in the House of Representatives; but the Senate may propose or concur with amendments as on other Bills.

Every bill which shall have passed the House of Representatives and the Senate, shall, before it become a law, be presented to the President of the United States; if he approve he shall sign it, but if not he shall return it, with his objections to that House in which it shall have originated, who shall enter the objections at large on their journal, and proceed to reconsider it. If after such reconsideration two thirds of that House shall agree to pass the bill, it shall be sent, together with the objections, to the other House, by which it shall likewise be reconsidered, and if approved by two thirds of that House, it shall become a law. But in all such cases the votes of both Houses shall be determined by yeas and nays, and the names of the persons voting for and against the bill shall be entered on the journal of each House respectively. If any bill shall not be returned by the President within ten days (Sundays excepted) after it shall have been presented to him, the same shall be a law, in like manner as if he had signed it, unless the Congress by their adjournment prevent its return, in which case it shall not be a law.

Every order, resolution, or vote to which the concurrence of the Senate and House of Representatives may be necessary (except on a question of adjournment) shall be presented to the President of the United States; and before the same shall take effect, shall be approved by him, or being disapproved by him, shall be repassed by two thirds of the Senate and House of Representatives, according to the rules and limitations prescribed in the case of a bill.

Section 8. The Congress shall have power to lay and collect taxes, duties, imposts and excises, to pay the debts and provide for the common defense and general welfare of the United States; but all duties, imposts and excises shall be uniform throughout the United States;

To borrow money on the credit of the United States;

To regulate commerce with foreign nations, and among the several states, and with the Indian tribes;

To establish a uniform rule of naturalization, and uniform laws on the subject of bankruptcies throughout the United States;

To coin money, regulate the value thereof, and of foreign coin, and fix the standard of weights and measures;

To provide for the punishment of counterfeiting the securities and current coin of the United States;

To establish post offices and post roads;

To promote the progress of science and useful arts, by securing for limited times to authors and inventors the exclusive right to their respective writings and discoveries;

To constitute tribunals inferior to the Supreme Court;

To define and punish piracies and felonies committed on the high seas, and offenses against the law of nations;

To declare war, grant letters of marque and reprisal, and make rules concerning captures on land and water;

To raise and support armies, but no appropriation of money to that use shall be for a longer term than two years;

To provide and maintain a navy;

To make rules for the government and regulation of the land and naval forces;

To provide for calling forth the militia to execute the laws of the union, suppress insurrections and repel invasions;

To provide for organizing, arming, and disciplining, the militia, and for governing such part of them as may be employed in the service of the United States, reserving to the states respectively, the appointment of the officers, and the authority of training the militia according to the discipline prescribed by Congress;

To exercise exclusive legislation in all cases whatsoever, over such District (not exceeding ten miles square) as may, by cession of particular states, and the acceptance of Congress, become the seat of the government of the United States, and to exercise like authority over all places purchased by the consent of the legislature of the state in which the same shall be, for the erection of forts, magazines, arsenals, dockyards, and other needful buildings;—And

To make all laws which shall be necessary and proper for carrying into execution the foregoing powers, and all other powers vested by this Constitution in the government of the United States, or in any department or officer thereof.

Section 9. The migration or importation of such persons as any of the states now existing shall think proper to admit, shall not be prohibited by the Congress prior to the year one thousand eight hundred and eight, but a tax or duty may be imposed on such importation, not exceeding ten dollars for each person.

The privilege of the writ of habeas corpus shall not be suspended, unless when in cases of rebellion or invasion the public safety may require it.

No bill of attainder or ex post facto Law shall be passed.

No capitation, or other direct, tax shall be laid, unless in proportion to the census or enumeration herein before directed to be taken.

No tax or duty shall be laid on articles exported from any state.

No preference shall be given by any regulation of commerce or revenue to the ports of one state over those of another: nor shall vessels bound to, or from, one state, be obliged to enter, clear or pay duties in another.

No money shall be drawn from the treasury, but in consequence of appropriations made by law; and a regular statement and account of receipts and expenditures of all public money shall be published from time to time.

No title of nobility shall be granted by the United States: and no person holding any office of profit or trust under them, shall, without the consent of the Congress, accept of any present, emolument, office, or title, of any kind whatever, from any king, prince, or foreign state.

Section 10. No state shall enter into any treaty, alliance, or confederation; grant letters of marque and reprisal; coin money; emit bills of credit; make anything but gold and silver coin a tender in payment of debts; pass any bill of attainder, ex post facto law, or law impairing the obligation of contracts, or grant any title of nobility.

No state shall, without the consent of the Congress, lay any imposts or duties on imports or exports, except what may be absolutely necessary for executing its inspection laws: and the net produce of all duties and imposts, laid by any state on imports or exports, shall be for the use of the treasury of the United States; and all such laws shall be subject to the revision and control of the Congress.

No state shall, without the consent of Congress, lay any duty of tonnage, keep troops, or ships of war in time of peace, enter into any agreement or compact with another state, or with a foreign power, or engage in war, unless actually invaded, or in such imminent danger as will not admit of delay.

Article II

Section 1. The executive power shall be vested in a President of the United States of America. He shall hold his office during the term of four years, and, together with the Vice President, chosen for the same term, be elected, as follows:

Each state shall appoint, in such manner as the Legislature thereof may direct, a number of electors, equal to the whole number of Senators and Representatives to which the State may be entitled in the Congress: but no Senator or Representative, or person holding an office of trust or profit under the United States, shall be appointed an elector.

The electors shall meet in their respective states, and vote by ballot for two persons, of whom one at least shall not be an inhabitant of the same state with themselves. And they shall make a list of all the persons voted for, and of the number of votes for each; which list they shall sign and certify, and transmit sealed to the seat of the government of the United States, directed to the President of the Senate. The President of the Senate shall, in the presence of the Senate and House of Representatives, open all the certificates, and the votes shall then be counted. The person having the greatest number of votes shall be the President, if such number be a majority of the whole number of electors appointed; and if there be more than one who have such majority, and have an equal number of votes, then the House of Representatives shall immediately choose by ballot one of them for President; and if no person have a majority, then from the five highest on the list the said House shall in like manner choose the President. But in choosing the President, the votes shall be taken by States, the representation from each state having one vote; A quorum for this purpose shall consist of a member or members from two thirds of the states, and a majority of all the states shall be necessary to a choice. In every case, after the choice of the President, the person having the greatest number of votes of the electors shall be the Vice President. But if there should remain two or more who have equal votes, the Senate shall choose from them by ballot the Vice President.

The Congress may determine the time of choosing the electors, and the day on which they shall give their votes; which day shall be the same throughout the United States.

No person except a natural born citizen, or a citizen of the United States, at the time of the adoption of this Constitution, shall be eligible to the office of President; neither shall any person be eligible to that office who shall not have attained to the age of thirty five years, and been fourteen Years a resident within the United States.

In case of the removal of the President from office, or of his death, resignation, or inability to discharge the powers and duties of the said office, the same shall devolve on the Vice President, and the Congress may by law provide for the case of removal, death, resignation or inability, both of the President and Vice President, declaring what officer shall then act as President, and such officer shall act accordingly, until the disability be removed, or a President shall be elected.

The President shall, at stated times, receive for his services, a compensation, which shall neither be increased nor diminished during the period for which he shall have been elected, and he shall not receive within that period any other emolument from the United States, or any of them.

Before he enter on the execution of his office, he shall take the following oath or affirmation:—
"I do solemnly swear (or affirm) that I will faithfully execute the office of President of the United States, and will to the best of my ability, preserve, protect and defend the Constitution of the United States."

Section 2. The President shall be commander in chief of the Army and Navy of the United States, and of the militia of the several states, when called into the actual service of the United States; he may require the opinion, in writing, of the principal officer in each of the executive departments, upon any subject relating to the duties of their respective offices, and he shall have power to grant reprieves and pardons for offenses against the United States, except in cases of impeachment.

He shall have power, by and with the advice and consent of the Senate, to make treaties, provided two thirds of the Senators present concur; and he shall nominate, and by and with the advice and consent of the Senate, shall appoint ambassadors, other public ministers and consuls, judges of the Supreme Court, and all other officers of the United States, whose appointments are not herein otherwise provided for, and which shall be established by law: but the Congress may by law vest the appointment of such inferior officers, as they think proper, in the President alone, in the courts of law, or in the heads of departments.

The President shall have power to fill up all vacancies that may happen during the recess of the Senate, by granting commissions which shall expire at the end of their next session.

Section 3. He shall from time to time give to the Congress information of the state of the union, and recommend to their consideration such measures as he shall judge necessary and expedient; he may, on extraordinary occasions, convene both Houses, or either of them, and in case of disagreement between them, with respect to the time of adjournment, he may adjourn them to such time as he shall think proper; he shall receive ambassadors and other public ministers; he shall take care that the laws be faithfully executed, and shall commission all the officers of the United States.

Section 4. The President, Vice President and all civil officers of the United States, shall be removed from office on impeachment for, and conviction of, treason, bribery, or other high crimes and misdemeanors.

Article III

Section 1. The judicial power of the United States, shall be vested in one Supreme Court, and in such inferior courts as the Congress may from time to time ordain and establish. The judges, both of the supreme and inferior courts, shall hold their offices during good behaviour, and shall, at stated times, receive for their services, a compensation, which shall not be diminished during their continuance in office.

Section 2. The judicial power shall extend to all cases, in law and equity, arising under this Constitution, the laws of the United States, and treaties made, or which shall be made, under their authority;—to all cases affecting ambassadors, other public ministers and consuls;—to all cases of admiralty and maritime jurisdiction;—to controversies to which the United States shall be a party;—to controversies between two or more states;—between a state and citizens of another state;—between citizens of different states;—between citizens of the same state claiming lands under grants of different states, and between a state, or the citizens thereof, and foreign states, citizens or subjects.

In all cases affecting ambassadors, other public ministers and consuls, and those in which a state shall be party, the Supreme Court shall have original jurisdiction. In all the other cases before mentioned, the Supreme Court shall have appellate jurisdiction, both as to law and fact, with such exceptions, and under such regulations as the Congress shall make.

The trial of all crimes, except in cases of impeachment, shall be by jury; and such trial shall be held in the state where the said crimes shall have been committed; but when not committed within any state, the trial shall be at such place or places as the Congress may by law have directed.

Section 3. Treason against the United States, shall consist only in levying war against them, or in adhering to their enemies, giving them aid and comfort. No person shall be convicted of treason unless on the testimony of two witnesses to the same overt act, or on confession in open court.

The Congress shall have power to declare the punishment of treason, but no attainder of treason shall work corruption of blood, or forfeiture except during the life of the person attainted.

Article IV

Section 1. Full faith and credit shall be given in each state to the public acts, records, and judicial proceedings of every other state. And the Congress may by general laws prescribe the manner in which such acts, records, and proceedings shall be proved, and the effect thereof.

Section 2. The citizens of each state shall be entitled to all privileges and immunities of citizens in the several states.

A person charged in any state with treason, felony, or other crime, who shall flee from justice, and be found in another state, shall on demand of the executive authority of the state from which he fled, be delivered up, to be removed to the state having jurisdiction of the crime.

No person held to service or labor in one state, under the laws thereof, escaping into another, shall, in consequence of any law or regulation therein, be discharged from such service or labor, but shall be delivered up on claim of the party to whom such service or labor may be due.

Section 3. New states may be admitted by the Congress into this union; but no new states shall be formed or erected within the jurisdiction of any other state; nor any state be formed by the junction of two or more states, or parts of states, without the consent of the legislatures of the states concerned as well as of the Congress.

The Congress shall have power to dispose of and make all needful rules and regulations respecting the territory or other property belonging to the United States; and nothing in this Constitution shall be so construed as to prejudice any claims of the United States, or of any particular state.

Section 4. The United States shall guarantee to every state in this union a republican form of government, and shall protect each of them against invasion; and on application of the legislature, or of the executive (when the legislature cannot be convened) against domestic violence.

Article V

The Congress, whenever two thirds of both houses shall deem it necessary, shall propose amendments to this Constitution, or, on the application of the legislatures of two thirds of the several states, shall call a convention for proposing amendments, which, in either case, shall be valid to all intents and purposes, as part of this Constitution, when ratified by the legislatures of three fourths of the several states, or by conventions in three fourths thereof, as the one or the other mode of ratification may be proposed by the Congress; provided that no amendment which may be made prior to the year one thousand eight hundred and eight shall in any manner affect the first and fourth clauses in the ninth section of the first article; and that no state, without its consent, shall be deprived of its equal suffrage in the Senate.

Article VI

All debts contracted and engagements entered into, before the adoption of this Constitution, shall be as valid against the United States under this Constitution, as under the Confederation.

This Constitution, and the laws of the United States which shall be made in pursuance thereof; and all treaties made, or which shall be made, under the authority of the United States, shall be the supreme law of the land; and the judges in every state shall be bound thereby, anything in the Constitution or laws of any State to the contrary notwithstanding.

The Senators and Representatives before mentioned, and the members of the several state legislatures, and all executive and judicial officers, both of the United States and of the several states, shall be bound by oath or affirmation, to support this Constitution; but no religious test shall ever be required as a qualification to any office or public trust under the United States.

Article VII

The ratification of the conventions of nine states, shall be sufficient for the establishment of this Constitution between the states so ratifying the same.

Done in convention by the unanimous consent of the states present the seventeenth day of September in the year of our Lord one thousand seven hundred and eighty seven and of the independence of the United States of America the twelfth.

Go. WASHINGTON — Presidt. and deputy from Virginia

[Signed also by the deputies of twelve States.]

The Conventions of a number of the States having, at the time of adopting the Constitution, expressed a desire, in order to prevent misconstruction or abuse of its powers, that further declaratory and restrictive clauses should be added, and as extending the ground of public confidence in the Government will best insure the beneficent ends of its institution;

Resolved, by the Senate and House of Representatives of the United States of America, in Congress assembled, two-thirds of both Houses concurring, that the following articles be proposed to the Legislatures of the several States, as amendments to the Constitution of the United States; all or any of which articles, when ratified by three-fourths of the said Legislatures, to be valid to all intents and purposes as part of the said Constitution, namely:

Amendment I

Congress shall make no law respecting an establishment of religion, or prohibiting the free exercise thereof; or abridging the freedom of speech, or of the press; or the right of the people peaceably to assemble, and to petition the government for a redress of grievances.

Amendment II

A well regulated militia, being necessary to the security of a free state, the right of the people to keep and bear arms, shall not be infringed.

Amendment III

No soldier shall, in time of peace be quartered in any house, without the consent of the owner, nor in time of war, but in a manner to be prescribed by law.

Amendment IV

The right of the people to be secure in their persons, houses, papers, and effects, against unreasonable searches and seizures, shall not be violated, and no warrants shall issue, but upon probable cause, supported by oath or affirmation, and particularly describing the place to be searched, and the persons or things to be seized.

Amendment V

No person shall be held to answer for a capital, or otherwise infamous crime, unless on a presentment or indictment of a grand jury, except in cases arising in the land or naval forces, or in the militia, when in actual service in time of war or public danger; nor shall any person be subject for the same offense to be twice put in jeopardy of life or limb; nor shall be compelled in any criminal case to be a witness against himself, nor be deprived of life, liberty, or property, without due process of law; nor shall private property be taken for public use, without just compensation.

Amendment VI

In all criminal prosecutions, the accused shall enjoy the right to a speedy and public trial, by an impartial jury of the state and district wherein the crime shall have been committed, which district shall have been previously ascertained by law, and to be informed of the nature and cause of the accusation; to be confronted with the witnesses against him; to have compulsory process for obtaining witnesses in his favor, and to have the assistance of counsel for his defense.

Amendment VII

In suits at common law, where the value in controversy shall exceed twenty dollars, the right of trial by jury shall be preserved, and no fact tried by a jury, shall be otherwise reexamined in any court of the United States, than according to the rules of the common law.

Amendment VIII

Excessive bail shall not be required, nor excessive fines imposed, nor cruel and unusual punishments inflicted.

Amendment IX

The enumeration in the Constitution, of certain rights, shall not be construed to deny or disparage others retained by the people.

Amendment X

The powers not delegated to the United States by the Constitution, nor prohibited by it to the states, are reserved to the states respectively, or to the people.

Amendment XI (1798)

The judicial power of the United States shall not be construed to extend to any suit in law or equity, commenced or prosecuted against one of the United States by citizens of another state, or by citizens or subjects of any foreign state.

Amendment XII (1804)

The electors shall meet in their respective states and vote by ballot for President and Vice-President, one of whom, at least, shall not be an inhabitant of the same state with themselves; they shall name in their ballots the person voted for as President, and in distinct ballots the person voted for as Vice-President, and they shall make distinct lists of all persons voted for as President, and of all persons voted for as Vice-President, and of the number of votes for each, which lists they shall sign and certify, and transmit sealed to the seat of the government of the United States, directed to the President of the Senate;—The President of the Senate shall, in the presence of the Senate and House of Representatives, open all the certificates and the votes shall then be counted;—the person having the greatest number of votes for President, shall be the President, if such number be a majority of the whole number of electors appointed; and if no person have such majority, then from the persons having the highest numbers not exceeding three on the list of those voted for as President, the House of Representatives shall choose immediately, by ballot, the President. But in choosing the President, the votes shall be taken by states, the representation from each state having one vote; a quorum for this purpose shall consist of a member or members from two-thirds of the states, and a majority of all the states shall be necessary to a choice. And if the House of Representatives shall not choose a President whenever the right of choice shall devolve upon them, before the fourth day of March next following, then the Vice-President shall act as President, as in the case of the death or other constitutional disability of the President. The person having the greatest number of votes as Vice-President, shall be the Vice-President, if such number be a majority of the whole number of electors appointed, and if no person have a majority, then from the two highest numbers on the list, the Senate shall choose the Vice-President; a quorum for the purpose shall consist of two-thirds of the whole number of Senators, and a majority of the whole number shall be necessary to a choice. But no person constitutionally ineligible to the office of President shall be eligible to that of Vice-President of the United States.

Amendment XIII (1865)

Section 1. Neither slavery nor involuntary servitude, except as a punishment for crime whereof the party shall have been duly convicted, shall exist within the United States, or any place subject to their jurisdiction.

Section 2. Congress shall have power to enforce this article by appropriate legislation.

Amendment XIV (1868)

Section 1. All persons born or naturalized in the United States, and subject to the jurisdiction thereof, are citizens of the United States and of the state wherein they reside. No state shall make or enforce any law which shall abridge the privileges or immunities of citizens of the United States; nor shall any state deprive any person of life, liberty, or property, without due process of law; nor deny to any person within its jurisdiction the equal protection of the laws.

Section 2. Representatives shall be apportioned among the several states according to their respective numbers, counting the whole number of persons in each state, excluding Indians not taxed. But when the right to vote at any election for the choice of electors for President and Vice President of the United States, Representatives in Congress, the executive and judicial officers of a state, or the members of the legislature thereof, is denied to any of the male inhabitants of such state, being twenty-one years of age, and citizens of the United States, or in any way abridged, except for participation in rebellion, or other crime, the basis of representation therein shall be reduced in the proportion which the number of such male citizens shall bear to the whole number of male citizens twenty-one years of age in such state.

Section 3. No person shall be a Senator or Representative in Congress, or elector of President and Vice President, or hold any office, civil or military, under the United States, or under any state, who, having previously taken an oath, as a member of Congress, or as an officer of the United States, or as a member of any state legislature, or as an executive or judicial officer of any state, to support the Constitution of the United States, shall have engaged in insurrection or rebellion against the same, or given aid or comfort to the enemies thereof. But Congress may by a vote of two-thirds of each House, remove such disability.

Section 4. The validity of the public debt of the United States, authorized by law, including debts incurred for payment of pensions and bounties for services in suppressing insurrection or rebellion, shall not be questioned. But neither the United States nor any state shall assume or pay any debt or obligation incurred in aid of insurrection or rebellion against the United States, or any claim for the loss or emancipation of any slave; but all such debts, obligations and claims shall be held illegal and void.

Section 5. The Congress shall have power to enforce, by appropriate legislation, the provisions of this article.

Amendment XV (1870)

Section 1. The right of citizens of the United States to vote shall not be denied or abridged by the United States or by any state on account of race, color, or previous condition of servitude.

Section 2. The Congress shall have power to enforce this article by appropriate legislation.

Amendment XVI (1913)

The Congress shall have power to lay and collect taxes on incomes, from whatever source derived, without apportionment among the several states, and without regard to any census of enumeration.

Amendment XVII (1913)

The Senate of the United States shall be composed of two Senators from each state, elected by the people thereof, for six years; and each Senator shall have one vote. The electors in each state shall have the qualifications requisite for electors of the most numerous branch of the state legislatures.

When vacancies happen in the representation of any state in the Senate, the executive authority of such state shall issue writs of election to fill such vacancies: Provided, that the legislature of any state may empower the executive thereof to make temporary appointments until the people fill the vacancies by election as the legislature may direct.

This amendment shall not be so construed as to affect the election or term of any Senator chosen before it becomes valid as part of the Constitution.

Amendment XVIII (1919)

Section 1. After one year from the ratification of this article the manufacture, sale, or transportation of intoxicating liquors within, the importation thereof into, or the exportation thereof from the United States and all territory subject to the jurisdiction thereof for beverage purposes is hereby prohibited.

Section 2. The Congress and the several states shall have concurrent power to enforce this article by appropriate legislation.

Section 3. This article shall be inoperative unless it shall have been ratified as an amendment to the Constitution by the legislatures of the several states, as provided in the Constitution, within seven years from the date of the submission hereof to the states by the Congress.

Amendment XIX (1920)

The right of citizens of the United States to vote shall not be denied or abridged by the United States or by any state on account of sex.

Congress shall have power to enforce this article by appropriate legislation.

Amendment XX (1933)

Section 1. The terms of the President and Vice President shall end at noon on the 20th day of January, and the terms of Senators and Representatives at noon on the 3d day of January, of the years in which such terms would have ended if this article had not been ratified; and the terms of their successors shall then begin.

Section 2. The Congress shall assemble at least once in every year, and such meeting shall begin at noon on the 3d day of January, unless they shall by law appoint a different day.

Section 3. If, at the time fixed for the beginning of the term of the President, the President elect shall have died, the Vice President elect shall become President. If a President shall not have been chosen before the time fixed for the beginning of his term, or if the President elect shall have failed to qualify, then the Vice President elect shall act as President until a President shall have qualified; and the Congress may by law provide for the case wherein neither a President elect nor a Vice President elect shall have qualified, declaring who shall then act as President, or the manner in which one who is to act shall be selected, and such person shall act accordingly until a President or Vice President shall have qualified.

Section 4. The Congress may by law provide for the case of the death of any of the persons from whom the House of Representatives may choose a President whenever the right of choice shall have devolved upon them, and for the case of the death of any of the persons from whom the Senate may choose a Vice President whenever the right of choice shall have devolved upon them.

Section 5. Sections 1 and 2 shall take effect on the 15th day of October following the ratification of this article.

Section 6. This article shall be inoperative unless it shall have been ratified as an amendment to the Constitution by the legislatures of three-fourths of the several states within seven years from the date of its submission.

Amendment XXI (1933)

Section 1. The eighteenth article of amendment to the Constitution of the United States is hereby repealed.

Section 2. The transportation or importation into any state, territory, or possession of the United States for delivery or use therein of intoxicating liquors, in violation of the laws thereof, is hereby prohibited.

Section 3. This article shall be inoperative unless it shall have been ratified as an amendment to the Constitution by conventions in the several states, as provided in the Constitution, within seven years from the date of the submission hereof to the states by the Congress.

Amendment XXII (1951)

Section 1. No person shall be elected to the office of the President more than twice, and no person who has held the office of President, or acted as President, for more than two years of a term to which some other person was elected President shall be elected to the office of the President more than once. But this article shall not apply to any person holding the office of President when this article was proposed by the Congress, and shall not prevent any person who may be holding the office of President, or acting as President, during the term within which this article becomes operative from holding the office of President or acting as President during the remainder of such term.

Section 2. This article shall be inoperative unless it shall have been ratified as an amendment to the Constitution by the legislatures of three-fourths of the several states within seven years from the date of its submission to the states by the Congress.

Amendment XXIII (1961)

Section 1. The District constituting the seat of government of the United States shall appoint in such manner as the Congress may direct:

A number of electors of President and Vice President equal to the whole number of Senators and Representatives in Congress to which the District would be entitled if it were a state, but in no event more than the least populous state; they shall be in addition to those appointed by the states, but they shall be considered, for the purposes of the election of President and Vice President, to be electors appointed by a state; and they shall meet in the District and perform such duties as provided by the twelfth article of amendment.

Section 2. The Congress shall have power to enforce this article by appropriate legislation.

Amendment XXIV (1964)

Section 1. The right of citizens of the United States to vote in any primary or other election for President or Vice President, for electors for President or Vice President, or for Senator or Representative in Congress, shall not be denied or abridged by the United States or any state by reason of failure to pay any poll tax or other tax.

Section 2. The Congress shall have power to enforce this article by appropriate legislation.

Amendment XXV (1967)

Section 1. In case of the removal of the President from office or of his death or resignation, the Vice President shall become President.

Section 2. Whenever there is a vacancy in the office of the Vice President, the President shall nominate a Vice President who shall take office upon confirmation by a majority vote of both Houses of Congress.

Section 3. Whenever the President transmits to the President pro tempore of the Senate and the Speaker of the House of Representatives his written declaration that he is unable to discharge the powers and duties of his office, and until he transmits to them a written declaration to the contrary, such powers and duties shall be discharged by the Vice President as Acting President.

Section 4. Whenever the Vice President and a majority of either the principal officers of the executive departments or of such other body as Congress may by law provide, transmit to the President pro tempore of the Senate and the Speaker of the House of Representatives their written declaration that the President is unable to discharge the powers and duties of his office, the Vice President shall immediately assume the powers and duties of the office as Acting President.

Thereafter, when the President transmits to the President pro tempore of the Senate and the Speaker of the House of Representatives his written declaration that no inability exists, he shall resume the powers and duties of his office unless the Vice President and a majority of either the principal officers of the executive department or of such other body as Congress may by law provide, transmit within four days to the President pro tempore of the Senate and the Speaker of the House of Representatives their written declaration that the President is unable to discharge the powers and duties of his office. Thereupon Congress shall decide the issue, assembling within forty-eight hours for that purpose if not in session. If the Congress, within twenty-one days after receipt of the latter written declaration, or, if Congress is not in session, within twenty-one days after Congress is required to assemble, determines by two-thirds vote of both Houses that the President is unable to discharge the powers and duties of his office, the Vice President shall continue to discharge the same as Acting President; otherwise, the President shall resume the powers and duties of his office.

Amendment XXVI (1971)

Section 1. The right of citizens of the United States, who are 18 years of age or older, to vote, shall not be denied or abridged by the United States or any state on account of age.

Section 2. The Congress shall have the power to enforce this article by appropriate legislation.

Amendment XXVII (1992)

No law varying the compensation for the services of the Senators and Representatives shall take effect until an election of Representatives shall have intervened.

Appendix C

Map of Federal Circuits

Index